Lecture Notes in Computer Science 10595

Commenced Publication in 1973
Founding and Former Series Editors:
Gerhard Goos, Juris Hartmanis, and Jan van Leeuwen

More information about this series at http://www.springer.com/series/7407

Arpan Kumar Kar · P. Vigneswara Ilavarasan
M.P. Gupta · Yogesh K. Dwivedi
Matti Mäntymäki · Marijn Janssen
Antonis Simintiras · Salah Al-Sharhan (Eds.)

Digital Nations – Smart Cities, Innovation, and Sustainability

16th IFIP WG 6.11 Conference on
e-Business, e-Services, and e-Society, I3E 2017
Delhi, India, November 21–23, 2017
Proceedings

 Springer

Editors
Arpan Kumar Kar (iD)
Indian Institute of Technology Delhi
New Delhi
India

P. Vigneswara Ilavarasan
Indian Institute of Technology Delhi
New Delhi
India

M.P. Gupta
Indian Institute of Technology Delhi
New Delhi
India

Yogesh K. Dwivedi
Swansea University
Swansea
UK

Matti Mäntymäki
University of Turku
Turku
Finland

Marijn Janssen (iD)
Delft University of Technology
Delft
The Netherlands

Antonis Simintiras
Gulf University for Science and Technology
West Mishref
Kuwait

Salah Al-Sharhan
Gulf University for Science and Technology
West Mishref
Kuwait

ISSN 0302-9743   ISSN 1611-3349 (electronic)
Lecture Notes in Computer Science
ISBN 978-3-319-68556-4   ISBN 978-3-319-68557-1 (eBook)
DOI 10.1007/978-3-319-68557-1

Library of Congress Control Number: 2017955726

LNCS Sublibrary: SL1 – Theoretical Computer Science and General Issues

This Springer imprint is published by the registered company Springer Nature Switzerland AG
The registered company address is: Gewerbestrasse 11, 6330 Cham, Switzerland

Preface

This volume presents the proceedings of the 16th International Federation of Information Processing (IFIP) Conference on e-Business, e-Services and e-Society (I3E) held at the Indian Institute of Technology, Delhi, during November 21–23, 2017. The IFIP-I3E conference is highly interdisciplinary in nature and focuses on academic contributions in varied domains of electronic business, services, and society. It had great participation from academia, industry, and practitioners who are either working directly in the domain or are in the process of exploring it. The central theme of the 16th edition of the conference was "Digital Nations – Smart Cities, Innovation, and Sustainability." The idea of digital nations perfectly aligns with the three Es of the conference series. As you get through the following pages, you will discover interesting ideas in the domains of governance, social media, and analytics that are shaping our lives today or most likely will alter the digital nations of tomorrow (Zuiderwijk and Janssen 2014; Rana et al. 2017). From any benchmark, the trajectory of technology developments in the post-Internet period is extraordinary and never seen before (Khatwani et al. 2014). It is complex but fascinating; it is bringing people and communities together, enterprises to collaborate on strengths to grab opportunities as competition becomes intense and nations to break boundaries allowing societies to interoperate across different domains and communities. It is producing an amalgamation of various cultures and the emergence of a new way of living – a society that is truly global with global citizenship (Carter et al. 2016).

In the digital society, the issues emerging are plenty and complicated due to the networkedness and possibilities of understanding the complexities through big data analytics (Janssen et al. 2012; Chauhan et al. 2016). The governance is not so much about digital spread as access is fast bridged by expanding mobile networks and broadband as it is about ability in enabling digital-based services to everyone to their expectations. The literacy gap around the globe will remain a cause of concern in the use and adoption of new media, even though the younger generation is fast in adoption. Digital literacy programs will need continuous monitoring and revision to keep pace with the technology change. The underpinning factor in leveraging the new media is having clarity about the culture and community where one is operating. This has not been explored much. Social media has fast become a widespread fascination for everyone, much more than normal social life, raising new challenges and opportunities related to community, culture, and business (Rathore et al. 2016; Lakhiwal and Kar 2016). Understanding variability in cross-cultural boundaries, particularly East vs. West, is necessary in developing a social media strategy for different contextual settings. It hardly needs any emphasis how trust plays a major role in allowing people to overcome the perception of risk and insecurity. Gender effect is also found to play a key role in social media use.

The use of information and communication technologies (ICTs) is greatly impacting the economy (Chew et al. 2010) and governance (Gupta and Jana 2003). Citizens across the globe are adapting to the changing e-government systems for smart and sustainable digital nations (Carter et al. 2016; Rana et al. 2017). These advancements have empowered citizens and have been a major driver for e-participation and e-democracy (Alathur et al. 2016). Despite these advances toward digital nations in the areas of e-governance, e-democracy, e-participation, and open government data (Janssen et al. 2012; Dwivedi et al. 2012; Zuiderwijk and Janssen 2014; Janssen et al. 2015), there are many issues that remain unexplored in greater detail. This includes the use of the Internet, social media, analytical frameworks, and smart services that are still developing each day with the burst of data in the Web 3.0 space (Joseph et al. 2017). Furthermore, with the huge inflow of data, concepts surrounding big data, their impact, and challenges come into the picture that need a deeper understanding (Grover and Kar 2017). Several advanced analytical and meta-heuristic approaches have emerged to address such highly complex computational problems that have arisen with this explosion of data (Kar 2016; Chakraborty and Kar 2017).

The previous IFIP I3E 2016 Conference had a focus on social media, its benefits and pitfalls (Dwivedi et al. 2016), and addressed them in greater detail. The I3E-2017 conference circumscribes the overall broader domain of digital nations including e-services, e-governance, social media, and data analytics with a focus on recent trends. The call for papers sought full-length papers as well as short communication articles. Extended versions of selected submissions also had a chance for fast-track publication in*Information Systems Frontiers*by Springer and in the *e-Service Journal*published by Indiana University Press.The conference received 96 high-quality submissions from 14 countries. Each article was sent for a blind peer review to at least two experts. After a rigorous review process, 44 submissions were accepted for presentation at IFIP I3E 2017 and are included in the proceedings. These are grouped into five themes or tracks, each of which is outlined here.

The articles appearing in Track I primarily cover discussions on the adoption of smart services focusing on various domains and sectors across nations. The vision of digitization can only be successful if the relevant stakeholders adopt, use, and embrace the ICT-enabled technologies, processes, and outcomes. Sahu and Singh explore the factors that may influence a consumer's behavior to adopt mobile applications with a specific focus on the IRCTC connect mobile application. Tuikka and Sachdeva highlight the experiences surrounding the assistive technology services and their delivery. Hoque, Islam, and Talukder further investigate the factors that may affect the adoption of e-commerce in the readymade garment industry at the B2B level. The exploratory study by Mustafa and Kar evaluates multidimensional risk factors for digital services catering to smart cities. Klimova uses the studies in the existing literature to highlight the use of smart phones in managing dementia. Tamilmani, Rana, and Dwivedi present a systematic review of citations surrounding UTAUT2 and the usage trends. Svobodová and Hedvičáková demonstrate the use of social networks with a primary focus on elderly people in various countries. Patil, Dwivedi, and Rana also present an exploratory study reviewing the existing literature on the adoption of digital payments. Guo and Gao's article concludes Track I with a case-based article exploring the barriers of adoption of e-commerce specifically in rural China. Track I thus comprises articles that present a holistic view of discussions surrounding the adoption of e-services for promoting digital nations. The studies present insights from different countries including India, Bangladesh, China, and Finland.

The Track II submissions focus on assessing the impacts of ICT-enabled smart initiatives. Assessment of ICT-enabled initiatives is critical in understanding the shortcomings of current approaches, and it paves the way for potential improvements. The first article by Praditya and Janssen focuses on the assessment of factors that have an influence on information sharing using the best–worst method. Ramalingam, Christophe, and Samuel assess the potential of the Internet of Things (IoT) in the aerospace domain. Spil, Effing, and Kwast compared the smart city participatory strategies of Hamburg, Berlin, and Enschede. Svobodova and Cerna explore the benefits and pitfalls faced by elderly people while using the Internet. The advances in the adoption of e-government research by SAARC countries are demonstrated in an exploratory study by Rana et al. The work by Mishra et al. assesses the open government data initiative using a perception-driven approach. Singh, Grover, and Kar focus their study on the quality of mobile payment service in India. Finally, the work of Svobodová, Černá, and Hruša explores the use of advanced technology to support smart cities with a focus on identifying simple and composite indicators that impact the tourism sector.

Track III of the proceedings shares insights into the analytical aspects surrounding smart initiatives. Here, the main focus was on providing insights into the governance of the new era of digitization in domains like Web 3.0 and digital literacy. Aswani et al. develop a semantic-based mechanism for exploring the vitality of content in Facebook. Maresova and Klimova highlight the use of the Internet for searching health-related information. Joseph, Kar, and Ilavarasan proposed a model to prioritize and predict the impact of digital literacy training programs along with validation. Joseph et al. use Twitter as a medium for analyzing public conversations proving insights for policy makers. The study by Aswani et al. identifies outliers among influencer blogs using web analytics. Dabrowski, Weippl, and Echizen propose a community-based method for the protection and privacy of photographed subjects on various social networks. Kumar et al. on the other hand developed a profile-based mechanism that mitigates fake orders. AlSabeeh and Moghrabi investigate the utilization of programmatic advertising and real-time bidding. Track III concludes with the intelligent vehicle tracking and prediction system proposed by Dhanasekar et al. in their research.

The papers in Track IV focus on the domain of social media and web 3.0 for promoting smartness in digital nations. These studies have highlighted interesting approaches that have used bio-inspired computing, text analytics, machine learning, and big data analytics for key insights. Amirkhanyan and Meinel propose a grouping mechanism that clusters based on density and intensity for fixed distance and time radius. Bühler, Murawski, and Bick discuss the impact of negative word of mouth on social media pertaining to consumer trust in fashion presentations with arguments surrounding the disabling of the comment function. Grover et al. present interesting insights from Twitter analytics on the USA presidential elections. The impact of trust and network ties on word of mouth is further discussed by Mikalef, Pappas, and Sharma, where they explore the social commerce sector. Findings surrounding demonetization and its impact on the Indian economy are highlighted by Mohan and Kar in their study using social media. User satisfaction surrounding fsQCA is explored by analyzing the motivations and emotions in social media as presented by Pappas et al. in their work. Mikalef et al. explore the information available on social commerce, being reviews or marketer information. Gaurav and Kumar propose a mechanism to gauge consumer satisfaction based on the rating using sentiment analysis. Finally, Singh et al. present their forecast on the US presidential elections using sentiment analysis.

Track V continues the central theme of the conference with a focus on smart solutions for the future. This track focuses on the discussions surrounding smart solutions that may have a great impact in varied domains to support smart cities, innovation, and sustainability. Kumar et al. propose a digitized residential address system that provides faster service delivery for smart city development in India. Hyrynsalmi, Mäntymäki, and Baur discuss the concepts of multi-homing and software firm performance as a primary research agenda in their work. Sahu and Singh explore the case of India for explaining the paradigm shift from a cash-based to cash-less economy. The benefits and challenges faced by using reference architecture for processing statistical data are highlighted by Wahyudi, Matheus, and Janssen in their paper. Kumar, Grover, and Kar examine the existing literature surrounding IT consulting by giving an extensive systematic review. Giannakos, Pappas, and Mikalef extend the FsQCA approach to further demonstrate the role of contemporary skills in information technology professionals. The insights from roadway breakdown services for gauging complexity and productivity in e-mobility is another interesting study presented by Baur et al. The final article in the I3E 2017 proceedings explores the effective use of the Internet by elderly people.

In addition to the contributions of the aforementioned authors, we were delighted to have Prof. Luís Soares Barbosa and Prof. Jeremy Millard as our keynote speakers. Prof. Luís Soares Barbosa is Head of UNU-EGOV – the Operational Unit on Policy-Driven Electronic Governance of the United Nations University – Professor of Computer Science at the University of Minho, Portugal, and a senior researcher at INESC TEC. His research interests include formal modeling techniques and logics, applied to the rigorous design of complex systems and digital governance processes. He coordinates the PT-FLAD Chair on Smart Cities and Smart Governance, a recently established chair on the development of foundations, methods, and reliable technologies to support the development of smart cities and intelligent governance infrastructures.

Prof. Jeremy Millard has over 40 years' global experience on issues ranging from governance, ICT, open data, open and social innovation, participation, sustainable and socio-economic development, the new economy, urbanization, and nature-based solutions for growth. He has published extensively in these and related fields and his clients include governments, the European Commission, the United Nations, the OECD and World Bank, as well as many non-profit organizations and companies around the world. Recent assignments include mapping European Smart Cities for the European Parliament, designing the World Bank's Knowledge Exchange Platform for Indian Smart Cities, and an EC project on the maker movement and new forms of distributed manufacturing for FabCities.

The success of the 16th IFIP I3E conference is due to the efforts of numerous people and organizations involved. We thank the WG 6.11 for the conference series and their continuous support. We are grateful to them for selecting the Indian Institute of

Technology, Delhi, for the IFIP I3E-2017 conference. We further thank the authors from across the globe for choosing I3E 2017 to submit their manuscripts. We were overwhelmed with the response and felt privileged to receive a large number of high-quality manuscripts for the conference. We would also like to take this moment to extend our sincere gratitude to the keynote speakers for offering their valuable time and sharing their knowledge with the conference attendees. The conference would not have been a success with the members of the Program Committee who devoted their valuable time to give input for improving the quality of the manuscripts. We would also like to thank the Department of Management Studies, Indian Institute of Technology, Delhi, and the members of the Organizing Committee for hosting and supporting the conference in every possible way. The other faculty members of the department were extremely supportive towards our academic endeavors while trying to organize this mammoth conference. We are also thankful to the conference secretaries who dedicated a lot of time and effort to support us in organizing this program. Without the continuous support of our research scholars, we, the faculty chairs, would have found it impossible to organize a conference of this stature. Finally, we thank Springer LNCS for publishing the proceedings and helping the I3E series to disseminate and impart the collective knowledge across the globe in the form of this book.

References

Alathur, S., Ilavarasan, P. V., & Gupta, M. P. (2016). Determinants of e-participation in the citizens and the government initiatives: Insights from India. *Socio-Economic Planning Sciences*, *55*, 25-35.

Carter, L., Weerakkody, V., Phillips, B., & Dwivedi, Y. K. (2016). Citizen adoption of e-government Services: Exploring citizen perceptions of online services in the United States and United Kingdom.*Information Systems Management*, *33*(2), 124-140.

Chakraborty, A., & Kar, A. K. (2017). Swarm intelligence: A review of algorithms. In*Nature-Inspired Computing and Optimization* (pp. 475–494). Springer International Publishing.

Chauhan, S., Agarwal, N., Agarwal, N., & Kar, A. K. (2016). Addressing big data challenges in smart cities: a systematic literature review.*info*, *18*(4), 73–90.

Chew, H. E., Ilavarasan, P. V., & Levy, M. R. (2010). The economic impact of information and communication technologies (ICTs) on microenterprises in the context of development.*The Electronic Journal of Information Systems in Developing Countries*, *44*.

Dwivedi, Y. K., Mäntymäki, M., Ravishankar, M. N., Janssen, M., Clement, M., Slade, E. L., & Simintiras, A. C. (Eds.). (2016). *Social Media: The Good, the Bad, and the Ugly: 15th IFIP WG 6.11 Conference on e-Business, e-Services, and e-Society, I3E 2016, Swansea, UK, September 13–15, 2016, Proceedings* (Vol. 9844). Springer.

Dwivedi, Y. K., Weerakkody, V., & Janssen, M. (2012). Moving towards maturity: challenges to successful e-government implementation and diffusion. *ACM SIGMIS Database*, *42*(4), 11–22.

Grover, P., & Kar, A. K. (2017). Big Data Analytics: A Review on Theoretical Contributions and Tools Used in Literature.*Global Journal of Flexible Systems Management*, 1–27.

Gupta, M. P., & Jana, D. (2003). E-government evaluation: A framework and case study.*Government information quarterly*, *20*(4), 365–387.

Janssen, M., Charalabidis, Y., & Zuiderwijk, A. (2012). Benefits, adoption barriers and myths of open data and open government.*Information systems management*, *29*(4), 258–268.

Janssen, M., Mäntymäki, M., Hidders, J., Klievink, B., Lamersdorf, W., Van Loenen, B., & Zuiderwijk, A. (Eds.). (2015).*Open and Big Data Management and Innovation: 14th IFIP WG 6.11 Conference on E-Business, E-Services, and E-Society, I3E 2015, Delft, the Netherlands, October 13–15, 2015, Proceedings* (Vol. 9373). Springer.

Joseph, N., Kar, A. K., Ilavarasan, P. V., & Ganesh, S. (2017). Review of discussions on internet of things (IoT): insights from twitter analytics.*Journal of Global Information Management (JGIM)*, *25*(2), 38–51.

Kar, A. K. (2016). Bio inspired computing–A review of algorithms and scope of applications. *Expert Systems with Applications*, *59*, 20-32.

Khatwani, G., Anand, O., & Kar, A. K. (2014, December). Evaluating internet information search channels using hybrid MCDM technique. In*International Conference on Swarm, Evolutionary, and Memetic Computing* (pp. 123–133). Springer, Cham.

Lakhiwal, A., & Kar, A. K. (2016, September). Insights from Twitter Analytics: Modeling Social Media Personality Dimensions and Impact of Breakthrough Events. In*Conference on e-Business, e-Services and e-Society* (pp. 533–544). Springer International Publishing.

Rana, N. P., Dwivedi, Y. K., Lal, B., Williams, M. D., & Clement, M. (2017). Citizens' adoption of an electronic government system: towards a unified view.*Information Systems Frontiers*, *19*(3), 549–568.

Rathore, A. K., Ilavarasan, P. V., & Dwivedi, Y. K. (2016). Social media content and product co-creation: an emerging paradigm.*Journal of Enterprise Information Management*, *29*(1), 7–18.

Zuiderwijk, A., & Janssen, M. (2014). Open data policies, their implementation and impact: A framework for comparison.*Government Information Quarterly*, *31*(1), 17–29.

October 2017

Arpan Kumar Kar
P. Vigneswara Ilavarasan
M. P. Gupta
Yogesh K. Dwivedi
Matti Mäntymäki
Marijn Janssen
Antonis Simintiras
Salah Al-Sharhan

Organization

IFIP I3E 2017 Conference Chairs

Salah Al-Sharhan	Gulf University for Science and Technology (GUST), State of Kuwait
Yogesh K. Dwivedi	Swansea University, UK
M.P. Gupta	IIT Delhi, India
Marijn Janssen	Delft University of Technology, The Netherlands
Arpan Kumar Kar	IIT Delhi, India
Vigneswara llavarasan	IIT Delhi, India
Matti Mäntymäki	Turku School of Economics, Finland
Antonis C. Simintiras	Gulf University for Science and Technology (GUST), State of Kuwait

IFIP I3E 2017 Program Chairs

Salah Al-Sharhan	Gulf University for Science and Technology (GUST), State of Kuwait
Yogesh K. Dwivedi	Swansea University, UK
M.P. Gupta	IIT Delhi, India
Marijn Janssen	Delft University of Technology, The Netherlands
Arpan Kumar Kar	IIT Delhi, India
Vigneswara llavarasan	IIT Delhi, India
Matti Mäntymäki	Turku School of Economics, Finland
Antonis C. Simintiras	Gulf University for Science and Technology (GUST), State of Kuwait

IFIP I3E 2017 Organization Chairs

Yogesh K. Dwivedi	Swansea University, UK
M.P. Gupta	IIT Delhi, India
Arpan Kumar Kar	IIT Delhi, India
Vigneswara llavarasan	IIT Delhi, India
Nripendra P. Rana	Swansea University, UK
G.P. Sahu	MNNIT Allahabad, India
Emma L. Slade	Swansea University, UK

IFIP I3E 2017 Keynote Speakers

Luis Soares Barbosa	United Nations University, Portugal
Jeremy Millard	Danish Technological Institute, Denmark

IFIP I3E 2017 Conference Administrators

Reema Aswani	IIT Delhi, India
Purva Grover	IIT Delhi, India
Nimish Joseph	IIT Delhi, India
Vimal Kumar	IIT Delhi, India
Harish Kumar	IIT Delhi, India
Abbas Singapurwala	IIT Delhi, India

IFIP I3E 2017 Program Committee

Dolphy Abraham	Alliance University, India
Reema Aswani	AKGEC, India
Aaron W. Baur	ESCP Europe Business School Berlin, Germany
Khalid Benali	LORIA, Université de Lorraine, France
Peter De Bruyn	University of Antwerp, Belgium
Julian Bühler	ESCP Europe Business School Berlin, Berlin, Germany
Wojciech Cellary	Poznan University of Economics, Poland
Sheshadri Chatterjee	Microsoft, India
Sumedha Chauhan	IIM Rohtak, India
Joep Crompvoets	KU Leuven, Belgium
Ashraf Darwish	Helwan University, Egypt
Dipanjan Goswami	Daiichi Sankyo, Ranbaxy Laboratories Inc., India
Purva Grover	IIT Delhi, India
Mohammad Hossain	RMIT University, Australia
Marijn Janssen	Delft University of Technology, The Netherlands
Anand Jeyaraj	Wright State University, USA
Nimish Joseph	IIT Delhi, India
Abhishek Kumar	IIT Delhi, India
Harish Kumar	IIT Delhi, India
Sudeep Kumar	IIT Delhi, India
Prabhat Kumar	NIT Patna, India
Winfried Lamersdorf	Universität Hamburg, Germany
Sven Laumer	University of Bamberg, Germany
Hong Xiu Li	University of Turku, Finland
José María Moreno-Jiménez	Universidad de Zaragoza, Spain
Syed Ziaul Mustafa	IIT Delhi, India
Nripendra P. Rana	Swansea University, UK
Ashish Rathore	IIT Delhi, India
Rishiraj Saha Roy	Max Planck Institute for Informatics, Germany
Bishal Dey Sarkar	IIT Delhi, India
Harjit Singh	Tata Consultancy Services, India
Reima Suomi	University of Turku, Finland
Anushruti Vagrani	IIT Delhi, India
Ravinder Kumar Verma	IIT Delhi, India

Hans Weigand   Tilburg University, The Netherlands
Hiroshi Yoshiura   University of Electro-Communications, Japan

IFIP I3E 2017 Authors

Shalabh Aggarwal   IIT Delhi, India
Mohammad Abdallah Ali   Al-Balqa' Applied University, Jordan
  Alryalat
Dalal A. AlSabeeh   Gulf University for Science and Technology, Kuwait
Aragats Amirkhanyan   University of Potsdam, Germany
Reema Aswani   AKGEC, India
Sunil Babbar   National Informatics Centre Delhi, India
Aaron W. Baur   ESCP Europe Business School Berlin, Germany
Markus Bick   ESCP Europe Business School Berlin, Germany
Shubhadip Biswas   Open Government Data Project, Delhi, India
Julian Bühler   ESCP Europe Business School Berlin, Germany
Miloslava Cerna   University of Hradec Kralove, Czech Republic
Satish Chandra   Jaypee University of Information Technology, Noida,
                              India
Benaroya Christophe   Toulouse Business School, France
Adrian Dabrowski   SBA Research, Austria
Yashwanth Dasari   National Institute of Technology Patna, India
Yogesh K. Dwivedi   Swansea University, UK
Isao Echizen   National Institute of Informatics, Japan
Robin Effing   University of Twente, The Netherlands
Shang Gao   Örebro University, Sweden
Jörg von Garrel   SRH Fernhochschule – The Mobile University,
                              Riedlingen, Germany
Kumar Gaurav   National Institute of Technology Patna, India
S.P. Ghrera   Jaypee University of Information Technology, Solan,
                              India
Michail N. Giannakos   Norwegian University of Science and Technology,
                              Norway
Purva Grover   IIT Delhi, India
Hong Guo   Anhui University, China
M.P. Gupta   IIT Delhi, India
Martina Hedvičáková   University of Hradec Kralove, Czech Republic
Petr Hruša   University of Hradec Kralove, Czech Republic
Sami Hyrynsalmi   Tampere University of Technology, Pori, Finland
Ayushi Jain   National Institute of Technology Patna, India
Marijn Janssen   Delft University of Technology, The Netherlands
Nimish Joseph   IIT Delhi, India
Karanjeet Singh Kahlon   Guru Nanak Dev University, Amritsar, India
Arpan Kumar Kar   IIT Delhi, India
Blanka Klimova   University of Hradec Kralove, Czech Republic
Panos E. Kourouthanassis   Ionian University, Corfu, Greece

Monika Singh	Motilal Nehru National Institute of Technology Allahabad, India
Naveen Kumar Singh	Motilal Nehru National Institute of Technology Allahabad, India
Prabhsimran Singh	Guru Nanak Dev University, Amritsar, India
Akash Sinha	National Institute of Technology Patna, India
Ton A.M. Spil	University of Twente, The Netherlands
Dhanasekar Sundararaman	SSN College of Engineering, Chennai, India
Libuše Svobodová	University of Hradec Kralove, Czech Republic
Pushp P. Patil	Swansea University, UK
Kuttimani Tamilmani	Swansea University, UK
Anne-Marie Tuikka	University of Turku, Finland
Christoph Meinel	University of Potsdam, Germany
P. Vigneswara Ilavarsan	IIT Delhi, India
Agung Wahyudi	Delft University of Technology, The Netherlands
Edgar Weippl	SBA Research, Austria

Contents

Analytics for Smart Governance

Social Media and Web 3.0 for Smartness

Smart Solutions for the Future

Adoption of Smart Services

Factors Influencing Consumer's Behavioral Intention to Adopt IRCTC Connect Mobile Application

Ganesh P. Sahu[(⊠)] and Monika Singh

Motilal Nehru National Institute of Technology Allahabad, Allahabad, India
{gsahu, rms1502}@mnnit.ac.in

Abstract. Indian Railway Catering and Tourism Corporation Ltd. (IRCTC) launched "IRCTC Connect" mobile application (app) for different mobile platforms for booking/cancellation tickets, but the app usage rate is very low in comparison to IRCTC website and Passenger Reservation System (PRS). This indicates a gap between implementation and adaption of IRCTC Connect. This paper explores the factors influencing the consumer's behavioral intention to use IRCTC Connect by adapting Unified Theory of Acceptance and Use of Technology 2 (UTAUT2) model. Regression analysis is used to analyze total 159 valid responses, collected through survey at MNNIT campus Allahabad, India. The findings of the study illustrate that only three factors Social Influence, Price Value and Habit of UTAUT2 model are significantly influencing the adoption of IRCTC Connect with adjusted R-Square value 0.699. This study will facilitate IRCTC Connect developers to encompass better understanding on consumers' desires and intention and encourages researchers in this area for longitudinal observation in different backgrounds.

Keywords: IRCTC apps · IRCTC mobile application · IRCTC Connect · UTAUT2 · Determinants of consumer's behavior intention · m-governance

1 Introduction

In today's lifestyle, all well educated, awarded and techno savoir-faire customers are highly cautious to adopt those applications and services which save their time and cost, and also applicable in the case of online Railway ticket booking [43, 44]. Indian Railways have enabled the customers to book/cancel ticket via website irctc.co.in and mobile app 'IRCTC Connect' instead of waiting in the ques at railways counters. Still approximately 54% of the Indian Railways tickets were reserved online and rest 46% were booked at the railway counters in 2014–15 financial year [34]. According to CRIS [11] report 54.4 million citizens booked tickets on railway counter in December 2015, whilst a total 183 billion tickets were booked through IRCTC website in 2014–15 and approximate 149 million tickets reserved till December 2015 [19].

Since, m-Government (mGov) is an approach and its realization concern the employment of various wireless and mobile technologies, facilities, applications and procedures for benefits of all [3]. However, in developing countries like India, it is in initial stage of enlargement. The scope of expansion of online ticket booking is 80% in

A.K. Kar et al. (Eds.): I3E 2017, LNCS 10595, pp. 3–15, 2017.
DOI: 10.1007/978-3-319-68557-1_1

near future if Indian Railways and IRCTC will make its portal better [34]. It is apparent that there is a gap between government developed facilities and customers' intentions to accept the IRCTC Connect [22, 24, 25], due to which customers resists to use mobile apps in comparison to access the Railways counters or portals.

The study focused on investigation of the factors influencing customers' intentions to use IRCTC Connect. The findings will be helpful for policy makers in Indian Railways' to develop the strategies and upgrade mobile apps accordingly, so that, the outcome will meet the customers expectation. Subsequently, this study will be helpful for Indian government to make Digital India. Further, this study will enrich the existing literature. There are limited studies on mobile applications using this model. Therefore, it is an opportunity to explore the applicability of this theory in a small area of m-governance i.e. IRCTC mobile app.

Following research methodology has been designed: A scrupulous Literature review followed by UTAUT2 model description and framing research model and hypotheses development. Afterward, Statistical Package for the Social Sciences (SPSS) is used for data analysis and interpretation. At the last discussion on results, and concluding remarks are laid down.

1.1   Motivation and Relevance of the Research and Its Contribution

As per the Telecom Regulatory Authority of India [48] records, till June 2015, there are 980.81 million peoples are wireless telephone (mobile phones) users with the 0.51% monthly development rate. The Urban mobile phones subscribers are 562.95 million (0.74% monthly growth rate) and Rural mobile phones subscribers are 417.85 million (0.22% monthly growth rate) making contribution of 57.40% and 42.60% respectively in mobile phone subscriber market. India is the second largest country after China which has crossed this milestone. Again India has more 213 million mobile internet users (above than 60%) out of 352 million internet users according to Internet and Mobile Association of India [20], which shows that in India there is a wide scope for online marketing and m- governance services. Indian government has launched huge number of mobile applications in various segments (Health, Education, Electrical etc.), like mSwasthya, mTranslatorIndian, AADHAAR, MPMKVVCL, Kissan, MEESEWA and the list goes on, to offer m-services more conveniently and to provide the citizen-centric platform empowering natives to hook up with the Indian Government and participate in building good governance [31, 33] (Table 1).

Table 1. Review of IRCTC Apps for multiple operating systems

IRCTC Connect	Android App	Apple's iOS App	Blackberry App	IRCTC Windows App
Launched	October, 2014	10th Jan 2015	August, 2014	July, 2013
Bookings	15,90,563 (2014-15)	67,086 (2014-15)	11,585 (2014-15)	3,11,381 (2014-15)

Source: IRCTC Annual Report 2014-15 and irctc.co.in

Among all various mobile applications, winner of National award for E-Governance Best Citizen Centric application of year 2007-08, Indian Railway Catering and Tourism Corporation Ltd., Public Sector Enterprise under Ministry of Railway, launched "IRCTC Connect" official mobile app in October'2014 for android and Blackberry Smartphone users in August'2014, after a year of hosting "IRCTC Windows 8 App" for Windows phone users in July, 2013 [19, 20]. IRCTC app is also available on Apple's iOS platform by January'2015. Mobillion 2015 award winner 'IRCTC Connect' under category of 'Best Use of mobile app' has the motive behind offering ticket booking through multiple platforms is to attract maximum travelers and generate revenue [20].

2 Literature Review

Islam et al. [21] defined mobile apps as a set of application programmes that are used to perform a certain defined task for the mobile users. A number of user acceptance models identifying various factors are developed to measure the acceptance of information systems and technologies indicating the system's achievement or malfunctions [30]. In Bomhold [40] study students were considered for mobile apps usages calculation; Kang [23] using the Unified Theory of Acceptance and Use of Technology (UTAUT) & Uses and Gratifications Theory (UGT) investigated the mobile apps usage intention.

Hew et al. [17] determined the factors that influence the mobile apps usage intention on the basis of UTAUT2 model. Oechslein et al. [36] and Raman and Dodds [14] found in their studies that UTAUT2 is the best fit model and all constructs taken for the study consistent with the model. Kapoor et al. [24] in their study analyzed and confirmed that 14 innovation attribute sets Image, Social Approval, Observability, Trialability, Visibility, Riskiness, Cost, Behavioral Intention, Voluntariness, Result Demonstrability, Compatibility, Communicability, Complexity, Relative Advantage from Diffusion of technology theory, Perceived Characteristics of Innovating theory [32], and meta-analysis [47] influences the adoption intention of IRCTC mobile ticketing.

2.1 Model Selection for the Study

Diffusion of technology (DOI) [41] suggested five factors of innovation influencing the adaption attitude: compatibility, complexity, observability, relative advantage, and trialability [53]. Though, Crabbe et al. [10] suggested that DOI is more appropriate to examine diffusion across inhabitants, in comparison to individual adoption decisions. As per the Theory of Reasoned Action (TRA) [2] theory individual's behavior is straightforwardly prejudiced by its Behavioral Intention (BI) to apply the behavior, and the causal factors of BI are attitude and subjective standards. Ajzen's [2] Theory of Planned Behavior (TPB) model accumulated perceived behavioral control into TRA.

Technology acceptance model (TAM) model, proposed by Davis et al. [13], was modified from TRA model and recommended that individual's BI affects the real usage of system. In 2003, new model UTAUT was proposed by Venkatesh et al. [51]

included eight different eminent IT acceptance and practice models. This model includes four key factors of BI and usage behavior (UB): Effort expectancy (EE), Facilitating conditions (FC), Performance expectancy (PE) and social influence (SI). Further, Venkatesh et al. [51] recommended that this model included the essences of those recognized models and is proficient to elucidate 70% of the variance in BI. In 2012, Venkatesh et al. [52] proposed extended theory UTAUT2 of UTAUT by including three more factors namely Hedonic Motivation (HM), Price Value (PV) and Habit (HA). Venkatesh et al. [52] claimed that UTAUT2 is the improved theory over UTAUT due to higher percentage value of variance in BI and technology uses. Therefore, we have adopted UTAUT2 model for this study. Also, there is limited study on mobile applications using this model.

3 Concepts, Hypotheses and Research Model

3.1 Direct Effects

PE: Rendering to Venkatesh et al. [51] Performance expectancy is the extent to which a person will achieve the expected goals in work performance by using the technology; EE is described as the extent to which a person will easily operate the system [54, 55]; SI is the degree to which a person is influenced by other individuals' believes that he should use that meticulous technology [32, 46, 52]. Pynoo et al. [38] highlighted that PE and EE are the combination of PU from TAM. Mobile devices especially smart phones are easy to operate [21], because of touch screen which provides more control [5, 7]. Also, if a system is easy to operate, learn and useful, intention to use that system increases [37]. Factors PE, EE and SI have direct positive impact on BI of accepting technology [8, 12, 13, 29, 45, 49–52]. Therefore, the hypotheses are:

> H1: PE stands a direct positive impact on BI to use IRCTC Connect.
> H2: EE stands a direct positive impact on BI to use IRCTC Connect.
> H3: SI stands a direct positive impact on BI to use IRCTC Connect.

FC is described as the resources and technical support available to an individual to adapt the system [51]. In this study it is presumed that FC has a direct positive impact on BI. Moreover, in different studies of mobile apps uses, mobile banking it is revealed that FC has direct positive impact on BI [9]. So the hypothesis is:

> H4: FC stands a direct positive impact on BI to use IRCTC Connect.

3.2 Added Determinants and Moderating Effects

HM according to Brown and Venkatesh [6], is the associated pleasure with the usage of technology; PV according to Dodds et al. [15] is the consumers' intellective transaction among the apparent reimbursement of the applications and the expenses for using them; HA according to Venkatesh et al. [52] sculpted habit which affects directly or indirectly the use of the system and affected by BI; BI is the total efforts an individual is willing to made to achieve a goal and is the best predictor of real behavior. If a users feels pleasure and fun in using a technology, than they achieve enjoyment in using it [16, 27, 52].

According to Venkatesh et al. [52] the perceived benefits after expending the price (PV) on a technology affects the consumers intention to use to technology. Moreover, a user's experience to use similar technologies affect the acceptance of new technologies is able to influence the adoption of a new technology [11]. There is a major impact of HA on mobile technologies and apps [7, 35]. Therefore the next hypotheses are:

H5: HM stands a positive impact on BI to use IRCTC Connect.
H6: PV stands a positive impact on BI to use IRCTC Connect.
H7: HA stands a positive impact on BI to use IRCTC Connect.

There are some moderating factors: age, gender and education. Male and female have diverse viewpoints in technology adaption decisions [52, 56]. According to Li et al. [30], the role of Education level moderator is ignored in previous studies and it is not included in UTAUT [1] and UTAUT2 [52] as a mediator. Therefore the effect of education level is not considered in the study. The study is based on youngsters at MNNIT Allahabad, India campus therefore the impact of age is insignificant. Consequently, the impact of only gender moderator is hypothesized:

H8: The moderating factor gender stands influence on the constructs FC, HM, PV and HA of BI.

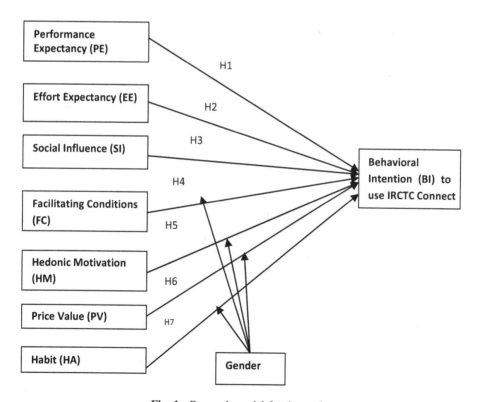

Fig. 1. Research model for the study

Research model developed for this study is shown in Fig. 1. The relationships between the constructs are shown in the research. In the research model all the seven factors (independent variables) are constructs and Gender is role out as the moderating variables. Due to the cross-sectional study, experience is not taken into account and for model simplicity use behavior of consumers is abolished.

4   Research Design

4.1   Data Collection and Sample

The target population was the current users of mobile Internet technology especially users of IRCTC Connect. The survey was conducted in MNNIT Allahabad campus, since the young customers are more interested in new technology and innovation [29] also they are keen to adapt technology related to their entertainment, life style, comfort, inexpensive and less time taken [4], in the context of mobile applications. It is assumed that all the samples taken for the survey are/were users of IRCTC Connect.

To conduct the effective survey, a questionnaire is developed from the original questionnaire published in Venkatesh et al. [52] including all the constructs PE, EE, SI, FC, HM, PV, HA and BI. All the items of the original established questionnaire were devised for researching customer's acceptance of technology.

4.2   Measures

For this study 28 items to measure the constructs were taken. The measure scale used was comprised of 8 constructs namely: PE (4 items), EE (4 items), SI (3 items), FC (4 items), HM (3 items), PV (3 items), HA (4 items) and BI (4 items). In the questionnaire seven-point Likert scale was used in based on, 1 being strongly disagreed and 7 being strongly agreed. 200 questionnaires were randomly distributed in MNNIT Allahabad campus in all departments.

5   Data Analysis

5.1   Demographic Attribute of Respondents

Out of 200 questionnaires, 183 filled questionnaires returned and 159 questionnaires found valid during analysis through SPSS. In 159 valid data maximum respondents were female (54.1%), age below 25 years (82.4%) and educational background of graduation (66%).

5.2   Statistical Analysis

5.2.1   Reliability of the Constructs

Reliability analysis conducted on constructs through evaluating Cronbach's alpha evaluating. Table 2 shows the results of all constructs. For all constructs Cronbach's alpha values are above 0.7. Therefore, all the construct's Cronbach's alpha values indicate the internal consistency of the scale used in the study, confirming the reliability of the scale.

Table 2. Cronbach's alpha value for all items

S.N.	Items	Cronbach's alpha value	S.N.	Items	Cronbach's alpha value
1	PE	0.923	5	HM	0.892
2	EE	0.815	6	PV	0.807
3	SI	0.843	7	HA	0.856
4	FC	0.792	8	BI	0.793

The correlation analysis result is shown in the Table 3. The results indicate that for all construct the correlation coefficients are above than 0.5 except for few constructs PV, HA and HM. Underneath the table it is mentioned that correlation is significant at the level 0.01 and in the results it is found that significance values for all correlation coefficients are 0.00 i.e. less than .01 Therefore there are statistically significant relationship for the behavior intention of the customer to use IRCTC Connect.

Table 3. Correlation table for all the dependent and independent variables

Constructs	Mean	Standard Deviation	PE	EE	SI	FC	HM	PV	HA	BI
PE	5.142	1.178	1							
EE	5.441	0.848	.798**	1						
SI	4.991	1.145	.625**	.538**	1					
FC	5.264	0.953	.721**	.740**	.639**	1				
HM	4.807	1.156	.450**	.393**	.530**	.447**	1			
PV	5.128	1.063	.499**	.504**	.438**	.498**	.405**	1		
HA	4.849	1.186	.499**	.441**	.641**	.536**	.576**	.524**	1	
BI	5.200	1.073	.576**	.535**	.636**	.571**	.530**	.650**	.778**	1

**Correlation is significant at the 0.01 level (2-tailed).

5.2.2 Regression Analysis and Result

a. Regression diagnostics.

The histogram drawn to test the normality, the distribution of residuals was approximately symmetric and unimodal fulfilling the normality test postulation and scatter-plot plot indicated the linearity of the distribution. The non-existence of multicollinearity and heteroscedasticity was examined through Bartlett test of sphericity, since the Barlett's significant value is less than .05 refer Table 4.

The Durbin-Watson value 2.097 found which is nearer to 2, indicating the freedom of error term. The nonexistence of outlier and influential observations examined through the normal p-p plot analysis presenting a straight line against the dependent observation.

Table 4. Bartlett's test results

Bartlett's Test of Sphericity	
Approx. Chi-Square	3270.642
Df	378
Sig.	.000

To determine the relationship between predictors linear regression conducted. The results are presented in Fig. 2 and Table 5. The regression results shows that Performance expectancy has no effect on Behavioral Intention to use IRCTC apps as the p-value of 0.407 is greater than 0.05. Hence, H1 is rejected. Again, the results show that "Effort expectancy" also has no effect on Behavioral Intention to use IRCTC Connect as its p-value = 0.465 (>0.05). Thus, H2 is also rejected. Likewise Facilities Condition and Hedonic motivation has no impact on Behavioral Intention to use IRCTC Connect since the p-values are 0.944 and 0.667 respectively which are greater that p = .05. Therefore, hypotheses H4 and H5 are also rejected. Whilst there is positive impact of Social Influence on Behavioral Intention to use IRCTC Connect as p = .048 (<0.05) which leads to acceptance of H3. Similarly, there are also positive impacts of PV and HA on Behavioral Intention to use IRCTC Connect as the p-values are 0.00 for both the constructs. Therefore, again, the results lead to the acceptance of hypotheses H6 and H7.

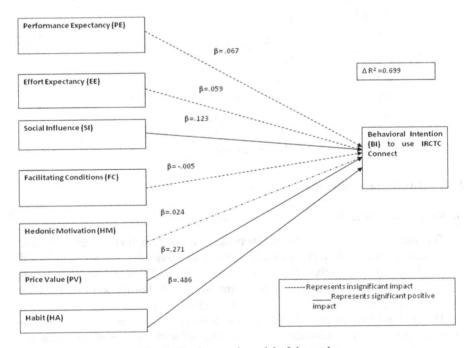

Fig. 2. Final research model of the study

In Table 5, the value of R2 = 0.71 indicates that the predictors account for 71% variation in the customer's Behavioral Intention to use IRCTC Connect. And rest of 29% variation explained by some other predictors. Since the value of F-ratio 53.377 is significant (as p-value = 0.00 is less than 0.05), therefore, there is less than a 0.1% chances that an F-ratio this big would occur if all the null hypotheses were true.

Table 5. Regression model summary

Model summary[b]				
Model	R	R Square	Adjusted R Square	Std. Error of the Estimate
1	.844[a]	.712	.699	.58861
F = 53.377, Sig. = 0.00				

[a]Predictors: (Constant), HA, EE, HM, PV, SI, FC, PE
[b]Dependent Variable: BI

5.2.3 Comparative Significance Based on Regression Output

The unstandardized β-coefficient for the predictors ranges from −0.006 to .440. It is necessary to examine the p-values of predictors before moving to standardized β coefficients. The results from the coefficient Table 5 presents that Habit, Price value and Social Influence have the significant standardized β-coefficients (as p-values are less than 0.05 at 5% significance level). Hence the "Habit" is the mainly essential factor influencing the customer behavioral intention to use IRCTC Connect (with standardized β of 0.486) followed by Price Value (with standardized β of 0.271) and with "Social Influence" having the least impact (with standardized β of 0.123). Table 6 presents the final results of the acceptance or rejection of hypotheses based on regression results.

Regression analysis is used to see the effect of moderator gender on constructs FC, HM, PV and HA. The results found were insignificant coefficients of moderators for four constructs Facilitating Condition, Hedonic Motivation, Price Value and Habit as the p values found was p = 0.200, .05, 0402 and 0.620 (always greater than p = 0.05) respectively. Therefore, it is concluded that the impact of gender is insignificant leading to rejection of hypothesis 8 (H8). Thus the final research model is presented in Fig. 2.

5.3 Discussion

On the basis of results of the regression analysis three constructs 'Social Influence', 'Price Value' and 'Habit' were established significant and direct positive impact on Behavioral Intention to use IRCTC Connect and rest of other four factors did not have any significant positive relationship with Behavioral Intention to use IRCTC Connect (Fig. 2). Also it was found that gender is not moderating the relationship between predictors and outcome.

PE, EE, FC and HM insignificantly influence Behavioral Intention to use IRCTC Connect which is contradiction to the previous studies done by Lewis et al. [25, 26, 28, 35, 52]. The reason for rejection of hypothesis H1, H2, H4 and H5 may be availability of other options. Since MNNIT Allahabad campus is fully Wi-Fi enabled and near to

Table 6. Hypotheses outcome

Hypotheses	β-coefficients	Conclusion
H1: PE stands a direct positive impact on BI to use IRCTC Connect	.067	Rejected
H2: EE stands a direct positive impact on BI to use IRCTC Connect	.059	Rejected
H3: SI stands a direct positive impact on BI to use IRCTC Connect	.123	Accepted
H4: FC stands a direct positive impact on BI to use IRCTC Connect	−.005	Rejected
H5: HM stands a positive impact on BI to use IRCTC Connect	.024	Rejected
H6: PV stands a positive impact on BI to use IRCTC Connect	.271	Accepted
H7: HA stands a positive impact on BI to use IRCTC Connect	.486	Accepted

Prayag Railway Station Allahabad, enables the students to easily access the irctc.co.in website on their mobile or laptop. The IRCTC website is easy to use not only for booking or cancelling tickets but also for other advanced features in comparison to IRCTC Connect. Also, many students prefer to book ticket via PRS because it is on walking distance and validity of waiting tickets booked on counter. Moreover, Tatkal reservation is still not available on IRCTC connect, directing students to book via IRCTC website or PRS. Therefore, the performance of IRCTC Connect, efforts made to use this app as well as resources availability for using this app do not influence student's intention. Additionally, in this competitive epoch when all commercial apps are offering various discounts, IRCTC Connect does not provide any reward points or discounts on booking tickets, creating the lack of interest and fun to use this. IRCTC does not offer any feature which attracts the customers to use this app presents the possible reason behind the insignificant impact of hedonic motivation on consumer's behavioral intention.

SI, PV and HA are the factors which effects the Behavioral Intention to use IRCTC Connect which is consistent with the previous studies. The reason may be youngsters follow their elders and influenced by their peers to use any services and applications. Youngsters use those applications which do not require extra amount to be paid, indicating the direct positive impact of PV on BI.

6 Concluding Remarks

This paper is an attempt to investigate the factors which leads to IRCTC Connect usage. The paper initially discuss the background and motivation of the study presenting how many number of citizens are using IRCTC apps and what factors influence consumer to use IRCTC Connect mobile app. Using UTAUT2 model, new model is proposed with a detailed account of factors of consumer intention to use IRCTC Connect. The results presented that Social Influence, Price Value and Habit are the three factors influence the behavioral intention of people to use IRCTC apps with coefficient β values 0.123, 0.271 and 0.486 respectively out of seven factors of UTAUT2 model rest four factors Performance expectancy, Effort expectancy, Facilitating Condition and Hedonic Motivation do not influence the Behavioral intention to use IRCTC Connect.

This study is useful for IRCTC managers to make strategies and develop and upgrade their apps accordingly. Further this study will be helpful for the researchers to replicate further concern in this area (Mygov APP) and will enrich the literature review. The limitation of the study was the samples (limited to only MNNIT Allahabad) and limited availability of resources for literature review.

References

1. Abu-Shanab, E.A.: Education level as a technology adoption moderator. In: 2011 3rd International Conference on Computer Research and Development (ICCRD), vol. 1, pp. 324–328. IEEE (2011)
2. Ajzen, I., Fishbein, M.: Understanding Attitudes and Predicting Social Behavior. Prentice-Hall, Englewood Cliffs (1980)
3. Antovski, L., Gusev, M.: M-government framework. In: Proceedings EURO mGov, 10–12 (2005)
4. Bigne, E., Ruiz, C., Sanz, S.: The impact of internet user shopping patterns and demographics on consumer mobile buying behaviour. J. Electron. Commerce Res. 6(3), 193 (2005)
5. Brasel, S.A., Gips, J.: Interface psychology: touchscreens change attribute importance, decision criteria, and behavior in online choice. Cyberpsychol. Behav. Soc. Netw. 18(9), 534–538 (2015)
6. Brown, S.A., Venkatesh, V.: Model of adoption of technology in households: a baseline model test and extension incorporating household life cycle. MIS Q. 29, 399–426 (2005)
7. Chang, C.C., Yan, C.F., Tseng, J.S.: Perceived convenience in an extended technology acceptance model: mobile technology and English learning for college students. Australas. J. Educ. Technol. 28(5), 809–826 (2012)
8. Chong, A.Y.L.: Predicting m-commerce adoption determinants: a neural network approach. Expert Syst. Appl. 40(2), 523–530 (2013)
9. Chuang, Y.F.: Pull-and-suck effects in Taiwan mobile phone subscribers switching intentions. Telecommun. Policy 35(2), 128–140 (2011)
10. Crabbe, M., Standing, C., Standing, S., Karjaluoto, H.: An adoption model for mobile banking in Ghana. Int. J. Mobile Commun. 7(5), 515–543 (2009)
11. CRIS: Progress of projects in CRIS. STATUS OF PROJECTS AT A GLANCE, New Delhi, India, January 2016. http://cris.org.in/CRIS/PDF/Progress_of_IT_projects.pdf. Accessed 29 Jan 2016
12. Davis, F.D.: Perceived usefulness, perceived ease of use, and user acceptance of information technology. MIS Q. 13, 319–340 (1989)
13. Davis, F.D., Bagozzi, R.P., Warshaw, P.R.: User acceptance of computer technology: a comparison of two theoretical models. Manage. Sci. 35(8), 982–1003 (1989)
14. Dodds, W.B., Monroe, K.B., Grewal, D.: Effects of price, brand, and store information on buyers' product evaluations. J. Mark. Res. 28, 307–319 (1991)
15. Dodds, W.K., Priscu, J.C.: An inexpensive device for sampling large volumes of lake water from discrete depths. Freshw. Biol. 20(1), 113–115 (1988)

16. Gu, J.C., Lee, S.C., Suh, Y.H.: Determinants of behavioral intention to mobile banking. Expert Syst. Appl. **36**(9), 11605–11616 (2009)
17. Hew, J.J., Lee, V.H., Ooi, K.B., Wei, J.: What catalyses mobile apps usage intention: an empirical analysis. Ind. Manag. Data Syst. **115**(7), 1269–1291 (2015)
18. IAMAI: Internet and Mobile Association of India 11th Annual Report 2014-15. Dr. Subho Ray on behalf of IAMAI, New Delhi, September 2015
19. IRCTC: IRCTC 16 Annual Report 2014-2015. 22. Vijaylakshmi Printing Works Pvt. Ltd., New Delhi, India, 9 July 2015. Accessed 23 Jan 2016
20. irctc.com.: IRCTC: A progress profile (2002). http://irctc.com/Company_Profile.html. Accessed Sunday Jan 2016
21. Islam, R., Islam, R., Mazumder, T.: Mobile application and its global impact. Int. J. Eng. Technol. IJET-IJENS **10**(6), 72–78 (2010)
22. Kailasam, R.: m-Governance… Leveraging Mobile Technology to extend the reach of e-Governance. In: Proceedings of the TRAI Conference on Mobile Applications for Inclusive Growth and Sustainable Development (2010)
23. Kang, S.: Factors influencing intention of mobile application use. Int. J. Mobile Commun. **12**(4), 360–379 (2014)
24. Kapoor, K.K., Dwivedi, Y.K., Williams, M.D.: IRCTC mobile ticketing adoption in an Indian context. Int. J. Indian Cult. Bus. Manage. **11**(2), 155–183 (2015)
25. Kapoor, K.K., Dwivedi, Y.K., Williams, M.D.: Empirical examination of the role of three sets of innovation attributes for determining adoption of IRCTC mobile ticketing service. Inf. Syst. Manage. **32**(2), 153–173 (2015)
26. Lewis, K.N., Palmer, A., Moll, A.: Predicting young consumer's take up of mobile banking services. Int. J. Bank Mark. **28**(5), 410–432 (2010)
27. Leong, L.Y., Ooi, K.B., Chong, A.Y.L., Lin, B.: Modeling the stimulators of the behavioral intention to use mobile entertainment: does gender really matter? Comput. Hum. Behav. **29**(5), 2109–2121 (2013)
28. Li, H., Kuo, C., Rusell, M.G.: The impact of perceived channel utilities, shopping orientations, and demographics on the consumer's online buying behavior. J. Comput.-Mediated Commun. **5**(2) (1999)
29. Luo, X., Li, H., Zhang, J., Shim, J.P.: Examining multi-dimensional trust and multi-faceted risk in initial acceptance of emerging technologies: an empirical study of mobile banking services. Decis. Support Syst. **49**(2), 222–234 (2010)
30. Melone, N.P.: A theoretical assessment of the user-satisfaction construct in information systems research. Manage. Sci. **36**(1), 76–91 (1990)
31. Mobile Seva: Mobile Seva Appstore, January 2016. https://apps.mgov.gov.in/liveapp.do. Accessed 25 Jan 2016
32. Moore, G.C., Benbasat, I.: Development of an instrument to measure the perceptions of adopting an information technology innovation. Inf. Syst. Res. **2**(3), 192–222 (1991)
33. MyGov: MyGov.in. https://mygov.in/overview/. Accessed 25 Jan 2016
34. mytrainstatus.com: IRCTC Makes 35 seconds to Wait to Book Tickets, January 2016. https://mytrainstatus.com/blog/irctc-makes-35-seconds-to-wait-to-book-tickets/. Accessed 28 Jan 2016
35. Nikou, S., Bouwman, H.: Ubiquitous use of mobile social network services. Telematics Inform. **31**(3), 422–433 (2014)
36. Oechslein, O., Fleischmann, M., Hess, T.: An application of UTAUT2 on social recommender systems: incorporating social information for performance expectancy. In: 2014 47th Hawaii International Conference on System Sciences (HICSS), pp. 3297–3306. IEEE (2014)

37. Pikkarainen, T., Pikkarainen, K., Karjaluoto, H., Pahnila, S.: Consumer acceptance of online banking: an extension of the technology acceptance model. Internet Res. **14**(3), 224–235 (2004)
38. Pynoo, B., Devolder, P., Tondeur, J., Van Braak, J., Duyck, W., Duyck, P.: Predicting secondary school teachers' acceptance and use of a digital learning environment: a cross-sectional study. Comput. Hum. Behav. **27**(1), 568–575 (2011)
39. Raman, A., Don, Y.: Preservice teachers' acceptance of learning management software: an application of the UTAUT2 Model. Int. Educ. Stud. **6**(7), 157 (2013)
40. Reese Bomhold, C.: Educational use of smart phone technology: a survey of mobile phone application use by undergraduate university students. Program **47**(4), 424–436 (2013)
41. Rogers, E.M.: Diffusion of Innovations: modifications of a model for telecommunications. Die Diffusion von Innovationen in der Telekommunikation **17**, 25–38 (1995)
42. Rogers, E.M.: Diffusion of Innovations, 5th edn. The Free Press, New York (2003)
43. Sahney, S., Ghosh, K., Shrivastava, A.: "Buyer's motivation" for online buying: an empirical case of railway e-ticketing in Indian context. J. Asia Bus. Stud. **8**(1), 43–64 (2013)
44. Sahney, S., Ghosh, K., Shrivastava, A: Conceptualizing consumer "trust" in online buying behaviour: an empirical inquiry and model development in Indian context. J. Asia Bus. Stud. **7**(3), 278–298 (2013b). http://dx.doi.org/10.1108/JABS-Jul-2011-0038
45. Taylor, S., Todd, P.A.: Understanding information technology usage: a test of competing models. Inf. Syst. Res. **6**(2), 144–176 (1995)
46. Thompson, R.L., Higgins, C.A., Howell, J.M.: Personal computing: toward a conceptual model of utilization. MIS Q. **15**, 125–143 (1991)
47. Tornatzky, L.G., Klein, K.J.: Innovation characteristics and innovation adoption-implementation: a meta-analysis of findings. IEEE Trans. Eng. Manage. **1**, 28–45 (1982)
48. TRAI: Telecom regulatory authority of India. TRAI, Delhi (2015)
49. Venkatesh, V., Davis, F.D.: A theoretical extension of the technology acceptance model: four longitudinal field studies. Manage. Sci. **46**(2), 186–204 (2000)
50. Venkatesh, V., Morris, M.G.: Why don't men ever stop to ask for directions? Gender, social influence, and their role in technology acceptance and usage behavior. MIS Q. **24**, 115–139 (2000)
51. Venkatesh, V., Morris, M.G., Davis, G.B., Davis, F.D.: User acceptance of information technology: toward a unified view. MIS Q. **27**, 425–478 (2003)
52. Venkatesh, V., Thong, J.Y., Xu, X.: Consumer acceptance and use of information technology: extending the unified theory of acceptance and use of technology. MIS Q. **36**(1), 157–178 (2003)
53. Yahya, M., Nadzar, F., Masrek, N., Rahman, B.A.: Determinants of UTAUT in measuring user acceptance of e-Syariah portal in syariah courts in Malaysia. In: The 2nd International Research Symposium in Service Management Yogyakarta, Indonesia, July 2011
54. Yang, K.C.: Exploring factors affecting the adoption of mobile commerce in Singapore. Telematics Inform. **22**(3), 257–277 (2005)
55. Zhou, T., Lu, Y., Wang, B.: Integrating TTF and UTAUT to explain mobile banking user adoption. Comput. Hum. Behav. **26**(4), 760–767 (2010)

Experiences from Assistive Technology Services and Their Delivery in Finland

Anne-Marie Tuikka[✉] and Neeraj Sachdeva

Turku School of Economics, University of Turku, Turku, Finland
amstou@utu.fi

Abstract. The purpose of this article is to understand and document the level and quality of assistive technology (AT) driven rehabilitative support offered to people with impairments within Finland. Availability, accessibility and adoption of assistive technologies are of interest to this study. Currently public institutions, such as city hospitals and national social security institution, offer AT services generally on the basis of age, employment and individual needs. The main research question is, how people with impairments and their relatives perceive assistive technology delivery, use as well as continued adoption? Based on data, the different aspects of AT service delivery model and its relationship to rehabilitation process are described.

The empirical data is gathered through interviews and official documents including appropriate laws and guidelines published by public institutions. Analysis of the data highlights stages within the current system where negative experiences create distrust and dissatisfaction among AT adopters. These experiences are categorized to themes and stages which may be used for analyzing AT services and its relation to rehabilitation in future research. Further research would be needed to compare the applicability of the defined stages in analyzing delivering AT services in other countries – both similar and different to Finland.

Keywords: Assistive technology · Service delivery model · Finland · Visual impairments · The autism spectrum

1 Introduction

People with impairments have found numerous uses for technologies in their lives – helping them live a normal life, regardless of their impairments. Often, technologies that "assist" in improving quality of life, especially for the people with impairments, are classified as "assistive technologies" (AT). Hersh [4] has defined the role of assistive technology in terms of social model as "overcoming the gap between what disabled people want to do and what the existing social infrastructure allows them to do". AT for people with severe visual impairments include screen and braille readers, walking sticks for navigation and hearing aids; whereas AT for people with neurobiological impairments (such as the autism spectrum) include electronic communication aids, communication books and function cards. However, knowing about, obtaining and continually

© IFIP International Federation for Information Processing 2017
Published by Springer International Publishing AG 2017. All Rights Reserved
A.K. Kar et al. (Eds.): I3E 2017, LNCS 10595, pp. 16–22, 2017.
DOI: 10.1007/978-3-319-68557-1_2

using these technologies is usually not as simple as walking into an Apple store and ordering a new device. Many devices don't have built-in assistance modules [5], which necessitates purchase and use of an additional technologies. Even though some communication applications can be accessed through Apple store, they are usually expensive and they often lack translation to smaller language groups such as Finnish or Swedish (both official languages of Finland).

This article presents preliminary results from an ongoing research project, which concentrates on studying the assistive technology service delivery model in Finland and experiences related to it. In this article, various assistive and rehabilitation technology service delivery models are evaluated to recognize current state of Finnish assistive technology service delivery model (later referred as AT service delivery model). Adya et al. [1] have previously analyzed different AT service delivery models, focusing on charity-based, community-based rehabilitation, individual empowerment, entrepreneurial, globalization and universal design model. Bartfai and Boman [2] have analyzed policies concerning AT and home modification services for impaired people in Sweden. The Finnish AT service delivery model – slightly different to previously mentioned models – is analyzed through empirical data which is collected as a part of this research project.

The main research question is, how people with impairments and their relatives perceive assistive technology delivery, use, and continued adoption? To answer to this question, three sets of stakeholders are interviewed – people with impairments who need and use assistive technology, parents of children with impairments, and service providers who recommend and provide assistive technology and relevant training. The semi-structured interviews focus on the experiences of accessing, applying and using assistive technology; before, during and after the rehabilitation process. At this point of the project, total amount of interviews and interviewees is ten. Most of the interviews were done face-to-face (n = 9) and one of them was done through phone.

In following section, we describe the context of delivering AT services in Finland. Then we continue by analyzing the experiences of Finnish assistive technology users, their parents and the professionals. We finish with the discussion about the future of Finnish AT service delivery model and its requirements in different stages of disability.

2 Assistive Technology Service Delivery Model in Finland

There are multiple AT service delivery models in Finland. Central to all the models is the main principle that a person should be able to get any assistive technology which is prescribed to them, for free. The AT and the training related to its use are paid by different organization in different cases.

In general, city is responsible for offering or covering the cost of AT for its citizen if AT is used for medical rehabilitation. This can be understood from the law on health care [8] which states that city is in charge of organizing medical rehabilitation for its citizens, when their rehabilitation is not covered by the national social security institution named as KELA. For this reason, city needs to organize AT for any person who is under the age of 13 or a person over 65 years, because their medical rehabilitation is never covered by KELA. In the case of the person who is 13 to 65 years old, KELA is responsible for covering the cost of the assistive technology which is needed to maintain person's abilities to work and to study [6, 9]. In the case of someone who has got impaired as a consequence of work accident, travel accident or another kind of accident covered by the private insurance, the private insurance company should pay for the prescribed assistive technology and the training related to it.

When city is responsible for organizing AT for its citizens, citizen usually has a possibility to get the AT through public hospital which is funded by the city or sometimes by multiple cities within same geographical area. To get the assistive technology, the patient needs to have prescription for certain kind of assistive technology from the doctor who is responsible for their rehabilitation. However, the final decision about the specific type of assistive technology such as certain device or particular application is often done by the professionals working in the unit which is specialized on AT services. Most often the assistive technology is loaned to the person who needs it. However, the loaning time may be so long that the assistive technology is never transferred to anyone else after it is returned. In these cases, the assistive technology is practically given to the person who needs it.

In the case of KELA, the process is quite different. To get KELA to support the cost of the assistive technology, the person needs to have prescription from a doctor to show that they need this technology for their medical rehabilitation. After receiving the prescription, they can apply funding from KELA. After they have received the positive decision from KELA, they can buy the technology and KELA will refund the purchase amount to them. In some cases, KELA can decide not cover the full cost of the technology because the person chose a technology which is too expensive compared with the technology which would have satisfied the requirements of their medical rehabilitation.

All of the previously mentioned cases focus on medical rehabilitation. In the case of AT which is not needed for medical rehabilitation, it is possible to get financial support from the social services within a certain city or a municipality. This type of AT might be covered if they are needed for free time activities or to support independent living. However, only half of the cost of the AT is covered by social services. The other half must be covered by the person who needs the technology [9].

3   Stakeholder Perspectives

This section shares perspectives on stakeholders' experience with assistive technology service delivery in Finland. These stakeholders include AT users who have sever visual impairment, parents of children within the autism spectrum and service providers. Some of the service providers are also visually impaired, and regular users of assistive technologies. The experiences of different stakeholder groups have been grouped based on three themes commonly identified in the data. These themes are availability, accessibility and adoption of AT. Availability refers to the knowledge about different technologies and services related to them. Accessibility refers to a person's possibilities to get the AT they need. Adoption refers to communication between service providers and the experiences from continued usage of AT. Each perspective is further classified as either positive, neutral or negative experience.

3.1   On Availability

Representatives of different stakeholder groups appear to disagree whether there is enough information about the AT services. It seems, that AT availability can be improved by making more resources and opportunities for AT education available. Here is what the participants had to say:

"There should be some resource/forum for blind people. E.g. the magazine for the blind association – it could have section about new technologies." - Legally blind assistive technology user 1, negative experience

"…the people in the rehabilitation group, they know exactly what they have (in reference to assistive technologies available)." - Service provider 4, positive experience

Finland is quite far ahead in terms of technology availability. But, there are restrictions. It's easier to get these technologies if you have a job or are studying. - Service provider 5, positive experience.

3.2   On Accessibility

Most people with impairments first learn about ways to access AT via a professional who offers more insights into what's accessible. In some cases, bureaucracy (and other factors) can be an impediment to assistive technology access, as shared here:

"2–3 different types of screen readers were available in the market. JAWS was a good choice, but it was not possible to buy, as it was expensive and I had to get reimbursement and permission from KELA or insurance company, which could take 2 months." - Legally blind assistive technology user 1, negative experience

"I don't think it (assistive technology design) is a question of attitude. I think they (designers and developers) don't know that there are also other groups that can't use them (assistive technology) the same way as normal users use them." - Legally blind assistive technology user 2, neutral experience

"If you have workplace or are studying at university, it's easy to get it (screen readers), otherwise it's not so easy." - Service Provider 3, negative experience

"The speak therapist (who is caring for the child and is a private entrepreneur) told us about the devices. She recommended them to the recommending therapist (who works in the city). Naturally, the process is really complicated." - Parent 1, negative experience.

3.3   On Adoption

Positive adoption and continued use is often the end goal of any assistive technology service. For this reason, there are IT trainers and installers for visually impaired people who need AT. We have interviewed one of them (Service Provider 1), who is the only Linux trainer in Finland, and therefore has customers from (different) parts of Finland. There is also portal related to accessibility, although, it "has been a little bit quiet" according to Service Provider 2, who is responsible for maintaining it.

The parents of children within the autism spectrum have got the training for their child's AT through public hospital, which has special unit focusing on AT services. Parent 1 had been very happy with their services whereas Parent 2 had faced problems when their AT got broken. She said: "It was a device which should not have got broken if the child is observed when using it. For this reason, we should have written a report to explain, how it got broken."

Experiences from the adoption of AT were generally positive, as stated here:

"He trained with the speak therapist. He trained with us. He is now hundred times better with the device than me or his father." - Parent 1, positive experience

"The screen reader is gives me independence in general tasks. You get access to internet and you can pay your bills in the bank or do just anything you want without help from someone else." - Service Provider 3, positive experience.

4   Discussion

Analysis of data highlights the three themes – availability, accessibility and adoption (Fig. 1) – which affect the delivery of assistive technologies and services (e.g. training) related to them. Availability affects people regardless of where they live. Accessibility pertains individually to people and is impacted by their ability to access an assistive technology. Finally, adoption refers to the frequency and continuity of assistive technology use, and can be impacted by quality of the technology and associated training. Each theme has a common element – interaction – between the stakeholders. In this scenario stakeholders include people, who need AT, care givers of people, who need AT, and people who provide AT and services related to it.

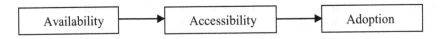

Fig. 1. Themes of assistive technology service delivery

Negative experiences can generally create distrust and dissatisfaction among technology adopters, which can create further negative impact on consumption decisions [3, 7]. While the interviews did not highlight any exclusive distrust or dissatisfaction, the interviewees were apprehensive of using new technology unless they had thoroughly reviewed it, or it had been strongly recommended by someone else. This is contradictory behavior when compared with the technology adoption generally visible in the modern world of annual cycle of new iPhones and operating systems. If type of behavior could be detected among other users of AT in different contexts, it might be possible to deduce that people with impairments and their parents generally need bigger time investment with assistive technologies, and hence prefer to access and adopt assistive technology as and when they need – and not when it becomes available.

Based on the interviews, a clearer insight into the delivery cycles of assistive technology services was obtained, and it can be classified into three stages:

Pre-Disability: In instances where a person is expected to face one or the other form of disability, they should be offered enough information and education on what to expect.

Ideally, this person should be able to consult with doctors and prepare for an easier transition post-disability, and ensure that they can continue living similar or even better quality of life. However, due to somewhat untimely nature of some disabilities, this might not apply in each case.

Immediately Post-Disability: During this stage, it is crucial to enable a person to receive easy access to AT. For example, someone who has just lost vision should be offered immediate support to purchase a screen reader or braille reader.

Support Post-Disability: Continued support for older and newer technologies and services is essential to keep adoption rate high as well as continue a level of comfort.

5 Conclusion

The Finnish society provides a rich level of assistive technology based rehabilitation to those that need it. This research project has started to study the experiences of different stakeholders on the accessibility, availability and adoption of AT in Finland. However, the current study is limited by the small number of representatives, who have been interviewed. Further interviews with people with impairments, their parents and service providers dealing with different impairments at different stages of AT lifecycle could offer more insights and further develop the three themes – availability, accessibility and adoption – to create a solid framework which could be employed to different contexts. Future research on the assistive technology service delivery model in the Finnish context is also needed, because the governance of health care and social care services are changing in Finland. How these changes affect the Finnish assistive technology service delivery model, remains to be seen.

References

1. Adya, M., Samant, D., Scherer, M.J., Killeen, M., Morris, M.W.: Assistive/rehabilitation technology, disability, and service delivery models. Cogn. Process. **13**(Suppl 1), S75–S78 (2012). doi:10.1007/s10339-012-0466-8
2. Bartfai, A., Boman, I.-L.: Policies concerning assistive technology and home modification services for people with physical and cognitive disabilities in Sweden. NeuroRehabilitation **28**(3), 303–308 (2011). doi:10.3233/NRE-2011-0658
3. Frankoff, D.J.: Experiences of families seeking funding for assistive technologies for children with disabilities: awareness of legal mandates. In: Efficacy of Assistive Technology Interventions. Advances in Special Education Technology, vol. 1, pp. 229–258. Emerald Group Publishing Limited (2015). doi:10.1108/S2056-769320150000001009
4. Hersh, M., Johnson, M.A.: Assistive Technology for Visually Impaired and Blind People. Springer, London. http://www.springer.com/gp/book/9781846288661. Accessed 26 Apr 2017
5. Hitchcock, C., Stahl, S.: Assistive technology, universal design, universal design for learning: improved learning opportunities. J. Special Educ. Technol. **18**(4), 45–52 (2003). doi:10.1177/016264340301800404
6. KELA: Vaativa lääkinnällinen kuntoutus ja palvelut. http://www.kela.fi/vaativan-laakinnallisen-kuntoutuksen-palvelut. Accessed 30 Apr 2017
7. Ou, C.X., Sia, C.L.: Consumer trust and distrust: an issue of website design. Int. J. Hum. Comput. Stud. **68**(12), 913–934 (2010). doi:10.1016/j.ijhcs.2010.08.003

8. Terveydenhuoltolaki 30.12.2010/1326. Section 3, 29 §. http://www.finlex.fi/fi/laki/ajantasa/2010/20101326?search[type]=pika&search[pika]=terveydenhuoltolaki#L3P29. Accessed 30 Apr 2017
9. THL: Apuvälinepalvelujen työnjako. In Vammaispalvelujen käsikirja. https://www.thl.fi/fi/web/vammaispalvelujen-kasikirja/itsenaisen-elaman-tuki/apuvalineet/apuvalinepalvelujen-tyonjako. Accessed 30 Apr 2017

Evaluating Multi-dimensional Risk for Digital Services in Smart Cities

Syed Ziaul Mustafa[1(✉)] and Arpan Kumar Kar[2]

[1] Center of Excellence in Cyber Systems and Information Assurance (CoE-CSIA),
Indian Institute of Technology Delhi, New Delhi 110016, India
mustafa.ziaul@gmail.com
[2] Department of Management Studies, Indian Institute of Technology Delhi,
New Delhi 110016, India
arpan_kar@yahoo.co.in

Abstract. In current times, emerging economies are providing digital services to its citizen through public or private organization. Literature indicates that digital services are facing major challenges with respect to its adoption among relevant users groups, largely due to the perceived risks surrounding digital services. A purposive sampling methodology was adopted for the empirical validation of the framework among user groups. With the use of Generalized Analytic Network Process (GANP), prioritization of different dimensions of risk has been illustrated. The result indicates that dimensions like privacy risk, performance risk and financial risk are the most important risk across digital services models. However physical risk, social risk, psychological risk and time risk are comparatively less important risk across digital services. This research also finds out that the end users are reluctant to provide their personal information. The sample size is relatively small which limits generalizability of results. However an application of GANP has been showcased for empirical research. The research outcome can help managers in deciding which dimensions of risk are more important for digital service delivery. This study focuses on the different facets of risk perceived by consumers towards the digital services available in smart cities. Perceived risk dimensions like privacy risk, performance risk, financial risk, physical risk, social risk, psychological risk and time risk, have shown that there is a need to prioritize these risk to the digital services which is offered to the residents of the smart cities.

Keywords: Information risk · Digital services · Smart cities · Perceived risk · Analytic Network Process · Emerging economies

1 Introduction

The concept of "smart city" has emerged from the concept of "Intelligent Cities". The basic idea of smart cities is to use the existing resources in a "smarter" way. Smart cities provide ICTs infrastructure and digital services which poses risk while sharing information with the third party [42]. These risk can be classified as privacy, performance,

A.K. Kar et al. (Eds.): I3E 2017, LNCS 10595, pp. 23–32, 2017.
DOI: 10.1007/978-3-319-68557-1_3

financial, physical, social, psychological, and time risk [30]. Smart cities are sustainable, creative and livable cities. It is part of government vision for the development of urban habitats through smart cities. In order to develop smart cities, experts from various fields are needed such as consultants, marketing specialists, corporations and officials [40]. These entities should take an active role in provisioning and delivering the digital services which are used by the citizens of the smart cities. The concept of smart cities can be seen as an assemblage of Information and Communication Technologies (ICTs), cyber-physical systems, urban infrastructure, sustainable process and the practices which aims to increase the administrative efficiency, competitiveness and socio-economic inclusion [9, 10]. A smart city needed to solve the issues such as ICTs and Digital services in order to improve the quality of life [42].

The world is moving towards the evolution of urbanization through smart cities. In order to make a smart city, various innovations related to information technology pose a threat to security and privacy. People in smart cities are already connected with various electronic gadgets such as mobile phones and laptops. The use of services are changing with new digital services introduced. In smart cities, many smart appliances, smart devices and smart energy meters have been used which makes the user reluctant to share the information through these digital services. As the number of digital services increases the risk associated with its use also increases [13]. Since 2011, the contribution to the smart cities has been critically scrutinized from different factors such as political economy, science and technology, ideological critiques and socio-economical [40]. In general smart cities create a relation between the usages of technology in a socio-economical ecosystem. In our study, we are focusing on the management of risk in digital services, where literature is still at a nascent stage. Integration of digital services in smart cities lengthy, complex and often requires dispersed resources. There are few publications which indicates the Integration of IT services such as digital services in smart city system [34].

In this study, multi-dimensional nature of risk such as privacy risk, performance risk, financial risk, Physical risk, social risk, psychological risk and time risk has been explored in the context of digital services. Further the study highlights an application of an emerging methodology based on the Generalised Analytic Network Process (GANP) for empirical research for prioritization, which has not been explored till now [44].

This paper Evaluate the raking of the different dimensions of the risk while suing digital services. The organization of the paper are as follows. Section 2 provides a review of the study done on Perceived risk to evaluate the various consumer related services. Sections 3 describe the methodology used to prioritize and rank the multi-dimensions of perceived risk. This section also provides data analysis and interpretation, Cronbach's alpha, exploratory factor analysis, inter-item correlation matrix of variables. Further it provides the ranking of the dimension of the perceived risk. Section 4 discusses the findings of the research, Sects. 5 concludes the paper.

2 Literature Review

A detailed review of literature has been conducted to understand the domain of risk in digital services better. With the increase in population of the urban area, the people are making strategies in order to improve the livings in urban areas. Further the use of digital services which makes the city to improve the existing information and communication technologies (ICTs). In subsequent sections, we first explore the literature surrounding smart cities, then explore the literature surrounding digital services and finally explore perceived risk [1] in such services.

2.1 Smart Cities

Smart city concept was introduced first in 1990s [2, 3, 12, 40]. There is no consistent definition of smart city till now which can fit the all the dimensions of smart city [2, 3, 5, 24, 25, 33, 41]. The concept of smart city has been explained as the utilization of human and technological capital for the development of urban agglomeration [3]. Various theoretical and managerial conceptualization has been introduced and the concepts of smart cities have gained the widest recognition among the urban researchers and the practitioners.

Major dimension of smart city are smart people, smart economy, smart mobility, smart living, smart governance and smart environment [2, 5, 9, 10, 24, 28, 42].

Digital services forms an integral part of smart cities, where residents are empowered to access these services using ICTs. Across all the dimensions of smart cities, digital services play an important role for the end consumers to realize the benefits envisioned from these smart cities.

2.2 Digital Services

There are various definitions of digital services in the literature [4, 7, 20]. The generic definition is "services or resources accessed and/or provided via digital transaction." [18]. With the use of digital services, the city will have a high quality of life which will lead to smart governance [25]. So the risk of sharing the personal information while using digital service make ends user afraid of data getting misused [22].

Digital services are accessed via internet with the use of an interactive software. It is generally referred as an information asset which is made available through internet. The most sought examples of digital services is online purchasing, banking and financial portfolio management. Digital services have been classified in literature based on the value they provide, their model of service delivery and parameters for assessment. For example, categorization of digital service as technology-assisted consumer contact, technology-facilitated consumer contact, technology-mediated consumer contact and technology generated consumer contact, based on the nature of interaction between the consumer, the service provider and technology [17]. The digital services may be categorised on the basis of delivery, maturity, malleability (provider and consumer of service), pricing and funding [43], which again strive to meet business, interaction and technological objectives. Again digital services classification done by the governments are often done on the nature of benefits. Across these digital services, it has been highlighted that adoption is significantly affected by the perception of risk in such services [15, 26]; which is why a deeper exploration is required in the domain of risk in digital services.

2.3 Risk in Digital Services

Bauer has introduced the concept of risk and defined it as "a combination of uncertainty plus serious of outcome involved" whereas "the expectation of losses associated with the purchase and act as an inhibitor to purchase behavior" has been defined by [36]. Perceived risk is generally thought of as felt uncertainty with respect to the negative consequences of using a product or service [15].

The consumers are also very much sensitive about the privacy and security of the products or services which they purchase or consume through the internet [6, 9, 39]. The reason behind it was the fear of getting theft of the product or getting personal information misused by the company [14, 31, 32, 35]. The seven dimensions of perceived risk are as follows.

1. Privacy risk. The risk associated with the loss of personal information without your permission.
2. Performance risk. The possibility that the services or products is not delivering the desired benefits as it was advertised and designed.
3. Financial risk. The price associated with the purchase of products or services and the subsequent maintenance cost associated with it.
4. Physical risk. The risk associated with the safety of consumers while using product or services.
5. Social risk. The risk associated with the use of product or service leads to embarrassment in social media.
6. Psychological risk. The risk that using of the product or services will decrease the self-image of the consumer.
7. Time risk. The lost time associated with bad purchase decision such as researching and purchasing a product or services.

3 Methodology

Each dimensions of risk such as privacy risk, performance risk, financial risk, physical risk, social risk, psychological risk and time risk has been mapped to digital services. The data has been collected from the end users who are using digital services in two form: online and offline. The survey forms has been circulated to the end users of the smart cities. For proceeding with the analysis, data on preferences needed to be elicited through structured questionnaires from experienced user groups of the digital services residing in smart cities. The data was captured from the smart cities in the national capital region of India, where the access and usage of digital services by the residents was among the top three in the country. The targeted user groups had used at least two different models of digital services out of the four models of service delivery proposed by [17].

A purposive sampling methodology was adopted so that the elicited responses would have more richness and represent the concerns of user groups who are more frequent in using the digital services. Over 441 respondents were approached for administering the questionnaire through a combination of online and offline channels of communication. Out of this, only 100 respondent data could be collected which had the requisite degree of consistency, needed for the subsequent analysis.

During the review of literature, it has been seen that various authors have used different methodologies to evaluate perceived risk in different contexts. Data on preferences needed to be elicited through structured questionnaires from user groups of the digital services residing in smart cities. After the collection of data, analysis has be done using Generalized Analytic Network Process (GANP) proposed by [44] for prioritization of perceived risk dimension. This study also highlights the application of the GANP for prioritization of empirical data. It is an extension of Analytic Network Process (ANP) methodology which is used for Multi Criteria Decision Making (MCDM) to obtain the priorities of the compared element in a network hierarchy [38].

By using the GANP, this study further highlights how empirically prioritization of alternatives, which may not be free of exigencies and internal influences, may be done using this approach. While such empirical prioritization based on surveys on specific user groups has been done in past literature [21, 27] using the Analytic Hierarchy Process (AHP), no study has attempted to do the same using the GANP. The use of AHP becomes restricted when alternatives may also have an impact on one other and are not mutually independent. Hence the proposed approach also highlights the application of a new methodology in the context of risk assessment of digital services.

While following the approach of the GANP, first the Complex Comparison Matrix (CCM) is developed based on the judgment on 1–9 scale [21, 27]. The decision maker's judgment is crisp value which describes the relationship between paired comparisons. Among similar approaches, there are over 20 approaches for prioritization of preferences or judgments [23], however very few of these recent approaches have been used for empirical case studies.

3.1 Data Analysis and Interpretation

It has been noticed that end user are reluctant to provide their personal information [6, 9, 39]. In the survey, 97% respondent are male where as 3% are females. The total respondents' age group varies in such a way that it is 24% from 16–20 years of age group, 53% from 21–25 years of age group, 15% from 26–30 years of age group, 4% from 31–35 years of age group and 2% from 46–50 years of age group. The education qualification of the responds are such that 41% are having bachelor degree, 39% are having Master's degree, 8% are having doctorate degree and 12% have done higher secondary only. The employment status of the respondent are such that 10% belongs to under employment, 4% belongs to self-employed, 86% are still student. The employment types of the respondent are such that 20% are in Government sector, 4% are in private sector, 3% are having their own business and NGOs while 70% are unemployed. The average duration (in months) during which the respondent were using digital services is 51 months.

Reliability analysis was conducted using Cronbach's alpha to evaluate the value of all the variables and it is found to be 0.830. The composite reliability and Cronbach's alpha values of 0.6 or greater are considered to the acceptable [19]. The values are as shown in the Table 1.

Table 1. List of variables

Risk dimension	Variable ID	Risk measurement indicators	Cronbach alpha
Privacy risk	V_C	What are the chances that your personal information and privacy will get compromised?	0.662
	V_D	What are the chances that the personal information will be used while using digital service without your knowledge?	
	V_E	If I use the digital service, hackers will take control of my account	
Performance risk	V_A	Services offered is not able to perform as designed and creates problem for you	0.603
	V_B	Service Provider may not perform well and process transactions correctly	
Financial risk	V_P	What are the chances that you will lose your money by using these services?	0.760
	V_Q	Using banking services will lead to financial loss for me	
	V_R	Using the service subjects your bank account to financial risk	
Physical risk	V_K	Using these digital service poses a threat to my health	0.871
	V_L	If you do NOT use service, you will live for a long time	
	V_M	If I use service, I will get ill	
	V_N	If I use service, I will be exposed to harmful radiation	
	V_O	If I use this service, I will damage my brain	
Social risk	V_H	What are the chances that others thinking will negatively affect by using the services?	0.797
	V_I	With the use of digital services, there will be social loss for me because my relatives and friends will think less highly of me	
Psychological risk	V_F	These digital services will not fit well with my self-image.	0.737
	V_G	With the use of digital services, there will be a psychological loss for me since it will not fit with my self-image	
Time risk	V_J	With the use of digital services there will be a loss of time because of inconvenience to me	0.825

After aggregating all the normalized value from the end user, we get the final priority. Sub-dimension specific priority and dimension level priority, computed using the GANP as illustrated in Table 2. It has been found that the privacy risk has first priority and time risk has the last priority. The priority of the risk are for the digital services from the end user perspective. The priority of the risk dimensions are illustrated in the Table 2.

Table 2. Priority of the different dimensions of Risk

Priority of variable	Priority value	Geometric mean	Type of risk	Rank
V_D	0.100899	0.096011	Privacy risk	1
V_C	0.095285			
V_E	0.092056			
V_B	0.065001	0.063244	Performance risk	2
V_A	0.061535			
V_R	0.062688	0.053748	Financial risk	3
V_P	0.061682			
V_Q	0.040156			
V_K	0.058852	0.043965	Physical risk	4
V_N	0.050532			
V_L	0.044987			
V_M	0.029691			
V_O	0.04135			
V_H	0.043696	0.040426	Social risk	5
V_I	0.037401			
V_F	0.040694	0.038126	Psychological risk	6
V_G	0.035721			
V_J	0.037773	0.037773	Time risk	7

4   Discussion

Previous research has focused on the different dimension of the risk for the adoption of e-services such as given by [11] has focused on the financial risk, social risk, privacy risk, and psychological risk for the adoption of technology has focused on the financial risk, psychological risk, privacy risk, time risk, performance risk, and overall risk in order to evaluate the adoption of e-services [15]. The study by [1] has taken financial risk, privacy risk, psychological risk, and performance risk dimensions of the perceived risk to illustrate how adoption of mobile banking influence the consumer.

In a study done by [8], privacy risk, source risk and performance risk were are first, second and third most important dimensions of risk while time risk, financial risk and social risk were the sixth, seventh and eight position in the raking of all the eight dimensions of risk. In contract to our findings says that privacy risk, performance risk and financial risk are the first, second and third most important dimensions of perceived risk as shown in Table 2. In a study done by [26], it shows that the security, time, financial, social, and performance risk negatively affects the adoption of online banking services. It also shows that security, financial and performance risk are the top most important risk factor where as social and time risk are fourth and fifth most important risk. The study has taken only four dimensions of the perceived risk and concluded that performance risk are the most important risk dimensions followed by financial risk, psychological risk and time risk during internet shopping [16].

A closer look into the prioritization of risks highlight that dominant cluster of risk would include privacy risk, performance risk and financial risk. This is a contrasting finding from that of previous literature [15] who highlighted that the dominant risks affecting adoption are time risk, psychological risk, privacy risk and financial risk. Probably due to the maturity of technology and processes, the aspect of time risk is lowered in the recent times. Connecting our findings to adoption related literature [26] it is understandable that privacy risk and financial risk affects the perceived usefulness of any digital service, while social risks affect social norms. However privacy risk, time risks and financial risks affect intention for adoption of digital services. It appears that our findings highlight that performance risk becomes a perceived usefulness which again drives adoption. The impact of social risks (and probably social norms) is noticeable in our findings. Hence it is possible that user groups is gradually losing its significance as more and more users of digital services are viewing it as a necessity due to its high utility rather than an alternative, and hence are less affected by social norms [29].

5   Conclusion

The output of the research can be useful for the policy makers, consultants, big enterprises and entrepreneurs in making the strategic, tactical and operational decisions. The research outcome can help managers in deciding which dimensions of risk are more important for digital service delivery. Also how different dimensions of risk affects consumption of digital services and affect failures will be provided, which will impact policies surrounding service management.

Further this study highlights how empirically prioritization of alternatives, which may not be free of exigencies and internal influences, may be done using the GANP. While such prioritization has been done in past literature using the Analytic Hierarchy Process [21, 27], no study has attempted to do the same using the GANP, since this methodological development is rather recent. Hence the proposed approach also highlights the application of a new methodology in the context of risk assessment of digital services. This approach may be adopted in future research for other prioritization problems when responses are elicited from user groups or experts and findings are validated empirically.

References

1. Alalwan, A.A., et al.: Consumer adoption of mobile banking in Jordan Examining the role of usefulness, ease of use, perceived risk and self-efficacy. J. Enterp. Inf. Manag. **29**(1), 118–139 (2016)
2. Albino, V., et al.: Smart cities: definitions, dimensions, performance, and initiatives. J. Urban Technol. **22**(1), 3–21 (2015)
3. Angelidou, M.: Smart cities: a conjuncture of four forces. Cities **47**, 95–106 (2015)
4. Barrett, M., et al.: Service innovation in the digital age: key contributions and future directions. MIS Q. **39**(1), 135–154 (2015)
5. Batty, M., et al.: Smart cities of the future. Eur. Phys. J. Spec. Top. **214**(1), 481–518 (2012)
6. Belanche-Gracia, D., et al.: Determinants of multi-service smartcard success for smart cities development: a study based on citizens' privacy and security perceptions. Gov. Inf. Q. **32**(2), 154–163 (2015)
7. Buchanan, S., McMenemy, D.: Digital service analysis and design: the role of process modelling. Int. J. Inf. Manage. **32**(3), 251–256 (2012)
8. Cases, A.-S.: Perceived risk and risk-reduction strategies in Internet shopping. Int. Rev. Retail. Distrib. Consum. Res. **12**(4), 375–394 (2002)
9. Chatterjee, S., Kar, A.K.: Smart cities in developing economies: a literature review and policy insights. In: International Conference on Advances in Computing, Communications and Informatics, pp. 2335–2340 (2015)
10. Chauhan, S., et al.: Addressing big data challenges in smart cities: a systematic literature review. info **18**(4), 73–90 (2016)
11. Cocosila, M., et al.: Early investigation of new information technology acceptance: a perceived risk - motivation model. Commun. Assoc. Inf. Syst. **25**(1), 339–358 (2009)
12. Crivello, S.: Urban policy mobilities: the case of Turin as a smart city. Eur. Plan. Stud. **23**(5), 909–921 (2015)
13. Elmaghraby, A.S., Losavio, M.M.: Cyber security challenges in smart cities: safety, security and privacy. J. Adv. Res. **5**(4), 491–497 (2014)
14. Featherman, M.S., et al.: Reducing online privacy risk to facilitate e-service adoption: the influence of perceived ease of use and corporate credibility. J. Serv. Mark. **24**(3), 219–229 (2010)
15. Featherman, M.S., Pavlou, P.A.: Predicting e-services adoption: a perceived risk facets perspective. Int. J. Hum Comput Stud. **59**(4), 451–474 (2003)
16. Forsythe, S.M., Shi, B.: Consumer patronage and risk perceptions in Internet shopping. J. Bus. Res. **56**, 867–875 (2003)
17. Froehle, C.M., Roth, A.V.: New measurement scales for evaluating perceptions of the technology-mediated customer service experience. J. Oper. Manag. **22**(1), 1–21 (2004)
18. Fung, W., et al.: Hedge funds: performance, risk, and capital formation. J. Finan. **63**(4), 1777–1803 (2008)
19. Gefen, D., et al.: Structural equation modeling and regression: guidelines for research practice. Commun. Assoc. Inf. Syst. **4**, 1–77 (2000)
20. Higgs, G., et al.: Investigating variations in the provision of digital services in public libraries using network-based GIS models. Libr. Inf. Sci. Res. **35**(1), 24–32 (2013)
21. Kar, A.K., Pani, A.K.: Exploring the importance of different supplier selection criteria. Manag. Res. Rev. **37**(1), 89–105 (2014)
22. De Kerviler, G., et al.: Adoption of in-store mobile payment: are perceived risk and convenience the only drivers? J. Retail. Consum. Serv. **31**, 334–344 (2016)

23. Khatwani, G., Kar, A.K.: Improving the Cosine Consistency Index for the analytic hierarchy process for solving multi-criteria decision making problems. Appl. Comput. Inform. **13**(2), 118–129 (2017)
24. Lazaroiu, G.C., Roscia, M.: Definition methodology for the smart cities model. Energy **47**(1), 326–332 (2012)
25. Lee, J.H., et al.: An integrated service-device-technology roadmap for smart city development. Technol. Forecast. Soc. Chang. **80**(2), 286–306 (2013)
26. Lee, M.: Factors influencing the adoption of internet banking: an integration of TAM and TPB with perceived risk and perceived benefit. Electron. Commer. Res. Appl. **8**, 130–141 (2009)
27. Lee, Y., Kozar, K.A.: Investigating the effect of website quality on e-business success: an analytic hierarchy process (AHP) approach. Decis. Support Syst. **42**, 1383–1401 (2006)
28. Lombardi, P., et al.: Modelling the smart city performance. Innov. Eur. J. Soc. Sci. Res. **25**(2), 137–149 (2012)
29. Lu, J.: Personal innovativeness, social influences and adoption of wireless Internet services via mobile technology. J. Strateg. Inf. Syst. **14**, 245–268 (2005)
30. Luo, X., et al.: Examining multi-dimensional trust and multi-faceted risk in initial acceptance of emerging technologies: an empirical study of mobile banking services. Decis. Support Syst. **49**(2), 222–234 (2010)
31. Mohd Nishat, F., et al.: Information risks management in supply chains: an assessment and mitigation framework. J. Enterp. Inf. Manag. **20**(6), 677–699 (2007)
32. Nazimoglu, Ö., Özsen, Y.: Analysis of risk dynamics in information technology service delivery. J. Enterp. Inf. Manag. **23**(3), 350–364 (2010)
33. Neirotti, P., et al.: Current trends in smart city initiatives: some stylised facts. Cities **38**, 25–36 (2014)
34. Orlowski, S., Orlowski, S.: Government initiatives in information technology security Government initiatives in information technology security. Inf. Manag. Comput. Secur. **5**(3), 111–118 (1997)
35. Özkan, S., et al.: Facilitating the adoption of e-payment systems: theoretical constructs and empirical analysis. J. Enterp. Inf. Manag. **23**(3), 305–325 (2010)
36. Peter, J.P., Ryan, M.J.: An investigation of perceived risk at the brand level. J. Mark. Res. **13**(2), 184–188 (1976)
37. Saaty, R.W.: The analytic hierarchy process-what it is and how it is used. Math. Model. **9**(3–5), 161–176 (1987)
38. Saaty, T.L., Vargas, L.G.: The analytic network process. Decis. Mak. Anal. Netw. Process. **195**, 1–40 (2013)
39. Singhal, H., Kar, A.K.: Information security concerns in digital services: literature review and a multi-stakeholder approach. In: International Conference on Advances in Computing, Communications and Informatics, pp. 901–906 (2015)
40. Söderström, O., et al.: Smart cities as corporate storytelling. City **18**(3), 307–320 (2014)
41. Steenbruggen, J., et al.: Data from mobile phone operators: a tool for smarter cities? Telecomm. Policy **39**, 335–346 (2015)
42. Tachizawa, E.M., et al.: How "smart cities" will change supply chain management. Supply Chain Manag. Int. J. **20**(3), 237–248 (2015)
43. Williams, K., et al.: Design of emerging digital services: a taxonomy. Eur. J. Inf. Syst. **17**(5), 505–517 (2008)
44. Zhu, B., et al.: Generalized analytic network process. Eur. J. Oper. Res. **244**(1), 277–288 (2015)

Mobile Phones and/or Smartphones and Their Use in the Management of Dementia – Findings from the Research Studies

Blanka Klimova[✉]

University of Hradec Kralove, Rokitanskeho 62, Hradec Kralove, Czech Republic
blanka.klimova@uhk.cz

Abstract. Nowadays, there are significant changes in the number of elderly people all over the world. This accelerating trend in the rise of elderly inevitably results in serious economic and social changes accompanied with a number of aging diseases such as dementia. The aim of the review study is to examine the exploitation of mobile phones and/or smartphones and their benefits and limitations for patients with dementia. The methods of this review involve literature search of accessible studies dealing with the topic on the exploitation of mobile phones and/or smartphones in dementia found in three acknowledged databases Science Direct, Web of Science, and MEDLINE. Furthermore, the results of the detected studies were compared and evaluated. The results of this article show that the use of mobile phones and/or smartphones by patients with dementia can provide support for the activities of daily life. In addition, they can reduce both mental and economic burden of their caregivers and help doctors in their assessments and diagnoses. Nevertheless, more original research studies, especially in the area of the effectiveness of their use should be conducted. The same is true for sustainable support in the use of mobile phones by patients with dementia.

Keywords: Mobile phones · Smartphones · Dementia · Patients · Benefits · Limitations

1 Introduction

Currently, demographic changes result in an increase in the number of older people worldwide. For instance, in Europe older people aged 55+ years represent 25% of the whole population [1]. This accelerating trend in the rise of elderly people groups inevitably results in serious economic and social changes accompanied with a number of aging diseases such as dementia.

Dementia, respectively Alzheimer's disease, together with heart diseases, cancer, and respiratory diseases, is one of the most common causes of death among older people [2]. Nowadays, dementia affects approximately 58 million people and it is estimated that this number of older people with dementia should triple by 2050 since each year there are about 9.9 million of new dementia cases worldwide [3, 4]. The key symptom of dementia is cognitive decline. Unfortunately, at the moment, there is no effective

A.K. Kar et al. (Eds.): I3E 2017, LNCS 10595, pp. 33–37, 2017.
DOI: 10.1007/978-3-319-68557-1_4

pharmacological treatment for this cognitive decline [5]. Thus, there is an increasing interest in non-pharmacological alternative approaches which may maintain or in some cases even enhance the quality of life of people living with dementia. And mobile devices appear to offer some benefits for enhancing the quality of life of these people, especially enabling them to stay independent and socially engaged in the early phases of this disease [6].

The aim of the review is to examine the exploitation of mobile phones and/or smartphones and their benefits and limitations/challenges for patients with dementia.

2 Methods

The methods of this review involve literature search of accessible studies dealing with the topic on the exploitation of mobile phones and/or smartphones in dementia found in three acknowledged databases Science Direct, Web of Science, and MEDLINE. Furthermore, the results of the detected studies were compared and evaluated. The search words were *mobile phone use* AND *dementia, mobile phone use* AND *Alzheimer's disease, smartphone use* AND *dementia, smartphone use* AND *Alzheimer's disease.*

Although the use of mobile phones is not that ubiquitous among patients with dementia, their use is moderately rising as it can been seen from the number of publications recorded on this topic in Science Direct from 2000 till 2016 (consult Fig. 1 below).

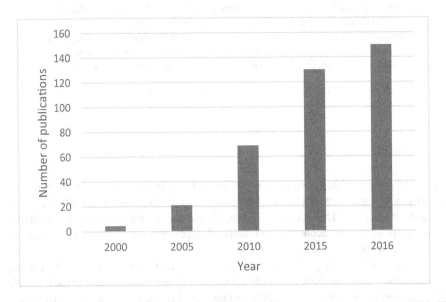

Fig. 1. A number of publications on the topic of mobile phone use in dementia from 2000 till 2016, based on the data from Science Direct [7]

3   Findings and Their Discussion

The detected studies concerning the exploitation of mobile phones and/or smartphones by patients with dementia can be divided into several areas according to their focus as follows:

- studies concentrating on the adoption and usability of these devices by patients with dementia [6, 8–11];
- descriptive studies depicting the development of potential mobile phone/smartphone apps for patients with dementia [12, 13];
- studies exploring the role of these mobile devices for the assessment and diagnostic purposes [14–16];
- studies focusing on the actual use of mobile phones and/or smartphones by patients with dementia [17–19].

Thorpe et al. [6] explored the adoption of smartphone and smartwatch use among people with mild dementia. In their study they discovered that the smartphone should be used for input and smartwatch for output, e.g., notifications, orientation and behavior sensing. The most appreciated function by patients was scheduling which reminded or notified them about the activities they should perform. The navigation or emergency support functions were not considered to be that much useful. The most important aspect for patients with dementia was personalization of both devices, i.e., tailoring the devices to their individual needs. This was in fact confirmed in other research studies as well. For example, Faucounau et al. [19] claim that it is a must to involve users in the designing process of new devices in order to develop a tailored gadget. Furthermore, Hedman et al. [10] on the amount and type of everyday technology use found out that people with cognitive impairment tended to decrease the use of everyday technology over time. This is quite common since patients with dementia are generally older people and they like to use what they already know. Therefore higher awareness of the benefits of these devices should be raised among patients and their caregivers.

In addition, mobile phones and/or smartphones have big potential in the assessment and diagnosis of dementia for the following reasons [20]:

- they have an ability to accurately record and measure the outcomes without manual operation;
- they can minimize the examiner's biases;
- they enable older people to remain independent in their tasks of daily living;
- they enable older people to understand conditions as well as terms and symptoms associated with their conditions from credible sources;
- they are cost-effective; they cut potential costs on treatment and hospitalization of older people;
- they can provide enhance access to healthcare for older people in remote areas;
- they target to enhance the overall quality of life of elderly; and
- they are ecological.

For instance, Sangha et al. [15] in their research study showed that before the intro-duction of the smartphone app for cognitive assessment, only one third of people aged

75+ years had been evaluated cognitively. The results revealed that when patients started to use the smartphone app, the number rose twice. In addition, this cognitive assessment was especially enhanced after training the young doctors in their use.

As far as the actual use of both devices is concerned, the most exploited applications according to the research findings seem to be reminders and tracking/positioning applications [6, 13, 18, 19]. Table 1 below then highlights the main benefits and limitations/challenges of the exploitation of mobile phones and/or smartphones for patients with dementia.

Table 1. Benefits and limitations/challenges of the exploitation of mobile phones and/or smartphones in the management of dementia

Benefits	Limitations/Challenges
• Potential cost savings of care, reduced mental burden for patient's caregiver;	• Not sufficient access to these devices;
• Activities of daily life become easier, which can lead to an improved quality of life for users and a reduced need for help from society and relatives;	• More evidence on the efficacy of technologies is required to improve coverage of these devices for patients with dementia by insurance companies;
• Patients and caregivers are positive and motivated to use technologies in the future;	• Unexpected ethical, as well as environmental and health consequences of new technologies used in medicine;
• Provide patients with safety and security;	• Improved knowledge and awareness of the benefits of these devices are needed
• Offer opportunities for early assessment and diagnosis of dementia	

4   Conclusion

The results of this article show that the use of mobile phones and/or smartphones by patients with dementia can provide support for their activities of daily life. In addition, they can reduce both mental and economic burden of their caregivers and help doctors in their assessments and diagnoses. Nevertheless, more original research studies, especially in the area of the effectiveness of their use should be conducted. The same is true for sustainable support in the use of mobile phones by patients with dementia.

Acknowledgments. This article is supported by the SPEV project 2017/2018 at FIM UHK. The author especially thanks Josef Toman for data processing.

References

1. Global AgeWatch index 2015: Insight report (2015). http://www.population.gov.za/index.php/npu-articles/send/22-aging/535-global-agewatch-index-2015-insight-report
2. Vann, M.R., Bass, P.F.: The 15 most common health concerns for seniors (2016). http://www.everydayhealth.com/news/most-common-health-concerns-seniors/
3. Langa, K.M.: Is the risk of Alzheimer's disease and dementia declining? Alzheimer's Res. Ther. **7**, 1–4 (2015)

4. WHO (2016). http://www.who.int/features/factfiles/dementia/en/
5. Karakaya, T., Fußer, F., Schroder, J., Pantel, J.: Pharmacological treatment of mild cognitive impairment as a prodromal syndrome of Alzheimer's disease. Curr. Neuropharmacol. **11**(1), 102 (2013)
6. Thorpe, J.R., Ronn-Andersen, K.V., Bien, P., Ozkil, A.G., Forchhammer, B.H., Maier, A.M.: Pervasive assistive technology for people with dementia: a UCD case. Healthc. Technol. Lett. **3**(4), 297–302 (2016)
7. Science Direct (2017). http://www.sciencedirect.com/science?_ob=ArticleListURL&_method=list&_ArticleListID=-1198558763&_sort=r&_st=13&view=c&md5=9c87fb919562daeed92c5141e26d971e&searchtype=a
8. Hartin, P.J., Nugent, C.D., McClean, S.I., Cleland, I., Norton, M.C., Sanders, C., Tschanz, J.T.: A smartphone application to evaluate technology adoption and usage in persons with dementia. Conf. Proc. IEEE Eng. Med. Biol. Soc. **2014**, 5389–5392 (2014)
9. van Osch, M., Rovekamp, A., Bergman-Agteres, S.N., Wijsman, L.W., Ooms, S.J., Mooijaart, S.P., Vermeulen, J.: User preferences and usability of iVitality: optimizing an innovative online research platform for home-based health monitoring. Patient Prefer. Adherence **9**, 857–867 (2015)
10. Hedman, A., Nygard, L., Almkvist, O., Kottorp, A.: Amount and type of everyday technology use over time in older adults with cognitive impairment. Scand. J. Occup. Ther. **22**(3), 196–206 (2015)
11. Malinowsky, C., Nygard, L., Kottorp, A.: Using a screening tool to evaluate potential use of e-health services for older people with and without cognitive impairment. Aging Ment. Health **18**(3), 340–345 (2014)
12. Weir, A.J., Paterson, C.A., Tieges, Z., MacLullich, A.M., Parra-Rodriguez, M., Della Sala, S., Logie, R.H.: Development of Android apps for cognitive assessment of dementia and delirium. Conf. Proc. IEEE Eng. Med. Biol. Soc. **2014**, 2169–2172 (2014)
13. McKinstry, B., Sheikh, A.: The use of global positioning systems in promoting safer walking for people with dementia. J. Telemed. Telecare **19**(5), 288–292 (2013)
14. Leurent, C., Ehlers, M.D.: Digital technologies for cognitive assessment to accelerate drug development in Alzheimer's disease. Clin. Pharmacol. Ther. **98**(5), 475–476 (2015)
15. Sangha, S., George, J., Winthrop, C., Panchal, S.: Confusion: delirium and dementia - a smartphone app to improve cognitive assessment. BMJ Qual. Improv. Rep. **4**(1), pii: u202580.w1592 (2015)
16. Brouillette, R.M., Foil, H., Fontenot, S., Correro, A., Allen, R., Martin, C.K., Bruce-Keller, A.J., Keller, J.N.: Feasibility, reliability, and validity of a smartphone based application for the assessment of cognitive function in the elderly. PLoS ONE **8**(6), e65925 (2013)
17. Hartin, P.J., Nugent, C.D., McClean, S.I., Cleland, I., Tschanz, J.T., Clark, C.J., Norton, M.C.: The empowering role of mobile apps in behavior change interventions: the gray matters randomized controlled trial. JMIR Mhealth Uhealth **4**(3), e93 (2016)
18. Olsson, A., Engstrom, M., Lampic, C., Skovdahl, K.: A passive positioning alarm used by persons with dementia and their spouses–a qualitative intervention study. BMC Geriatr. **13**, 11 (2013)
19. Faucounau, V., Riguet, M., Orvoen, G., Lacombe, A., Rialle, V., Extra, J., Rigaud, A.S.: Electronic tracking system and wandering in Alzheimer's disease: a case study. Ann. Phys. Rehabil. Med. **52**(7–8), 579–587 (2009)
20. Klimova, B., Valis, M., Kuca, K.: Potential of mobile technologies and applications in the detection of mild cognitive impairment among older generation groups. Soc. Work Health Care, 1–12 (2017). doi:10.1080/00981389.2017.1316339

A Systematic Review of Citations of UTAUT2 Article and Its Usage Trends

Kuttimani Tamilmani, Nripendra P. Rana[(⊠)], and Yogesh K. Dwivedi

Emerging Markets Research Centre (EMaRC), School of Management,
Swansea University Bay Campus, Swansea, SA1 8EN, UK
kuttimani.tamilmani@gmail.com,
{n.p.rana,y.k.dwivedi}@swansea.ac.uk

Abstract. Unified Theory of Acceptance and Use of Technology (UTAUT) is considered as the most comprehensive theory in Information Systems (IS) research to understand technology acceptance across various use contexts. The theory was extended to consumer context by incorporating three external constructs. This extended version is referred as UTAUT2. Although UTAUT2 is relatively new, the increasing number of citations is a testimony to the fact that it's popular amongst IS researchers especially for examining consumer- focused issues. However, none of the existing studies attempted to analyze the pattern of UTAUT2 citations. This study is aimed to undertake a systematic review of 650 citations with a motivation to fulfill this research gap. The study revealed that majority of the studies i.e. 77% cited UTAUT2 for general citation purpose. However, the remaining 23%, even if they utilized UTATU2, did so in combination with external theories where the moderators of UTAUT2 were rarely considered.

Keywords: Adoption · Acceptance · Citation analysis · Diffusion · Information systems · Information technology · Systematic review · UTAUT2

1 Introduction

Understanding individual acceptance and use of information technology (IT) is considered as one of the most mature streams of research in the field of information systems (IS) [1]. The adoption and use related issues have been constantly examined due to two reasons: new technologies are constantly evolving and finding their place both in organizations and society, and the IS failure rate continued to be high [2]. Due to constant effort to understand adoption and diffusion related issues, many theories have been developed, adopted or adapted in IS literature to explain technology acceptance and use in various contexts [3–5]. This plurality often poses a challenge to IS researchers when selecting an appropriate theory for undertaking a new study. Venkatesh et al. [6] noted that many of these existing theories used similar constructs with different names. Considering that Venkatesh et al. [6] developed the unified theory of acceptance and use of technology (UTAUT) by reviewing, mapping and integrating constructs from

© IFIP International Federation for Information Processing 2017
Published by Springer International Publishing AG 2017. All Rights Reserved
A.K. Kar et al. (Eds.): I3E 2017, LNCS 10595, pp. 38–49, 2017.
DOI: 10.1007/978-3-319-68557-1_5

eight dominant theories/models (generally utilized in organizational context) of technology adoption emphasizing on the utilitarian value of technology users [4, 5, 7]. The UTAUT theory postulates performance expectancy, effort expectancy and social influence as indirect determinants of use behavior through behavioral intention, whereas behavioral intention and facilitating conditions influence use behavior directly. The theory also hypothesized the relationship amongst the constructs are influenced through various combinations of its moderators namely: gender, age, experience and voluntariness of use [6, 8]. UTAUT explained about 70% of the variance in behavioral intention and about 50% of the variance in technology use [6, 9]. However, the review of 1,267 UTAUT cited papers since its publication revealed just 62 studies (approximately 5%) utilized UTAUT whereas remaining 1,205 studies (comprising 95%) just cited the article for general purposes without using UTAUT or its constructs [8]. This result was consistent with a similar earlier study by [7] on 450 UTAUT cited articles, which revealed only 43 articles (around 10%) utilized UTAUT and the remaining 407 articles (90%) employed it for general citation purpose.

Venkatesh et al. [9] extended their UTAUT for the consumer context emphasizing on hedonic value (intrinsic motivation) of technology users. The extended version of UTAUT is known as UTAUT2, which incorporated three new constructs such as hedonic motivation, price value and habit into original UATUT. However, in UTAUT2 voluntariness of use was dropped as moderator since consumers have no organizational mandate and in many situations, consumer behavior is voluntary [9]. UTAUT2 is gaining momentum in terms of its use to examine IS/IT adoption and diffusion related issues leading to a fast increase in its citations.

Besides UTAUT based theories, the most extensive theory used to study IS/IT adoption within the IS discipline was TAM [4, 6, 10]. Cross-disciplinary and extensive application of TAM since its existence attracted numerous researchers to analyze its actual performance through systemic literature review and meta-analysis approach. Instances of such efforts include Lee et al. [11], King and He [12] and Williams et al. [5, 7]. Similarly, the systematic review of UTAUT with more than 10 years of its existence revealed that UTAUT has been utilized as is or used in combination with other theories or was extended with additional constructs to evaluate a range of technologies in a variety of settings including both organizational and non-organizational [8]. The number of studies using UTAUT2 in various context of technology adoption has increased substantially in the last few years. However, none of the existing studies have conducted a systematic review of UTAUT2 citations for understanding the trend emerging from its use including its purpose of citation, its application and adaptation in various contexts. This study intends to fulfill that purpose.

Given the preceding discussion, the paper is structured as follows. Section 2 will describe the research method employed in this study; Sect. 3 will present the trend emerging from the systematic review of UTAUT2 cited articles into various categories. This will be followed by discussion in Sect. 4 and conclusion in final Sect. 5.

2   Research Method

In order to achieve objectives of this research, it was deemed appropriate to conduct a combined analysis of "cited reference search" and systematic review [4, 5, 7, 11, 13]. This study utilized "cited reference search" method in Scopus and Web of Science databases for identifying papers that cited the originating article (i.e. Venkatesh et al. [9]) of UTAUT2 theory from March 2012 to March 2017. The initial search resulted in 1320 total citations (497 from web of science and 823 citations from Scopus). Later it was found that 452 out of 1,320 total citations were overlapping amongst the two databases resulting in a total of 868 unique citations (see Fig. 1). After this step, these 868 citations were screened for the availability of full articles resulting in 650 fully downloaded articles. These articles were then systematically reviewed to reveal various patterns, application and types of UTAUT2 usage.

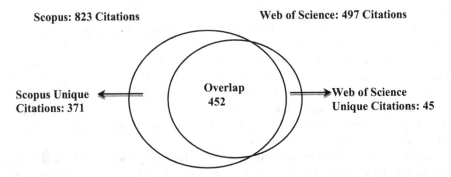

Scopus: 823 Citations   **Web of Science: 497 Citations**

Scopus Unique ← ← Overlap → → **Web of Science**
Citations: 371   452   **Unique Citations: 45**

Fig. 1. Total unique citations (C = 868) for Venkatesh et al. [9] article

3   Systematic Review Findings of UTAUT2 Citations

This section presents and explains results from the systematic review based on their purpose of UTAUT2 utilization. Following the approach of Williams et al. [7] the 650 downloaded articles were broadly classified into two categories: (1) General Citation – 503 studies; and (2) UTAUT2 Utilization – 147 studies.

3.1   General Citation

This category refers to studies which just cited Venkatesh et al.'s [9] article for general purposes but did not utilize the theory in any substantial manner. This category of citations included 503 studies. We adapted Williams et al.'s [7] classification to further categories studies with no actual use of UTAUT2. In the process, some of the existing categories were removed, modified and few new categories were introduced resulting in final eight general citation categories of UTAUT2 as summarized in Table 1 and briefly discussed hereafter.

Table 1. UTAUT2 general citation categories (Approach adapted from Williams et al. [7])

Category type	Frequency	Description	Example citations
1. Reference to the evolution of technology adoption theories in IS research	214	This category consists of studies which cited UTAUT2 to discuss about evolution of technology adoption theories in IS research mostly in the introduction and theory development section	[14, 15]
2. Development of constructs	118	Studies in this category cited UTAUT2 to define, compare and support the role of utilizing a construct or moderators or control variables during hypothesis development although they didn't employ same construct as used in UTAUT2. However, in some cases even if the studies employed few same constructs as in UTAUT2 they adapted measurement items fully or partially from other studies	[16, 17]
3. Supporting findings with UTAUT2	51	Studies included in this category cited UTAUT2 to support their findings	[18, 19]
4. Research methodology design	39	Studies in this category cited UTAUT2 in research method section as most of them adapted similar data collection methods or measurement scales as employed in UTAUT2. However, these studies did not utilize measurement items from UTAUT2 constructs	[20, 21]
5. Justification for application of UTAUT2 in various contexts	24	This category contains studies which justify the application of UTAUT2 in various contexts	[22, 23]
6. Criticism of TAM or UTAUT2	17	Studies in this category have criticised TAM or UTAUT2 theory on their various shortcomings	[24, 25]
7. Future research suggestion	15	Studies in the category Cited UTAUT2 referring that it should be used in future	[26, 27]
8. Others	25	This category contains studies which could not be readily classified into any of the previous seven categories	[28, 29]

3.1.1 Reference to the Evolution of Technology Adoption Theories in IS Research

The majority of the studies under general citation fell under this category 1. There were 214 studies in total which cited UTAUT2 article either in the introduction section on the discussion about the evolution of individual technology adoption or during the review of existing technology adoption theories in the theory development section. Gu et al. [15] is an example where Venkatesh et al. [9] is cited in the introduction section to support statement on the evolution of individual acceptance and use of IT. On the other hand, Chuah et al. [14] cited UTAUT2 alongside with various other technology acceptance models in the theory development section.

3.1.2   Development of Constructs

Category 2 titled development of constructs consists of 118 studies which cited UTAUT2 to define, compare and support the role of utilizing a particular construct or moderators or control variables during hypothesis development although they didn't employ the same construct as used in UTAUT2. For instance, Gao and Bai [16] cited UTAUT2 to define "perceived usefulness" construct which is similar to "Performance expectancy" construct of UTAUT2. However, in some cases even if the studies employ few same constructs as in UTAUT2 they adapted measurement items fully or partially from other studies. This phenomenon is observed in Matt et al. [17] study which utilized habit from the UTAUT2 construct. However, the study cited UTUAT2 to compare the construct alongside with other studies and adapted the measurement items for Habit from Limayem et al. [30].

3.1.3   Supporting Findings with UTAUT2

51 studies in this category cited UTAUT2 to support their findings. UTAUT2 is cited to support outcomes evolving from relationship amongst various constructs or moderators used in these studies. For instance, the positive significant effect of the habit construct on users IS continuing intention in Wang et al. [19] was consistent with the UTAUT2 study. On the other hand, the study of Shaikh and Karjaluoto [18] cited UTAUT2 to support the negative effect of experience as a moderating variable.

3.1.4   Research Methodology Design

39 studies fell under this category which cited UTAUT2 in research methodology section. These studies either adopted similar data collection methods or adopted measurement scales from UTAUT2. However, these studies did not utilize any measurement items from UTAUT2 constructs. The study of Stock and Schulz [21] cited UTAUT2 as they employed similar data collection methods by personally contacting consumers in large public places like malls and asked them whether they have used high-tech products. In the case of Alalwan et al. [20] the study adopted the seven-point measurement scale usage pattern from UATUT2 and cited it.

3.1.5   Justification for Application of UTAUT2 in Various Contexts

Category 5 contains 24 studies which justified the application of UTAUT2 in various contexts. Samples include Hess et al. [23], which criticized the extensive application of UTAUT in an institutional context and justified the need for adoption theories such as UTAUT2 in the consumer context. Similarly, Cimperman et al. [22] cited UTAUT2 and demanded the introduction of contextual predictors which could enable more accurate understanding of users of technology in specific domains.

3.1.6   Criticism of TAM or UTAUT2

Category 6 consists of 17 studies which cited UTAUT2 while criticizing TAM or UTAUT2 theory on their various shortcomings. Chandrasekhar and Nandagopal [24] criticized TAM related theories which do not account for many new technology adoption enablers and disablers. The study cited UTAUT2 by stating that in order to make TAM relevant to current day requirements it has to be revised with additional elements. Also, UTAUT2 is not without its criticism. Choi [25] found although hedonic motivation was included as the predictor of behavioral intention and use behaviour in UTAUT2, it failed to discuss factors that lead to enjoyment.

3.1.7   Future Research Suggestion

15 studies under category 7 cited UTAUT2 by referring that it should be used in future. The majority of them are UTAUT based studies insisting to include additional UTAUT2 constructs to their model and test them in consumer context as mentioned in Chang et al. [26]. There were also instances where studies (for example, Hoehle et al. [27]) attempted to integrate their model with existing IS theories like UTAUT2 in future.

3.1.8   Others

This category contains studies which could not be readily classified into any of the other 7 categories and provides brief references to Venkatesh et al. [9] under wider technology adoption research contexts. There were 25 such studies, instances range from McLean et al. [29] study citing UTAUT2 to refer mobile interface research to Brenner et al. [28] study citing UTAUT2 to refer 'human center design'.

3.2   UTAUT2 Utilization

This category refers to studies which utilized UTAUT2 in some form either standalone or in combination with external theories. There were 147 such studies.

3.2.1   UTAUT2 as Basis for Conceptual Model Development

15 among 147 UTAUT2 based studies were classified under this category. The studies under this category used UTAUT2 as base line model in combination with external theories and proposed a conceptual model to be empirically tested in future along various technology use contexts. The analysis of studies in Table 2 reveals ECT model and trust as most frequently used external theories alongside with UTAUT2- both of them were utilized on three occasions each. This is followed by TOE, TAM, TTF, MMT and SQM each of them being utilized twice with UTAUT2; the remaining theories were used on one instance in combination with UTAUT2. The exploration of remaining 134 UTAUT2 based studies is underway.

Table 2. Summary of external theories (Approach adapted from Dwivedi et al. [31])

Context	Frequency	Source	External theories utilized
Generic	1	[8]	Framework of Weber's [32]; Topology of context adapted from Johns' [33]
Organization	3	[34]	Trust in Storage Data Framework
		[35]	TOE; TTF
		[36]	TOE
Consumers	8	[37]	TAM
		[38]	ECT; MMT; SQM
		[39]	ECT; MMT; SQM
		[40]	TTF
		[41]	Mobile affinity (e.g. Mathews et al. [42]); DOI; Risk (e.g. Jacoby and Kaplan [43]); Trust
		[44]	ANT
		[45]	TAM
		[46]	Information Privacy Concerns, Relationship Expectancy, Espoused Cultural Values adapted from Hofstede's [47]
Society	3	[48]	Privacy calculus model adapted from Dinev et al. [49]
		[50]	Perceived Risk adapted from Susanto and Goodwin [51]; TPB; Use Satisfaction' adapted from Delone and McLean [52]
		[53]	CET; ECT; Service Quality Types; Trust factors adapted from Jøsang et al. [54]

LEGEND: ANT: Actor Network Theory; CET: Channel Expansion Theory; DOI: Diffusion of Innovations; ECT: Expectation Confirmation Theory; MMT: Marketing Mix Theory; SQM: Service Quality Model; TAM: Technology Acceptance Model; TOE: Technology-Organization-Environment framework; TPB: Theory of Planned Behavior; TTF: Task Technology Fit

Venkatesh et al. [8] provided generic baseline model for individual technology use at feature level for various cross–context research. The remaining studies proposed conceptual model to understand individual users of technology along three major contexts such as employees in organizations, consumers of various technologies and societal context - citizens using E-government services. Research on organizational technology users comprises of three studies: Alazzam et al. [34] study on Medical staffs Intention to use Electronic Health Records, Balaid et al. [35] conceptual model for examining knowledge maps adoption in software development organizations and Rosli et al. [36] study on factors influencing computer-assisted auditing tools (CAATs) acceptance in public audit firms. Two of these three studies employed TOE as an external theory alongside UTAUT2 in understanding organizational technology users signifying popularity of TOE theory in organizational context. Eight studies developed conceptual framework by utilizing UTAUT2 alongside external theories to understand consumers use intention of various technologies. These studies include consumer acceptance of smart mobile devices [37], customer repurchase behaviour in mobile service business

[38], customer retention framework in mobile telecommunication services [39], consumers behavioural intention of using autonomous vehicle (AV) [44], individual use of social network sites [46], consumer acceptance behavior of mobile shopping [41] and mobile technology acceptance for library information services [40, 45]. Whereas, Nwanekezie et al. [53] study on public sector online communication channel adoption, Hassan et al. [48] study on citizens' acceptance and use of health information application embedded in Smart National Identity Card (SNIC) and Kasaj [50] study on user's adoption of mandatory E-government explored individual use of technology from citizen's perspective.

4 Discussion

From the results section, it's observed out of 650 studies only 147 studies (23%) employed UTAUT2 theory in some form. The remaining 503 studies (77%) cited it for general purpose without employing the theory in any substantial manner. Although 23% UTAUT2 utilization is way higher than the application of UTAUT where it was employed by 5% of studies (see Venkatesh et al. [8]) and 10% of studies as reported by Williams et al. [7]. The marked increase in UTAUT2 utilization can be attributed to penetration of IT exploding across the globe touching every aspect of society giving rise to various individuals in the different context to use IT and UTAUT2 is focused on consumer context [8]. We assume given its focus on consumer context, UTAUT2 has not just been utilized by IS/IT researchers but in also other related academic disciplines such as marketing.

The general citation still comprises of 77% studies with majority of them citing UTAUT2 article in introduction section referring to the evolution of technology adoption theories in IS research or during the development of conceptual model as UTAUT and UTAUT2 theories are dominant theory in the field of IS research with similar constructs from major technology adoption theories. However, the higher citation doesn't correlate to actual usage of theory, which should serve as the caution for future researchers in IS [7].

One of the major limitations of UTAUT based theories is its complex interactions among the various attributes and moderators resulting in relatively less parsimony hindering its usage as such [8]. This shortcoming is still unaddressed in UTAUT2 as the majority of the 15 studies which utilized UTAUT2 didn't include moderating variables during conceptual model development. The irony of UTAUT/UTATUT2 theories is that since it is comprehensive in nature, it not only hinders efforts in extending the existing theory but also hampers the further theoretical advancement [8].

In terms of methodology this study employed combination of "cited reference search" and systematic review. The results of which partly revealed although UTAUT2 is comprehensive theory many studies utilized external theories alongside UTAUT2 in their research model. This pattern is similar to results shown by Lee et al. [11] in relation to TAM and Williams et al. [7] with respect to UTAUT. This reaffirms careful consideration is required in terms of selecting constructs while developing unified models such as UTAUT in order for them to be deployed as such across various technology use contexts.

5 Conclusion

The noteworthy outcomes of this study through systematic review and findings are listed as follows: (1) there has been a proportionate increase in UTAUT2 theory utilization amongst articles which cited it in comparison to UTAUT. However, most of the studies cited it for general purposes like supporting an argument, following research methodology design rather using the actual theory in substantial manner; (2) Majority of the 15 studies which utilized UTAUT2 omitted the moderating variables due to the complexity of their relationship amongst various constructs; (3) Although UTAUT2 is considered as the most comprehensive model in the field IS/IT adoption research with addition of three new constructs to UTAUT, still most of the studies which utilized UTAUT2, did so in combination with external theories signifying UTAUT2 cannot be used standalone across all technology use context and (4) the analysis of remaining 134 studies that utilized UTAUT2 is underway which could reveal more insightful results. This systematic review of UTAUT2 citations revealed various general citation categories; most frequently used external theories alongside UTAUT2 while developing conceptual model and individual users of technology along three major contexts such as employees in organizations, consumers of various technologies and citizens using e-government services. Although, this study didn't provide information on UTAUT2 model performance, it did provide understanding about various purposes of UTAUT2 citations which are of scholarly importance to future researchers.

References

1. Venkatesh, V., Davis, F.D., Morris, M.G.: Dead or alive? The development, trajectory and future of technology adoption research. J. Assoc. Inf. Syst. **8**(4), 268–286 (2007)
2. Dwivedi, Y.K., Wastell, D., Laumer, S., Henriksen, H.Z., Myers, M.D., Bunker, D., Elbanna, A., Ravishankar, M.N., Srivastava, S.C.: Research on information systems failures and successes: status update and future directions. Inf. Syst. Front. **17**(1), 143–157 (2015)
3. Morosan, C.: Toward an integrated model of adoption of mobile phones for purchasing ancillary services in air travel. Int. J. Contemp. Hosp. Manag. **26**(2), 246–271 (2014)
4. Williams, M.D., Dwivedi, Y.K., Lal, B., Schwarz, A.: Contemporary trends and issues in IT adoption and diffusion research. J. Inf. Technol. **24**(1), 1–10 (2009)
5. Williams, M.D., Rana, N.P., Dwivedi, Y.K.: The unified theory of acceptance and use of technology (UTAUT): a literature review. J. Enterp. Inf. Manag. **28**(3), 443–488 (2015)
6. Venkatesh, V., Morris, M.G., Davis, G.B., Davis, F.D.: User acceptance of information technology: toward a unified view. MIS Q. **27**(3), 425–478 (2015)
7. Williams, M.D., Rana, N.P., Dwivedi, Y.K., Lal, B.: Is UTAUT really used or just cited for the sake of it? A systematic review of citations of UTAUT's originating article. In: ECIS (2011)
8. Venkatesh, V., Thong, J.Y.L., Xu, X.: Unified theory of acceptance and use of technology: a synthesis and the road ahead. J. Assoc. Inf. Syst. **17**(5), 328–376 (2016)
9. Venkatesh, V., Thong, J.Y., Xu, X.: Consumer acceptance and use of information technology: extending the unified theory of acceptance and use of technology. MIS Q. **36**(1), 157–178 (2012)

10. Dwivedi, Y.K., Williams, M.D., Lal, B.: The diffusion of research on the adoption and diffusion of information technology. In: León, G., Bernardos, A.M., Casar, J.R., Kautz, K., De Gross, J.I. (eds.) TDIT 2008. ITIFIP, vol. 287, pp. 3–22. Springer, Boston, MA (2008). doi:10.1007/978-0-387-87503-3_1

11. Lee, Y., Kozar, K.A., Larsen, K.R.: The technology acceptance model: past, present, and future. Commun. Assoc. Inf. Syst. **12**(50), 752–780 (2003)

12. King, W.R., He, J.: A meta-analysis of the technology acceptance model. Inf. Manag. **43**(6), 740–755 (2006)

13. Legris, P., Ingham, J., Collerette, P.: Why do people use information technology? A critical review of the technology acceptance model. Inf. Manag. **40**(3), 191–204 (2003)

14. Chuah, S.H.W., Rauschnabel, P.A., Krey, N., Nguyen, B., Ramayah, T., Lade, S.: Wearable technologies: the role of usefulness and visibility in smartwatch adoption. Comput. Hum. Behav. **65**, 276–284 (2016)

15. Gu, R., Jiang, Z., Oh, L.B., Wang, K.: Exploring the influence of optimum stimulation level on individual perceptions of IT innovations. In: PACIS (2014)

16. Gao, L., Bai, X.: A unified perspective on the factors influencing consumer acceptance of internet of things technology. Asia Pac. J. Mark. Logist. **26**(2), 211–231 (2014)

17. Matt, C., Hess, T., Heinz, S.: Should we take a closer look? Extending switching theories from singular products to complex ecosystem structures. Paper presented at the 2015 International Conference on Information Systems: Exploring the Information Frontier, ICIS (2015)

18. Shaikh, A.A., Karjaluoto, H.: Mobile banking services continuous usage–case study of Finland. In: 49th Hawaii International Conference on System Sciences (HICSS), 2016, pp. 1497–1506. IEEE (2016)

19. Wang, Y.S., Li, H.T., Li, C.R., Zhang, D.Z.: Factors affecting hotels' adoption of mobile reservation systems: a technology-organization-environment framework. Tour. Manag. **53**, 163–172 (2016)

20. Alalwan, A.A., Dwivedi, Y.K., Rana, N.P., Williams, M.D.: Consumer adoption of mobile banking in Jordan: examining the role of usefulness, ease of use, perceived risk and self-efficacy. J. Enterp. Inf. Manag. **29**(1), 118–139 (2016)

21. Stock, R.M., Schulz, C.: Understanding consumers' predispositions toward new technological products: taxonomy and implications for adoption behaviour. Int. J. Innov. Manag. **19**(5), 1550056 (2015)

22. Cimperman, M., Brenčič, M.M., Trkman, P.: Analyzing older users' home telehealth services acceptance behavior—applying an Extended UTAUT model. Int. J. Med. Inform. **90**, 22–31 (2016)

23. Hess, T., Legner, C., Esswein, W., Maaß, W., Matt, C., Österle, H., Zarnekow, R.: Digital life as a topic of business and information systems engineering? Bus. Inf. Syst. Eng. **6**(4), 247–253 (2014)

24. Chandrasekhar, U., Nandagopal, R.: Mobile payments at retail point of sale-an Indian perspective. Life Sci. J. **10**(2), 2684–2688 (2013)

25. Choi, S.: The flipside of ubiquitous connectivity enabled by smartphone-based social networking service: social presence and privacy concern. Comput. Hum. Behav. **65**, 325–333 (2016)

26. Chang, H.H., Fu, C.S., Jain, H.T.: Modifying UTAUT and innovation diffusion theory to reveal online shopping behavior: familiarity and perceived risk as mediators. Inf. Dev. **32**(5), 1757–1773 (2016)

27. Hoehle, H., Zhang, X., Venkatesh, V.: An espoused cultural perspective to understand continued intention to use mobile applications: a four-country study of mobile social media application usability. Eur. J. Inf. Syst. **24**(3), 337–359 (2015)

28. Brenner, W., Karagiannis, D., Kolbe, L., Krüger, D.K.J., Leifer, L., Lamberti, H.J., Schwabe, G.: User, use & utility research. Bus. Inf. Syst. Eng. **6**(1), 55–61 (2014)

29. McLean, G., Al-Nabhani, K., Wilson, A.: The Customer Experience... Is there an App for that? A conceptual understanding of the customer experience with m-commerce mobile applications. In: Tiziana Russo-Spenaand Cristina Mele, 1088 (2016)

30. Limayem, M., Hirt, S.G., Cheung, C.M.: How habit limits the predictive power of intention: the case of information systems continuance. MIS Q. **31**(4), 705–737 (2007)

31. Dwivedi, Y.K., Rana, N.P., Chen, H., Williams, M.D.: A meta-analysis of the Unified Theory of Acceptance and Use of Technology (UTAUT). In: Nüttgens, M., Gadatsch, A., Kautz, K., Schirmer, I., Blinn, N. (eds.) TDIT 2011. IAICT, vol. 366, pp. 155–170. Springer, Heidelberg (2011). doi:10.1007/978-3-642-24148-2_10

32. Weber, R.: Evaluating and developing theories in the information systems discipline. J. Assoc. Inf. Syst. **13**(1), 1–30 (2012)

33. Johns, G.: The essential impact of context on organizational behavior. Acad. Manag. Rev. **31**(2), 386–408 (2006)

34. Alazzam, M.B., Basari, A.S.H., Sibghatullah, A.S., Ramli, M.R., Jaber, M.M., Naim, M.H.: Pilot study of EHRs acceptance in Jordan hospitals by UTAUT2. J. Theor. Appl. Inf. Technol. **85**(3), 378–393 (2016)

35. Balaid, A., Rozan, M.Z.A., Abdullah, S.N.: Conceptual model for examining knowledge maps adoption in software development organizations. Asian Soc. Sci. **10**(15), 118–132 (2014)

36. Rosli, K., Yeow, P.H., Siew, E.G.: Computer-assisted auditing tools acceptance using I-Toe: a new paradigm. Computer **7**, 15 (2012)

37. Ally, M., Gardiner, M.: The moderating influence of device characteristics and usage on user acceptance of Smart Mobile Devices. In: Proceedings of the 23rd Australasian Conference on Information Systems 2012, pp. 1–10 (2012)

38. Bhatti, H., Abareshi, A., Pittayachawan, S.: An evaluation of customer repurchase behaviour in mobile telecommunication services in Australia. In: IEEE International Conference on Industrial Engineering and Engineering Management, pp. 602–606 (2016a)

39. Bhatti, H., Abareshi, A., Pittayachawan, S.: An empirical examination of customer retention in mobile telecommunication services in Australia. In: Proceedings of the 13th International Joint Conference on e-Business and Telecommunications (ICETE 2016), vol. 2 (2016b)

40. Chaveesuk, S., Vongjaturapat, S., Chotikakamthorn, N.: Analysis of factors influencing the mobile technology acceptance for library information services: conceptual model. In: International Conference on Information Technology and Electrical Engineering (ICITEE), pp. 18–24 (2013)

41. Marriott, H.R., Williams, M.D.: Developing a theoretical model to examine consumer acceptance behavior of mobile shopping. In: Dwivedi, Y.K. (ed.) I3E 2016. LNCS, vol. 9844, pp. 261–266. Springer, Cham (2016). doi:10.1007/978-3-319-45234-0_24

42. Matthews, T., Pierce, J., Tang, J.: No smart phone is an island: the impact of places, situations, and other devices on smart phone use. IBM Research Report, pp. 1–10 (2009)

43. Jacoby, J., Kaplan, L.B.: The components of perceived risk. Adv. Consumer Res. **3**(3), 382–383 (1972)

44. Seuwou, P., Banissi, E., Ubakanma, G., Sharif, M.S., Healey, A.: Actor-network theory as a framework to analyse technology acceptance model's external variables: the case of autonomous vehicles. In: Jahankhani, H., Carlile, A., Emm, D., Hosseinian-Far, A., Brown, G., Sexton, G., Jamal, A. (eds.) ICGS3 2017. CCIS, vol. 630, pp. 305–320. Springer, Cham (2016). doi:10.1007/978-3-319-51064-4_24

45. Vonjaturapat, S., Chaveesuk, S.: Proposed mobile technology acceptance model of the information services in a library context. In: Proceedings of the 4th International Conference on Information Systems Management and Evaluation (Icime2013), Acad Conferences Ltd., England, pp. 385–388 (2013)

46. Zhao, Y., Srite, M.: Modeling online social network use: incorporating espoused national cultural values into an extended unified theory of acceptance and use of technology. In: Proceedings of International Conference on Information Systems, Milan, Italy (2013)

47. Hofstede, G.: Cultures and Organizations: Software of the Mind. McGraw-Hill, London (1991)

48. Hassan, I.B., Murad, M.A.A., Nor, R.N.H.B., Abdullah, S.B.: Towards developing a new IP technology adoption framework: a research road map. In: International Conference in Computer Assisted System in Health, pp. 77–83 (2014)

49. Dinev, T., Bellotto, M., Hart, P., Russo, V., Serra, I., Colautti, C.: Privacy calculus model in e-commerce–a study of Italy and the United States. Eur. J. Inf. Syst. 15(4), 389–402 (2006)

50. Kasaj, A.: User adoption of mandatory e-government systems: notarial system in Albania, an empirical analyse. In: CBU International Conference Proceedings, vol. 4, pp. 531–543 (2016)

51. Susanto, T.D., Goodwin, R.: User acceptance of SMS-based e-government services: Differences between adopters and non-adopters. Govern. Inf. Q. 30(4), 486–497 (2013)

52. Delone, W.H., McLean, E.R.: The DeLone and McLean model of information systems success: a ten-year update. J. Manag. Inf. Syst. 19(4), 9–30 (2003)

53. Nwanekezie, U., Choudrie, J., Spencer, N.: Public Sector Online Communication Channel Adoption and Usage amongst older adults: a UK local government perspective. In: Proceedings of Twenty-Fourth European Conference on Information Systems, İstanbul, Turkey (2016)

54. Jøsang, A., Keser, C., Dimitrakos, T.: Can we manage trust? In: Herrmann, P., Issarny, V., Shiu, S. (eds.) iTrust 2005. LNCS, vol. 3477, pp. 93–107. Springer, Heidelberg (2005). doi: 10.1007/11429760_7

The Use of the Social Networks by Elderly People in the Czech Republic and Other Countries V4

Libuše Svobodová$^{(\boxtimes)}$ and Martina Hedvičáková

Department of Economics, Faculty of Informatics and Management,
University of Hradec Králové, Rokitanského 62, 500 03
Hradec Králové, Czech Republic
{Libuse.svobodova,martina.hedvicakova}@uhk.cz

Abstract. In the article we will focus on the elderly people in the connection with the utilization of social networks in the Czech Republic, countries of Visegrad Group and the EU 28. Individuals use social networks for sharing materials, photos or videos, communication or posting messages. Very important is also a topic of social isolation that will be discussed in the article. The results of the statistics show that the share of seniors in the Czech Republic has an increasing trend. The utilization of social networks by elderly people has in the Czech Republic also increasing trend except for the second quarter of the 2015 year when a slight decrease was recorded. In comparison with other countries from Visegrad group and the EU 28 the Czech Republic reached lower results in the utilization of social networks. In two evaluated criteria from three the Czech Republic was comparable to Poland. The age groups show that with increasing age there is a declining trend for the use of social networks. 10.1% of the population from 55 to 64 years and 3.3% of the population over 65 use social networks in the second quarter of 2015. Data show that almost half of the elderly people that use social networks get connected almost every day.

Keywords: Elderly people · Social networks · Statistics · Utilization

1 Introduction

The discussed topic of the utilization and role of social software applications with the focus on the elderly people will be solved in the article. Elderly people have an impact not only on the economy, health care but also on social relations and other important areas. Despite the fact that ten years ago, there was no usual use of ICT by elderly people, the situation is in recent years evolving and changing.

Learning and using information and communication technologies (ICT) such as computer technologies and internet by the elderly is seen as an important demand for their integration in daily life and as a factor related to active aging. [1] Elderly people can on the Internet read online news, newspapers and magazines [17], find information about goods and services, travel and accommodation, health, or search information in the encyclopedias. They can also share information, communicate with others and obtain the above mentioned information via social networks. Also people that have

A.K. Kar et al. (Eds.): I3E 2017, LNCS 10595, pp. 50–60, 2017.
DOI: 10.1007/978-3-319-68557-1_6

medical or other problems and have problems to communicate face to face may thanks to these services get again engaged in an active lifestyle [7, 22]. Social networks help in the social isolation [16]. A lot of elderly people have problems with the movement. They can be in the connection with their families and other people via social networks. [8] Active ageing but also social isolation are the most important facts why elderly people use social networks.

Due to a growing number of elderly people, it is a necessity to create the cities that are aware of the special needs of all their citizens including the needs of aging populations. [2] Despite the fact that urban population is ageing, there is a paucity of studies exploring how ICTs can support older people's living in urban areas. Thus far, visions of smart cities for older people have focused on removing architectural barriers and making physical environments more age-friendly, by considering age-related declines in functional abilities, especially mobility. [3] The aging population comes with many challenges for smart cities— across social, financial, economic, and political dimensions. Managing healthcare quality and costs for this demographic is one of the key focus areas but there are other areas that our Smart Cities majors and municipal councils should consider. [4] The Internet of Everything will allow new business models based on Internet of Things technologies. Sensor technology is increasingly being used in cities to provide us with information about how traffic is flowing, where water pipes are leaking and how much rubbish is going in bins. How looks like the situation in utilization of social networks in the Czech Republic and in other countries of Visegrad four by elderly people will be solved in the next part of the article.

1.1 Development of Population in the Czech Republic

The share of seniors in the Czech population has been steadily increasing since 1985 (from the level of 12%). By the end of the 20th century, the growth was slow (to 13.9% in 2000–2003), but thereafter it accelerated. The share significantly rose especially since 2007, in the connection with baby boomers born in the 40s of the 20th century across the border 65 years of age. During the years 2004–2014, the share of seniors increased from 14% to almost 18% (Table 1).

Table 1. The characteristics of the age composition of 1984, 1994, 2004 and 2014 (to 31. 12.)

Index	1984	1994	2004	2014
The share of seniors (in%)	11,8	13,1	14	17,8
The share of persons aged 80+ on 65+ years (in%)	17,9	21,0	21,5	22,3
Age index	50,3	69,6	94,0	117,4
Average age (in years)	35,6	37,0	39,8	41,7
Median age (in years)	33,9	36,2	38,7	41,1
The number of seniors aged 65+ years (in mil.)	1,22	1,36	1,43	1,88
The number of seniors aged 80+ years (in thousands)	219	285	308	419

Source: [5]

The last presented data (to 31. 12. 2014) states that the proportion of people over 65 years of age is in the general population 17.8%. The current number of 1.88 million is about 243 thousands higher than at the beginning of 2011. Also the highest increases in the age groups were concentrated in the population of the age group of seniors over 65 years. Those increased by 54,900 during 2014. Due to the aging population this issue is very serious in solving economic, social and other areas.

2 Literature Review

Social software applications, social media and social networks play integral role in everyday life of a lot of people all over the world. This topic is also very often discussed but it is not so often connected with the elderly people.

Internet is an ever-growing communication net that connects the most computer systems of the world. It is also the growing technology which is used by people like the information storage, sharing, and easy access. Computer and internet are large communication vehicles of nowadays and future that provide an easy, quick, cheap and safe access to a lot of information [9].

A sociologist J. A. Barnes (1954) is considered to be the author of the definition of the social network. The term social network is associated with the Internet and directly with the social networks on the Internet [10].

Social network on the Internet is considered to be a group of people who communicate and share documents and information on users. The Social Network concept is described and defined by Boyd and Ellison: Social networking is defined as a web service that allows individuals to create a public or semi-public profile within the bounded system, create a group of users with whom they share a connection, and browse the list of own connections and that created by other users of the system. The nature and terminology of these connections may be different network from the net-work [11].

Social media refers to the means of interactions among people in which they create, share, and exchange information and ideas in virtual communities and networks. [12] Furthermore, social media depends on mobile and web-based technologies to create highly interactive platforms through which individuals and communities share, co-create, discuss, and modify user-generated content. It introduces substantial and pervasive changes to communication between organizations, communities, and individuals. [13] Kaplan and Haenlein [14] define social media as a group of Internet-based applications that build on the ideological and technological foundations of Web 2.0, and that allow the creation and exchange of user-generated content.

On Web 2.0 summit presented O'Reilly and Battelle Web Squared: Web 2.0 Five Years On [15]. Chief among our insights was that "the network as platform" means far more than just offering old applications via the network ("software as a service"); it means building applications that literally get better the more people use them, harnessing network effects not only to acquire users, but also to learn from them and build on their contributions. From Google and Amazon to Wikipedia, eBay, and craigslist, we saw that the value was facilitated by the software, but was co-created by and for the community of connected users. Since then, powerful new platforms like YouTube,

Facebook, and Twitter have demonstrated that same insight in new ways. Web 2.0 is all about harnessing collective intelligence. Collective intelligence applications depend on managing, understanding, and responding to massive amounts of user-generated data in real time.

Chen and Schulz [16] presented review study focused on utilization of social media in the connection with social isolation among elderly people. Evidence indicates that contemporary information and communication technologies (ICT) have the potential to prevent or reduce the social isolation of elderly people via various mechanisms. ICT was found to alleviate the elderly's social isolation through four mechanisms: connecting to the outside world, gaining social support, engaging in activities of interests, and boosting self-confidence.

Gonzalez et al. [17] focused on the analysis of the main habits of use and consumption of new technologies by older people, in particular, the level of knowledge and their level of education.

3 Methodology and Goals

Elderly people as a term doesn't have a single definition; there is no general agreement when the person is considered old. Most developed world countries have accepted the chronological age of 65 years as a definition of 'elderly' or older person. At the moment, there is no United Nations standard numerical criterion, but the UN agreed cut off is 60+ years to refer to the older population. [6] Casado-Munoz et al. presented in their paper [7] elderly people from 55 years. In our paper will be presented data from 55+ when data is known. Montaa et al. [8] classify in the research young olds from 61–70 years and middle olds (71 and over).

The goal of the article is to analyse the situation in the field of utilization of social software applications by elderly people in the Czech Republic and to compare the use of social networks in the Czech Republic with other countries V4. Visegrad group is the association composed of the Czech Republic, the Slovak Republic, Poland and Hungary. It focuses on foreign policy activities and the group aims to promote cooperation and stability in the broader region of Central Europe.

The following scientific questions will be solved in the article:

- At least 5% of elderly people in the Czech Republic were using social networks in 2015.
- The percentage of users of social networks by elderly people is increasing every year in the last three years.
- At least ½ of elderly people who use social networks attend them regularly.

While composing this article, especially secondary sources from the various authors but also official statistics by the Eurostat and Czech Statistical Office were used. Information was also obtained from expert press, conferences, seminars and other sources. The obtained data were further sorted, processed in custom tables, clearly set-out diagrams, and further analysed to provide a basic overview of the relevant problem area.

Data that were gained from Eurostat [18] refer to the last 3 months before the survey, for private purposes. Participating in social networks: creating user profile, posting messages or other contributions to facebook, twitter, etc. Data given in this domain [18] are collected annually by the National Statistical Institutes and are based on Eurostat's annual model questionnaires on ICT (Information and Communication Technologies) usage in households and by individuals. The aim of the European ICT surveys is the timely provision of statistics on individuals and households on the use of Information and Communication Technologies at European level. Data for this collection are supplied directly from the surveys with no separate treatment. The survey is a general population/household survey.

The detailed description of methodology and data are discussed directly by tables and graphs.

4   Results

4.1   International Comparison

Statistics were obtained from Eurostat sources. Data are always stated for years that were statistically processed. Always refer to all "All Individuals". Data only for 65+ are not available at the moment. Selected data for the EU 28 and the Czech Republic together with the countries of the Visegrad Group were chosen for comparison because those countries are close to the Czech Republic. Data [18] are always given in %. Tables are completed with graphs which will help in faster-after straightening.

The Fig. 1 contains data about Participating in social networks. It includes creating user profile, posting messages or other contributions to Facebook, Twitter etc. Even though the use of social networking is still growing, data shows that the Czech Republic was in a comprehensive comparison almost always in the last position. Social networks are being used the most over the evaluated period in Hungary, followed by Slovakia, EU 28 and similar results as the Czech Republic reached Poland. If we additionally add into comparison professional networks, percentages are slightly raised. There are not significant changes in the comparison of the trend, see Fig. 2. Only 0.5% of pensioners in the Czech Republic use professional networks, see Fig. 2.

Posting messages to social media sites or instant messaging is the next researched topic, see Fig. 3.

At first glance is it is evident from the graph and table in Fig. 3 that the Czech Republic is again on the last place and lags behind other countries. Despite the fact that from 2009 to 2012 posting messages increased by 3%, other countries grew much more. The highest increase was 12% in the EU 28, but the EU 28 reached in the 2012 the second lowest percentage in the reference sample. About 18% to 47% increased messaging in Slovakia, 9% to 43% in Hungary and increase by 7% to 42% in Poland.

The connection of social networks with elderly people will be solved in the next part of the article.

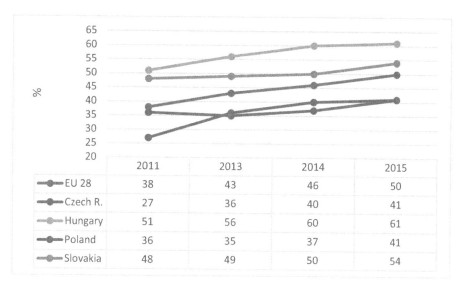

Fig. 1. Participating in social networks (creating user profile, posting messages or other contributions to Facebook, Twitter, etc.). Source own elaboration based on [18]

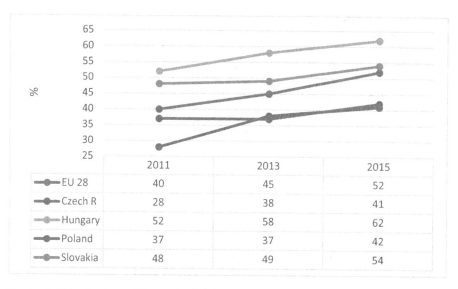

Fig. 2. Participating in social or professional networks. Source: own elaboration based on [18]

4.2   Czech Republic

The Table 2 shows the reasons for utilization of the Internet with focus on the use of social networks. Presented results are divided for citizens over 16 years. Furthermore, according to gender over 16 years and then by age and according to economic activity status. Two age groups - from 55 to 64 years and 65 years were chosen for comparison.

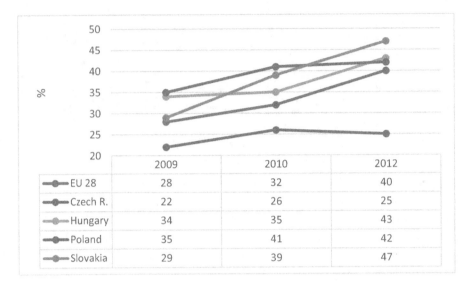

	2009	2010	2012
EU 28	28	32	40
Czech R.	22	26	25
Hungary	34	35	43
Poland	35	41	42
Slovakia	29	39	47

Fig. 3. Posting messages to social media sites or instant messaging. Source own elaboration based on [18]

Furthermore, statistics are given for employed, unemployed and pensioners. Both age groups in all economic activity statuses can be represented in the Czech Republic. It can also for example happen that pensioner is employed.

In detailed table at Czech Statistical Office is at the first glance evident that young adults are still the most likely to use social media. 37.4% of the population over 16 years uses social networks according to the Czech Statistical Office. 40.7% individuals aged 16 to 74 years uses social networks according to the Eurostat. In the event that we focus on the individuals who use the Internet, the percentage will rise. 49.5% of the population that uses the Internet, uses social networks according to the Czech Statistical Office. For gender, there were no significant differences. Data shows that women and men use social networking sites at comparable rates. The similar results were gained also in the Pew Research Center [20]. A slightly higher percentage of men, 37.6% use social networks. Women's use is smaller by 0.3%. In case that we focus again on the group using the Internet, the percentage will rise again. 48.2% of men using the Internet are also using social networks. Representation of women stand higher by 50.8%.

The age groups shows that with increasing age is a declining trend for the use of social networks. While 88.7% of the population from 16 to 24 years benefited in 2015 from utilization of social networks, in the age group 15–34 it was 72.3%, from 35–44 it was 23.9%. 10.1% of the population from 55 to 64 years and 3.3% of the population over 65 use social networks.

Other statistics show that nearly 68% of users who use social networks attend these application every day or almost every day. For older population this percentage decreases by almost a third, to 45.4%. A similar percentage, 45.7% are also listed among pensioners. From the data it is evident that almost half of the elderly people that use social networks are connected each or almost every day.

Table 2. Individuals in the Czech Republic using the Internet for private purposes for selected activities in the field of communication; Q2 2015

	Participation in social networks - total		From that every day or almost every day				
	in thous.	%[a]	%[b]	in thous.	%[a]	%[b]	%[c]
Total 16+	3 284,6	37,4	49,5	2 218,8	25,3	33,4	67,6
Total 16–74[d]	3 282,5	40,7	50,0	2 218,8	27,5	33,8	67,6
Gender							
Male 16+	1 609,3	37,6	48,2	1 103,0	25,7	33,0	68,5
Female 16+	1 675,3	37,3	50,8	1 115,8	24,9	33,8	66,6
Age group							
55–64 years	144,1	10,1	14,9	66,0	4,6	6,8	45,8
65+	60,1	3,3	11,7	27,3	1,5	5,3	45,4
Economic activity status							
Employed	2 164,4	43,3	47,2	1 340,7	26,8	29,2	61,9
Unemployed	100,2	38,6	52,2	72,4	27,9	37,8	72,3
Pensioners	83,2	3,7	11,4	38,0	1,7	5,2	45,7

Source [19]
[a]As a % of total number of individuals in a given socio-demographic group
[b]As a % of total number of Internet users in a given socio-demographic group
[c]As a % of total number of social network users
[d]The data presented by Eurostat for the Czech Republic covers only individuals aged 16 to 74 years.

In the case that we will focus on the development in time it is from Table 3 evident that in almost all of the analysed groups in the article increased using the social networks. The exception is the last year when in the last two age groups has slightly decreased using of social networks, as well as a decline among pensioners. The available statistical data from the Czech statistical office from 2011 used social networks 6% of people 55 to 64 years, and only 1% of the population over 65 years.

Table 3. Individuals using social networks in the Czech Republic

	2013	2014	2015
Total 16+	34,3	36,9	37,4
Total 16–74 years	36,3	40,0	40,7
Age groups			
55–64 let	9,7	10,5	10,1
65+	2,0	3,5	3,3
Pensioners	3,3	4,1	3,7

Source [19]
Share in the total number of individuals in a given group

Another interesting statistics shows that a small percentage of the population uses professional networks, see Table 4. Only 4.1% of the population over 16 years use professional networks by the Czech Statistical Office. Men outnumber women from 5.1% to 1.9%. In the case that we focus on elderly people, only 0.4% over 65 use professional social networks and 1.9% from 55 to 64 years. In the event that we will focus on economic activity status, 0.5% of pensioners use social networks. The table also shows the data for employed and unemployed. Results are surprising. 2.4% unemployed uses social networks.

Table 4. Individuals using professional social networks in the Czech Republic

	Participation in professional networks		
	in thous.	%[a]	%[b]
Total 16+	362,6	4,1	5,5
Total 16–74*	359,8	4,5	5,5
Gender			
Males 16+	216,7	5,1	6,5
Females 16+	145,9	3,2	4,4
Age group			
55–64 years	27,7	1,9	2,9
65+	6,7	0,4	1,3
Economic activity status			
Employed	285,4	5,7	6,2
Unemployed	6,2	2,4	3,2
Pensioners	10,5	0,5	1,4

Source [19]
[a]As a % of total number of individuals in a given socio-demographic group
[b]As a % of total number of Internet users in a given socio-demographic group

5 Conclusion and Discussion

The user group of elderly people is a still growing group and hence depicts an interesting research area. Individuals 55 to 74 years old has the growing trend from 2007 in the indicator last internet use: in last 3 months.

The results show that even though social software applications are used by a small percentage of elderly people, their number and percentage increases. 3.7% individuals 65+ used the social networks in the second quarter of 2015. 11.4% individuals 65+ who use the Internet visit also social networks. 1.7% of all elderly people regularly attend social networks. 5.2% who use the Internet at the same time use social networks regularly and 45.7% who visit social networks access networks each or almost every day.

Participating in social networks (creating user profile, posting messages or other contributions to Facebook, Twitter, etc.) was in the compared years in the Czech Republic and in Poland on the lowest levels in Visegrad 4 and in EU 28 (mean). In the Czech Republic and in Poland participate on social networks more than 35%, in EU28 it was 50%, in Slovakia 54% and the highest use presented Hungary with 61%. The development was in all countries similar instead Poland. Due to the above mentioned facts it is not possible to confirm scientific questions which were stated in the second chapter of the article. In the Czech Republic is also rising the percentage of the individuals aged 65 to 74 old people that have to use internet.

The next researched topic was the utilization of social networks in the Czech Republic and in other countries of Visegrad Group and the EU28 average. It was found out that social networks were used in the followed period less often in the Czech Republic than in other countries involved into the comparison. The question can be why? Do pensioners have digital literacy or necessary equipment? Are there the courses for seniors in the large cities like Hradec Králové?

Also for these reasons we recommended to promote information and digital literacy to citizens and to invest in further education in this field. Information on the courses that are focused on the elderly people and computer literacy in Hradec Králové are presented in [23]. Most elderly people watch TV and read newspapers and for that reason promotion could focus on those channels, but also on other sources. This topic is also interesting due the SMART cities.

The question in the discussion is whether the increasing number of pensioners in the Czech Republic will increase the number of Internet users and social networking for 65+ or will be still personal communication significantly more used. It is expected that the increase in percentage of elderly people who will use advanced technologies will continue. Therefore, the next question might be, whether growing population in 55–64 group which currently uses advanced technologies by 20% more than the 65+ group will keep this trend. The influence of family and health status on the utilization of social networks to communicate with other people or more detailed mentioned benefits gained from utilization of advanced technologies by elderly people may be other areas of research. Next important topic can be social networks and clustering [21].

Acknowledgment. This study is supported by internal research project No. 2103/2017 Investment evaluation within concept Industry 4.0 at Faculty of Informatics and Management, University of Hradec Kralove, Czech Republic. We would like to thank student Marta Martinova for cooperation in the processing of the article.

References

1. Sitti, S., Nuntachampoo, S.: Attitudes towards the use of ICT training curriculum for Thai elderly people. Procedia Soc. Behav. Sci. **103**, 161–164 (2013)
2. Skouby, K.E., Kivimäki, A., Haukipuro, L., Lynggaard, P., Windekilde, I.: Smart Cities and the Ageing Population. http://www.wwrf.ch/files/wwrf/content/files/publications/outlook/Outlook12.pdf
3. Righi, V., Sayago, S., Blat, J.: Urban ageing: technology, agency and community in smarter cities for older people. http://www.dtic.upf.edu/~ssayag/pre-print/C&T15_UrbanAgeing_AAV.pdf
4. Smart Cities Are Vital to Cope with the Aging Population. https://datafloq.com/read/smart-cities-vital-cope-with-aging-population/1205

5. Statistics about population. http://www.statistikaamy.cz/2015/05/praha-uz-neni-nejstarsim-krajem/
6. Health statistics and information systems, Definition of an older or elderly person. http://www.who.int/healthinfo/survey/ageingdefnolder/en/
7. Casado-Munoz, R., Lezcano, F., Rodriguez-Conde, M.J.: Active ageing and access to technology: an evolving empirical study. Comunicar **45**, 37–46 (2015)
8. Montaa, M., Estanyol, E., Lalueza, F.: Our seniors' challenge to the new media: uses and opinions. Profesional de le Informacion **24**(6), 759–765 (2015)
9. Ramazan, A., Kazaz, N., Basa, B.: The internet addiction of Kosovo and Turkey elderly people. Procedia Soc. Behav. Sci. **103**, 1104–1117 (2013)
10. Barnes, J.: Class and committees in a Norwegian Island Parish. Hum. Relat. **7**, 39–58 (1954)
11. Boyd, D.M., Ellison, N.B.: Social network sites: definition, history, and scholarship. J. Computer-Mediated Commun. **13**(1), 210–230 (2007)
12. Ahlqvist, T., Bäck, A., Halonen, M., Heinonen, S.: Social media road maps exploring the futures triggered by social media. VTT Tiedotteita - Valtion Teknillinen Tutkimuskeskus **2454**, 13 (2008)
13. Kietzmann, H.J., Hermkens, K.: Social media? Get serious! Understanding the functional building blocks of social media. Bus. Horiz. **54**, 241–251 (2011)
14. Kaplan, A.M., Haenlein, M.: Users of the world, unite! The challenges and opportunities of social media. Bus. Horiz. **53**(1), 61 (2010)
15. O'Reilly, T., Battelle, J.: Web Squared: Web 2.0 Five Years On. http://www.web2summit.com/web2009/public/schedule/detail/10194
16. Chen, Y.R.R., Schulz, P.J.: The effect of information communication technology interventions on reducing social isolation in the elderly: a systematic review. J. Med. Internet Res. **18**(1), 11 (2016)
17. Gonzalez-Onate, C., Fanjul-Peyro, C., Cabezuelo-Lorenzo, F.: Use, consumption and knowledge of new technologies by elderly people in France, United Kingdom and Spain. Comunicar **45**, 19–27 (2015)
18. Eurostat. http://ec.europa.eu/eurostat/statistics-explained/index.php/Digital_economy_and_society_statistics_-_households_and_individuals
19. Czech Statistical Office (2015). https://www.czso.cz/csu/czso/cinnosti-provadene-jednotlivci-na-internetu
20. Pew Research Center. Social Media Usage 2005–2015. http://www.pewinternet.org/2015/10/08/social-networking-usage-2005-2015/
21. Hedvicakova, M., Pozdilkova, A., Stranska, P.K., Svobodova, L.: Analysis of mobile social networks using clustering. Adv. Sci. Lett. **22**(5–6), 1273–1277 (2016)
22. Llorente-Barroso, C., Vinaras-Abad, M., Sancher-Valle, M.: Internet and the elderly: enhancing active ageing. Comunicar **45**, 29–36 (2015)
23. Autumn Internet courses for seniors - seniorhk.cz. http://www.hradeckralove.org/urad/internet-pro-seniory

Digital Payments Adoption: An Analysis of Literature

Pushp P. Patil, Yogesh K. Dwivedi[✉], and Nripendra P. Rana

Emerging Markets Research Centre (EMaRC), School of Management,
Swansea University Bay Campus, Swansea, SA1 8EN, UK
Pushpppatil@gmail.com, {y.k.dwivedi,n.p.rana}@Swansea.ac.uk

Abstract. Digital payments (mainly enabled by mobile devices) have huge potential to change lives of millions of people in developing countries by offering financial services to the unbanked masses. Despite its potential digital payment methods have not been widely and successfully adopted in the developing countries. In order to ascertain the various drivers and inhibitors behind digital payment adoption, this study did a review of research on digital and mobile payment adoption and use. Results of this literature analysis revealed performance expectancy/perceived usefulness as most significant determinant of consumer's behavioral intention to use mobile payments followed by perceived ease of use (PEOU). Perceived risk was found as major inhibitor to the adoption of mobile payments. Also majority of studies employed TAM and its extension to understand consumer adoption to mobile payment followed by UTAUT.

Keywords: Adoption · Cashless payments · Digital payments · Diffusion · Literature review · Mobile payments · TAM · UTAUT

1 Introduction

Internet has changed the way business is conducted in recent years in terms of wireless communication. This emerging trend is more powerful than anything internet used to offer before as this allows consumers an anywhere and anytime paradigm [1]. In the history of mankind no other innovation has influenced the lives of people in ways as Mobile devices [2]. These hand held devices have gradually shifted daily activities from real world circumstances to mobile phone-based virtual world. In the entire consumer technology adoption history the rate of adoption of Mobile phone was the fastest and to the deepest level [3].

The global spread and use of mobile devices provide prominent role to digital payments in the payment market. This wide penetration of mobile devices bring world of opportunities to transform the manner in which people manage and move money through secure mobile transactions [4]. Consumers are slowly moving towards changing their payment method from traditional ways to contactless devices due to emergence of these new mobile and other digital payment technologies. The rapid development in technology has enabled innovation in payment methods resulting in applications such as Near Field Communication (NFC), mobile wallets, P2P apps, quick response code and wearable [5].

A.K. Kar et al. (Eds.): I3E 2017, LNCS 10595, pp. 61–70, 2017.
DOI: 10.1007/978-3-319-68557-1_7

Despite their popularity as an emerging service mobile payments have not as widely adopted as expected in the developing countries [4]. This could to attribute to the fact that in the developed countries Mobile Payment systems have to compete with range of alternative payment methods with longstanding history [6]. However, the scenario is quite different in the emerging markets. Mobile Payments are readily accepted in the countries like Kenya and Philippines where penetration of formal banking system is low [7].

Given the background, it is undoubted mobile payments have potential to bring financial inclusion especially in the emerging markets by offering financial services to the unbanked masses and improve their lives for better. Recently there have been huge drives to promote various digital payment systems including mobile payments by Government of India (GoI) for enhancing transparency in financial transactions, reducing tax envision and improving public welfare and delivery systems. GoI has not only made variety of digital payment systems available to cater need of all segments (affluent vs. non affluent; rural vs. urban) of society, but widespread training and financial incentives also offered to equip and encourage people to use these systems. Despite the advantages of digital payment systems and widespread promotion there is reluctance among consumers to use various digital payment systems including mobile payment not only in India but also in other countries. This provides motivation and relevance to undertake research in this area. An examination of existing literature suggest that a number of studies have already been conducted to examine factors influencing mobile payments adoption largely in the context of developed countries and there are some in developing countries context. Before undertaking any further empirical work on this topic, it was deemed appropriate to undertake review of existing studies for synthesizing the results reported, identifying their limitations and directions of further work in this important and emerging area.

Considering the discussion presented above, the aim of this study is to undertake analysis and synthesis of relevant research exist on issues related to the mobile payments adoption. In order to achieve this, the remaining part of this submission is structured as follows: next section briefly describe literature search and analysis approach followed by a brief review relevant studies is presented in Sect. 3. Section 4 briefly outlines the main limitations of existing work followed by future research directions in Sect. 5 and finally, key conclusions are outlined in the last section.

2   Literature Search Approach

It was deemed appropriate to do keyword search in order to achieve objectives of this research. This study utilized following keywords to undertake search for relevant work using the Scopus database: "Digital Payment" OR "Cashless Payment" OR "Mobile Payment" OR "Adoption" OR "Acceptance" OR "Diffusion" OR "Usage" OR "Intention" OR "Success" OR "Satisfaction" in order to identify papers relevant to digital payment. The keyword search returned 109 articles. We were able to download 47 full articles. Then Adobe Reader's advanced search function was employed using keywords such as "consumer" and "adoption" for all 47 full articles on mobile payment in order to narrow down articles on consumer adoption of mobile payment. The downloaded mobile payment articles were deemed to be relevant for this study if they met one of the following two criteria: (1) the data collection of research took place among consumers, or (2) the studies developed conceptual model to be empirically tested on consumers at later stage. The articles were screened out if the data was collected from merchants or focusing on organizations aspect. In the end 21 papers were found relevant for inclusion in this review. This study looked into these 21 articles which specifically focused on consumer adoption of mobile payment. Then a detailed review of these articles was conducted to identify theories utilized in this area and various drivers and inhibitors of mobile payment.

3   Systematic Literature and Findings

This section presents review summary of mobile payment adoption research. The review is classified broadly under two categories: (1) frequently used theories in research addressing consumer adoption of mobile payment; and (2) drivers and inhibitors of mobile payment adoption.

3.1   Frequently Used Theories in Consumer Mobile Payment Adoption

A large number of Information Technology (IT)/Information Systems (IS) projects and systems continue to fail leading to adverse impact of such investments on individuals, organizations and society [8–10]. This provides reasonable impetus to researchers for repeatedly examining factor influencing adoption and use of new technologies and systems in the contexts of individual, organization and society. Consequently, multiple theories have been employed in IS field to determine individual technology acceptance in various use contexts. Table 1 reveals frequently used theories for understanding issues related to consumer adoption of mobile payment systems. These studies were either used standalone or in combination with other dominant technology adoption theories and models.

Table 1. Frequently used theories and model in consumer Mobile payment adoption.

Theory/Model	Freq	Citations
TAM	14	[4, 11, 17, 21–30, 33]
UTAUT	5	[6, 19–21, 33]
DOI	3	[12, 15, 19]
IDT	3	[4, 15, 33]
Mallat (2007)	1	[13]
Dahlberg and Oorni Factor (2007)		
Tornatzky and Klein (1982)	1	[15]
Trust based acceptance model [36]	1	[16]

LEGEND: DOI: Diffusions of Innovations Theory; IDT: Innovation Diffusion Theory; TAM: Technology Acceptance Model; UTAUT: Unified Theory of Acceptance and Use of Technology

With 14 studies Technology Acceptance Model (TAM) and its extension have been most utilized technology adoption theory/model in this domain. These studies adopted, adapted and extended TAM across various use contexts. For instance the study by Jack and Suri [2] utilized TAM alongside with Innovation Diffusion Theory (IDT) to explore adoption of mobile payments and value added services (VAS). Whereas Zhanga et al. [11] employed TAM standalone to explore factors affecting the adoption of mobile payment in particular cultural settings. The Unified Theory of Acceptance and Use of Technology (UTAUT) emerged as the second most utilized theory (originating from Venkatesh et al. [34]) with five studies employing it. Slade et al. [6] utilized UTAUT to examine consumer adoption of proximity mobile payments in the UK and Zhanga et al. [11] utilized it to examine consumer adoption of mobile payments in China. This is followed by Diffusion of Innovation Theory (DOI) utilized thrice in studies including Pham and Ho [12] who examined consumer adoption of NFC-based mobile payments. IDT was employed on two occasions by Augsburg and Hedman [4] and Zhanga et al. [11]. More than 50% of studies reviewed by Slade et al. [20] have drawn on Davis' (1989) TAM as a theoretical base.

The remaining four theories/models were employed only once. The study of Keramati et al. [13] employed combinative model of Mallat N. factors [14] and Dahlberg and Oorni Factor model [35] to explore factors affecting 'mobile'-payment services adoption, whereas Kapoor et al. [15] utilized Tornatzky and Klein's theory and Moore and Benbasat's perceived characteristics of innovating theory to determine adoption of the interbank mobile payment service and finally Gong et al. [16] utilized trust based acceptance model to study the effects of cognitive and emotional trust on mobile payment adoption.

3.2 Drivers and Inhibitors of Mobile Payment Adoption

Review also revealed that majority of the studies have reported performance expectancy (PE) construct from UTAUT and perceived usefulness (PU) from TAM as most significant determinant of consumer's behavioral intention to use mobile payments whereas perceived risk was found as inhibitor to the adoption of mobile payments. Study of Augsburg and Hedman [4] on value added services (VAS) and adoption of mobile payments found PU can influence the consumer intention to adopt mobile payments. Consumers see payment process being easier and more efficient when VAS is integrated with the mobile payment service. Compatibility and convenience were also found as critical factors of intention to adopt mobile payments [4].

Other studies that have reported PE/PU as major predictor of consumer mobile payments were Chandrasekhar and Nandagopal [17]; Koenig-Lewis et al. [18]; Oliveira et al. [19]; Pham and Ho [12]; Slade et al. [20]; Staykova and Damsgaard [21]. Apart from PU the study of Chandrasekhar and Nandagopal [17] found consumers will adopt mobile payment use behavior if it fits into their lifestyle. Whereas Koenig-Lewis et al. [18] study revealed social influence and perceived enjoyment can reduce perceived risk of using mobile payment.

Four studies [13, 22–24] have reported Perceived Ease of Use (PEOU) as major driver to consumer mobile payment adoption. These studies found in terms of consumers' willingness to adapt to mobile payment, the impact of usability issues are more important than those pertaining to usefulness. In addition to PEOU, the study of [23] noted that implementation of mobile payment technology needs substantial considerations in terms of infrastructure availability, partnerships between various stakeholders such as banks and phone operators and quality of the business model. Whereas, Keramati et al. [13] revealed an interesting lifestyle as a driver for adoption, finding people who travel often and reside in other countries are more inclined to use M-payment services.

Apart from PEOU and PU the following studies found other significant drivers of consumer mobile payment adoption. Liébana-Cabanillas et al. [25, 26] have reported role of external influence (that is derived from the social influence and subjective norms) as the strongest driver of consumer adoption towards mobile payment. Gao and Waechter [27] found perceived information quality, perceived system quality, and perceived service quality as major drivers of initial trust formation while examining user adoption of mobile payment services. Emotional trust was found to have stronger effect on consumers' intention to use mobile payment [16]. Moreover, Hossain and Mahmud [28] results found cognitive style significantly related to perceived ease of use in determining mobile payment adoption. Whereas Kapoor et al. [15] found Rogers' diffusion of innovation attributes as significant predicator for determining adoption of the interbank mobile payment service in India and Lee et al. [29] found perceived benefits as significant factor of mobile payment service acceptance.

Perceived risk (PR) was found as inhibitor by majority of the studies. Andreev et al. [22] found PR as a major inhibitor of user willingness to M-Pay for LBS. They also found magnitude of PR's negative impact could be at least twice the magnitude of any other positive driver's impact. Apart from Andreev et al. [22] studies such as Koenig-Lewis et al. [18], Liébana-Cabanillas et al. [25], Pham and Ho [12], Slade et al. [20] and Slade et al. [6] also found Perceived risk as the major inhibitor to consumer adoption to mobile payment. Whereas, Augsburg and Hedmann [4] found an interesting fact that insignificant effect of VAS on Perceived Ease of Use can become an inhibitor. Apart from PR, perceived uncertainty was found as major initial trust inhibitor that exerts a significant negative effect on building initial trust in user adoption of mobile payment services. Information privacy is another inhibitor to consumer adoption of mobile payment services for "fintech". Whereas network externalities, security, and payment transaction information were found as major inhibitors to consumers 'mobile'-payment services adoption by Keramati et al. [13].

4   Research Limitations

Augsburg and Hedman [4] research on value added service (VAS) and mobile payment have chosen three VAS but does not differentiate between them and presents them all to the experimental group. Limitation of this study is that VAS offer different value propositions and different consumers may be more attracted to some propositions than others. Gao and Waechter [27] examined the role of initial trust in user adoption of mobile payment service empirically in Australia which, in terms of national characteristics, is different from other mobile technology advancing nations such as South Korea, Japan, and Finland. Also, the results of this study may or may not be applicable to emerging markets context such as India. Individual user characteristics is also a factor which might affect but not been used in this study. The study examined ·initial trust formation, which may demonstrate different trust behavioral pattern with time in future [27]. Gong et al. [16] examined the effects of cognitive and emotional trust on mobile payment adoption. The limitation of this study Gong et al. [16] is that sample size was relatively small and participants were Chinese university students or faculties, which require further research in different regional/national settings with a larger sample size. Hossain and Mahmud [28] studied influence of cognitive style on mobile payment system adoption with an extended technology acceptance model. The limitation of this study is that sample size is too small and study used questionnaire which was completed by educated people with prior use experience of mobile payment. Another limitation of this study Hossain and Mahmud [28] is that it has not examined actual usage behavior.

Kapoor et al. [15] examined role of three sets of innovation attributes for determining adoption of the interbank mobile payment service. The limitation of this study is that the data collection was geographically restricted to only four largest Indian cities. Given that the culture and geographical locations do impact the diffusion of an innovations, Kapoor et al. [15] work should be tested using data from smaller cities. Kim et al. [24] studied the adoption of mobile payment services for "fintech" and the limitation of this study is that the samples of the survey were limited to Seoul, the capital area, and certain age groups were predominantly represented, giving way to regional and age biases. Liébana-Cabanillas et al. [25] examined antecedents of the adoption of the new mobile payment systems with moderating effect of age. Limitation of this study is that it was focused only on one mobile payment system (SMS), while there are other technologies such as the NFC payment systems that also need attention. Oliveira et al. [19] examined mobile payment to understand the determinants of customer adoption and intention to recommend the technology. Limitation of this study is that it hasn't used some factors that some may consider important to the adoption of mobile payment, such as trust [30, 31] and risk [32]. Limitation of this research also concerns the age and location of the questionnaire respondents; more than 88% were aged 45 years or less from Portugal.

5   Future Research Directions

Augsburg and Hedman [4] was conducted in Denmark, which has very high mobile usage and very high maturity in credit and debit card usage; hence the high intention to use mobile payment with or without VAS is not surprising. Further research can focus in Western countries as well as in the context of emerging markets (such as India) with high cash usage. Gao and Waechter [27] study suggest that future research should compare pre-adoption and post-adoption of m-payment trust behavior to find out whether trust behaviors changes over time. Gao and Waechter [27] also recommended examining role of additional constructs such as perceived value, perceived justice and perceived risk. Gong et al. [16] study primarily focuses on the trust transfer mechanism from one source (web payment) to mobile payment (MP) as one target. This study only examined the effects of emotional trust in web payment, perceived similarity, and cognitive trust in MP on emotional trust in MP. As emotional trust in really important in consumer decision-making, future studies could empirically examine other valid mechanisms to build consumers' emotional trust in MP [16].

Hossain and Mahmud [28] recommended undertaking further research in the context of rural areas in Bangladesh and testing an extended model by incorporating the actual usage, cognitive style or any other relevant variables based on the recent literature on this topic. Kapoor et al. [15] study can be extended by collecting more representative data from other states and smaller towns. The future studies may want to focus more on the influences of image as an innovation attribute. Also, the future studies might want to test the various risk types associated to IMPS in order to arrive at a more convincing explanation on the influences that riskiness may have on the diffusion of IMPS in the Indian context [15].

Follow-up studies to Kim et al. [24] should analyze the impact on the acceptance of groups classified into more specific age groups, income and device through a multi-group model. Future research of Liébana-Cabanillas et al. [26] can be directed towards in various technologies such as QR codes, a two dimensional bar code, biometric fingerprints, voice payment, Google Goggles. Oliveira et al.'s [19] work can be furthered by examining age and cultural differences. Studies with a larger sample size from other geographical settings can help to confirm validity and establish generalizability of Pham and Ho [12]. Longitudinal studies should be conducted in future to test same research model at different points of time, which will allow comparisons and will help to provide further insights towards consumers' adoption behavior towards NFC mobile payments. In addition, the future research should also validate the modified UTAUT model developed by some recent studies (e.g. Dwivedi et al. [37, 38]; Rana et al. [39, 40]) in the areas of technology and e-government adoption.

6   Conclusions

This study conducted a review of literature on consumer adoption of mobile payments. The salient points emerged from this literature analysis suggest that TAM and its extension as most utilized technology adoption theory/model for understanding consumer adoption of mobile payments. Performance expectancy and perceived usefulness emerged as most significant determinant of consumer's behavioral intention to use mobile payments whereas perceived risk was found as inhibitor to the adoption of mobile payments in majority of studies.

Although this review presents a concise summary of mobile payment adoption research, insight provide by it should be interpreted in light of the following limitations. This review was based on literature search using only Scopus database, so studies that are not indexed in this database may have been excluded. Future literature reviews should consider other databases to address the limitations of this study. Also, only a subset of studies identified was reviewed, remaining studies would be reviewed in this ongoing work to explore if there are drivers and inhibitors that needs to be considered by future studies. Also, this study only presented review about theories; drivers and inhibitors, there are other aspects that require further detailed analysis. This work mainly reviewed studies on mobile payment adoption; future reviews should also include studies on other digital payment methods. The other limitation is that this study focused on consumer adoption of mobile payment excluding organization adoption and other stakeholders.

References

1. Barnes, S.: The mobile commerce value chain: analysis and future developments. Int. J. Inf. Manage. **22**(2), 91–108 (2002)
2. Jack, W., Suri, T.: Mobile money: the economics of M-PESA (No. w16721). National Bureau of Economic Research (2011)
3. Thakur, R., Srivastava, M.: Adoption readiness, personal innovativeness, perceived risk and usage intention across customer groups for mobile payment services in India. Internet Research. **24**(3), 369–392 (2014)
4. Augsburg, C., Hedman, J.: Value added services and adoption of mobile payments. In: Sixteenth International Conference on Electronic Commerce (2014)
5. De Kerviler, G., Demoulin, N., Zidda, P.: Adoption of in-store mobile payment: are perceived risk and convenience the only drivers? J. Retail. Consum. Serv. **31**, 334–344 (2016)
6. Slade, E., Williams, M., Dwivedi, Y., Piercy, N.: Exploring consumer adoption of proximity mobile payments. J. Strat. Mark. **23**, 209–223 (2014)
7. Mobile financial services development report (2011). http://www3.weforum.org/docs/WEF_MFSD_Report_2011.pdf
8. Dwivedi, Y., Wastell, D., Laumer, S., Henriksen, H., Myers, M., Bunker, D., Elbanna, A., Ravishankar, M., Srivastava, S.: Research on information systems failures and successes: status update and future directions. Inf. Syst. Front. **17**, 143–157 (2014)
9. Hughes, D., Dwivedi, Y., Rana, N., Simintiras, A.: Information systems project failure – analysis of causal links using interpretive structural modelling. Prod. Plan. Control **27**, 1313–1333 (2016)
10. Hughes, D.L., Dwivedi, Y.K., Simintiras, A.C., Rana, N.P.: Success and Failure of IS/IT Projects. SIS. Springer, Cham (2016). doi:10.1007/978-3-319-23000-9
11. Zhanga, A., Yue, X., Kong, Y.: Exploring culture factors affecting the adoption of mobile payment. In: Tenth International Conference on Mobile Business, pp. 263–267 (2011)
12. Pham, T., Ho, J.: The effects of product-related, personal-related factors and attractiveness of alternatives on consumer adoption of NFC-based mobile payments. Technol. Soc. **43**, 159–172 (2015)
13. Keramati, A., Taeb, R., Larijani, A., Mojir, N.: A combinative model of behavioural and technical factors affecting 'Mobile'-payment services adoption: an empirical study. Serv. Ind. J. **32**, 1489–1504 (2012)
14. Mallat, N.: Exploring consumer adoption of mobile payments – a qualitative study. J. Strateg. Inf. Syst. **16**, 413–432 (2007)
15. Kapoor, K., Dwivedi, Y., Williams, M.: Examining the role of three sets of innovation attributes for determining adoption of the interbank mobile payment service. Inf. Syst. Front. **17**, 1039–1056 (2014)
16. Gong, X., Zhang, K.Z., Zhao, S.J., Lee, M.K.: The effects of cognitive and emotional trust on mobile payment adoption: a trust transfer perspective. In: Proceedings of Pacific Asia Conference on Information Systems (PACIS), Taiwan (2016)

17. Chandrasekhar, U., Nandagopal, R.: Mobile payment usage intent in an Indian context: an exploratory study. Asian J. Inf. Technol. **15**(3), 542–552 (2016)
18. Koenig-Lewis, N., Marquet, M., Palmer, A., Zhao, A.: Enjoyment and social influence: predicting mobile payment adoption. Serv. Ind. J. **35**, 537–554 (2015)
19. Oliveira, T., Thomas, M., Baptista, G., Campos, F.: Mobile payment: understanding the determinants of customer adoption and intention to recommend the technology. Comput. Hum. Behav. **61**, 404–414 (2016)
20. Slade, E., Dwivedi, Y., Piercy, N., Williams, M.: Modeling consumers' adoption intentions of remote mobile payments in the united kingdom: extending UTAUT with innovativeness, risk, and trust. Psychol. Mark. **32**, 860–873 (2015)
21. Staykova, K., Damsgaard, J.: Adoption of mobile payment platforms: managing reach and range. J. Theor. Appl. Electron. Commerce Res. **11**, 66–85 (2016)
22. Andreev, P., Pliskin, N., Rafaeli, S.: Drivers and inhibitors of mobile-payment adoption by smartphone users. Int. J. E-Business Res. **8**, 50–67 (2012)
23. Berrado, A., Elfahli, S., El Garah, W.: Using data mining techniques to investigate the factors influencing mobile payment adoption in morocco. Paper Presented at the 2013 8th International Conference on Intelligent Systems: Theories and Applications, SITA (2013). doi:10.1109/SITA.2013.6560791
24. Kim, Y., Park, Y.J., Choi, J.: The adoption of mobile payment services for "Fintech". Int. J. Appl. Eng. Res. **11**(2), 1058–1061 (2016)
25. Liébana-Cabanillas, F., Sánchez-Fernández, J., Muñoz-Leiva, F.: Antecedents of the adoption of the new mobile payment systems: the moderating effect of age. Comput. Hum. Behav. **35**, 464–478 (2014)
26. Liébana-Cabanillas, F., Sánchez-Fernández, J., Muñoz-Leiva, F.: The moderating effect of experience in the adoption of mobile payment tools in Virtual Social Networks: the m-Payment Acceptance Model in Virtual Social Networks (MPAM-VSN). Int. J. Inf. Manage. **34**, 151–166 (2014)
27. Gao, L., Waechter, K.: Examining the role of initial trust in user adoption of mobile payment services: an empirical investigation. Inf. Syst. Front. **19**, 525–548 (2015)
28. Hossain, R., Mahmud, I.: Influence of cognitive style on mobile payment system adoption: an extended technology acceptance model. Paper presented at the 2016 International Conference on Computer Communication and Informatics, ICCCI (2016). doi:10.1109/ICCCI.2016.7479973
29. Lee, J.B., Lee, S.B., Park, C.: A study on the individual and environmental factors affecting mobile payment service acceptance-a focus on NFC-based payment ServicesJae-Beom. Int. Inf. Inst. (Tokyo) Inf. **18**(4), 1185 (2015)
30. Liébana-Cabanillas, F., Muñoz-Leiva, F., Sánchez-Fernández, J.: Influence of age in the adoption of new mobile payment systems. Revista Brasileira de Gestão de Negócios **17**(58), 1390 (2015)
31. Guillén, A., Herrera, L., Pomares, H., Rojas, I., Liébana-Cabanillas, F.: Decision support system to determine intention to use mobile payment systems on social networks: a methodological analysis. Int. J. Intell. Syst. **31**, 153–172 (2015)
32. Slade, E., Williams, M., Dwivedi, Y.: Devising a research model to examine adoption of mobile payments: an extension of UTAUT2. Market. Rev. **14**, 310–335 (2014)
33. Zhong, J., Dhir, A., Nieminen, M., Hämäläinen, M., Laine, J.: Exploring consumer adoption of mobile payments in china. Paper presented at the Proceedings of the 17th International Academic MindTrek Conference: "Making Sense of Converging Media", MindTrek, pp. 318–325 (2013)

34. Venkatesh, V., Morris, M.G., Davis, G.B., Davis, F.D.: User acceptance of information technology: toward a unified view. MIS Q. **27**(3), 425–478 (2003)
35. Dahlberg, T., Oorni, A.: Understanding changes in consumer payment habits-do mobile payments and electronic invoices attract consumers? In: 40th Annual Hawaii International Conference on System Sciences (2007)
36. Komiak, S.Y., Benbasat, I.: The effects of personalization and familiarity on trust and adoption of recommendation agents. MIS Q. **30**(4), 941–960 (2006)
37. Dwivedi, Y.K., Rana, N.P., Jeyaraj, A., Clement, M., Williams, M.D. Re-examining the Unified Theory of Acceptance and Use of Technology (UTAUT): towards a revised theoretical model. Inf. Syst. Front. (2017a). doi:10.1007/s10796-017-9774-y
38. Dwivedi, Y.K., Rana, N.P., Janssen, M., Lal, B., Williams, M.D., Clement, M.: An empirical validation of a Unified Model of Electronic Government Adoption (UMEGA). Gov. Inf. Q. (2017b). doi:10.1016/j.giq.2017.03.001
39. Rana, N.P., Dwivedi, Y.K., Lal, B., Williams, M.D., Clement, M.: Citizens' adoption of an electronic government system: toward a unified view. Inf. Syst. Front. **19**(3), 549–568 (2017)
40. Rana, N.P., Dwivedi, Y.K., Williams, M.D., Weerakkody, V.: Adoption of online public grievance redressal system in India: toward developing a unified view. Comput. Hum. Behav. **59**, 265–282 (2016)

Barriers to Adopting E-commerce in Chinese Rural Areas: A Case Study

Hong Guo[1(✉)] and Shang Gao[2]

[1] School of Business Administration, Anhui University, Hefei, China
homekuo@gmail.com
[2] School of Business, Örebro University, Örebro, Sweden
shang.gao@oru.se

Abstract. Although e-commerce has been adopted and developed rapidly in rural areas in China during the past two years, serious issues have been encountered as well. Practitioners and scientists proposed lists of barriers. However, such lists differ with each other for different regions and at different time. Fixed lists may not help much practically. Present research proposes a framework named N3F4 to structure and formalize such barriers. Based on the framework, researchers could make a list of barriers for a given region, perform surveys among interested people, prioritize the barriers, analyze reasons and propose solutions. In this paper, we introduce the N3F4 framework, and present a case study of applying the framework in one small county in China. The result shows that the N3F4 framework helps structure barriers before performing the survey, and it also helps analyze the result and come up with solutions afterwards, both effectively and efficiently.

Keywords: E-commerce · Chinese rural areas · Barriers

1 Introduction

As e-commerce has been developed rapidly and gained huge achievement in Chinese cities, e-commerce giants such as Alibaba and JD.com accelerated their business expansion in Chinese rural areas. During this process, experiences in cities were copied to rural areas. However, due to huge differences between developed cities and rural villages in China, many challenges have been met. Chinese practitioners and experts reflected on their practices and proposed barrier lists as well as corresponding solutions. But limitations exist in such lists. Firstly, in such lists, it is often not clear from which perspective these lists have been proposed. For instance, when "lack of talented people" is proposed, it is not clear that such a barrier is meaning for business owners, consumers, or government. Therefore it is not clear which *subject* should pay attention to (and come up with solutions for) this barrier. Secondly, it is often confused that, what is the reason that has caused a barrier. For instance, when "logistics cost is high" is referred to, we are not sure if this is the reason why e-commerce has not been developed as well as expected, or this is the result of low development level of e-commerce. It is not clear that we should take steps to improve the infrastructure like roads, or try to increase the e-commerce volume. In another word, it is difficult to

A.K. Kar et al. (Eds.): I3E 2017, LNCS 10595, pp. 71–82, 2017.
DOI: 10.1007/978-3-319-68557-1_8

analyze *reasons* and come up with *solutions*. Thirdly, it is often not clear that what is the result such a barrier will lead to. For regions where "logistics cost is high", the degree of "high" may differ a lot. As a result, different *priorities* should be granted to. To summary, such barrier lists may not help much in practice.

Despite various barrier lists proposed by experts, practitioners have been struggling for long time in many rural areas. This is primarily because of the huge differences between urban and rural areas in China. In addition, there is huge difference among different villages as well. A general barrier list does not make sense for different areas, different people, and at different stages. In this research, we propose a conceptual framework to generate barriers for a given region. We expect that barrier lists can be made in a more structured and efficient way. More importantly, solutions can be proposed more effectively.

The rest of this paper is organized as below. Section 2 introduces background knowledge about Chinese rural areas, e-commerce development in Chinese urban and suburban areas. In Sect. 3, we introduce some related work. Section 4 presents the N3F4 framework and how to apply the framework to structure a barrier list. Then we introduce a case study of applying N3F4 framework in Sect. 5. Later in Sect. 6, we discuss how N3F4 framework can be utilized in similar contexts. Limitations and future work are also discussed. And lastly, we conclude this paper in Sect. 7.

2 Background

2.1 Chinese Rural Areas: Subjects, Regions and Industries

In China, there are around 39789 towns (townships) [1], and more than 500 thousands villages. According to statistics in 2015, population in Chinese villages are 603.46 million, counting for 43.9% overall population of China. In such areas, primary industry is performed which refers to agriculture, forestry, animal husbandry, fishery, and services in support of these industries. In 2015, gross output value of primary industry was 10705 billion [1]. Most residents in villages are engaged in primary industry, especially agriculture.

There is a huge difference between urban and rural areas in China, both from the natural perspective and the social perspective. Therefore, issues regarding agriculture, countryside and farmers have been traditionally important for economy increase and social development in China. Such issues are characterized as "Three Nong" issues meaning "NongYe" (agriculture), "NongCun" (countryside) and "NongMin" (farmers) [2].

2.2 E-commerce in Chinese Developed Cities and Rural Areas

As the world's largest online market, Chinese e-commerce sales at $750 billion in 2016 sales [3]. Nearly 25% of all sales are apparel, footwear, and accessories. Another 20% is electronics and appliances. All these sales are about living industrial goods.

Meanwhile, internet [4] and e-commerce were perceived as a new engine for rural empowerment and a number of experimental projects were initiated in recent years.

From 2015, e-commerce giants started their businesses in Chinese rural areas. Businesses mainly include selling industrial products in countryside, selling agricultural products to cities, agricultural materials e-commerce, and etc. Despite huge achievement in some rural areas [5], problems have also been encountered in many other areas.

3 Related Work

There are many scientific papers where barriers, difficulties, challenges and issues that hinders the adoption and diffusion of e-commerce in developed countries are enumerated [6–11]. However, as indicated in [12], the development route of Chinese e-commerce may not follow that in US and other developed countries. Many such barrier lists may not fit well in China.

Chinese researchers have proposed various barrier lists for rural e-commerce adoption, at different time and in different perspectives. In [13], the author thought that the difference between residents in rural areas and cities is one of the most prominent issues for e-commerce adoption in China. For instance, residents in rural areas are more conservative and do not trust new things like electronic payment. Residents in rural areas are less educated and may not be qualified for running e-commerce. In addition, low level of logistics services, low level of standardization of agricultural products, and food safety issues bring difficulties for e-commerce development also. Similarly, in [14], high-cost logistics, small scale and unprofessional online shops, and low standardization level of agricultural products are thought to be important barriers for developing e-commerce in Chinese rural areas. While in [15], the authors emphasized on issues for e-commerce of fresh agricultural products in China. Such issues include lack of cold-chain logistics, weak supply chain management, high loss, and slow business expansion at grass roots level. As introduced in Sect. 1, most of such barriers were proposed without detailed description about their subjects, reasons and corresponding results. This is because such barriers were usually proposed at a high theoretical level and did not intend to provide concrete solutions to a given area at a specified time.

In [16], thirty barriers to e-commerce were gathered from literature and put into six groups as social and culture barriers, technical barriers, economical barriers, political barriers, organizational barriers, and legal and regulatory barriers. Some business runners of small and medium enterprises in Egypt were asked to indicate the factors which inhibited e-commerce adoption. A similar case study was introduced in [17]. However, as indicated in [18], issues inhibiting SMEs in their uptake of e-commerce have largely remained the same for many years. Researches should focus more on how to overcome barriers instead of reinventing barrier lists. In our research, we try to formalize barriers in a structured way, so that it is possible to identify and prioritize top barriers for a given situation in order to overcome them.

4 N3F4 Framework Formalism

4.1 "Three Nong" Issues

"Three Nong" issues are issues concerning "NongYe" (agriculture), "NongCun" (countryside) and "NongMin" (farmers). "Three Nong" consists of subjects, region and major industry. There are complicated relationship among these issues. And such issues consist of not only natural issues, but also social issues. As a large agricultural country, "Three Nong" issues have being traditionally very important for China as they concerns national quality, economic development, social stability, national prosperity, and etc.

"Three Nong" issues are very important for e-commerce adoption and development in Chinese rural areas as well. This is because when e-commerce were firstly advocated in rural areas, practitioners copied their experiences of operating e-commerce of industrial products in urban areas. The difference between "Three Nong" and their correspondences in urban areas represented reasons why new barriers are met in rural areas.

1. "Nong" Region (NR): NR is referred to as rural areas, villages or countryside. When NR is compared with urban areas, geographical features, infrastructure levels, supporting services, and etc. may differ a lot. For instance, it is usually less developed in NR than in cities.
2. "Nong" People (NP): In Chinese, NP is primarily refers to people who perform agriculture (farmers). Most of the residents of NR is NP. In this research, we refer to residents in NR as NP.
3. "Nong" Industry (NI): Traditionally, agriculture is the major industry which is performed in NR. In this research, we include forestry, animal husbandry, fishery and etc. that most NP are engaged in.

4.2 Four Flows of E-commerce

E-commerce includes exchange of goods, cash, information among businesses and consumers [19]. In addition, e-commerce usually makes it easier to exchange information, cash and goods than traditional commercial behavior. In Chinese literature, it is referred to as "Four Flows of E-commerce".

If e-commerce is developed well in some areas, we can see that the "Four flows" should run smoothly and efficiently. On the country, if e-commerce is not developed well in some areas, one or more of the "Four flows" must not run well. Therefore, whether the "Four flows" runs smoothly can be used to judge the level of e-commerce development in one area to some extent.

1. IF (Information Flow): Information flows among businesses and consumers during the whole process of a transaction. Such information includes commodity information, marketing information, asking price information, payment status information, consumer services information, and etc. When E-commerce is utilized, information flows much more easily than before (when mail, telephone, and face-to-face communication were used);

2. CF (Cash Flow): A transaction is formally executed when a buyer pays (cash flows from the buyer to the seller) and gets the product. For E-commerce, it is easy for cash to flow (payment or transaction) owing to the usage of electronic payment means and Electronic Funds Transfer (EFT);

3. GF (Goods Flow): When a buyer pays, he gets the product (goods flows from the seller to the buyer). In another word, GF refers to logistics. Some kinds of commodities such as electronic books, software and tickets can be transferred virtually via network. Most commodities still need to be transferred physically. However, utilizing information technologies makes GF more effectively and efficiently than before;

4. TF (Trade Flow): In addition to information flow, cash flow and goods flow, TF includes a series of activities during the whole transaction process. Such activities are like: (sellers) market positioning, (sellers) market promoting, (consumers) acquiring commodity information, (sellers and buyers) negotiating, and (sellers and buyers) contract signing. TF is the base of CF and GF. TF also includes some activities that CF, IF and GF do not cover. For E-commerce, most of such activities can be eased by utilizing electronic means and information technologies.

4.3   N3F4 Framework Formalism

To develop the N3F4 framework, we reviewed more than thirty scientific papers regarding barriers (sometimes called as challenges, problems, difficulties or issues) that have been met when e-commerce were promoted in Chinese rural area. As indicated in [12], the development route of Chinese e-commerce may not follow that in US and other developed countries. Thus these scientific papers are mostly written in Chinese and published in notable Chinese journals. Corresponding solutions are often proposed in such papers as well. Considering the limited space, the detailed review method and process will be presented in another paper. We collected barriers and solutions, analyzed commonalities and differences among them. It was found that such barriers are often proposed from different perspectives and at different levels as introduced in Sect. 1. We identified two important factors for each barrier: reasons and results. While "SanNong" can be used to characterize reason categories (what kind of urban-rural differences caused the barrier), "Four Flow" can be thought as which part of e-commerce is hindered by such a barrier as a result. We constructed the N3F4 framework therefore as Table 1 shows. This table can be used as a container of barriers as we introduce in the next section.

Table 1. A two-dimension issue space structured by N3F4 framework

	TF	IF	CF	GF
NR				
NP				
NI				

4.4   Applying N3F4 Framework to Structure Barriers

By following this idea, we collected, reconstructed the barriers in one list as Table 2 shows.

Table 2. Barriers of adopting and developing e-commerce in Chinese rural areas

Barriers in one list:	
B1. Lack of related services;	B2. Lack of platform and cooperation atmosphere;
B3. Lower income and living conditions in rural area;	B4. Bad coverage of network, or bad signal;
B5. Lack of local information broadcasting;	B6. Lack of information consulting channel;
B7. Fewer bank offices;	B8. Lack of local channel to get finance support;
B9. Mobile payment, payment through online banks, electronic banks, and telephone banks are not widely available;	B10. Lack of space for production and storage;
B11. Road network is not developed and convenient enough;	B12. Expensive and inconvenient logistics;
B13. Lack of cold-chain logistics;	B14. Lack of computer and mobile phone skills;
B15. Lack of electronic commerce knowledge;	B16. Lack of operation management capability;
B17. Fierce competition due to many similar products;	B18. Low margin due to high production and operation cost;
B19. Lack of market information;	B20. Difficulty of finding buyers;
B21. Difficulty of selling with a desirable price;	B22. Difficulty to ensure similar quality level;
B23. Difficulty to ensure supply quantity;	B24. Difficulty of recruitment;
B25. Inconvenient of communication due to few internet users;	B26. Difficulty of getting information and operation without computers;
B27. Lack of funds;	B28. Lack of financing channels;
B29. High logistics cost due to remote and decentralized production& living area;	B30. Low consumer trust in food safety;
B21. Quality fluctuation due to different season and types of farm products;	B32. Price fluctuation due to different season and types of farm products;
B33. Difficulty of scale up due to features of specified farm products;	B34. Taobao and Wechat [20] platforms are not suitable for selling farm products;
B35. Selling agricultural products demands more funds;	B36. Difficulty of storage and transportation because farm products are perishable;
B37. Requirement of cold-chain logistics because farm products are perishable;	B38. High logistics cost because farm products are produced in small scale and scattered;
B39. Difficulty to ensure supply quantity due to small scale and scattered production;	

By putting all the barriers in N3F4 according to which aspects such barriers are caused by, and which flow such barriers may hinder, the barrier list is structured as Table 3 shows. Such a structured barrier list can be used for surveys in order to collect user attitudes. We will introduce this in Sect. 5.

Table 3. Barriers in N3F4 framework

	TF	IF	CF	GF
NR	B1, B2, *B3*	*B4*, **B5**, B6	*B7*, B8, *B9*	B10, *B11*, B12, B13
NP	B14, B15, B16, B17, B18, B19, B20, B21, *B22*, B23, B24	*B25*, *B26*	B27, B28	B29
NI	B30, B31, B32, B33	*B34*	*B35*	B36, B37, B38, B39

5   Case Study

In this section, we present how we apply N3F4 framework to prepare a survey, analyze data, and propose solutions in one case study.

5.1   Method and Process

In April 2017, more than one hundred farmers took part in an e-commerce training course in a mountainous country in Anhui province of China. Few of them have utilized e-commerce tools to sell their agricultural or farm products online. While most of them only have intention or interests to adopt e-commerce for their businesses (if there are) in future. We prepared a survey and asked these farmers to give a score (from 1 to 5) for each barrier listed in Table 2. 75 valid questionnaires have been received afterwards.

5.2   Data Analysis and Discussion

By counting the average score each barrier was, we came up with top ten barriers and bottom ten barriers for the participants. We observe where each barrier locates (due to which "Nong" and bring impact to which "Flow"), analyze possible reasons, and propose corresponding solutions.

Top Ten Barriers and Bottom Ten Barriers for All Participants

Firstly, we come up with top and bottom ten barriers for all participants as Table 4 shows. By highlighting such barriers (top ten in red and bolded, while bottom ten in green and italic) in N3F4 framework as shown in Table 3, some interesting facts were found:

Table 4. Identified top ten barriers and bottom ten barriers from the case study

Top Ten Barriers			Bottom Ten Barriers		
4	B1	3.92	9	B3	3.14
8	B5	3.86	4	B4	2.64
10	B15	3.73	2	B7	2.58
9	B17	3.82	1	B9	2.50
3	B18	3.93	8	B11	3.09
5	B19	3.9	6	B22	2.96
7	B20	3.87	7	B25	3.04
1	B29	3.96	5	B26	2.65
6	B38	3.89	3	B34	2.61
1	B39	3.96	10	B35	3.19

1. Five of the top ten barriers (B15, B17, B18, B19 and B20) are located in the cell of NP-TF. Which means, such barriers are due to the population quality of NP (farmers primarily), and the result of such may be somehow devastating (for TF): buyers cannot be found or products cannot be sold with a desirable price. As a consequence, business contract may not even be signed. This is in accordance with the fact that most of the participants said they were aware of their shortcomings, so they took part in the training. Such talents issues are also highlighted in many Chinese scientific papers that we have reviewed.

2. Both B25 and B26 are within the bottom ten barriers. Although B25 and B26 are also caused by NP, they only bring impacts to information flow, and are thought as not important as other barriers. This might be because they are about lower-level computer skills. While broadband is popularized in Chinese rural areas, more and more people in such area get in touch with computers, mobile phones and become more skillful to utilize such IT tools to get information and communicate with others. According to CNNIC [21], there have been 201 million internet users in Chinese rural areas, accounting for 33.1 of total population in such areas. At the training site, almost every participants used mobile phone and Wechat, and when a Wechat group was established, many participants chat actively. This fact supports the hypothesis to some extent.

3. In all CF related cells, there is no top ten barriers. Instead, two barriers (B7 and B8) within these cells are thought as not quite important (in bottom ten barriers). This may indicate that, in rural areas where mobile phone have been popularized, traditional bank offices and payment methods may not be quite important for people to adopt e-commerce. Thanks to the e-payment technologies and platforms such as Wechat payment and Alipay, it is possible for rural areas to develop e-commerce without some traditional infrastructure construction. And it makes it possible for a "corner overtaking" for such an area.

4. Compared with CF and IF related cells, there are more top ten barriers (B29, B38, and B39) in GF related cells. This is in accordance with reports from scientific papers and practitioners that high cost and bad quality of logistic services seriously

hindered e-commerce development in many rural areas. We can further identify reasons that might have caused such issues by looking at other barriers in GF related cells. Despite fine road network (B11 is in bottom ten barriers), high logistics cost might be primarily caused by remote and decentralized population and production (B38).

Top Ten Barriers for Business Owners

Compared with general people who have interests or intention to run a business, it may be important to pay more attention to the needs of existing business owners.

We also look at the situation of participants who have already utilized e-commerce tools for their businesses. 5 such valid questionnaires are included. The corresponding top ten barriers differ a lot with that of all participants. These barriers are: B5, B6, B15, B16, B17, B18, B25, B27, B28, B29, B32, B38 and B39 (several barriers have the same score). By comparing this list with the top ten barriers of all participants, we found that:

1. In addition to B5, B6 is also in top ten barriers. That is to say, information turns out to be more important for business holders than general people. Business owners might not be satisfied with access to general information. They have further requirements such as consulting on specified and personalized topics. This is reasonable because as long as people have begun businesses, various concrete issues might be met.
2. Many top ten barriers (B15, B16, B17 and B18) are still found in NP-TF. Compared with the general situation, B19 and B20 are no longer thought as quite important because business runners could find market information and sell their products out better. However, these business runners find operation skills are very important (B16 is one of the top ten barriers).
3. B27 and B28 are new barriers that appear in top ten barriers. Both of them are about CF indicating that people may not feel the pressure of money until they have really run an e-commerce.

Top Ten Barriers for Returnees

Urbanization has partly led to serious population loss in many Chinese villages. When most young adults move to big cities to work, large proportion of residents are children, women of childbearing age, and elders. As a result, "lack of talents, technician or labor" becomes a general issue in many areas. When e-commerce is promoted in such areas, governments often introduce policies to lure returnees and great expectations are placed on them.

Among all our 75 valid questionnaires, 25 are from returnees. When we focus on these people, we have the top ten barriers as: B2, B5, B6, B12, B17, B18, B19, B20, B21, B29. By comparing this list with the general one, we found that:

1. B2 appears in top ten barriers now. In cities, talented people often worked and studied together. While in rural areas, such platform is quite rare. Returnees realize this difference because they have seen or experienced that;

2. In addition to B5, B6 is also in top ten barriers. Similar to business owners, returnees might have a wider view and think about e-commerce in an independent way. As a result, they require channels to consult on personalized topics more than other people;

Top Ten Barriers for College Graduates

In addition to returnees, college graduates are better educated and more innovative. Thus, they are often thought as another important force for rural areas to develop E-commerce.

Five college graduates participated in our survey, and their correspondent top ten barriers are: B2, B12, B13, B18, B19, B20, B24, B29, B36, and B37. Findings are:

1. B2 also appears in top ten barriers as it is in the list for returnees. This might be caused by similar reasons: college graduates have sights or experience which make them feel it is important to work and study together with others;
2. B13 and B37 appear in top ten barriers as never before. Both items are about cold-chain logistic services. Both items do not appear in top ten lists for general people, business owners, or returnees. We consider the reason is that college graduates think highly of advanced and new things. However, it is difficult to judge for a given area whether applying cold-chain logistic is a practical choice as cold-chain logistic services charge much more than general logistic services.

6 Discussion

A list of top ten barriers implies information of what blocks the adoption or hinders the diffusion of e-commerce. Surveys can be conducted to help scientists and practitioners identify particular barriers for a given region, from perspective of a given demographic and at a given stage. By doing so, requirements can be analyzed and prioritized, and solutions can be proposed correspondingly.

However, such lists vary under different conditions. **Firstly**, different demographics possess different top ten barriers. This helps us analyze and infer what caused the issues, and what the issues will bring impacts on from corresponding perspectives as we discussed in the case study. **Secondly**, it is obvious that top ten barriers also differ from each other for different areas. For instance, in more remote mountainous regions where Internet is not populated and few people use mobile phones, people may probably pay more attention to infrastructure related barriers such as B11 (road), B4 (internet signal), and etc. **Thirdly**, such lists differ for different industries. For instance, when online shopping (living industrial goods) is considered, the top ten barriers might differ from that when online shopping (agricultural supplies) is considered. **Lastly**, such lists differ with time. As time goes on, roads and Internet would be populated, people would grow to be more knowledgeable and skillful, industries would be developed, and barrier list would change as well.

As a result, barriers should be observed for different regions and different industries, from perspectives of different demographics, and at different time. By doing so, the prioritized barriers can be thought as reflective, constructive and instructive. From the case study presented in Sect. 4, we can see that N3F4 framework helps us generate and structure barrier lists, as well as analyze barrier reasons and results, both effectively and efficiently.

Limitations and Future Work

There are limitations of current research. Barriers enumerated in Table 2 are not formalized well. Some of them have similar meanings and have confused survey participants. Correspondingly, we identify some possible future work. Firstly, we plan to refine the current barrier list by reviewing and analyzing recent literature. Secondly, we will collect and analyze barriers which have been met and reported in related subdomains such as agricultural materials e-commerce, living industrial goods e-commerce, and etc. Thirdly, we plan to carry out more formal and large-scale surveys to evaluate the N3F4 framework.

7 Conclusions

In this paper, we introduce the N3F4 framework to structure barriers encountered when e-commerce is adopted in Chinese rural areas. The framework is based on two traditional theories in China. The first is the N3 theory which refers to three key feature categories of Chinese rural areas: agriculture, farmers, and countryside. And another is the F4 theory which characterizes that when a transaction happens, information, cash, goods and transaction activities "flow" among stakeholders. Such flows can be eased by utilizing IT tools in e-commerce transactions. We introduce both the N3F4 framework and how to apply it to generate and structure prioritized barrier lists for a particular purpose. A case study of applying N3F4 is presented. And the result shows that, the N3F4 framework helps us not only when barriers are enumerated and structured, but also when result is analyzed, and solutions are proposed.

References

1. National Bureau of Statistics of the People's Republic of China (2017). http://www.stats.gov.cn/
2. Lin, W., Wong, C.: Are Beijing's equalization policies reaching the poor? An analysis of direct subsidies under the "Three Rurals" (Sannong). China J. **67**, 23–46 (2012)
3. Chinese Ecommerce Market Pegged at $1.7 Trillion by 2020 (2017). http://multichannelmerchant.com/news/chinese-ecommerce-market-pegged-1-7-trillion-2020/
4. Zhao, J.: ICT4D: Internet adoption and usage among rural users in China. Knowl. Technol. Policy **21**(1), 9–18 (2008)
5. Leong, C.M.L., et al.: The emergence of self-organizing e-commerce ecosystems in remote villages of China: a tale of digital empowerment for rural development. MIS Q. **40**(2), 475–484 (2016)
6. Kshetri, N.: Barriers to e-commerce and competitive business models in developing countries: a case study. Electron. Commer. Res. Appl. **6**(4), 443–452 (2008)
7. Kapurubandara, M., Lawson, R.: Barriers to adopting ICT and e-commerce with SMEs in developing countries: an exploratory study in Sri Lanka, pp. 2005–2016. University of Western Sydney, Australia (2006)

8. Lawrence, J.E., Tar, U.A.: Barriers to e-commerce in developing countries. Inf. Soc. Justice J. **3**(1), 23–35 (2010)
9. MacGregor, R.C., Vrazalic, L.: E-commerce adoption barriers in small businesses and the differential effects of gender. J. Electron. Commerce Organ. **4**(2) (2009)
10. MacGregor, R.C., Vrazalic, L.: A basic model of electronic commerce adoption barriers: a study of regional small businesses in Sweden and Australia. J. Small Bus. Enterp. Dev. **12** (4), 510–527 (2005)
11. MacGregor, R.C., Kartiwi, M.: Perception of barriers to e-commerce adoption in SMEs in a developed and developing country: a comparison between Australia and Indonesia. J. Electron. Commerce Organ. **8**(1), 61–82 (2010)
12. Haley, G.T.: E-commerce in China: changing business as we know it. Ind. Mark. Manage. **31**(2), 119–124 (2002)
13. Lai, X.Y.: Problems and countermeasures in the development of agricultural electronic commerce. Chinese J. Agric. Res. Reg. Plan. **37**(3), 180–183 (2016)
14. Li, J.B., Chen, W.: Problems and innovative countermeasures in the development of agricultural electronic commerce. Commercial Times **34**, 89–90 (2014)
15. Liu, J.X., Wang, K.S., Zhang, C.L.: Main problems and countermeasures in the development of fresh agricultural products electronic commerce. China Bus. Market **30**(12), 57–64 (2016)
16. Zaied, A.N.H.: Barriers to e-commerce adoption in Egyptian SMEs. Int. J. Inf. Eng. Electron. Bus. **4**(3), 9–18 (2012)
17. Sandberg, K.W.: Barriers to adapt eCommerce by rural Microenterprises in Sweden: a case study. Int. J. Knowl. Res. Manag. E-Commerce **4**(1), 1–7 (2014)
18. Chitura, T., et al.: Barriers to electronic commerce adoption in small and medium enterprises: a critical literature review. J. Internet Bank. Commerce **2**, 1–13 (2010)
19. Ying, W., Dayong, S.: Multi-agent framework for third party logistics in E-commerce. Expert Syst. Appl. **29**(2), 431–436 (2005)
20. Gao, S., Krogstie, J.: Understanding business models of mobile ecosystems in China: a case study. In: The Proceedings of the 7th International Conference on Management of Computational and Collective IntElligence in Digital EcoSystems (MEDES 2015), Caraguatatuba/Sao Paulo, Brazil. ACM (2015)
21. CNNIC, China Statistical Report on Internet Development (2017)

Assessment of ICT enabled Smart Initiatives

Digital Governance for Sustainable Development

Luís Soares Barbosa[✉]

UNU-EGOV, United Nations University, Campus de Couros, Guimarães, Portugal
barbosa@unu.edu

Abstract. This lecture discusses the impact of digital transformation of governance mechanisms as a tool to promote sustainable development and more inclusive societies, in the spirit of the United Nations 2030 Agenda. Three main challenges are addressed: the pursuit of *inclusiveness*, *trustworthiness* of software infrastructures, and the mechanisms to enforce more transparent and *accountable* public institutions.

1 Introduction

The answer is yes, but would you mind to repeat the question? This excited reply verbalised in a scene of a famous Woody Allen's movie from the Eighties, sums up quite precisely the way societies, States and citizens face the tide of digitization with its ever-growing spectrum of applications and possibilities.

Actually, governments cannot ignore the huge potential of digital technologies and of their progressive integration with unsuspected social dynamics. In particular, new tecnologies provide innovative tools to enhance communication, coordination, and participation in social and political life [8]: their effective harnessing will indeed shape the future of governance and democracy in the years to come.

On the other hand, the global spread of digital technologies has often increased inequality, and the poorest and most marginalised have frequently failed to benefit from it. For example, the absence of a reliable internet infrastructure can further entrench inequality and exclusion, as it is increasingly difficult for people to participate in the digital economy and new forms of civic engagement without proper internet connection, and, of course, without the corresponding literacy.

The Sustainable Development Goal 16 of the United Nations 2030 Agenda calls for effective, accountable and inclusive institutions at all levels in the framework of peaceful and inclusive societies [14]. We believe that digital transformation of governance processes and procedures has a role to play in achieving such a goal. After reviewing what *electronic governance* (EGOV) means in the current context, and highlighting some characteristics of digitization in Sects. 2 and 3, this lecture opens the discussion on digital transformation as a tool to promote sustainable development and more inclusive societies. Three main challenges are discussed in Sect. 4: the pursuit of *inclusiveness*, the *trustworthiness* of software infrastructures, and the mechanisms to enforce *accountability* of public institutions.

Published by Springer International Publishing AG 2017. All Rights Reserved
A.K. Kar et al. (Eds.): I3E 2017, LNCS 10595, pp. 85–93, 2017.
DOI: 10.1007/978-3-319-68557-1_9

Although the views expressed below are strictly personal, they are based on empirical evidence collected from our current work within UNU-EGOV, the new United Nations University unit on *Policy-Driven Electronic Governance*[1], established in Guimarães, Portugal, in 2014. As part of the 'research branch' of the United Nations, the Unit aims at transforming the mechanisms of governance through the strategic application of digital technologies, and building effective capabilities for technology-enabled governance at the global, national and local levels. It takes an integrative, holistic view of governance networks focused on articulating macro-level development policies with micro-level, bottom-up participation.

2   EGOV: From Electronic Government to Digital Governance

The reader is certainly familiar with standard definitions of EGOV: for the World Bank it refers to *the use of information and communication technologies by government agencies that have the power to transform the relations of citizens, businesses and other government sectors*; for the European Union it focuses on the use of such technologies *in public administrations combined with organizational change and new skills to improve public services, democratic processes and increase support for public policy.*

In practice, EGOV is a main component in the process of strengthening the performance of government and public administration [16]. Traditionally associated with the (digital) provision of public services, it also relates directly to questions of democracy, leveraging new information, consultation, or communication possibilities, for example, in regard to proposed legislation or in planning processes. Actually, its impact on the re-organization of public services and participation processes cannot be underestimated. For example, the separation between *front* and *back* offices, a typically favoured EGOV service structure, not only requires a readjustment of working processes, but leads to numerous institutional changes. In particular, this makes possible to reduce or eliminate the institutional fragmentation of public administration, giving citizens access to public services from a single location and interface.

Over the past two decades, EGOV both as an application area and a research domain, evolved from a straight use of technology in public administration, to a multidisciplinary understanding of governance, and an integrative, holistic view of administrative processes. Its initial focus on establishing and maintaining a technological environment in government quickly evolved into the use of technology to transform its internal working and organization, and later expanded to also cover transformation of the relationships between government and citizens, businesses and other non-state actors [7]. New designations such as *digital governance* or *policy-driven electronic governance* are currently used to highlight its broad scope, encompassing the impact of emerging technologies, in the former case, or to emphasise that investment into technology is expected, not only to

---

[1] egov.unu.edu.

transform the working of government, but also to directly support public policy goals in specific contexts, in the latter.

At the verge of such new development, EGOV becomes a catalyst for change with the public administration and its relationships with the civil society [20], raising the overall efficiency, effectiveness, and legitimization of administrative structures and decision-making processes.

3   The Rise of Everyware

At different levels, governance and public administration, and consequently EGOV processes, are facing the huge impact of ever new digital technologies and the progressive integration of digital, physical and biologial systems [5,10,11]. The rise of *everyware*, an expression capturing the fact that our devices are increasingly part of our personal ecosystem, is leading not only to flexible production schemes, customization of products and highly competitive markets operating via digital platforms [19], but also to a huge manancial of data, as well as new ways of living [4], heterogenous societies, and better informed citizens, increasingly demanding in their expectations.

In particular, as noticed in [12], digitization is removing from the State the information monopoly, which was once one of its main sources of power. At the same time it acts as a catalyst of change in the nature of the relationships between the civil society and the State, enforcing their evolution from a hierarchical to a network structure. The impact of social media [1], defining new, unsuspected forms of socio-interaction at all levels of society, should not be underestimated. In such a context, in an increasing number of countries, governments are regarded as public-service centers, and evaluated on their abilities to deliver through the most efficient and individualized channels.

The governance function and, consequently, EGOV processes, need to follow or, better still, to anticipate such moves to be able to harness digital technology to address really complex problems and permanently assess and control its side-effects.

Clearly, such technologies are a source of empowerment for citizens, providing new ways to voice their opinions, coordinate efforts, and possibly circumvent governmental supervision. As for the reverse of the coin, new surveillance systems and data mining, if uncontrolled, may give rise to all-too-powerful public authorities.

Yet a more precise example is given by the blockchain technology, which enables a network of computers to jointly verify a transaction before it can be recorded and approved. As such, blockchain has the potential to create trust between independent, non familiar actors which become entitled to collaborate without requiring any kind of central authority. Currently its most common use is on recording financial transactions made with digital currencies. However, if blockchain-based, descentralised payment systems can lead to easier and more transparent transactions, they could also hinder the ability for public authorities to trace their origin and destination. Notice, in passing, that other application areas for blockchain are emerging, namely in the EGOV domain, to record different sorts of administrative transactions, such us certificates of birth, academic degrees or ownership.

Indeed, when essential public functions and data migrate to digital platforms, clear regulatory frameworks need to be enforced to guarantee reliability, trustworthiness and, in general, the defence of public interest. The process, however, is never linear: most of the time new policies are triggered by the rapid pace of change and the dynamics of societies[2].

4 Challenges

In a changing world, no *one-fits-all* recipe [6] can be suggested to strengthen EGOV processes and ensure their articulation with more general societal aims of sustainable development. Digitization itself has different faces and impacts in different regions of the world. This section discusses three challenges which are, from our perspective, critical for the future.

4.1 EGOV for Inclusiveness

We do not live in inclusive societies nor in an inclusive world. The statistical evidence is overwhelming: Half of all assets around the world are controlled by the richest 1% of the global population, while the lower half own less of 1% of global wealth. Extreme poverty places a challenge to the way governance is conceptualized: good governance should provide for the basic human needs of everyone, in particular to people and communities extremely vulnerable to poverty. And yet digital transformations may be a net contributer to meet the sustainable development goals. Thus the challenge to EGOV systems and policies is to pursue a rights-based approach to service delivery and universal access [13,16].

In the developing world this means first of all the ability to set up processes and services supporting the State activity and society dynamics under the rule of law. However, it also means to harness technology to facilitate access to public services over rent, distance, and literacy rates. The use of mobile channels in regions whose first, and often unique, contact with the Internet is precisely the mobile phone is a classical example. Mobile devices acting over a reliable, extensive and, of course, affordable communications infrastructure help marginalised communities build stronger networks, open new opportunities, and eventually find their way out of economic hardship. For example, mobile banking, providing mobile money for 'unbanked' people[3], can foster new localised services to e.g. facilitate family remits or micro-credit which is consensually an important catalyst in alleviating poverty. A specific, associated technology, that of voice recognition as a certification device, has been successfully and widely implemented

---

[2] An illustrative example is provided by the fragmented emergence of data protection laws in most countries, somehow pushed by the growing digital, global economy.

[3] People who lack bank services in their communities or even fail have a home address or other documents required to open an account.

in rural areas in India, allowing to overcome low literacy rates still dominant in several regions of the planet.

Designing EGOV for inclusiveness also means a progressive involvement of communities in the construction of relevant EGOV processes to improve access to sustainable livelihoods, entrepreneurial opportunities and information resources. For example, our experience in Africa shows the relevance of digital platforms for land registration and price alerts for framers, as well as for promoting bottom-up participation in community-level development plans.

4.2 Trustworthy Infrastructures

The existence of a reliable and effective communications infrastructure is a precondition to any EGOV development project, namely within the developing world where cost is the biggest obstacle to access digital technologies and the internet. Actually, broadband access must be viewed as the most critical resource within an ecosystem that touches all aspects of life (devices, skills, infrastructure).

But technological infrastructures, to begin with the EGOV platforms at national, regional and local levels, also need to operate in a reliable, trustworthy mode. This concerns general issues on the top of the mediatic agenda, such as security and data privacy, but goes beyond. Puting it simple, the software underlying EGOV processes and platforms cannot fail and should ally simplicity of use with reliable operation.

In Computer Science this calls for software design and development methodologies in which the correctness of a system, i.e. its strict conformance with the specification of the intended behaviour, is established and checked in a rigorous way by mathematical reasoning. This is an area of research, going back to the Seventies, suggestively entitled *formal methods* [2,9]. There is nothing surprising here: the engineering of a complex software system requires the same level of rigour necessary to build a bridge or establish an electric network.

Indeed, the use of precise and mathematically sound techniques to design and engineer software is advantageous for a variety of reasons. A well-defined notation allows an expression of requirements in a manner that is both clear and comprehensive, resulting in a formal specification. A model of the system can then be developed and checked for correctness with respect to it. This is achieved by a variety of means. One approach is to use theorem-proving where logical axioms and inference rules are used to construct a proof, usually in a semi-automatic procedure. Another approach is to use model-checking whereby an exhaustive search of all possible states of the system is performed to demonstrate whether it is correct; one advantage of this approach is that in case the system is flawed then a counter-example is produced, which can be helpful in determining where the flaw is in the system. Of interest here is not only correctness, but also (usually intricate) properties of the system that need to be established. For example, system designers are often interested to check whether a concurrent system is deadlock-free. Such questions have to be answered before a system is implemented and operational, and, in most cases, this can only be done if the system is modelled and designed formally.

As a research agenda, trustworthy development of software is at the centre of a debate which is no longer a technical one. Actually, for ICT industry correctness is not only emerging as a key concern: it is simply becoming part of the business. Companies are becoming aware of the essential role played by proofs and formal reasoning in this process. At present, at least in what concerns safety-critical systems, *proofs pay the rent*: they are no more an academic activity or an exotic detail.

The same applies to State run information systems which more and more can be regarded as critical infrastructures providing resilient platforms for connecting the State and citizens, public administration and the private sector.

4.3 Accountable Institutions

It was already mentioned in the Introduction that Sustainable Development Goal 16 of the United Nations 2030 Agenda calls for effective, accountable and inclusive institutions at all levels. Actually, it marks the recognition that institution-building for sustainable development is critical for realizing the Agenda's underlying vision.

The impact of digitization at this level should be made clear. There are, of course, direct benefits in terms of efficiency of service delivery and the potential to increase transparency at all levels of administration. To be effective, however, an objective and intentional course of action is required to enforce the necessary re-organization of procedures and processes, and build on the move to develop a new institutional culture. Digitization can make public administrations more responsive through new participation channels. Citizen participation, for example in city-level budgetary decisions or the development of land-use plans, also contributes to *legitimization* of political decisions and adds credibility to public institutions.

The digitization of service processes in public administration also requires a degree of formalization, which may act as a mechanism to impose a certain level of *formalization* upon the work of State institutions. In countries where informal, poorly controlled administrative behaviours are one of the essential problems, this sort of EGOV 'side-effect' becomes particularly important. A specific relevant example comes from the introduction of electronic procurement, which is not only a way of combining purchases, thereby reducing expenditures, but has also the potencial of reducing the possibility for corruption in the tendering process.

In general, as recent research at UNU-EGOV has shown [17], EGOV offers a particular potential to improve financial and taxation systems. The introduction of integrated tax systems not only allows to control expenditures, but also to better supervise taxpayers, increasing internal revenues, dramatically reducing the shadow economy, and better monitoring financial flows within the State.

Nevertheless, technology, as such, has a limited direct impact upon the organization change towards more transparent and accountable institutions. It has all the potential, but real impact depends on the way it is introduced and managed by political actors whose ways of thinking often reflect power interests (e.g. neopatrimonial leadership styles, rent-seeking behaviours, etc.). Some experience reports on EGOV remark that *although process transparency and reducing the autonomy of offices which deal directly with citizens could reduce corruption, new channels of corruption could also arise, in particular through the delegation of front office functions to third parties.* [18].

A low-performance, rigid, and centralised public administration with correspondingly low resources is a typical problem in several developing countries. Within a proper environment, EGOV development may contribute to its development and democratization, which is a necessary prerequisite for economic and social development. A word of caution makes sense here: digital technology cannot compensate for weakly developed administrative and management capacities, unmotivated, poorly-trained staff or for a poor democratic culture.

5   Conclusions

In a famous, lucid essay, Ha-Joon Chang, a Korean economist, argues that in relative terms, digitization has not yet proved as revolutionary as what happened in the late nineteenth century with wired telegraphy and later with the emergence of household appliances, as well as electricity, piped water and piped gas, which *totally transformed the way women, and consequently men, live* [3]. This is certainly a most interesting debate, but clearly, in pragmatic terms digitization opens the opportunity to 'do government better' and, if correctly planned, contributes to achieving the sustainable development agenda which is crucial in the years to come [15]. In particular, it can put more power in the hands of citizens and communities, starting with so simple things like allowing people to rate their health or educational services, as well as building a direct, suitably formalised relationship with the State.

The State itself is becoming less uniform, with a diversity of internal organizations, dynamics and culture. Local administration, namely at city level, is increasingly determinant, as the proportion of the world's population living in urban areas has grown from 14 to 50% in about a century. As always, their best regulators are the citizens themselves. We have already illustrated this by mentioning the potential of EGOV in procurement to promote accountable procedures. But it also helps to increase supplier diversity so that local suppliers can be provided with business opportunities and communities actively involved.

On the other hand, and although digitization is a global phenomenon, simply transferring EGOV solutions from developed to developing countries seems inappropriate. Actually, the different initial institutional, cultural, and wider administrative contexts must be considered to avoid unintended effects. In particular, the development potential of digitization in public administration can only be realized in the presence of certain preconditions, and may therefore require longer implementation periods for pilot projects and a stronger focus on capacity building. In any case, almost irrespective of geography, it requires strong political initiative and a serious debate on the different roles the State may play and the corresponding understandings of governance.

We believe that the retreat of governments from many areas where they used to play a major role in the past, and their redefinition as enablers of private initiatives, may limit their impact on leading a sustainable development agenda and supporting the poorest segments of the population. Digital technologies may bring new instruments to this arena, catalysing new alliances within societies, reinventing the State roles and helping us formulate new answers to old, pressing problems, such as development, environmental sustainability, and the eradication of poverty.

Aknowlegdments. This paper is a result of the project SMARTEGOV - *Harnessing EGOV for Smart Governance (Foundations, methods, Tools)*/NORTE-01-0145-FEDER-000037, supported by Norte Portugal Regional Operational Programme (NORTE 2020), under the PORTUGAL 2020 Partnership Agreement, through the European Regional Development Fund (EFDR).

References

1. Alarabiat, A., Soares, D.S., Estevez, E.: Electronic participation with a special reference to social media - a literature review. In: Tambouris, E., et al. (eds.) ePart 2016. LNCS, vol. 9821, pp. 41–52. Springer, Cham (2016). doi:10.1007/978-3-319-45074-2_4
2. Bjørner, D., Havelund, K.: 40 years of formal methods. In: Jones, C., Pihlajasaari, P., Sun, J. (eds.) FM 2014. LNCS, vol. 8442, pp. 42–61. Springer, Cham (2014). doi:10.1007/978-3-319-06410-9_4
3. Chang, H.-J.: 23 Things They Don't Tell You About Capitalism. Bloomsbury Press, New York (2010)
4. Cowen, T.: Average is Over: Powering America Beyond the Age of the Great Stagnation. Penguin, New York (2013)
5. Gubbi, J., Buyya, R., Marusic, S., Palaniswami, M.: Internet of things: a vision, architectural elements, and future directions. Future Gener. Comput. Syst. **29**(7), 1645–1660 (2013)
6. Hill, H., Schuppan, T., Walter, K.: Rethinking e-government from below: new skills for the working level? In: Bertot, J.C., Luna-Reyes, L.F., Mellouli, S. (eds.) 13th Annual International Conference on Digital Government Research, dg.o 2012, College Park, MD, USA, June 4–7, 2012, pp. 264–265. ACM (2012)
7. Janowski, T.: Digital government evolution: from transformation to contextualization. Gov. Inf. Quart. **32**(3), 221–236 (2015)
8. Janssen, M., Estevez, E.: Lean government, platform-based governance - doing more with less. Gov. Inf. Quart. **30**((Supplement-1)), S1–S8 (2013)
9. Jones, C.B., O'Hearn, P.W., Woodcock, J.: Verified software: a grand challenge. IEEE Comput. **39**(4), 93–95 (2006)
10. Kim, K.-D., Kumar, P.R.: Cyber-physical systems: a perspective at the centennial. In: Proceedings of the IEEE, vol. 100(Centennial-Issue), pp. 1287–1308 (2012)
11. Lee, E.A.: The past, present and future of cyber-physical systems: a focus on models. Sensors **15**(3), 4837–4869 (2015)
12. Mickelthwait, J., Wooldridge, A.: The Fourth Revolutions: The Global Race to Reinvent the State. The Penguin Press, New York (2014)
13. Picot, A., Lorenz, J. (eds.): ICT for the Next Five Billion People. Springer, Heidelberg (2010)

14. United Nations Development Programme. Building Inclusive Societies and Sustaining Peace through Democratic Governance and Conflict Prevention. United Nations Development Programme (2016)
15. United Nations Development Programme. Final Report on illustrative work to pilot governance in the context of the SDGs. United Nations Development Programme (2016)
16. United Nations Development Programme: UN E-Government Survey. E-Government in Support of Sustainable Development, United Nations Department of Economic and Social Affairs (2016)
17. Rohman, I., Veiga, L.: Against the shadow: the role of e-government. In: 18th Annual International Conference on Digital Government Research, pp. 319–328. ACM (2017)
18. Schuppan, T.: E-government in developing countries: experiences from sub-saharan Africa. Gov. Inf. Quart. **26**(1), 118–127 (2009)
19. Schwab, K.: The Fourth Industrial Revolution. World Economic Forum, Cologny (2016)
20. Veiga, L., Janowski, T., Barbosa, L.S.: Digital government and administrative burden reduction. In: Bertot, J.C., Estevez, E., Mellouli, S. (eds.) Proceedings of the 9th International Conference on Theory and Practice of Electronic Governance, ICEGOV 2016, Montevideo, Uruguay, March 1–3, 2016, pp. 323–326. ACM (2016)

Assessment of Factors Influencing Information Sharing Arrangements Using the Best-Worst Method

Dhata Praditya[✉] and Marijn Janssen

Faculty of Technology, Policy and Management, Delft University of Technology,
Jaffalaan 5, 2628 BX Delft, Netherlands
{D.Praditya,M.F.W.H.A.Janssen}@tudelft.nl

Abstract. Governments and companies exchange various kinds of data. The methods to exchange data are evolving and becoming more and more advanced, supported by the rapid development of information and communication technology (ICT). Although some research has been carried out on the adoption of ICT-based information sharing, there is still very little understanding of enablers for information sharing arrangements between private and public organisations. Developing an information sharing arrangement often requires complex interactions among parties resulting in negotiated arrangements. This paper aims to derive factors of information sharing arrangements by assessing the importance of factors in shaping information sharing from public and private organisations perspectives. Factors found in previous studies were analysed using the Best-Worst method by collecting experts' opinions. While private sector's expert was much focussed on the Perceived Benefits, the public sector's experts considered Trust, Investment, Perceived Costs and Relationship as the most important factors in shaping the information sharing arrangement between public and private organisations. Identifying which factors are crucial in shaping information sharing arrangements can help in reducing potential conflicts during planning, implementation and usage, and bringing benefits to all stakeholders.

Keywords: Information sharing · Big data · Open data · E-Government · Interorganisational Information System (IOS) · Information sharing arrangement · System architecture · System governance · Best worst method

1 Introduction

In the era of big data, more and more emphasis is put on information to support better decisions [1]. For this reason, information sharing intra and interorganisational are required. Interorganisational information arrangements are typically more complex system compared to intraorganisational, because these arrangements have to deal with a variety of stakeholders, multi-level interactions, vertically and horizontally, which makes it is more difficult to reach negotiated solutions [2].

Pardo et al. [3] highlighted the importance of understanding factors influencing the adoption of interorganisational information sharing. Consequently, many studies have

© IFIP International Federation for Information Processing 2017
Published by Springer International Publishing AG 2017. All Rights Reserved
A.K. Kar et al. (Eds.): I3E 2017, LNCS 10595, pp. 94–106, 2017.
DOI: 10.1007/978-3-319-68557-1_10

been investigating factors affecting the interorganisational information sharing [4–7], and especially involving public and private organisations [8–11].

Work on information sharing have been conducted in various domains, including supply chain [12, 13], public safety network [14, 15], disaster management [16, 17] and financial reporting system [18, 19]. These studies emphasized several challenges that complicates the implementation and adoption of information sharing arrangements. These challenges ranging from organisational aspects, such as difference viewpoints, goals, organisational structure, and the availability of resources, to technological aspects, such as interoperability, IT complexity, IT maturity and IT capability [20]. Moreover, there is also imbalance of benefits perceived between stakeholders, one stakeholder might profit, whereas another might bear the cost, which might add complexity and could result in unwillingness to join the project.

To deal with the aforementioned challenges, a proper arrangement which can bridge the interest of the involved stakeholders needs to be developed. An information sharing arrangement can be conceptualised by the interplay between system architecture for information sharing and its accompanying governance [18]. There is a whole range of factors influencing the shape of an information sharing arrangement.

The selection of information sharing arrangement factors can be considered as a type of Multi Criteria Decision Making (MCDM) problem since it influenced by several factors. It is crucial to know which factors influence the shaping of an information sharing arrangement to a large extent and which factors have less influence. This paper aims to derive factors of information sharing arrangements by assessing the importance of factors in shaping information sharing collected from previous studies. To reach that objective, a MCDM method called Best-Worst Method (BWM) was applied in analysing the expert's opinions. The experts were selected from both private and public organisations as well as academia. This results in a list of weighting factors from both the public and private sectors perspective.

BWM is a relatively new method in MCDM area [21]. BWM uses a pairwise comparison to find the optimal weights of the criteria and their consistency ratios. BWM can produce highly consistent and reliable results in more efficient way by provides a pairwise comparison using two vectors instead of a full pairwise matrix and by using only integer value [22]. By using these two characteristics, the result will be reliable even using a few respondents and easier to interpret compared to other methods that utilising fractions. According to [21], BWM is statistically better than AHP (Analytic Hierarchy Process) in term of the consistency ratio, minimum violation, total deviation and conformity.

Understanding which factors and how important they are in arranging information sharing can be beneficial for involved public and private organisations as well as potential users. This can help them to focus on the factors that matter during the development of an information sharing arrangement. The results of this research can be used as a point of reference to reduce potential conflicts which may occur between organisations during negotiating processes. This can increase the acceptance and usage of the system, and bringing benefits to all stakeholders.

This document is structured as follows: the literature review is presented in the next section, including the explanation of information sharing between public and private organisations, and its arrangements. Following that, the research methodology is described. Next, the findings of the research are provided, followed by the discussion of the findings. Finally, conclusions, which consists of contributions of the paper, limitations of the research and future research directions are presented.

2   Literature Review

2.1   Information Sharing Between Public and Private Organisations

Based on [10, 16, 23], information sharing between public and private organisations is defined as *an act to exchange data through a mutual agreement with the objective to improve public services and organisation performances for involved government agencies and private organisations*. Points to be underlined are that enabling the information sharing requires agreements, and the implications of information sharing for public and private organisations should be considered. Further in this study, information sharing refers to above definition.

A high-level conceptualisation of information sharing is presented in the Fig. 1. In the relationship with businesses regarding the market, the government has main function to maintain the market by ensuring competitiveness and equal opportunity for firms. The governments (could be national, regional or local level) create regulations, for example regarding trading or fiscal policy, which should protect the customers, the employees, companies and investors. These regulations are then integrated by the private organisations in their routines, in trading activities or other companies' actions. As an assurance that these businesses activities comply with regulations, the companies must report. These reports are then evaluated and analysed by the public organisations.

Fig. 1. High-level conceptualisation of information sharing between governments and businesses

2.2   Information Sharing Arrangement

According to Orlikowski [24], technology adaptation and organisation affects each other. Organisational setting and condition may need to be restructured by adapting technology. Organisation, on the other hand, have a privilege to select some technologies in accordance with their objectives, in which could affect the diffusion of those technologies in internal organisation and the market. Further, study from Tiwana and Konsynski [25] provided explanation about how the interplay between architecture and IT governance ensures the use of IT in supporting organisational objective. From a different perspective, the institutional arrangement proposed by Koppenjan and Groenewegen [26] which "designed to coordinate specific transactions among multiple actors concerning labour, capital, intermediate goods, information and the like" [26, p. 246]. For the IOS, this arrangement is important to facilitate the functioning of the network.

These three approaches are used to conceptualise the arrangement, which is defined as the interplay between architecture and governance of interorganisational system which facilitate information sharing. The importance of information sharing arrangement has been discussed in previous studies. As an example, four essential components of cross-boundary information sharing developed by Gil-Garcia [27] consists of an organised setting between the infrastructure, shared and standardised data, and trusted social network. Another example, principles in implementing the IOS proposed by Fedorowicz et al. [28] were also highlighting the need of IOS arrangement which encompasses organisational and technological issues.

Further, to have a better understanding of information sharing arrangement, this study will use several design variables: (1) Network Archetype, which comprises the type of infrastructure used to share information; (2) Data Management, including all process of collecting, processing, storing and distributing the data for sharing intention; (3) Process alignment, which related to how the users aligning their business process to support the sharing objectives; and (4) System Governance, which encompass the decision-making structure in the IOS and the communication between users.

3 Research Methodology

This paper aims to assess the importance of influential factors in information sharing arrangements. Prior research from Praditya et al. [18] provided 26 factors categorized using Technological, Organisational and Environment (TOE) framework from [29]. Some factors, for example management support and level of adoption, were left-out since they were not relevant for influencing the type of arrangements. Some other factors were combined, including firm size, firm structure, firm governance, firm strategy into organisational compatibilities; standardised data, amount of data and number of transactions into types of data; and all technological factors grouped into IT Capabilities, and IT Compatibility and Interoperability. There are also some factors added based on recent development in the research, for example, perceived benefits, perceived costs, perceived risks, experience and interorganisational relationship. This resulted in 16 factors which grouped into factors belonging to the internal organisation, to the interorganisational and to the technical level as shown in Fig. 2.

The BWM was applied as the main method in this study to find the weight of each factor. Data were collected via four expert interviews conducted from April 21st to 26th 2017. Each interview took between 45 min to 1 h. The selected respondents have at least 5 years' experience working in the information sharing system. From the interaction during

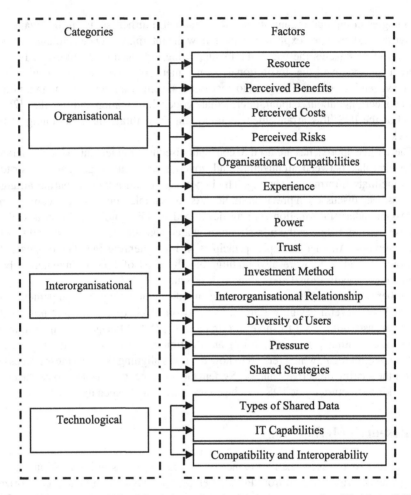

Fig. 2. List of factors influencing information sharing arrangements (modified from [18])

the interviews, these experts showed their broad knowledge regarding the system, especially the ability to analyse the problem from multi-level and multi-contextual perspectives. The overview of the profile of each respondent is presented in Table 1. Based on this selection, this study takes into consideration various viewpoints in prioritising the factors.

Table 1. Profile of the experts

Variables	A	B	C	D
Position	Consultant	Researcher	Researcher	IT Architect
Experience	E-Government projects	Open data infrastructure and information sharing mechanism	Data sharing mechanism to solve societal problems	Information systems in private organisations
Region	South America	Europe	Europe	Europe

Interviews were conducted using the steps provided by BWM [21]. However, this study did not follow all the BWM steps because this study aims to weighting the factors, and not to find the best alternative.

The steps to determine the preference and the weight of each factor in this method were as follows: First, a set of criteria (or factors) was defined. In this step, factors that should be used to arrive at a decision were selected. In the second step, the best and worst factors were selected. In this study, each respondent had to select the most important and least important factor in all categories. Because of in this study the factors divided into three groups, it was also necessary to select the best and least important category.

In the third step, each respondent was asked to select the preference of the best factor over all the other factors using a number between one (no preference) and nine (extreme preference). Then, step four was aimed to determine the preference of all the criteria over the worst criterion using the similar way with the previous step. This step performs a role in checking the consistency of respondents' preferences. From these 4 steps, data were collected, and added into 'Microsoft Excel' as the calculation tool. Hence, the weights of factors were determined.

The categorisation aims to simplify the data collection and analysis in the BWM. Instead of comparing 16 factors in one phase, which may confuse the interviewees, this study was divided into two phases. The first phase aimed to determine the weight of factors in each category, or local weighting. At the end of this phase, the weight of each category was determined. The local weight of each factor then multiplied with the weight of correspondent category to determine the global weights. An average of the global weights of the four experts was used as the final results. The result of each phase, the consistency ratio and the patterns or variations in the personal weights of the experts are presented and discussed in the next section.

4   Results

As already mentioned in the research methodology, the first step in the first phase aimed to assess each factor locally, or in each category, per expert. Later, the importance of each category is evaluated per expert. As shown in the Table 2, each expert has their own opinion regarding the importance of each factor as they have experiences in different situations.

Table 2. Results of weighting factors per category

	Factor	A	B	C	D		Factor	A	B	C	D
Category	O	0.45	0.31	0.25	0.57	Organisational	R	0.15	0.12	0.27	0.12
	IO	0.45	0.58	0.42	0.29		PB	0.37	0.17	0.27	0.56
	T	0.09	0.11	0.33	0.14		PC	0.37	0.11	0.21	0.08
	Ksi*	0.00	0.03	0.08	0.00		PR	0.00	0.52	0.10	0.05
Interorganisational	P	0.29	0.10	0.19	0.22		OC	0.12	0.05	0.11	0.05
	T	0.17	0.46	0.09	0.15		E	0.00	0.04	0.04	0.13
	I	0.03	0.18	0.42	0.11		Ksi*	0.37	0.19	0.06	0.18
	IOR	0.37	0.11	0.09	0.05	Technological	TD	0.08	0.70	0.33	0.09
	DoU	0.02	0.04	0.07	0.06		Cap	0.29	0.10	0.33	0.32
	IP	0.08	0.06	0.09	0.08		CI	0.63	0.20	0.33	0.59
	SS	0.03	0.05	0.05	0.33		Ksi*	0.25	0.10	0.00	0.05
	Ksi*	0.21	0.12	0.15	0.10						

4.1 Local Weighting

For the **Organisational factors**, the perceived benefits is considered as the most important factor for almost all experts, excluded expert B which considered this factor as the second most important factor after perceived risks. On the other hand, perceived risks and organisational compatibilities are selected as the least important factors.

For the **Interorganisational factors**, the experts have different opinion regarding the most influential factor. Interorganisational relationship is selected by expert A; trust is selected by expert B; investment is selected by expert C; and shared strategies is selected by expert D. This suggests that there is no dominating factor in this category.

Regarding the **Technological factors**, expert A and D have similar opinions, they consider compatibility and interoperability as the main factor, while expert B select type of data as the most important factor. For this category, expert C found it difficult to select the best criteria and gave all factors the same importance.

In the last step of local weighting, all experts were asked to rank the importance of the category. All experts agreed that technological factors are less important for influencing the information sharing arrangement. Expert B and C selected Interorganisational as the most influential category, while expert D picked out Organisational. In this step, expert A considered both Organisational and Interorganisational as the most important category.

In addition, the BWM results of this local weighting also shows the consistency ratio (CR) of each expert in each category. CR is determined by dividing the Ksi from the BWM results (in Table 2) with the maximum possible of Ksi for the number of factors (consistency index) (in Table 3). The CR is ranging from 0 to 1. The lower CR means more consistent of the comparisons, hence more reliable results. The CR for this research is shown in the Table 4 below. The average CR per expert shows that, in general, all experts has CR close to zero which means the BWM results used in this research are consistent and reliable.

Table 3. Consistency Index based on the number of criteria [30]

α	1	2	3	4	5	6	7	8	9
Consistency index	0.00	0.44	1.00	1.63	2.30	3.00	3.73	4.47	5.23

Table 4. Consistency ratio of each expert

Consistency ratio	A	B	C	D
Organisational	0.12	0.06	0.02	0.06
Interorganisational	0.06	0.03	0.04	0.03
Technological	0.25	0.10	0.00	0.05
Average	**0.11**	**0.06**	**0.04**	**0.03**

The local weights of all factors and the weights of the categories then will be used to calculate the global weights of all factors. These results are presented in the next part.

4.2 Global Weighting

The global weighting of each factor calculated by multiplying the weight of each factor and the weight of its corresponding category. The final calculation of global weighting is shown in Table 5. Dark grey indicates the most important factor(s) for each expert,

Table 5. Results of the global weighting phase

Factors	A	B	C	D	Avg.
PB	0.17	0.05	0.07	0.32	0.15
T	0.08	0.27	0.04	0.04	0.11
P	0.13	0.06	0.08	0.06	0.08
I	0.02	0.10	0.17	0.03	0.08
PC	0.17	0.03	0.05	0.04	0.07
IOR	0.17	0.07	0.04	0.01	0.07
CI	0.06	0.02	0.11	0.08	0.07
R	0.07	0.04	0.07	0.07	0.06
PR	0.00	0.16	0.03	0.03	0.05
TD	0.01	0.08	0.11	0.01	0.05
Cap	0.03	0.01	0.11	0.05	0.05
SS	0.02	0.03	0.02	0.09	0.04
IP	0.04	0.03	0.04	0.02	0.03
OC	0.06	0.01	0.03	0.03	0.03
E	0.00	0.01	0.01	0.07	0.02
DoU	0.01	0.02	0.03	0.02	0.02

while light grey indicates their top-5 important factors. The results show that the importance factors of each experts varied which might be explained by the variety of experiences with the IOS and their background. The variations can be seen in the selection of Top-5 influential factors per each expert and the weight per factor.

The average weights of criteria from all experts shows that perceived benefits, trust, power, investment method, perceived costs, interorganisational relationship, and compatibility and interoperability are the most important factors influencing information sharing arrangement. These factors are the focus of the next section.

5   Discussion

The objective of this paper is to assess the importance of factors influencing information sharing arrangement. BWM provided a structured approach to weighting each factor based on experts' opinions. Based on the average calculation of global weighting by each expert, seven most important factors were selected: two factors are included in organisational, four factors are from interorganisational and one factor is from technological. Three of the top-ranking factors are related to economic aspects, including perceived costs, investment and perceived benefits; although perceived benefits could also be measured by other parameters. The other three factors are about the intangible factors, including power, trust and interorganisational relationship. Only one factor categorized as technological factors which implies the experts rate this category is not as challenging as the other two factors.

Perceived benefits is selected as the most important factor of the information sharing arrangement. This factor has often been found as a significant factor in IT adoption [31, 32], including in the adoption of EDI [33]. The expert from private organisation was heavily prioritising this factor even though it is not straightforward to quantify perceived benefits. This may reflect the main motivation of private organisation in the economic aspect of technology adoption. In business-and-government IOS, some benefits might have perceived as less prominent by businesses in comparison to in business-and-business IOS. Example of such benefits are the strengthening customer and business partner relationship [33].

IOS depends on the power relation between involved users [34]. A powerful party can dictate on how the infrastructure should be developed and what kind of governance should be created for the IOS. In the business-and-government setting, government agencies may be considered as the powerful players, but also market leaders or big companies might have more power. Power may also dependent on the investment method being used. Usually, higher investments correspondent with the higher power in system-related decision-making. Power can be used to accelerate the decision-making process; however, this may also lead to unwillingness of some potential users to involve in the information sharing. The importance of power in the information sharing arrangements or IOS is widely recognized, see for example [35–37].

Interorganisational trust is defined as "*a company's belief that another company will perform actions that will result in positive outcomes, as well as not taking unexpected actions that would result in negative outcomes for the company*" [38, p. 522].

It is considered as a control mechanism of interorganisational relationship [39]. Trust influences the information sharing arrangements for example in the development of a decentralised system. This network archetype requires higher-level trust compare to a centralised system. In the implementation of Standard Business Reporting (SBR) as an example, trust is reflected in the strong contribution of involved users in the decision-making process [18].

The choice of network archetype can be influenced by the investment method. For example, using the public-private partnership for financing the implementation project may lead to centralisation, which makes the investment easier to manage. In many cases of IOS implementation, the main investor is the government. Because of the government has strong resemblance in centralisation, this may lead to the adoption of centralisation system. The importance of investment method in the IOS adoption is consistent with the findings from [40, 41].

Perceived costs were found as a significant factor in IOS adoption [33, 42]. Perceived costs is not only determined during the implementation project, but also during the use and maintenance of the system. Higher costs may be perceived in the implementation of centralised system, especially if the organisation need to improve their internal IT system in order to be compatible with the IOS. However, during the use of the system, centralisation may imply less costs. This kind of trade-off need to be considered carefully by the involved parties.

To achieve objectives which may transcend the organisational boundary and difficult to resolve by individual organisation, it is necessary to develop and maintain the inter-organisational relationship [43]. Related to the information sharing and IOS adoption, the established interorganisational relationship plays an important role as discussed by Praditya et al. [18]. In the case of SBR implementation, the interorganisational relationship between Tax Office and its auditees influences the adoption of previous system's governance to the new system's governance. The adoption of previous system's governance was beneficial in reducing the conflict which potentially occurs, especially, during the early phase of implementation project.

Compatibility and interoperability were found as one of the significant factor in the adoption of information sharing and IOS [44, 45]. The importance of this factor can be seen in the implementation of SBR. Standardisation of data, technology and processes are needed to deal with the heterogeneity and the fragmentation of existing IIT systems owned by involved users [18]. This compatibility and interoperability within the system can resulted in the decision of using certain network archetype.

6   Conclusions

This study aimed to derive factors of information sharing arrangements by assessing the importance of factors influencing information sharing between public and private organisations identified from previous study. To achieve the objective, BWM was applied in the experts' opinions analysis.

From the seven most important factors: two factors are from the organisational category; four factors are from interorganisational category; and one factor is from technological category. These factors are: perceived benefits, trust, power, investment method, perceived costs, interorganisational relationship, and compatibility and interoperability. The results of this study also showed the different opinions from experts which may influenced by their background and experience in information sharing. While other experts selected various of important factors, the expert from private organisation emphasized the importance of perceived benefits above the other factors. Further, the results are found to be consistent with the prior studies in the interorganisational information sharing and IOS adoption.

The results of this study can be used in multiple ways. First, the users and developers of the system can understand which factors that are relatively important and ensure they are fulfilled during the development of information sharing system. Second, the differences between private and public organisations' viewpoints can be used as inputs for developing a strategy, for example, to create different narratives when providing information to a particular organisation. Third, scientifically, the results can be used as an input for future studies if, for example, the factors are tested using other MCDM method or other statistical analysis. Different statistical analysis may capture the possibilities of mutually influence and dependencies between factors, for example, between trust and power or between perceived costs, benefits and investment.

However, there are also some limitations. Although the BWM does not require a minimum number of respondents, there might be an issue regarding the generality and reliability of the results. The results could be better if the stakeholder analysis were also applied. Hence, comprehensive viewpoints from both businesses and governments would be better captured. Another limitation is the absence of alternatives, as one of the main elements for MCDM, and this resulted in the BWM was not being fully utilised.

References

1. Janssen, M., van der Voort, H., Wahyudi, A.: Factors influencing big data decision-making quality. J. Bus. Res. **70**, 338–345 (2017)
2. Treku, D.N., Wiredu, G.O.: Information Systems Implementation and Structural Adaptation in Government-Business Inter-Organization (2016)
3. Pardo, T.A., et al.: Modeling the social & technical processes of interorganizational information integration. In: Proceedings of the 37th Annual Hawaii International Conference on System Sciences. IEEE (2004)
4. Samaddar, S., Nargundkar, S., Daley, M.: Inter-organizational information sharing: the role of supply network configuration and partner goal congruence. Eur. J. Oper. Res. **174**(2), 744–765 (2006)
5. Dawes, S.S.: Interagency information sharing: expected benefits, manageable risks. J. Policy Anal. Manage. **15**(3), 377–394 (1996)
6. Barrett, S., Konsynski, B.: Inter-organization information sharing systems. MIS Quart. **6**, 93–105 (1982)
7. Landsbergen Jr., D., Wolken Jr., G.: Realizing the promise: government information systems and the fourth generation of information technology. Public Adm. Rev. **61**(2), 206–220 (2001)
8. Yang, T.-M., Maxwell, T.A.: Information-sharing in public organizations: a literature review of interpersonal, intra-organizational and inter-organizational success factors. Gov. Inf. Quart. **28**(2), 164–175 (2011)

9. Gil-Garcia, J.R., Sayogo, D.S.: Government inter-organizational information sharing initiatives: understanding the main determinants of success. Gov. Inf. Quart. **33**, 572–582 (2016)
10. Yang, T.-M., Wu, Y.-J.: Exploring the determinants of cross-boundary information sharing in the public sector: an e-Government case study in Taiwan. J. Inf. Sci. **40**(5), 649–668 (2014)
11. Sayogo, D.S., Gil-Garcia, J.R.: Understanding the determinants of success in inter-organizational information sharing initiatives: results from a national survey. In: Proceedings of the 15th Annual International Conference on Digital Government Research. ACM (2014)
12. Olesen, P.B., Damgaard, C.M., Hvolby, H.-H., Dukovska-Popovska, I., Sommer, A.F.: Framework for information sharing in a small-to-medium port system supply chain. In: Grabot, B., Vallespir, B., Gomes, S., Bouras, A., Kiritsis, D. (eds.) APMS 2014. IAICT, vol. 438, pp. 257–264. Springer, Heidelberg (2014). doi:10.1007/978-3-662-44739-0_32
13. Engel, T., et al.: Investigating information sharing behavior in supply chains: evidence from an embedded single case study. In: 2014 47th Hawaii International Conference on System Sciences (HICSS) (2014)
14. Fedorowicz, J., Gogan, J.L., Williams, C.B.: A collaborative network for first responders: lessons from the CapWIN case. Gov. Inf. Quart. **24**(4), 785–807 (2007)
15. Kożuch, B., Sienkiewicz-Małyjurek, K.: Information sharing in complex systems: a case study on public safety management. Procedia Soc. Behav. Sci. **213**, 722–727 (2015)
16. Crowther, K.G.: Understanding and overcoming information sharing failures. J. Homel. Secur. Emerg. Manage. **11**(1), 131–154 (2014)
17. Lee, J., et al.: Group value and intention to use—a study of multi-agency disaster management information systems for public safety. Decis. Support Syst. **50**(2), 404–414 (2011)
18. Praditya, D., Janssen, M., Sulastri, R.: Determinants of business-to-government information sharing arrangements. Electron. J. E-Gov. **15**(1), 44–55 (2017)
19. Bharosa, N., et al.: Developing multi-sided platforms for public-private information sharing: design observations from two case studies. In: Proceedings of the 14th Annual International Conference on Digital Government Research. 2013, New York, USA, pp. 146–155. ACM (2013)
20. Praditya, D., Janssen, M.: Benefits and challenges in information sharing between the public and private sectors. Academic Conferences Limited (2015)
21. Rezaei, J.: Best-worst multi-criteria decision-making method. Omega **53**, 49–57 (2015)
22. Rezaei, J., et al.: A supplier selection life cycle approach integrating traditional and environmental criteria using the best worst method. J. Clean. Prod. **135**, 577–588 (2016)
23. Gil-Garcia, J.R., Chun, S.A., Janssen, M.: Government information sharing and integration: combining the social and the technical. Inf. Polity **14**(1,2), 1–10 (2009)
24. Orlikowski, W.J.: The duality of technology: rethinking the concept of technology in organizations. Organ. Sci. **3**(3), 398–427 (1992)
25. Tiwana, A., Konsynski, B.: Complementarities between organizational IT architecture and governance structure. Inf. Syst. Res. **21**(2), 288–304 (2010)
26. Koppenjan, J., Groenewegen, J.: Institutional design for complex technological systems. Int. J. Technol. Policy Manage. **5**(3), 240–257 (2005)
27. Gil-Garcia J.R., Pardo, T.A., Burke, G.B.: Conceptualizing information integration in government. In: Scholl, H.J. (ed.) E-Government: Information, Technology, and Transformation, pp. 179–202. M.E. Sharpe, Armonk, NY (2010)
28. Fedorowicz, J., et al.: Design observations for interagency collaboration. Gov. Inf. Quart. **31**(2), 302–316 (2014)
29. Depietro, R., Wiarda, E., Fleischer, M.: The context for change: organization, technology and environment. Process. Technol. Innov. **199**, 151–175 (1990)

30. Rezaei, J.: Best-worst multi-criteria decision-making method: some properties and a linear model. Omega **64**, 126–130 (2016)
31. Iacovou, C.L., Benbasat, I., Dexter, A.S.: Electronic data interchange and small organizations: adoption and impact of technology. MIS Quart. **19**, 465–485 (1995)
32. Akbulut, A.Y., et al.: To share or not to share? Examining the factors influencing local agency electronic information sharing. Int. J. Bus. Inf. Syst. **4**(2), 143–172 (2009)
33. Chau, P.Y., Hui, K.L.: Determinants of small business EDI adoption: an empirical investigation. J. Organ. Comput. Electron. Commer. **11**(4), 229–252 (2001)
34. Boonstra, A., de Vries, J.: Analyzing inter-organizational systems from a power and interest perspective. Int. J. Inf. Manage. **25**(6), 485–501 (2005)
35. Hart, P., Saunders, C.: Power and trust: critical factors in the adoption and use of electronic data interchange. Organ. Sci. **8**(1), 23–42 (1997)
36. Chang, C.L.: The relationship among power types, political games, game players, and information system project outcomes—a multiple-case study. Int. J. Proj. Manage. **31**(1), 57–67 (2013)
37. Nicholls, A., Huybrechts, B.: Sustaining inter-organizational relationships across institutional logics and power asymmetries: the case of fair trade. J. Bus. Ethics **135**(4), 699–714 (2016)
38. Neergaard, H., Ulhøi, J.P.: Government agency and trust in the formation and transformation of interorganizational entrepreneurial networks. Entrep. Theor. Pract. **30**(4), 519–539 (2006)
39. Gil-Garcia, J.R., et al.: Trust in government cross-boundary information sharing initiatives: identifying the determinants. In: 2010 43rd Hawaii International Conference on System Sciences (HICSS) (2010)
40. Han, K., Kauffman, R.J., Nault, B.R.: Relative importance, specific investment and ownership in interorganizational systems. Inf. Technol. Manage. **9**(3), 181–200 (2008)
41. Iubatti, D., Masciarelli, F., Simboli, A.: Inter-organizational design: exploring the relationship between formal architecture and ICT investments. In: Passiante, G. (ed.) Evolving Towards the Internetworked Enterprise, pp. 163–174. Springer, Boston (2010)
42. Lin, H.-F.: Understanding the determinants of electronic supply chain management system adoption: using the technology–organization–environment framework. Technol. Forecast. Soc. Chang. **86**, 80–92 (2014)
43. Cheng, J.-H.: Inter-organizational relationships and information sharing in supply chains. Int. J. Inf. Manage. **31**(4), 374–384 (2011)
44. Premkumar, G., Ramamurthy, K., Crum, M.: Determinants of EDI adoption in the transportation industry. Eur. J. Inf. Syst. **6**(2), 107–121 (1997)
45. Tornatzky, L.G., Klein, K.J.: Innovation characteristics and innovation adoption-implementation: a meta-analysis of findings. IEEE Trans. Eng. Manage. **EM-29**(1), 28–45 (1982)

Assessing the Potential of IoT in Aerospace

Thirunavukkarasu Ramalingam[1(✉)], Benaroya Christophe[2],
and Fosso Wamba Samuel[2]

[1] Indian Institute of Management, Bangalore 560 076, Karnataka, India
thirunavukkarasur15@iimb.ernet.in
[2] Toulouse Business School, 31068 Toulouse, France
{c.benaroya,s.fosso-wamba}@tbs-education.fr

Abstract. Internet of Things – Aerospace (IoTA): IoT in Aerospace sector? Is
it really happening? This is what industry experts think while talking about
Internet of Things in Aerospace! IoTA is the Ninth letter of Greek alphabet, which
means 'extremely small amount'. Will it impact the nine letter 'AEROSPACE'
industry? In the Aerospace & Defense industry, split-second decisions can mean
a difference between success and failure as there is longer product life cycle.

This exploratory research is targeted towards identifying the various IoT
characteristics and its maturity level. A methodology was developed using House
of Quality (HoQ) to identify the potential system which will be impacted by IoT
in future. HoQ helped in identifying the positive and negative correlation between
the IoT characteristics and its linkage with various aerospace systems. This investigative research can be used by aerospace system suppliers to make qualitative
decisions before investing in IoT for their system/product enhancements.

Keywords: Internet of Things (IoT) · Aerospace systems · IoT characteristics ·
House of Quality (HoQ)

1 Introduction

Aerospace and Defense (A&D) industry is poised for growth despite economic down-
turns. Increase in travel demand, development of new technologies and security threat
for nations are fueling increase in aircraft production, defense budgets and the need for
global supply chain [1]. Airbus global market forecast predicts that air traffic will grow
at 4.5% annually and more than 30,000 aircrafts will be required over the next 20 years
[2]. Aircraft manufacturers and operators are always in the lookout to improve the
vehicle performance by providing more connected and smarter systems to achieve the
Fuel Efficiency, Zero downtime and Route optimization.

The phrase Internet of Things (IoT) was first used in 1999 by Kevin Ashton. The
concept of IoT is to connect the real-world objects with speech, vision, hearing, smell
and touch, so inanimate things can perform jobs more accurately, responsively, collab-
oratively with learnings. IoT transformation is possible only when set of technologies
are created that are broadly applicable to industry with relevant IoT characteristics

© IFIP International Federation for Information Processing 2017
Published by Springer International Publishing AG 2017. All Rights Reserved
A.K. Kar et al. (Eds.): I3E 2017, LNCS 10595, pp. 107–121, 2017.
DOI: 10.1007/978-3-319-68557-1_11

maturity [3]. IoT characteristics defined as a set of capabilities encompasses in a system which can be increased or reduced based on design decisions and tradeoffs.

Prior studies suggest that IoT may transform various industries and services including healthcare [4–6], construction [7], territories management [8], predictive maintenance [9] and manufacturing shop floors [10].

Nowadays digital transformation is the heart of business strategies and it begins with the executive mandate. There is a strong sense of urgency among executives as the threat of digitally enabled competitors and disruptive technologies remain high on the list of concerns. Internet of Things (IoT) is becoming more and more important in many industry sectors and domains. Digital Technology evolution is happening rapid fast, within no time this will impact every business. However, it is essentially a commitment by organizations to innovate which would add value to their customers.

SAP research on digital transformation (see Fig. 1) shows that 33% of industry leaders will be disrupted in this way by 2018 and 58% of companies' think IoT is strategic [11]. Though the IoT evolution happened more than a decade ago, its impact on aerospace systems are limited due to IoT characteristics maturity, its adaptability and ease of implementation in safety critical aerospace systems.

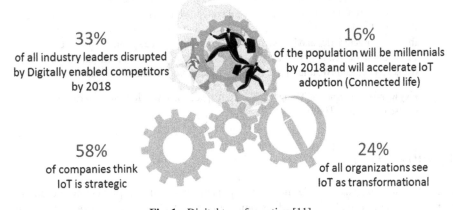

33%
of all industry leaders disrupted by Digitally enabled competitors by 2018

16%
of the population will be millennials by 2018 and will accelerate IoT adoption (Connected life)

58%
of companies think IoT is strategic

24%
of all organizations see IoT as transformational

Fig. 1. Digital transformation [11]

1.1 Objective of the Paper

Aerospace industries are currently in search of minimum viable systems/products and are investing heavily to develop IoT technologies which can yield long term value. IoT technologies are evolving faster than predicted which can change the product landscape in aerospace industry as well. However, there is no established approach to identify such systems/products. This investigative research paper can help aerospace system suppliers identify the IoT characteristics maturity. The methodology developed using HoQ will help them narrow down the system/product to focus.

According to the research paper [12] findings, it is indicated that the IoT research field is immature, with experimental methods dominating research outputs. No research paper covers IoT characteristics maturity and its impact on aerospace systems. Therefore, objectives of this exploratory research are as follows:

- Identify and list the aerospace relevant IoT characteristics
- Find out the IoT characteristics maturity
- Connect the IoT characteristics with aerospace systems

1.2 Author Definition of IoT and IoTA

Based on literature survey and its applicability to the context of this research, IoT is defined as "A system with in-built computing devices which can communicate with other such devices through secured network and take the decisions based on intelligence and can work on centralized and decentralized model".

Extending this definition to Internet of Things for Aerospace (IoTA), "IoTA is defined as aircraft systems with in-built computing devices which can communicate with other such devices through secured deterministic network and take the decisions based on swarm intelligence and works on centralized and decentralized model".

1.3 IoT Potential in Aerospace

There are more than 20 IoT characteristics which can complement and add value in aerospace systems in many ways by reducing customer pain points such as flight cancellation, flight delays etc., Direct cost of air transportation delay is USD 32.9 billion which incurs a loss of USD 8.3 billion to airlines [13]. As per IATA report it is mentioned that USD 15 billion was spent on direct maintenance, with average maintenance cost of USD 295 million per airline and USD 1087 per flight hour [14]. Identification of potential systems and its relevant characteristics maturity is the key to develop and implement IoT products/systems in aerospace.

2 Methodology

Methodology followed in this project (see Fig. 2) was to first identify the various general IoT characteristics which are not relevant to any specific industry or domain. Each characteristics maturity was understood by conducting a targeted IoT audience market survey with varied experience level (Beginner, Intermediate & Expert) across demographics (USA, Europe & APAC). Two IoT experts were interviewed to validate the survey results and to confirm the IoT characteristics maturity. House of Quality (HoQ) tool was used to establish the correlation between the IoT characteristics and relations between the various aerospace systems. HoQ also helped to identify the relative weights between the characteristics and to identify potential IoT system.

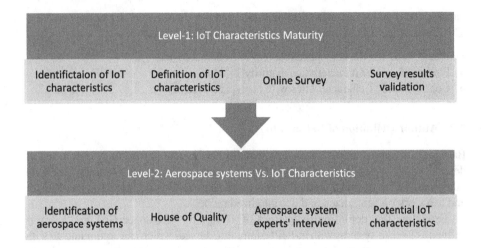

Fig. 2. Step by step methodology for IoTA

2.1 Level-1: IoT Characteristics Maturity

Step-1: Identification of IoT characteristics using various published papers/articles
Step-2: Definition of each IoT characteristics based on the literature survey
Step-3: Online survey
- Develop interview questions with appropriate rating scale
- Circulate the online survey to targeted IoT audience across demographics
- Plot the survey results and analyze

Step-4: Survey result validation
- Conduct IoT experts' interview
- Co-relate the survey results and record findings

Limitations of Level-1

- IoT characteristics definition and its understandability by survey audience
- Ratings by audience depends on their own perspective
- IoT experts' opinions based on their industry experience may/may not align with aerospace systems

2.2 Level-2: Aerospace Systems Vs. IoT Characteristics

Step-1: Identification of top level aerospace systems
Step-2: Develop House of Quality
Step-3: Aerospace system experts' interview
- Identify system level experts'
- Explain the context of the discussion and conduct focused interview
- Use House of Quality (HoQ) to establish the linkages between the aerospace systems and IoT characteristics

Step-4:   Potential IoT characteristics
- Establish the correlation between the IoT characteristics

In this project, Authors have rated each characteristic to establish the correlation (Triangular shaped Roof) based on insight, gained through the literature survey.

- Identification of potential IoT characteristics for each aerospace system

Limitations of level-2

- Experts' idea on future aerospace system using IoT was limited
- Definition of IoT characteristics and its explanations to the system level experts'
- IoT experts rating and its validation of results

3   IoT Characteristics

Table 1 shown below lists the IoT characteristics that are fundamental and emerging new characteristics mentioned/referred in published articles. Online survey participants suggested characteristics are also listed.

Table 1. IoT characteristics

Fundamental IoT characteristics [15]	Mentioned/referred in published articles
• Interconnectivity	• Intelligence
• Things-related services	• Sensing /Sensor
• Heterogeneity	• Expressing
• Dynamic changes	• Energy
• Enormous scale	• Computing/Processors
• Safety	• Quality & Reliability
• Connectivity	• Cost effectiveness
	• Consumption
	• Conversion
	• Centralization
	• Cognition
	• Configuration
	• Coordination
	• Deterministic
	• Mobility
	• Security
Suggested by online survey participants	
• Miniaturization & Composability	
• Standards and Protocols	

Though 25 IoT characteristics were identified, all of them may not contribute to aerospace systems. Definition of 11 IoT characteristics are explained in Sect. 3.1 that have scored a relative weight above 4 in HoQ and are favorable for IoT systems/products in aerospace industry.

3.1 Definition of IoT Characteristics

Definitions of potential IoT characteristics for aerospace systems development are listed below:

Safety: IoT can yield lot of benefits, however safety should be the prime concern. Design for safety is the key aspect to be considered both by creators and recipients of the IoT. This includes the safety of personal data and physical well-being [15].

Connectivity: It enables network compatibility and accessibility. Compatibility provides the common ability to consume and produce data while accessibility is getting on a network. Connectivity in the IoT can very soon get rid of the Wi-Fi module [15].

Intelligence: Product experiences are made smarter with the help of software and hardware algorithms and its computing power provides the "intelligent spark" [16].

Expressing: Expressing provides a way to create products that interact intelligently with people and real world, not just rendering beautiful user interface [16].

Energy-Efficiency: Energy harvesting, power efficiency and charging infrastructure are the necessary parts of a power intelligent ecosystem that we must design. Today, it is woefully inadequate and lacks the focus in many product teams [16].

Computing/Processors: Certain degree of computing power is needed for all the devices connected in the network so that IoT devices can relay and transmit gathered data. Like any other computing device, this will require a processor as well [17].

Quality & Reliability: Devices in the IoT may be operating in extreme weather conditions and tough environments. As the IoT devices might be exposed to such an environment it is important that they are made with the highest quality and reliability [17].

Cognition: This is not the same as plain old data conversion it is more of an analytical process where we apply context to the data in hand. Cognition makes sure that we get the right perception of the data [18].

Deterministic: Time Sensitive Networking (TSN) features are currently being developed by The IEEE standards organization by including standard 802.1 and 802.3. To allow Ethernet to be deployed in mission critical applications, it is necessary to add specific features including time synchronization, scheduled traffic, ingress policing and seamless redundancy. This is to ensure that specific data traffic can flow, on time and throughout the entire network topology [16].

Security: This is concerned with safeguarding IoT connected devices and networks. Security is a wide concept which covers everything from authenticity, authority, integrity and confidentiality. Security paradigm will scale up when IoT would need securing the endpoints, the networks and the data moving across the network [19].

Standards & Protocols: A standard document has all rules and procedures developed by a regulatory party and agreed upon to be followed by many parties. A protocol is a particular set of rules that enables conversation between two computers to convey a specific set of information. Such well known communication technologies are Wi-Fi, Bluetooth, ZigBee and 2G/3G/4G cellular [20].

3.2 IoT Characteristics Maturity

More than 20 IoT characteristics were identified by going through various whitepapers, technical papers and published articles on Internet of Things. As these characteristics have evolved over several years, it is not easy to measure its maturity from those data sources. Hence authors have decided to conduct market research using targeted IoT audience and validate the survey results by interviewing IoT experts'.

A survey questionnaire is formulated for the target audience with explanation of the identified IoT characteristics and a four-point scale rating to assess the maturity (i.e. New, Improving, Maturing & Aging). The target audience/survey participants were carefully chosen (with IoT experience of 2 years at least) across the globe as there are not many IoT industry experts. Figure 3 show the percentage of participants across demographics.

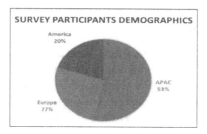

Fig. 3. Survey demographics

About 30 responses were received from across the globe and its results are shown in Fig. 4. More than 10 characteristics have scored above 50% rating on 'Improving' scale (see Fig. 4). Two characteristics (connectivity and computing & processor) have scored above 30% on 'Mature' scale (see Fig. 5). Online survey respondents helped in identifying two more characteristics - Miniaturization & Composability and Standards & Protocols. These two characteristics were later included for rating during the IoT experts' interview.

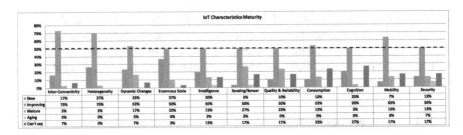

	Inter-Connectivity	Heterogeneity	Dynamic Changes	Enormous Scale	Intelligence	Sensing/Sensor	Quality & Reliability	Consumption	Cognition	Mobility	Security
New	17%	27%	23%	37%	20%	3%	10%	10%	20%	7%	13%
Improving	73%	70%	53%	50%	50%	50%	50%	53%	50%	63%	50%
Mature	3%	3%	17%	10%	13%	27%	23%	13%	3%	13%	13%
Aging	0%	0%	0%	0%	3%	3%	0%	0%	0%	0%	7%
Can't say	7%	0%	7%	3%	13%	17%	17%	23%	27%	17%	17%

Fig. 4. IoT characteristics ≥50% in 'Improving' scale

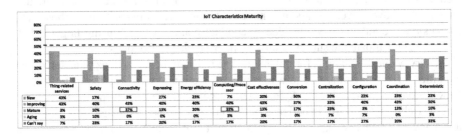

	Thing-related services	Safety	Connectivity	Expressing	Energy efficiency	Computing/Processor	Cost effectiveness	Conversion	Centralization	Configuration	Coordination	Deterministic
New	43%	17%	3%	27%	23%	7%	20%	30%	20%	23%	23%	23%
Improving	43%	40%	43%	40%	40%	40%	43%	37%	33%	40%	43%	30%
Mature	3%	10%	37%	13%	20%	33%	13%	17%	23%	3%	13%	10%
Aging	3%	10%	0%	0%	0%	3%	3%	0%	7%	7%	0%	3%
Can't say	7%	23%	17%	20%	17%	17%	20%	17%	17%	27%	20%	33%

Fig. 5. IoT characteristics <50% in 'Improving' scale

3.3 Survey Result Validation

To validate survey results, two industry experts were interviewed by the author. Expert-1 is a Senior Director of leading USA multinational company pioneer in Industrial Internet of Things (IIoT). Expert-2 is a Product Marketing Manager in USA aerospace company which is actively pursuing the IoT journey in aerospace industry.

There are differences between survey results and experts' ratings due to the following reasons.

- Personal interviews provide more subjective data than surveys. It was very evident from the two sets of charts that depicted the similarities and differences in perspectives of IoT experts online survey participants.
- Experts were asked to rate in the scale of 1–5 to reduce the ambiguity. Results of interview might not be statistically reliable, but closer ratings were grouped together.
- Experts' interviews yielded valuable insights into customer attitudes and unfolded issues related to new IoT products development in their respective industry.

Similarities in ratings by experts' and survey (see Fig. 6) were observed for the characteristics such as Inter-connectivity, Dynamic changes, Things related services, Sensing/Sensor, Expressing, Quality & Reliability, Cost-effectiveness, Consumption, Conversion, Centralization, Cognition and Standards & Protocols.

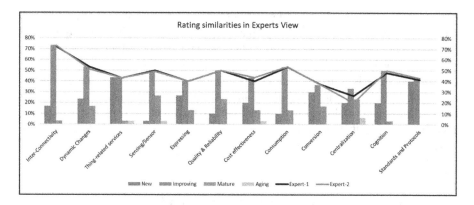

Fig. 6. Similarities in survey result & experts' view

Expert-1 ratings on maturity have largely varied from survey results for the characteristics such as Heterogeneity, Safety, Connectivity, Energy efficiency, Computing/processor and Security. Whereas, IoT Characteristics such as Enormous scale, Intelligence, Configuration, Coordination, Deterministic, Mobility and Standardization & Composability have closely aligned rating on maturity levels with the survey results (see Fig. 7).

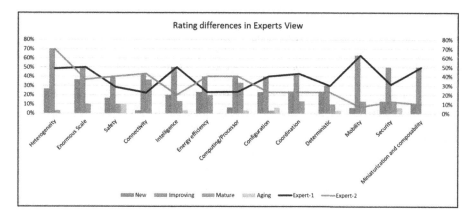

Fig. 7. Differences in survey result & experts' view

As per Expert-2, Enormous scale, Intelligence, Configuration, Coordination, Deterministic, Mobility, Security and Standardization & Composability have different maturity ratings compared to the survey results. IoT characteristics such as Heterogeneity, Safety, Connectivity, Energy efficiency and Computing/processor rating of Expert-2 on maturity ratings have aligned with survey results (see Fig. 7).

IoT characteristics 'Mobility' has received completely varied Maturity ratings from expert-1 and expert-2 (See Fig. 7). Industrial IoT expert has rated 'Mobility' on 'Improving' scale whereas Aerospace IoT expert has rated the same as 'New'. This may be due to their different industries of work and limited use of 'Mobility' characteristics except for its application in Fight Entertainment (IFE) and ground handling equipment, in aerospace domain. It means that this particular characteristic 'Mobility' needs lot of improvement before adopting it to the aerospace industry. It is rightly pointed out by expert-1 that there is a need for 'Mobility' characteristics and lot of development/ improvement efforts are happening in that area. According to the experts', more number of characteristics have aligned with Industrial IoT than with aerospace IoT industry, which makes it clear that Industrial IoT products are yielding more value than aerospace IoT products. It shows that safety critical aerospace industry has just started off the IoT journey.

4   Aircraft Avionics, Systems and Equipment

There are many aircraft systems and sub systems behind every successful flight. To establish the relationship between the IoT Characteristics and aircraft systems, the authors have decided to use research areas listed (see Table 2) in European Aeronautics Science Network (EASN) [21].

Table 2. List of aircraft avionics, systems and equipment

• Avionics	• Electronic Library System
• Cockpit Systems, Visualization & Display Systems	• Aircraft health and usage monitoring system
• Navigation /Flight Management /Auto-land	• Smart maintenance systems
• Warning System	• Lighting systems
• Electronics & Microelectronics for on-board systems	• Aircraft Security
• Sensors integration	• Electrical Power Generation & Distribution
• Flight Data/Flight Recording	• Pneumatic systems
• Communications Systems	• Hydraulic power generation & distribution
• Identification of Aircraft by ATM (Air traffic Management)	• Passenger and freight systems
• Avionics Integration	• Environmental control System
• Optics - Optronic - Lasers - Image processing and data fusion	• Water and waste systems
	• Fuel systems
	• Landing gear and braking systems
	• Fire protection systems

5   Integrating All

'House of Quality' (HoQ), the basic design tool for the management approach known as Quality Function Deployment (QFD), originated in 1972 at Mitsubishi's Kobe ship-yard site. Toyota and its suppliers developed it in numerous ways. HoQ is a kind of conceptual map that provides the means for inter-functional planning and communication. People with different industrial problems and responsibilities can thrash out design priorities while referring to patterns of evidence on the house's grid [22].

HoQ is one of the matrices of an iterative process called QFD. It is the nerve center that drives the entire QFD process which is most recognized and widely used tool for

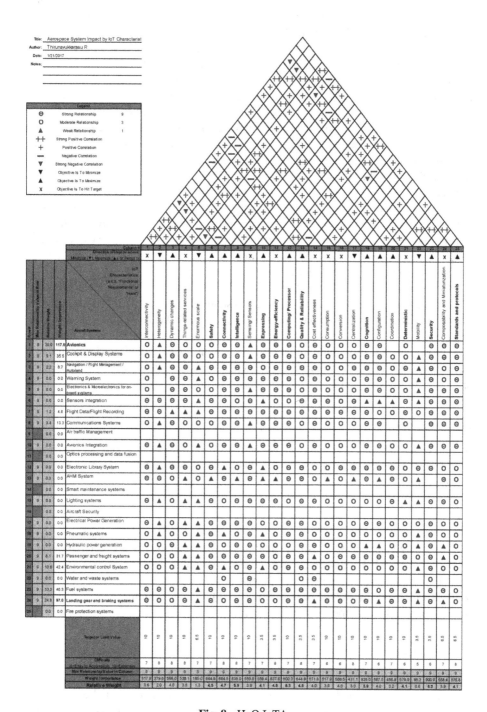

Fig. 8. HoQ IoTA

new product design. It translates customer requirements, based on market research data, into an appropriate number of engineering targets to be met by a new product design. It is performed by a multidisciplinary business critical team [23].

Customer attributes for aircraft systems are listed on the left of the matrix (Horizontal). Meaningful, measurable and global IoT characteristics are listed in the top column of HoQ. Relationship matrix (Central portion) between aircraft systems and IoT characteristics are established (scale of strong, medium and weak relationships) using the discussion outcome with aerospace system experts' (17 interviews with experience levels in the range of 7–30 years) who are working for Tier-1 aircraft system companies. End user views from Pilots, Maintenance Engineers & Airlines executives (3 interviews with experience levels in the range of 10–20 years) are also considered. Five system relationships are not evaluated due to lack of time with system experts' and are marked in red color.

Determined Co-relationship matrix (Triangular shaped Roof) with potential positive and negative interactions between IoT characteristics. Too many positive interactions imply possible redundancy in aircraft systems IoT characteristics. Negative interactions suggest to consider the trade-offs in establishing target values for aircraft systems concepts or technology (see Fig. 8).

As per the survey results and experts' interview, most of the characteristics are difficult and risky to implement in aerospace systems as the maturity levels are still new and improving. 15 Out of 25 characteristics have scored relative weight $\geq$ 4 (Dynamic changes, Safety, Connectivity, Intelligence, Expressing, Energy efficiency, Computing and processor, Quality and Reliability, Cognition, Configuration, Deterministic, Security and Standards & Protocols). These characteristics can potentially impact aerospace systems design and its perceived value in future.

5.1 Assumptions

- Survey participants' knowledge level on IoT characteristics maturity is moderate
- Aerospace systems experts understand the basics of IoT and its impact
- Selection of Aerospace system is based on the research interest

5.2 Limitations

- Use of HoQ alone to establish the relationship between the IoT characteristics
- Perspective of IoT impact on aerospace systems can vary among experts
- IoT characteristics maturity are evolving every day
- Risk factor of using weak relationships in HoQ rows or columns
- Too many relationships between the characteristics

5.3 Results of HoQ

HoQ reveals the relative weight of the IoT characteristics. Four characteristics have scored more than 5 (Intelligence, Computing/Processor, Cognition, and Security). It would encourage companies to invest in developing technologies which can mature on these characteristics. Characteristics such as Intelligence & Computing/Processor have evolved over a period of time and have benefited other industries. It's time for aerospace industry to develop IoT products using the available technologies. Cognition remains as a challenge for IoT products as data is still being interpreted and perceived. Currently less than 1% of data is used for decision making. Security is another challenge for IoT in aerospace industry as the standards and protocols are still evolving and yet to be established.

6 Recommendations

By collating the ratings on IoT characteristics maturity on aerospace systems provided by IoT and Aerospace systems experts', the weightage/importance are evaluated. Avionics and Landing systems have scored high among the aerospace systems. Also, these systems have strong relationship with 50% of the IoT characteristics, which are on improving scale. Aircraft system suppliers should look out for the opportunities in & out of their domain to develop IoT systems/products which can yield long term value to their organizations. Based on this exploratory research, paper authors recommend the following:

- Methodology can help in identifying the potential aerospace system for implementing IoT
- HoQ will help to develop relationship between various IoT characteristics and aircraft system
- When the maturity scale for an IoT characteristic increases, the ease of its implementation in aircraft system also increases

HoQ also helps in establishing the relationship between the characteristics and aircraft systems. Aircraft system development companies are likely to focus on co-relations between the IoT characteristics shown in Triangular shaped roof (see Fig. 8).

7 Conclusions

This research project has established the relationship between IoT Characteristics maturity and its impact on Aerospace systems. HoQ has helped in identifying the potential aerospace systems where IoT can be implemented. The methodology referred in this paper can help aerospace systems companies to understand the IoT characteristics and its related impact on aerospace systems. This paper has identified IoT characteristics which are relevant to aerospace industry. IoT characteristics maturity was determined by an online survey with targeted audience and by interviewing IoT experts. Finally, the IoT Characteristics were connected, relatively weighed and its relationship with system was established by interviewing aerospace system experts'. As per research findings, characteristics such as Intelligence, Computing/Processor, Cognition and Security have scored relative weight > 5. This means that these characteristics are key for implementing IoT in aerospace systems. Aerospace companies should analyze the maturity of these characteristics before considering to invest in developing IoT products.

Future scope of research is to develop a robust methodology to find out the IoT characteristics maturity with increased number of target audience. Aerospace systems experts' interviews can be strengthened further by framing the questionnaire targeting their proficiency level and its relevance to IoT. Research can be extended further on the lines of identifying the impact of IoT elements like sensing, communicating etc., on aerospace systems. HoQ shall be developed for each aerospace system with IoT elements which can help companies move forward in developing IoT enabled aerospace systems.

References

1. Bénaroya, C., Malaval, P.: Aerospace Marketing Management. Springer, Berlin (2013)
2. Global Market Forecast 2016–2035. Airbus
3. Trappeya, A.J.C., Trappey, C.V., Govindarajana, U.H., Chuanga, A.C., Suna, J.J.: A review of essential standards and patent landscapes for the IoT: Key enabler for Industry 4.0. In: Advanced Engineering Informatics, p. 3 (2016)
4. Wamba, S.F.: Rfid-enabled healthcare applications, issues and benefits: an archival analysis (1997–2011). J. Med. Syst. **36**, 1–6 (2012)
5. Rahmani, A.M., Gia, T.N., Negash, B., Anzanpour, A., Azimi, I., Jiang, M., Liljeberg, P.: Exploiting smart e-health gateways at the edge of healthcare internet-of-things: a fog computing approach. Future Gener. Comput. Syst. (2017, in press)
6. Wamba, S.F., Ngai, E.W.T.: Internet of things in healthcare: the case of RFID-enabled asset management. Int. J. Biomed. Eng. Technol. **11**(3), 318–335 (2013)
7. Zhong, R.Y., Peng, Y., Xue, F., Fang, J., Zou, W., Luo, H., Ng, S.T., Lu, W., Shen, G.Q.P., Huang, G.Q.: Prefabricated construction enabled by the internet-of-things. Autom. Constr. **76**(4), 59–70 (2017)
8. D'Angelo, G., Ferretti, S., Ghini, V.: Multi-level simulation of internet of things on smart territories. Simul. Model. Pract. Theor. **73**(4), 3–21 (2017)
9. Civerchia, F., Bocchino, S., Salvadori, C., Rossi, E., Maggiani, L., Petracca, M.: Industrial internet of things monitoring solution for advanced predictive maintenance applications. J. Ind. Inf. Integr. **7**, 4–12 (2017)
10. Tan, Y.S., Ng, Y.T., Low, J.S.C.: Internet-of-things enabled real-time monitoring of energy efficiency on manufacturing shop floors. Procedia CIRP **61**, 376–381 (2017)
11. Dunbrack, L., Ellis, S., Hand, L., Knickle, K., Turner, V.: White Paper "IoT and Digital Transformation: A Tale of Four Industries". Sponsored by: SAP (2016)
12. Vos, M.: Maturity of the internet of things research field: or why choose rigorous keywords. In: Australasian Conference on Information Systems, Adelaide, p. 1 (2015)
13. Ball, M., Barnhart, C., Dresner, M., Hansen, M., Neels, K., Odoni, A., Peterson, E., Sherry, L., Trani, A., Zou, B.: Research Report published by The National Centre of Excellence for Aviation Operations Research titled "Total Delay Impact - A Comprehensive Assessment of the Costs and Impacts of Flight Delay in the United States, p. 14 (2010)
14. An Exclusive Benchmark Analysis (FY2014 data) by Maintenance Cost Task Force published by IATA. https://www.iata.org/whatwedo/workgroups/Documents/MCTF/AMC-Exec-Comment-FY14.pdf
15. Patel, K.K., Patel, S.M.: Internet of things-iot: definition, characteristics, architecture, enabling technologies, application & future challenges. Int. J. Eng. Sci. Comput. **6**, 6123 (2016)
16. http://www.electronicsweekly.com/news/ethernet-goes-deterministic-for-iot-2016-02/
17. https://www.webchoiceonline.com.au/blog/?post=63

18. http://www.forbes.com/sites/adrianbridgwater/2016/01/12/the-7-cs-of-the-internet-of-things/#124784ce59f4
19. Jara, A.J., Ladid, L., Skarmeta, A.: The internet of everything through IPv6: an analysis of challenges, solutions and opportunities. J. Wirel. Mob. Netw. Ubiquit. Comput. Dependable Appl. **4**(3), 97–118 (2013)
20. https://www.rs-online.com/designspark/eleven-internet-of-things-iot-protocols-you-need-to-know-about
21. https://easn.net/, https://easn.net/research-technology-areas/4/#60
22. https://hbr.org/1988/05/the-house-of-quality
23. Shrivastava, P.: House of quality: an effective approach to achieve customer satisfaction & business growth in industries. Int. J. Sci. Res. (IJSR) **5**(9), 1365 (2016)

Smart City Participation: Dream or Reality?
A Comparison of Participatory Strategies
from Hamburg, Berlin & Enschede

Ton A.M. Spil[1(✉)], Robin Effing[2], and Jaron Kwast[1]

[1] University of Twente, Saxion, P.O. Box 217 7500 AE Enschede, The Netherlands
`a.a.m.spil@utwente.nl`
[2] University of Applied Sciences, Saxion, P.O. Box 70.000 7500 KB Enschede, The Netherlands
`r.effing@utwente.nl`

Abstract. Urbanization is forcing local government to revisit their way of communicating with citizens. By using Information Technology, cities can become smarter, more livable and more sustainable. The purpose of this study is to identify critical success factors for local government regarding smart city strategy and participation. The literature study consists of concepts such as smart city, participation and digital strategy. The qualitative study shows that the city of Hamburg defined a digital vision while the other two cities lacked setting such strategies. Bottom-up planning was their primary approach for smart city activities. Regarding the topic of participation we recognize that Hamburg can be recognized as a best practice example. Although the participatory practices were still in its infancy, they showed promising results. Remarkably, all three cities stress the importance of collaboration of different types of stakeholders. The quadruple helix structure ensures effective participation of citizens, companies, universities and government.

Keywords: Smart cities · Participatory governance · Intelligent city · Digital strategy · Urban planning

1 Introduction

In 2050, about two-thirds of the world population will live in cities [1, 2]. The urbanization rate of cities within the European Union even exceeds that. In the year 2010, already 75% of all EU citizens were living in urban areas and it is anticipated that in the year 2050 this number will increase to approximately 85% [3].

However, increasing urbanization provides the world with new challenges. Challenges include providing affordable living space, environmental care, health conditions, and the protection of human rights [4, 5]. Cities include many different actors that influence the city future. The focus of this paper is the topic of participation. Cities and their local government layers need to interact closely with their citizens, companies and other stakeholders. In many societies, the role of the government is changing from a leading authority to a contributory partner [5]. However, local city government struggles

© IFIP International Federation for Information Processing 2017
Published by Springer International Publishing AG 2017. All Rights Reserved
A.K. Kar et al. (Eds.): I3E 2017, LNCS 10595, pp. 122–134, 2017.
DOI: 10.1007/978-3-319-68557-1_12

with keeping up with new technology trends. One of the underlying reasons is that existing regulations and laws do not effectively support the implementation of new technologies [6]. People, companies and public authorities can now easily connect and cooperate via the Internet and social media more efficiently than ever before [7]. The transformation of governance is changing towards more co-creation of all stakeholders [8]. This paper aims to synthesize the topics of digital strategy [9] and participatory governance from empirical cases [8].

This research paper is structured as follows. Firstly, a literature review will be presented including related concepts and literature gaps. Secondly, the chosen methodology for retrieving qualitative information is explained. Thirdlu, we present qualitative findings from the three cities and describe their e-participation strategies and implementation experiences. Finally, we will analyze these cases and draw some important conclusions.

2   Theoretical Background

2.1   Structured Literature Research Method

First, the keywords related to the topic were defined: smart city, governance, government, strategy and success factors. The database Scopus was used to search relevant literature. The result of the first queries resulted in a list of over 500 items. The results were limited to both conference papers and articles in order to exclude other document types. This resulted in 420 items. After careful reading of the title, abstract and keywords, 22 publications were identified as relevant for our study. This was a useful set to study and this led to the development of this theoretical background section.

2.2   The Smart City Concept

In recent years, a new city model, called smart city, has emerged and has gained attractiveness among many scholars [1, 3, 7, 8, 10–14]. As Van den Bergh and Viaene [13] have pointed out, the smart city concept evolved from already existing concepts such as eco-city, digital city and wireless city. The concept of smart city is not completely a new concept. In 1989, Castells [15] already mentioned the importance of an informational city and the potential power of technology for reshaping the social life in our cities. In the last decades, various innovative city concepts have entered the policy discourse such as sustainable city, green city, livable cities, digital cities, intelligent cities, knowledge cities, information cities and resilient cities [11]. As Zubizarreta et al. [14] propose, the smart city model could help addressing the main challenges of cities and attempts to avoid the new issues that will come. Those challenges include population- related problems, mobility, energy and environmental issues. Some authors claim that the smart city concept will eventually improve the city regarding social, environmental, economic and sustainable performance [16, 17]. A city has to interrelate social, economic and environmental dimensions with each other to keep the overall city in balance and create benefits for all stakeholders [11]. According to Caragliu et al. [3] a city is smart: *"when the investment in human and social capital and traditional (transport) and modern (ICT) communication infrastructure fuel sustainable economic growth and a high quality of life, with a wise management of natural resources, through participatory governance".* There "is neither a single template of framing it, nor a-one-size-fits-all definition" on what a smart city should look like [18]. For example, smart cities in Japan have been focusing on a technical-intensive approach such as using smart grid technologies for energy control [8]. In Europe, cities such as Amsterdam, Copenhagen, Manchester and Milan were combining both the technological approach with a more citizen-centric approach [13].

2.3 Participation in Cities

Participation includes all activities that are conducted voluntarily, without a statutory obligation to involve citizens in the political decision-making process [19]. Informal participation practices can be used in addition to formal practices or used separately for individual projects, but not as a replacement for formal participation [20]. Government project requirements could be met more effectively by increasing informal ways of participation [20]. This way of including citizens can be considered as more discursive and cooperative since citizens are able to exchange their opinions among each other and get in touch with other stakeholders involved. A wide range of informal participation tools is available such as stakeholder workshops, citizen juries, focus groups, electrical forums, web polling, public conversations, participatory budgeting, study circles and collaborative policy making [21]. A shift from formal to informal participation can be considered as a shift from hierarchical structures to dialog-oriented participation practices [20]. As companies are increasingly changing their management systems to bottom-up approaches, government want to adopt a similar change [1, 7, 8]. The premise for effective governance in smart cities is that, by having the right information at the right time, citizens can be included in decision making. That eventually results in an increased quality of life for residents and the overall sustainability of the city [22]. However, local city councils and city administration officials still struggle to decide when citizens should get involved in political decision-making and to what extent they should be involved [23].

2.4 Digital Strategies for Cities

In recent years, the rise of Web 2.0 and social media has greatly changed the way people communicate with each other [24–26]. Because of the many developments in the field of Information and Communication Technology (ICT), it should be easier for municipalities and citizens to communicate with each other [27, 28]. ICT provides citizens with new opportunities to create user generated content and exchange it via social media [29]. For government "it is necessary to change government perspective [of the citizens] from a content consumer to a content producer" [30–32]. ICT is considered by many scholars as a powerful means to promote and improve public participation [8]. There is still significant change that needs to happen within the government because traditional modes of public participation like public meetings are not beneficial according to Evans-Cowley and Hollander [33]. Traditional modes are limited in their scope and duration and therefore limited in their learning process. Public knowledge can enhance the outcome of projects that have a reason for citizen engagement [34]. Many cities keep improving their digital performance and move many services from offline media to online media. ICT is being employed for involving citizens in the decision-making process [28]. In many cases, different branches of the government initialiate different ICT initiatives. As a result, there is a lack of a central point of overview where citizens can identify all current participation opportunities [19]. Generally it is expected that the input that was generated by asking the input of citizens enriches the decision-making process [8], eventually leading to a better outcome of the project. Therefore, the use of ICT will become even more important in the future [21]. Moreover, new ICT strategies that make use of the Internet provides government with a more cost-effective way of public administration [19, 27]. The ICT infrastructures in current cities support and enable the concept of smart governance [35]. Particularly social media is expected to play a key role in digital participation because of its unique opportunities for fostering public debates and exchanging opinions [19]. However, many city government employees still lack skills to effectively employ these social media for within the decision-making process [36].

2.5   E-Participatory Smart Cities

This paper uses the concepts of Effing and Groot [37] and Spil et al. [9, 51] in the analysis to combine the degree of engagement that citizens have with government, citizen or network initiatives of a smart city that can be taken in order to improve and develop the overall city to become smart.

Citizens are increasingly **engaged** into the concept through their mobile devices that enable direct involvement [8]. E-commitment [37] can be seen as part of the engagement [9]. To be engaged the cities have to identify the target groups, set their goals and determine the channels that they want to use. Furthermore, is it important for cities to integrate their habitants since they are the protagonist of a city, the most important feature, and belong to the site and everything that is being done concerns them [14].

Governments need to **enable** the capacity to be able to manage the amount of new possibilities of participation [9]. Cities need to adapt to the fact that citizens want to be able to actively take part into governmental decisions [38]. They have to allocate resources, decide and communicate policies. Cities have already implemented many online participation tools, but there is still capacity in integrating real time data from sensors and activators [39] into participatory governance. Overall smart cities have a high interest in integrating sensors, smart devices and real-time data into every aspect of human life [40]. Cities have often not realized the potential of participatory governance, and is still an underestimated factor [41]. Also the concept of the quadruple helix is increasingly important [42] since the innovation benefits from the involvement of citizens, companies, government and universities.

Finally Cities have to **evaluate** their digital strategy [9]. Although it is hard to measure Return on Investment quantitatively, the cities can monitor and listen to its citizens and cities need to use evaluation tool to measure this.

3   Results

3.1   Empirical Research Method

This study consists of three cases that were selected for the following reasons. First, we searched for best practice examples. Hamburg is considered as one of the smartest and most livable cities in Germany according to several rankings [43–45]. A case study of Hamburg was conducted. A contemporary phenomenon (a "case") was studied in-depth within its real-world context. Hamburg has been classified as a critical case as former research has shown, that it provides a critical reason to investigate Hamburg more intensively when this holds true according to Yin [46]. Especially when the boundaries between phenomenon and context may not be clearly evident, a case study can create new insights [46]. Remenyi and Williams [47] claim that a single case study is quite limited in business and management research for drawing general conclusions. Therefore we selected two additional cities for case study research. These are Berlin, the capital and largest city of Germany, and the city of Enschede, in the Eastern part of the Netherlands, with the potential to become a smart city. Eisenhardt and Graebner [48] claim that insights drawn from cases often result in highly cited publications. Furthermore, Zainal [49] states that case studies, in their true essence, are aimed at investigating contemporary real-life phenomenon through detailed contextual analysis of a limited number of events or conditions and their relationships. The qualitative interviews were carried out with two employees of each city. They were, at the time of writing, working on the smart city development at the municipalities of the included cities. All interviewees were highly familiar with the main concepts and had practical knowledge to serve the potential of this research. For this qualitative part of the study, we conducted semi-structured interviews. This type of interview combines the benefits of both unstructured interviews and structured interviews. On the one hand, these interviews served as evidence for the validation of our literature findings. On the other hand, these interviews were open for the possibility for adding additional knowledge regarding the subject matter of smart cities [50]. The interviews were recorded and transcribed to warrant that all information said was included in this paper.

3.2   Hamburg

Respondent 2 (R2) mentioned: "everybody is talking about the smart city concept. However, the ultimate smart city is an utopia and does not exist". The smart city concept is not a single concept. It includes many different ways for cities to become smart. In January 2015, a visionary paper about Hamburg´s digital future, entitled "Digitale Stadt" (digital city), was approved by The Senate of the Free and Hanseatic city of Hamburg. Within this vision it was especially important to "establish an innovation climate that enables citizens to make public data openly accessible and support companies and institutions in networking" (R1) as well as "achieving a higher quality of living" (R2). In the online communication and public services, there is great potential to exploit since offline communication channels are already exploited to the maximum within the city of Hamburg (R2). Therefore, the Internet can serve as a new opportunity for increasing the number of participating citizens. Furthermore, Respondent 2 stressed that it is important for governments to increasingly work in a citizen-centric way and try to reach out for citizens. For example, when citizens say that "if Hamburg sends a multiple-choice list on my mobile device, then I am willing to respond" (R2), then Hamburg is obligated to serve them multiple-choice lists to increase their participation.

In recent years, governance has changed and became a bottom-up approach. Citizens are empowered by letting them actively engage in the decision-making process (R1). Information flow and accessability of information is considered as important in Hamburg. Therefore, the city of Hamburg has decided to implement the "Transparenz-gesetz" (transparency law) in 2012. This includes creating an online platform, the so called "Transparenzportal" (transparency portal), in order to give the public online access to data created by the local government.

Another tool Hamburg is using to drive up innovation with companies is embedded into the Transparenzportal and provides open data for companies to use. Yet companies have not showed much interest in these datasets. Predominantly, the academic stake-holders are interested in using those datasets (R2).

Additionally, Hamburg wants to promote the implementation of various informal participation tools in the decision-making processes. The city of Hamburg already recognized this trend and gained some positive results from using informal participation practices. For example, the "Weltquartier Wilhelmsburg" and the "Hamburger Deckel". Through the early recognition of the value of informal participation, one best practice has evolved over time (R2). An important smart strategy is: "including citizens as early and as active as possible" (R1), even before the projects are tendered to business... Everything regarding participation in Hamburg, including phase zero, is joined in the online platform called Stadtwerkstatt. The Stadtwerkstatt "is an integral part of citizen participation" (R1). This is considered as the "central place to receive information" (R1) regarding projects initiated by the government. Another important topic of digital partic-ipation is the use of social media, However, effective social media use is very time-consuming and many resources are necessary. Employees are in charge of the content and serve as contact persons. "The Senate of Hamburg is using many social media plat-forms and online appearances" (R1). However, there is not enough budget to participate on social media for projects regarding decision making for special projects (R2).

An important part of online tools is that they empower citizens much more than offline tools do (R2). Empowering is a very important part of smart governance and needs to be implemented in one way or another. But as the interviews showed, "real empowerment does not exist since municipalities are always in need for expert knowl-edge" (R2). However, it is important that the government should not limit citizens in their creativity or manipulate their decision-making abilities (R2). Hence, empowerment is important but it needs to be tailored for the citizens in such a way that it does not disable their creativity and free expression.

Network collaboration represents another key part of the smart city concept. Hamburg tries to encourage innovation through a variety of collaborative practices. One possibility is "to encourage innovation using the triple helix structure, which brings together companies, universities and the government" (R1).

3.3 Berlin

According to Berlin's Smart City Strategy, the city can only be smart if the following three key aspects are fulfilled:

1. The city combines various sources of information;
2. The city achieves a significant increase in efficiency and use of resources through integrated approaches and;
3. The city actively involves citizens and investors in the process of shaping the city in order to make it attractive, viable for the future, resilient and dedicated to the common good, eventually increasing the quality of life.

The smart city strategy is a proposal of actions that Berlin needs to undertake in order to become a smart city. This strategy plan includes all aspects that appear in the smart city conceptualization: environment, safety, innovation, network, infrastructure and social participation. In addition, they emphasize the goals of making Berlin more competitive as a capital region internationally and the marketing of Berlin's innovativeness. The actions proposed are aimed at digitalizing the way Berlin's government and public administration works. However, an implementation plan or schedule is lacking. When asked about the most important aspects of the Smart City Berlin, the respondent 3 (R3) mentioned the Smart City Berlin Network. "This network has 100 members, comprising innovative companies and research institutes in Berlin. They already developed a lot of creative ideas for applications in order to make the city smarter". She says, so far these applications have only been applied abroad and Berlin has not implemented their own ideas yet. The city's senate was too constrained for applying a strategy in order to test it. As for the social aspect of the smart city, the smart city strategy Berlin supports the idea of earlier mentioned literature: the citizens of Berlin are the most important component for making the strategy work. It argues that, for digital strategies and applications to be successful, citizens of Berlin have to approve of them. In order to achieve that, marketing has to convince them of the strategies' usefulness, for which they want to communicate with citizens via social media platforms. The strategy proposes ways to enable e-participation, which will be elaborated on in the next section. However, an implementation plan was lacking.

The most elaborated e-participation strategy in Berlin is the use of Open Data as an innovation strategy. The webpage enables citizens who are interested in Berlin's city development and decisions about all senate solutions, official documents and dates regarding all components of the capital. However, for empowering, Berlin's smart city e-participation strategy "Mein Berlin" (My Berlin) is presented in the Smart City Strategy Berlin as Berlin's main participatory instrument for the future. Furthermore, Berlin's Smart City Strategy suggests that their open data policy, guided towards transparency and open decision-making, will encourage citizen participation in the future. Nonetheless, the same chapter of the strategy states that, no matter how evolved these platforms might be, it is important that they do not replace democratic decision making. As an agenda for 2016, a unifying platform of contact was planned to facilitate administrative services and "create a unified point of contact for citizens and business".

This represented a digital strategy for citizens to involve themselves with the government, but was still lacking the participatory element.

One of the innovations that came from companies working on smart governmental solutions is called the "DIALOG BOX". It was found during the analysis of Berlin's governmental webpages. The innovation claims to be an ideal way for communication between citizens and government. It is software that was developed for the sole purpose of citizen participation. Nonetheless, there is no evidence for a link with Berlin's smart city strategy, neither a sign of collaboration (R3). This suggests that the progress of implementation of these strategies is taking place quite slowly and an implementation schedule is lacking. This was also confirmed by respondent 3. Nevertheless, she emphasized that the Smart City Berlin Network is regularly discussing strategies and proposals to make participatory action reality. This means that in their annual meetings, they consider the Smart City Berlin Strategy as a basis of their actions and they come up with ideas to implement e-participation, based on the senate's strategy.

The only informative digital platform that is implemented from the strategy is Berlin's Open Data page, giving citizens access to administrative documents and data. However, this platform does not provide visitors with any participatory functions for commenting and sharing their opinions. The beta version of "Mein Berlin" is the closest Berlin gets to an empowering e-participation strategy at this moment. According to R3, the chamber of Industry and Commerce Berlin and other network partners expressed critique towards the lacking implementation schedule. Her department did publish a brochure stating that participatory instruments need to be implemented. She further explained that the Smart City Berlin Network also proposed solutions for participatory action. However, in order to implement a strategy, the final decision lies within the senate department of urban development and environment. During an interview with the smart city strategist R4 of that department, it was expressed that any kind of such a strategy in practice would be "Zukunftsmusik" (Still up in the air) in Berlin and that there will be no implementation regarding that matter soon. This respondent also made very clear, that there is nothing to talk about regarding that matter. According to R3, the important missing piece in this endeavor right now is an implementation plan with exact steps to take in the future, published by the senate and their strategists.

3.4 Enschede

"Enschede describes a smart city as: making the city smarter, with smart people and doing things smarter as a government". The key questions of the municipality are: how can we make better use of the already available data? "And how can we use technology in a better way?" This can then be used for monitoring, user experience, and the development of policies. Enschede did focus on the opportunities of the use of big data. They described their key challenge as: "How can we use the already available data in a better, more smarter way for creating policies?" Another project is focusing on the city centre that is employed as a living-lab in cooperation with local universities. In Enschede, collaboration with large companies was mostly avoided, since this could lead to a vendor lock-in. Instead, local businesses were contacted and involved. According to respondent 5, the municipality shifted towards a bottom-up approach, starting with small projects in the Enschede community. There are entrepreneurs and citizens working on this. Their quest according to respondent 5 is: "how can we make a transition in means of communication in order to activate these people?"

Enschede is labelling itself as a smart city (R5). "We are focussing on this topic and we recognise the importance. We make room for it and act on this topic. We are in anyway planning on providing more open data. (R5)" An example of this is the cooperation with the German city of Heidelberg and the American city of Palo Alto in Silicon Valley. Furthermore, the municipality is a member of different collaboration platforms regarding smart city strategies such as the Open and Agile Smart Cities Initiative. The interviewee did explore the subject of smart city and what it can do for the city. However, a smart city strategy was at the time of research not defined in a policy plan. Furtermore, the implementation budget for smart cities was relatively small. Instead, investments are part of on-going maintenance and existing policy programs: Investments are always required within cities. For example Enschede has recurring investments in street lights, asphalt or traffic lights giving them the opportunity to innovate. "If you think smart on those moments about what you want and what is possible, you can invest in new technology that might not be needed now, but that can be uses in the near future. (R5)"

Enschede currently does not have a detailed vision on smart city. The respondent 6 had defined something that could be seen as a vision, but this is not really useful according to the interviewee: "from the moment you write down your vision it is obsolete". For now they want to focus on participating citizens, knowledge centres and businesses: "we want to give space to companies to do things, create a living-lab environment. Not only for knowledge institutes, but also for businesses, to make things happen."

4   Analysis

In this section, we compare the three cities by using relevant digital strategy models [9, 37, 51].

A digital strategy cannot be effective without engagement of people. While both the dialog box in Berlin and "Enschede stad" provide us with participatory examples, they still lack real commitment. In Hamburg, they use social media in an effective way for engaging their citizens, companies and knowledge institutes. E-commitment is quite a remarkable practice in Hamburg but is still starting up in the "Stadtwerkstatt" environment. Effing and Groot [37] emphasise the importance of commitment as part of the smart city. "Mein Berlin" is a good example but you could expect more similar initiatives in a big capital city such as Berlin. In Enschede, small companies are involved for building commitment. We also recognize the quadruple helix collaboration structure being beneficial there. In Hamburg, there was actually a digital strategy in place but it was not incorporated in a formal governance cycle. Evaluation of the smart city progress was lacking as shown in Table 1. In Berlin and Enschede, the respondents did not mention a specifically defined digital strategy. All three cities formulated goals for their smart cities. However, these goals were not quantified and difficult to measure. In theory, enabling citizens by digital solutions means much more than having a website. The aspect of effective enabling citizens and companies requires also resources and policies as part of the strategy [9]. Yet all respondents refer to the basic website of the cities when they talk about enabling. A share of the included respondents stressed that the capacity and resources of the "smart" departments were quite limited. Finally, evaluation of progress regarding the smart city strategy is not specifically developed at these three cities [9]. The emphasis of the smart cities Hamburg, Berlin and Enschede clearly was aimed at developing digital engagement with the public as first priority.

Table 1. Analysis overview

City/Stage of participation	Enable	Engage	Evaluate
Hamburg	Hamburg.de	Social media Stadtwerkstatt	None
Berlin	Berlin.de	Dialog box Mein Berlin	None
Enschede	Enschede.nl	Enschede stad Small companies	None

5 Conclusion

Cities in Europe are still struggling with the smart city concept. In most cities, digital strategies and visions still have to be developed. Furthermore, the evaluation and monitoring of smart city results is not yet operational. As a result, the government policy cycle is not working effectively. However, there is awareness that the quadruple helix collaboration structure is necessary; involving citizens, companies, knowledge institutes and government for creating and fostering a livable society.

The empirical results show that smart cities are still a dream but that reality is winning fast and the possibilities seem endless. Hamburg is a pioneering city with participation tools at the operational level and their experiences can lead the way for other cities, but experiences and learning are not yet developed well.

As a theoretical contribution, evaluation should be added to the smart city concept model to create a knowledge-learning loop and to create a basis for future digital strategies. The new concept encompasses: Enablement, Engagement and Evaluation.

Future studies have to address evaluation, can explore ICT more specifically the Internet of Things [51] and can explore more cities for a more general view on smart cities.

Acknowledgements. We express our gratitude for students who have contributed to this paper. We want to thank Julia Steinke and Johann Rick Harms who helped collecting case material. Their thesis projects were part of the broader research collaboration regarding smart city strategy of both University of Twente and Saxion University of Applied Sciences (Project TFF Brid.ge).

References

1. Niaros, V.: Introducing a taxonomy of the "smart city": Towards a commons-oriented approach? (2016)
2. World Health Organization. Global Report on Urban Health, equitable cities for sustainable development (2016). www.who.int/kobe_centre/measuring/urban-global-report/ugr_full_report.pdf. Accessed 30 Apr 2017
3. Caragliu, A., Del Bo, C., Nijkamp, P.: Smart cities in Europe. J. Urban Technol. **18**(2), 65–82 (2011)
4. Cohen, B.: Urbanization in developing countries: current trends, future projections, and key challenges for sustainability. Technol. Soc. **28**(1–2), 63–80 (2006). doi:10.1016/j.techsoc.2005.10.005
5. Gil-Garcia, J.R., Pardo, T.A., Nam, T.: What makes a city smart? Identifying core components and proposing an integrative and comprehensive conceptualization. Inf. Polity **20**(1), 61–87 (2015)
6. Kettl, D.F.: The Transformation of Governance: Public Administration for the Twenty-First Century. JHU Press, Baltimore (2015)
7. Schaffers, H., Komninos, N., Pallot, M., Trousse, B., Nilsson, M., Oliveira, A.: Smart cities and the future internet: towards cooperation frameworks for open innovation. Future Internet Assem. **6656**(31), 431–446 (2011)
8. Granier, B., Kudo, H.: How are citizens involved in smart cities? Analysing citizen participation in Japanese "Smart Communities". Inf. Polity **21**, 1–16 (2015). (Preprint)
9. Spil, T.A.M., Effing, R., Both, M.P.: Enable, engage and evaluate: introducing the 3E social media strategy canvas based on the european airline industry. In: Dwivedi, Y.K., et al. (eds.) I3E 2016. LNCS, vol. 9844, pp. 15–30. Springer, Cham (2016). doi:10.1007/978-3-319-45234-0_2
10. Chourabi, H., Nam, T., Walker, S., Gil-Garcia, J. R., Mellouli, S., Nahon, K., Scholl, H.J.: Understanding smart cities: an integrative framework. In: Paper presented at the 2012 45th Hawaii International Conference on System Science (HICSS) (2012)
11. De Jong, M., Joss, S., Schraven, D., Zhan, C., Weijnen, M.: Sustainable–smart–resilient–low carbon–eco–knowledge cities; making sense of a multitude of concepts promoting sustainable urbanization. J. Clean. Prod. **109**, 25–38 (2015)
12. Hollands, R.G.: Will the real smart city please stand up? Intelligent, progressive or entrepreneurial? City **12**(3), 303–320 (2008)
13. Van den Bergh, J., Viaene, S.: Unveiling smart city implementation challenges: the case of Ghent. Inf. Polity **21**, 1–15 (2016). (Preprint)
14. Zubizarreta, I., Seravalli, A., Arrizabalaga, S.: Smart city concept: what it is and what it should be. J. Urban Plan. Dev. **142**, 04015005 (2015)
15. Castells, M.: The Informational City: Information Technology, Economic Restructuring, and The Urban-Regional Process. Blackwell Oxford, Oxford (1989)
16. SG Network, ICCM Association: Getting to smart growth: 100 policies for implementation: Smart Growth Network (2002)
17. SG Network, ICCM Association: Getting to Smart Growth II: 100 more policies for implementation: Smart Growth Network (2003)
18. Albino, V., Berardi, U., Dangelico, R.M.: Smart cities: definitions, dimensions, performance, and initiatives. J. Urban Technol. **22**(1), 3–21 (2015)
19. Vogt, S., Förster, B., Kabst, R.: Social media and e-participation: challenges of social media for managing public projects. Int. J. Public Adm. Digit. Age (IJPADA) **1**(3), 85–105 (2014)
20. Klages, H., Vetter, A.: Bürgerbeteiligung auf kommunaler Ebene: Perspektiven für eine systematische und verstetigte Gestaltung, vol. 43, edition sigma (2013)

21. Vogt, S., Haas, A.: The future of public participation in Germany: empirical analyses of administration experts' assessments. Technol. Forecast. Soc. Chang. **98**, 157–173 (2015)
22. Khansari, N., Mostashari, A., Mansouri, M.: Impacting sustainable behavior and planning in smart city. Int. J. Sustain. Land Use Urban Plan. (IJSLUP) **1**(2) (2014)
23. Rowe, G., Frewer, L.J.: Public participation methods: a framework for evaluation. Sci. Technol. Hum. Values **25**(1), 3–29 (2000)
24. Greenhow, C., Robelia, B., Hughes, J.E.: Learning, teaching, and scholarship in a digital age Web 2.0 and classroom research: What path should we take now? Edu. Res. **38**(4), 246–259 (2009)
25. Hoffman, D.L., Novak, T.P., Venkatesh, A.: Has the Internet become indispensable? Commun. ACM **47**(7), 37–42 (2004)
26. Leiner, B.M., Cerf, V.G., Clark, D.D., Kahn, R.E., Kleinrock, L., Lynch, D.C., Wolff, S.: A brief history of the Internet. ACM SIGCOMM Comput. Commun. Rev. **39**(5), 22–31 (2009)
27. Åström, J.: Should democracy online be quick, strong, or thin? Commun. ACM **44**(1), 49–51 (2001)
28. Medaglia, R.: eParticipation research: moving characterization forward (2006–2011). Gov. Inf. Quart. **29**(3), 346–360 (2012). doi:10.1016/j.giq.2012.02.010
29. Kaplan, A.M., Haenlein, M.: Users of the world, unite! the challenges and opportunities of Social Media. Bus. Horiz. **53**(1), 59–68 (2010)
30. Brabham, D.C.: Crowdsourcing the public participation process for planning projects. Plan. Theor. **8**(3), 242–262 (2009)
31. Ornebring, H.: The Consumer as Producer* of What? User-generated tabloid content in The Sun (UK) and Aftonbladet (Sweden). Future Newspapers **142** (2013)
32. Rebillard, F., Touboul, A.: Promises unfulfilled? 'Journalism 2.0', user participation and editorial policy on newspaper websites. Media Cult. Soc. **32**(2), 323–334 (2010)
33. Evans-Cowley, J., Hollander, J.: The new generation of public participation: internet-based participation tools. Plan. Pract. Res. **25**(3), 397–408 (2010)
34. Schweizer, P.-J., Renn, O., Köck, W., Bovet, J., Benighaus, C., Scheel, O., Schröter, R.: Public participation for infrastructure planning in the context of the German "Energiewende". Util. Policy **43**, 206–209 (2014)
35. Scholl, H.J., AlAwadhi, S.: Creating smart governance: the key to radical ICT overhaul at the city of munich. Inf. Polity **21**, 1–22 (2016). (Preprint)
36. Dameri, R.P.: Searching for Smart City definition: a comprehensive proposal. Int. J. Comput. Technol. **11**(5), 2544–2551 (2013)
37. Effing, R., Groot, B.P.: Social smart city: introducing digital and social strategies for participatory governance in smart cities. In: Scholl, H.J., et al. (eds.) EGOVIS 2016. LNCS, vol. 9820, pp. 241–252. Springer, Cham (2016). doi:10.1007/978-3-319-44421-5_19
38. Städtetag, D.: Culture of Participation in Integrated Urban Development: Working Paper of the Working Group on Public Participation by the German Association of Cities, Deutscher Städtetag (2013)
39. Zygiaris, S.: Smart city reference model: assisting planners to conceptualize the building of smart city innovation ecosystems. J. Knowl. Econ. **4**(2), 217–231 (2013)
40. Cretu, L.-G.: Smart cities design using event-driven paradigm and semantic web. Informatica Economica **16**(4), 57 (2012)
41. Bingham, L.B., Nabatchi, T., O'Leary, R.: The new governance: practices and processes for stakeholder and citizen participation in the work of government. Public Adm. Rev. **65**(5), 547–558 (2005)
42. Afonso, Ó., Monteiro, S., Thompson, M.J.R.: A growth model for the quadruple helix innovation theory (2010)

43. Cohen, B.: The 10 Smartest Cities in Europe (2014). http://www.fastcoexist.com/3024721/the-10-smartest-cities-in-europe/8
44. Mercer. Quality of living ranking (2016). https://www.imercer.com/content/mobility/quality-of-living-city-rankings.html-list
45. Numbeo. Quality of Life Index 2016 (2016). http://www.numbeo.com/quality-of-life/rankings.jsp
46. Yin, R.K.: Case Study Research: Design and Methods. Sage publications, Thousand Oaks (2013)
47. Remenyi, D., Williams, B.: Doing Research in Business and Management: An Introduction to Process and Method. Sage, London (1998)
48. Eisenhardt, K.M., Graebner, M.E.: Theory building from cases: opportunities and challenges. Acad. Manag. J. 50(1), 25 (2007)
49. Zainal, Z.: Case Study as a Research Method. Jurnal Kemanusiaan 9, 1–6 (2007)
50. Hove, S.E., Anda, B.: Experiences from conducting semi-structured interviews in empirical software engineering research. In: Paper presented at the 2005 11th IEEE International Symposium Software Metrics (2005)
51. Spil, T.A.M., Pris, M., Kijl, B.: Exploring the BIG Five of e-leadership by developing digital strategies with mobile, cloud, big data, social media, and the Internet of things. In: E-proceedings IC Management Leadership &Governance, Johannesburg South Africa (2017)

Benefits and Pitfalls in Utilization of the Internet by Elderly People

Libuse Svobodova[✉] and Miloslava Cerna

Faculty of Informatics and Management, University of Hradec Kralove,
Rokitanskeho 62, Hradec Kralove, Czech Republic
{libuse.svobodova,miloslava.cerna}@uhk.cz

Abstract. The role of advanced technologies is being discussed in public, academic and government environments. The paper deals with the current issue of computer literacy in the elderly people with focus not only on benefits but also on pitfalls connected with their use. The paper brings an insight into the technical literature review. It strives to summarize key beneficial outcomes and contrary unexpected obstacles which elderly people face when they use information and communication technology. A set of examples as practical demonstrations of real computer usage by elderly people illustrates the issue on the national scene. The research was run to explore the computer literacy in elderly people from three perspectives, roughly corresponding to three kinds of elderly people reflecting their physical and mental state. Findings from the surveys which were conducted with a group of elderly respondents in the senior homes and findings from the interview with a young lector teaching old generation show the issue in the local city environment. A question on benefits of organized course for the elderly from the questionnaire explores the survey from four perspectives and brings enriching findings. Findings from literature review correspond to findings gained from the research. Positive attributes of active utilization of the Internet contribute to active ageing, to the combat of the feelings of social isolation and loneliness.

Keywords: Benefits · Elderly people · Expectation · Pitfalls · Realization · Research

1 Introduction

Population is growing old which is a general fact scientifically validated by statistics of individual countries, see statistics of the national Czech Statistical Office of the Czech Republic (CZSO) [1]. Percentage of the population classified as elderly people is steadily increasing.

Elderly people as a term doesn't have a single definition; there is no general agreement when the person is considered old. Its definition slightly varies according to the environment it is used or discussed, e.g. state economic system or sociological disciplines. Applied chronological age of 65 years in this paper stems from statement of the World Health Organization which is a widely recognized health expert in 150 countries within the United Nations' system.

© IFIP International Federation for Information Processing 2017
Published by Springer International Publishing AG 2017. All Rights Reserved
A.K. Kar et al. (Eds.): I3E 2017, LNCS 10595, pp. 135–146, 2017.
DOI: 10.1007/978-3-319-68557-1_13

"Most developed world countries have accepted the chronological age of 65 years as a definition of 'elderly' or older person. While this definition is somewhat arbitrary, it is many times associated with the age at which one can begin to receive pension benefits. At the moment, there is no United Nations standard numerical criterion, but the UN agreed cutoff is 60+ years to refer to the older population." [2]

Casado et al. [3] discuss the issue of active ageing in their recent empirical study on technology and elderly people in the research conducted with the 55 to 94 years old group of people. So, as the starting point they defined the age 55. There is no strict point defining the beginning phase of the age category called elderly people in statics and charts in sources processed in this paper that is why the inhere presented charts also work with not strictly unified beginning of the senior age.

There are two inexorably developing trends; population is ageing and new technology is constantly evolving and improving. Utilization of technology by elderly people is being a current topic, with solutions lagging behind or coming ad-hoc. It is true that there are attempts or even established a kind of tradition in training older people how to gain computer literacy, e.g. within U3A (the university of the Third Age) in the UK [4] but there is no comprehensive and functional system.

2   Materials and Methods

The aim of the paper is to analyse the current computer literacy in elderly people with a focus on benefits and possible difficulties and pitfalls which go along with utilization of computers and the Internet.

The research procedure consisted of the following phases:

- The first phase dealt with the introduction to the topic and defining the key term 'elderly people'.
- Methodological frame encompassed goal setting, description of the study procedure and literature review.
- Literature review consists of two sections. The first one brings the results from official statistical recordings' so that via this way the width of the issue is visualized and serves as a starting point to the insight into the later main section dealing with benefits and pitfalls in utilization of ICT elderly people.
- In the next phase the issue of computer literacy in elderly people on the local scene was discussed based on the real programmes which had been organized for the elderly people and on the outcomes which were consequently published. This phase forms a kind of a balance to the 'cold' statistical data and 'remote' academic studies as it focuses on real tangible events in the local circumstances. Due to the fact that during the work in the field which means in the home for elderly people or in the course of computer literacy for retired people organized by the Municipality of the regional city, it was instantly revealed that the utilization of social network is too narrow topic, mostly neglected by the accessible sample. The perspective of benefits and pitfalls got extended to the wider topic to the computer literacy.
- Following stage deals with processing and publishing results and findings from the survey. The survey was conducted in November and December 2016 in 12 primary

schools which have been engaged in the long-term "intergeneration" project "Internet for Senior Citizens" with the Municipality of Hradec Kralove in organizing courses of computer literacy for the elderly.

Primary and secondary sources were used. As for secondary sources, they comprised websites of selected surveys and also official statistics from the Czech Statistical Office and Eurostat, technical literature, information gathered from professional journals, discussions or participation at professional seminars or conferences. Then it was necessary to select, categorize and update available relevant information from the collected published material.

Work in the field followed: elderly people were contacted both in their senior homes and at home with home care, then appointments and one interview with a young lecturer participating in the training course for the elderly people were done.

Data from the project "Internet for the Senior Citizens" were gained from discussions, interviews, questionnaires and from the Presentation at the graceful closing ceremony where participants of the courses were awarded with diplomas. *In total 173 senior citizens graduated* in the last term – they successfully completed one of three kinds of courses: Internet for beginners, Internet for advanced and Digital photography course. Researchers distributed questionnaires to the Elderly participants – "Students", to primary school pupils – "Lecturers", to primary school teachers who ensured smooth run in each course – "Tutors" and to the Directors of project involved schools. Researchers gained filled in questionnaires from all directors, from 15 teachers - "Tutors", 99 pupils -"Lecturers", and 82 senior citizens – "Students". It means that nearly half of "Students" provided researchers with the valuable response.

2.1 Literature Review – Utilization of Telephones, Computers and the Internet by Elderly People

In spite of the fact that advanced technologies are in the Czech Republic commonly used for communication, in case of the analysed category of elderly people telephones are commonly used but as for utilization of computers and the Internet they are used to much lesser extent, see Fig. 1. Data are collected from the national Czech Statistical Office and Eurostat. The graph in Fig. 1 shows that the Internet use is very closely related to the computer use.

In the use of computers and their services to communicate with other people we still don't achieve or even do not come close to the level of their utilization as is the average of the EU 28 [6], it is necessary to clarify that the data referring to pure communication reasons aren't available for elderly people, the data in this case refer to 16+ [7].

When it comes to utilization of the Internet by the group 65+ (elderly people) in the United States there were 58% users but in comparison with the Czech Republic the number was just half, only 28.4%. It is interesting to follow the time-line and the trends; in 2005 28% of elderly people used the Internet in the United States but as for the Czech Republic, there were only 2.2% of 65+ people using the Internet.

In 2010, the Internet was used in the States by 43% of elderly people but in the Czech Republic there was an incredible six fold increase in users meaning that 13.2% 65+

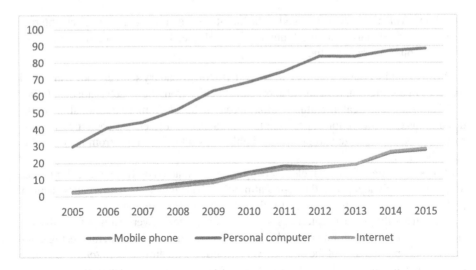

Fig. 1. Individuals aged 65+ years old that use information and communication technology in the Czech Republic. Data are given in percentages. Source: [5]

people were using the Internet. Five years later in 2015 the rise wasn't as steep as in previous years, but the number of Czech elderly users doubled and reached 28.4%, in the States more than half of the elderly people to be precise 58% use the Internet.

The increase in Internet users in connection with the development and expansion of advanced technology is evident. Its share may have seniors who have become seniors in recent years and got into contact with information and communication technology e.g. in their work, which for the previous older generation was not very common.

2.2   Literature Review - Benefits and Pitfalls

The other part of the literature review deals with the key issue of the paper; it focuses on computer literacy in the elderly people, on the aspects of benefits and pitfalls of ICT utilization, especially of the Internet and media.

The pros and contras, positives and negatives of Internet utilization are widely discussed in the academic sphere. But as for the age category of 'elderly people' the offer of academic studies gets narrower, selected studies follow.

Chen, Schultz [8] discussed in their review study beside other topics the issue of *social isolation* in the use of social networks by elderly people. Evidence indicates that contemporary information and communication technologies (ICT) have the potential to prevent or reduce the social isolation of elderly people via various mechanisms. The findings of this review suggest that the elderly can benefit from ICT interventions and will use them (sometimes frequently) after proper training.

Gonzalez [9] work deals with main habits when new technologies are used by older people. The *level of knowledge* and their *level of education* are highlighted. The purpose was to analyse whether the technological skills of elderly people are sufficient, as well as to know if the audio-visual resources are appropriate. This study strives to find out if the ageing society is prepared to handle everything the Internet has to offer. This study took place in three countries of the European Union: the United Kingdom, France and Spain. The worst results were found in Spain. In 2013 and 2014 the Internet was used by one third of elderly people (33%). Nearly the same number about one fifth of the elderly people used tablet pc (21%), WhatsApp (20%) and Facebook (19%). Mobile phone is used by 81%. As for social networks, 85% of Spanish elderly people stated they had never participated, 14% participated from time to time and only 1% claimed that they participated online regularly.

The other presented study comes also from Spain. Montaa [10] claims that Spanish elderly people show considerable interest in the Internet and more than 60% of them check their email daily. Their *use of the Internet*, however, is eminently pragmatic, so they tend not to explore and use its potential as social media, as means of social communication.

Active Ageing is a term which accompanies the elderly people theme in academic papers as well as in texts written for the general public. Llorente-Barroso [11] explores active ageing in elderly people within the research on utilization of the Internet and its potential. Global ageing has led European and international organizations to develop programs for active ageing, in order to reconstruct the role of the elderly in society. Active ageing includes social communication aspects which have been the subject of less research than other more pressing ones linked to physical and economic characteristics. The results of the qualitative content analysis of discussion indicate that the Internet is a source of opportunities for the elderly, and this potential may be divided into four categories: Information, communication, transactions and administration, together with leisure and entertainment. This potential improves the quality of life for the elderly and contributes to their active ageing. However, to maximize this, e-inclusion programs and methodologies are needed to make the Internet user-friendlier for the elderly and provide them with training in digital skills.

Casado-Munoz [3] conducted a research with 419 people aged between 55 and astonishing 94 who participated in the "Inter-university Programs of Experiences" from the University of Burgos) The Internet served as the platform which increases ways of communication, enables to *avoid isolation and loneliness via active ageing.*

Williams [12] also highlight attributes of the elderly age like *loneliness* and *social isolation*. Feelings of loneliness and social isolation can occur in many older adults and impairments that may occur in old age, such as reduced mobility, deteriorating sight, and deteriorating hearing, can prevent elderly adults from visiting their friends and family. Interpersonal communication software such as Facebook Messenger and Skype - can be very useful in keeping bonds with loved ones strong over long distances. However, sometimes these applications can be confusing and difficult for elderly people to use. A design created with considerations for the variety of abilities and older user might prompt more elderly users to use interpersonal communication software, and assist in the fight to reduce loneliness and social isolation in older adults.

3   Computer Literacy in Elderly People on the Local Scene – Awareness, Courses and Instant Outcomes from Research

In the original plan there was an intention to explore utilization of social network by elderly people: what programmes and courses were offered to this age group by local authorities, by senior homes, senior center and Home Charity care service in the regional city. But there was rather limited or no awareness of the social networks among the elderly. The research had to be adapted to exploration of the computer literacy in elderly people from three perspectives, roughly corresponding to three kinds of elderly people reflecting their physical and mental state:

• Programmes and courses organized by local authorities for retired people.
• Possession of ICT devices and use of information and communication technology by people staying in the senior homes in the city.
• Home health care service and Home Charity care service in the regional city

The first group represented independent mobile retired or semiretired people who were able to move and come to the place where the course was supposed to be organized which is mostly in some city primary school. The second group was formed by the people who were of the older age category who lived in a senior home where service corresponding to their specific needs was provided who practically didn't leave the premises of the walls very often. The last group was represented by the most disabled people who were dependent on assistance of other people.

3.1   Latest Findings from the Local Scene

There has been a long ten years long commendable tradition in the city of Hradec Králové. Its municipality regularly organizes free courses on computer literacy for elderly people. The awareness of this event got established among the city population due to systematic promotion on the websites of the city in the section designed for the elderly people [13] and in reports in local media [14]. Deputy Mayor responsible for education and social area stated … we can truly say that it is meaningful activity and brings a lot of good fruit. It is run in the spirit of intergenerational dialogue, but also improves the quality of life of our seniors. Contributes to their activation and prevents social isolation [15]. Twelve city primary schools are currently involved into the project 'The Internet for seniors'. Pupils from the lower secondary schools teach elderly people how to work with the computer in a ten-week course one hour weekly. The teacher emphasises the value of communication between two generations, she enjoys watching how 'her' pupils cope with their new role. She has sober expectations in the progress in computer literacy in the elderly people. She states that there is no possible generalization in the technical achievements, because participants of the course differ. But several times she has mentioned that pupils change in perceiving the computer – from predominantly useful thing for gaming to useful device of everyday use (organizing files, searching for information, e-mails. internet banking, etc.)

Current state in selected senior or nursing homes and opportunities for improvement follow. People in three nursing homes in Hradec Králové which provide home to 2 hundred elderly people were interviewed and contacted. In nursing homes there is no special ICT equipment provided; no free ICT devices, no organized courses or ICT support. Few residents own a computer or tablet, but it is rather exceptional. Thus, people usually do not use computers. They like the situation as it is, people are satisfied, and the expert care is provided to them, they somehow do not need to search for information, explore or communicate with the outer world or study. Personal communication with people in the senior house or telephone call with the family they find satisfactory.

In case that caregivers visit of their elderly clients in their homes, the situation in the use of computers significantly differs. People tend to live a more active life and communicate more with others, if health state allows. Another criterion may be age. Computers are usually used to view photos of the family. The Internet is used by not very big deal of elderly people, and social networks even smaller. As for Home Charity care service in the regional city, it presents itself on the Internet on their modest websites [16]. Home Charity Care service helps people care for themselves and for their own household when they already cannot cope with the situation. Home Charity assists in a wide range of services but all are linked to physical or mental assistance in a serious health state, no motivating activities relating to active ageing are presented.

3.2   Findings from the Internet for Senior Citizens Survey

The issue of computer literacy explored from four perspectives. There are four groups of people who participate in the project who differ in cognitive and affective areas, they differ in knowledge and experience, and they differ in interest and expectations. Four kinds of modified questionnaires were created. Some questions were same. One of these will be analysed in this paper not only that it forms one of the pillars of the paper but because all stakeholders can learn from comparison of these findings. The discussed question: In your opinion What benefits arise to the seniors from attending the course? Results from all four groups follow in Figs. 2 and 3.

Findings are worth further discussion as they vary in groups.

Most positive responses were gained from teachers who coordinate the individual courses. They are responsible for administration of the course and provide assistance to the attendees and to pupils if is needed. They expected that the positive outcomes will be very high.

Then there were Directors of schools and pupils-lecturers who were also very positive about the benefits arising to attendees of the course.

The least positive were the attendees - senior citizens about potential benefits.

Teachers expressed greatest expectations in computer literacy skills. 14 teachers out of 15 believed in improvement of attendees' computer literacy. 13 teachers stressed potential positives to the attendees which were related to social and socializing sphere: development of other ways of communication with family. 12 teachers mentioned 'advanced' skills which relate to uploading and downloading videos and photos. Teachers expressed that there was no interest in gaining information from various disciplines, no interest in medical science. Interest in medicine was very low in analysed groups: 6 directors out of 12 expected interest in medicine discipline in the attendees, 39 lecturers out of 99 but as for seniors only 13 out of 82 had found it beneficial.

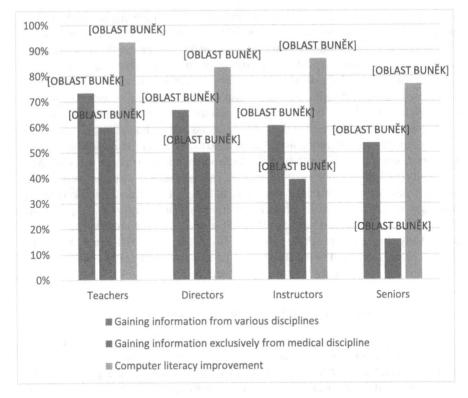

Fig. 2. Benefits – computer literacy skills

Directors could see the biggest benefits in improvement of computer literacy and meeting other people with similar interests. Other positive expectations follow: other ways of communication with family, gaining information from various disciplines, sharing and uploading photos.

Lecturers had the greatest expectations in improvement if computer literacy, opportunities to develop further communication with the family, sharing and uploading photos, gaining information from various disciplines and meeting people with similar interests. These expectations were formulated by 50 out of 99 lecturers.

Senior attendees (63 out of 82) stated that most important area is improvement of computer skills.

Other frequently ticked options were: gaining information from a variety of disciplines, an opportunity to develop new ways to communication with family and sharing information. One third of them marked the option meeting other people with similar interests. The lowest interest is in the already mentioned category - Getting information from the medical field.

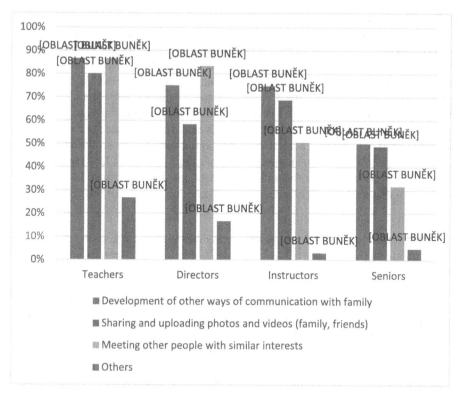

Fig. 3. Benefits – social perspective

3.3   Findings from the International Studies

Study from the France, United Kingdom and Spain research [9] presented more fields such as owned and used technologies, sources of information, skills of elderly people, participation of social networks etc. In our here presented research we focus on two selected parts – why the elderly people use advanced technologies and whether and how they improve their ICT skills.

France
Elderly people in France mainly use the devices to keep being informed (29%) and connected to their families by sharing photos and videos with them (14%). Entertainment is another one of the reasons they include to explain their use (13%). Adapting to new technologies is considered a trend and a tendency that the elderly in France are actively participating in. the results of the survey in France highlight that most (66% of those surveyed) are self-learners in relation to learning and improving their knowledge of ICT. Therefore, older users are willing to adapt and improve their knowledge in this field. The platform that they most commonly use to improve their knowledge is with tutorial videos. The mobile applications are also appealing to them but they only use them for personal leisure.

United Kingdom

There is a high level of interest to learn and improve in this field, especially because most British people are aware of their needs, their surroundings and the potential of new technologies to improve their living conditions. The need to feel independent is the main incentive for this increase in using and consuming technology in the UK. That is the reason we understand that for the 55 to 65 age group, studying is the main use of ICT (54%). On the contrary, in people over 65, the main use is still the need to keep being informed (24%) and entertainment (22%). Moreover and as is the case in France, despite the high interest and degree of adaptation of this profile with ICT, most of those surveyed are self-learners (69%) or learn through the help of a family member (22%), with tutorials being the most used platform for self-learning amongst those between the ages of 55 and 65 (72%). In the Great Britain there are ICT training courses for this audience.

Spain

The Spanish mainly use this device to keep being informed and to keep in touch (69%), for entertainment (18%) and to talk (10%). Only 2% claimed to have used it for education or training. This is a result that contrasts with the data obtained in France and in the United Kingdom, since we observe that in Spain there is not high adaptation to new technologies and the elderly are unaware of the actual possibilities. The elderly in Spain primarily learn about new technologies from family members and friends (61%) followed by self-learning (26%) and only 13% have attended a course as a way of learning about new technologies. On the contrary, Spaniards are very interested in learning about new technologies (87% want training and only 13% don't) through class-room courses (62%) and specific conferences about this subject and in accordance with their needs (38%).

4   Conclusion and Discussion

Creation of suitable conditions for elderly people could be the proper way to finding solution for greater use of advanced technology, the internet, social networks, etc. As an inspiring and promising example of this approach the case study from Spain might serve. [11] The authors claim that although the Spanish elderly people are equipped with new technologies, they aren't able to use them to full extent they use only fragment of offered options and possibilities.

Elderly people in the Czech Republic widely use mobile phones but when it comes to computers, the Internet or even social network the percentage of active users is small. The surprising finding comes from senior homes in which elderly people use advanced technologies only scarcely with any need to activate themselves in further studies or adventurous exploration in the on-line communication raised the question how to moti-vate them. In comparison to them there are people who are even less mobile who need care assistance but still stay in their homes are much more active. The situation in senior houses might be improved via improvement in facilities, creation of centers where seniors could meet and work with technology. Hand in hand with these improvements goes the need to create enough opportunities for education in this area.

Results of the questionnaire investigation which was done by the authors of the paper are presented. Researchers applied a collaborative approach; they explored the argued project "Internet for Senior citizens" as it was a kind of orchestra where participants have specific roles; in this case those were attendees, lecturers, teachers and directors. All of them had to participate, all of them had their experience as well as expectations and all of them were after the same goal. For the successful run of the project it is not only desirable but definitely it necessary to collaborate, discuss the problems, needs, achievements and expectations within the community of stakeholders. As it was found out, expectations and belief differ; individual people perceive things differently, with different intensity. Most positive responses on the benefits were gained from teachers who coordinate the individual courses. Then there were Directors of schools and pupils-lecturers who were also very positive about the benefits arising to attendees of the course. The least positive were the attendees - senior citizens about potential benefits.

As findings show the most beneficial is when several missions combine like learning and socializing which was clearly illustrated in the case of organized computer courses where young and old generations met, gained and shared information and experience.

The following work might focus an analyzing the gained data from another perspective, for example, based on the methodology of [17].

Acknowledgement. This paper is supported by specific project No. 2103/2017 "Investment evaluation within concept Industry 4.0" at Faculty of Informatics and Management, University of Hradec Kralove, Czech Republic. We would like to thank student Marta Martinova for cooperation in the processing of the article.

References

1. Age structure. https://www.czso.cz/csu/czso/animated-life-pyramids
2. Health statistics and information systems, Definition of an older or elderly person. http://www.who.int/healthinfo/survey/ageingdefnolder/en/. Accessed 10 Apr 2017
3. Casado-Munoz, R., Lezcano, F., Rodriguez-Conde, M.J.: Active ageing and access to technology: an evolving empirical study. Comunicar **45**, 37–46 (2015)
4. The University of Third Age. http://www.u3a.org.uk/. Accessed 10 Apr 2017
5. Czech statistical office. Information Society in Figures. https://www.czso.cz/csu/czso/information_society_in_figures
6. Americans' Internet Access: 2000–2015. http://www.pewinternet.org/2015/06/26/americans-internet-access-2000-2015/
7. Eurostat. http://ec.europa.eu/eurostat/statisticsexplained/index.php/Digital_economy_and_society_statistics_-_households_and_individuals
8. Chen, Y.R.R., Schulz, P.J.: The effect of information communication technology interventions on reducing social isolation in the elderly: a systematic review. J. Med. Internet Res. **18**(1), e18 (2016)
9. Gonzalez-Onate, C., Fanjul-Peyro, C., Cabezuelo-Lorenzo, F.: Use, consumption and knowledge of new technologies by elderly people in France, United Kingdom and Spain. Comunicar **45**, 19–27 (2015)
10. Montaa, M., Estanyol, E., Lalueza, F.: Our seniors' challenge to the new media: uses and opinions. Profesional de le Informacion **24**(6), 759–765 (2015)

146 L. Svobodova and M. Cerna

11. Llorente-Barroso, C., Vinaras-Abad, M., Sancher-Valle, M.: Internet and the elderly: enhancing active ageing. Comunicar **45**, 29–36 (2015)
12. Williams, D., Ahamed, S.I., Chu, W.: Designing interpersonal communication software for the abilities of elderly users. In: 38th Annual IEEE International Computer Software and Applications Conference (COMPSAC), Sweden, pp. 282–287 (2014)
13. Autumn Internet courses for seniors - seniorhk.cz. http://www.hradeckralove.org/urad/internet-pro-seniory
14. Pupils in the role of real teachers. http://www.hradeckralove.org/noviny-a-novinky/zaci-v-roli-opravdovych-lektoru
15. Pupils in the role of real teachers. They teaches seniors how to use the Internet. http://www.maclova.cz/aktualne/aktuality/2013/zaci-v-roli-opravdovych-lektoru-uci-seniory-jak-s
16. Domestic charity care service. http://www.charitahk.cz/nase-strediska/charitni-pecovat elska-sluzba/
17. Khatwani, G., Anand, O., Kar, A.K.: Evaluating Internet Information Search Channels Using Hybrid MCDM Technique. In: Panigrahi, B.K., Suganthan, P.N., Das, S. (eds.) SEMCCO 2014. LNCS, vol. 8947, pp. 123–133. Springer, Cham (2015). doi:10.1007/978-3-319-20294-5_11

Advances in Electronic Government (e-Government) Adoption Research in SAARC Countries

Nripendra P. Rana[1], Yogesh K. Dwivedi[1(✉)], Sunil Luthra[2], Banita Lal[3], and Mohammad Abdallah Ali Alryalat[4]

[1] School of Management, Emerging Market Research Center (EMaRC),
Swansea University Bay Campus, Fabian Way, Swansea, SA1 8EN, UK
{n.p.rana,y.k.dwivedi}@swansea.ac.uk
[2] Department of Mechanical Engineering, Government Engineering College, Nilokheri 132117,
Haryana, India
sunilluthra1977@gmail.com
[3] Nottingham Business School, Nottingham Trent University, 50 Shakespeare St,
Nottingham, NG1 4FQ, UK
banita.lal@ntu.ac.uk
[4] Faculty of Business, Al-Balqa' Applied University, Salt, 19117, Jordan
mohammad.alryalat@hotmail.com

Abstract. This paper profiles the research activities that have been published on e-government adoption in the context of South Asian Association for Regional Cooperation (SAARC) countries. Our analysis includes variables such as the years of publication, journals most often publishing papers on e-government adoption, countries in which the research activity was conducted, the authors most active in the subject area, keywords analysis, methodological analysis, technology and respondents contexts, analysis of theories or models used and analysis of limitations and future research directions extracted from 48 research papers that were extracted from Scopus database using some key terminologies related to e-government, adoption and eight SAARC countries. This is the first study that has comprehensively examined the analysis of e-government adoption literature in these eight countries' context. The results of this research provide some promising lines of inquiry that have been largely neglected along with those that have received a much larger attention.

Keywords: Adoption · Afghanistan · Bangladesh · Bhutan · e-Government · eGov · Digital government · India · Literature review · Maldives · Nepal · Online government · Pakistan · SAARC countries · Sri Lanka

1 Introduction

Electronic government (hereafter, e-government) is one of the most fascinating concepts to have appeared in the area of public administration and has become a substantially evident aspect of governance in the last few years [1, 2]. The introduction of e-government is a move undertaken by various governments across the world toward becoming

© IFIP International Federation for Information Processing 2017
Published by Springer International Publishing AG 2017. All Rights Reserved
A.K. Kar et al. (Eds.): I3E 2017, LNCS 10595, pp. 147–158, 2017.
DOI: 10.1007/978-3-319-68557-1_14

more service oriented and focused for their widespread implementation of digital services to its users [3]. E-government can be defined as the delivery of government information and services to citizens through the Internet (as the Internet is one of the preconditions to the acceptance and use of e-government services) or other digital means [4, 5]. It provides citizens with convenient access to such information and services [6], the ability to search and acquire them at their own convenience.

E-government provides a number of benefits to its users including reducing administrative burdens and corruption, delivering more accountable, transparent and easily accessible cost-effective delivery of public services, employing citizen empowerment, improving convenience, and ensuring quicker adaptation to meet citizens' needs and better governance that help the government to become more result-oriented [3, 7]. Nowadays, as governments are increasingly turning to e-government led administrative reforms, citizens' slow uptake or adoption of governments' online services poses a great threat for reform managers who are not only responsible for improving the quality of public service delivery but also cutting down on operating expenses [8]. Citizens who do not use these services end up wasting their valuable time in government offices, which could have well be used in the economically productive activity. Moreover, under-utilisation of e-government services also results in a low rate of return on government funds that were invested to develop those services. Considering that it takes substantial funds for a government to create new e-government services, it might be difficult to sustain severely under-utilised e-government service [9, 10]. A number of studies (e.g. [7, 11, 12]) both in context of developed and developing countries' contexts have emphasized the slow adoption of e-government services right from the early days of its evolution. This is the reason why a number of studies have explored the reasons behind the slow adoption of e-government services particularly in developing countries' context through research dispersed in the various outlets.

This study will focus on the analysis of literature on e-government adoption emerging from the countries that are members of South Asian Association for Regional Cooperation (SAARC), which consists of eight countries namely India, Pakistan, Sri Lanka, Bangladesh, Afghanistan, Bhutan, Nepal and Maldives. We have selected the research on e-government adoption from these member countries from SAARC because they represent a part of Asian continent and agreed to work on five areas including telecommunication, which could be considered as a backbone for effective e-government implementation. They also share socioeconomic, demographic and cultural practices and they all share some attributes of developing countries. Hence, analysis of literature from these countries would provide insights that would be applicable to them. Furthermore, combining literature from other countries would provide a mix picture and outcomes may not be fully applicable these countries.

The remaining sections of the paper are structured as follows: Sect. 2 will describe the literature search approach. Section 3 will perform literature analyses using metadata analysis in terms of years of publications of research, journals where such research studies were published, countries of research publication and list of prolific authors who published research on e-government adoption. The following subsections will evaluate the keyword analysis, methodological analysis, technology context, types of respondents and analysis of theories and models in these e-government adoption studies.

Section 4 will provide brief discussion of findings, limitations of existing studies, their future research agenda, contribution of this research to literature and recommendations provided to government based on this literature analysis. The final section (i.e. Sect. 5) will provide conclusive remarks of this research including limitations and future research directions for this study.

2 Literature Search Approach

We used the set of keywords such as "electronic government", "e-government", "eGov", "eGovernment", "mobile government", "m-government", "digital government" and "online government" using the logical OR operator supported with other sets of keywords on the major theme of adoption/acceptance including "adoption", "intention", "behavior", "acceptance" and list of eight SAARC countries in context for which the available literature have to be considered for this study including "India", "Pakistan", "Sri Lanka", "Bangladesh", "Afghanistan", "Bhutan", "Nepal" and "Maldives" using AND operator in Scopus database. We gathered 54 articles from different journals based on the above search. However, we discarded six studies because either they were not related to e-government research in SAARC countries' context or their theme was not quite related to e-government adoption/context. This way we left out with 48 articles that made the basis for the literature analysis for this study.

3 Literature Analysis

This section will present analysis on meta-data, keywords, methodology, technology context, respondent types and use of theories/models gathered from 48 articles on e-government adoption research in the context of SAARC countries.

3.1 Meta-Data Analysis

The number of papers published on e-government adoption in context of SAARC countries indicates that the trend of publications was quite tentative over the years with 2016 being the most productive year with highest 11 studies published in one or the other research outlets. However, the lowest one paper was published in year 2006. The collective trend of publications of research in the last two years indicates increasing levels of interest and research activity in this area in the recent time [13].

As far as the breakdown of our search output according to the journals in which the papers on e-government adoption appeared during 2006–2017 period. A total of 21 journals were found as the appropriate outlets for e-government adoption research. The largest number of papers (8) on e-government adoption appeared in the journal called *Electronic Government, an International Journal* and least one paper each published in 10 different journals. Other journals have published something between two to six papers on e-government adoption. Our finding reveals that research outlets are quite diverse and in addition to journals that largely publish issues related to government and public sector, they are largely related to information systems and technology.

The findings regarding countries where the research studies were piloted indicated that the largest numbers of research studies were conducted in India (23) followed by Pakistan (10), Bangladesh (7) and Sri Lanka (4). However, only one study each was conducted in context of Afghanistan and Nepal and no research on e-government adoption has yet been conducted in the context of Bhutan and Maldives. Given that Sri Lanka holds the highest rank in terms of e-government development index among the SAARC countries, it is surprising that there has not been much research based on this country. Hence, there is an opportunity for additional research based in such countries where there is no research or only a handful of research available in order to further expand the existing knowledge base.

So far as authors actively involved in conducting and publishing e-government adoption related research is concerned, it appears that the most productive author in e-government adoption research is Dwivedi with 13 papers closely followed by two authors Gupta and Rana both with six papers each and Williams and Shareef with five and four papers respectively. Thereafter, four authors contributed three papers each and 13 authors contributed two papers each while 72 authors published just one paper in the set of journals comprising our search data. Due to space limitations the authors with one publication has not been listed.

3.2 Keyword Analysis

In order to assess the most frequently used keywords, all the keywords from 48 studies were gathered. A total of 30 keywords were used two or more times. E-government in its various forms including m-government was the most frequently used keywords with all 48 papers utilized them. This is followed by adoption (19), India (14), communication technologies (13), trust (9) and developing countries (9) are some of the other more frequently used keywords used in e-government adoption research here. The use of keywords such as e-government and adoption as the two leading keywords is not surprising as these keywords are related to the major themes of the research. We have also found some of the obvious keywords related to countries where such research has been conducted and linked to the use of key theories/models, factors, research methods and analysis techniques related to this area of research. We also found 75 keywords with only one occurrence and have not included them in the text because of space limitations. Moreover, even though some other keywords such as digital divide, citizen satisfaction, corruption, Internet usage are relatively less frequently occurring they seem more interesting and hold significance in terms of their further exploration in context of SAARC countries.

3.3 Research Methods Analysis

Research methods include research approach, methodology, analysis techniques and analysis tools used by these e-government adoption studies (see Table 1). The findings indicate that majority (i.e. 27 studies) of the research (e.g. [3, 7]) on e-government adoption are quantitative in nature followed by eleven studies (e.g. [14]) using qualitative research. However, only one study each was found under the category of conceptual

[15], descriptive [16], and interpretive research [17]. Therefore, it quite clearly indicates that e-government research in SAARC countries is slowly moving from informational to transactional stage. As far as methodologies are concerned, survey (33) was found as the most commonly used methodology (e.g. [18]). This was followed by some others but relatively less frequently used methodologies including case study (5) (e.g. [19]), interview (2) (e.g. [14]) and content analysis (2) (e.g. [20]), literature review (2) (e.g. [21]) and interpretive structural modelling (ISM) (e.g. [17]) as some others. Survey was commonly used in different forms including questionnaire survey, online survey, email survey and field survey. The scrutiny of analysis techniques and tools indicates that the studies have mainly used regression analysis (14) (e.g. [22, 24]) and structural equation modelling (12) (using AMOS (8), Smart PLS (1) and LISREL (3)) (e.g. [7, 18, 23]) as the key techniques to evaluate their results.

Table 1. Research methods used

Research methods	Details	Example reference(s)
Research approach	Quantitative [27]	[3, 7, 10, 18, 32]
	Qualitative [11]	[14, 20, 31, 36]
	Conceptual [1]	[15]
	Descriptive [1]	[16]
	Interpretive [1]	[17]
Methodology	Survey (Online, Questionnaire, Email, Field survey etc.) [33]	[7, 18, 27, 32]
	Interview [3]	[14, 21]
	Content analysis [2]	[20]
	Case study [5]	[16, 19, 40]
	ISM [1]	[17]
	Literature review [2]	[21, 25]
Analysis technique	Regression (i.e. multiple regression, hierarchical regression) analysis [14]	[10, 22, 35]
	Structural equation modelling [12]	[3, 7, 32]
	Factor analysis [1]	[30]
Analysis tool	SPSS [14]	[22, 30, 31]
	AMOS [8]	[3, 7]
	Smart PLS [1]	[41]
	LISREL [3]	[18, 33]

3.4 System or Technology Context

This section presents different systems or technologies examined across 48 studies that formed our search results. It is clear from the investigation that e-government in its generic (e.g. [8, 20]) and specific forms (e.g. [3, 7]) make the most of systems. However, some studies have also examined other technologies such as cloud computing, information and communication technology (ICT) or online services in government context. For example, MdYusof et al. [25] and Gupta et al. [26] examined adoption of cloud computing and ICT in context of government of public sector organisations whereas Manandhar et al. [27] explored success factors of online services in the Nepalese perspective. The findings indicate that despite of e-government development in SAARC countries in last few years, research is largely limited to the evaluation of generic e-government and m-government services and less effort has been paid toward evaluating specific e-government or m-government applications.

3.5   Respondent Type

This section presents different types of respondents from whom the data for studies were gathered (see Table 2). The analysis indicated that largest 26 studies (e.g. [7, 28]) used citizens' data whereas 10 studies (e.g. [10, 26]) utilized employees as their respondents. Only two studies (e.g. [29]) used student data and the remaining 10 studies (e.g. [19, 20]) were based on literature reviews, content analysis of e-government portals, descriptive research or case studies. Given that development of e-government in SAARC countries is not very old they have started riding on the wagon wheel of evaluating their e-government initiatives using primary data however as some research studies are still trying to understand the development of e-government initiatives using literature review, case studies, content analysis and descriptive research before the performance of systems could be evaluated using primary data.

Table 2. Respondent type

Respondent type	N	Example source(s)
Citizenl consumer	26	[7, 8, 18, 22, 30, 32, 35]
Employeel professional	10	[10, 21, 27]
Student	2	[24, 29]
Content analysis, descriptive, literature reviews, case study	10	[19, 20, 40]

3.6   Theories/Models Used

This section provides account for different theories and/or models that have been used across the studies on e-government adoption in SAARC countries context (see Table 3). The findings indicated that the unified theory of acceptance and use of technology (UTAUT) (10) (e.g. [7, 30]) has been used the most number of times closely followed by the technology acceptance model (TAM) (9) (e.g. [8]). The theories like diffusion of innovation (DOI) (e.g. [31]) and IS success model (e.g. [27]) have been used five times each. However, the theories/models such as TRA [32], TPB [33], SCT [3], trustworthiness model [34], transaction cost theory [31] and perceived characteristics of innovating

[8] have been used only once. The findings clearly indicate that the studies of e-government adoption are largely dependent on information systems/technology (IS/IT) adoption models.

Table 3. Theories/Models used

Theory/Model used	N	Example sources
UTAUT	10	[7, 19, 29, 30]
TAM	9	[8, 33]
DOI	5	[10, 31, 33, 39]
IS success model	5	[23, 24, 27]

3.7   Limitations and Recommended Future Research of Reviewed Studies

The findings related to limitations of existing research indicate that the largest number of limitations is related to context specific sample collected from one or limited number of organisations, cultures, countries, communities or settings (i.e. G2C, G2E) (e.g. [2, 3, 35]) followed by limitations related to generalizability of findings to the other contexts or settings [7, 32]. Some studies have also highlighted the issues of cross-sectional data (e.g. [8]), data collected from non-adopters of the system (e.g. [7]), lack of additional and more suitable variables in the proposed model (e.g. [36]), student sample (e.g. [8]), small or inadequate sample and limited variance obtained by the model on dependent variables (e.g. [30]). In addition, there are some other limitations that have occurred only once or twice and so have not been included into text due to space limitations. Some of these limitations include lower response rate [18], no use of moderating variables [30], no validation for conceptual model [37], exploratory research or research in progress [18] and the qualitative nature of study [14] to name a few.

The largest number of studies proposed their future research directions in terms of the need for diverse sample (e.g. [22, 30]), which are aligned with the limitations of existing research as presented earlier where the highest 14 studies articulated that their sample was context specific. This is followed by some other future research directions including the need for the proposed model to be tested using longitudinal data (e.g. [28]), use of additional, new and more specific constructs (e.g. [3]), testing models in some other similar contexts (e.g. [18]), need of examining more specific cultural and geographical contests (e.g. [28]) and extending the model to be tested using adopters data (e.g. [7]) to name a few. The other future research directions, which occurred only once or twice include the need of using non-student data [36], need of embedding use behavior in the proposed model [32], need for quantitative approach in the research [14] and need for larger sample [29] to name a few.

4   Discussion

The findings presented above explored a number of dimensions of the analysis of literature on e-government adoption in SAARC countries. The findings suggest the increasing levels of interest in e-government adoption research in last two years. The further analysis of it indicates that majority of research in last few years have been published repeatedly by a very small group of researchers on the various emerging e-government systems in context of India, Bangladesh, Pakistan and Sri Lanka. However, this effort needs to be diversified and more researchers should join hands in publishing research in this area. The findings along the journals most often published paper on e-government adoption indicates that in addition to the government and/or public sector related journals the papers have also highly diversely published across IS/IT, information management and human behavior related journals. The findings also revealed that majority of studies on e-government adoption in SAARC countries context have not quite been able to find their homes in internationally respected peer reviewed journals. The natural and obvious reason for this could be less mature e-government related research in these countries' perspectives [38]. In terms of country analysis, it was found that India was the leading country for which the e-government adoption research was conducted whereas no research was undertaken for countries like Bhutan and Maldives. Hence, there are ample opportunities to conduct research for such countries, which are completely untapped and also those (e.g. Nepal and Afghanistan), which are under researched.

The findings also suggest that the most productive authors in terms of number of papers published in last 11 years were Dwivedi, Gupta, Rana, Williams and Shareef. The Google Scholar citation for Dwivedi also suggests that he has had the largest number of citation counts for his research. Moreover, only one out of these most productive authors is based in India and others are from the UK or Bangladesh. This clearly indicates that even though the e-government adoption research is being conducted for the SAARC countries, the authors belong to the academic institutions of other countries. Hence, there is a need for more authors within the countries to highlight and explore research agenda related to e-government, as it is one of the most relevant ways in which government services could be delivered from the government to its citizens. The regular appearance of certain related keywords such as e-government in general and specific e-government services such as e-District, e-Pension, income tax filing etc. and m-government clearly suggests that majority of these studies are focused on investigating e-government and m-government services. However, a large body of under-represented keywords (i.e. 75) such as digital divide, citizen satisfaction, D&M model, corruption, Internet usage are worthy of further exploration in the future research. For example, the less frequent use of keywords such as satisfaction and D&M model also indicates that the e-government adoption research has not quite reached to its maturity in SAARC countries whereby the research could examine the citizens' satisfaction using D&M model.

In terms of research methods, our investigation revealed that quantitative approach has dominated the e-government adoption research in context of SAARC countries. Similarly, survey methodology appears to have been much preferred over other available alternatives. As the e-government research is still in its nascent state in the eight developing countries of SAARC, there is a further need to have some more literature review, case study, focus group, observation, and interview based research to establish the boundary of e-government research particularly in the countries where such research is under-published or not published at all. It is also very evident that the majority of research used quantitative analysis techniques such as regression analysis or structural equation modeling using tools including SPSS, AMOS, Smart PLS and LISREL. The further exploration of qualitative techniques and tools is also needed to have the in-depth analysis of the research questions. Exploring the system or technology for e-government adoption research indicates that majority of studies examined generic e-government services. Given the substantial growth of mobile use by all classes of people throughout the world and its very nature of providing alternative way of providing public services through online wireless media [18], there is further need to explore the success of such services in delivering government services to end users in SAARC countries as well. The analysis of respondent types also indicates that individual context/unit of analysis including citizens, customers, students and employees with citizen/customer as the most frequently researched context. The more research is needed to further examine how e-government adoption for professionals is different to citizens. The analyses of theories and models have revealed that most of the quantitative studies on e-government adoption have inherited the IS/IT theories of adoption (e.g. UTAUT) [42] into e-government context and there has hardly been any effort of theory development for this type of research. A very recent effort has been made by few studies (e.g. [2, 7, 28]) toward developing specific theories/models particularly applicable to e-government context in India. However, these theories/models need further validation for establishing their generalisability using diverse datasets from other countries as well. Limitations acknowledged by the studies included in our investigation appear to center on the nature of collected data and data collection issues – such as context specific or biased sample, non-generalisable findings or results, only non-user's or non-adopter's views, student sample and small sample to name some of such frequently used limitations. Therefore, there would appear to be much scope for researchers to undertake the future research on e-government adoption that addresses these limitations [38]. This recommendation is also supported by the investigation of future research agenda of 48 studies in question where two most frequently occurring research agendas are related to data collection. However, the other most relevant and common research agenda emerging from the analysis of future research was largely related to extending the existing models with new constructs and testing them in some other similar contexts. The future research should contribute to the existing literature by doing so.

5   Conclusion, Limitations and Future Work

The intention of this paper is to provide an overview of the current state of e-government adoption research by presenting the results of comprehensive analysis of 48 papers appearing across 21 journals during a period of last 11 years in the context of SAARC countries. We have presented the results of our investigation along a series of dimensions including the years of publication, journals most often publishing papers on e-government adoption, countries in which the research activity was conducted, the authors most active in the subject area, keywords analysis, methodological analysis, technology and respondents contexts, analysis of theories or models used and analysis of limitations and future research directions extracted from all the papers.

In keeping with previous research of this nature, we posit that our findings demonstrate some promising lines of inquiry and also those that were largely neglected along with those that have received a much larger attention. The overall analysis of literature on e-government adoption clearly indicates that this research is still in its early stage of development with very little area of maturity. Our results on country analysis indicate that majority of research have been published in Indian context so there are ample opportunities for researchers from other countries to embark on performing research for some least or under-represented countries. Also only few studies (e.g. [39, 40]) have researched e-government adoption in context of SAARC countries along Western countries. Given that Western countries have very developed infrastructure and implementations and their citizens are much aware about the use of such services, more such multicultural studies would be very helpful to undertake in the future as well. The exploration of limitations and future research agenda for the existing research studies in SAARC countries also provided us to avoid those limitations and follow the suggested research plan to perform original research studies on e-government adoption in the future.

We very much believe that this paper can prove to be a useful source of information for the readers who want to undertake e-government adoption research in context of any SAARC country in the future. However, we also acknowledge that this study has a number of limitations as well. Firstly and most obvious of all is that our research is limited to the exploration of existing research published only in journals and not considered a volume of research published in conferences and book chapters. The future research can incorporate all possible research to perform the analysis. Secondly, this research is a literature analysis and not the actual review of studies on e-government adoption in SAARC countries' context. The future research can perform systematic literature review of all existing studies to set the research agenda for the future. Finally, this research has not analysed the quantitative research for weight- and meta-analysis to understand the significant factors across the countries that have most significant and non-significant impact on e-government adoption. The future research can perform such analysis considering only all empirical studies available in these eight countries context. The future research can also look at community analysis and association mining among e-government adoption constructs gathered from the studies in SAARC countries' context [43].

References

1. Morgeson III, F.V., Van Amburg, D., Mithas, S.: Misplaced trust? Exploring the structure of the e-government-citizen trust relationship. J. Public Adm. Res. Theor. **21**(2), 257–283 (2010)
2. Rana, N.P., Dwivedi, Y.K., Lal, B., Williams, M.D., Clement, M.: Citizens' adoption of an electronic government system: towards a unified view. Inf. Syst. Front. **19**(3), 549–568 (2015)
3. Rana, N.P., Dwivedi, Y.K.: Citizen's adoption of an e-government system: validating extended social cognitive theory (SCT). Gov. Inf. Q. **32**(2), 172–181 (2015)
4. Joseph, R.C.: A structured analysis of e-government studies: trends and opportunities. Gov. Inf. Q. **30**(4), 435–440 (2013)

5. West, D.: E-Government and the transformation of service delivery and citizen attitudes. Public Adm. Rev. **64**(1), 15–27 (2004)
6. Schaupp, L.C., Carter, L.: The impact of trust, risk and optimism bias on e-file adoption. Inf. Syst. Front. **12**(3), 299–309 (2010)
7. Dwivedi, Y.K., Rana, N.P., Janssen, M., Lal, B., Williams, M.D., Clement, M.: An empirical validation of a unified model of electronic government adoption (UMEGA). Gov. Inf. Q., 1–20 (2017) doi:10.1016/j.giq.2017.03.001
8. Ojha, A., Sahu, G.P., Gupta, M.P.: Citizens' adoption of pay-to-use e-government services: an empirical study. Int. J. Electron. Gov. Res. **7**(2), 15–35 (2011)
9. Bertot, J.C., Jaeger, P.T.: The e-government paradox: better customer service doesn't necessarily cost less. Gov. Inf. Q. **25**(2), 149–154 (2008)
10. Ojha, A., Sahu, G.P., Gupta, M.P.: Antecedents of paperless income tax filing by young professionals in India: an exploratory study. Transform. Gov. People Process Policy **3**(1), 65–90 (2009)
11. Akkaya, C., Obermeier, M., Wolf, P., Krcmar, H.: Components of trust influencing egovernment adoption in Germany. In: Janssen, M., Scholl, Hans J., Wimmer, Maria A., Tan, Y.-h. (eds.) EGOV 2011. LNCS, vol. 6846, pp. 88–99. Springer, Heidelberg (2011). doi: 10.1007/978-3-642-22878-0_8
12. Williams, M.D., Dwivedi, Y.K., Lal, B., Schwarz, A.: Contemporary trends and issues in IT adoption and diffusion research. J. Inf. Technol. **24**(1), 1–10 (2009)
13. Bwalya, K.J., Healy, M.: Harnessing e-government adoption in the SADC region: a conceptual underpinning. Electron. J. e-Gov. **8**(1), 23–32 (2010)
14. Kumar, R., Sachan, A., Mukherjee, A.: Qualitative approach to determine user experience of e-government services. Comput. Hum. Behav. **71**, 299–306 (2017)
15. Diwan, S.A., Perumal, S., Siber, D.S.: Smart e-service implementation as mobile agent in a smart e-government platform. Int. J. Appl. Eng. Res. **11**(7), 5250–5255 (2012)
16. Hasan, S.: ICT policies and their role in governance: the case of Bangladesh. Sci. Technol. Soc. **19**(3), 363–381 (2014)
17. Faisal, M.N., Rahman, Z.: E-government in India: modelling the barriers to its adoption and diffusion. Electron. Gov. **5**(2), 181–202 (2008)
18. Shareef, M.A., Dwivedi, Y.K., Stamati, T., Williams, M.D.: SQ mGov: a comprehensive service-quality paradigm for mobile government. Inf. Syst. Manag. **31**(2), 126–142 (2014)
19. Ahmed, M.A., Janssen, M., Van Den Hoven, J.: Value sensitive transfer (VST) of systems among countries: towards a framework. Int. J. Electron. Gov. Res. **8**(1), 26–42 (2012)
20. Tripathi, R., Gupta, M.P., Bhattacharya, J.: Interoperability adoption among government and corporate portals in India: a study. J. Enterprise Inf. Manag. **25**(2), 98–122 (2012)
21. Tripathi, R., Gupta, M.P., Bhattacharya, J.: Identifying factors of integration for an interoperable government portal: a study in Indian context. Int. J. Electron. Gov. Res. **7**(1), 64–88 (2011)
22. Dwivedi, Y.K., Khan, N., Papazafeiropoulou, A.: Consumer adoption and usage of broadband in Bangladesh. Electron. Gov. **4**(3), 299–313 (2007)
23. Rehman, M., Kamal, M.M., Esichaikul, V.: Adoption of e-government services in Pakistan: a comparative study between online and offline users. Inf. Syst. Manag. **33**(3), 248–267 (2016)
24. Rehman, M., Esichaikul, V., Kamal, M.: Factors influencing e-government adoption in Pakistan. Transform. Gov. People Process Policy **6**(3), 258–282 (2012)
25. MdYusof, M.I.B., Baharudin, A.S., Karkonasasi, K.: Factors affecting the cloud computing technology adoption among public organizations. Int. J. Appl. Eng. Res. **11**(14), 8145–8148 (2016)

26. Gupta, B., Dasgupta, S., Gupta, A.: Adoption of ICT in a government organization in a developing country: an empirical study. J. Strateg. Inf. Syst. **17**(2), 140–154 (2008)

27. Manandhar, S.P., Kim, S., Hwang, J.: Success factors of online services in Kathmandu, Nepal: an empirical analysis. Int. J. Bus. Inf. Syst. **18**(4), 422–436 (2015)

28. Rana, N.P., Dwivedi, Y.K., Williams, M.D., Weerakkody, V.: Adoption of online public grievance redressal system in India: toward developing a unified view. Comput. Hum. Behav. **59**, 265–282 (2016)

29. Azam, A., Qiang, F., Abdullah, M.I.: Determinants of e-government services adoption in Pakistan: an integrated model. Electron. Gov. Int. J. **10**(2), 105–124 (2013)

30. Gupta, K.P., Bhaskar, P., Singh, S.: Critical factors influencing e-government adoption in India: an investigation of the citizens' perspectives. J. Inf. Technol. Res. **9**(4), 28–44 (2016)

31. Shareef, M.A., Kumar, U., Kumar, V., Dwivedi, Y.K.: Identifying critical factors for adoption of e-government. Electron. Gov. Int. J. **6**(1), 70–96 (2009)

32. Alryalat, M.A.A., Rana, N.P., Dwivedi, Y.K.: Citizen's adoption of an e-government system: validating the extended Theory of Reasoned Action (TRA). Int. J. Electron. Gov. Res. **11**(4), 1–23 (2015)

33. Shareef, M.A., Dwivedi, Y.K., Laumer, S., Archer, N.: Citizens' adoption behavior of mobile government (mGov): a cross-cultural study. Inf. Syst. Manag. **33**(3), 268–283 (2016)

34. Sultana, M.R., Ahlan, A.R., Habibullah, M.: A comprehensive adoption model of M-government services among citizens in developing countries. J. Theoret. Appl. Inf. Technol. **90**(1), 49–60 (2016)

35. Rana, N.P., Dwivedi, Y.K., Williams, M.D., Weerakkody, V.: Investigating success of an e-government initiative: validation of an integrated IS success model. Inf. Syst. Front. **17**(1), 127–142 (2015)

36. Ahmad, M.O., Markkula, J., Oivo, M.: Factors affecting e-government adoption in Pakistan: a citizen's perspective. Transform. Gov. People Process Policy **7**(2), 225–239 (2013)

37. Ranaweera, H.M.B.P.: Perspective of trust towards e-government initiatives in Sri Lanka. SpringerPlus **5**(1), 1–11 (2016)

38. Williams, M.D., Rana, N.P., Dwivedi, Y.K.: The unified theory of acceptance and use of technology: a systematic review. J. Enterp. Inf. Manag. **28**(3), 443–488 (2015)

39. Shareef, M.A., Kumar, V., Dwivedi, Y.K., Kumar, U.: Service delivery through mobile-government (mGov): driving factors and cultural impacts. Inf. Syst. Front. **18**(2), 315–332 (2016)

40. Weerakkody, V., Dwivedi, Y.K., Kurunananda, A.: Implementing e-government in Sri Lanka: lessons from the UK. Inf. Technol. Dev. **15**(3), 171–192 (2009)

41. Chauhan, S., Kaushik, A.: Evaluating citizen acceptance of unique identification number in India: an empirical study. Electron. Gov. **12**(3), 223–242 (2012)

42. Dwivedi, Y.K., Rana, N.P., Jeyaraj, A., Clement, M., Williams, M.D.: Re-examining the Unified Theory of Acceptance and Use of Technology (UTAUT): towards a revised theoretical model. Inf. Syst. Front., 1–16 (2017). doi:10.1007/s10796-017-9774-y

43. Grover, P., Kar, A.K.: Big data analytics: a review on theoretical contributions and tools used in literature. Glob. J. Flex. Syst. Manag., 1–27 (2017). doi:10.1007/s40171-017-0159-3

Assessment of Open Government Data Initiative - A Perception Driven Approach

Alka Mishra[1], D.P. Misra[1], Arpan Kumar Kar[2], Sunil Babbar[1], and Shubhadip Biswas[3(✉)]

[1] National Informatics Centre, Delhi, New Delhi, India
[2] DMS, Indian Institute of Technology, Delhi, New Delhi, India
[3] Open Government Data Project, Delhi, New Delhi, India
shubhadip.biswas@live.com

Abstract. Evolution of Information and Communications Technologies (ICT) and digital governance became the key enablers for open data initiative of the government to become more open, responsive, inclusive, transparent, accountable and efficient. Through the e-governance initiatives governments worldwide are focusing on the concept of open data and its huge potential to bring positive changes to the socio-economic value by developing and disseminating information within a vibrant mixed economy comprising of open source, government bodies, business houses, and hybrid solutions of various forms fueled with the sharp elevation of digitization. This study demonstrates assessment of open government data initiatives by the geometric mean method (GMM) of analytical hierarchy process (AHP). Few key factors i.e. people, technology scope, policy, economic and institution were identified which have a very strong impact for any e-governance initiative.

Keywords: E-governance · Open data · Analytic Hierarchy Process · Impact assessment · Feature prioritization

1 Introduction

The digital space is increasing rapidly throughout the world. Public and organizations are using more and more digital mechanism to interact with each other, and to transact day to day business. Nowadays, the focus of the governments across the world are mainly to develop competences to deliver public services using ICT to various stakeholders [19]. E-governance works as a catalyst to improve the public service quality, effectivity, and efficiency, to improve the decision-making process and to promote citizen centric governance. To promote access of publicly held information, promoting transparency and enabling wider socio-economic gain, need has been realized in India that there must be a mechanism for proactive share and free access of the data originated from public funds and which are available with various government bodies. As a result, in 2012, the open government data initiative in India moved towards a new dimension with the notification of the National Data Sharing and Accessibility Policy (NDSAP), & in pursuance of the policy, the Open Government Data (OGD) platform - India (https://data.gov.in) was developed and launched to facilitate share and free access of data through an efficient and dynamic process.

© IFIP International Federation for Information Processing 2017
Published by Springer International Publishing AG 2017. All Rights Reserved
A.K. Kar et al. (Eds.): I3E 2017, LNCS 10595, pp. 159–171, 2017.
DOI: 10.1007/978-3-319-68557-1_15

Many assessment frameworks have been developed, primarily with an objective to address e-governance initiatives. According to various studies, user perspectives, scope of information technology, government policies and regulations, economic benefit and government are very important parameters to understand any e-governance initiative [22]. In this study, the analytical hierarchy process (AHP) has been applied to assess open government data initiatives by group decision making approach for the prioritization among assessment factors and constructs. This study illustrates the application of the geometric mean method (GMM) and its theories to prioritize the assessment criterions of Indian open government data initiative.

2   Review of Literature

2.1   E-governance Project Assessment

E-governance can have a major impact in socio-economic development by transforming the public administration mechanism. E-Governance is the process to enable government using ICT to make governance effective for citizens in terms of effectiveness and efficiency in public service, decision-making process, transparency, citizen centric governance, socio-economic development and cost-effectiveness [42].

According to reviews of literature on assessment of e-governance projects [22] various constructs may be clubbed in to factor groups like people, technology scope, policy, economic and institution. Within these factors, constructs were identified based on prominence and dominance in existing literature. Clubbing of these constructs were also done within these factors based on having the similar dimensions and characteristics. The Table 1 provide information of each constructs in the factor group.

2.2   Open Government Data Initiative

The concept of open government data has been popularized significantly, with the demand being placed on all kinds of government bodies to release the data for open access [47]. Open access to government data, can help government to become more open, responsive, inclusive, transparent, accountable and efficient, can provide greater returns from the public-sector investment [33], can create new economy through the downstream use of outputs, can help policy makers in data driven decision making [7], and can motivate the citizens in proactive innovation using government data [25] or participate in policy-making [8]. Participatory governance would evolve into a heightened accountability that in result curbs corruption [35]. Open government data has the potential to increase productivity, to improve products and services by value addition to the original open government data and most importantly to make way for the data-driven innovation with new age products and services [34]. Moreover, it galvanizes creation of new firms and companies. In 2012, Indian government had formulated National Data Sharing and Accessibility Policy (NDSAP) [37] and under the mandate of NDSAP, the Open Government Data (OGD) platform - India (https:// data.gov.in/) was developed and launched. Though there is a drastic increase in open datasets across the world, it is still a big hurdle to reach to the full potency of this

Table 1. Details of construct groups for e-governance Assessment

Factor group	Construct subgroup	Construct item	Cross-reference of Construct to publications
People	Individual perceptions	Adoption	31
		Ease of use	5
		Perceived usefulness	31
		User satisfaction	2
	Social perceptions	Social benefits and influence	18
	Awareness	User awareness	43
Technology scope	Technological	Accessibility	38
		Infrastructure	44
		Reliability	32
		Technological risks	12
	System maturity	Website maturity	3
Policy	Information governance	Laws and policies	44
		Privacy	16
		Security	43
		Transparency	5
		User trust	39
	Outcome based	Effectiveness	23
		Empowerment	4
Economic	Individual	Affordability	32
		Cost of service	9
		Cost saving	40
	Government	Cost	46
		Funding sustainability	49
Institution	Management	Management support	44
	Operational	Availability	20
		Operational efficiency	43
		Performance	16
	Quality	Information quality	5
		Service quality	2

initiative and actively engage all stakeholders with the initiative [47, 48]. Several factors, including stakeholder engagement, technical scope, regulations and policies, economical and institutional [13], contribute to this obstacle [51].

The factor groups i.e. people, technology scope, policy, economic and institution, which have been emerged for e-governance project assessment have been detailed below in the context of open government data initiative India.

People. India's Open Government Data (OGD) platform has a rich framework for citizen engagement, which could help government bodies to prioritize the release of open government data. The platform also acts as a knowledge-sharing platform through online communities. Citizens with specific interests are encouraged to contribute blogs and join online sector specific forums of their domain of interest, it enables communities to express their requirement for datasets or applications, to rate the dataset quality, provide suggestions and feedbacks, and seek clarification or information. Indian open government data initiative also engaged with various stakeholders through various citizen and community collaboration initiatives by organizing various workshops, hackathons, application challenges, etc.

As per open government data initiative constructs under 'people' group are engagement and adaptation of open government data by civil society, participatory governance for social benefit through collaboration with all stakeholders i.e. government bodies, academia, private organizations and people, awareness of open government data among citizens, user friendly and ease of use of platform, perceived usefulness of open government data among users & user satisfaction on open government data.

Technology Scope. The OGD platform was developed using open source stack, with focus on proactive dissemination of open government resources i.e. data, applications, tools, etc. in open format. The platform has a configurable multilevel workflow module to be used by government bodies to contribute, review, approve and publish open data, it has configurable and scalable modules i.e. data management, content management, visitor relationship management, community, blog, visualization, dataset conversion tool, APIs etc. [34]. The OGD platform is also offering the platform under software as a service (SaaS) model, which has helped states and urban local bodies to create their own open government data portal. As per open government data initiative constructs under 'technology scope' group are accessibility of open government data, infrastructure of Open Government Data (OGD) platform and to build new products/services based on open government data, reliability of open government data, website maturity/stability of Open Government Data (OGD) platform & technological risk for uninterrupted access of open government data.

Policy. Under open government data initiative, the National Data Sharing and Accessibility Policy (NDSAP) was designed to apply to all sharable and non-sensitive data available and generated using public funds by government bodies. Open data & NDSAP implementation guidelines [24] provide guidelines on data, metadata, and implementation methodologies, role of chief data officer (CDO), NDSAP cell, data contributor, publishing & management of resources, etc. [36]. Government Open Data License - India [21] was gazette notified on 10th February 2017, to provide a legal framework to the data users wishing to use and build on top of public data. License also gives assurance of what they legally can and can't do with the data both commercially and non-commercially. In NDSAP and Government Open Data License, special care has been taken to protect privacy, security and sensitive information. As per open government data initiative constructs under 'policy' group are existence of open government data sharing policy and open government data license, policy to empower citizens to take informed and data driven decision, effectiveness of open government data, policy to make data authentic and reliable to build trust of the users, security policies for website and data, accountable and transparent governance by sharing open government data & protection of privacy and sensitive information in open government data.

Economic. Open data can be described as a data which anyone is free to use, reuse, and redistribute. So, freeness is an integral part of open data, users can easily avail free of cost open government data from OGD platform. Ready availability of open government data in a single centralized platform is not only saving the monetary cost but also the time cost. Following the mandate of the National Data Sharing and Accessibility Policy (NDSAP), in the Government Open Data License - India, all users have been provided a worldwide, royalty-free, non-exclusive license to use, adapt, publish (either in original, or in adapted and/or derivative forms), translate, display, add value, and create derivative works (including products and services), for all lawful commercial and non-commercial purposes. As per open government data initiative constructs under 'economic' group are cost of accessing open government data, affordability of using open government data services, cost saving due to open government data, cost to government for sharing open government data and sustainable funding for open government data initiative.

Institution. To implement NDSAP policy under open government data initiative rich sharing framework has been developed to manage contribution, approval and publishing process of open government data. As per the mandate of NDSAP, a senior officer is to be nominated as the nodal officer or chief data officer from the departments/organizations/states. The responsibility of chief data officer is to spearhead the initiative of the respective department/organization/state. For operation efficiency and for proactive share of the data, there is provision for chief data officer to nominate several data contributors who would contribute datasets along with the metadata on the OGD platform. Special care has been taken in NDSAP guidelines to maintain quality of data and metadata. As per open government data initiative constructs under 'institution' group are management support for open government data initiative, availability of datasets, operational efficiency to share the datasets, performance of open government data sharing mechanism, quality of services provided by Open Government Data (OGD) platform & quality of open government data/metadata.

3 Computational Approach Using Analytic Hierarchy Process

Analytic Hierarchy Process (AHP) is one of the robust multi criteria decision making method, in short, it is a process to derive ratio scales from paired judgments based on psychology and mathematics. The analytical hierarchy process (AHP) has been applied in this study to assess open government data initiatives by providing group decision support [6, 26–30]. This study explores the suitability and applicability of the geometric mean method (GMM) and its theories to prioritize the assessment criterions of Indian open government data initiative.

3.1   Measurement of Individual Decisions

Let $B = (b_1, b_2, ..., b_5)$ be the consensus vector where b_i represents the "i_{th}" criterion's priority, estimated as $\sum b_i = 1$. Let $V = (v_1, v_2, ..., v_n)$ be the set of n expert decision makers with a relative importance of ϕ_i and $\phi = (\phi_1, \phi_2, ..., \phi_n)$ is the weight vector of the decision makers and $\sum \phi_i = 1$ [26].

Shanon function maximization approach for the middle element can be used to optimize the unpredictability of an individual preference as $S(\mu) = \mu \ln \mu - (1 - \mu) \ln (1 - \mu)$ [50]. The pairwise comparison approach [10] has been used for fuzzy set operations and for the operator $\Diamond$ used as an illustration, it has been shown for the fuzzy sets

$$\tilde{b}_i \text{ and } \tilde{b}_j : \tilde{b}_i \Diamond \tilde{b}_j = (\tilde{b}_{i,1}, \tilde{b}_{i,2}, \tilde{b}_{i,3}) \Diamond (\tilde{b}_{j,1}, \tilde{b}_{j,2}, \tilde{b}_{j,3})$$
$$= ((\tilde{b}_{i,1} \Diamond \tilde{b}_{j,1}), (\tilde{b}_{i,2} \Diamond \tilde{b}_{j,2}), (\tilde{b}_{i,3} \Diamond \tilde{b}_{j,3})) \tag{1}$$

3.2   Measurement of Individual Condition of Consistency

The pair wise matrix i.e. $K = (\tilde{k}_{ij})_{n \times n}$ is an n $\times$ n real matrix, for a decision maker v_i, where n is the number of evaluation criteria considered and $\tilde{k}_{ij} \geq 0$. The entries $\tilde{k}_{ij}$ and $\tilde{k}_{ji}$ satisfy the constraint: $\tilde{k}_{ij} \times \tilde{k}_{ji} = 1$. In the eigenvector method (EVM) it derives values (priorities) $(w_1, w_2, ...w_n)$ of comparable elements as the linear solution of the eigenvalue problem [41]:

$$\sum_{i=1}^{n} \tilde{k}_{i,j} w_i = \lambda_{max} w_i, \ e^T w = 1 \text{ where } i = 1, 2, ..., n \tag{2}$$

Equation for the individual decision vector:

$$\min \sum_{i=1}^{n} \sum_{j>i}^{n} \left(\ln \tilde{k}_{i,j} - (\ln \tilde{w}_i - \ln \tilde{w}_j)^2 \right) \text{ such that } \tilde{w}_i \geq 0 \text{ and } \sum \tilde{w}_i = 1 \tag{3}$$

$$\text{The solution is obtained by } \tilde{w}_i = \frac{\sqrt[1/n]{\prod_{j=1}^{n} \tilde{k}_{i,j}}}{\sum_{i=1}^{n} \sqrt[1/n]{\prod_{j=1}^{n} \tilde{k}_{i,j}}} \tag{4}$$

where $\tilde{w}_i$ is the judgement criteria's weight so that $\tilde{W}_i = \{\tilde{w}_1, \tilde{w}_2, ..., \tilde{w}_7\}$ for i_{th} decision maker.

$$\text{GCI} (K^{v_i}) [14] = \frac{2}{(n-1)(n-2)} \sum_{j>i}^{n} \left(log|\tilde{k}_{i,j}| - (log|\tilde{w}_i| - log|\tilde{w}_j|)^2 \right) \tag{5}$$

Aguarón and Moreno-Jiménez [1] has proposed a corresponding threshold for GCI_n i.e. $\text{GCI}_3 < 0.0314$, $\text{GCI}_4 < 0.0352$, $\text{GCI}_n < 0.037$ (for n > 4). The analysis of the Saaty's criterion exhibits that this criterion is not an acceptable EM error indicator [45]. The condition for consistency can be $\text{GCI} (K^{v_i}) \leq \overline{GCI}$ [11].

3.3   Aggregation of Individual Priorities

$$\text{Aggregation of preferences of individual: } \tilde{k}_{ij}^{(c)} = \prod_{m=1}^{t} \left(\tilde{k}_{ij}^{(m)} \right)^{\phi m} \quad (6)$$

A vector can be formulated by GMM where $w_i^{(c)}$ is the vector such that $w_i^{(c)} = \{\tilde{w}_1^{(c)}, \ldots \tilde{w}_7^{(c)}\}^T$ and ϕ_i is the importance of expert decision maker v_i. The equation of conversion of the fuzzy weights to crisp weights has been shown below:

$$|\tilde{w}_i| = \left[(w_{i,1} \times 0.25) + (w_{i,2} \times 0.50) + (w_{i,3} \times 0.25) \right] \quad (7)$$

3.4   Achieving Consensus in Priorities of User Groups

$$\text{GCCI}(K^{v_{(c)}}) = \frac{2}{(n-1)(n-2)} \sum_{j>i}^{n} \left(log|\tilde{k}^{(c)}_{ij}| - (log|w^{(c)}_i| - log|w^{(c)}_j|)^2 \right) \quad (8)$$

Consensus is achieved if $\text{GCCI}(K^{v_{(c)}}) \leq \overline{GCCI}$ for, $\text{GCCI}_n < 0.037$ (for $n > 4$) [17]. If $\text{GCCI}(K^{v_{(c)}}) \geq \overline{GCCI}$, to achieve group consensus following computations need to be completed [15]: Assume $\text{GCCI}(K^{v_{(\tau)}}) = max_c \{\text{GCCI}(K^{v_{(c)}})\}$ where $z = max_n z + 1$,

$$\text{Let } K_{z+1}^{(m)} = \left(k_{ij, \ z+1}^{(m)} \right)_{n \times n}, \text{ Where } k_{ij, \ z+1}^{(m)} = \begin{cases} \left(k_{ij,z}^{(m)} \right)^b \left[\frac{(k_{ij,z}^{(m)})}{(k_{ij,z}^{(m)})} \right]^{1-b} & \text{if } m = \tau \\ \left(k_{ij,z}^{(m)} \right) & \text{if } m \neq \tau \end{cases}$$

1. If $\text{GCCI}(K_z^{v_{(c)}}) \leq \overline{GCCI}$, $X = K_z^{v_{(c)}}$ else return to 1st process.

4   Data Collection and Analysis

After studying various literatures on assessment of e-governance project important constructs were identified and those have been clubbed in to factor groups like people, technology scope, policy, economic and institution.

The data for AHP for assessment of open data initiatives, were collected from fifty-eight senior government officials, and experienced open data activist, these domain experts were very actively engaged in the open data activities at least for last six years. The priorities of these fifty-eight domain experts had equal importance in decision making. These group of experts were asked to prioritize the, factor groups and, they have been asked to choose the constructs' importance in a 5-point Likert scale, through on line questionnaire. Finally, the priorities were measured using GMM methodology. GCI of individual responses were also measured to check the consistency. Consensus has been achieved as GCI $(K^{v_i}) \leq 0.037$. Priority vector has been obtained after aggregating the individual judgements using GMM methodology i.e. (0.4425, 0.2226, 0.1540, 0.1244, 0.0565). In the next level, aggregated judgements were also checked for the consistency and group Consensus has been achieved as GCCI $(K^{v(e)}) \leq 0.037$. All the constructs were also analyzed and weightages within the group and aggregated weightages have been estimated.

5   Results

Based on the individual judgements, weightage of all the factor groups and constructs weightages have been estimated. The result has been provided below in Table 2.

Table 2. Result of group decision on assessment of open government data initiative

Factor groups	Factor groups weight	Constructs	Constructs weight
People	0.4425	Perceived usefulness of open government data among users	0.0749
		Awareness of open government data among citizens	0.0747
		Engagement and adaptation of open government data by civil society	0.0736
		User friendly and ease of use of platform	0.0736
		User satisfaction on open government data	0.0736
		Participatory governance for social benefit through collaboration with all stakeholders i.e. government bodies, academia, private organizations and people	0.0720
Economy	0.2226	Cost saving due to open government data	0.0454
		Cost of accessing open government data	0.0451
		Affordability of using open government data services	0.0449
		Sustainable funding for open government data initiative	0.0437
		Cost to government for sharing open government data	0.0435

(*continued*)

Table 2. (*continued*)

Factor groups	Factor groups weight	Constructs	Constructs weight
Technology scope	0.1540	Accessibility of open government data	0.0325
		Infrastructure of Open Government Data (OGD) platform and to build new products/services based on open government data	0.0313
		Website maturity/stability of Open Government Data (OGD) platform	0.0305
		Reliability of open government data	0.0299
		Technological risk for uninterrupted access of open government data	0.0298
Policy	0.1244	Existence of open government data sharing policy and open government data license	0.0198
		Protection of privacy and sensitive information in open government data	0.0197
		Accountable and transparent governance by sharing open government data	0.0186
		Effectiveness of open government data	0.0175
		Policy to make data authentic and reliable to build trust of the users	0.0169
		Security policies for website and data	0.0164
		Policy to empower citizens to take informed and data driven decision	0.0154
Institution	0.0565	Quality of open government data/metadata	0.0106
		Availability of datasets	0.0106
		Management support for open government data initiative	0.0094
		Quality of services provided by Open Government Data (OGD) platform	0.0092
		Operational efficiency to share the datasets	0.0087
		Performance of open government data sharing mechanism	0.0080

In the above table, factor groups weight column provides the result based on individual prioritization using GMM method and constructs weight column shows the outcome of their weightage based on the factor groups weight and their individual weight. The implications have been discussed in detail in the next section.

6 Conclusions

ICT is the key enabler of open data initiative of the government to become more open, responsive, inclusive, transparent, accountable and efficient. Evidence based planning process is essential for socio-economic development and all this depends on availability of up-to-date and quality government data. In the result of the assessment factor people has the highest weightage on open government data initiative. Apparently, citizen centricity becomes the key factor for determining success of such an initiative. Economy and technology has the second and third weightage respectively. Concerns about policy and institution were found to have lower impact in successful implementation of open government data initiative.

As per the study, foremost priority of the open government data initiative should be on adopting a citizen centric model. This model needs a clear comprehension of human elements to understand why citizens (user groups) would proactively use open data and engage with the initiative. Core-essence of this model is to focus on the requirement of citizens from the perspectives of citizens themselves, on building value & awareness of the people on the importance of leveraging the open data, to enable participatory governance by citizen engagement activities. Second priority should be to build economic model by providing competent and cost effective services i.e. open data and data related services, to the citizens. Focus should also be on sustainable funding for the initiative and economic benefit of the government through participatory governance by sharing open data, and extensive data sharing mechanism across various government bodies, which will automatically save time and cost and will also benefit decision makers to take quick action for nation building. Next priority should be on technology scope, technology plays a major role to provide uninterrupted and quality services to the citizen, special focus should be on accessibility and in developing robust infrastructure to provide uninterrupted services. When data is being made open for public, need is there for implementing a policy & regulatory framework, which grants access, use and distribute the open data without much restrictions. So, there should be a strong policy framework while implementing open government data. Last but not the least there is always a need of positive intent from the government bodies to share the data in open domain, hence availability & quality of data/metadata with management support plays a big role in open government data initiative.

References

1. Aguarón, J., Moreno-Jiménez, J.M.: The geometric consistency index: approximated thresholds. Eur. J. Oper. Res. **147**(1), 137–145 (2003)
2. Al Hujran, O., Aloudat, A., Altarawneh, I.: Factors influencing citizen adoption of e-government in developing countries: the case of Jordan. Int. J. Technol. Hum. Interact. (IJTHI) **9**(2), 1–19 (2013)
3. AlBalushi, T.H., Ali, S.: Evaluation of the quality of E-government services: quality trend analysis. In: 2015 International Conference on Information and Communication Technology Research (ICTRC), Abu Dhabi, pp. 226–229. IEEE (2015)

4. Alenezi, H., Tarhini, A., Sharma, S.K.: Development of quantitative model to investigate the strategic relationship between information quality and e-government benefits. Transform. Gov. People Process Policy **9**(3), 324–351 (2015)

5. Amritesh, C., Misra, S., Chatterjee, J.: Conceptualizing e-government service quality under credence based settings: a case of e-counseling in India. Int. J. Qual. Reliab. Manag. **31**(7), 764–787 (2014)

6. Anand, O., Mittal, A., Moolchandani, K., Kagzi, M.M., Kar, A.K.: Evaluating travel websites using WebQual: a group decision support approach. In: Buyya, R., Thampi, S.M. (eds.) Intelligent Distributed Computing. AISC, vol. 321, pp. 151–160. Springer, Cham (2015). doi:10.1007/978-3-319-11227-5_14

7. Arzberger, P., et al.: An international framework to promote access to data. Science **303** (5665), 1777–1778 (2004)

8. Attard, J., et al.: A systematic review of open government data initiatives. Gov. Inf. Q. **32**(4), 399–418 (2015)

9. Bhatnagar, S.C., Singh, N.: Assessing the impact of e-government: a study of projects in India. Inf. Technol. Int. Dev. **6**(2), 109–127 (2010). Information Technologies & International Development, Los Angeles

10. Buckley, J.J.: Fuzzy hierarchical analysis. Fuzzy Sets Syst. **17**(3), 233–247 (1985)

11. Cao, D., Leung, L.C., Law, J.S.: Modifying inconsistent comparison matrix in analytic hierarchy process: a heuristic approach. Decis. Support Syst. **44**(4), 944–953 (2008)

12. Chan, F.K., Thong, J.Y., Venkatesh, V., Brown, S.A., Hu, P.J., Tam, K.Y.: Modeling citizen satisfaction with mandatory adoption of an e-government technology. J. Assoc. Inf. Syst. **11** (10), 519–549 (2010)

13. Conradie, P., Choenni, S.: Exploring process barriers to release public sector information in local government. In: Proceedings of the 6th International Conference on Theory and Practice of Electronic Governance, ICEGOV, pp. 5–13. ACM, New York (2012)

14. Crawford, G., Williams, C.: A note on the analysis of subjective judgment matrices. J. Math. Psychol. **29**(4), 387–405 (1985)

15. Dong, Y., et al.: Consensus models for AHP group decision making under row geometric mean prioritization method. Decis. Support Syst. **49**(3), 281–289 (2010)

16. Economides, A.A., Terzis, V.: Evaluating tax sites: an evaluation framework and its application. Electron. Gov. Int. J. **5**(3), 321–344 (2008)

17. Escobar, M.T., Aguarón, J., Moreno-Jiménez, J.M.: A note on AHP group consistency for the row geometric mean priorization procedure. Eur. J. Oper. Res. **153**(2), 18–322 (2004)

18. Fan, J., Zhang, P., Yen, D.C.: G2G information sharing among government agencies. Inf. Manag. **51**(1), 120–128 (2014)

19. Fitsilis, P., Anthopoulos, L., Gerogiannis, V.: Assessment frameworks of e-government projects: a comparison. In: The Proceedings of the 13th Panhellenic Conference on Informatics (PCI 2009), PCI, Corfu Island, pp. 10–12 (2009)

20. Funilkul, S., et al.: An evaluation framework for e-government services based on principles laid out in COBIT, the ISO 9000 standard, and TAM. In: ACIS 2006 Proceedings, 3, Adelaide (2006)

21. Government Open Data License – India. https://data.gov.in/sites/default/files/Gazette_ Notification_OGDL.pdf. Accessed 12 May 2017

22. Singh, H., Kar, A.K., Vigneswara Ilavarasan, P.: Assessment of e-Governance projects: an integrated framework and its validation. In: ICEGOV 2017 SCII, New Delhi (2017)

23. Heeks, R.: Benchmarking e-government: improving the national and international measurement, evaluation and comparison of e-government. In: Evaluating Information Systems, p. 257. Elsevier, Hungary (2006)

24. Implementation Guidelines for National Data Sharing and Accessibility Policy (NDSAP) of India. https://data.gov.in/sites/default/files/NDSAP_Implementation_Guidelines_2.2.pdf. Accessed 12 May 2017

25. Janssen, M., Charalabidis, Y., Zuiderwijk, A.: Benefits, adoption barriers and myths of open data and open government. Inf. Syst. Manag. **29**(4), 258–268 (2012)

26. Kar, A.K., Rakshit, A.: Flexible pricing models for cloud computing based on group decision making under consensus. Global J. Flex. Syst. Manag. **16**(2), 191–204 (2015)

27. Kar, A.K., Rakshit, A.: Pricing of cloud IaaS based on feature prioritization - a value based approach. In: Thampi, S., Abraham, A., Pal, S., Rodriguez, J. (eds.) Recent Advances in Intelligent Informatics. AISC, vol. 235, pp. 321–330. Springer, Cham (2014). doi:10.1007/978-3-319-01778-5_33

28. Kar, A.K.: Integrating websites with social media–an approach for group decision support. J. Decis. Syst. **24**(3), 339–353 (2015)

29. Khatwani, G., Kar, A.K.: Improving the Cosine Consistency Index for the analytic hierarchy process for solving multi-criteria decision making problems. Appl. Comput. Inform. (2016). Elsevier, Hungary

30. Kar, A.K., Pani, A.K.: Exploring the importance of different supplier selection criteria. Manag. Res. Rev. **37**(1), 89–105 (2014)

31. Kumar, V., Mukerji, B., Butt, I., Persaud, A.: Factors for successful e-government adoption: a conceptual framework. Electron. J. e-government **5**(1), 63–76 (2007)

32. Mates, P., Lechner, T., Rieger, P., Pěkná, J.: Towards e-government project assessment: European approach. J. Econ. Bus. **31**(1), 103–125 (2013). ZbornikradovaEkonomskog-fakulteta u Rijeci, časopiszaekonomskuteorijuipraksu-Proceedings of Rijeka Faculty of Economics

33. Mennis, E.A.: The wisdom of crowds: why the many are smarter than the few and how collective wisdom shapes business, economies, societies, and nations. Bus. Econ. **41**(4), 63–65 (2006)

34. Misra, D.P., Mishra, A.: Societal and economical impact on citizens through innovations using open government data: Indian initiative on open government data. In: Handbook of Research on Cultural and Economic Impacts of the Information Society, pp. 147–178. IGI Global, Salamanca (2015)

35. Misra, D.P., Verma, N.: Enabling public participation through e-governance: an Indian context. IJeN **2**(1), 20–41 (2014)

36. Misra, D., Mishra, A., Babbar, S., Gupta, V.: Open government data policy and Indian ecosystems. In: ICEGOV 2017 SCII, New Delhi (2017)

37. National Data Sharing and Accessibility Policy-2012. https://data.gov.in/sites/default/files/NDSAP.pdf. Accessed 12 May 2017

38. Panopoulou, E., Tambouris, E., Tarabanis, K.: A framework for evaluating web sites of public authorities. In: ASLIB Proceedings, vol. 60, no. 5, pp. 517–546. Emerald Group Publishing Limited, Bingley (2008)

39. Porumbescu, G.A.: Placing the effect? Gleaning insights into the relationship between citizens' use of e-government and trust in government. Public Manag. Rev. **18**(10), 1504–1535 (2016)

40. Rotchanakitumnuai, S.: Measuring e-government service value with the E-GOVSQUAL-RISK model. Bus. Process Manag. J. **14**(5), 724–737 (2008)

41. Saaty, T.L.: Multicriteria Decision Making: The Analytic Hierarchy Process. McGraw-Hill, New York (1980)

42. Sapru, R.K., Sapru, Y.: Good governance through e-governance with special reference to India. Indian J. Public Adm. **60**(2), 313–331 (2014)

43. Sharma, S.K., Govindaluri, S.M., Gattoufi, S.: Understanding and predicting the quality determinants of e-government services: a two-staged regression-neural network model. J. Model. Manag. **10**(3), 325–340 (2015)
44. Singh Kalsi, N., Kiran, R.: E-governance success factors: an analysis of e-governance initiatives of ten major states of India. Int. J. Public Sector Manag. **26**(4), 320–336 (2013)
45. Tomashevskii, I.L.: Eigenvector ranking method as a measuring tool: formulas for errors. Eur. J. Oper. Res. **240**(3), 774–780 (2015)
46. Tsohou, A., Lee, H., Irani, Z., Weerakkody, V., Osman, I.H., Anouze, A.L., Medeni, T.: Proposing a reference process model for the citizen-centric evaluation of e-government services. Transform. Gov. People Process Policy **7**(2), 240–255 (2013)
47. Ubaldi, B.: Open Government Data: Towards Empirical Analysis of Open Government Data Initiatives. OECD Working Papers on Public Governance, No. 22, 0_1. OECD Publishing, Paris (2013)
48. Verma, N., Gupta, M.P.: Open government data: beyond policy & portal, a study in Indian context. In: Proceedings of the 7th International Conference on Theory and Practice of Electronic Governance, Seoul, pp. 338–341. ACM (2013)
49. Xu, J.: Measurement of public satisfaction evaluation on e-government: based on structural equation model. In: 2009 IITA International Conference on Control, Automation and Systems Engineering, Zhangjiajie, pp. 418–421. IEEE (2009)
50. Zimmermann, H.-J.: Fuzzy set theory—and its applications, 4th edn. Springer Science & Business Media, New York (2011). doi:10.1007/978-94-010-0646-0
51. Zuiderwijk, A., Janssen, M.: Barriers and development directions for the publication and usage of open data: a socio-technical view. In: Gascó-Hernández, M. (ed.) Open Government. PAIT, vol. 4, pp. 115–135. Springer, New York (2014). doi:10.1007/978-1-4614-9563-5_8

Selected Simple Indicators in the Field of Advanced Technologies as a Support of SMART Cities and Their Impact on Tourism

Libuše Svobodová[✉], Miloslava Černá, and Petr Hruša

Faculty of Informatics and Management, University of Hradec Králové,
Rokitanského 62, 500 03 Hradec Králové, Czech Republic
{libuse.svobodova,miloslava.cerna,petr.hrusa}@uhk.cz

Abstract. The paper discusses the issue of SMART cities in the context of tourism with a focus on utilization of technologies for travel purposes. Using the Pearson correlation coefficient, dependencies are calculated and analyzed between relative outbound tourism and selected simple indicators which are percentage of the internet users, availability of latest technologies, percentage of people speaking English at the communication level and mobile telephone subscriptions. All four correlated coefficients reached positive values. According to the theoretical bases we can state that there is dependence in all four cases. But mobile telephone subscriptions have a weak dependence. Percentage of the internet users reached the highest dependence. It is positive also for SMART cities. Official data from technical sources were used when working on the paper.

Keywords: Tourism · Internet · Simple indicators · Smart cities · Advanced technologies

1 Introduction

Tourism is one of the indivisible areas of individual economies. While 20 years ago people used as main source of information materials of travel agencies, travel books, television documentaries, etc., nowadays travelers use advanced technology as the main sources of information. On the Internet and social networks, they search information on destinations, places to visit, accommodation, transport and many other. Technologies seem to be in tourism of vital importance as they are irreplaceable. Citizens get new mobile phones, tablets, computers, and so on. This way they also support the concept of SMART cities. Travelling and SMART cities as the key terms of this paper will be defined in the first chapter. Then environmental indicators will be described and characterized based on SMART concept.

In the main part of the paper, four simple indicators dealing with the use of advanced technologies will be discussed, e.g. individuals using internet, % availability of latest technologies, English at the communication level and mobile phone subscriptions/100 pop. These indicators will be correlated with outbound tourism and

A.K. Kar et al. (Eds.): I3E 2017, LNCS 10595, pp. 172–182, 2017.
DOI: 10.1007/978-3-319-68557-1_16

through the Pearson correlation coefficient the impact of these indicators on tourism will be examined.

1.1 Tourism and Smart Cities

Tourism is a complex phenomenon comprising a wide range of disciplines. Due to that fact, defining tourism varies; definition of tourism is significantly influenced by its scope into other disciplines. Stating the appropriate definition is based on the intention of the technical report [1], research [2] or academic papers [3].

For the purposes of this paper the most frequently cited definition of 'Tourism' was selected. It is the definition from 1995 [4] created by the leading international organization in the field of tourism in the global scale [5] by The World Tourism Organization UNWTO which is still repeatedly used in UNWTO reports, e.g. Statistics of UNWTO [6].

The World Tourism Organisation UNWTO definition of Tourism is: "Tourism comprises the activities of persons travelling to and staying in places out-side their usual environment for not more than one consecutive year for leisure, business and other purposes not related to the exercise of an activity remunerated from within the place visited." [4]. This is a demand side definition, not a supply side definition [6].

As for the Czech Tourism [7] it is classified according to kinds and forms of tourism.

The most significant factor influencing the forms of tourism in the Czech Republic is motivation of visitors. The kinds of tourism are determined by the applied methodology. Zelenka and Pásková [8] state that individual forms and kinds of tourism can get combined as well as overlap each other.

Smart city is defined at Business Dictionary [9] as "a developed urban area that creates sustainable economic development and high quality of life by excelling in multiple key areas; economy, mobility, environment, people, living, and government. Excelling in these key areas can be done so through strong human capital, social capital, and/or ICT infrastructure."

Next definition is used from Innovation city. [10] Smart Cities is a vendor /city term commonly used to refer to the creation of knowledge infrastructure. Smart City, in everyday use, is inclusive of terms such as 'digital city' or 'connected cities'. Smart Cities as an applied technology term often refers to smart grids, smart meters, and other infrastructure for electricity, water supply, waste and what 2thinknow refer to as, 'city basics'.

Times of India [11] used brief and the simplest definition. Smart city is "a city equipped with basic infrastructure to give a decent quality of life, a clean and sustainable environment through application of some smart solutions."

Smart city is reffered [28] as Using ICTs to connect systems to fulfil complex tasks that involve multiple areas in the context of a city. In the study of [29] smart city is defined as an ecosystem that is more than the sum of its parts, where sustainability is maintained through the interactions of urban functions.

Thompson [30] states that the answer to "What a smart city is?" is complex and it is not easy to define it. The answer depends on where the focus is and who is giving the answer. Although still a definitive definition is lacking, in many aspects this is by no means a terrible void. Smart City concept is wide and many players and notions are involved and therefore capturing all these elements in one definition might not be possible.

Albino, Berardi, and Dangelico's [31] paper is a great resource. They analysed several different definitions and clarified that perceiving and understanding of smart city phenomenon is changing and the smart city concept is no longer limited to the diffusion of ICT, but it looks at people and community needs. With this in mind the definition generated by the British Standards Institution [32] was selected; it focuses on integrating diverse systems namely, physical, digital and human systems is our preferred definition: Smart city is an effective integration of physical, digital and human systems in the built environment to deliver a sustainable, prosperous and inclusive future for its citizens. It is good to point out at this stage that as Gil-Garcia, Pardo, and Nam [33] explain being smart is not an end state, but rather can be an enabling condition that may lead to other desirable social, economic, or environmental outcomes. It is clear that, data and ICT play a big part in the smart future urbanism. But equally there are other major concepts contributing towards creation of smart cities. As Neirottio et al. [34] highlights, ICT is unable to transform cities without the human capital which brings the liveability of a city to attention. Angelidou [35] explains that, smart cities represent a conceptual urban development model based on the utilization of human, collective and technological capital for the enhancement of development and prosperity in urban agglomerations.

1.2   The Environmental Indicator

The paper discusses selected simple indicators. As an entry into this issue, the fundamental environmental indicator will be explained via definitions and characteristics gathered from local sources as well as international ones.

The first definition is taken from the local source. The environmental indicator is approached as a kind of information. The definition is descriptive, widely explanatory and easily understandable.

Hák [12] defined the environmental indicator as a type of information that provides a benchmark for assessing (mostly for quantitative assessing) of environmental trends, ecological policy goals, or health or ecosystem status. Indicators offer information which is simpler and easier to understand in comparison with information than we can find in statistics. Numeric indicators simplify information about complex phenomena, so they are clearly understandable and communicable. They are generated by the processing of primary data and thus constitute an empirical model of reality. Their calculation has to be justified and must be made in a clear way and preferably by an established method.

The following definition of the environmental indicator formulated by the Organization for Economic Cooperation and Development (OECD) might be considered as the fundamental definition accepted and frequently referred to by e.g. researchers or environmental policy makers in their countries [13].

The OECD [14] definition of the environmental indicator is: "An environmental indicator is a parameter, or a value derived from parameters, that points to, provides information about and/or describes the state of the environment, and has a significance extending beyond that directly associated with any given parametric value. The term may encompass indicators of environmental pressures, conditions and responses."

Saunders et al. [15] state that environmental indicators can be described as physical, chemical, biological or socio-economic measures that best represent the key elements of a complex ecosystem or an environmental issue.

1.3 Characteristics of Indicators Based on SMART Concept

Authors of the document Environmental indicators for reporting approached the issue basically to fit the needs of State of the Environment (SoE) reporting so that it could be possible to track environmental policy, its performance and results. They highlighted the importance of clearly stated objectives of what will be measured and that the indicators should be administratively practical and cost-effective to populate.

A SMART concept of indicators was designed. Characteristics of indicators in brief according to the "SMART" abbreviation concept follow:

- 'S' stands for Simple (easily interpreted and monitored),
- 'M' means Measurable (statistically verifiable, reproducible and show trends),
- 'A' is Accessible (easily monitored, cost effective and consistent),
- 'R' stands for Relevant (directly address agreed objectives
- and 'T' means Timely (for the purposes of State of the Environment reporting it should provide early warning of potential problems) [13].

The indicators can be categorized according to various criteria. The standard division of indicators is division into simple and complex indicators.

Simple indicator
Hák [12] defines a simple indicator as one-dimensional magnitude. It aims to give information about only one single phenomenon and its context. Most indicators are derived from primary data and are in the form of a simple indicator.

Composite indicator
Composite indicators group are more variables or different variables into one index. The goal of merging variables with the same properties into a single number is to describe their aggregate properties. Composite indicators can be created by different methodologies and include various components. Changes in index construction often cause confusion because indexes can give different information as compared to one another or even when refer-ring to long-term trends [12].

2 Methodology and Objectives

The paper focuses on comparison of the degree of dependence between the inbound tourism and four selected simple indicators from the field of advanced technologies.

The aim is to introduce simple indicators that are most closely linked to tourism and advanced technologies that support the concept of SMART cities.

Hypothesis: Due to the importance of advanced technology in everyday life, tourism is related to the availability and use of advanced technologies in selected countries of the European Union.

2.1 Statistical Data Processing

Statistical correlation was used for statistical data processing.

Skalská [16] argues that correlation analysis deals with the measurement of relations between variables. Correlation analysis is used to quantify the association between two continuous variables i.e. between an independent and a dependent variable or between two independent variables. [17]. But Skalská [16] explains that the correlation is the degree of linear association between variables, when none of the variables needs to be labeled as dependent or independent.

Crossman [18] explains the Correlation as a term that refers to the strength of a relationship between two variables. A strong, or high, correlation means that two or more variables have a strong relationship with each other, while a weak or low correlation means that the variables are hardly related. Correlation analysis is the process of studying the strength of that relationship with available statistical data.

According to Litschmann [19] the tightness of linear dependence is assessed by a correlation coefficient. "The assessed relationship is the stronger and the regression function is the better, the more the monitored values of the variable are concentrated around the estimated regression function, and contrary the weaker, the more the values are distant from balanced values."

Pearson correlation coefficient

The correlation coefficient is a measure of the linear dependence and is denoted. It can be explained as a share of covariance and the square root of the product of the scattering of variables, where the covariance expresses the relationship X and Y, and the population scattering describes how much the data are scattered around the population average [16, 20].

Formula for calculating the correlation coefficient:

$\rho(X,Y) = (C(X,Y))/\sqrt{(D(X)D(Y))}$, where $D(x)$, $D(Y)$ denote population scattering. According to Skalská [13], the range of values is approximately

$0,1 < |\ | \leq 0,3$ indicates a weak dependence,
$0,3 < |\ | \leq 0,6$ mean medium dependence,
$0,6 < |\ | \leq 0,8$ we speak of strong dependence
$0,8 < |\ | \leq 0,9$ suggests a very strong dependence

$|\ | \geq 0,9$ almost linear dependence direct or indirect, according to the sign of the correlation coefficient.

Skalská [16] warns that the general problem of observation and measurement can be the assumption of an association between two variables if the changes of both variables prove a certain connection. Skalská [16] points out that "the observed association (link) may be true, or it may be mediated by another variable (s) that is hidden". The author also states that a variable that is hidden or not included in the observation can affect the observed variables, which then appear to be related. For the interpretation of associations, it is necessary to know the context and the events that may influence the data compared.

2.2   Statistics in Tourism

The content of the statistics in tourism is described in this chapter from global and local perspectives, from the international UNWTO perspective and from the national perspective represented by Czech Statistical Office of the Czech Republic.

The statistics in tourism deals with the collection of statistical data from various areas of tourism, their processing and comparison, both at the regional and as well as at the international level. Statistical data refer to the profile of tourism participants, occupancy of accommodation facilities or means of transport, outbound tourism or customer satisfaction with the services provided. Statistics deals not only with collection of data but it deals also with the creation of statistical methodologies and their processing. Gained data are available and used by both professional and general public in private and public spheres.

The UNWTO as the United Nations agency responsible for the promotion of responsible, sustainable and universally accessible tourism defines the content of Statists in tourism as follows:

"The UNWTO systematically gathers tourism statistics from countries and territories around the world into a vast database that constitutes the most comprehensive statistical information available on the tourism sector. The database, updated regularly, is composed by the following sets of data [21]:

- Compendium of Tourism Statistics - The Compendium provides statistical data and indicators on inbound, outbound and domestic tourism, as well as on the number and types of tourism industries, the number of employees by tourism industries, and macroeconomic indicators related to international tourism.
- Yearbook of Tourism Statistics - The Yearbook focuses on data related to inbound tourism (total arrivals and overnight stays), broken down by country of origin.
- Outbound tourism data (estimates) tourism of resident visitors outside the economic territory of the country of reference".

The Czech Republic is a member of the European Union. In the Czech Republic, Tourism statistics is coordinated by the Czech Statistical Office. Websites of this state important body are systematically updated and coordinated with Statistical offices of other European countries as well as the UNWTO. Websites bring Data encompassing Latest figures in News Releases, Time series, Tourism Satellite Account, Selected tables from the Public Database, another large section represents Methodology covering Tourism - Methodology and Metadata and quality reports, the last section brings a wide range of analyses [22].

Tourism has an enormous economic potential. In the EU the role of tourism is discussed in its social and environmental implications. Eurostat statistics websites provide recent statistics from Tourism in individual states of the European Union as well as the EU as a whole [23].

3   Correlation of Simple Indicators

A total of 60 simple indicators from the fields of economics, sociology and ecology were analyzed in the research. Selected results from the research are presented in this paper. The strength of dependence on the relative outbound tourism for 2014 was determined. The analysed EU states do not include Croatia, Ireland, Malta, Bulgaria, Greece, Slovenia, Luxembourg and Cyprus. Data for the results of the indicators come from the Global Competitiveness Index [24], the OECD Better Life Index 2014 [25], Wikipedia [26] and Numbeo [27] websites, all data relate to 2014. Data for relating to the share of English-speaking inhabitants are from to 2012 for France, Italy, Austria, Denmark, Finland, the Czech Republic, Hungary, Slovakia, Lithuania, Latvia, Estonia, Romania, the Netherlands, Spain and Sweden, as for the United Kingdom of Great Britain and Northern Ireland the data relate to 2011 and older data coming from 2006 relate to Germany and Belgium. As for Poland the data are recorded but without the year of their collection.

All data of the outbound tourism were drawn from Eurostat and consequently processed by authors. The data relate to 2014.

The following part discusses four simple indicators. Three of them demonstrated the highest rates of dependency and ranked among the top ten indicators. The crucial reason for selection of these specific indicators was their relation to the advanced technologies which represent fundamental area for the development of the Information and communication (ICT) literacy and for the creation and efficient operation of SMART cities.

The results of the correlations of the analyzed simple indicators are shown in the table below. There are analysed relative outbound tourism with percentage of the internet users, availability of latest technologies, percentage of people speaking English at the communication level and mobile telephone subscriptions. All four correlated coefficients reached positive values as is illustrated in the Table 1. According to the theoretical bases we can state that it is in the first three cases the strong or medium dependence. In the last one case is the dependence weak.

The highest rate of dependence on the relative outbound tourism out of the 60 simple indicators analysed was achieved by a simple indicator of **the percentage of users using the Internet.** The correlation coefficient was 0.71. This is, therefore, a **strong dependence** between investigated items. It can be interpreted that the outbound tourism per person increases with a higher number of Internet users. It is understandable, because these days the Internet is the main source of information in general as well as for the purposes of tourism. In addition, gaining information on foreign destinations, weather, exchange rates and prices is very cheap, fast, convenient and accessible at anytime from anywhere thanks to the internet.

The indicator of **the latest technology availability** shows **moderate dependence** on the outbound tourism. It can be deduced that the outbound tourism is more or less growing with better access to the latest technology. Modern technology moves human possibilities, whether it is information, security or accessibility. The latest technologies push the boundaries of the tourism and have a significant impact on its quality of service. This naturally leads to an increase in the number of tourists.

Table 1. Correlation of the relative outbound tourism and four selected simple indicators related to the use of advanced technologies with the highest correlation rate. Source: wwn processing based on data from Schwab [24], organization for economic cooperation and development [25], Wikipedia [26] and Numbeo [27]

Country	Individuals using Internet, %	Availability of latest technologies	English at the communication level	Mobile telephone subscriptions/100 pop.
Belgium	85	6,2	38	114,3
Czech Republic	79,7	5,6	27	130
Denmark	96	6	86	126
Estonia	84,2	5,8	50	160,7
Finland	92,4	6,6	70	139,7
France	83,8	6	39	100,4
Germany	86,2	6,2	56	120,4
Great Britain	91,6	6,5	98	123,6
Hungary	76,1	5,1	20	118,1
Italy	62	5,1	34	154,2
Latvia	75,8	5,8	46	124,2
Lithuania	72,1	5,8	38	147
Netherlands	93,2	6,3	90	116,4
Poland	66,6	4,6	33	156,4
Portugal	64,6	6,1	27	110
Romania	54,1	4,6	31	105,9
Slovakia	80	5,5	26	116,9
Spain	76,2	5,5	22	107,8
Sweden	92,5	6,5	86	127,8
Correlation	0,713338809	0,576664394	0,55514043	0,057982463

The ten strongest correlation relationships are concluded by the indicator of **the percentage of people speaking English** at least at the communicative level. The correlation coefficient is 0.55. From these results it can be concluded that the number of foreign visits will increase more or less with the increasing number of people who can speak English. **The dependence is medium.** The authors claim that the ability to communicate in English can break the anxiety from cultural barriers, the unfamiliar environment, and the unexpected situations that can happen during a trip abroad. The authors believe that the ability to communicate in a foreign language abroad significantly affects people's decision whether to travel beyond the borders of the state or not.

Even though there are more than one **Mobile phone subscriptions** in each monitored country and mobile phones are actively used, they have a **very low correlation** with tourism. To give an example, in Austria, Estonia, Italy, Poland there is more than 1.5 accounts per capita. On the contrary, the lowest share was recorded in France, Romania and Spain. Individuals using internet, availability of latest technologies and mobile telephone subscriptions are also solved in the technological readiness that is evaluated each year by World bank [36]. Level of the technological readiness of the Czech Republic was also solved by Svobodova, Hedvicakova [37].

4 Conclusion

The paper discusses the basic concepts and principles of tourism, economy and the use of technologies and language competences in travel as a support for utilization of SMART technology and impact on destinations. Knowledge of basic concepts of mentioned areas and understanding their interconnectedness is necessary for the subsequent exploration of their relationships. In order to compare the dependencies between the items, the relevant issues from statistics and the Pearson correlation coefficient are explained.

Theoretical knowledge was applied to the correlation of the relative outbound tourism and selected simple indicators. The correlation results were processed into tables, compared, analyzed and interpreted. All correlated coefficients reached positive values as is illustrated in the Table 1. According to the theoretical bases we can state that there is the dependence in all four cases.

The first place in the top ten simple indicators with the highest coefficient belongs to users of the Internet. The eight position out of ten belongs to the availability of advanced technologies and the tenth place the percentage of people speaking English at least at the communicative level. A note should be made on incorporation of the mobile telephones indicator into the paper; mobile phones are not linked to tourism but majority of people use them as a standard device when they are travelling.

Given the above results, the assumed hypothesis can be accepted. Due to the importance of advanced technology in everyday life, tourism is related to the availability and use of advanced technologies in selected countries of the European Union.

The percentage of users using the Internet gained a correlation of 0.71, the availability of the latest technologies 0.58, the percentage of people speaking at a communicative level of 0.56. The number of mobile phones per 100 inhabitants showed only 0.16 which is a weak dependence.

The crucial reason for selection of specific indicators was their relation to the advanced technologies which represent fundamental area for the development of the Information and communication (ICT) literacy and for the creation and efficient operation of SMART cities.

As a theoretical contribution of the paper might be perceived following, users of the Internet, availability of the latest advanced technologies and the percentage of people speaking English at least at the communicative level have a significant impact on tourism. Mobile phones have lesser influence than other categories. The results and findings are beneficial not only for the academic area but also for the business entities that sell or provide the given products and as well as for the general public. By linking two areas that are tourism and technology and communication, the issue can be of interest to both urban experts and people in tourism. Not only tourist destinations, but also travel agencies, information centers, towns, castles, castles or chateaus should nowadays use advanced technologies to promote their attractions, thus boost tourism that has a positive impact on the economic situation and development. In conclusion, this is an interesting issue with great potential for the future.

Acknowledgement. This paper is supported by internal grant No. 1907/2017 "Transformation of knowledge from the field of kinanthropology into geography and tourism" at the Faculty of Informatics and Management, University of Hradec Kralove, Czech Republic and by the Specific Research Project "Information and knowledge management and cognitive science in tourism" of FIM UHK. We would like to thank student Jan Hruška for active involvement.

References

1. UNWTO - Tourism Highlights (2016). http://fac.ksu.edu.sa/sites/default/files/tourism_high lights_2016-_unwto.pdf
2. Jennings, G.: Tourism research - CAB Direct (2001). https://www.cabdirect.org/cabdirect/ abstract/20023031452
3. Progress in Tourism and Hospitality Research. http://onlinelibrary.wiley.com/journal/ 10.1002/(ISSN)1099-1603
4. UNWTO (1995:1–2): Concepts, Definitions, and Classifications for Tourism Statistics. Technical Manual: Technical Manual. Madrid: World Tourism Organization (1995)
5. UNWTO - Who we are. http://www2.unwto.org/content/who-we-are-0
6. World Tourism Organisation - Statistics and Tourism Satellite Account (2011). http:// statistics.unwto.org/sites/all/files/pdf/unwto_tsa_1.pdf
7. CZECHTOURISM: Charakteristika a význam cestovního ruchu v Česku. In: CzechTourism: 20 let s vámi (2016). http://old.czechtourism.cz/didakticke-podklady/1-charakteristika-a-vyznam-cestovniho-ruchu-v-cesku/
8. Zelenka, J., Pásková, M.: Výkladový slovník cestovního ruchu. Kompletně přeprac. a dopl. 2. vyd. Praha: Linde Praha (2012)
9. Smart city. Definition of SMART city. http://www.businessdictionary.com/definition/smart-city.html
10. Innovation cities. Definition of SMART city. http://www.innovation-cities.com/a-definition-of-a-smart-cities-compared-with-an-innovation-city/1322
11. Times of India. Definition of SMART city. http://timesofindia.indiatimes.com/What-is-a-smart-city-and-how-it-will-work/listshow/47128930.cms
12. Hák, T.: Indikátory blahobytu: všechno, co jste kdy chtěli vědět o štěstí (ale báli jste se zeptat) (2010). http://www.zelenykruh.cz/o-nas/publikace/edice-apel
13. Department of the Environment and Heritage, Environmental indicators for reporting (2006). https://www.environment.gov.au/node/22551
14. Environmental Indicator OECD Glossary of statistical terms. https://stats.oecd.org/glossary/ detail.asp?ID=830
15. Saunders, D.C., Margules, C., Hill, B.: Environmental indicators for national state of the environment reporting-Biodiversity, Australia: State of the Environment (Environmental Indicator Reports), Department of the Environment, Canberra (1998)
16. Skalská, H.: Aplikovaná statistika. Hradec Králové: Gaudeamus (2013)
17. Multivariable Methods. http://sphweb.bumc.bu.edu/otlt/mph-modules/bs/bs704_multi variable/bs704_multivariable5.html
18. Crossman, A.: Understanding Correlation Analysis (2016). https://www.thoughtco.com/ what-is-correlation-analysis-3026696

19. Litschmannová, M.: Úvod do statistiky: interaktivní učební text (2012). http://mi21.vsb.cz/sites/mi21.vsb.cz/files/unit/interaktivni_uvod_do_statistiky.pdf

20. Hudecová, Š.: Matematická statistika (2012). http://www.karlin.mff.cuni.cz/~hudecova/education/archive11/download/chem_predn/predn_slides_05.pdf

21. Statistics and Tourism Satellite Account (2013). http://statistics.unwto.org/content/data-1

22. Tourism: Czech Statistical Office (2016). https://www.czso.cz/csu/czso/tourism_ekon

23. Tourism statistics (2016). http://ec.europa.eu/eurostat/statistics-explained/index.php/Tourism_statistics

24. Schwab, K. (ed.): The Global Competitiveness Report 2015–2016: Insight Report (2015). http://www3.weforum.org/docs/gcr/2015-2016/Global_Competitiveness_Report_2015-2016.pdf

25. Organisation for Economic Co-operation and Development. Average annual hours actually worked per worker (2016). https://stats.oecd.org/Index.aspx?DataSetCode=ANHRS

26. Wikipedia: List of countries by English-speaking population (2016). https://en.wikipedia.org/wiki/List_of_countries_by_English-speaking_population

27. Numbeo: Quality of Life Index for Country 2016 Mid Year (2016). http://www.numbeo.com/quality-of-life/rankings_by_country.jsp?title=2016-mid

28. Gottschalk, M., Uslar, M.: Using a use case methodology and an architecture model for describing smart city functionalities. Int. J. Electron. Gov.Res. 12(2), 1–17 (2016)

29. Rochet, C., Correa, J.D.P.: Urban lifecycle management: a research program for smart Government of smart cities. Revista de Gestão e Secretariado 7(2), 1–20 (2016)

30. Thompson, E.M.: Smart city: adding to the complexity of cities a critical reflection. In: 34th eCAADe Conference: Complexity & Simplicity (eCAADe 2016), Finland, University Oulu, pp. 651–660 (2016)

31. Albino, V., Berardi, U., Dangelico, R.M.: Smart cities: definitions, dimensions, performance, and initiatives. J. Urban Technol. 22(1), 3–21 (2015)

32. BSI standards publication. http://shop.bsigroup.com/upload/PASs/Free-Download/PAS180.pdf

33. Garcia, G., Pardo, T.A., Nam, T.: Smarter as the New Urban Agenda. A Comprehensive View of the 21st Century City, vol. 11. Springer, Heidelberg (2016)

34. Neirotti, P., De Marco, A., Cagliano, A.C., Mangano, G., Scorrano, F.: Current trends in smart city initiatives: some stylised facts. Cities 38, 25–36 (2014)

35. Angelidou, M.: Smart city policies: a spatial approach. Cities 41, 3–11 (2014)

36. Technological Readiness (2016). https://tcdata360.worldbank.org/indicators/inn.tech.ready

37. Svobodova, L., Hedvicakova, M.: Technological readiness of the Czech Republic and the use of technology. In: Themistocleous, M., Morabito, V. (eds.) Information Systems, EMCIS 2017. LNBIP, vol. 299, pp. 670–678. Springer, Cham (2017). doi: 10.1007/978-3-319-65930-5_53

Quality in Mobile Payment Service in India

Bhartendra Pratap Singh[✉], Purva Grover, and Arpan Kumar Kar

Department of Management Studies, Indian Institute of Technology Delhi,
New Delhi, India
singhbp.dms.iitd@gmail.com

Abstract. This study seeks to determine the dimensions of quality from the perspective of "voice of the consumer". It uses the Total Interpretive Structural Modelling (TISM) with construct of Usefulness, Ease of Use, Security &Trust, Visual Appeal, Complementary Relationship and Customer Service. The general theoretical framework of the Theory of Reasoned Action (TRA), Technology Acceptance Model (TAM), SERVQUAL, WebQual and Quality Function Deployment have been used to develop a questionnaire for Mobile Payment Service (MPS) quality. Individual's response to questions about the quality in MPS, they are using were collected and analysed with TISM. Though, the analysis confirms with the classical theory of TAM (i.e. Usefulness and Ease of Use), additionally the results also shows the consumers perceived concern about trust and security. There is also existence of significant relationship observed between demographics of the respondents and variables measured. The study intended to analyse the service quality in MPS in light of extant research on Technology Acceptance and Service Quality via construct of behavioural interaction to use and actual usage.

Keywords: Mobile payments · WebQual · Quality Function Deployment (QFD) · Total Interpretational Structural Model (TISM)

1 Introduction

Nowadays the wireless feature of mobile phones is continuously inspiring creation of value added services and functionalities which surpass telephony needs [8]. Due to the exponential growth in the subscribers and wider coverage in India, mobile has offered an option of delivering banking and payment services. A Mobile Payments Service (MPS) is a usage of mobile device supported with wireless and communication technology for payment bills, goods and services [3]. Further, demonetization of Rs. 500 and 1,000 currency tenders on November 08, 2016 by Government of India and highest emphasis on cashless economy has put digital payment on forefront. Among other digital payment modes, MPS has an increasing importance and development in essential mode of low value and high frequency money transactions. Therefore, field of MPS is already witnessing the increasing competition in India, post demonetisation and only providing service will not be adequate to gain competitive advantage. The mobile payment transaction volume is likely to register a compound growth rate of 90% to reach 15 billion by year 2022 (Mint 10 November 2016).

© IFIP International Federation for Information Processing 2017
Published by Springer International Publishing AG 2017. All Rights Reserved
A.K. Kar et al. (Eds.): I3E 2017, LNCS 10595, pp. 183–193, 2017.
DOI: 10.1007/978-3-319-68557-1_17

This study determines the dimension of quality in MPS and their effect on customer satisfaction. The study will determine the dimensions of quality with respect to the perspective of the customer. Service quality in MPS is determined by TISM, on the basis of survey undertaken. On the integrated theoretical framework of SERVQUAL [31], WebQual [5, 13, 30], QFD; the current study undertakes an empirical assessment using the research model in context of the MPS.

2   Literature Review

MPS is a mobile phone based application, provided with the utilities of a bank credit card/debit card and other features of financial transactions capable to replace person's wallet [20]. As per [19], in mobile payment at least a payer engages mobile device to carry out payment transaction. The rapid mobile technology evolution followed by mobile phone users expanding base, it has been identified that the commercial industry of mobile applications is having a high growth potential [2]. MPS can support both C2C and C2B transactions on all type of Point-of-Sales (PoS). Evaluating the quality in MPS can be approached from three major methods - machine, expert analysis and customer evaluation. Since the customer point of view gets ignored in machine or expert approach, asking customer is desirable [12, 13].

2.1   Service Quality

The quality of any service from the view point of consumer is considered as judgment of overall excellence or superiority [6, 29]. According to SERVQUAL scale [17] service quality is a gap between perceived service expectation and perceived service performance. Therefore, service quality may be explained in a form of a simple equation as:

$$SQ = P - E$$

Where: SQ = service quality, P = perceived delivery of the service by the individual, E = expected delivery of the service by the individual

2.2   Website Service Quality

Consumers' perception of quality and their usage behavior [1] towards MPS can better explained using Unified Theory of Acceptance and Use of Technology (UTAUT) model [23]. In current study paper following aspects: perceived usefulness, perceived ease of use, perceived security& Trust, self-efficacy and social influence. Further, this paper examines three moderating variables (age, earning, and location type) that have varying influences on the primary constructs. MPS application is founded on the contention of internet service or MIS, therefore theories related to WebQual [12] are applicable. In a mobile based service, the employment of software, hardware, networking, storage, display, process or transfer are information system element [26].

2.3   Additional Aspects of Mobile Payment Service

Ubiquity. The most cited example of network effect is the telecommunications, which is the leveraging on mobile phones platform effect. Therefore, success of MPS is also depends upon the management of ubiquity at the similar levels as the mobile phone. Ubiquity is the reason behind persistence of high expectation from MPS in future [18]. There are two dimensions of ubiquity: ubiquity of availability and ubiquity of use.

Security and Trust. Security is the subjective issue and depends on user specific perception affected by cultural and socio-economic parameters. In context of payment, brand name has a better chance to gain trust due to familiarity gained through frequent exposure and has high potential to motivate trust [27].Customer loyalty and satisfaction towards mobile modes positively influenced by trust factor [11].

2.4   Total Interpretive Structural Model (TISM)

Interpretive Structural Model (ISM) [25] can effectively derive the interrelation among elements and their level of association. ISM has been used to articulate disjointed and ambiguous rational system models to visible, well-defined models [22]. In the ISM diagraph can be interpreted at two levels i.e. nodes and links. Though ISM defines nodes in terms of the elements representing it, however the interpretation of link direction is inadequate. The links simply indicate the directional relationship between nodes but, it does neither captured nor represented the causal thinking behind the interrelation of paired comparison. Therefore, there is a requirement to interpret the casual thinking behind the paired interrelationship. Total interpretive structural mod-elling (TISM) [22, 28] by using the tool of Interpretive Matrix [21] evolves method-ology and framework for conceptualizing scantily articulated mental models. The TISM model in present study is developed on the basis of the work done by researchers on WebQual [4, 5, 12] and mobile wallet [20]. On the basis of literature review, a questionnaire was prepared to validate the assumptions. The TISM is used to develop a hierarchical structure of the set variables, which helps transform poorly articulated mental models into systematic form.

3   Study Design

The study design largely follows the MPS survey design used by method used by [4, 12]. The survey method adopted was through a questionnaire consisting of 46 questions. Prior commencement of full-fledged survey, the questionnaire was tested by administering a pilot survey undertaken to examine test–retest reliability and construct reliability before conducting the fieldwork. At the end by minimizing the uncertainty in syntax and semantics, the final survey through a questionnaire consisting of 24 ques-tions (Exhibit 1) was administered online as well as offline in January and February 2017. By the end of survey total 266 responses were captured. Of the submitted responses 12 were omitted because of incomplete answers, balance of which 254 were complete responses and considered for analysis.

In order to improve validity and generalizability, respondents were selected from various class of the cities i.e. Class A, B and C (classification by Government of India for the purpose of House Rent Allowance on the basis of cost of living). However, it was observed during analysis that the sample is unbalanced in in terms of brand of MPS subscription (Fig. 1). It has been observed the subscription of PayTm brand within the sample is as high as 94% (239 responses). The subscription of all other brands (i.e. ICICI, Airtel, BHIM, iMobile and MobiKwik) was only 15 (6%) in the sample of 254 good responses. So, it was decided during the study that the quality evaluation in Mobile Payment Service will be undertaken only for PayTm brand with a sample size of 239.

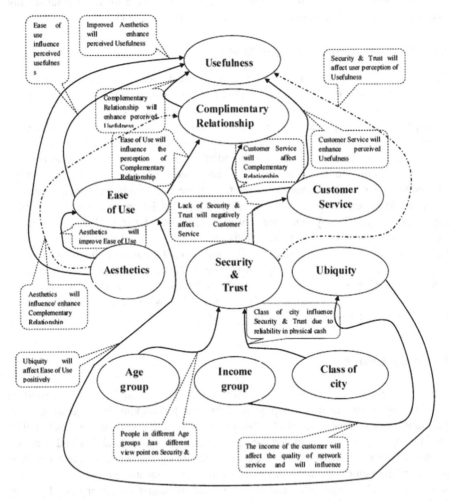

Fig. 1. Solid arrows are direct links and dotted arrows are significant Transitive Links

The final sample demographics presented in Table 1 is rather unbalanced with respect to city class, age and income group. This may have resulted due to proximity of survey efforts concentration to National Capital Region (NCR). Additionally, considering the nature of mobile payment, this unbalance is understandable because a large number of smart phone users are young and from middle income group.

Table 1. Characteristics of respondents (total = 239)

City class	Number	%
Class A	123	51
Class B	75	31
Class C	41	17
Age (years)	Number	%
Under 25	62	26
25–35	130	54
35–45	28	12
Above 45	19	8
Income group (INR,000)	Number	%
Less than 25	89	37
25–75	101	42
75–150	32	13
More than 150	17	7

3.1 Data Analysis

The respondents indicated their agreement or disagreement with a set of statements, using a 5-point Likert-type scale (ranging from "strongly agree" to "strongly disagree"). Since, option 1 was given to "strongly agree" and option 5 to "strongly disagree" on 5-point Likert-type scale, the points closer to the center are indicative of agreement and points on periphery are indicative of disagreement. The questions were further grouped to form elements, which can be co-related to the attributes the MPS quality (**Exhibit 2**) (Table 4).

4   Development of Total Interpretive Structural Model

For the development of TISM model, help of past studies [14, 15] has been taken to identify the elements and moderators. The pioneer work of TISM [22] is used to build up a hierarchical structure of the set of variables of interest.

4.1   Elements and Contextual Relationship

Perceived Usefulness and Perceived Ease of Use. Above are two distinct but interrelated beliefs as per TAM. Among these two variables, perceived usefulness have the stronger influence [7]. Which is the degree to which a consumer believes that the service will satisfy his/her need. However, perceived ease of use refers believe of the consumer to use the service will be effortless [24].

E1: Perceived usefulness has a positive effect on attitude toward the MPS.

E2: Perceived ease of use has a positive effect on attitude toward the MPS.

Aesthetics. This dimension concerns with the visual characteristics of the of the application design that attracts the user's attentions and encourages them to reuse the payment service. This dimension is covered by most of the IS studies due to its importance. All the mobile application companies give a great emphasis on this aspect. The combined appeal of the application will make the user happy, pleasant, enjoyable and cheerful [4].

E3: Aesthetics is positively related to intension to use MPS.

Security & Trust. The degree to which a customer believes that using MPS will be secure [20]. Perception of lack of security in digital payments is the most common reason for a refusal to use. Trust is the predecessor variable to the intention to use a MPS. Therefore, it is vital for mobile payment service provider to build trust through website and risk assessments.

E4: Security & Trust has a positive effect on the intention to use MPS.

Ubiquity. MPS application fulfills the customer need of accessing information and service for payment at anytime from anywhere [18].

E5: Ubiquity of MPS has a positive effect on intension to use.

Complimentary Relationship. How the usage of MPS application is better than other modes of transactions and better than other applications? Des it also allows all or most necessary payment transactions to be completed? These are important aspects.

E6: Complementary Relationship positively related to intention to use MPS.

Customer Service. The customer response to feedbacks, inquiries and comments is an essential aspect of MPS quality [10, 16]. This is also a deciding factor for customer loyalty.

E7: Quality of Customer Service in MPS affects the customer's intention to use.

Demographic Factors. These are the variables that represent association between other variables. The direction and strength of various relationships is shaped by the crucial role of age, gender, income etc. As per TAM research, age is an important parameter of market segmentation. Age also moderates technology adoption-related relationships [23]. Classification of city of MPS user is considered in current study as a vital personal characteristic. The impact of class of the city on adoption behavior has been a point of interest. Class 'C' city MPS customers is found to be strongly influenced by their perception of security.

E8: Age group of the user affects the intention to use MPS.

E9: Income group of the user has positive effect on attitude towards the MPS.

E10: The class of city of residence and usage of customer affects attitude towards MPS.

4.2   Defining Contextual Relationship

All the elements that affects the customer attitude towards MPS are subject to paired comparison to evolve the interpretive logic – knowledge base, which is converted into reachability matrix. The contextual relationship identified was 'Attribute A will influence /enhance attribute B'. Since, there was 10 attributes, the total number of rows in the knowledge base was 90 (= 10*9). The relationship in the knowledge base were designed with the help of Cronbach Alfa and established relationship in previous studies. The value of Cronbach Alfa above 0.7 was considered Y, otherwise N was marked in pairwise comparison. It has been observed that the high value of Alfa from survey in current study is also supported by previous research in case of most of the pairs. The final Knowledge base was developed for all the paired relationships.

4.3   Reachability Matrix

Further, transitivity concept is introduced to develop final reachability matrix so that some of the cells of initial reachability matrix are filled by inference [9]. The concept of transitivity can be explained as follows:-

If, (($Element_i \rightarrow Element_j$) and ($Element_j \rightarrow Element_k$))

then: ($Element_i \rightarrow Element_k$)

Transitivity is the ground assumption in ISM and be always used in modeling approach [21]. Transitivity also strengthens the consistency of the model. Final reachability matrix with transitive links is shown in Table 2. The antecedents and reachability of each element of enablers are drawn from the final reachability matrix. Reachability set consists of a group of enablers itself and other enablers, which may help in realizing the enabler. On the other hand antecedents set consists of a group of enablers itself and other enablers, which may help achieving it. Further, elements present in both reachability set as well as antecedent set are positioned as intersection set. The elements having same reachability set and interaction set are positioned at top spot. The elements already secured position in levels are removed to recognize next level and the cycle is repeated until all elements are placed hierarchical levels. These levels are utilized for formation diagram. The final level matrix is shown at Table 3.

Table 2. Final reachability matrix with transitivity (Transitive relation are shown with *)

Elements	E1	E2	E3	E4	E5	E6	E7	E8	E9	E10
E1	1	0	0	0	0	0	0	0	0	0
E2	1	1	0	0	0	1	0	0	0	0
E3	1	1	1	0	0	1*	0	0	0	0
E4	1*	0	0	1	0	1	1	0	0	0
E5	1*	1	0	0	1	1*	0	0	0	0
E6	1	0	0	0	0	1	0	0	0	0
E7	1	0	0	0	0	1	1	0	0	0
E8	1	0	0	1	0	1*	1*	1	0	0
E9	1	1*	0	0	1	1*	1	0	1	0
E10	1	1*	0	1	1	1*	1*	0	0	1

Table 3. Level Matrix

Element code	Enablers	Level
E1	Perceived usefulness has a positive effect on attitude toward the MPS.	I
E2	Perceived ease of use has a positive effect on attitude toward the MPS.	III
E3	Aesthetics is positively related to intension to use MPS.	IV
E4	Security & Trust has a positive effect on the intention to use MPS.	IV
E5	Ubiquity of MPS has a positive effect on intension to use.	IV
E6	Complementary Relationship positively related to intention to use MPS.	II
E7	Quality of Customer Service in MPS affects the customer's intention to use.	III
E8	Age group of the user affects the intention to use MPS.	V
E9	Income group of the user has positive effect on attitude towards the MPS.	V
E10	The class of city of residence and usage of customer affects attitude towards MPS.	V

4.4   Developing Diagraph

The meaning of diagraph is directed graph, which illustrates the relationship between the elements of enablers [9].The relationship between element i to j can be represented with an arrow for i to j, which signifies element i influence/enhance element j. The diagraph with significant transition links for current study is shown at Fig. 1. A binary interaction matrix is developed from the digraph.

4.5   Total Interpretive Structure Model

Figure 1 depicts the hierarchical structure of TISM showing driving force behind users' perception of quality in Mobile Payment Service by PayTm and causal relationship towards reusability. Demographic factors have a direct influence on users' perceived trust. Towards end all the enablers are influencing and also having impact on the perception of usefulness.

5   Conclusion

There is a widespread acceptance of mobile payment service, specifically among the young population. However, the concern of security, lack of trust, awareness and infrastructure is precluding percolation of the service to the masses. Further, the features internal to the service providers, like aesthetics, customer service and complimentary relationship will influence the perception of usefulness by the customer. The perceived usefulness by the customer is also the indicator of attitude to reuse. Therefore, the present study provides prescriptive advice concerning, how a service provider of MPS can improve the offering, which was not true in the case of WebQual and WebQual/M. Given that 'Usefulness' was most highly ranked dimension of the quality in MPS and has a considerable implications for the perception of quality, the same can be influenced by factors like trust and customer relationship.

Exhibit 1: Questionnaire

1. The OS on my mobile is -
2. Mobile Payment App I am using frequently is -
3. The App is always available for payment.
4. The App loads quickly.
5. Learning to operate the App is easy for me.
6. I find the App easy to use.
7. The display pages within the App are easy to read.
8. When I use the App there is very little waiting time between my actions and the response.
9. The App design is visually pleasing and innovative.
10. The App's impression (image) matches that of the company.
11. The App has interactive features, which help me accomplish my task.
12. All my payments can be completed via the App.
13. It has useful links to other Apps and sites.
14. It is easier to use the App to complete my payments than it is to conventional means.
15. The payment through this Mobile Payment App is more convenient than using internet banking.
16. I trust the App to keep my personal information safe.
17. I consider mode of payment through Mobile App safer than cash/card payment.
18. I use this Mobile App because it is better than other popular Mobile Payment Apps.
19. The App makes easy to contact the service provider/give feedback.
20. The App service provider quickly resolves the payment transaction problems/errors.
21. I also use below Mobile Payment Apps in addition to mentioned above at serial 2-
22. Please select your age group (years).
23. Please select your monthly income group (INR, 000).
24. Which city you are residing in?

Exhibit 2

Table 4. Mobile payment service quality items by construct

Usefulness
4. The App loads quickly
8. When I use the App there is very little waiting time between my actions and the response
11. The App has interactive features, which help me accomplish my task
12. All my payments can be completed via the App
13. It has useful links to other Apps and sites
Ease of use
5. Learning to operate the App is easy for me
6. I find the App easy to use
7. The display pages within the App are easy to read

(continued)

Table 4. (*continued*)

Aesthetics

9. The App design is visually pleasing and innovative

Security & trust

10. The App's impression (image) matches that of the company

16. I trust the App to keep my personal information safe

17. I consider mode of payment through Mobile App safer than cash/card payment

Ubiquity

3. The App is always available for payment

Complementary relationship

14. It is easier to use the App to complete my payments than it is to conventional means

15. The payment through this Mobile Payment App is more convenient than using internet banking

18. I use this Mobile App because it is better than other popular Mobile Payment Apps

Customer service

19. The App makes easy to contact the service provider/give feedback

20. The App service provider quickly resolves the payment transaction problems/errors

References

1. Aizen, I., Fishbein, M.: Understanding Attitudes and Predicting Social Behaviour. Prentice-Hall, Englewood Cliffs (1980)
2. Au, Y.A., Kauffman, R.J.: The economics of mobile payments: Understanding stakeholder issues for an emerging financial technology application. Electron. Commer. Res. Appl. **7**(2), 141–164 (2007)
3. Balasubramanian, S., Peterson, R.A., Janvenpaa, S.L.: Exploring the implications of m-commerce for markets and marketing. J. Acad. Mark. Sci. **30**(4), 348–361 (2002)
4. Barnes, S.J., Vidgen, R.: WebQual: An exploration of web-site quality. Int. J. Electron. Commer. **6**(1), 11–30 (2001)
5. Barnes, S.J., Vidgen, R.: Evaluating WAP news sites: The WEBQUAL/M approach. In: The 9th European Conference on Information Systems, vol. 17 (2001)
6. Cronin, J.J., Taylor, S.A.: Measuring service quality: a re-examination and extension. J. Mark. **56**(3), 55–68 (1992)
7. Davis, F.: Perceived usefulness, perceived ease of use, and user acceptance of information technology. MIS Q. **13**(3), 319–340 (1989)
8. Dahlberg, T., Mallat, N., Ondrus, J., Zmijewska, A.: Past, present and future of mobile payments research: A literature review. Electron. Commer. Res. Appl. **7**(2), 165–181 (2008)
9. Jayalakshmi, B., Pramod, V.R.: Total interpretive structural modelling (TISM) of the enablers of a flexible control system for industry. Glob. J. Flex. Syst. Manage. **16**(1), 63–85 (2015)
10. Kreyer, N., Pousttchi, K., Turowski, K.: Standardized payment procedures as key enabling factor for mobile commerce. In: Bauknecht, K., Tjoa, A.M., Quirchmayr, G. (eds.) EC-Web 2002. LNCS, vol. 2455, pp. 400–409. Springer, Heidelberg (2002). doi:10.1007/3-540-45705-4_41

11. Lin, H.-H., Wang, Y.-S.: An examination of the determinants of customer loyalty in mobile commerce contexts. Inf. Manage. **43**(3), 271–282 (2006)
12. Loiacono, E.T., Watson, R.T., Goodhue, D.L.: WebQual: A measure of website quality. Mark. Theory Appl. **13**(3), 432–438 (2002)
13. Loiacono, E., Chen, D., Goodhue, D.: WebQual TM revisited: predicting the intent to reuse a Web site. In: AMCIS 2002 Proceedings, vol. 46 (2002)
14. Lu, Y., Zhang, L., Wang, B.: A multidimensional and hierarchical model of mobile service quality. Electron. Commer. Res. Appl. **8**(5), 228–240 (2009)
15. Mallat, N.: Exploring consumer adoption of mobile payments – A qualitative study. J. Strateg. Inf. Syst. **16**(4), 413–432 (2007)
16. Ozer, A., Argan, M.T., Argan, M.: The effect of mobile service quality dimensions on customer satisfaction. Procedia Soc. Behav. Sci. **99**, 428–438 (2013)
17. Parasuraman, A., Zeithaml, V.A., Berry, L.L.: SERVQUAL: a multiple-item scale for measuring consumer perceptions of service quality. J. Retail. **64**(1), 12–40 (1988)
18. Pousttchi, K., Selk, B., Turowski, K.: Enabling mobile commerce through mass customization. In: Proceedings of the EIS 2002 Workshop on Information Systems for Mass Customization, Malaga 2002, pp. 1–6 (2002)
19. Pousttchi, K.: Conditions for acceptance and usage of mobile payment procedures. In: Giaglis, G.M., Werthner, H., Tschammer, V., Foeschl. K. (eds.) mBusiness 2003 - The Second International Conference on Mobile Business, Vienna, pp. 201–210 (2003)
20. Shin, D.-H.: Towards an understanding of the consumer acceptance of mobile wallet. Comput. Hum. Behav. **25**(6), 1343–1354 (2009)
21. Sushil.: Interpretive matrix a tool to aid interpretation of management and social research. Glob. J. Flex. Syst. Manage. **6**(2), 27–30 (2005)
22. Sushil.: Interpreting the interpretive structural model. Glob. J. Flex. Syst. Manage. **13**(2), 87–106 (2012)
23. Venkatesh, V., Morris, M., Davis, G.B., Davis, F.D.: User acceptance of information technology: Toward a unified view. MIS Q. **3**, 425–478 (2003)
24. Viehland, D., Leong, R.: Acceptance and use of mobile payments. In: 18th Australasian Conference on Information Systems Acceptance and Use of Mpayments, vol. 16, pp. 665–671 (2007)
25. Warfield, J.N.: Intent structures. IEEE Trans. Syst. Man Cybern. SMC **3**(2), 133–140 (1973)
26. Wolfinbarger, M., Gilly, M.C.: eTailQ: Dimensionalizing, measuring and predicting etail quality. J. Retail. **79**, 183–198 (2003)
27. Wu, J.H., Wang, S.C.: What drives mobile commerce? An empirical evaluation of the revised technology acceptance model. Inf. Manage. **42**(5), 719–729 (2005)
28. Yadav, M., Rangnekar, S., Bamel, U.: Workplace flexibility dimensions as enablers of organizational citizenship behaviour. Glob. J. Flex. Syst. Manage. **17**(1), 41–56 (2016)
29. Zeithaml, V.A.: Defining and Relating Prices, Perceived Quality and Perceived Value. Marketing Science Institute, Cambridge (1987)
30. Anand, O., Mittal, A., Moolchandani, K., Kagzi, Munezasultana M., Kar, A.K.: Evaluating travel websites using WebQual: a group decision support approach. In: Buyya, R., Thampi, Sabu M. (eds.) Intelligent Distributed Computing. AISC, vol. 321, pp. 151–160. Springer, Cham (2015). doi:10.1007/978-3-319-11227-5_14
31. Kalelkar, G.R., Kumbhare, G., Mehta, V., Kar, A.K.: Evaluating E-Commerce Portals from the Perspective of the End User – A Group Decision Support Approach. In: Thampi, Sabu M., Gelbukh, A., Mukhopadhyay, J. (eds.) Advances in Signal Processing and Intelligent Recognition Systems. AISC, vol. 264, pp. 107–117. Springer, Cham (2014). doi:10.1007/978-3-319-04960-1_10

Selected Composite Indicators in the Field of Advanced Technologies and the Internet as a Support of SMART Cities and Their Impact on Tourism

Miloslava Černá[✉], Libuše Svobodová, and Petr Hruša

Faculty of Informatics and Management, University of Hradec Králové,
Rokitanského 62, 500 03 Hradec Králové, Czech Republic
{miloslava.cerna,libuse.svobodova,petr.hrusa}@uhk.cz

Abstract. The article discusses the possible relationships between the outbound tourism of the European Union countries and selected composite indicators from the social, economic and environmental areas. Three indicators have been selected, analyzed and evaluated. The choice of the indicators was based on their relation to the use of advanced technologies and the Internet and to their close interconnectedness with SMART cities. Namely following Indices were analyzed: the Social Progress Index, part of the Wellbeing of Nations Index – the Human Wellbeing Index and the Index of Quality of Life and Sustainable Development. The first part of the paper explains the different concepts of tourism, sustainable development, indices and statistics. Then three examined indicators are described. The core part is devoted to the research on the relationships between relative outbound tourism of individual European Union countries and the three indicators. The analysis is performed using the Pearson correlation coefficient. The highest correlation between outbound tourism and three analyzed indices was reached in the Social Progress Index which was closely followed by the Index of Quality of life and Sustainable Development. In both cases we speak about strong dependence.

Keywords: Advanced technologies · Composite indicator · Internet · Smart cities · Sustainable development

1   Introduction

The article discusses the possible relationships between the outbound tourism of the European Union countries and selected composite indicators from the social, economic and environmental areas. Three indicators have been selected, analyzed and evaluated. The choice of the indicators was based on their relation to the use of advanced technologies and the Internet and to their close interconnectedness with SMART cities.

The structure of the paper follows: the methodological frame, description of the analyzed indices: the Social Progress Index, part of the Wellbeing of Nations Index – the Human Wellbeing Index and the Index of Quality of Life and Sustainable

A.K. Kar et al. (Eds.): I3E 2017, LNCS 10595, pp. 194–205, 2017.
DOI: 10.1007/978-3-319-68557-1_18

Development, the core part - correlation of the outbound tourism and the composite indicators and conclusion.

1.1 Composite Indicator

The definitions of the composite indicator were drawn from globally accepted Organisation for economic cooperation and development (OECD) documents and from the Czech author whose categorisation of composite indicators is presented, as well as, an entry into the issue. Definition given by OECD follows: "A composite indicator is formed when Indicators are compiled into a single index, on the basis of an underlying model of the multi-dimensional concept that is being measured (e.g. competitiveness, e-trade or environmental quality)" [1].

According to Hák [2] composite indicators group more variables or different variables into one index. The goal of compiling variables with the same properties into a single figure is to describe their aggregate properties. Composite indicators can be constructed by different methodologies and include different components. Changes in the index construction often cause confusion, as indices can give different information as compared to one another or when referring to long-term trends." Hák [2] states that composite indicators are further divided into aggregated, compounded and indices.

- Aggregated indicator
  Aggregated indicators compile together several components or indices which are in the same units. They are created, for example, by summing or averaging the results of individual components. GDP is a typical example of this kind of indicator.
- Compounded indicator
  Compounded indicators combine various aspects of an individual phenomenon into one numeral expression. The result is usually a number with a common unit. The author illustrates this kind of indicator on the following examples: global hectares in ecological trail or amount of years in life expectancy [2].
- Index
  Indices are composite indicators which are at the top of the information pyramid. The index is a dimensionless number for which the data are often transformed before counting, for example, in the form of a deviation from the average. As an example might be give the human development index, the environmental performance index or the air quality index [2].

1.2 SMART Cities and Advanced Technologies

According to Duran [22] a city is smart when the social investment, human resources, communications and the building infrastructure, coexist harmoniously and get systematically developed through the use of Information and Communication Technologies (ICT). All that generates better quality of life and natural resources; efficient management is conducted through the citizens' participation.

As already highlighted above, utilization of the Internet and latest technologies play the crucial role in the development of SMART cities. Based on this matter of fact, researchers have focused, analyzed and explained a set of selected composite indicators which contain utilization of advanced technologies and communication channels, like Access to basic knowledge, Access to information and communication, Technology and information sharing, communication - accessibility and reliability of the telephone connection, Internet access.

2 Methodology and the Objective of the Paper

A set of composite indicators which comprise a component on utilization of advanced technologies and the Internet, which represent one of fundamental basis for smart cities, was selected.

The objective of this paper was to find out which of selected composite indicators relate to tourism.

2.1 Structure of the Research

Firstly, selected indices are introduced. Secondly, the degree of correlation between the indicators and the relative outbound tourism is examined. Finally, the findings are presented and explained.

Statistical data processing

Statistical correlation was used for statistical data processing.

Skalská [3] argues that correlation analysis deals with the measurement of relations between variables. Correlation analysis is used to quantify the association between two continuous variables i.e. between an independent and a dependent variable or between two independent variables [4]. But Skalská [3] explains that the correlation is the degree of linear association between variables, when none of the variables needs to be labeled as dependent or independent.

Crossman [5] explains the Correlation as a term that refers to the strength of a relationship between two variables. A strong, or high, correlation means that two or more variables have a strong relationship with each other, while a weak or low correlation means that the variables are hardly related. Correlation analysis is the process of studying the strength of that relationship with available statistical data.

According to Litschmann [6] the tightness of linear dependence is assessed by a correlation coefficient. "The assessed relationship is the stronger and the regression function is the better, the more the monitored values of the variable are concentrated around the estimated regression function, and contrary the weaker, the more the values are distant from balanced values."

Pearson correlation coefficient

The correlation coefficient is a measure of the linear dependence and is denoted. It can be explained as a share of covariance and the square root of the product of the scattering of variables, where the covariance expresses the relationship X and Y, and the population scattering describes how much the data are scattered around the population average. [3, 7].

Formula for calculating the correlation coefficient:

ρ $(X,Y) = (C (X,Y))/\sqrt{(D(X)D(Y))}$, where D (x), D (Y) denote population scattering.

According to Skalská [13], the range of values is approximately

0,1 < | | ≤ 0,3 indicates a weak dependence,

0,3 < | | ≤ 0,6 mean medium dependence,

0,6 < | | ≤ 0,8 we speak of strong dependence

0,8 < | | ≤ 0,9 suggests a very strong dependence

| | ≥ 0,9 almost linear dependence direct or indirect, according to the sign of the correlation coefficient."

Skalská [3] warns that the general problem of observation and measurement can be the assumption of an association between two variables if the changes of both variables prove a certain connection. Skalská [3] points out that "the observed association (link) may be true, or it may be mediated by another variable (s) that is hidden". The author also states that a variable that is hidden or not included in the observation can affect the observed variables, which then appear to be related. For the interpretation of associations, it is necessary to know the context and the events that may influence the data compared.

3 Description of Composite Indicators

14 composite indicators of sustainable development and one indicator of economic performance were selected for the research. Dependency between these indicators and relative outbound tourism for the year 2014 was examined. The results of the correlation of each indicator as well as the results of the ranking of countries within the individual indicators were analyzed in detail and described in the following subchapters.

Only three indicators were used in the comparison because only these three contain utilization of technologies, the Internet and other Smart cities support.

Online banking or online shopping might be presented as areas, apart from plenty of others, where the Internet and advanced technologies can be used to efficiently support SMART.

3.1 The Social Progress Index

As stated by Wikipedia [8], the Social Progress Index (SPI) evaluates how much each country satisfies the social and environmental needs of its citizens. According to Bishop [9], the authors were encouraged to create an index that would interpret social progress differently than all the existing indicators. As noted on the Social Progress Imperative [10], the authors believe that combining economic and social factors can not properly explain the relationship between economic and social progress. Therefore, it was desirable to develop an indicator that would put emphasis on the social and environmental spheres. Thus, the Social Progress Index does not include any economic measurement. By measuring social progress independently of economic development, it differs from all other indicators.

As stated in the Social Progress Index 2: "SPI focuses exclusively on indicators of social impacts and outcomes from results, instead of input measurements, of the country's efforts. It focuses on the level of social progress that countries have already achieved. For example, how much money countries spend on health care is far less important than the level of health actually achieved by the state" [11].

The Web further states [11], that the Social Progress Index is an aggregate index comprised of social and environmental indicators that capture the three dimensions of social progress. Individual dimensions consist of four indicators. Overall, the index is composed of 56 indicators.

This Index was selected because it contains Foundations of Wellbeing section with the subsection Access to Information and Communications. Within this section mobile telephone subscriptions, internet users and press freedom index were assessed.

The Social Progress Imperative [12] explains that the resulting SPI is calculated by the average of the values of each dimension.

As stated in the Social Progress Imperative [13], the social progress index was first published in 2014 and rated 133 countries. Since then, the index has been updated and published annually. The Social Progress Imperative [12] explains that the annual results of the surveyed countries are ranked according to the social progress from highest to lowest and further categorized into six categories: very high social progress, high social progress, moderate, medium, low and very low social progress.

3.2 Wellbeing of Nations Index

The Wellbeing of Nations (WN) was created by the International Union for Conservation of Nature (IUCN). As IUCN [14] states that this is the first global sustainability rating. The index compares a total of 180 countries. WN consists of four indicators that together provide a comprehensive picture of sustainable development. The IUCN [14] claims, that WN's main goal is to promote a high level of human and ecosystem well-being. It is striving to show the practicality and potential of this method of assessing well-being and, last but not least, aims to persuade states, communities and associations to run evaluation of their well-being (Table 1).

Table 1. Construction of the Social Progress Index.

Basic human needs	Basics of well-being	Opportunities
Nutrition and basic medical care	*Access to basic knowledge*	Personal rights
Water cleanliness and hygiene facilities	*Access to information and communication*	Access to higher education
The roof overhead	Overall health	Personal freedom and freedom of choice
Personal security	Sustainability of the ecosystem	Justice and inclusion

Source: Social Progress Index [10]

"Nováček [15] explains that the rating scale ranges from 0 to 100 where the value of 100 means the maximum sustainability of a given country."

Wellbeing Index

According to the International Union for Conservation of Nature [14], Wellbeing Index (WI) consists of two parts:

- the Human Wellbeing Index (HWI) and
- the Index of Ecosystem Wellbeing (EWI).

The same weight is attributed to both components. Wellbeing Index shows the point at which the HWI and EWI values intersect. This point is depicted on the so-called sustainability barometer.

Human Wellbeing Index

The International Union for Conservation of Nature [14] argues that Human Wellbeing Index is a much more accurate indicator of socio-economic conditions than gross Domestic Product (GDP) or HDI (Human Development Index), as GDP is focused on monetary indicators only, and HDI does not include as many aspects of human well-being as Human Wellbeing Index (HWI).

Human Wellbeing index consists of five thematic areas; gained results are consequently averaged in the overall HWI rating. Altogether it contains 36 indicators which are compared. Three indicators out of them are of key importance to us; they are found in the section Knowledge culture, to be precise they are placed in the sub-section Communication – accessibility and reliability of the telephone connections and internet access.

Ecosystem Wellbeing Index will not be discussed in this paper. It doesn´t contain analysed topics [14].

3.3 Index of Quality of Life and Sustainable Development

The most successful attempt to compare quality of life and sustainable development from the home environment seems to be the Index of Quality of Life and Sustainable Development, the so-called SD Index. As reported by Viturka [16] and Nováček [15], the Sustainable Development Index was developed by Nováček, Mederly and Topercer in 1999–2004 for a total of 179 countries and is an alternative to the HDI indicator (Table 2).

The goal of the index is to express the state's progress towards sustainable development, based on generally available data, so that the results can be regularly evaluated Nováček [15]. According to the author, the results make it possible to compare countries in the seven areas of sustainable development. Each area consists of two sub-areas that contain a total of 64 examined indicators. This indicator was selected because it contains technology and information segment.

The calculation of the overall index is based on averaged results of individual areas. As the author states, sub-indices for individual areas are to be transformed into one scale in the range from zero to one, with zero being equal to the least favorable value and one equals the most favorable, and then the values are to be averaged Nováček [15].

Table 2. Construction of the Human Wellbeing Index.

Health and population	Wealth	Knowledge and culture	Community	Equality
Life expectancy in good health (1 indicator)	The degree of satisfaction of needs relating to income, food, safe water and sanitary equipment (6 indicators)	Education (basic, secondary, higher education) and *communication - accessibility and reliability of the telephone connection, Internet access* (6 indicators)	Freedom and good governance - political rights, civil liberties, freedom of the press, corruption (4 indicators)	Equality of households - difference in income among the richest and poorest fifth of the population (1 indicator)
Family size stability (1 indicator)	Size and status of national economy, inflation, unemployment, debt ratio (8 indicators)		Peace coexistence - army spending, deaths due to military conflicts and terrorism (2 indicators)	Gender Equality - Gender in Income, Education and Representation in Legislative Bodies (3 indicators)
			Violent crime (4 indicators)	

Source: [14]

Nováček [15] appreciates that the advantage of this method of calculation is in its simplicity and comprehensibility for the wider public; it enables the public to apprehend the results. On the other hand, significant simplification of reality can lead to misleading results.

4   Correlation of Composite Indicators

4.1   Correlation of Relative Outbound Tourism and the Social Progress Index

The data for the Social Progress Index were obtained from the Social Progress Imperative site and are related to 2014. The Web unfortunately does not provide data for the states Cyprus, Luxembourg and Malta. Thus, the correlation of the EU states was done without their influence. Data for the relative outbound tourism were drawn from Eurostat and then they were processed by authors (Table 3).

As can be seen from the correlation result, the coefficient denotes direct linear dependence and reached the value of 0.69. According to theoretical rules, this shows a strong dependence. In addition, the SPI indicator achieved the second highest correlation rate of all composite indicators examined.

Table 3. Construction of the Quality of Life Index and Sustainable Development.

Human rights, freedom. Equality	Demographic indicators and life expectancy	Health status and health care	Education, *technology and information*	Economic Development and Foreign Debt	Consumption of resources and ecological efficiency	Quality of the environment
Politics and human rights	Demographic indicators	Health care	Education	Economy	Economy - net domestic savings	Environment - natural resources, land use
Equality	Life expectancy, mortality	Diseases and Nutrition	*Technology and information sharing*	Indebtedness	Economy - Consumption of resources	Environment - problems of cities and rural landscape

Source: [15]

- Thus, it can be interpreted that with the increasing Social progress Index of individual EU countries, the number of people traveling abroad also increases.
- Based on the composition of the index, it is also possible to state that the number of trips is related to the quality of basic human needs, well-being and the opportunities of the population.

Table 4 shows that the top level of the Social Progress Index in the EU countries was reached by the Northern countries in the order of Sweden, Finland and Denmark.

Table 4. Correlation of relative outbound tourism with the Social Progress Index.

Country	Relative outbound tourism	SPI	Country	Relative outbound tourism	SPI
Austria	2,64141646	85,11	Ireland	2,586063379	84,05
Belgium	1,16309194	82,63	Italy	0,904744585	73,93
Bulgaria	0,520833751	70,24	Latvia	2,308240545	73,91
Croatia	1,924605662	73,31	Lithuania	1,505686265	73,76
Cyprus	2,907724432		Luxembourg	3,357062686	
Czech Republic	3,109905016	80,41	Malta	1,199364198	
Denmark	5,63962351	86,55	Netherlands	2,512258005	87,37
Estonia	3,038291812	81,28	Poland	1,279130596	77,44
Finland	6,898412248	86,91	Portugal	1,405518987	80,49
France	3,433958429	81,11	Romania	0,87621287	67,72
Germany	2,933234972	84,61	Slovakia	1,30416196	78,93
Great Britain	2,477244213	84,56	Slovenia	2,198127086	81,65
Greece	0,57971176	73,43	Spain	2,75053499	80,77
Hungary	1,753224974	73,87	Sweden	4,039785131	87,08
Correlation		0,6885			

Source: [17]

Of the remaining countries, Austria was best placed. The last places were occupied by Romania and Bulgaria. Before them there were Croatia, Greece, Lithuania, Hungary and Latvia ranked within one point.

4.2   Correlation of Relative Outbound Tourism and the Wellbeing Index

Data for Wellbeing Index for all EU countries were drawn from The Wellbeing of Nations book [18]. The data are from 1996–1999. Newer data could not be retrieved. The data for the relative outbound tourism refer to 2014. The data were processed by authors who used the data on the Eurostat website [19].

The final value of the correlation coefficient is 0.56. According to the theory, it shows the direct linear moderate dependence.

- It can be interpreted that the growing number of Wellbeing in individual EU countries corresponds to growing number of people traveling abroad.
- On the other hand, the resulting value of the correlation rate belongs to the lowest ones among the all 14 analyzed indicators.

As for the results, Sweden reached the very top; it was followed by Finland, Austria occupied the third highest position. The worst Wellbeing Index among the EU countries had Romania, but Malta with France with the same score got only one place better (Table 5).

Table 5. Correlation of the relative outbound tourism with the Wellbeing Index.

	Relative outbund tourism	WI	HWI		Relative outbund tourism	WI	HWI
Austria	2,64141646	61	80	Ireland	2,586063379	54	76
Belgium	1,16309194	51,5	80	Italy	0,904744585	52	74
Bulgaria	0,520833751	44,5	58	Latvia	2,308240545	54	62
Croatia	1,924605662	45	57	Lithuania	1,505686265	52,5	61
Cyprus	2,907724432	52,5	67	Luxembourg	3,357062686	50,5	77
Czech Republic	3,109905016	51,5	70	Malta	1,199364198	42	70
Denmark	5,63962351	56	81	Netherlands	2,512258005	50	78
Estonia	3,038291812	48	62	Poland	1,279130596	47,5	65
Finland	6,898412248	62,4	81	Portugal	1,405518987	51,5	72
France	3,433958429	42	75	Romania	0,87621287	40	50
Germany	2,933234972	56,5	77	Slovakia	1,30416196	50,5	61
Great Britain	2,477244213	51,5	73	Slovenia	2,198127086	53	71
Greece	0,57971176	51,5	70	Spain	2,75053499	46,5	73
Hungary	1,753224974	49	66	Sweden	4,039785131	64	79
Correlation		0,5591	0,5602				

Source: Own processing based on data drawn from PRESCOTT-ALLEN [20]

4.3   Correlation of Relative Outbound Tourism with the Index of Quality of Life and Sustainable Development

Data for the Sustainable Development index for all EU countries were obtained from the Quality of Life and Sustainable Development Indicators. Data are from 1998–2001. Since then, the SD index has not been re-evaluated. The relative outbound tourism data related to 2014 were processed by the authors and were based on data from Eurostat. [19]

The final value of the correlation coefficient value is 0.68. According to the theory, it shows direct strong linear dependence. In addition, the final correlation value is one of the highest among the indicators presented.

- It can be interpreted that with the rising Sustainable Development Index of individual EU countries the number of people traveling abroad also increases.
- Based on the SD index track, it can be deduced that the outbound tourism of the given country will increase with the increasing quality of its environment, with greater eco-efficiency, economic development, better healthcare and health state of its population, with access to education, technology and information, with a longer life expectancy and with freedom and equality of the population.

The results of the index came first in Sweden, followed by Finland and Luxembourg was the third highest. The worst Sustainable development index among the EU states gained Bulgaria, before Bulgaria only one place better was Romania trying to overtake Croatia and Poland [21].

5   Discussion, Limitations and Future Research

The outputs, here presented findings are limited by the composition of each composite indicator. Each of the three selected composite indicators encompasses in itself a kind of advanced technology. Given that the indicators are complex, technologies and their use play only a partial role in them. The key phenomenon in the issue of SMART cities is and will be the Internet. Another area that might be of interest for the future research is, for example, the idea to link the research with the use of online banking, online purchase or some other activity connected to the use of Internet or IT. Gained data could be processed via other statistical methods. As for the future, it would be certainly interesting to correlate data of the outbound tourism which are not counted on the population with the composite indicators of sustainable development and compare the results with the correlation of the outbound tourism and GDP. In the further research, it would be appropriate to work with the data of all EU countries (Table 6).

Table 6. Correlation of relative outbound tourism with the Sustainable Development index.

Country	Relative outbound tourism	SD index	Country	Relative outbound tourism	SD index
Austria	2,64141646	0,847	Ireland	2,586063379	0,855
Belgium	1,16309194	0,826	Italy	0,904744585	0,803
Bulgaria	0,520833751	0,663	Latvia	2,308240545	0,758
Croatia	1,924605662	0,714	Lithuania	1,505686265	0,74
Cyprus	2,907724432	0,79	Luxembourg	3,357062686	0,873
Czech Republic	3,109905016	0,763	Malta	1,199364198	0,793
Denmark	5,63962351	0,858	Netherlands	2,512258005	0,848
Estonia	3,038291812	0,782	Poland	1,279130596	0,725
Finland	6,898412248	0,882	Portugal	1,405518987	0,781
France	3,433958429	0,832	Romania	0,87621287	0,678
Germany	2,933234972	0,843	Slovakia	1,30416196	0,783
Great Britain	2,477244213	0,817	Slovenia	2,198127086	0,824
Greece	0,57971176	0.755	Spain	2,75053499	0,821
Hungary	1,753224974	0,773	Sweden	4,039785131	0,885
Correlation		0,67787			

Source: Custom processing based on data from [15]

6   Conclusion

Predominately northern countries like Denmark, Finland and Sweden achieved the best results in individual Sustainable Development Indicators. This reflects their complex maturity, high quality of life and good sustainable development. Romania and Bulgaria mostly gained the worst ranking; these countries should aim at improvement of their economic, social and environmental situation.

The analysis was performed using the Pearson correlation coefficient. The highest correlation between outbound tourism and three analyzed indices was reached by the Social Progress Index, closely followed by the Index of Quality of Life and Sustainable Development. In both cases it is possible to speak about strong dependence. The Human Wellbeing Index as the last analyzed index reached medium dependence but if it reached just a few tenths more we could also speak about strong dependence.

The ideal situation would be if the data were available for the current year or the previous year. However, such an ideal situation is likely to remain only a pious desire.

Acknowledgement. This paper is supported by internal grant No. 1907/2017 "Transformation of knowledge from the field of kinanthropology into geography and tourism" at Faculty of Informatics and Management, University of Hradec Kralove, Czech Republic.

References

1. Handbook on construction of composite indicators – Methodology and User´s Guide. OECD (2004). http://www.oecd.org/std/42495745.pdf
2. Hák, T.: Indikátory blahobytu: všechno, co jste kdy chtěli vědět o štěstí (ale báli jste se zeptat) Praha 2010, pp. 10–19 (2010). http://www.zelenykruh.cz/o-nas/publikace/edice-apel
3. Skalská, H.: Aplikovaná statistika. Gaudeamus, Hradec Králové (2013)
4. Multivariable Methods (2013). http://sphweb.bumc.bu.edu/otlt/mph-modules/bs/bs704_multivariable/bs704_multivariable5.html
5. Crossman, A.: Understanding Correlation Analysis (2016). https://www.thoughtco.com/what-is-correlation-analysis-3026696
6. Litschmannová, M.: Úvod do statistiky: interaktivní učební text. In: MI21: Matematika pro inženýry 21. Století (2012)
7. Hudecová, Š.: Matematická statistika. In: Matematická sekce: Matematicko-fyzikální fakulta Univerzita Karlova v Praze (2012). http://www.karlin.mff.cuni.cz/~hudecova/education/archive11/download/chem_predn/predn_slides_05.pdf
8. Wikipedia. List of countries by Social Progress Index. In: Wikipedia: the free encyclopedia. San Francisco, CA, Wikimedia Foundation (2015). https://en.wikipedia.org/wiki/List_of_countries_by_Social_Progress_Index
9. Bishop, M.: Social progress: Beyond GDP. In: The Economist (2013). http://www.economist.com/blogs/feastandfamine/2013/04/social-progress
10. Social progress imperative: Social Progress Indexes: A new way to define what it means to be a successful community. In: Social Progress Imperative (2016). http://www.socialprogressimperative.org/social-progress-indexes/
11. Social progress imperative: Social Progress Indexes: Methodological report (2016). http://www.socialprogressimperative.org/wp-content/uploads/2016/07/SPI-2016-Methodological-Report.pdf
12. Social progress imperative: Findings. In: Social Progress Imperative (2016). http://www.socialprogressimperative.org/findings/
13. Social progress imperative: Frequently Asked Questions. In: Social Progress Imperative (2016). http://www.socialprogressimperative.org/faqs/
14. The Wellbeing of Nations at a Glance. In: International Union for Conservation of Nature (2016). http://cmsdata.iucn.org/downloads/wonback.pdf
15. Nováček, P.: Udržitelný rozvoj, 2nd edn. Univerzita Palackého v Olomouci, Olomouc (2012)
16. Viturka, M.: Regionální hodnocení kvality sociálního prostředí – případová studie české republiky. In: XVI.mezinárodní kolokvium o regionálních vědách. Valtice, pp. 65–71 (2013)
17. Porter, M., Stern, S., Green, M.: Social progress index (2016). http://www.socialprogressimperative.org/wp-content/uploads/2016/06/SPI-2016-Main-Report.pdf
18. The Wellbeing of Nations at a Glance. 2016. In: International Union for Conservation of Nature (2016). http://cmsdata.iucn.org/downloads/wonback.pdf
19. Tourism Eurostat (2016). http://ec.europa.eu/eurostat/web/tourism/data
20. Prescott-Allen, R.: The wellbeing of nations: a country-by-country index of quality of life and the environment Washington. Island Press, International Development Research Centre, Ottawa (2001)
21. Šimková, J.: Correlation of sustainable development indicators with outbound tourism in countries of the European Union, Bachelor thesis, University of Hradec Králové, Faculty of Informatics and Management (2016)
22. Duran, J., Perez, V.: Smart, innovative and sustainable cities for the future income: caracas city. In: 35th IEEE Central American and Panama Convention. IEEE, Honduras (2015)

Analytics for Smart Governance

Exploring Content Virality in Facebook:
A Semantic Based Approach

Reema Aswani[✉], Arpan Kumar Kar, Shalabh Aggarwal,
and P. Vigneswara Ilavarsan

Indian Institute of Technology, Delhi, India
reemaswani@gmail.com

Abstract. In the current era of digitization specifically with the advent of Web 2.0, social media has become an imposing force in shaping up the way people perceive and react to the information around them. Social media platforms have empowered people to share almost instant feedback on the content posted by individuals and organizations facilitating two way interaction and better engagement among them. This continuous interaction among individuals and organizations creates huge amount of user-generated content (UGC) and associated tokens. This study attempts to understand various semantics that might affect the virality of Facebook posts. Several pages have been identified and shortlisted from domains including e-commerce, manufacturing, services and media. A total of 53,340 Facebook posts comprising of 37, 38, 168 words have been extracted using Facebook Graph API from each of the mentioned domains and subsequently analyzed using NOSQL databases. Further, the derived tokens are semantically grouped and used to gather insights by mapping to existing virality frameworks for identifying and ranking the ones that might be affecting the virality of a post. Findings indicate the virality of content shared has positive correlation with direct brand engagement, promotional offers, freebies and direct user mentions.

Keywords: Social media · Information propagation · Content virality · Semantic analysis · Facebook analytics

1 Introduction

Today, in the digital world circling around social media with recent advancements in web 2.0, the ways and means of marketing and promoting content are concentrated completely around how certain content becomes popular and subsequently "viral" [1, 2]. In other words, making sure that the shared content reaches out to as many people as possible and subsequently attracts user attention in the form of likes, comments and shares. Social media comprises of wide variety of platforms to enable users to engage with each other, dominant platforms include Facebook, Twitter, LinkedIn, Google, YouTube, etc. In terms of traffic, Facebook is the most popular website, as given by its Alexa ranking in April 2017. With the widespread use of social media specifically Facebook, the generic verb "Facebooking" has become prevalent and is often used to describe the process of browsing profiles of oneself and others [3, 4]. Within a span of

© IFIP International Federation for Information Processing 2017
Published by Springer International Publishing AG 2017. All Rights Reserved
A.K. Kar et al. (Eds.): I3E 2017, LNCS 10595, pp. 209–220, 2017.
DOI: 10.1007/978-3-319-68557-1_19

10 years, Facebook's active user base grew to more than 1 Billion users which is around 1/7th of the planet's population. This vast user base makes Facebook a very attractive marketing platform for marketers across the globe. Facebook is used by people across all age groups in most of the geographies and this makes the platform much more important than other social platforms. With time, it has grown to provide a lot more features and services that enable different media type; be it text, images, audio or video to be shared and promoted amongst current and potential consumers [5]. This rampant growth of interactive social media platforms like Facebook has not only benefited individuals for better communication and engagement but has also attracted the attention of organizations, public figures, news portals and e-commerce portals [6–8]. With the huge user base Facebook commands, it has become an important and cost effective tool for various organizations to introduce, promote, market, collect feedback about, the products and services, while engaging with the consumers in the virtual world [9].

These organizations and web portals have started leveraging the immense power of these platforms to maximize their visibility and customer outreach [10–12]. This has led to a widely used concept of 'viral marketing' that was first coined in 1997 to describe Hotmail's idea of promotion by inserting advertisements about its free email service in the end of users' outgoing emails [13]. In last two decades, virality of online content has gone through multiple transformations and different scholars have different views about the same but the basic premise remains the same where "virality" means that certain content has reached a good number of people and is being talked about. There are several factors that affect popularity of individuals and organizations on these social media platforms [14, 15].

Companies often create online ad campaigns and encourage UGC with discussions on social media anticipating that the content would be shared among others leading to popularity [16]. However, this does not happen always and some of these promotion efforts fail miserably and are not able to attract user attention. This makes us wonder whether virality is just random or are there specific characteristics that govern whether the content will be highly propagated and shared [17]. Facebook defines 'virality' as the percentage of people creating a story from a certain page post out of the total number of unique people who have actually seen the post. This becomes a good indicator of virality from the perspective of Facebook and can be very effectively explained in terms of likes, comments and shares a page post receives. The more the number of likes, comments and/or shares a post receives, the more popular or viral the post may be considered.

This study thus uses 53,340 publically available posts from Facebook (comprising of 37, 38, 168 words) from different industry domains with an aim to identify drivers of content virality [18]. Certain set of pages are selected from each domain where each page is exceptionally popular in its respective domain and has large number of followers. This study will thus prove to be beneficial in identifying various semantics that make a post in a certain domain popular or viral among the targeted audience. None of the existing studies explore content virality using a semantic token based approach with a focus on what tokens present in a post are likely to make the post go viral. The possible reasons of lack of such studies aiming at content virality semantics may be limited application scope in traditional marketing from social media, limited dataset availability and scope of focus.

However, plethora of semantic analysis contributes towards causing the posts to be concealed from the target audience. Actual empirical data analysis will point to practical semantics and can be good pointer for marketers in planning their promotional content. Throughout the study, we also outline the data collection techniques which allow to get substantial data from an otherwise closed and restricted ecosystem of Facebook.

2 Literature Review

Literature highlights the emerging importance of social media in the current age of digitization [19]. Social media enables sharing and promotion of content on variety of topics including politics, technology, business, media and e-commerce to name a few [20, 21]. Studies also explore social media's business value and discussions surrounding selection process for selecting a platform for content promotion [22]. The impact of content shared amongst the users increases even more if the content becomes popular or goes viral. Several studies in literature highlight insights in social media marketing and content virality. Some of the studies focus on a single social media platform for the analysis of virality while others take into consideration multiple platforms and domains for the understanding of viral marketing [1]. Facebook has had its own large share of studies that have been conducted since its successful inception around a decade back. The growing sophistication of social media has opened new avenues for advertisers and marketers. This has resulted in a quest for reliable metrics to quantify the effectiveness of online messages [23]. Virality is thus considered as a combination of viral reach, effective evaluation, and message deliberation.

Social networks have become a great source of sharing opinions, ideas, information and beliefs [24]. With the availability of huge amount of data, the analysis of information diffusion has become an interesting area to explore [25]. Virality has thus become an indicator of online ad effectiveness [26]. Literature highlights several user behavior characteristics that greatly affect the popularity and subsequent virality of content [27–29]. The virality aspect includes posts [17, 30, 31], links and images/memes [32–36] that get popular.

Studies further focus on analysis of social posts and messages on popular social media platforms. However, only a couple of them focus on engagement metrics while others mostly deal with the communication aspects of the social media posts. Metrics surrounding virality on social platforms focus on analyzing buzz, appreciation, content traction and controversy [30]. Further, network structures and community metrics [37] also play a vital role in popularity and virality of content [38]. Studies demonstrate the importance of network retweets, follower networks and homophily when social contagions is spread [24]. Besides these, SPIN Framework [31] demonstrates the four metrics for viral content categorization as spreadability, propagativity, integration and nexus. Coursaris et al. [39] highlight how consumer engagement may be strategized using brand Facebook page messages. However, no study in literature focuses on the semantics derived from the UGC that enables brands to identify drivers of to content virality using Facebook brand pages. There are no discussions that explore the linkage between the motivation to propagate and the virality of the content. This study thus attempts to identify content semantics for four selected domains using Facebook brand pages under the listed categories. These semantics are known to attract user attention when present in the shared content.

3 Research Methodology

This study uses a tokenization-based approach for mining semantics from the public content available on Facebook pages under four broad domains of e-commerce, manufacturing, media and services. A set of popular pages have been identified for each domain for the purpose of data extraction. Further, a semantic token-based approach is adopted to capture top 10 topics that apparently gain traction when it comes to popularity of content on the platform. We detail these activities in the subsequent subsections:

3.1 Domain and Page Selection

In order to understand virality semantics on a broader level, it would be unjust to single out a domain resulting in nullification of generalizability of the findings. The study thus considers four broad domains for the analysis are e-commerce, manufacturing, media and services. The domains selected are strictly business domains that deal with customer engagement on a regular basis. From each of the selected domains, Facebook pages of a list of dominant firms are identified and subsequently analyzed. The minimum criteria considered for page selection for the relevant domains is a minimum of 100,000 fans per followers. Considering multiple pages provides a deeper look at the content that is promoted and shared helping in an in depth analysis and comparison. A total of 53,340 posts have been considered for the analysis. Table 1 lists all the pages considered for analysis of virality per domain with number of followers/fans and number of pages per post.

The number of followers of each page is very dynamic and changes at a very significant rate. The count provided above is recorded at the time of data collection. The data collection for the pages selected from every domain is conducted using Facebook's Graph API which is the primary way to extract data out of Facebook's platform. This HTTP-based API can be used for querying data, posting stories, managing advertisements, uploading photos and a variety of other tasks that are an essential part of any application. For the scope of this study, only the data query and read aspects of the API are used. Certain pre-requisites and conditions are considered while extracting the relevant data including a unique follower/fans threshold of 1,00,000, a minimum of 140 characters of textual content and availability of posts for more than a year at least. A python script is used to collect the data. Table 2 describes the attributes collected for each post including the domain name, page name, the actual content, likes, shares and comments. Post analysis an inference column is appended depending on the semantic analysis for popularity of the content.

Computation of "inference" is done with the underlying consideration that the data collected for each post has associated count of likes, shares and comments for it. From a manual analysis of the sorted posts data, it is evident that the number of likes and

Table 1. Data description of selected pages in each domain.

Domain	Page	Followers/Fans	Number of posts
E-Commerce	Amazon	26,653,543	6122
	AmazonIN	5,213,009	2127
	Flipkart	5,429,434	2083
	Myntra	3,166,625	1758
	Shopclues	2,708,682	2738
	Snapdeal	3,964,189	1978
	Total		16806
Manufacturing	Honda	4,061,973	2905
	Toyota	2,814,599	3474
	Ford	3,432,091	3625
	HeroMotoCorp	1,756, 770	935
	TVS Motor Company	242,078	1168
	Total		12,107
Media	channelvindia	5,644,539	3383
	MTV	48,397,370	4248
	MTV India	11,600,934	2345
	TEDxEvents	1,415,214	1120
	Yahoo	13,726,619	1723
	ScoopWhoop	3,355,158	2378
	Total		15,197
Services	AmericanExpressIndia	6,243,134	934
	amazonwebservices	140,340	1156
	FacebookIndia	170,811,531	1357
	Google	19,656,574	625
	LinkedIn	1,121,976	924
	oyorooms	330,918	2395
	TataConsultancyServices	537,169	1839
	Total		9230

shares and comments are mostly directly proportional to each other, i.e., as the number of likes increase, the number of shares increase and so the number of comment. It is hence safe to assume that we can rest our inference based on likes on the post. Exceptions occurring do not have an effect on the overall results due to minimal frequency. Further, for the purpose of this study if the number of likes on any post is greater than 1000 (which is 0.1% of our lower limit criteria for the number of likes any page should have), then the post is tagged as "viral". Similarly, if the number of likes is more than 100 then, the post is considered as "popular" (it may become viral over a period). In case that does not happen, the post seems to have been "ignored" by the fans/followers of the page.

Table 2. Description of attributes collected Facebook posts.

Field name	Description
Domain	Predefined value out of E-Commerce, Media, Manufacturing and Services
Page name/ID	Name/ID of the Facebook page for which the data is being collected, example: Amazon, MTV, Honda etc.
Post message	Actual complete content of concerned post
Number of likes	Total number of likes for the concerned post
Number of shares	The total number of shares for the concerned post
Number of comments	The total number of comments on the concerned post
Inference	A computed value that specifies whether the post is "viral", "popular" or "ignored"

3.2   Data Cleaning and Token Generation

The collected data (37, 38, 168 words from 53,340 posts) comprising of UGC from various pages grouped under different domains is further analyzed for identification tokens that primarily affect the virality of the post. The NOSQL database (here MongoDB) facilitates a quick read and write of the volume and structure of the data being handled. Python's inbuilt NLTK (Natural Language Toolkit) library tokenizes the post messages based on words. The number of token words for each post depends on the length of the post message. An initial cleaning process eliminates all tokens with length less than 3 characters including common words like 'is', 'if', 'in' and 'an' to name a few. The frequency for final tokens is computed and a semantic token map is created. Individual frequencies of "viral", "popular" and "ignored" posts are computed for the pages in every domain. Further, semantic ranking based on their relevance is captured by considering the following short listing criteria:

1. Remove the tokens (words) with relatively high "ignored" count. Their count in other two frequencies can also be high but a higher ignored count suggests that this is a commonly used word as the number of ignored posts was much higher than the other two combined.
2. Shortlist top 10 tokens to be rated if:
   The viral count is more than 100; or
   The popular count is more than 500.
3. The criteria for ranking the top 10 is a weight based approach:
   For each count of viral frequency, a weight of 1 is given;
   For each count of popular frequency, a weight of 0.25 is given;
   For each count of ignored frequency, a weight of −0.1 is given.

Figure 1. demonstrates the top 10 tokens for every domain with their respective weights have been shortlisted. The weights for similar tokens may vary across domains as the number of posts collected pertaining to it across domains also vary. On the other hand, Fig. 2. depicts a wordcloud of the popular discussions in each of the domain.

E-Commerce Token	Frequency Ignored	Frequency Popular	Frequency Viral	Weight
http	3625	4032	2230	2875.50
win	314	569	526	636.85
comment	97	187	479	516.05
see	792	362	450	461.30
ends	44	199	412	457.35
here	1579	854	375	430.60
rules	69	170	394	429.60
official	97	161	395	425.55
chance	238	375	352	421.95
deal	717	512	271	327.30

Media Tokens	Frequency Ignored	Frequency Popular	Frequency Viral	Weight
you	820	2080	349	787
for	797	1180	196	411.30
your	363	1031	138	359.45
with	331	776	151	311.90
http	601	827	158	304.65
this	321	651	158	288.65
channel	163	603	67	201.45
here	382	598	70	181.30
her	88	299	101	166.95
image	3	119	114	143.45

Manufacturing Token	Frequency Ignored	Frequency Popular	Frequency Viral	Weight
http	2722	3490	1277	1877.30
ford	978	266	423	391.70
fans	89	391	287	375.85
show	475	566	254	348
honda	1135	390	353	337
mustang	538	334	243	272.70
our	486	236	244	254.40
toyota	788	467	190	227.95
racing	660	546	127	197.50
see	773	326	165	169.20

Services Tokens	Frequency Ignored	Frequency Popular	Frequency Viral	Weight
http	3177	2677	1270	1621.55
your	1720	591	398	373.75
search	321	626	231	355.4
facebook	40	171	258	296.75
tcs	798	361	213	223.45
google	6	339	115	199.15
new	504	216	189	192.6
digital	260	354	127	189.5
linkedin	287	134	167	171.8
india	187	146	104	121.8

Fig. 1. Domain - wise token identification.

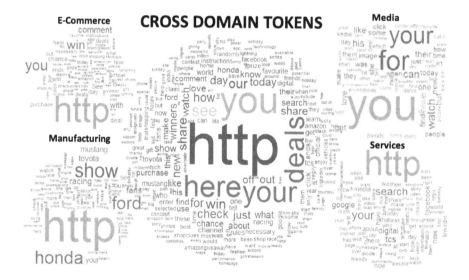

Fig. 2. Wordcloud for domain-wise and cross-domain tokens.

3.3 Cross-Domain Semantic Analysis

Post semantic analysis for each domain, the identification of top tokens across all domains is done. The subsequent discussions analyze the relevance and impact of the top cross-domain semantics. Further, each token is analyzed using the SPIN Framework [31] to identify the impact of various parameters and how concepts of virality map to the same. The framework introduces four key factors for viral campaigns: spreadability, propagativity, integration and nexus. The metrics relevant to this study are subsequently mapped to the identified tokens. In context with Facebook only spreadability comes into picture, since a single social media platform is considered (negating the relevance of integration) having a low cycle time (just a few clicks to share/like), high network size (limited by security features though), high level of content richness (allows multiple type of content amalgamation) and good content proximity (the options to share/like are visible very near to actual content that negates the need of considering propagativity. Further, the lack of enough data due to Facebook's security and privacy settings limits us for not considering nexus considers causal effect to future campaigns. Thus, spreadability is captured in the context of this study referring to the ability of the content of the message to appeal to the consumer in some way and prompt/motivate the consumer to take action on the same. Spreadability comprises of both likeability and shareability:

Likeability refers to the willingness of a consumer to use the content. This is often influenced by the degree to which the consumer finds the message stimulating and engaging.

Shareability is the willingness of the consumer to distribute the content. This is influenced the degree to which the consumer thinks that the content will impact others in their network as well.

From the analysis of the extracted data, it is evident that the shares of a post are directly proportional to the number of likes on a post. Further, Facebook specific findings in literature have emphasized consumers' expressing greater intentions to like a post and then subsequently sharing and commenting on it. This premise further strengthens the basis of the empirical data analysis that has been undertaken in this study of considering likeability as the primary metric of analysis [23].

Hence, an analysis on the basis of likeability may be a good indicator of shareability as well. Further, the identified tokens are semantically categorized into groups with their associated likeability. Table 3 demonstrates a list of semantics into which these token are grouped and captured across domains with their associated likeability ratings and a brief description as to why these semantics have an impact on virality.

It is evident from the likeability ratings of the cross-domain semantics that the posts containing URLs are most liked and shared by the users on social media indicating that http links have a "high" likeability rating. Further, the posts containing popular brand names like ford, honda, toyota, mustang, google, facebook, linkedin and tcs to name a few in our study also manage to get user attention and subsequent popularity. In addition to this, high content likeability is seen when the users are directly addressed and engaged by using words like "you/your" and offered promotional deals, offers, chances to win something. Besides these, posts offering something by using tokens like "here/this", reference to current content, explicit mention of sharing, promoting and commenting and images in posts also gain some traction. Further, call to action words like "comment/share/like" also explicitly motivate users to propagate the content. The remaining content seems to have "low" likeability rating and thus is unlikely to be shared and propagated among the user social networks.

Table 3. List of cross-domain semantics and associated likeability rating.

Semantics	Likeability	Description
Links	High	Posts which contain links get more attention
Brand name	High	Posts which include the brand name give a feeling of inclusion to the consumer
See/show/check/know/watch	High	Posts which prompt the consumer to go ahead and see something more, point to an interesting content ahead
Your/you	High	Addressing the consumer directly tend to get more engagement.
Win/chance/deal/ends/claim/prize	High	Engage the consumers by telling them that they can win something by liking this content/post.
Here/this	Medium	Such posts might be offering a good deal to the consumer on the current page itself.
Call to action	Medium	Prompting the consumers explicitly to share or comment on the post might trigger the action.
Image	Medium	Posts containing images get more attention in a limited time span as compared to textual content

4 Conclusion

Social media platforms specifically have gained immense popularity not just for communication among individuals but also as a two-way interactive platform for online marketing and content promotion. In this era of digitization, the target of each marketer is now to produce content that gets as much attention as possible. These firms not only want their content to be consumed but also shared and propagated in the consumers' respective social networks for greater popularity and outreach. The popularity of content not only depends on its inherent value or usefulness of the information but also several other factors as discussed in literature including network dynamics, nature of propagators, user behavior and lastly the content semantics as discussed in this study.

In this study, a total of around 53,340 Facebook posts' comprising of 37,38,168 words from various domains is captured and analyzed to form tokens and subsequently rank relevant semantics associated with it that might affect the virality of the post. The domains under consideration comprise of e-commerce, media, manufacturing and services. Each domain has its own way of attracting consumers based on the content shared by them. Further, the consumers of each domain may not necessarily be interested in similar content and thus the analysis generates different set of tokens for each domain depending on the traction of the content among the consumers. A total of top 10 semantics (in the form of word tokens) are further shortlisted from each domain with assigned weight metrics depending on whether the content is tagged as "popular", "viral" or "ignored". A cross-domain semantic analysis is subsequently done by mapping the metrics to the SPIN framework to explore whether the identified semantics belong to multiple domains. Facebook specific findings in literature have emphasized consumers' expressing greater intentions to like a post, followed by sharing and commenting on it. This premise further strengthens the basis of the empirical data analysis that has been undertaken in this study of considering likeability as the primary metric of analysis.

The results indicate that posts that have more to offer to the consumer than just a simple text get more traction and have a higher likeability among the consumers. This "more" content may be in the form of web URL links or images or simple direct referencing to the content or the user in person. Also, it is seen that when the brand engages itself directly in the post via its name, then the probability of the content getting viral increases. This is indicative of the trust factor that the brand brings with itself and promotes engagement within the consumers. Findings also indicate that virality further depends on factors like explicitly telling people to like/comment/share a post or by providing lucrative offers to the consumers about discounts, deals, freebies etc., especially for a limited time. Hence, it is seen that virality over social media, specifically Facebook, is a broad area of study and one cannot be always sure whether the content will get the desired popularity and subsequent virality but a few semantic based incorporations in the content may attract significant user attention.

5   Implications and Future Scope

This study is an empirical study for identifying semantics that may have an effect on virality of Facebook posts. A number of semantics are identified and ranked as using the data collected from 53,340 posts comprising of 37,38,168 words across four prominent business domains. This study also brings out potential linkage between motivation and virality metrics/semantics. Previous literature also focuses largely psychographics primarily personality dimensions of users. However, there are no discussions that highlight the motivation behind users' propagating the content resulting into popularity and subsequently virality on the social networks. Thus, motivation is an important and interesting topic of research in the domain of social media virality. This study thus highlights the motivation for content shareability from Facebook posts that became popular and subsequently viral using empirical and factual metrics.

Future studies may focus on combining user related metrics like age groups, user reputation, demographics, etc. along with their user behavior characteristics, usage and consumption patterns. Further this may subsequently be used for improvising the understanding of how virality can be impacted by fine tuning the content to get best results. Future work may also focus more on improvised semantic analysis to correlate motivation and virality aspects. This may be done by considering network specific metrics like centrality, betweenness, cliques, reciprocity and propinquity to name a few. Network analytics may be beneficial in providing useful insights surrounding causality of drivers for content shareability and virality.

References

1. Leskovec, J., Adamic, L.A., Huberman, B.A.: The dynamics of viral marketing. ACM Trans. Web (TWEB) **1**(1), 5 (2007)
2. Mangold, W.G., Faulds, D.J.: Social media: the new hybrid element of the promotion mix. Bus. Horiz. **52**(4), 357–365 (2009)
3. Facebooking, the rage on college campuses. The Seattle Times. http://www.seattletimes.com/business/facebooking-the-rage-on-college-campuses/. Accessed 31 Mar 2017
4. Junco, R.: The relationship between frequency of Facebook use, participation in Facebook activities, and student engagement. Comput. Educ. **58**(1), 162–171 (2012)
5. Lampe, C., Ellison, N.B., Steinfield, C.: Changes in use and perception of Facebook. In: Proceedings of the 2008 ACM Conference on Computer Supported Cooperative Work, pp. 721–730. ACM, San Diego (2008)
6. Hennig-Thurau, T., Gwinner, K.P., Walsh, G., Gremler, D.D.: Electronic word-of-mouth via consumer-opinion platforms: what motivates consumers to articulate themselves on the internet? J. Interact. Mark. **18**(1), 38–52 (2004)
7. Waters, R.D., Burnett, E., Lamm, A., Lucas, J.: Engaging stakeholders through social networking: how nonprofit organizations are using Facebook. Pub. Relat. Rev. **35**(2), 102–106 (2009)
8. Hanna, R., Rohm, A., Crittenden, V.L.: We're all connected: the power of the social media ecosystem. Bus. Horiz. **54**(3), 265–273 (2011)
9. Viswanath, B., Mislove, A., Cha, M., Gummadi, K.P.: On the evolution of user interaction in facebook. In: Proceedings of the 2nd ACM Workshop on Online Social Networks, pp. 37–42. ACM, Barcelona (2009)
10. Qualman, E.: Socialnomics: How Social Media Transforms the Way We Live and Do Business. Wiley, New Jersey (2010)
11. Handayani, P.W., Lisdianingrum, W.: Impact analysis on free online marketing using social network Facebook: case study SMEs in Indonesia. In: 2011 International Conference on Advanced Computer Science and Information System (ICACSIS), pp. 171–176. IEEE, Jakarta (2011)
12. Stelzner, M.A.: Social media marketing industry report. Soc. Media Exam. **41**, 1–10 (2011)
13. Beeler, A.: Virus without a cure. Advert. Age **71**(17), 54–55 (2000)
14. Quercia, D., Lambiotte, R., Stillwell, D., Kosinski, M., Crowcroft, J.: The personality of popular facebook users. In: Proceedings of the ACM 2012 Conference on Computer Supported Cooperative Work, pp. 955–964. ACM, Seattle (2012)
15. Sabate, F., Berbegal-Mirabent, J., Cañabate, A., Lebherz, P.R.: Factors influencing popularity of branded content in Facebook fan pages. Eur. Manag. J. **32**(6), 1001–1011 (2014)
16. Berthon, P.R., Pitt, L.F., Plangger, K., Shapiro, D.: Marketing meets Web 2.0, social media, and creative consumers: implications for international marketing strategy. Bus. Horiz. **55**(3), 261–271 (2012)
17. Berger, J., Milkman, K.: Social transmission, emotion, and the virality of online content. Wharton research paper 106 (2010)
18. Berger, J., Milkman, K.L.: What makes online content viral? J. Mark. Res. **49**(2), 192–205 (2012)
19. Kaplan, A.M., Haenlein, M.: Users of the world, unite! The challenges and opportunities of Social Media. Bus. Horiz. **53**(1), 59–68 (2010)
20. Shirky, C.: The political power of social media: technology, the public sphere, and political change. Foreign Aff. **90**, 28–41 (2011)

21. Patino, A., Pitta, D.A., Quinones, R.: Social media's emerging importance in market research. J. Consum. Mark. **29**(3), 233–237 (2012)
22. Nagle, T., Pope, A.: Understanding social media business value, a prerequisite for social media selection. J. Decis. Syst. **22**(4), 283–297 (2013)
23. Alhabash, S., McAlister, A.R., Rifon, N.J., Quilliam, E.T., Sternadori, M., Richards, J.I.: A different take on virality: the relationship among motivations, uses, and viral behavioral intentions on Facebook and Twitter. In: American Academy of Advertising. Conference, Proceedings (Online), p. 24. American Academy of Advertising (2013)
24. Weng, L., Menczer, F., Ahn, Y.Y.: Virality prediction and community structure in social networks. Scientific reports 3 (2013)
25. Iribarren, J.L., Moro, E.: Affinity paths and information diffusion in social networks. Soc. Netw. **33**(2), 134–142 (2011)
26. Tucker, C.: Virality, Network Effects and Advertising (2011)
27. Centola, D.: The spread of behavior in an online social network experiment. Science **329** (5996), 1194–1197 (2010)
28. Morales, A.J., Borondo, J., Losada, J.C., Benito, R.M.: Efficiency of human activity on information spreading on Twitter. Soc. Netw. **39**, 1–11 (2014)
29. Roelens, I., Baecke, P., Benoit, D.F.: Identifying influencers in a social network: the value of real referral data. Decis. Support Syst. **91**, 25–36 (2016)
30. Guerini, M., Strapparava, C., Özbal, G.: Exploring text virality in social networks. In: Proceedings of the Fifth International AAAI Conference on Weblogs and Social Media (ICWSM 2011). AAAI Publications, Barcelona (2011)
31. Mills, A.J.: Virality in social media: the SPIN framework. J. Publ. Aff. **12**(2), 162–169 (2012)
32. Ienco, D., Bonchi, F., Castillo, C.: The meme ranking problem: maximizing microblogging virality. In: IEEE International Conference on Data Mining Workshops, pp. 328–335. IEEE, Sydney(2010)
33. Weng, L., Flammini, A., Vespignani, A., Menczer, F.: Competition among memes in a world with limited attention. Sci. Rep. **2**, 1–8 (2012)
34. Guerini, M., Staiano, J., Albanese, D.: Exploring image virality in google plus. In: International Conference on Social Computing (SocialCom), pp. 671–678. IEEE, Alexandria (2013)
35. Weng, L., Menczer, F., Ahn, Y.Y.: Predicting successful memes using network and community structure. In: Proceedings of the Eighth International AAAI Conference on Weblogs and Social Media, pp. 535–544. AAAI Publications (2014)
36. Deza, A., Parikh, D.: Understanding image virality. In: Proceedings of the IEEE Conference on Computer Vision and Pattern Recognition, pp. 1818–1826. IEEE, Boston (2015)
37. Zubcsek, P.P., Chowdhury, I., Katona, Z.: Information communities: the network structure of communication. Soc. Netw. **38**, 50–62 (2014)
38. Harrigan, N., Achananuparp, P., Lim, E.P.: Influentials, novelty, and social contagion: the viral power of average friends, close communities, and old news. Soc. Netw. **34**(4), 470–480 (2012)
39. Coursaris, C.K., Van Osch, W., Balogh, B.A.: A social media marketing typology: classifying brand facebook page messages for strategic consumer engagement. In: Proceedings of the 21st European Conference on Information Systems (ECIS), p. 46. Association for Information Systems, Utrecht (2013)

Selected Aspects in Searching for Health Information on the Internet Among Generation Y

Petra Maresova[✉] and Blanka Klimova

Faculty of Informatics and Management, University of Hradec Kralove,
Hradec Kralove, Czech Republic
petra.maresova@uhk.cz

Abstract. Good health conditions are very important for quality of life not only for an individual but for the whole society. Many people try to do their best in order to be fit, others do not care. Currently, people also try to use the Internet to find the information about health they need. In fact, the information about health is the third most searched information on the Internet after goods and services and travelling information. The purpose of this study is to analyze selected aspects of the search for health information on the Internet and verify dependence between sex, health condition and family relationships with respect to healthcare in the search of health information on the Internet. The methods used in this study include an online survey in form of a questionnaire. The target research group are people aged 20–35 who are the so-called digitally literate generation. The survey was conducted from 29 November 2015 till 29 February 2016 and involved 120 respondents in the selected age group. The findings confirm that the dependence between the search for health information on the Internet and sex, the existence of chronic disease, and the psychic disorder and preference of the Internet advice was proved.

Keywords: Generation Y · Information · Internet · Search · Benefits · Limitations

1 Introduction

Modern technologies penetrate in many areas of human activities and health is not an exception [1, 2]. People also try to use the Internet to find the information about health they need. In fact, the use of the Internet in the European Union (EU) countries reaches 78% among people aged 16–74 years [3]. The use of the Internet for different purposes differs among its users in many aspects. The majority of researchers state that the gender gap in Internet use has considerably narrowed with the university age group [4], as well as with the general population [5]. Nevertheless, some gender differences have been discovered with respect to technology, intensity of the Internet use, online applications and experience in cyberspace. In addition, research shows that technologies are not used in similar ways by men and women [16]. Furthermore, Zhang [7] presents that female

The original version of this chapter was revised: An incorrect grant number was published in the acknowledgement. This has been corrected. The correction to this chapter is available at https://doi.org/10.1007/978-3-319-68557-1_46

A. K. Kar et al. (Eds.): I3E 2017, LNCS 10595, pp. 221–226, 2017.
https://doi.org/10.1007/978-3-319-68557-1_20

university students have more positive attitudes towards its use than male students. Trifonova et al. [6] add that men seem to like to try out new things in comparison with women. Gender differences can be also seen in the use of web applications. Fox [8] shows that one in four internet users who suffers from a chronic disease such as high blood pressure, diabetes, heart conditions, lung conditions, cancer, or some other chronic ailment (23%) has accessed the Internet to find others with a similar health problem. On the contrary, 15% of the Internet users who report no chronic conditions have sought such help online.

The information described above shows that there are several dependences which can be researched. Thus, the purpose of this study is to analyze selected aspects of the search for health information on the Internet and verify dependence between sex, health condition and family relationships with respect to healthcare in the search of health information on the Internet.

2   Used Methods and Tools

The sample of the respondents include people aged 20–35 years since this group of people should have an influence on future development of different fields. It is also considered to be generation Y in dependence on the year when they were born, usually around the year of 1980. In addition, these are people who are digital natives and are used to exploiting the Internet information on a daily basis. Altogether 200 respondents participated in the questionnaire survey. Nevertheless, the selected group of the Y generation respondents comprised only 120 people. The questionnaire survey consisted of 22 questions that were divided into three main areas: demographic data of the whole sample (i.e. age, sex, employment and education); respondents´ state of health; and the use of the Internet, especially for health purposes. However, only the most important results are presented in this study due to its limited scope. The questionnaire was distributed via click4survey in the course of three months, from 29 November 2015 till 29 February 2016. 51% of the respondents completed the secondary school education with school leaving exam (51%) and 41% of the respondents had a university education degree. Most of them were already employed (57%). Just a small percentage of people (3%) either studied medical field or worked in it, which did not really have any significant impact on the survey.

3   Health Information on the Internet Among Generation Y

The results of this study show that the search for the health information on the Internet comes fourth because young generation like to search for fun as well (Fig. 1).

As Fig. 2 below illustrates, people are quite interested in searching for the information about alternative medicine, which is most likely connected with following the right lifestyle and trying out something new. People also search for the information about different types of allergies, and psychic problems.

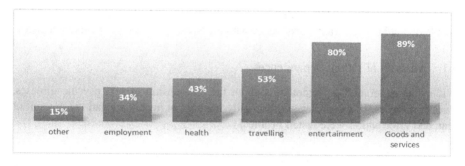

Fig. 1. An overview of the search for the information on the Internet

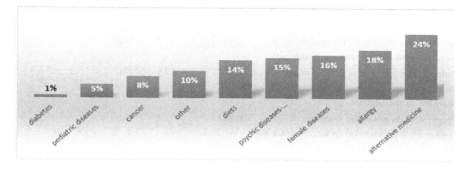

Fig. 2. Patients and their search for the information about a specific health problem

Most often the respondents search for the information about health via Google search engine. The findings also show that 43% of the respondents are willing to spend between 18-36 EUR per month on drugs or medical devices recommended to them on the Internet. Students usually are ready to spend about 7EUR. As far as the time spent on the Internet is concerned, the respondents (71%) usually spend one hour per day on searching for the health information on the Internet. 11% of the respondents spend between 2 and 5 h. In most cases these are the people who suffer from some chronic disease. The findings of this study also indicate that people are a bit suspicious of the information found on the Internet, which is, on the other hand, a quite positive observation since currently one cannot believe everything that is published on the Internet pages. Only 10% of the respondents do not see any negatives when searching for the health information. These are mainly men who often buy products on the Internet, however, they do not search for the health information, they do not suffer from any chronic disease and they trust their doctor. The specific negative aspects mainly include the distortion of information (56%) and a lack of relevant information (23%). In addition, more respondents (63%) think that doctor's advice cannot be compared with the Internet information, particularly the university students and women. 38% of the respondents who think that the Internet advice is as good as doctor's advice are the patients who are not satisfied with their doctor, which results in searching for the information on the Internet and they consider this information trustworthy. Nevertheless, the findings show that people generally prefer doctor's advice as 83% of the respondents confirmed. And in majority cases (90%) people do have a negative experience with the advice provided on the Internet pages.

3.1 Analysis of Other Dependences

Within the generation Y, hypotheses about the relationship of sex, psychic diseases, chronic diseases, or the presence of a family member in healthcare and the amount of searched information were tested (Table 1).

Table 1. Results of the statistical testing

Indicator Hypothesis H0: P1 = P2 versus H1: P1 <>P2*	Test statistic value	P-value	Conclude H1 at 5% Significance?
Searching for the health information (men X women)	0.075	0.433	No
Searching for the health information (family members work/do not work in healthcare)	0.351	0.43	No
Patients suffering from a psychic disorder trust their doctor less and they prefer advice provided on the Internet	0.117	0.15	No
People who do not suffer from any chronic disease are less interested in searching for the information about alternative medicine	0.842	0.23	No

The results in Table 1 show that within the generation Y, the search for this information is not connected with the aspects stated above. These results need further investigation, especially the difference in the approach of the generation Y and other respondents, which will be a subject of further research after the expansion of the sample outside the generation Y.

4 Discussion

The fact that men search for the health information less frequently than women have bee also confirmed by the findings of foreign research studies. A German study [12] states that this is particularly true for the women with the university degree and higher income. The findings of this study about the female prevalence in searching for the health information on the Internet, or the fact that people who do not suffer from a chronic disease are less interested in searching for the health information on the Internet, also correspond to the results of the study performed by Fox [8] or Economides and Grousopoulou [13] in which these issues were also discussed.

In addition, the empirical findings of this study confirm that although many respondents do not understand the medical reports, they do not search for further information. Furthermore, health application, which could help in the prevention and treatment are not fully exploited either. People prefer to use general search engines to discover the needed health information. If people use specific web pages, they are usually influenced by their design. The findings also indicate that each user of the Internet should evaluate the reliability of the health web pages for the following aspects to make sure that s/he receives a trustworthy piece of information: author's credibility; author's expertise; topicality of the page; possibility of the verification of the provided information.

As Murray et al. [9] claim, the quality of information on the Internet is paramount because inaccurate information can cause a lot of harm both to the doctor and his/her patients in terms of doctor-patient relationship, quality of care, health outcomes, and time efficiency. Murray et al. [9] also emphasize the need to develop doctor's skills in the area of reacting to patients' enquiries about the health information they find on the Internet.

5 Conclusion

Overall, the Y generation aged 20–35 years is a digitally literate generation, members of which rely on their own opinions and they are more independent. Almost all the respondents use the Internet and 82% have mobile access to the Internet [11]. The findings analyzed among this generation demonstrate that more respondents do not suffer from any chronic disease and they are satisfied with their doctor. Altogether 43% of the respondents search for the health information on the Internet and 35% of people use mobile health applications such as pressure measurement or pedometer. Despite this fact, only a few use applications aimed at the check-ups or prevention of their health. A vast majority of people compares the results of their search for the health information with other web pages by using general search engines such as Google or Seznam. Furthermore, 90% of the respondents see the negative aspects when searching on the Internet and they rather trust their doctor than to the Internet information. This is a positive sign since the respondents seem to be cautious and careful when they use the Internet while comparing the results of their search.

Acknowledgement. This study was supported by the research project The Czech Science Foundation (GACR) 2017 No. 17- 03037 Investment evaluation of medical device development run at the Faculty of Informatics and Management, University of Hradec Kralove, Czech Republic.

References

1. Maresova, P., Kacetl, J.: Innovations in ICT in the Czech Republic with focus on a chosen region. Procedia Soc. Behav. Sci. **109**, 679–683 (2014)
2. Marešová, P.: Knowledge Management in Czech Companies. E&M Econ. Manag. **13**(1), 131–143 (2010)
3. CSO (Czech Statistical Office): Využívání informačních a komunikačních technologií v domácnostech a mezi jednotlivci (The use of information and communication technologies in households and among individuals) (2015). https://www.czso.cz/documents/ 10180/20568879/062004-15a.pdf/c5df6b-e412-48ed-8129-082d8cad914d?version=1.0. Accessed 17 Apr. 2016

4. Goodson, P., McCormick, D., Evans, A.: Searching for sexually explicit materials on the internet: an exploratory study of college students. Arch. Sex. Behav. **30**(2), 101–118 (2001)
5. Brenner, V.: Psychology of computer use: XLVII - parameters of internet use, abuse and addiction: the first 90 days of the internet usage survey'. Psychol. Rep. **80**(3), 879–882 (1997)
6. Trifonova, A., Ronchetti, M.: Hoarding content for mobile learning. Int. J. Mobile Commun. **4**(4), 459–476 (2006)
7. Zhang, Y.X.: Comparison of internet attitudes between industrial employees and college students. Cyberpsychol. Behav. **5**(2), 143–149 (2002)
8. Fox, S.: Peer-to-peer Health Care. Pew Reserch Center (2011). http://www.pewinternet.org/2011/02/28/peer-to-peer-health-care-2/. Accessed 17 Apr. 2016
9. Murray, E., Lo, B., Pollack, L., Donelan, K., Catawa, J., Lee, K., Zapet, K., Turnes, R.: The Impact of health care and the physician-patient relationship: national U.S. survey among 1,050 U.S. physicians. JMIR **5**(3) (2003). PMC1550564
10. Lapacek, J.: Zdraví na internetu. (Health on the Internet) Praha:Computer Press a.s (2002)
11. IBM: Myths, exaggerations and uncomfortable truths-The real story blind Millennials in the workplace (2015). http://www-01.ibm.com/common/ssi/cgi-bin/ssialias?subtype=WH&infotype=SA&appname=GBSE_GB_TI_USEN&attAchment=GBLO03032USEN.PDF. Accessed 17 Apr. 2016
12. Zschorlich, B., Gechter, D., Janssen, I., et al.: Gesundheits informationen im Internet: Wer sucht was, wann und wie? Zeitschrift fur Evidenz. Fortbildung und Qualitat im Gesundsheitswessen **109**(2), 144–152 (2015)
13 Economides, A.A., Grousopoulou, A.: Use of mobile phones by male and female Greek students. Int. J. Mob. Commun. (IJMC) **6**(6), 729–749 (2008)

A Model for Prioritization and Prediction of Impact of Digital Literacy Training Programmes and Validation

Nimish Joseph$^{(\boxtimes)}$ ⓘ, Arpan Kumar Kar ⓘ,
and P. Vigneswara Ilavarasan ⓘ

Department of Management Studies, IIT Delhi, New Delhi, India
nimishjoseph@gmail.com

Abstract. The Government of India through its various programmes like Digital India aims to provide digital literacy to all its citizens. Towards this mission, National Digital Literacy Mission and Digital Saksharata Abhiyan conducted various training programmes throughout the country. The authors collected details of 5 lakh participants, who successfully completed the training programme and to learn the quality of the training and identify its impact 30,003 participants were interviewed based on a systematic sampling. This study based on the survey and interview identifies a model to predict and validate the impact of similar Digital Literacy training programmes in India. The various components identified in this study were then ranked based on the participant responses using the analytical hierarchy process. The various constructs identified for assessing the quality of training includes conduct, delivery and content, and perceived value. The impact of training was measured using knowledge gained, comfort level achieved and frequency of usage. To identify the impact of training a simple linear regression technique was also used.

Keywords: Digital India · Digital literacy · National digital literacy mission · Knowledge · Comfort · Frequency · Training · Impact · Linear regression · AHP

1 Introduction

Digital India is a flagship programme of Government of India with a vision to transform India into a digitally empowered society and knowledge economy. It is evolved with a vision of providing digital infrastructure as a core utility to every citizen, governance and service on demand, and digital empowerment of citizens [1] and to empower the citizens the key areas of focus include digital literacy, digital resources, and collaborative digital platforms. Digital Literacy helps the citizens to exploit digital technologies and thus helping them to lead a better life, becoming economically more secure. The major focus of the government lies in making at least one person from every house hold e-literate. The major achievements of Digital India include National Digital Literacy Mission and Digital Saksharata Abhiyan [2]. There are other activities related to the Digital India under various stages of implementation and related transformational processes to achieve the desired objectives [3]. Under the National Digital Literacy Mission, approximately 12.25 lakh persons have been trained and 10 lakh candidates have been certified by National Institute of Electronics & Information Technology (NIELIT), National Institute of Open Schooling (NIOS), Haryana Knowledge Corporation Limited (HKCL), ICT Academy of Tamil Nadu (ICTACT) and National Institute for Entrepreneurship and Small Business Development (NIESBUD).

In support of above, CSC e-Governance Services India Limited (CSCSPV) is implementing a mass information and communication technology (ICT) literacy programme that provides ICT training to 52.5 lakh citizens in the country. The broad objective of the training is 'to make a person IT literate, so that he or she can operate a computer or any other digital devices like tablet to perform various tasks including the sending and receiving of emails and searching information in the internet. The programme, consists of 20 h of training, which provides trainees basic familiarity with using computer hardware and IT skills like Internet browsing, emailing etc. After the training, there is an online examination for the trainees. The beneficiaries are selected from households where none of the members in the age group of 14 to 60 years are IT literate. Adequate representation of disadvantaged groups (SC/ST) and below poverty line (BPL) is to be made in the coverage of the programme. The training was mainly provided through CSCSPV's service centres. Some part of the training was also provided through a PPP mode with following partners: adult literacy centers, D/o School Education & Literacy, MHRD; NIELIT Centers and their accredited Centers; IGNOU Centers and their authorized centers; Rural Self Employment Training Institutes (RSETI); NGOs involved in IT Literacy; and Companies with CSR provisions.

The hands on training received can help the individuals to learn the role of online communities in driving innovation. In particular "peer-produced" knowledge goods like open source software, Wikipedia and crowd-science have been shown to contribute significantly to national growth and productivity [4]. Relevance of social media platforms for professional networking and job portals needs to be introduced to the participants. Digitization has a proven impact on reducing unemployment, improving quality of life, and boosting citizens' access to public services [5].

Governments use ICTs to strengthen political participation of citizens in policy and politics. Online platforms can bring their voices to the higher levels [6]. In a country like India, where the major share of population is below the age of 35 [7], the involvement of youth adds value by participation than its outcome. In fact, online platforms like social media have reinforced the potential for expressive participation. Training programme of this kind is therefore targeted to help the participants become digitally literate. Digital literacy is not just about the ability to handle a software or a digital device, it includes a large variety of complex cognitive, motor, sociological, and emotional skills, which users need in order to function effectively in digital environments [8]. Hence, the evaluation of this training programme includes an impact study which tries to capture information from different perspectives like the level of comfort, confidence and knowledge levels, the frequency of usage and difficulties experienced.

A part of the project is already implemented and a questionnaire was circulated amongst the beneficiaries. 30,003 respondents were contacted for data collection and is then used to learn the training programme and its impacts. This study focusses to predict the impact of this training and to project a model for prioritization and prediction of the impact of Digital Literacy Training programmes and its validation.

The survey included various parameters to capture the different aspects of the training and its impacts. The components of training identified include conduct, content and perceived usefulness. The different parameters based on which the impacts of study measured are knowledge gained, comfort level achieved and the frequency of usage post training. Based on the survey results we are framing a model that could be used for the prioritization and prediction of the training impacts. This study identifies if there is any significant relationship between the training provided in terms of conduct, content and perceived value; and the priorities of choices made with respect to impact of the training based on knowledge, comfort and frequency.

2 Literature Review

Digitization across the globe is creating tremendous opportunities for economies [9] and India is one great example which understood, this need and started preparing the workforce for future to emerge as a technology powerhouse. However, achieving this is not an easy task and involves overcoming of multiple barriers [10]. The rise in internet and mobile subscription in recent years has generated hope but, concrete efforts at multi agency levels are required. For speeding up the economic growth and to improve the human development indices, creativity is a very important resource [11] and digitization practices can help in the creation of such innovative societies. Digital literacy involves many components and establishing the benefits of this diverse view of digital literacies [12] that can help the participants to progress. Digital literacy is not only a key factor in enabling employment and participation in education, but also, a means of acquiring some understanding of the world [13].

Many of the countries in the west have adopted information and communication technologies (ICT) for multiple purposes [14, 15]. A study conducted in the UK shows how ICT is widely being used in the education sector and it cross examines whether society really desires a transformed, technologically-mediated relation between teacher and learner [16]. ICT training for the residents of Austin emphasizes that such programmes should provide affordable internet, computers and training to its participants [17]. Since last 2–3 years ICT have been widely used for various governance related activities in India [18]. The establishment of portals like myGov [19] and multiple mobile applications have helped the citizens to connect with the government and other service providers. However, to enhance the use of ICT among citizens, the digital literacy should be improved.

3 Data Collection

A questionnaire based telephonic survey was conducted for the study using a database of five lakhs people who have completed the training and have received the certificates across the country. This was treated as population. The beneficiaries were clubbed on the basis of e-readiness [20] of the state, gender, SC/ST status and religion. A sample of

5000 each from one lakh was selected. The sample selection followed a mix of quota and systematic sampling technique methods. From the database, every eight person was selected. The number eight was arrived at adding digits in the year, 2015, when the project was initially conceptualized. A telephonic survey was carried out for 30, 003 participants using a systematic approach.

A structured questionnaire was used for the survey for data collection from the respondents. The questionnaire was finalized with inputs from the terms of reference and the CSCSPV, especially on the parameters on which the programme could be assessed. Inputs from the stakeholders helped in improving the constructs and the items. The questionnaire collected information on gender, community, religion, age group, employment status, average monthly household income, marital status, educational qualification, language abilities and ICT access (computers/mobiles/tablet/ internet connections). Further, the training was assessed with respect to content delivery; impact on individuals' knowledge, comfort, and frequent usage; and benefits for employability and employment, personal usage.

3.1   Training Details

The study assessed training on three major components: conduct, delivery and the perceived value. Each of the components was examined with some questions. All three components are interrelated to each other and might impact the outcome of the other. In all three components, the training programme was found to be impacting beneficiaries.

The conduct of the training was understood in terms of regularity, facilities in the class, uninterrupted classes, power supply, and distance of the training center. The study assumed that inadequacy in conduct of the training classes shall result in failure despite a good conduct and might not be perceived as useful by the trainees. The delivery of the training was examined by the clarity of content, pedagogy, easiness of online assessment, and ability to impart what was taught in class to others. The perceived usefulness of the programme was measured by asking possible referrals and willing to attend similar programs. Conduct of the training, delivery of the training and perceived values are identified from the responses and have been explained in the subsequent sections.

Conduct of the training. The conduct of the training was examined using the following indicative questions:

- Was the training regular?
- Did you attend the training regularly?
- Were the training facilities good?
- Were the classes uninterrupted?
- Was the power supply regular to the class?
- Was the training center far from your house?

Training Delivery. This section questions whether the content is understandable and delivered appropriately. The study used the following indicative questions:

- Did you understand the content?
- Did you like the teaching methods?
- Was the trainer attentive to your queries?
- Were the doubts cleared effectively?
- Did you practice after the theory class?
- Did you find the Online Assessment easy?

Perceived Value. The third component of training examined the perceived usefulness of the course. When someone wants to repeat the similar training programme, it indicates the value of the relevance and usefulness of the content. Referrals for the training programme also indicate the perceived value for the same. This was understood by asking the following questions:

- Do you plan to attend similar trainings?
- Would you like to recommend the same kind of training to others?
- Are you confident of teaching others about computer and internet?

3.2   Training Impact

For the 29,834 trained respondents, impact of training on individuals' knowledge, comfort and frequency of usage were also determined. The study tried to understand the impact of the training programme on the following domains: impact on the individual capabilities and the usage of ICT post training. Impact on the individual capabilities covers whether the beneficiaries gained knowledge and comfort in using the stand alone ICTs and the interactive ones. Usage of ICT post training includes the frequent usage of various products.

Impact on individual capabilities. We study the post training responses regarding knowledge and comfort while using standalone and interactive ICTs. Any use of Internet ICTs where request and response of actions are involved is treated as interactive ICTs.

Use of stand-alone ICTs identified whether beneficiaries possess knowledge and feel comfortable using the following indicative questions:

- Basic computer skills (connecting peripherals)
- Using computer/laptop/mobile/smartphone/tablet
- Adding contacts in mobile phone
- Connecting to Wi-Fi in mobile phone/tablet
- Using search engines for information query
- Viewing YouTube and accessing Wikipedia

It's also important to learn whether the beneficiaries are frequently using or accessing the ICTs learnt from the training programme. The interactive ICTs include but is not limited to:

- Sending and receiving emails
- Using WhatsApp and other social media websites
- Using audio/video calls
- Boking tickets and paying bills online
- Accessing government websites and filling online applications

4 Experimental Details

Analysis was conducted using the Analytic Hierarchy Process (AHP) on each of the user data followed by a linear regression model to derive the required relationship. The user responses were marked in a scale of 1 to 4 for each of the questions, 1 being the lowest and 4 highest. Based on the users responses mean of the values were derived for all 3 parameters identified for both training and its impacts. After the determination of mean value, AHP was performed for each of the participant to identify the weights and priorities of each component.

The Analytic Hierarchy Process (AHP), introduced by Thomas Saaty (1980), is an effective tool for dealing with complex decision making process [21]. AHP for checking the consistency of the decision maker's evaluations, also incorporates a technique, that can improve the decision making process by reducing the bias. There will be a set of evaluation criteria and choices or alternatives from which the AHP makes the decision of best choice. The evaluation criteria might be contrasting and hence it is not true that some choice which optimizes independent criterion is going to be the best. Rather, the choice which achieves the maximum value amongst others will be declared as the best choice. Based on the decision maker's choice AHP initially assigns weight for every pair of choices. One criteria with a higher weight will have a higher impact on the results compared to others. Further based on the weights, scores are computed for every criteria pairwise. Finally, the AHP combines the criteria weights and the options scores, thus determining a global score for each option, and a consequent ranking [22].

AHP can be considered as a simple, flexible and powerful tool that is capable to translate both qualitative and quantitative evaluations made by the decision maker into a multi criteria ranking. The weights are assigned based on the decision makers choice and hence, making it flexible. However, as the number of criteria and evaluation increases, it requires a large amount of decision making as every pair in a criteria need to be given separate weights. The number of comparisons increase as the criteria increases. The number of pairwise comparisons increases quadratically.

Implementation of the AHP. The first step involved was identifying the hierarchy and also calculating the weighted matrix for each component. Figure 1 represents the hierarchy for training. It gives the components identified as part of collecting the training details. A hierarchy was also formed based on the identified components that was used to measure the impact. Figure 2 represents this hierarchy.

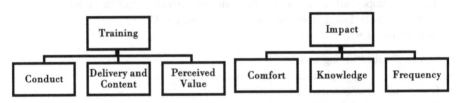

Fig. 1. Hierarchy for training   **Fig. 2.** Hierarchy for impact

The mean values obtained were used to compare the pairwise criteria and was then mapped to the scale of 1 to 9. Both training and impact have 3 evaluation criteria. For estimation of the individual consistent priorities using the row geometric mean method, the individual vector is obtained by solving the following system [23]. Let $M = (\tilde{m}_{ij})_{n*n}$, be the judgement matrix

$$min \sum_{i=1}^{n} \sum_{j>i}^{n} (\ln \tilde{m}_{ij} - (\ln \tilde{w}_i - \ln \tilde{w}_j)^2) \tag{1}$$

such that $\tilde{w}_i \geq 0$ and $\sum \tilde{w}_i = 1$. The solution is obtained by [24]

$$\tilde{w}_i = \frac{\frac{1}{n}\sqrt{\prod_{j=1}^{n} \tilde{m}_{ij}}}{\sum_{i=1}^{n} \frac{1}{n}\sqrt{\prod_{j=1}^{n} \tilde{m}_{ij}}} \tag{2}$$

where $\tilde{w}_i$ is the weight of the decision criteria i. To estimate the consistency of parameters geometric consistency index is being used [25]

$$GCI(M^{d_i}) = \frac{2}{(n-1)(n-2)} \sum_{j>i}^{n} \left(\log|\tilde{m}_{ij}| - (\log|\tilde{w}_i| - \log|\tilde{w}_j|)^2\right) \tag{3}$$

Aggregation of individual judgments:

$$\tilde{m}_{ij}^{(c)} = \prod_{k=1}^{t} (\tilde{m}_{ij}^{(k)})^{\varphi k} \tag{4}$$

The weighted matrix Y was identified separately for each hierarchy. For example, mean values of user$_i$ for conduct, content and perceived value are 3.4285, 3.285 and 4 respectively. The values here are arrived after performing the above computations. Table 1 gives the weighted matrix Y for Training data of user$_i$.

To collect obtain the normalized weights for each component geometric mean is calculated for each row. The normalized weights were then used to prioritize different components. Conduct, content and perceived value were ranked based on their contribution to the user responses. Table 2 denotes the prioritization of various components with respect to the training of user$_i$.

Table 1. Weighted matrix Y for training: user$_i$

	Conduct	Content	Perceived value
Conduct	1	1.380952	0.396226
Content	0.72413	1	0.344262
perceived value	2.52381	2.904762	1

Table 2. Prioritization of training components: user$_i$

Conduct	Content	Perceived value
0.241279	0.185659	0.573062

The authors performed a linear regression to develop a model to predict the components of impact based on the components of Training. The training components acted as the independent variables and the impact components as the dependent variable. Subsequent section discuss the findings of this regression model using SPSS [26].

5 Results and Discussions

The various findings of performing regression using SPSS are as follows. The independent variables entered to generate the regression chart for dependent variables knowledge gained, comfort level achieved and frequency of usage are perceived value and content. Tables 3 and 4 gives the simple correlation (R) and variation in dependent variables that can be explained by the independent variable (R Square). This also gives the F Test value which explains the relevance of linear relationship between two variables for different models.

Table 4 give the significance of this F Change where the dependent variable varies for model 1, model 2 and model 3 as knowledge gained, comfort level achieved and frequency of usage respectively.

Table 5, analysis of variance explains how well prediction is possible and whether the regression equation fits the data or not. Here, dependent variable b used for model 1 is the knowledge gained, for model 2 is the comfort level achieved and for model 3 is the frequency of usage.

Table 6 gives the regression coefficients and its significance along with the intercept. It helps us to derive the model for linear regression. The equations derived towards the end of this section are calculated. The residual values derived also gives clear indication on why this model is important.

Table 7 indicates the variable that are excluded and are not used as predictors in the model. This also explains the significance of excluded variable and its partial correlation value for the dependent variables knowledge gained, comfort level achieved and frequency of usage using model 1, model 2 and model 3 respectively. Figures 3 and 4 depicts the histogram for dependent variable knowledge gained where the regression standard residual is mapped with frequency and P-P plot of regression standardized residual respectively. Figures 5 and 6 are for comfort level achieved and Figs. 7 and 8 are for the frequency of usage.

The regression model developed above was successful in identifying relationships between the dependent and independent variables and the various relationships obtained is as follows:

- Knowledge = 0.415−0.079 Content + 0.080 Perceived Value,
- Comfort = 0.343 + 0.063 Content + 0.019 Perceived Value,
- Frequency = 0.243 + 0.016 Content −0.099 Perceived Value

Table 3. Model summary

Model	R	R square	Adjusted R square	Std. error of the estimate
1	.173a	.030	.030	.10496946
2	.066a	.004	.004	.07748532
3	.137a	.019	.019	.11440536

Table 4. Model Summary change statistics

Model	R Square change	F change	df1	df2	Sig. F change
1	.030	461.121	2	29831a	.000
2	.004	64.586	2	29831a	.000
3	.019	286.541	2	29831a	.000

a. Predictors: (Constant), Perceived Value, Content

Table 5. Analysis of Variance$_a$

Model	Sum of sq.	Df	Mean sq.	F	Sig.	
1	Regression	10.162	2	5.081	461.12	.000b
	Residual	328.695	29831	.011		
	Total	338.857	29833			
2	Regression	.776	2	.388	64.586	.000b
	Residual	179.105	29831	.006		
	Total	179.880	29833			
3	Regression˙	7.501	2	3.750	286.54	.000b
	Residual	390.446	29831	.013		
	Total	397.946	29833			

Table 6. Coefficients

Model		Unstandardized coefficients		Standardized coefficients	T	Sig.
		B	Std. Error	Beta		
1	(Constant)	.415	.004		103.354	.000
	Content	−.079	.008	−.077	−9.986	.000
	Perceived Value	.080	.006	.111	14.330	.000
2	(Constant)	.343	.003		115.712	.000
	Content	.063	.006	.085	10.775	.000
	Perceived Value	.019	.004	.036	4.642	.000
3	(Constant)	.243	.004		55.550	.000
	Content	.016	.009	.015	1.864	.062
	Perceived Value	−.099	.006	−.127	−16.292	.000

Table 7. Excluded Variables

Model	Beta in		T	Sig.	Partial correlation	Collinearity statistics
						Tolerance
1	Conduct	3921.646a	.11	.908	.001	2.797E-014
2	Conduct	−12429.6a	−.36	.719	−.002	2.797E-014
3	Conduct	4738.117a	.13	.890	.001	2.797E-014

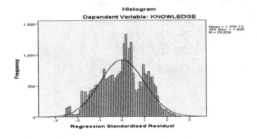

Fig. 3. Histogram for dependent variable knowledge

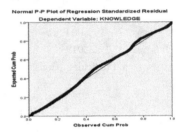

Fig. 4. Normal P-P plot of regression standard residual

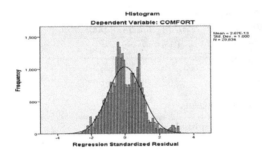

Fig. 5. Histogram for dependent variable comfort

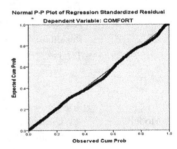

Fig. 6. Normal P-P plot of regression standard residual

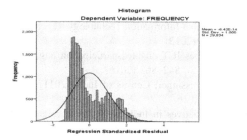
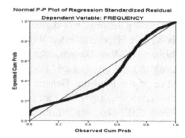

Fig. 7. Histogram for dependent variable frequency

Fig. 8. Normal P-P plot of regression standard residual

6   Conclusions

India, since independence is trying to achieve self-reliance and is looking forward to a 'Digital Revolution'. Many scientific and technical institutes and initiatives were started to make supreme contributions in this area. To become digitally literate, the programmes like this must reach every corner of the country and must bridge this digital divide. Learning and use of ICTs must also provide the users employment opportunity. The trainings like this have a great impact in our society and therefore, this study is focused to predict the impacts based on training and its components.

This study was successful in capturing the linear relationship for various components of digital literacy training with its impacts. This model can help us to predict what the impact of training could be based on the conduct, content and value perceived from the training. Knowledge, comfort and frequency - plots were obtained against the independent variables. The p-value statistics indicate that the results obtained are significant. This study also gives a model of how the survey results can be converted as a prediction model based on the priorities of user input. AHP used in this study helped the authors to identify the user priorities and also to determine its value against the responses, considering the differentiation from other responses. The successful combination of AHP and linear regression model can thus help in identifying a prediction model based on the survey responses. Hence, this study gives a model for prioritization and prediction of impact of digital literacy training programmes and validation.

References

1. Ministry of Electronics & Information Technology, Government of India. In: Digital India Programme, http://www.digitalindia.gov.in/. Last accessed 16 Sep 2016
2. Prasad, R.S.: Digital India – The Vision and the Mission. https://blog.mygov.in/editorial/digital-india-the-vision-and-the-mission/. Last accessed 08 Sep 2016
3. Sharma, S.K., Lama, V., Goyal, N.: Digital India: a vision towards digitally empowered knowledge economy. Indian J. Appl. Res. 5(10), 715–716 (2016)
4. Nagaraj, A.: Essays on the Impact of Digital Information on Innovation. http://papers.ssrn.com/sol3/papers.cfm?abstract_id=2810758. Last accessed 30 Sep 2016

5. Sabbagh, K., Friedrich, R., El-Darwiche, B., Singh, M., Ganediwalla, S., Katz, R.: Maximizing the impact of digitization. In: The Global Information Technology Report 2012: Living in a Hyperconnected World, pp. 121–133 (2012)
6. Thijssen, P., Van Dooren, W.: Going online. Does ICT enabled-participation engage the young in local governance? Local Gov. Stud. **42**(5), 842–862 (2016)
7. Office of the Registrar General & Census Commissioner, Census of India (2011). http://www.censusindia.gov.in/. Last accessed 28 Nov 2016
8. Ghosh, S.B., Das, A.K.: Information literacy initiatives in India with special reference to emerging knowledge economy. In: International Conference on Information Literacy (icil 2006), Kualalumpur, Malaysia, 12 p. (2006)
9. Chambers, J.: Bringing digital india to life. Bus. Today **26**(1), 52–54 (2017)
10. Khokhar, A.S.: Digital literacy: how prepared is india to embrace it? Int. J. Digit. Lit. Digit. Competence (IJDLDC) **7**(3), 1–12 (2016)
11. Khandwalla, P.: Designing a creative and innovative India. Int. J. Hum. Resour. Manage. **25**(10), 1417–1433 (2014)
12. Lankshear, C., Knobel, M.: Digital literacies Concepts Policies and Practices, vol. 30. Peter Lang, New York (2008)
13. Martin, A., Grudziecki, J.: DigEuLit: concepts and tools for digital literacy development. Innov. Teach. Learn. Inf. Comput. Sci. **5**(4), 1–19 (2006)
14. Mitrović, Ð.: Broadband adoption, digital divide, and the global economic competitiveness of western balkan countries. Ekonomski Anali/ Economic Annals **60**(207), 95–115 (2015)
15. Chew, H.E., Ilavarasan, P.V., Levy, M.R.: The economic impact of information and communication technologies (ICTs) on microenterprises in the context of development. Electron. J. Inf. Syst. Developing Countries 44 (2010)
16. Livingstone, S.: Critical reflections on the benefits of ICT in education. Oxford Rev. Educ. **38**(1), 9–24 (2012)
17. Richie Jr., C.S.: Digital inclusion. J. Hous. Commun. Dev. 72(4), 6–9 (2015)
18. Marathe, M., O'Neill, J., Pain, P., Thies, W.: ICT-enabled grievance redressal in central India: A comparative analysis. In: Proceedings of the Eighth International Conference on Information and Communication Technologies and Development (ICTD 2016), vol. 4. ACM, New York (2016)
19. Lamba, A., Yadav, D., Lele, A.: CitizenPulse: A text analytics framework for proactive e-governance-a case study of mygov.in. In: Proceedings of the 3rd IKDD Conference on Data Science 2016, Article no. 16. ACM (2016)
20. Government of India, Department of Information Technology, India e-Readiness Assessment Report (2008). http://meity.gov.in/sites/upload_files/dit/files/e-ReadinessReport_230410.pdf. Last accessed 28 Nov 2016
21. Satty, T.L.: The Analytical Hierarchy Process: Planning, Priority Setting, Resource Allocation. RWS Publication, Pittsburg (1980)
22. Mocenni, C., Casini, M., Paoletti, S., Giordani, G., Viaroli, P., Comenges, J.M.Z.: A Decision Support System for the management of the Sacca di Goro (Italy). In: Marcomini, A., Suter II, G., Critto, A. (eds.) Decision Support Systems for Risk-Based Management of Contaminated Sites, pp. 1–24. Springer, Heidelberg (2009)
23. Kar, A.K., Pani, A.K.: How can a group of procurement experts select suppliers? An approach for group decision support. J. Enterp. Inf. Manage. **27**(4), 337–357 (2014)
24. Crawford, G., Williams, C.: A note on the analysis of subjective judgment matrices. J. Math. Psychol. **29**(4), 387–405 (1985)
25. Aguaron, J., Moreno-Jiménez, J.M.: The geometric consistency index: approximated thresholds. Eur. J. Oper. Res. **147**(1), 137–145 (2003)
26. Norušis, M.J.: SPSS/PC + for the IBM PC/XT/AT. 1. SPSS (1986)

Deep Analyzing Public Conversations: Insights from Twitter Analytics for Policy Makers

Nimish Joseph$^{(\boxtimes)}$ ⓘ, Purva Grover ⓘ, Polaki Kishor Rao ⓘ,
and P. Vigneswara Ilavarasan ⓘ

Department of Management Studies, IIT Delhi, Delhi, India

Abstract. The paper argues for use of Twitter analytics in the study of public policy. Twitter as a social media platform is widely used by many users to express their emotions on various issues. Governments are now realizing the need for social media for administrative purposes and information proliferation to the general public. However, the extent of knowledge among policy makers, about gathering insights from citizen conversations on various social media platforms needs improvement. This research discusses Twitter analytics for two different use cases namely 'Demonetization' and 'GST', where citizen engagement and conversations are monitored, to gain insights. These use cases vary in terms of focus, volume, velocity, veracity, time frame, location, and networked-ness. Possible inferences are presented to gain insights and to help in the policy making process.

Keywords: Analytics · Social media analytics · Descriptive analytics · Content analytics · Network analytics · Hashtag · Demonetization · GST

1 Introduction

1.1 Social Media Analytics

Social media is facing an exponential growth and encapsulating almost every citizen across geographies. Social media analytics by definition comprehends filtering of useful insights from the huge data that is available in the form of semi-structured and unstructured public opinion or user generated content [1].

Social media has changed the manner in which we communicate for years now. It is no longer treated as a niche segment for early adopters. Status quo suggests that every possible brand irrespective of size and target audience is capitalizing to make higher profits for better understanding their customers need through continuous public engagement. Gradually, government and public policy makers have realized the importance of social media [2] and are endeavoring to move towards better adoption. Immediate and transparent, social media has provided the public with greater control, participation, and influence over governmental issues and initiatives over the past few years [3]. For example, a pothole on a road leading to transport inconvenience is now directly uploaded on Facebook to draw the attention of the authorities by either making it a matter of mockery or emphasizing the risks that are faced by the public. With the advent of social media, politician/government and policy makers can no more get away

A.K. Kar et al. (Eds.): I3E 2017, LNCS 10595, pp. 239–250, 2017.
DOI: 10.1007/978-3-319-68557-1_22

with their false promises as public is actively engaged to evaluate and suggest government through immediate feedback. Surprisingly, contemporary political elections are promoted and run through digital media to get more traction and understand public emotions and demands. While many government agencies still tend to employ the "broadcast" model when using social media, some are engaging through hashtags, community building initiatives, and geo-location analysis [4]. These efforts are helping to better inform the public and alert them to public safety emergencies in real-time. Government organizations often struggle with social media. With legal regulations, privacy concerns, risks in general and lack of knowledge for effective use, policy makers in India are finding it difficult to incorporate social media into their routine decision making formats [5]. A proper guidance from the field experts is required to show policy makers as how social media could be used by them and suggest methods to assess the impact of government social media interactions, but require demonstration on how various tools could be used to capture the insights from online conversations [6]. Therefore, the study shall undertake Twitter analytics for two real issues or cases where citizen engagement or conversations could be monitored and insights can be gathered through various analysis which policy makers can refer to for any future endeavors.

Social Media Analytics is rapidly emerging as an important aspect to drive business [7]. Despite the importance of social media analytics, manuals for easy use by the public officials are not readily available. As the required skillsets are short among the government officials, policy decision making processes seem to miss insights from the social media sources. These platforms can be very well leveraged to understand the people perception about an issue/trend or a policy and utilize the information to revise or amend such policies.

The information sharing can occur in two different ways based upon the insights so generated. Any government while formulating its policies and structures, endeavors to spread awareness and information about the new policies or changes in policies to the intended citizen [8]. Social media can be proven to be a great tool to share the information to an amplified population at a much cheaper cost and effectiveness [9]. One major advantage of social media is that the information sharing is bidirectional i.e. the citizen can respond to these changes [10]. People can post their queries, feedback or complaints directing it to a specific a government department.

Similarly, different government departments can interact with each other for general information or campaigning [11]. This can also be extended to international boundaries as well. For instance, Department of External Affairs interacts with different global governments to resolve issues possibly every other second.

In this study, we are analyzing two most recent and relevant topics through hashtag analysis. The cases studied in this paper are-Demonetization and GST.

Demonetization: On 8 November 2016, the Government of India announced the demonetization of all ₹ 500 and ₹ 1,000 banknotes which means that they ceased to be legal tender [12]. The government claimed that the action would curtail the shadow economy and crack down on the use of illicit and counterfeit cash to fund illegal activity and terrorism [13].

GST: Goods and Service Tax is an attempt to unify all taxation of goods and services to provide a seamless tax system for the entire country. The possible advantages of GST are that it will remove multiple taxation system to create a single market [14].

In our study, we have used Twitter, the fastest emerging social media network, as a social media platform for our analysis. The tweet count for Demonetization is 159433 and GST is 33570 tweets respectively. Comparison of the two issues depicts significant differences in terms of focus, volume, velocity and time frame. The data has been collected from November, 2016 to February, 2017. Figures 1 and 2 give the details of tweets collected.

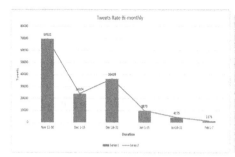
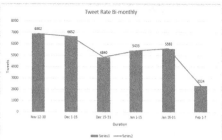

Fig. 1. Tweet rate for demonetization   **Fig. 2.** Tweet rate for GST

Demonetization addresses and outreaches almost all the population of the country irrespective of the class or group [15]. This is due to the simple fact the money (currency notes) are used by everyone almost every day for transactions and therefore, any manipulation in such policies would affect the whole country. On the other hand, subject like GST, interests economists, analytics and businesses more when compared to the general population. Even though the issue scales at national level but not everyone is well aware about it and even if they are not many tend to express their views on social media.

From the above 2 figures it is very much evident that demonetization is more impulsive in nature considering the fact that the tweet rate steeply decreased from 69531 in the initial 15 days of announcement to 1175 by the starting week of Feb, 2107. On the other hand, tweet rate for GST is more or less consistent and continuous over the weeks of data collection period. These graphs help to understand the scale of the discussion and the engagement rate of the people during that time period. Demonetization has clearly higher scale and people are discussing about it in the initial phases but the engagement is fading away gradually over a period of time. GST, the scale is low but the engagement is fairly constant for the period. The probable reason might be the fact that GST is yet to be implemented so people are not well aware of what consequences it might have after it is practically implemented. So, people are discussing more generically based on their expectations and knowledge about the subject.

2 Research Method

The analysis of the tweets has been done using R and NodeXL. Twitter API was used to extract the data. The study was divided into three major stages [16].

- Data Collection: Collection of data using relevant hashtags, i.e. tweets with #Demonetization and #GST were extracted.
- Data Cleansing: This involved cleansing of tweets as it is important from the analysis standpoint. The extracted tweets were first converted to lowercase text, post which the hashtags and hyperlinks were removed, along with punctuations, stop words and chains, retweets, special characters and @usernames etc.
- Data Analysis: The filtered data was then used for the analysis. Subsequent section discuss about the various analysis performed.

3 Analysis

Three different types of analysis were performed to extract insights from the data.

3.1 Descriptive Analytics

Tweet Statistics. The total number of tweets collected for count for Demonetization is 159433 and GST is 33570. For demonetization the tweets contained #Demonetization or #Demonetisation and each such tweet most probably included multiple related hashtags. Similarly, for GST, all the tweets included #GST and most probably had multiple related hashtags.

Inference for policy makers. These data allows the policy makers to comprehend the scope and scale of the issue. Demonetization with total tweet count of 159433 when compared to that of GST with 33570 tweets is a clear demonstration of the fact that demonetization impacts a larger audience and therefore has a larger scale of engagement. This data can also be used for prioritization of things from the task list. If the engagement is larger, more people will participate in the discussion and therefore there is higher probability of noise. Under such scenario, the authorities can control the noise and ensure right information is spread. With limited resources and infrastructure available, government can direct and concentrate more towards topics with higher engagement.

User Statistics. User analysis depicts the number of unique users, their activity, influencing characteristics etc. The details about the user metrics is given in Table 1.

Inference for policy makers. Knowledge about issue - The ratios like tweets/user, unique tweets/user, retweet/user give a relative idea about the engagement and spread of the issue but not the absolute values. For example, unique tweets/user is 1.04 and 1.5 for demonetization and GST respectively which shows a comparison that for policy change like demonetization, more people have knowledge about it as more retweets

Table 1. User Statistics

	#Demonetization	#GST
Users	61698	12722
Tweets/User	2.584087	2.638736
Unique tweet/User	1.040974	1.509904
Retweet/user	1.543113	1.128832

have been generated (60%) whereas knowledge/information about GST is concentrated to only few users and not many users tend to retweet (43%).

User profiling (most visible/influencers) - Policy makers can get deeper useful insights by understanding the demography of these users. They can be segregated into clusters based upon commonalities and differences. Example, male/female users, who are the influencers, most visible users, location of people posting the tweets, etc.

Influencers by retweets - An influencer can be categories as anyone with large number of retweets in the network. There are two categories of influencers, some being positive and others negative. Brands target and use these influencers to manipulate decision making of their customers [17]. Similarly, policy makers can utilize such influencers to spread the message to the population in a way that they intended. On the other hand, negative influencers need to consistently monitor to analyze the criticism and respond in a way that minimizes information asymmetry and damage control. This can make the followers to perceive information in opposite way of what actually was intended.

For each of the case under consideration, two of the influencers have been figured out and few of their respective tweets have been analyzed to determine if the users are positive or negative influencers. @YRDeshmukh and @RituRathaur were identified as the top two influencers with respect to #Demonetization and @ sachin_rt and @arunjaitley for GST [18].

Most visible users - By definition, most visible users are the users who tend to participate in the discussion more. These users might not have a great network of followers but they have their visibility in the discussion more often than influencers. Visibility is quantified as number of times a specific user has tweeted within a stipulated time.

Most visible users for Demonetization include user names 'Sreehari', 'mishr sanjay', 'adrenna', etc. and for #GST include 'GST Tracker', GlobalSmallTalk', etc. [18].

Inference for policy makers:. These users tend to take part in the discussion more often and therefore probability of their availability over a certain time frame is more. Similarly, policy makers can optimize the selection of most visible influencer to outspread information to the public in a quick and timely manner. From the above case tweets made by the user suggest their stance towards the issue which needs to be understood to categorize them into positive and negative most visible users.

- SHREEHARI- #Demonetization is solving unexpected problems. no funding for stone pelters and maoists! (Positive)
- Mishr_sanjay- @manjari__ @iSirArnab india knows that only BJP mercinaries are spreading these lies. After @MamataOfficial opposed #demonetization (Negative)

- GST_TRACKER- GST to create Rs. 36,000 crore software market in MSME segment.
- Globalsmalltalk: Centre, states gearing up for GST, says CBEC member (Information and statistics- Neutral)

3.2   Content Analytics

Most Frequent Hashtags
Figure 3 gives the most frequently hashtags for both Demonetization and GST.

#Demonetization		#GST	
#Demonetization	45000	#GST	18726
#Demonitisation	15256	#GSTbill	1543
#BlackMoney	1790	#DeMonetisation	1272
#India	1108	#GSTCouncil	857
#Modi	1032	#Budget	720
#cashless	564	#tax	499
#IAmWithModi	510	#GSTNews	423
#BJP	449	#GSTIndiaExpert	401
#CashlessEconomy	441	#ArunJaitley	397
#RBI	384	#RunSimple	391

Fig. 3. Most frequent hashtags

Inference for policy makers. Most frequent hashtags [19] allows policy makers to understand the trend among the citizen about a particular issue or policy. They can determine the most frequent words that are there in a discussion and are attached along with a specific issue or policy. The inclusion of these words will make the information reach the target population more effectively and efficiently. For example, if there is any new policy amendment that the government has made in the existing ones and it wants to dissipate the information to general/target population then it can refer to the most commonly used hashtags about the particular issue and post tweets including some of these hashtags to have an amplified outreach.

From the above data, one interesting information that can be gathered is that both the topics have Demonetisation as one of the top frequent words.

Few of tweets are:

- @ShekharGupta @ndtv Would be real shame if GST gets delayed because of demonetisation. Too much pain and very little gain so far #GST
- #Demonetisation, #GST to transform India's business ..

- can #Country suffer double #destabilisation of #Demonetisation/#GST at one go - the #GST should wait till States economy improves #Mitra
- #GST is good economics, #demonetisation is not.

The above tweets indicate that demonetization will have direct impact on GST implementation. People are apprehensive that GST might get delayed because of demonetization which has created instability in the economy. Government needs to provide clarifications and analyze the effect of demonetization on GST with appropriate data.

Word Cloud.
A word cloud was generated, so as to visually depict [20] the most frequent words and is depicted using Figs. 4 and 5

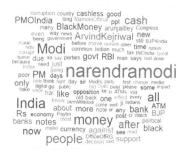

Fig. 4. Word cloud –Demonetization

Fig. 5. Word cloud –GST

Inference for policy makers. Here, some of the words that stand out as potentially usable keywords for a Twitter promoted tweets or promoted account campaigns can be used. Also, each word in the word cloud can be analyzed to understand people requirements, their complaints or response to an issue.

For example: In the word cloud for Demonetization, Paytm has been widely used. A critical analysis of the word through respective tweets can be done. Few of the tweets that mention Paytm have been extracted to understand if there is any possible insight that can be drawn:

- Inquired if they accept card at a small shop. "No sir, no card only @Paytm" was the response. Great penetration by the wallet. #Demonetization
- @Paytm guys please improve your service. Lakhs of ppl started using paytm due #Demonetization lot of errors while processing any requests.

From the above tweets it is evident that digital platforms penetration has increased due to demonetization and services provided by Paytm needs improvement to handle scale of people. Therefore government needs to act upon this and design similar apps to help people cope up with the situation.

The government soon launched its own app to help people. This was probably planned way before by the government but if it had not then it could have used insights from such word cloud analysis to address people needs.

Another similar example is that the word "Banks" have been appearing in the word cloud for Demonetization. If we deeply analyze by extracting some of the tweets:

- @arunjaitley Still no cash on Sbi bank- pin 385520 #Demonetization

We can see that in this particular tweet the user is directing his concern to authorities by stating that there is no cash available in ATM. Government can use such information for resolving the concerns of the citizen or giving them an update.

- #Demonetization has come as bliss for indian #PSU banks which have had been marred by #NPA. #SBI has got 35% of total cash deposits

This tweet depicts that the banks have been happy about the policy changes as it has led to reduction of NPAs.

If we also extract tweets for hospitals, the following tweets were found:

- @HospitalsApollo when whole India is moving towards cashless economy your doctors are asking for cash #Demonetization

Clearly, citizen are facing problem with healthcare services at Apollo hospitals. People are not denied treatment because of lack of cash. Government needs to address such issues by monitoring, interpreting and responding immediately to prevent public pain. Government can use such analysis for emergency management services and mitigate potential crisis, social unrest can be managed effectively through active listening, identifying noises and false information, and taking action to defuse or suppress them, such as issuing clarifying statements as necessary to dispel rumors.

Sentiment Analysis.
For sentimental analysis sentiment package for R has been used for classifying tweets by emotion, and polarity.

Negative polarity is defined as for any tweet that has negative emotion like sadness, anger, fear or disgust. Positive polarity is for the tweets including emotions like joy and trust. For, neutral emotions like surprise and anticipation tweets are classified as neutral. P-Positive, N-Negative, NTL-Neutral respectively.

Sentiment Analysis by polarity (words): The overall sentiment for each case has been graphically represented using Fig. 6.

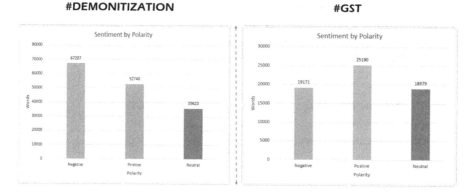

Fig. 6. Sentiment by words polarity

Sentiment Analysis by polarity (tweets): The overall sentiment for each case has been graphically represented using Fig. 7.

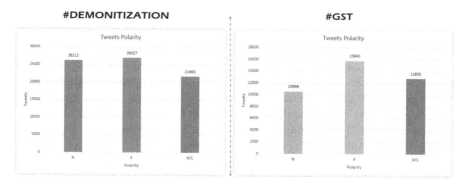

Fig. 7. Sentiment by tweet polarity

Demonetization.

- Negative tweets - 35.07%
- Positive tweets - 36%
- Neutral tweets - 28.9

Inference. Positive and negative tweet count by percentage is almost same suggesting that there is an ambiguity and people are not very much satisfied with the policy change.

GST.

- Negative tweets - 26.98%
- Positive tweets - 40.33%
- Neutral tweets - 32.69%

Inference. Positive tweet percentage is 40.33% whereas negative tweet count by percentage is 26.98% suggesting that there is overall positive emotions among the people about the policy change/implementation.

Sentiment by emotion for both the cases are depicted using Fig. 8

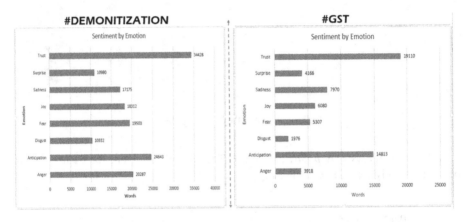

Fig. 8. Sentiment Analysis by emotion

From both the graphs two specific emotions are reciprocated very clearly. Trust and anticipation word count are more when compared with other emotions. Usage of more trust words suggests that people are supportive of the policy. But, is not a true measure because, considering tweet polarity, negative tweets are more in number.

Demonetization: Trust + Anticipation (34428 + 24643) words

GST: Trust + Anticipation (19110 + 14813) words

Inference for policy makers. Sentiment analysis is one of the most effective way to gauge public response of a policy by the government. Understanding emotions of a tweet/content helps policy makers to classify people into groups and take actions according to their responses on an issue. Figure 9 explains how sentiment analysis could be used.

Some of the questions that can be very effectively answered through such analysis are:

- What do citizens feel about the new policies and initiatives?
- What are the most talked about the new policies/amendments?
- What are the most positively talked about attributes in the new policies?
- Who are advocates and skeptics of the new policies?
- Where the government should be actively listening?

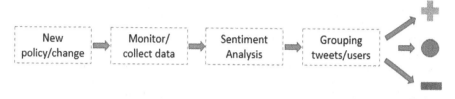

Fig. 9. Sentiment Analysis

3.3 Network Analytics

Topological Analysis
A social network of the influencers was created to understand their network and relationship. The network include followers, followers of, etc. Lay out was done by Fruchterman & Reingold representation. Influencers like @YRDeshmukh and their network was identified for #Demonetization and the influencers in the #GST network identified are BJ4India, Sachin_Kingdom, Bambamroy1980.
Inference for policy makers. Government can use such analysis to determine the largest networks of discussion for an issue and monitor the users to see their behavior and how they are influencing the network and act accordingly by taking corrective measures or using the positive influencers to enhance the reach of the message.

4 Conclusion

With the advent of technology and social media, Government is endeavoring to capitalize on this and use it for improvement in policy making and overall public service. This study is limited to the data from Twitter. However, with more people going online and expressing their opinion (citizen journalism), it becomes more difficult and important to filter out noise form the useful insights that the policy makers can make use of. Hence, it is imperative to build infrastructure and knowledge building in regards with the tools and frameworks. This study explains how government can use social media to improve governance and policy making by enhancing transparency, participation, collaboration and engagement.

Transparency can be achieved by making necessary information available to the public. Governments can use social media platforms to keep its citizens informed about the policies and amendments. Participation of citizen in the discussion allows the government to interpret and comprehend public opinion about the policies. Collaboration of various governmental departments and various public private institutions is possible through the social media. Each department can leverage the power of social media analytics for cross functional insights and better governance. Engagement happens when the information sharing occurs in all the possible direction.

References

1. Omitola, T., Ríos, S.A., Breslin, J.G.: Social Semantic Web Mining. Morgan & Claypool Publishers, San Rafael (2015)
2. Lee, G., Kwak, Y.H.: An open government maturity model for social media-based public engagement. Gov. Inf. Q. **29**(4), 492–503 (2012)
3. Zhang, W., Johnson, T.J., Seltzer, T., Bichard, S.L.: The revolution will be networked: The influence of social networking sites on political attitudes and behavior. Soc. Sci. Comput. Rev. **28**(1), 75–92 (2010)
4. Kaplan, A.M., Haenlein, M.: Users of the world, unite! The challenges and opportunities of social media. Bus. Horiz. **53**(1), 59–68 (2010)
5. Magro, M.J.: A review of social media use in e-government. Adm. Sci. **2**(2), 148–161 (2012)
6. Hoffman, D.L., Fodor, M.: Can you measure the ROI of your social media marketing? MIT Sloan Manage. Rev. **52**(1), 41 (2010)
7. Peters, K., Chen, Y., Kaplan, A.M., Ognibeni, B., Pauwels, K.: Social media metrics—A framework and guidelines for managing social media. J. Interact. Mark. **27**(4), 281–298 (2013)
8. Stoneman, P., Diederen, P.: Technology diffusion and public policy. Econ. J. **104**(425), 918–930 (1994)
9. Antcliff, V., Saundry, R., Stuart, M.: Networks and social capital in the UK television industry: The weakness of weak ties. Hum. Relat. **60**(2), 371–393 (2007)
10. Java, A., Song, X., Finin, T., Tseng, B.: Why we twitter: understanding microblogging usage and communities. In: Proceedings of the 9th WebKDD and 1st SNA-KDD 2007 workshop on Web mining and social network analysis, pp. 56–65. ACM (2007)
11. Kavanaugh, A.L., Fox, E.A., Sheetz, S.D., Yang, S., Li, L.T., Shoemaker, D.J., Natsev, A., Xie, L.: Social media use by government: From the routine to the critical. Gov. Inf. Q. **29**(4), 480–491 (2012)
12. Sherline, T.I.: Demonetisation as a prelude to complete financial inclusion. Int. Educ. Res. J. **2**(12) (2016)
13. Nag, A.: Lost due to demonetization. Econ. Polit. Wkly. **51**(48), 18–21 (2016)
14. Poddar, S., Ahmad, E.: GST reforms and intergovernmental considerations in India. Ministry of Finance, Government of India (2009)
15. Singh, P., Singh, V.: Impact of demonetization on Indian economy. In: 3rd International Conference on Recent Innovation in Science, Technology, Management and Environment (2016)
16. Joseph, N., Kar, A.K., Ilavarasan, P.V., Ganesh, S.: Review of discussions on internet of things (IoT): Insights from twitter analytics. J. Glob. Inf. Manage. (JGIM) **25**(2), 38–51 (2017)
17. Zhang, Y., Moe, W.W., Schweidel, D.A.: Modeling the role of message content and influencers in social media rebroadcasting. Int. J. Res. Mark. **34**(1), 100–119 (2017)
18. Twitter. http://www.twitter.com. Last accessed 05 Mar 2017
19. Stieglitz, S., Dang-Xuan, L.: Emotions and information diffusion in social media—sentiment of microblogs and sharing behavior. J. Manage. Inf. Syst. **29**(4), 217–248 (2013)
20. McNaught, C., Lam, P.: Using wordle as a supplementary research tool. Qual. Rep. **15**(3), 630 (2010)

Outlier Detection Among Influencer Blogs Based on off-Site Web Analytics Data

Reema Aswani[1], S.P. Ghrera[2], Satish Chandra[3(✉)], and Arpan Kumar Kar[1]

[1] Indian Institute of Technology, Delhi, India
reemaswani@gmail.com, arpan_kar@yahoo.co.in
[2] Jaypee University of Information Technology, Waknaghat, Solan, India
sp.ghrera@juit.ac.in
[3] Jaypee Institute of Information Technology, Noida, India
satish.chandra@jiit.ac.in

Abstract. In the current scenario, with the exponential increase in the use of internet, organizations are continuously thriving for visibility on the web. This has opened new avenues in influencer marketing. Several portals encourage these marketers to build content for the purpose of digital marketing. However, the content building process produces a lot of spam within these websites when done in bulk. This is often done in order to establish their presence by using techniques including article spinning and keyword stuffing. This study thus attempts to identify these spam websites using a dataset comprising 2751 websites using bio inspired outlier detection approaches. We use publically available key performance indicators (KPIs) through which websites that create spam content to boost the amount of text in the domain are identified. A hybrid wolf search algorithm (WSA) and bat algorithm (BA) integrated with K-means are used to classify these websites into spam. Findings indicate that metrics including Domain Authority, Page Authority, Moz Rank, Links In, External Equity Links, Spam Score, Alexa Rank, Citation Flow, Trust Flow, External Back Links, Referred Domains, SemRush URL Links and SemRush Hostname Links play an important role in identifying spam. The proposed approach may prove beneficial in segregating spam influencer websites for effective influencer marketing.

Keywords: Outlier detection · Bio inspired computing · Wolf search algorithm · Bat algorithm · Web analytics · Spam detection · Machine learning

1 Background

The exponential increase in the use of internet in this era of digitization across the world has become an important source of competitive edge for the marketing of products and services [1]. This explosion of digital marketing has completely revamped the way business is done and also affects the brand positioning strategy of the

© IFIP International Federation for Information Processing 2017
Published by Springer International Publishing AG 2017. All Rights Reserved
A.K. Kar et al. (Eds.): I3E 2017, LNCS 10595, pp. 251–260, 2017.
DOI: 10.1007/978-3-319-68557-1_23

organizations [2]. Organizations have realized the importance of web visibility for better customer engagement [3]. These organizations have thus started adopting ways to artificially boost their presence on the web using digital marketing specifically opening new avenues for influencer marketing. Influencer marketing is an approach to marketing that focuses on individuals that advise the decision-making consumers. Such people are referred to as influencers and often play a critical role in the customer engagement process [4]. These influencers often need to build huge amount of content in order to maximize web visibility.

The use of web analytics for enhancing digital marketing has been in practice for the last few decades. However, organizations are still not able to fully utilize the core potential of these techniques for improvising their web visibility. Studies highlight opportunities and practices in web analytics that organizations may adopt for better online marketing [5]. The optimization comprises of two primary categories of on-site (a measure of actual visitors on the website) and off-site web analytics (comprising of tools measuring website audience) [6]. One primary reason for failing to achieve the desired promotion from web analytics in online marketing is inexperienced and unskilled influencers. These influencers in order to expedite the process use unethical practices like artificially generating keywords and links to build low quality content. This not only results in that result ineffective off-site analytics but may even prove to be detrimental to the customer if detected by search engines [6, 7]. After the Google's Panda and subsequent updates such malpractices for artificially boosting the web site rank on search engines results page have resulted penalization and website delisting from search engines [8]. This study thus primarily focuses on identifying outlier influencer websites for the purpose of effective off-site web analytics.

There are several freelancing platforms including Blogmint, Influencer, Upwork and Craiglist that offer freelancers to build content on topics that may be utilized for generating back links and keywords for the customer website [9, 10]. These techniques attract traffic to the customer website and artificially boost the website rank. However, the influencers in the process to expedite the process generate low quality content that is often not original and use techniques like article spinning, keyword stuffing, link building and link farming [6] making the website quality a key driver for successful e-business [11]. The customer is often not aware of the adverse effects of such techniques and thus in the long run these may even lead to penalization by search engines. Studies in literature also discuss about website selection for advertising campaigns [12]. To avoid such spam within the website, our study proposes an outlier detection approach that uses website KPIs to identify spam influencer websites that indulge in low quality content building. Metrics like page rank, page authority, domain authority, alexa rank, google index, social shares, trust flow, citation flow, links, external equity link; external back links, referred domains and domain age are used as indicators for identifying spam influencer websites. A spam score is further associated with each of the 2751 websites considered for the analysis. A bio inspired wolf search and bat algorithm integrated with K-Means is used for subsequently segregating the outlier websites.

2 Research Methodology

This study uses a mixed research methodology where in the data collected surrounding the website KPIs for 2751 influencer blogs on unique domains. A statistical t-test is conducted on the normalized data for the two sets of influencer web domains, with low and high spam score. Further, the significant metrics are used as KPIs for analyzing whether the influencer is spam or not using bio inspired optimization approaches integrated with K-Means for mining outliers. The subsequent sub-sections highlight detailed discussions surrounding the analysis.

2.1 Data Collection and Metric Identification

The data is extracted through an API from the SEO Rank website (https://seo-rank.my-addr.com/) that provides a holistic list of selected metrics provided by various data providers like Majestic [13], Ahref [14], Moz [15], SemRush and Webmaster tools. These data providers have developed ranking mechanisms that are used worldwide for identifying the position of a page in organic search. A list of metrics considered for the analysis is demonstrated in Table 1.

Table 1. Description of website metrics for off-site analytics and digital marketing.

	Data provider	Metric	Description
1.	Moz	Domain Authority	Prediction of the ranking of domain on search engines. Depends on links, Moz Rank and other metrics
2.		Page Authority	Prediction of how a given URL may be ranked on search engines, associated with number of links, Moz Rank, and others
3.		Moz Rank	Link popularity score indicative of importance of the page on the web
4.		Moz Trust	Link trust checks for links from trustworthy sources
5.		Links In	Links to the web page, includes equity, or non-equity both internal and external links
6.		External Equity Links	Number of external equity links to the URL
7.		Spam Score	Based on number of sites penalized (de-listed) containing links to the web page
8.	Alexa	Alexa Rank	Global Alexa rank of webpage
9.		Alexa Links number	Number of links to the web page
10.		Country Rank	Alexa Rank in the popular country

(*continued*)

Table 1. (*continued*)

	Data provider	Metric	Description
11.	Majestic SEO	Citation Flow	Uses site link counts to the web page to see how influential the page is
12.		Trust Flow	Trustworthiness of the page based on link to trustworthy neighbours
13.		External Back Links	Total external back links to the web page
14.		Referred Domains	Total unique domains having links to the website
15.	SemRush	SemRush Rank	Domain rank by SemRush
16.		URL Links	Links to the mentioned web page
17.		Hostname Links	Links to the domain
18.	Ahrefs	URL Rating	Strength of web pages' back link profile and its chances of being ranked high in Google
19.		Domain Rating	Strength of website's domain back link profile
20.		Ahrefs Rank	Ranking based on size and quality back link profile
21.		Live & Fresh Index	List of live and dead links for the website

A total of 21 metrics are considered for the study, the data providers are mentioned along the metrics. This study uses a collective list of the metrics as KPIs for detecting spam influencer websites. The spam score is used as the criteria for dividing the data set into two for identifying the statistical significance of the metrics for subsequent analysis.

2.2   Statistical Analysis

The dataset is divided into two equal sets and 500 influencer websites each having a spam score less than 5 and greater than 5 are taken as sample for conducting a statistical t-test to identify metrics that are significantly different in the two sets. Since, the range of values of each of the metrics is considerably varied; min-max normalization is used to standardize the data to a 0–1 range. Subsequently t-test is conducted and the metrics having a p-value less than 0.05 are considered insignificant for further analysis. A list of remaining 12 significant metrics is highlighted in Table 2.

Table 2. Statistically significant metrics having a p-value greater than 0.05

Metric	P-value	Metric	P-value
Domain authority	0.038	Citation Flow	7.23E-28
Page authority	0.030	Trust Flow	0.0003
Moz rank	1.03E-15	External Back Links	0.002
Links in	0.048	Referred Domains	3.94E-32
External equity links	1.25E-05	SemRush URL Links	7.12E-28
Alexa rank	9.23E-15	SemRush Hostname Links	0.045

The final dataset for analysis thus comprises of the 13 significant attributes namely Domain Authority (DA), Page Authority (PA), Moz Rank (MR), Links In (LI), External Equity Links (ELL), Alexa Rank (AR), Citation Flow (CF), Trust Flow (TF), External Back Links (EBL), Referred Domains (RD), SemRush URL Links (UL) and SemRush Hostname Links (HL) for 2751 influencer websites. Subsequent sub-sections model the identified metrics to segregate outliers using bio inspired computing algorithms [16].

2.3   Outlier Detection

After the statistical t-test that identifies significant metrics, a hybrid bio inspired approach is used for detecting outlier influencer websites. Outlier detection is a popular approach when identifying data points that do not comply with majority of the data set based on selective metrics. There are several studies in literature that demonstrate various outlier detection approaches. An exhaustive list of outlier detection approaches with a comparison of motivation, comparison and disadvantages is highlighted with a categorization into statistical models, neural networks, machine learning and hybrid systems [17]. Chandola et al. [18] further provide an exhaustive review of the techniques by grouping the existing studies into six main categories based on classification, clustering, nearest neighbor, statistical, information theoretic and spectral. They further highlight the widespread applications of these approaches across domains encompassing cyber-intrusion detection [19], fraud detection [20], medical anomaly detection [21], image data [22], textual anomaly detection and sensor networks [23].

With the huge data influx, there are studies for outlier detection in high dimensional data [24–26]. However, these approaches are computationally intensive often NP hard and may even lead to a locally optimum solution [27]. Since the data under consideration is huge and may also be unstructured textual data. This is creates need of integrating approaches that do not converge to a local optima. The meta-heuristic approaches are known to help in reaching to a globally optimum system [28]. Further, bio inspired algorithms have been one of the most popular optimization techniques and mimic swarm behavior for optimization problems [16, 29, 30]. Tang et al. [31] thus integrate a few popular bio inspired algorithms with K-means to avoid the local convergence. This study thus utilizes the integrated bio inspired wolf search algorithm for outlier detection. We thus use the 2751 influencer websites comprising of 14 attributes including KPIs for each website for identifying these outliers.

The wolf search algorithm (WSA) is one such optimization approach that is said to overcome local optima by imitating the wolf preying behavior [31, 32]. Another similar wolf hunting approach for grey wolves is used in literature for detecting outliers integrated with k-nearest neighbor [33]. In the current study, the number of clusters is identified as 2 for normal and outlier data points. The wolf population is initialized with visual distance and escape probability. The initial centroids are assigned for the two clusters. The fitness for the centroid in each wolf is calculated and the best solution is identified. The random preying behavior of the wolf is done by selecting a companion having the best solution within the visual distance. If the fitness of the companion is better than the self fitness of the wolf the companion is selected and is thus approached. After the prey is hunted the wolf randomly selects a position beyond the visual range and the process is repeated from the new location. The centroids with the best fitness are considered as the final solution.

Further, the results are compared with the integrated bat algorithm (BA) which uses the echolocation behavior of bats to find the prey and differentiate between different insects even in the dark [31, 34]. The bat algorithm is one of the most popular algorithms used for several engineering, multi-objective and constrained optimization problems [35–37]. For the integrated bat approach along with the two clusters, the bat population, frequency factor and loudness are initialized. The initial clusters are randomly assigned or the bat population. For each bat, the initial centroids are similarly identified. The fitness of the centroids is computed and the best solutions are identified. Further, the new solution is generated by adjusting the frequency and velocity. If the randomly generated solution is greater than the defined pulse rate, a new best solution is selected from the best solutions from each of the bats. The new solutions are accepted by adjusting pulse rate and loudness for subsequent iterations. The pulse rate is increased and the loudness is decreased for the next iteration.

Thus the bio-inspired algorithms help in identifying the best cluster centroids over iterations. The formulation of centroids is mainly iteratively guided by the search agents in the mentioned approaches. Since the dataset considered for this study requires only two clusters and has a total of 14 attributes for which the centroid values need to be computed. The $Centroid_{ij}$ is value of the centroid for i^{th} cluster and j^{th} attribute. Thus, the $Centroid_{ij} = \sum_{k=1}^{SolSpace} weight_{ki} datapoint_{kj} / \sum_{k=1}^{SolSpace} weight_{ki}$. The centroids largely depend on the weight that tells whether the data point belongs to the cluster or not. $weight_{ki} = 1$, if $datapoint_k \in cluster_i$; else $weight_{ki} = 0$. Once the best cluster centroids are identified for the two clusters of outliers and normal data points, a distance measure is subsequently used segregate the outliers. The subsequent section demonstrates the findings.

3   Findings

The K-means integrating WSA and BA algorithms have been used in this study for detecting outliers. The use of bio-inspired algorithms avoids locally optimum solutions. The study demonstrates the segregation of outlier influencer websites based on certain KPIs that have been extracted for a set of 2751 influencer websites using APIs. A total of 13 attributes are considered for detecting the outlier influencers for off-site web analytics. The spam score is excluded for the classification and is used for the validation. Table 3 highlights the cluster centers for the remaining 12 metrics. The table lists the cluster centroids for the authentic blogs (A) and outlier blogs (O) for both WSA and BA.

Table 3. Cluster centers for K-Means Integrated WSA and BA

		DA	PA	MR	LI	ELL	AR	CF	TF	EBL	RD	UL	HL
WSA	A	0.12	0.19	0.18	0.69	0.32	0.74	0.55	0.76	0.84	0.58	0.46	0.75
	O	0.08	0.11	0.09	0.45	0.17	0.31	0.48	0.36	0.61	0.24	0.13	0.31
BA	A	0.20	0.27	0.24	0.81	0.39	0.96	0.59	0.97	0.98	0.40	0.31	0.50
	O	0.11	0.12	0.09	0.33	0.17	0.01	0.51	0.06	0.49	0.35	0.21	0.44

The results for the two approaches used for the purpose show that the bat algorithm shows higher accuracy. Out of 2751 influencer websites, 1254 websites were identified as outliers based on their spam score and manual examination. The bat algorithm correctly identified 1218 giving an accuracy of 97.12% while the wolf search algorithm correctly identified 1203 with an accuracy of 95.93%. However, time taken to converge to the optimum solution is 22.61 s for BA while it is just 16.18 s for WSA. The Fig. 1. demonstrates the outlier plots for WSA and BA.

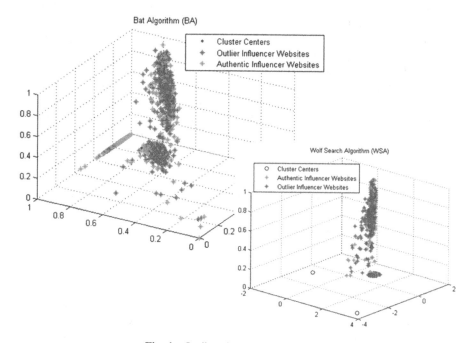

Fig. 1. Outlier plots for WSA and BA

Thus, the findings indicate that a large number (45.58%) of influencer websites are actually outliers. The reason behind this is that majority of influencer websites being categorized as outliers is because these blogs are heavily dependent on techniques like article spinning, link farming and keyword stuffing for content building and subsequent promotion. They often pick up original content and spin/manipulate the content by paraphrasing and including keywords related to the consumer domain to gain traction. These practices are often deemed unfit when it comes to digital marketing. However, the customers adopting these services are often not aware of such malpractices adopted by the websites. This has adverse effects on the consumer website in the long run and may even result in penalization. The use of KPIs in identifying such outlier influencers thus segregates these websites on the basis of publically available metrics from several service providers.

4 Conclusion

With the increased internet use and online marketing opportunities, organizations have realized the importance of web visibility and have started leveraging the power of internet to reach a larger audience for their products and services. This has opened new avenues for digital marketing especially influencer marketing where on several portals have emerged to encourage these influencers to build content for customer businesses. However, this process of content building generates a lot of spam content within these websites when done in bulk for a large consumer base and often involves techniques like article spinning and keyword stuffing for user traction. Such practices are not considered ethical as per the search engine guidelines and affect the consumers adversely. This study thus attempts to use publically available influencer website KPIs, a total of 13 attributes including Domain Authority, Page Authority, Moz Rank, Links In, External Equity Links, Spam Score, Alexa Rank, Citation Flow, Trust Flow, External Back Links, Referred Domains, SemRush URL Links and SemRush Hostname Links for 2751 influencer websites. Further, K-means integrated bio-inspired computing techniques are used for detecting and segregating outliers from the extracted data. Findings indicate that such approaches overcome local optima problems and give globally optimum solutions for such NP hard and computationally extensive data. Further, it is seen that the integrated bat algorithm gives better accuracy than wolf search algorithm as demonstrated in existing literature when the approach is used for clustering [31]. Our study re-establishes the same for the web analytics data set under consideration for outlier detection by extending the proposed approach.

5 Implications and Future Scope

This study uses KPIs and segregates outlier influencer websites that is beneficial for off-site web analytics. This may be useful for preventing consumer investments to such spam influencers that may adversely affect the websites position on search engines in the long run. Apart from the KPIs, content based analytics including keyword density, lexical diversity, meta information and topic modeling may also be incorporated in the analysis.

Future studies can be extended to using social media analytics for further validation of the results since social media platforms are utilized by consumers for raising concerns regarding the services used by them. These platforms specially Twitter and Facebook profiles of such influencer websites provide a lot of information in the form of user generated content that may be integrated with the existing metrics to reinforce the findings. An empirical validation of the results can also be done using a structured questionnaire for the consumers opting for such influencer marketing services and the short term and long term impact of the same on their visitors and web visibility. An existing study surrounding an analysis of results suggested by search engines for market share establishment can also be extended for influencer marketing [38].

References

1. Leeflang, P.S., Verhoef, P.C., Dahlström, P., Freundt, T.: Challenges and solutions for marketing in a digital era. Eur. Manag. J. **32**(1), 1–12 (2014)
2. Dou, W., Lim, K.H., Su, C., Zhou, N., Cui, N.: Brand positioning strategy using search engine marketing. MIS Q. **34**(2), 261–279 (2010)
3. Sawhney, M., Verona, G., Prandelli, E.: Collaborating to create: The Internet as a platform for customer engagement in product innovation. J. Interact. Mark. **19**(4), 4–17 (2005)
4. Brown, D., Hayes, N.: Influencer Marketing: Who Really Influences Your Customers?. Routledge, London (2008)
5. Chaffey, D., Patron, M.: From web analytics to digital marketing optimization: Increasing the commercial value of digital analytics. J. Direct Data Digital Mark. Pract. **14**(1), 30–45 (2012)
6. Malaga, R.A.: Worst practices in search engine optimization. Commun. ACM **51**(12), 147–150 (2008)
7. Moreno, L., Martinez, P.: Overlapping factors in search engine optimization and web accessibility. Online Inf. Rev. **37**(4), 564–580 (2013)
8. A Complete Guide to Panda, Penguin, and Hummingbird. Search Engine Journal. http://www.searchenginejournal.com/seo-guide/google-penguin-panda-hummingbird. Last accessed 15 Feb 2017
9. Jain, A., Dave, M.: The role of backlinks in search engine ranking. Int. J. Adv. Res. Comput. Sci. Softw. Eng. 3(4) (2013)
10. Zuze, H., Weideman, M.: Keyword stuffing and the big three search engines. Online Inf. Rev. **37**(2), 268–286 (2013)
11. Lee, Y., Kozar, K.A.: Investigating the effect of website quality on e-business success: An analytic hierarchy process (AHP) approach. Decis. Support Syst. **42**(3), 1383–1401 (2006)
12. Kar, A.K.: A decision support system for website selection for internet based advertising and promotions. In: Sengupta, S., Das, K., Khan, G. (eds.) Emerging Trends in Computing and Communication. LNEE, vol. 298, pp. 453–457. Springer, New Delhi (2014). doi:10.1007/978-81-322-1817-3_48
13. Positive link building using Majestic tools and metrics. Majestic Blog. https://blog.majestic.com/training/positive-link-building-with-majestic-tools/. Last accessed 10 Feb 2017
14. Ahrefs' SEO Metrics Explained (Finally). Ahrefs Blog. https://ahrefs.com/blog/seo-metrics/. Last accessed 10 Feb 2017
15. A Practical Guide to Content and Its Metrics. Moz Blog. https://moz.com/blog/practical-guide-content-metrics. Last accessed 15 Feb 2017
16. Kar, A.K.: Bio inspired computing–A review of algorithms and scope of applications. Expert Syst. Appl. **59**, 20–32 (2016)
17. Hodge, V., Austin, J.: A survey of outlier detection methodologies. Artif. Intell. Rev. **22**(2), 85–126 (2004)
18. Chandola, V., Banerjee, A., Kumar, V.: Anomaly detection: A survey. ACM Comput. Surv. (CSUR) **41**(3), 15 (2009)
19. Patcha, A., Park, J.M.: An overview of anomaly detection techniques: Existing solutions and latest technological trends. Comput. Netw. **51**(12), 3448–3470 (2007)
20. Ngai, E.W.T., Hu, Y., Wong, Y.H., Chen, Y., Sun, X.: The application of data mining techniques in financial fraud detection: A classification framework and an academic review of literature. Decis. Support Syst. **50**(3), 559–569 (2011)

21. Laurikkala, J., Juhola, M., Kentala, E., Lavrac, N., Miksch, S., Kavsek, B.: Informal identification of outliers in medical data. In: Fifth International Workshop on Intelligent Data Analysis in Medicine and Pharmacology, pp. 20–24 (2000)

22. Stein, D.W., Beaven, S.G., Hoff, L.E., Winter, E.M., Schaum, A.P., Stocker, A.D.: Anomaly detection from hyperspectral imagery. IEEE Signal Process. Mag. 19(1), 58–69 (2002)

23. Basu, S., Meckesheimer, M.: Automatic outlier detection for time series: an application to sensor data. Knowl. Inf. Syst. 11(2), 137–154 (2007)

24. Aggarwal, C.C., Yu, P.S.: Outlier detection for high dimensional data. In: ACM SIGMOD Record, pp. 37–46. ACM (2001)

25. Kriegel, H.P., Zimek, A.: Angle-based outlier detection in high-dimensional data. In: Proceedings of the 14th ACM SIGKDD international conference on Knowledge discovery and data mining, pp. 444–452. ACM (2008)

26. Zhou, X.Y., Sun, Z.H., Zhang, B.L., Yang, Y.D.: Fast outlier detection algorithm for high dimensional categorical data streams. Ruan Jian Xue Bao(Journal of Software) 18(4), 933–942 (2007)

27. Chawla, S., Gionis, A.: k-means–: A unified approach to clustering and outlier detection. In: Proceedings of the 2013 SIAM International Conference on Data Mining, pp. 189–197. Society for Industrial and Applied Mathematics (2013)

28. Blum, C., Roli, A.: Metaheuristics in combinatorial optimization: Overview and conceptual comparison. ACM Comput. Surv. (CSUR) 35(3), 268–308 (2003)

29. Binitha, S., Sathya, S.S.: A survey of bio inspired optimization algorithms. Int. J. Soft Comput. Eng. 2(2), 137–151 (2012)

30. Chakraborty, A., Kar, A.K.: Swarm intelligence: a review of algorithms. In: Patnaik, S., Yang, X.-S., Nakamatsu, K. (eds.) Nature-Inspired Computing and Optimization. MOST, vol. 10, pp. 475–494. Springer, Cham (2017). doi:10.1007/978-3-319-50920-4_19

31. Tang, R., Fong, S., Yang, X.S., Deb, S.: Integrating nature-inspired optimization algorithms to K-means clustering. In: Seventh International Conference on Digital Information Management (ICDIM), pp. 116–123. IEEE, Macao (2012)

32. Tang, R., Fong, S., Yang, X.S., Deb, S.: Wolf search algorithm with ephemeral memory. In: Seventh International Conference on Digital Information Management (ICDIM), pp. 165–172. IEEE, Macao (2012)

33. Aswani, R., Ghrera, S.P., Chandra, S.: A novel approach to outlier detection using modified grey wolf optimization and k-nearest neighbors algorithm. Indian J. Sci. Technol. 9(44) (2016)

34. Yang, X.S.: A new metaheuristic bat-inspired algorithm. In: González, J.R., Pelta, D.A., Cruz, C., Terrazas, G., Krasnogor, N. (eds.) Nature inspired cooperative strategies for optimization (NICSO 2010), Studies in Computational Intelligence, vol. 284, pp. 65–74. Springer Springer, Heidelberg (2010)

35. Yang, X.S., Gandomi, A.H.: Bat algorithm: a novel approach for global engineering optimization. Eng. Comput. 29(5), 464–483 (2012)

36. Yang, X.S.: Bat algorithm for multi-objective optimisation. Int. J. Bio-Inspired Comput. 3 (5), 267–274 (2011)

37. Gandomi, A.H., Yang, X.S., Alavi, A.H., Talatahari, S.: Bat algorithm for constrained optimization tasks. Neural Comput. Appl. 22(6), 1239–1255 (2013)

38. Utsuro, T., Zhao, C., Xu, L., Li, J., Kawada, Y.: An empirical analysis on comparing market share with concerns on companies measured through search engine suggests. Global J. Flex. Syst. Manage. 1–17 (2017)

PrivacyTag: A Community-Based Method for Protecting Privacy of Photographed Subjects in Online Social Networks

Shimon Machida[1(✉)], Adrian Dabrowski[2(✉)], Edgar Weippl[2(✉)], and Isao Echizen[3(✉)]

[1] SAP Japan, Tokyo, Japan
shimon.machida@sap.com
[2] SBA Research, Vienna, Austria
{adabrowski,eweippl}@sba-research.org
[3] National Institute of Informatics, Tokyo, Japan
iechizen@nii.ac.jp

Abstract. Online social networks, such as Facebook, have become popular with people of all ages, and online communication with friends and acquaintances via messages that include photos has become very common. With the increasing ease with which users can take and post photos, the unintentional disclosure of sensitive information of various kinds through mistakes made while posting has become a problem. In this work, we focused on the privacy of people appearing in photos and developed a method called "PrivacyTag" for adaptively blurring their facial area in accordance with the communities to which they belong by using tags embedded with community-based privacy policies. We also evaluated a newly designed privacy tag and developed a prototype application for Facebook that uses this tag.

Keywords: Photo Privacy · Privacy tag · Online social network

1 Introduction

Online social networks (OSNs), such as Facebook and Instagram, have become popular with people of all ages, and online communication with friends and acquaintances via messages that include photos and videos has become very common.

As it has become very easy for users to take and post photos, the inadvertent disclosure of sensitive information through mistakes made while posting has become a problem [1]. A message containing sensitive information can be passed along by the user or by the user's friends to acquaintances and strangers. Disclosure of such information can trigger unexpected problems such as loss of credibility. In a survey on awareness of information security ethics in Japan [4], researchers found that 70% of the respondents were not aware of the problems related to posting in OSNs photos containing other people. In response to this situation, and in order to avoid unnecessary trouble when making OSN posts [5], it was recommended that photos be processed before posting, specifically by (1) deleting location and other metadata, (2) obtaining

A.K. Kar et al. (Eds.): I3E 2017, LNCS 10595, pp. 261–275, 2017.
DOI: 10.1007/978-3-319-68557-1_24

permission from subjects before posting, and (3) preventing the identification of people that are unnecessarily included in the photos. However, since it is complicated to carry out all these measures every time a post is made, there is a need for a procedure that can be implemented easily.

People have different policies regarding privacy in daily life. Additionally, one person might have different policies depending on the communities to which he or she belongs [6]. Similarly, OSN users have subjective judgment criteria corresponding to the contents of the message being posted [8]. Moreover, they can belong to multiple OSN communities, which are created using social access control lists (SACLs) that classify friends into subsets that are used to determine which messages they can see. When posting a message or photo, the user can choose the target community appropriate for the situation and content of the post [7]. Users can share their posts more effectively by using SACLs to control disclosure to the particular individuals or communities that they think would be interested in the post [8, 9]. However, users are sometimes unhappy about unintentional people such as different community people on the SACL and people not on the SACL seeing their photos or finding out about their activities and other information included in the post, which can happen if a post is unintentionally or unthinkingly shared with a certain community [10]. Many people are sensitive about privacy and believe that they always make correct privacy-related decisions. However, it is not easy to make the right choice for every situation. For example, users tend to make wrong decisions about posting when undergoing changes in feelings and emotions [14], meaning that it is difficult to always make correct decisions when posting in OSNs. Therefore, a function is needed that can easily reflect privacy policies matching the user's communities or situation instead of merely relying on the user's subjective decision criteria. While there are several kinds of sensitive information that a user may unintentionally disclose in a posted message or photo, this study focused on protecting the privacy of people appearing in photos that are to be posted.

We have developed a method (PrivacyTag) for adaptively protecting (blurring) the facial area of people appearing in photos to be posted within and outside the communities to which they belong by using tags embedded with community-based privacy policies. The application of this method enables the protection of privacy based on the privacy policy of the photographed subject instead of relying on the subjective judgment of the OSN poster or photographer.

2   Related Work

2.1   OSN User Privacy

OSNs offer various privacy settings and functions to prevent the disclosure of users' sensitive information. However, privacy management is not only complicated, maintaining it requires a lot of effort [7]. This has prompted many studies on information disclosure boundaries, including proposals for access control for posts [7, 11, 12]. However, many of these studies focused on the privacy of the poster while ignoring the privacy of others in a photo. In fact, problems resulting from posting personally identifiable photos without permission have been reported in case studies about regrets of

OSN users after posting [8, 13, 14], showing that there is a need to also consider the privacy of everyone appearing in photos posted in OSNs. Therefore, we developed a method for reflecting the privacy policies of the subjects rather than protecting privacy only on the basis of the judgment criteria of the poster.

2.2 Privacy Protection for Photographed Subjects

Before the privacy policy of a subject can be respected, the policy first has to be determined. This can be achieved by methods that use (1) facial recognition, (2) radio frequency identification, or (3) tag recognition. Methods that use facial recognition involve linking facial features and privacy policies in advance, conducting facial recognition when a user posts photos, and applying and notifying the user of the subject's privacy policy [15, 16]. While these measures have the benefit of working without always having to wear tags, they require potential subjects to register their facial features and other physical characteristics to the system, which may be rejected due to privacy concerns [17]. With methods that use radio frequency identification, a person who is a candidate for privacy protection carries an RFID tag containing his privacy policy. When an RFID tracking system detects the person, he is anonymized on the basis of the privacy policy [3, 24]. These methods need to integrate unified tag specifications so that the RFID readers can recognize any tag. The tag recognition methods require wearing tags that show one's policies, conducting tag analysis when photos are to be posted, and applying the policies of the photographed subjects. In a previous study, Dabrowski et al. [2] proposed using a personal photo policy framework based on a simplified symbol/ accessory or button with a 2D barcode containing the subject's privacy policy. Pallas et al. [18] proposed wearing and displaying simplified tags that can be easily distinguished by people as well as machines. Other proposed methods control privacy by embedding many different kinds of policies in QR codes [6, 19]. Bo et al. [6] proposed using a QR-code-based tag (Privacy.Tag) embedding the subject's flexible privacy policy including allowed and disallowed domains. However, since such simplified tags cannot contain a large amount of information, it is difficult to use them to express varying community-based privacy policies. Conversely, with QR codes and other complex tags that contain large amounts of information, there are problems with detection accuracy and analysis depending on the distance to the photographed subject. Thus, none of these methods are practical for OSN application.

Also, in the method that uses tag recognition, when a person wears a policy tag, that person displays their policy to people around them. Since that policy can also be considered sensitive information, some people believe it should be hidden. Making them visible to people taking photos, however, promotes respect for the subject's policy [16]. Thus, in our proposal, we adopted a method that uses tag recognition, does not require the registration of physical attributes into the system, and applies policies acquired from tags worn by photographed subjects.

3 Method Overview

Our PrivacyTag method protects the privacy of people appearing in photos by adaptively blurring their facial area in photos to be posted within and outside the community to which that person belongs by using tags embedded with the community-based privacy policies. This method makes it possible to detect and analyze tags worn by individuals appearing in a photo and to blur and anonymize their facial areas in accordance with the policies acquired through analysis of the tags. Additionally, users can define to which communities they belong, and users can be assigned to those communities by using community information included in the tags. This enables subjects to wear tags that contain policies that differ for each community and to implement different privacy policies depending on the situation. Further, by specifying a particular community as the intended audience of a post, the user can restrict access to posted messages and thereby prevent inadvertent disclosure of sensitive information.

Figure 1 shows a simple example of how the proposed method works when the subject has a policy for only one community. In this case, he does not want his face shown to the community members, so he wears a privacy tag containing "Do not show my face" as his privacy policy. If a photographer using our smartphone application takes a photo of him, the application detects the subject's face and the tag being worn and analyzes the embedded policy. It then blurs his facial area in accordance with the policy and publishes a message including this photo in an OSN. The community members who are friends of the photographer can see the message with the anonymized photo. Other community members such as acquaintances and strangers cannot even see the message.

Fig. 1. Simple example of how proposed method works

This method is composed of three main functions: (1) Privacy Tag, (2) Photo Privacy Realizer, and (3) Privacy Wall. The following sub-sections explain these functions and the flow of the proposed method.

3.1 Privacy Tag

A privacy tag contains the wearer's privacy policy for each community to which she belongs. The tag is worn as a fashion accessory and displays the wearer's privacy policy. The design, analysis algorithm, and evaluation of the privacy tag are explained in Sect. 4.

3.2 Photo Privacy Realizer

The Photo Privacy Realizer (PPR) is a Web application that detects a person in a photo being posted in an OSN, detects and analyzes the privacy tag that the person is wearing, and performs protection measures for the facial area of the person in accordance with the policy acquired through the tag analysis. It is designed for use on smartphones and other devices and consists of two functions: (1) community management and (2) photo taking and anonymization. The PPR blurs the facial area on the basis of the acquired policy to anonymize the subject. It then posts the anonymized photo and message in the OSN, and they are visible only to the community members. Section 5 discusses a prototype PPR.

3.3 Privacy Wall

Privacy Wall is a function for protecting the privacy of a subject wearing a privacy tag in photos taken with ordinary digital cameras and devices that do not have the PPR installed. It is to be configured as a function offered by OSN providers. When a post is made, it detects the privacy tags and anonymizes the facial areas in accordance with the tags being worn. This function is only a proposal at the moment; it will be addressed in a future study.

3.4 Process Flow

Figure 2 shows the process flow of the proposed method. The numbers in red correspond to the following steps.

(1) **Tag acquisition:** Tags are bought from participating stores in a pack with three types of tags: public, private, and within community that include common community IDs. The user can also print her own tags.
(2) **Tag activation and community registration:** After purchasing the tags, the user uses the PPR to activate a tag and register a new community. She can then select the members of the community from her OSN friend list. All community members are asked to wear a tag with their own privacy policy.
(3) **Photo taking and anonymization:** A photo is taken using the PPR, which analyzes the tags worn by the subjects. If a subject is wearing a tag with a "private" policy, his facial area is blurred (Fig. 2, M5). Moreover, if people who are not members of the community appear in the photo, they are also anonymized to respect their privacy even though their policy cannot be acquired since they are not wearing tags (Fig. 2, S1). Likewise, if a tag is detected for someone but cannot be analyzed due to distance or other reasons, that person is anonymized as well.
(4) **OSN Posting:** After processing the photo to protect the privacy of the subjects, the user posts the photo in the OSN along with a message. The post is restricted to members of the community and they can see the anonymized photo.
(5) **Taking photos and posting from non-PPR devices:** If a person outside the community posts a photo taken using a device or application without the PPR, the Privacy Wall of the OSN provider detects only the presence of tags and anonymizes all subjects wearing tags.

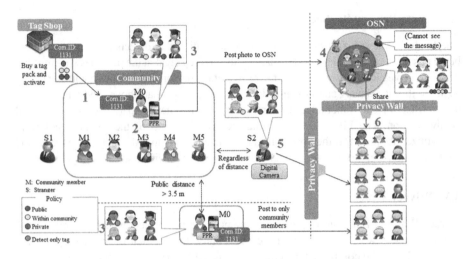

Fig. 2. Process flow of proposed method

(6) **Reposting outside the community:** When messages already posted are shared in the community or reposted outside the community, the privacy policies are acquired from the photo metadata, and anonymization is carried out on the basis of those policies.

3.5 Effect of Distance from Photographer

Protection of the facial area of the subject depends on (1) the distance between the photographer and subject and (2) whether the device used to take the photo was equipped with the PPR. According to a classification of photos posted on Instagram [20], photos fall into eight categories such as selfies, food, and pets. Selfies and group photos with two or more friends comprised 46.6% of the photos posted. To determine the distance within which tag detection and analysis should be accurate, we referred to the classification of personal space by Hall [21]. As shown in Table 1, he defined four distance categories. Since many of the photos posted on Instagram are either selfies or group photos with two or more friends, we assumed that many of the photos posted in OSNs fall into the categories of intimate, personal, and social. This means that the detection and analysis of tags should work accurately up to a distance of 350 cm from the photographer.

Table 1. Personal space classification by Hall

Distance category	Description	Distance
Intimate	Distance where only very close people are permitted	0–45 cm
Personal	Distance when talking to friends	45–120 cm
Social	Distance when talking to acquaintances and unrelated people	120–350 cm
Public	Distance in public intercourse	350–750 cm

4   Tag Realization

This section explains the design and the detection and analysis algorithm of the privacy tag we are proposing. We also compare our proposed tag with a QR-code-based tag used in conventional methods and demonstrate improvements in detection and analysis accuracy, which was previously limited by the distance to the subject.

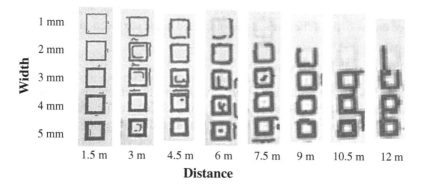

Fig. 3. Comparison of 5 × 5 cm outline detection for different frame line widths and distance

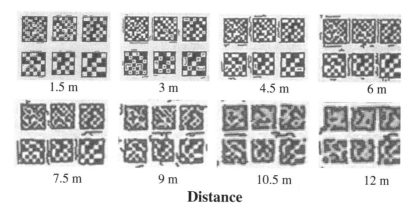

Fig. 4. Comparison of 5 × 5 cm bit pattern reading at different distances

4.1   Preliminary Evaluation

The design of the privacy tag takes into account the method used for tag detection and analysis. We created a frame to enclose the tag and assumed the following steps: detection of the frame, reading of the bit pattern inside the frame, and determining whether it is a privacy tag or not. On the basis of these assumptions, we performed a preliminary evaluation of (1) detection accuracy based on frame line width and distance and (2) accuracy of reading bit patterns depending on distance. For both tests, we used 5 × 5 cm tags and took photos of them with a digital camera (resolution of 20.9 megapixels).

Photo taking was considered successful when the frame or bit outline was clearly captured in the photo.

Figure 3 compares detection accuracy for different frame line widths (1 mm to 5 mm) and distances (in 1.5 m increments up to 12 m). For a frame line width of 2 mm or less, the farther the subject from the photographer, the more difficult it was to detect the frame outline. A frame line width of 3 mm or more could be detected up to a distance of 12 m. Figure 4 shows the results for reading bit patterns with 7 bits/surface. The bit patterns were mostly readable at distances of 6 m or less from the photographer. The tags were designed on the basis of these results, as discussed in the next section.

4.2 Disclosure Policy Design

Preventing inadvertent disclosure of sensitive information in photos does not require complex settings, so it is possible to carry out protection using only a few bits for expressing face information, tags, and disclosure/non-disclosure of location, etc. [22]. As shown in Table 2, we defined three privacy policies: (1) private, (2) within community, and (3) public.

Table 2. Disclosure policies

Disclosure policy	Description
Private	Do not show facial area either within or outside community
Within community	Show facial area within particular community
Public	Show facial area regardless of community

4.3 Bit Pattern Design

The pattern of the bits in the tag used to store the disclosure policy and applicable community information was designed as shown in Fig. 5(a). A sample tag is shown in Fig. 5(b).

Two requirements were set: (1) the bits should be readable regardless of tag orientation, and (2) error correction should be carried out based on burst error. To meet these requirements, we assumed that burst errors occur within the tag in the following order of likelihood: upper left/right → lower left/right → middle area. In accordance with these assumptions, we placed the bit pattern indicating the tag orientation as the header part in the two center columns to enable the system to quickly detect the tag and determine its orientation (Fig. 5(a), bits 0–11). Next, we placed the community ID and the disclosure policy, i.e., the privacy policy, in the central and lower part on the left and right sides (Fig. 5(a), bits 12–25, 26–27). We use the Reed-Solomon Code as the error-correcting code, meaning that error correction is possible for each symbol (=4 bits). The header part is excluded from error correction. The error-correcting code is located in the upper left and right corners (Fig. 5(a), bits 28–34).

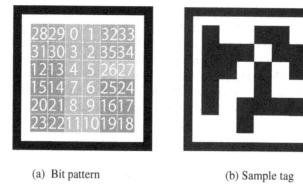

(a) Bit pattern   (b) Sample tag

Fig. 5. Privacy Tag

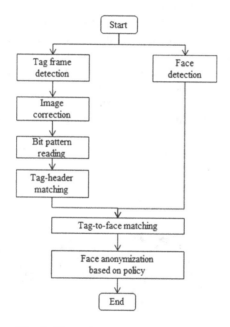

Fig. 6. Flow of tag detection and analysis

4.4   Detection and Analysis

As shown in Fig. 6, tag detection/analysis and face detection are carried out in parallel. The first step in tag detection/analysis is to detect the tag frame. Next, image correction is carried out to adjust the tag orientation, after which the bit pattern inside the tag is read. Finally, the decision of whether it is a privacy tag is made on the basis of matching with the header part, which indicates the orientation of the tag. For face detection, we use a method based on the Viola-Jones face detection algorithm [23]. The error-correction code is used to complement bits that cannot be read, if there are any.

After tag detection and analysis, the system identifies the subject wearing a tag. Matching is carried out under the assumptions that the subject is wearing the tag on the upper part of his or her body directly under the face and that the tag is three times the width and four times the height of the detected face (3–W × 4–H). Finally, the facial area is blurred or not blurred in accordance with the policy embedded in the tag. Moreover, if several faces are detected in a photo, the process can find a suitable tag for each one and blur the faces in accordance with the acquired policies.

4.5   Experimental Evaluation

To compare the performance of our proposed tag with that of QR-code-based tags used in conventional methods, we first measured the accuracy of tag detection and analysis for tags with a width and height of 2 cm to 10 cm at distances of 45 cm to 1050 cm from the photographer. We used a version-1 QR code and a digital camera with a resolution of 20.9 megapixels. The photos were taken outdoors in sunny conditions. Photos of a person wearing the QR-code-based tag and the proposed tag are shown in Fig. 7. As shown in Fig. 8, for tags 5 × 5 cm or smaller, which is considered to be a realistic size with regards to wearability, our tag could be detected and analyzed at a greater distance. For sizes between 2 and 5 cm, the QR code could be read from 120 cm up to a maximum of 350 cm while our proposed tag could be read up to 450 cm. As shown in Fig. 7(b), the bits in the proposed tag (3 cm in size) were clear and could be read at 350 cm while those in the QR code tag were blurred and could not be read. As discussed above, the intended scope of privacy protection ranges up to the social distance (350 cm), and these results show that it is possible to detect and analyze reasonably sized tags within the social distance. Furthermore, as shown by the photos of someone wearing a 10 cm tag in Fig. 7(a), a practical size for the tag is 5 cm or less.

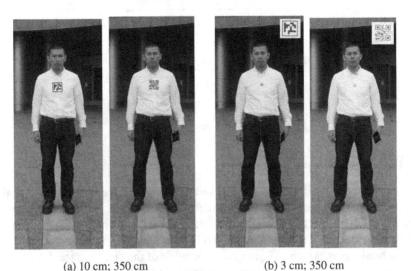

(a) 10 cm; 350 cm   (b) 3 cm; 350 cm

Fig. 7. Photos showing wearing of proposed tag (left photos) and QR code tag (right photos)

Proposed tag   (cm)

Size/Dist.	45	82.5	120	235	350	450	550	650	750	850	950	1050
2 cm	✓	✓	✓	✓	✓	ND	ND	ND	ND	ND	ND	ND
3 cm	✓	✓	✓	✓	✓	✓	ND	ND	ND	ND	ND	ND
5 cm	✓	✓	✓	✓	✓	✓	ND	ND	ND	ND	ND	ND
7.5 cm	✓	✓	✓	✓	✓	✓	✣	ND	ND	ND	ND	ND
10 cm	✓	✓	✓	✓	✓	✓	✓	ND	ND	ND	ND	ND

Intimate Distance	Personal Distance	Social Distance	Public Distance

✔ - Tag detection & analysis
✣ - Tag detection
ND - No detection

QR code tag   (cm)

Size/Dist.	45	82.5	120	235	350	450	550	650	750	850	950	1050
2 cm	✓	✓	✓	ND	ND	ND	ND	ND	ND	ND	ND	ND
3 cm	✓	✓	✓	✓	ND	ND	ND	ND	ND	ND	ND	ND
5 cm	✓	✓	✓	✓	✓	ND	ND	ND	ND	ND	ND	ND
7.5 cm	✓	✓	✓	✓	✓	✓	✓	ND	ND	ND	ND	ND
10 cm	✓	✓	✓	✓	✓	✓	✓	✓	ND	ND	ND	ND

Fig. 8. Results of comparison of the proposed tag and QR code tag

5 Application Implementation

In this section, we present a high-level application of our proposed Photo Privacy Realizer (PPR) and a prototype implementation.

5.1 Overview

The purpose of the PPR is to reflect a photographed subject's privacy policy acquired through analysis of the subject's privacy tag before publishing an original photo in an OSN. Figure 9 shows the PPR process flow.

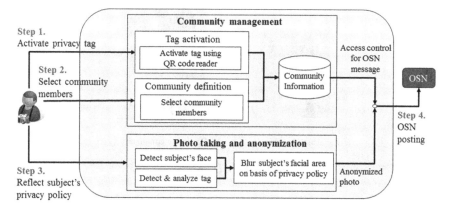

Fig. 9. Photo Privacy Realizer process flow

The PPR is composed of two modules: (1) community management and (2) photo taking and anonymization. The community management module creates a community and assigns OSN users to the community. First, the photographer activates a tag and creates a community. The PPR sets an expiration date for the tag automatically. The photographer then assigns users to the created community by using his OSN friend list. The PPR can create and manage several communities. After the community is activated, the photo-taking and anonymization module is used to take a photo and reflect the subject's privacy policy in accordance with the result of analyzing the privacy tag. Finally, the PPR is used to publish a message with the anonymized photo only to community members.

5.2   Prototype Implementation

We developed a prototype implementation of the PPR designed for Facebook. The user interface is shown in Fig. 10, and the operation flow is as follows.

(a) Community management

(b) Photo taking

(c) Facial area blurring

(d) Posting to community

Fig. 10. Flow of operation

Community management: The community management function of the PPR is used to activate a community and assign users to the community. The user first logs into her Facebook account through the PPR interface (Fig. 10(a)). After the user has logged in, her Facebook friend list is displayed. To activate (create) a community, the user presses the "Activate new community" button and registers the community ID attached to the purchased tag pack. After registering the community, the user then selects users to be included in the community by tapping on the respective friends' names. Users can be deleted from the community in the same way. After adding members, the user saves the community information. The community pull-down menu can be used to switch between communities and manage friends belonging to different communities.

Photo taking and anonymization: This function detects faces in new or old photos, detects and analyzes tags, and blurs faces depending on the acquired policies and the community specified in the PPR. First, the user inputs the message and takes the photo (Fig. 10(b)); at this point, the tag has not yet been detected or analyzed). Next, the user presses the "Anonymize" button to analyze the tags in the photo, and anonymization is performed in accordance with the results of the analysis. Anonymization is also carried out when communities in the tags do not match. Finally, the user presses the "Post" button to post the message and the anonymized photo in the OSN (Fig. 10(c)). They are visible only to members of the selected community (Fig. 10(d)).

6   Conclusions and Future Work

We have developed a method called "PrivacyTag" for adaptively blurring the facial area of a photographed subject in accordance with the communities to which the subject belongs by using privacy tags embedded with community-based privacy policies. We also evaluated the tag used for this by performing a preliminary evaluation of tag frame detection and bit reading and comparing the performance of our proposed tag with a QR-code-based tag for different tag sizes and distances from the photographer. We were able to demonstrate improved detection and analysis accuracy, which was previously limited by the distance to the subject. Furthermore, we created a prototype application (Photo Privacy Realizer) designed for Facebook using the proposed tag that can be used to publish an OSN message with an anonymized photo to only community members.

One open question is whether blurring the subject's face is sufficient for protecting the subject's privacy because a person who knows the subject may be able to recognize him or her from the subject's clothing or another simple factor. Another question regarding anonymization is whether, if all the subjects in a photo have a tag, is there is a possibility of blurring all the faces. If so, no one may want to post photos in OSNs. However, the basic concept of our method is that maximum safety measures are taken in cases where the subject's policy cannot be acquired and applied.

Also, we compared the performance of the proposed privacy tag with that of a QR-code-based tag in terms of detection and analysis accuracy for tags of various sizes and at various distances. Since the comparison with QR code tags was limited, future work includes more evaluation to improve the tag design. Finally, we showed as a first step that our method can protect the privacy of people appearing in photos without relying on subjective decisions by OSN posters and photographers.

Acknowledgment. This work was supported by JSPS KAKENHI Grants (JP16H06302 and JP15H01686).

References

1. Bosker, B.: The Twitter Typo That Exposed Anthony Weiner. http://www.huffington post.com/2011/06/07/anthony-weiner-twitter-dm_n_872590.html. Accessed 10 May 2017
2. Dabrowski, A., Weippl, E.R., Echizen, I.: Framework based on privacy policy hiding for preventing unauthorized face image processing. In: Proceedings of 2013 IEEE International Conference on Systems, Man and Cybernetics, pp. 455–461 (2013)
3. Wickramasuriya, J., Datt, M., Mehrotra, S., Venkatasubramanian, N.: Privacy protecting data collection in media spaces. In: Proceedings of the 12th Annual ACM International Conference on Multimedia, pp. 48–55 (2004)
4. Survey research regarding ethics of information security in 2014 (in Japanese). https://www.ipa.go.jp/files/000044094.pdf. Accessed 10 May 2017
5. Be careful when you post a photo during your vacation (in Japanese). http://www.ipa.go.jp/security/txt/2015/05outline.html. Accessed 10 May 2017
6. Bo, C., Shen, G., Liu, J., Li, X.-Y., Zhang, Y., Zhao, F.: Privacy.tag: privacy concern expressed and respected. In: Proceedings of the 12th ACM Conference on Embedded Network Sensor Systems, pp. 163–176 (2014)
7. Mondal, M., Liu, Y., Viswanath, B., Gummadi, K.P., Mislove, A.: Understanding and specifying social access control lists. In: Proceedings of the Tenth Symposium on Usable Privacy and Security, pp. 271–283 (2014)
8. Sleeper, M., Balebako, R., Das, S., McConahy, A.L., Wiese, J., Cranor, L.F.: The post that wasn't: exploring self-censorship on facebook. In: Proceedings of the 2013 Conference on Computer Supported Cooperative Work, pp. 793–802 (2013)
9. Besmer, A., Lipford, H.R.: Privacy perceptions of photo sharing in facebook. In: Proceedings of the Fourth Symposium on Usable Privacy and Security (2008)
10. Kumar, P., Schoenebeck, S.: The Modern day baby book: enacting good mothering and stewarding privacy on facebook. In: Proceedings of the 18th ACM Conference on Computer Supported Cooperative Work & Social Computing, pp. 1302–1312 (2015)
11. Egelman, S., Oates, A., Krishnamurthi, S.: Oops, I did it again: mitigating repeated access control errors on facebook. In: Proceedings of the SIGCHI Conference on Human Factors in Computing Systems, pp. 2295–2304 (2011)
12. Machida, S., Kajiyama, T., Shigeru, S., Echizen, I.: Analysis of facebook friends using disclosure level. In: Proceedings of the Tenth International Conference on Intelligent Information Hiding and Multimedia Signal Processing, pp. 471–474 (2014)
13. Sleeper, M., Cranshaw, J., Kelley, P.G., Ur, B., Acquisti, A., Cranor, L.F., Sadeh, N.: "I read my Twitter the next morning and was astonished": a conversational perspective on Twitter regrets. In: Proceedings of the SIGCHI Conference on Human Factors in Computing Systems, pp. 3277–3286 (2013)
14. Wang, Y., Norcie, G., Komanduri, S., Acquisti, A., Leon, P.G., Cranor, L.F.: "I regretted the minute I pressed share": a qualitative study of regrets on Facebook. In: Proceedings of the Seventh Symposium on Usable Privacy and Security, p. 10 (2011)

15. Henne, B., Szongott, C., Smith, M.: SnapMe if you can: privacy threats of other peoples' geo-tagged media and what we can do about it. In: Proceedings of the Sixth ACM Conference on Security and Privacy in Wireless and Mobile Networks, pp. 95–106 (2013)

16. Pappachan, P., Yus, R., Das, P.K., Finin, T., Mena, E., Joshi, A.: A semantic context-aware privacy model for faceblock. In: Proceedings of the 2nd International Conference on Society, Privacy and the Semantic Web - Policy and Technology, pp. 64–72 (2014)

17. Li, Y., Xu, K., Yan, Q., Li, Y., Deng, R.H.: Understanding OSN-based facial disclosure against face authentication systems. In: Proceedings of the 9th ACM Symposium on Information, Computer and Communications Security, pp. 413–424 (2014)

18. Pallas, F., Ulbricht, M.-R., Jaume-Palasí, L., Höppner, U.: Offlinetags: a novel privacy approach to online photo sharing. In: Proceedings of CHI 2014 Extended Abstracts on Human Factors in Computing Systems, pp. 2179–2184 (2014)

19. Cammozzo, A.: TagMeNot. http://tagmenot.info/. Accessed 10 May 2017

20. Hu, Y., Manikonda, L., Kambhampati, S.: What we instagram: a first analysis of instagram photo content and user types. In: Proceedings of the 8th International AAAI Conference on Weblogs and Social Media (2014)

21. Hall, E.T.: The Hidden Dimension. Anchor Books/Doubleday, New York (1966)

22. Ashok, A., Nguyen, V., Gruteser, M., Mandayam, N., Yuan, W., Dana, K.: Do not share!: invisible light beacons for signaling preferences to privacy-respecting cameras. In: Proceedings of the 1st ACM MobiCom Workshop on Visible Light Communication Systems, pp. 39–44 (2014)

23. Viola, P., Jones, M.J.: Robust real-time face detection. Int. J. Comput. Vis. **57**(2), 137–154 (2004). Springer

24. Cheung, S.-C.S., Venkatesh, M.V., Paruchuri, J.K., Zhao, J., Nguyen, T.: Protecting and managing privacy information in video surveillance systems. In: Senior, A. (ed.) Protecting Privacy in Video Surveillance, pp. 11–33. Springer, London (2009)

Fake Order Mitigation: A Profile Based Mechanism

Prabhat Kumar, Yashwanth Dasari, Ayushi Jain, and Akash Sinha[✉]

Computer Science and Engineering Department, National Institute of Technology Patna,
Patna, India
{prabhat,dasari134763,ayushi.cspg16,akash.cse15}@nitp.ac.in

Abstract. The ever-increasing need and interest of the consumers in online purchases has been a major driver in shaping the persistent and prominent role of e-commerce industry. Business – Consumer trust is a very important factor which should be harnessed for the well-being of this e-commerce community. Such a relationship can be easily hampered owing to the fraudulent behavior of either the consumer or the seller. From a consumer point of view, placement of fake orders can be considered as a breach of trust relationship which may attribute to the losses incurred to the e-commerce industry. Fake orders are those orders which are intentionally cancelled post the packaging and shipment stage. Motivated from this idea, this paper proposes an efficient mechanism to mitigate the fake orders, thereby, reducing the loss of packaging and shipment cost and improving the Business – Consumer relationship. The necessity to reduce the number of fake orders has been discussed eloquently in this paper. A qualitative analysis has been performed to elucidate the efficiency of the proposed mechanism. This mechanism, if implemented, has the potential to mitigate the fake orders which will inherently increase the profit of a company.

Keywords: Fake order · E-commerce · Trust · E-wallet · Virtual cash · Business-Consumer trust

1 Introduction

In the present world where everyone is running behind their goals with a busy schedule, no one has the time for offline shopping. This is one of the prime reasons behind the wider acceptance of the e-commerce platforms in the present context. E-commerce platforms provide a greater advantage with a variety of options by providing millions of brands on a single platform. The range of discounts provided by them is also a vital point which cannot be neglected especially in the consumer context. The global B2C e-commerce turnover is expected to reach \$2.352 trillion in the year 2017 [12]. Day by day the users of the e-commerce community are increasing. Taking this into account, the e-commerce industry must withstand with the problems which it is facing today.

One of the major challenge of the e-commerce industry is that there is no unified model to correlate various factors which affect the trust and trade between the seller and the consumer. Also with reference to the Indian context, fake orders are one of the key problems being faced by the industry. Fake orders can be considered as those orders that

© IFIP International Federation for Information Processing 2017
Published by Springer International Publishing AG 2017. All Rights Reserved
A.K. Kar et al. (Eds.): I3E 2017, LNCS 10595, pp. 276–288, 2017.
DOI: 10.1007/978-3-319-68557-1_25

have been placed initially but are intentionally cancelled by the consumers as a later stage. Such an activity can be considered as an intentional attack upon the economy of the target e-commerce industry since the cost incurred in packaging and shipping the order is wasted. This problem has a serious adverse effect on the industry resulting in the net decrease of the profit and hampering the trust between the seller and the consumer community.

In the Indian context, most of the users prefer the option of the Cash on Delivery (COD) [28]. This option of payment has both pros and cons. The consumer always wants to stay on the safe side with this option and as such, the essence of this option of payment in attracting the large number of consumers to an e-commerce portal cannot be overlooked. However, the COD mode of payment is also a significant antecedent of the loss incurred due to fake orders. If the number of fake orders increases the seller may be at a risk. The magnitude of this problem can be understood by the fact that FLIPKART, the Indian e-commerce tycoon that has banned the orders above INR 10,000 in the states of Bihar and Uttar Pradesh [8]. It is, hence, high time to find a consumer effective solution so that this problem doesn't reach its zenith. Further, it is required that the solution should not be only consumer friendly but also seller friendly. The remaining paper is organized as follows: Sect. 2 gives the motivation of this work; Sect. 3 reviews the existing literature in this field of research; the proposed system has been discussed in Sect. 4; Sect. 5 presents a qualitative analysis of the proposed mechanism; a case based on the proposed strategy has been discussed in Sect. 6; Sect. 7 provides a discussion about the research findings; and finally, Sect. 8 presents the concluding remarks and future works.

2 Background

Human behavior cannot be judged because it is subjected to many variations under different contexts, different scenarios and different perspectives [17]. What is of prior importance in one's view may be a subject of post importance in others view. This human incognito tendency is uncertain and varies in an uncanny fashion [17]. The present e-commerce trading system lacks a unified model for evaluating the trustworthy behavior of the consumers. A customer may show his order choice to his friends or family members and ask for their opinion and if the opinion is positive he won't cancel the order. However, if the opinion is negative there is a high chance that he may cancel the order because he has got a negative response from his known people.

It is also important to consider the economic issues which is very vital in the business-consumer community. A consumer may find a low price of the same product on a different platform or he may change his mind considering that the product may not be worthy enough for investing large amount of money on it. Consequently, this shall ultimately result in the rejection or cancellation of the order. This type of abnormal behavior is very common in the e-commerce community and as stated above it varies in an uncanny fashion. Hence there is no chance of getting to know which type of orders are cancelled the most and by what type of users even by applying data mining or statistical analysis.

The above discussed scenarios consider the case of genuine and honest users. However, an adverse user may plan a targeted attack on the e-commerce industry with the intention of hampering the financial gains of the merchant sellers. Such users tend to place the order and later cancel it post-shipment, thereby reducing the net profit of the retailers. Prabhat et al. [19] proposed a mechanism to deal with such socio-technical attacks on the ecommerce business. The authors considered the behavior of the fake users that aim to defame the product retailers thereby, instigating financial loss to the retailers. Such users shall intentionally order those products which involve high packaging and shipment cost. This may incur a good amount of loss to the product seller. If such attacks are made on large scales, it may attribute to a substantial amount of financial loss to the e-commerce industry when considered massive. It is for this reason that, the Indian E-commerce tycoon "Flipkart" decided not to accept high value orders from the states of Bihar and Uttar Pradesh if the payment mode is chosen to be COD [8]. It is vital to state that there are obvious possibilities that these states also incorporate honest users. If such users genuinely require to order valuable goods, then it is a loss to the retailers since the e-commerce platform has restricted the acceptance of such orders. In this context, the mechanism proposed in this paper will play an effective role in controlling the behavior of such untrusted users.

3   Literature Review

Internet has changed the face of business industry enormously. Consequently, the e-commerce industry witnessed an exponential growth in the past few years and as such has attracted the attention of many researchers and practitioners [21]. Several important studies [1, 4] [5] have emphasized upon the need to cater the security and privacy issues of the e-commerce industry. This can be attributed to the fact that the consumers are still not willing to perform high value transactions on the e-commerce portal owing to the security concerns. Moreover, these concerns can be considered to be the significant drivers of the business-consumer trust [12, 14, 22] which is an essential factor for the success of any business activity. In the case of e-commerce, trust becomes even more necessary since the online services and products are not immediately verifiable. Salam et al. [23] indicated in their study that the consumers just don't trust online merchants to take part in exchanges including cash and personal information. Owing to the lack of direct interactions [22] in the e-commerce industry, the authors in [16] investigate the significance of the established dimensions of trust for interpersonal relationships and traditional business-to-consumer (B2C) commerce in shaping the consumer trust in online merchants (e-trust).

Significant research has been performed in the past years regarding the e-commerce trust in various domains of Management, Economics, Sociology and Computer Science. The authors in [9, 18] debated that fraudulent vendors artificially increase their reputations by trading positive feedback ratings on eBay. Xiong and Liu [28, 29] proposed an adaptive trust model, PeerTrust, for quantifying and comparing the trustworthiness of peers. The model relies upon a weighted sum of the factors including feedback records, feedback scope, credibility, transaction context and community context. Bizer and

Oldakowski [6] outlined a trust architecture that has trust policies combining reputation, context and content-based trust mechanisms. It can be clearly observed that most of the work has been performed to mitigate the fraudulent activities of the online sellers. However, not much consideration has been given to the fraudulent behavior of the consumers on the e-commerce portal. As such, there is hardly any literature catering the issue discussed in this paper.

In fact, several works such as [7, 11] that aim to simplify the e-commerce experience of the consumers have inadvertently increased the risk of fake orders. Cameron et al. [7] devised a computerized order entry system and method for placing an order by a user using display mounted terminal. Eggebraaten and Prentice [11] patented a mechanism to add the last order list or a default order list to cart in an automated manner. However, simplifying the modification of the placed orders has led to an increase in the number of fake orders, thereby, posing a serious challenge to the ecommerce companies.

Certain attempts have been made to cater the challenges arising due to the fraudulent behavior of the consumers on the e-commerce portals. A 4D authentication mechanism have been discussed in [24] that considers the importance of comprehensive validation of the consumers upon the placement of any order on the e-commerce portal. The validation may include the verification of the consumer's email address, contacting the consumer over call for verifying the order, confirming the order before shipment, and finally using certain software to perform security checks. Such type of validation can be helpful in establishing the credibility of the consumers to certain extent. Sussman in [26] devised a system to electronically verify a customer using Address Verification Service (AVS). These attempts clearly highlight the urge of incorporating suitable mechanisms to counter the dishonest behavior of the consumers on the e-commerce portals.

4   Proposed Methodology

This section discusses the proposed mechanism which shall facilitate the e-commerce portals to limit the number of fake orders and maximize their financial gains. The objective of this research is neither to demoralize the customers nor disprove their loyalty. This research aims to help the e-commerce organizations to maintain benign relations with the customers so as to make these platforms more reliable.

The proposed mechanism considers the notion of adding certain amount of "virtual cash" to the e-wallet of a user. This virtual cash cannot be used for purchasing purpose unlike the present e-wallet cash. This virtual cash acts as a delimiter to stop the fake orders.

Let X is the amount in rupees credited to the account of the customer when he creates the account for the first time. For placing an order, the software will first check the amount of virtual cash present in the e-wallet. If the amount is sufficient, the order will proceed to the payment option. Else the order will be declined. After the payment is done through the available options the same amount will also be deducted from the e-wallet too. Without loss of generality, it is required that some virtual amount should also be credited to the e-wallet of the users in case of successful orders. However, in case of fake orders the users shall be penalized in terms of virtual cash. The above six are grouped into three pairs in which every case is dealt separately. By intuition in every case the amount returned will also vary. The Algorithm is as follows:

Proposed Algorithm

1. Place Order
2. Order_Payment_Options(order_amount)
3. Debit_Money_From_Ewallet (order_amount)
4. Update_Ewallet()
5. Exit ()

The proposed algorithm considers the following Global Variables:
g_ewallet_amt, g_total_orders, g_total_fake_orders

Pseudocode for Order_Payment_Options
The following function is used to investigate which payment option is applicable for the order. The function requires the value of the order being placed (order_amount) to evaluate the applicability of COD for that order. If ewallet_amt_status is 1 and the number of fake orders by the consumer is less than the threshold value, then the option for COD along with other pre-payment method shall be available for the customer. Otherwise, the COD option shall be disabled and only pre-payment is allowed. Customer can pay through debit/credit card, net-banking etc. in pre-payment option.

```
ORDER_PAYMENT_OPTION (order_amount)
{
  F = g_total_fake_orders;
  S = ewallet_amt_status(order_amount);
  If (S==YES && F<=25 || F*100/no_of_items<60)
  {
        Payment Options Available:
        Cash on Delivery (COD)
        Pre-payment Methods (Debit/Credit Card, Net Bank-
        -ing, Payment Gateway)
  }
  Else
  {
        Cash on Delivery (COD) unvailable.

        Payment Options Available:
         Pre-payment Methods (Debit/Credit Card, Net Bank-
         -ing, Payment Gateway)
  }
}
```

Auxiliary Function required by the Algorithm for ORDER_PAYMENT_OPTION().

```
boolean ewallet_amt_status order_amount)
{
 if (order_amount <= g_ewallet_amt)
        return 1;
 else
        return 0;
}
```

The above function compares the value of the order being placed with the amount of virtual cash available in the e-wallet. If the virtual cash present in the e-wallet is greater than the value of the current order, it returns 1 else 0.

Pseudocode for Debit_Money_From_Ewallet

This function deducts the virtual cash equal from the Ewallet upon placing an order. The amount of virtual cash to be deducted is equal to the value of the placed order.

```
Debit_Money_From_Ewallet (order_amount)
{
        g_ewallet_amt-=order_amount;

}
```

Pseudocode for Update_Ewallet

The Update_Ewallet function shall be used to credit/debit virtual cash to the ewallet as per the status of the order. The variable 'order' can be considered as a structure containing the value of the items comprising the order. The variable T refers to the threshold value for classifying the order as real or fake.

```
Update_e_wallet ()
initialize i=0;
If (Item status = Accepted/exchange)
          add_money_to_ewallet (2*order. item [i].value)
          amt = amt +2* order. item[i].value
Else if (item status = Cancelled before Shipment)
          add_money_to_ewallet (order.item[i].value)
             amt = amt + order. item[i].value
Else
/* Case of cancellation after
Shipment / Rejection */
          add_money_to_ewallet (0)
End If
i=i+1
Repeat step 1to 12 until i<=no_of_items
If (amt<T)
/*fake order*/
          g_total_fake_orders= g_total_fake_orders +1
End If
End If.
End.
```

Auxiliary Function required by the Algorithm for Update_Ewallet().

```
add_money_to_ewallet (float amt)
{
          g_ewallet_amt+=amt;
}
```

The above function is used to credit virtual cash to the ewallet.

Deciding the Initial Amount (X)

Originally, the option of COD was made available for the customers who do not own a credit card or do not have access to online payment modes. Later, it increased impulse purchases as payment was not due at the time of ordering.

The initial amount X is set to the maximum limit of COD amount offered by a particular online purchasing site. This maximum amount differs from one website to other. For instance, the maximum COD limit of FLIPKART is 50000 [13] while that for AMAZON is 30000 [2].

The choice was kept to a maximum and not any other intermediate value. Consider a scenario where the value of X is set to be 10,000. If a customer purchases goods worth 1,000 then the initial amount deducted from e-wallet is 1000. Upon acceptance of the order by the customer, the amount credited to his e-wallet is 2,000 and the total available virtual cash becomes 11,000. Subsequently, he purchases goods worth 7,000 and cancels his order after shipment due to some genuine reason. After deducting 7,000 he is left with virtual cash amounting to 4,000. Now, if he wants to buy an item worth 10,000 and has no access to any online payment mode then in that case he cannot purchase it.

5   Qualitative Analysis

This section presents a qualitative analysis of the proposed algorithm. The following discussion explains the efficacy of the proposed algorithm under different circumstances. There can be five types of situations which may arise when an order is placed. The order can be accepted, exchanged, cancelled before shipment, cancelled after shipment, or rejected. These situations have been analyzed under two different conditions: *virtual cash is sufficient* and *virtual cash is insufficient.*

5.1   Virtual Cash Is Sufficient

For an item, there can be three cases if the virtual cash present in the user's e-wallet is sufficient, i.e. the total value of the virtual cash is equal to or exceeds the value of the order that needs to be placed.

Case 1. If the status of the item is "accepted" then the amount credited to the e-wallet of the customer will be twice the value of the order. Also, there can be a case that the customer has some issues such as fit, colour, style, size etc. In that case, he opts for an "exchange" request. Even in that case the amount that will be credited to the wallet is twice because penalizing the customer in this case is not genuine since the order is eventually accepted.

Case 2. If the status of the item is "cancelled before the shipment" then also the deducted amount will be returned to his wallet. This type of cancellations happens due to human incognito tendency, cash issues etc.

Case 3. If the status of the item is "cancelled after shipment" then the deducted amount will not be returned to his wallet. If the status of the item is "rejection" then also the deducted amount will not be returned to his wallet. For an order, there can be following cases:

Case 3a. If "total" of all items in an order is greater than threshold value 'T' then the order is not fake order. It will be considered as a real order.

Case 3b. If "total" of all items in an order is less than threshold value 'T' then this type of orders can be termed as fake orders because these have high chances of cancellation or rejection. These types of orders can be placed by the adversaries to reduce the net profit. This can also be termed as a planned attack to waste the resources of a particular e-commerce site. In this case the customer is penalized because nothing is returned to his e-wallet.

5.2   Virtual Cash Is Insufficient

If the customer doesn't have enough amounts in his e-wallet and still he wants to proceed for the payment through cash on delivery, then the order is declined. In this case the e-commerce organizations cannot take the risk of accepting an order from a fake user. Intuitively if he doesn't have enough balance he can be termed as a Sybil user. Consequently, the user shall be provided only with the payment options which do not include Cash on Delivery. Generally, this case has less chance of cancellation as customer has already paid the amount.

The policy for updating the virtual cash in the user's e-wallet will be the same as discussed above.

The analysis of the proposed mechanism clearly reveals that if someone is giving fake orders by continuously cancelling/rejecting them, it will eventually lead to that instance where virtual cash will not be left in the wallet. In this way, the targeted economic attacks by the adversaries and fake orders may be controlled up to a maximum extent and thereby increasing the net profit percentage.

6   Case Study

Suppose that the initial amount he has in his wallet is 5,000. The first order contains 3 items. The total amount of order is 2,000. He rejected or cancelled all the items after shipment. So as per the algorithm we won't return anything to his e-wallet. It will be a fake order according to algorithm. Now presently he is having 3,000 in his wallet. Now he wants to order 2 items of total worth 2,700 from the store. Even this time he repeated the same thing mentioned above. So, the amount in his e-wallet will come down to 300. It is also a fake order. Now he wants to order some items again but as per the algorithm, percentage of fake orders and total orders is greater than 60%. So, cash on delivery (COD) is disabled. He can place a COD order only when he will do pre-payment. Otherwise he can't place an order. Hence, we clearly state that within a short span of 2 orders we have been able to restrict him. The span may increase if he orders the articles of low cost. But still in that case the cost of transport and packaging will be nominal. Even in that case he may be restricted within a few orders albeit it is greater than 2. Now we see the other side of the coin. Here it can be assumed that, in the earlier stages he pretends to be an honest customer and he has increased the amount in his e-wallet by making certain number of successful orders. In this he has a chance to make more number of fake orders. But still the profit gained through the successful orders will compensate this loss making the net loss almost zero. In this way, the loss is compensated.

7   Discussion

The proposed mechanism aims to mitigate the number of fake orders placed as a result of fraudulent behavior of the consumers on the e-commerce portals. The algorithm proposed as a part of the mechanism runs in $O(n)$ time and has the space complexity of

O(n). Incorporating the proposed mechanism into the e-commerce portals requires minimal changes in the current implementation of the portals.

The proposed mechanism may induce certain variations in the total number of real orders that are being currently placed on the e-commerce portal. However, it can easily be deduced, that there shall be a high rate of decrease in the number of fake orders on the portal. The following equation can be used to evaluate the percentage of reduction in the number of fake orders.

$$\text{Decrease in percentage of Fake orders} = \left(\left(F - F' \right) / F \right) * 100\% \tag{1}$$

In the above equation, F refers to the original number of fake orders while F' denotes the reduced number of fake orders.

Considering the above mentioned facts, it is vital to state that there will be a substantial decrease in the financial losses of the e-commerce retailer incurred due to fake orders. Consequently, the proposed mechanism will essentially increase the net profit of the e-commerce industry.

7.1   Contribution

The e-commerce industry is growing faster day by day [22]. However, the exponential growth of the e-commerce industry is being hampered by many challenges such as, fake orders. To the best of our knowledge. this is the first study of its type, which not only explores the context of fake users and orders but has proposes a formal mechanism to mitigate the financial loss incurred by the e-commerce industry due to such fake orders. Online purchasing offers an efficient and hassle free shopping experience to the customers. Owing to the facilities of returning, exchanging or cancelling the order at any time, this mode of shopping is being preferred by the most of the customers. However, it is not necessary that the seller gets profit all the time. If the customer is non-reliable or fake, then the seller may incur substantial loss. This research proposes a novel mechanism with the aim of minimizing the financial loss borne by the online retailers due to fake orders. The proposed mechanism ensures that the online retailer may not suffer any loss due to the order cancellation after the product has been shipped. In the context of the e-commerce industries, this research can be utilized for increasing the net profit of the ecommerce retailers.

The proposed mechanism introduces the concept of virtual cash for limit the fraudulent behavior of the consumers. A customer must have sufficient virtual cash in the e-wallet in order to procure a product using COD option. Online shopping portals, such as Flipkart, Amazon, etc. can utilize this mechanism in their current portals to minimize the cases where orders are deliberately cancelled after shipment due to which the online retailer has to bear the expenses involved packaging, shipment, etc., since the payment option was chosen to be COD. Application of the proposed mechanism will help in minimizing such financial loss, thereby improving the net profit of the retailer as well as the e-commerce industry.

This research clearly differentiates the honest users from the fake users. If a person has a record of successful orders, the amount in his e-wallet increases substantially. He can be termed as a reliable customer. In this way, the e-commerce retailers can make a set of reliable and non-reliable users. The proposed mechanism also ensures that there is no sign of "Mathew Effect" [20] which is deeply rooted in the e-commerce industry. Although, a consumer may have earlier cancelled few orders due to human incognito tendency, he can still rebuild his reputation by making some successful orders and thereby, increasing the virtual cash in his e-wallet. Hence this model can be seen as a Meta model because risk handling is inherent in this model.

8   Conclusions and Future Work

With the evolution of the e-commerce industry the requirement to sustain the Business–Consumer trust has become the focal point of many research work. The work proposed in this paper considers the behavior of the online consumers for mitigating the losses of the e-commerce industry incurred due to the placement of fake orders. The concept of virtual cash as an indicator of the customers' reputation is an effective strategy to cater the issue of the targeted economic attacks in the form of fake orders. The proposed mechanism is generic and as applicable to all platforms. Further, the implementation of the proposed model requires minimal change in the present architecture of the e-commerce portals. This aspect can be considered to be a significant determinant for the adoption of the proposed method by the e-commerce industry.

Due to the unavailability of the real-time data sets required for testing the model, we have qualitatively analyzed the proposed solution. Future research work may concentrate on upon implementing the proposed solution as a service and exposing the corresponding APIs to be integrated into the existing framework. Additionally, the algorithm can be fine-tuned by considering the other attributes of the consumers in terms of age, gender and location. A more generic solution can be suggested for the recently proposed scenario of Social Internet of Things [25] where the Business – Consumer trust builds upon the past transactions.

References

1. Ahuja, M., Gupta, B., Raman, P.: An empirical investigation of online consumer purchasing behavior. Commun. ACM **46**(12), 145–151 (2003)
2. Amazon: About Cash/Card on Delivery. https://www.amazon.in/gp/help/customer/display.html/ref=hp_gt_pt_cod?nodeId=201818150. Accessed 20 Apr 2017
3. Baabdullah, A., Dwivedi, Y., Williams, M., Kumar, P.: Understanding the adoption of mobile internet in the saudi arabian context: results from a descriptive analysis. In: Janssen, M., Mäntymäki, M., Hidders, J., Klievink, B., Lamersdorf, W., van Loenen, B., Zuiderwijk, A. (eds.) I3E 2015. LNCS, vol. 9373, pp. 95–106. Springer, Cham (2015). doi: 10.1007/978-3-319-25013-7_8
4. Basu, A., Muylle, S.: Authentication in e-commerce. Commun. ACM **46**(12), 159–166 (2003)
5. Bingi, P., Mir, A., Khamalah, J.: The challenges facing global ecommerce. Inf. Syst. Manage. **17**(4), 26–34 (2000)

6. Bizer, C., Oldakowski, R.: Using context- and content-based trust policies on the semantic web. In: Proceedings of the Thirteenth International World Wide Web Conference, New York, NY, May 17–24, 2004, pp. 228–229. ACM Press, New York (2004)
7. Cameron, P.S., Nash, J.C., Bloomer, R.C., Wollan, R.E., Kreutter, K.M., Olmstead, M.A.A. Renner, D.H., Bourne, R.D., Carnish, K.M., Jones, D.R.: U.S. Patent No. 5,592,378. U.S. Patent and Trademark Office, Washington, DC (1997)
8. Capitalmind: Flipkart Won't Deliver Orders More than 10 K to Uttar Pradesh (2013). https://capitalmind.in/2013/06/flipkart-wont-deliver-orders-more-than-10k-to-uttar-pradesh/. Accessed 27 June 2017
9. Dini, F., Spagnolo, G.: Buying reputation on eBay: do recent changes help? Int. J. Electr. Bus. 7(6), 581–598 (2009)
10. Dwyer, F.R., Schurr, P.H., Oh, S.: Developing buyer–seller relationships. J. Mark. 51(2), 11–27 (1987)
11. Eggebraaten, T., Prentice, J.: U.S. Patent Application No. 09/910,534 (2003)
12. eMarketer: Worldwide Retail Ecommerce Sales Will Reach $1.915 Trillion This Year (2016). https://www.emarketer.com/Article/Worldwide-Retail-Ecommerce-Sales-Will-Reach-1915-Trillion-This-Year/1014369. Accessed 27 June 2017
13. Flipkart: Help Center. https://www.flipkart.com/helpcentre/search?query=cash%20on%20delivery. Accessed 20 April 2017
14. Fukuyama, F.: Trust: The social virtues and the creation of prosperity (No. D10 301 c. 1/c. 2). Free Press Paperbacks (1995)
15. Gangeshwer, D.K.: E-commerce or internet marketing: a business review from Indian context. Int. J. u-and e-Service Sci. Technol. 6(6), 187–194 (2013)
16. Gefen, D.: E-commerce: the role of familiarity and trust. Omega Int. J. Manage. Sci. 28(6), 725–737 (2000)
17. Harre, R., Secord, P.F.: The Explanation of Social Behaviour. Rowman & Littlefield, Lanham (1972)
18. Jøsang, A., Ismail, R., Boyd, C.: A survey of trust and reputation systems for online service provision. Decis. Support Syst. 43(2), 618–644 (2007)
19. Kumar, P., Dasari, Y., Nath, S., Sinha, A.: Controlling and mitigating targeted socio-economic attacks. In: Dwivedi, Y.K., et al. (eds.) I3E 2016. LNCS, vol. 9844, pp. 471–476. Springer, Cham (2016). doi:10.1007/978-3-319-45234-0_42
20. Merton, R.K.: The matthew effect in science. Science 159(3810), 56–63 (1968)
21. Puthiran, S.H.H.: A study on impact of E-Commerce on Indian economy. Int. J. Commer. Manage. Res. 2(10), 39–41 (2016)
22. Reichheld, F.F., Schefter, P.: E-loyalty: your secret weapon on the web. Harvard Bus. Rev. 78(4), 105–113 (2000)
23. Salam, A.F., Rao, H.R., Pegels, C.C.: Consumer-perceived risk in ecommerce transactions. Commun. ACM 46(12), 325–331 (2003)
24. ShipRocket: How to Avoid Fake Orders on Your eCommerce Website (2015). https://www.shiprocket.in/avoid-fake-orders-ecommerce-website/. Accessed 27 June 2017
25. Sinha, A., Kumar, P.: A novel framework for social internet of things. Indian J. Sci. Technol. 9(36), 1–6 (2016)
26. Sussman, L.: U.S. Patent No. 6,836,765. U.S. Patent and Trademark Office, Washington, DC (2004)
27. Wikipedia: Cash on Delivery. https://en.wikipedia.org/wiki/Cash_on_delivery. Accessed 27 June 2017

28. Xiong, L., Liu, L.: A reputation-based trust model for peer-to-peer ecommerce communities. In: Proceedings of the 2003 IEEE International Conference on ECommerce, Newport Beach, CA, June 24– 27, 2003, pp. 275–284. IEEE Computer Society Press, Los Alamitos (2003)
29. Xiong, L., Liu, L.: Peer trust: supporting reputation-based trust for peer-to-peer electronic communities. IEEE Trans. Knowl. Data Eng. **16**(7), 843–857 (2004)

Programmatic Advertisement and Real Time Bidding Utilization

Dalal A. AlSabeeh and Issam A.R. Moghrabi[(✉)] [ID]

Gulf University for Science and Technology, Kuwait City, Kuwait
dalal-alsabeeh@outlook.com, moughrabi.i@gust.edu.kw

Abstract. This paper focuses on the use of Real Time Bidding in Programmatic Advertisement and its utilization with a focus on Kuwait. Real Time Bidding is a new marketing technique that uses information collected from web users and exploits this information in targeting them. This technique, though it saves both time and cost, is neither well known nor utilized in Kuwait. The paper sheds light on some research done on Real Time Bidding and its applications. A two-step study is presented here that aims at testing the efficiency of Real Time Bidding. The first step evaluates the relevance of the used advertisements. The second step uses a survey to assess if the technique may prove effective in Kuwait. Our findings indicate that Real Time Bidding is the closest thing to achieve efficient marketing, yet in order for it to work in Kuwait the technology infrastructure needs to be updated and upgraded in order to achieve the benefits of Programmatic Advertisement.

Keywords: Programmatic advertising · Real-Time Bidding (RTB) · Marketing

1 Introduction

Technology is continuously evolving and this makes it much easier to collect more information about the user. For example, cookies stored by visited web sites on the user's drive constitute an information collection mechanism. Having access to such information is very beneficial to not just governments, but also to the marketing agencies. In order for companies to upgrade their profit figures, efficiency in marketing is the key. Efficient marketing means reaching the right audience at the right time, a thing that requires the possession of enough information about the potential customers.

Nowadays, there are countless online advertising platforms. Programmatic advertising is an automated technique that publishers utilize to promote their advertising space to advertisers interested in exploiting that space to reach out to more potential customers. Programmatic advertising promises to improve the targeting of ads, decreasing costs on advertisers and making the web less annoying to users by maximizing the probability of showing them ads that are more likely to be of interest to them [5, 9, 11]. There are two types of programmatic advertisement the first one is direct advertising which is directly buying the advertising slots from the publisher, while the other kind is Real Time Bidding (RTB) which is based on bidding for advertisement spots. This paper

A.K. Kar et al. (Eds.): I3E 2017, LNCS 10595, pp. 289–297, 2017.
DOI: 10.1007/978-3-319-68557-1_26

focuses on RTB type of Programmatic Advertising, the objective of this paper is to find if RTB works in Kuwait and how acceptable is it.

Prior to RTB, display ads were sold in a reservation contract which is based on a negotiation between the publisher, who is displaying the ad on their website, and the advertiser, who wants to put an ad on that website. After signing on the reservation contract, a Direct Buy is made based on number of ads required, the target audience of those ads and their location [6, 13]. An example of a Direct Buy between an advertiser and publisher is advertising specifically for women aged 18–21 who live in Kuwait. RTB basically is marketers bidding on empty advertisement slots on real-time basis to achieve efficient marketing. Fernandez-Tapia et al. [2] emphasize that this defines a new model in the way digital inventory is purchased: advertisers can buy online inventory through real-time auctions for displaying a banner (or a short video). This model enables advertisers to target individual customers based on their website surfing by using browser cookie information. Based on Google's White Paper Review of the RTB, it is a system that has two intersecting layers, the RTB API and the Real Time Bidder; the "Pipe" and the "Brain". The job of the RTB API the "Pipe" is to provide empty ad slots in a real-time stream to eligible buyers. As soon as an ad slot becomes available for purchase, it is announced. Then, the "Brain" is connected to several "Pipes" which allow them to assess every ad slot announced in order to acquire the best slot for its advertiser. Bidding for advertisement slots, bidders become selective as to which slots they want to buy. That causes them to place premium bids on the audiences that are valuable for the advertiser; the highest bidder gets the slot [3]. Real-Time Bidding enables marketers to customize their ads for each individual. So, basically RTB bundles auctions that ascertain that the premium a bidder is willing to pay is exhausted for every ad impression, in milliseconds. This is certain to work to the advantage of the premium publisher [7]. It can be deduced that the bidder has the upper hand in controlling such a market, but it can also be equally beneficial to the publisher if the demand for their ad space turns out to be high. More than 85% of marketers believe that Programmatic Advertisement provides more Return on Investment (ROI) than traditional marketing [1].

2   How Does It Work?

As programmatic advertising aims to reach the right audience at the right time, it uses online Big Data repositories that contain data on millions of consumers (a good example of such data source are social networking platforms [5]). When an ad is revealed to a web visitor on a particular website (or the ad publisher's site), tracking the visitor's click behavior and, in some cases, whether the click converts to a desired action becomes possible, such as a sale or a sign-up [7]. This platform also has analytical software to excavate the targeted consumers and online shoppers in the database. Machine learning techniques are employed to test out combinations of consumer characteristics that optimize the chance of a purchase resulting from exposure to an ad [8, 12]. The inventory (ads) can be bought programmatically and may also be bought algorithmically by unit, in the hope of achieving the intended goal of programmatic advertisement of being an efficient marketing tool. This technology requires two sides, the supply side and the demand side. The supply side, which is the publisher, connects to a virtual ad exchange marketplace to offer each ad slot separately and start an auction for each slot. On the other side lies the ad trading desk which is a demand side platform where it receives an auction request, user information, type of website and the bid level that best matches their marketing strategy. Once all bids are processed in the system, the bidder with the highest bidding price gets the ad slot and then pays the price depending on the auction type. The entire process, from the user entering the website to displaying the banner, consumes around 100 ms [2]. Google explains that the first layer of the "Pipe" which is the RTB API, is available for use, but needs the second layer which is the "Brain" which is the bidder to connect to the "Pipe". Not many companies can afford the acquisition of the technology for building one. So, many of them are having contracts with ad exchange platforms in order to utilize ad slots. It also suggests that there are three ways to do Real-Time Bidding: First, a partner with an ad network that does real time buying on its own inventory that is connected to an RTB API. Second, a partner who wants to place an ad, would bid for it through an intermediary's Real Time Bidder, instead of building its own, and can access several RTB APIs. Third, a party who builds own real-time bidding platform which is mostly done by ad networks whose business model is based on targeting ads. It is also used by marketing agencies that retarget providers and customers as well [3, 13]. The first study presented in this paper explores if RTB has proven its effectiveness in Kuwait in terms of cookies collection relevance of displayed ads.

3   The Platforms

There are several Ad Exchange arenas that provide several types of platforms depending on the company's use of the platform. Some want to hire someone to do the whole process for them, bid and buy slots, others want to do the bidding through an intermediary and some want to build the whole thing and host it. Some Ad Agencies have access to several programmatic ad platforms that Google, AOL, Facebook, and many smaller firms make available to interested parties [8]. Google has three different RTB platforms Google Display Network, DoubleClick Ad Exchange and Invite Media; each is targeted for different users. First, the Google Display Network (GDN) is designed for advertising agencies to do real time buying of ad slots with full transparency, but the intermediary is GDN instead of buying directly from the publisher. Bidders can choose their audience based on demographics and geographical location as well as retargeting potential clients based on their surfing history. For example, someone enters a website to buy an item but does not proceed to check out. The website collects cookies and other data that reflect visitor's behavior, click pattern and interests. When the surfer visits any other website that placed their ad slots on the Google Display Network, advertisers are able to get this data and bid for the spot. They can then show the person the items relevant to what they searched for or the items that are exact matches to what they searched for, that is retargeting. The second platform provided by Google is the DoubleClick Ad Exchange (ADX), this platform gives the option for the Ad Slot Buyer can directly buy the ad slot from the publisher directly. On this platform, advertisers bring their own data and strategy and based on that they can choose their optimal ad spot, in order to achieve their marketing goal. The third platform which was acquired by Google is Invite Media platform. Invite Media deals with high volume transactions and deals with the demand side, it also allows buyers to create bidding rules and optimizations. It connects bidders with several ad exchanges and suppliers [3].

4   Our Study

Instead of spending fortunes to advertise on the television, newspaper or radio stations, whose effectiveness and efficiency in reaching their targeted audience cannot be assessed easily, RTB seems to be a more attractive option. As this type of advertisements requires two sides, a supply side and a demand side, it cannot be fully accomplished on the company side. RTB has demanding technological requirements, a dedicated server to store the data and an information system that organizes the data in order for it to be useful. So, a company could usually be on one of the three sides, the supplier, intermediary or the bidder. The supplier could directly work with the bidder in a reservation agreement, but in order to start an auction they need to use a platform in which an algorithm is in use to make sure the advertisement slot goes to the highest bidder in less than a second. A company can build and host its own RTB API but this company would only specialize in providing the bidders with the supply of the publishers to auction. Using these Platforms to bid for advertisements, based on available data, consumers will eventually get advertisements relevant to their interests. Once the right person is reached with the right message at the right time, and clicking on the advertisement then the goal of programmatic advertising has been achieved. This is a step closer to efficient marketing. This can only happen if all the collected data is accurate. In order to know if the collection of cookies gets the right ads to the users, a two-step study is conducted here. The first step involves visiting several websites and ranking the ads that appear on those sites based on relevance. The second part is conducting a survey to assess if RTB is channeling to users ads that are relevant to their target product or service, and if it is acceptable or not. The objective of this study is to know if it is accurately working in Kuwait or not? And is there an opportunity in the Kuwaiti market or not.

4.1   The First Part

The first part of our investigation aims at assessing, after picking a target product on a specific website by a group of users, whether that product resembles any of those appearing in the ads on other subsequently visited websites or not. To carry out this part of the study, the following steps are followed

- Clear all cookies and history (to start fresh)
- Search for a certain product on one site (to test a target product)
- Search for the same product on a different other website using the same client computer or the same local server (to test the tracking accuracy)
- Visit ten other websites and count the number of ads on the opening page

- Count the number of ads of interest on the website, and calculate the percentage of those in comparison to the total ads displayed
- If the relevant ads constitute 50% or more, then the result would advocate the fact that RTB and programmatic advertisements do work in that they collect the right information. (relevant ads are ads that are related to the item searched for, or the exact same product.)

For example, among others considered by each user, a search for *GoPro Hero 5* camera was done. First, the actual GoPro website was visited, and then a redirection is made to the website of the official provider of the product in Kuwait. Then, several sites that reviewed the GoPro were accessed. Other websites related to that product were also entered in order to give the chance for different websites to collect cookies. Most websites offered to access cookies in order to exploit those to show customized ads. After that, other different websites were accessed and the total number of ads displayed was counted. Specifically, the ads of interest were counted and then the percentage of those. Based on the results obtained, there were no ads relevant to the GoPro Hero 5 product seen in any of the websites accessed, but most ads were relevant to the surfer location instead. An example is a KLM ad that offers great deals from Kuwait to Amsterdam, or of no relevance at all like a university in America. The total number of ads spotted was 38, collected from 10 different websites of which only 8 ads were interesting, although they were not relevant to the searched product. Only 4 out of the 10 sites accessed scored more than 50% on the ads that were interesting to the user. This was repeated for several other products (a total of 45). The results did not change much. Hence, based on the results of this part of the study, RTB fails to a good extent to target the right audience. It must be kept in mind that this study was centered on Kuwait. The results of this first part are summarized in Table 1.

Table 1. A measure of the relevance of displayed ads to users' interests.

Website	Number of advertisements	Relevance
investopedia.com	4	0.00%
marketwatch.com	1	0.00%
youtube.com	1	100.00%
tweakandtrick.com	2	50.00%
finance.yahoo.com	1	0.00%
alwatan.kuwait.tt	3	66.67%
electronics.howstuffworks.com	5	0.00%
makeuseof.com	13	23.08%
instructables.com	6	16.67%
mirror.co.uk	2	50.00%
Total	38	21.05%

4.2   The Second Phase

The second component of the study is done in order to validate the results obtained from the first component of the investigation. It uses a survey of nine questions. Seventy-two responses were collected. The survey details are presented in the Appendix. Females constituted 65% of the respondents, and 55% of the respondents were between the age of 18 and 27. A percentage of 49% of the respondents spend 4–7 h online. Of the 72 responses, only 11% always shop online, while 40% rarely do so. Having this data, classifies the respondents as frequent internet users, and their age is the most targeted as they are the trendsetters, looking at this data it is expected that the cookies collected from them are valuable and most will bid for this market, depending on what they are looking for as well. Most of the respondents claim that they see 1–10 ads online, yet only 7% of the respondents claim that the ads are always relevant, while 40% answered rarely. 70% of the respondents answered that they do not click on any ad whether it is of interest to them or not. 15% of the respondents actually bought something as a result of seeing an online ad. Also, 36% of the respondents answered that yes, they do get inspired to buy products online. Thus, this shows that less people click on ads and buy anything through clicking such ads. This is done mainly to escape spam material. It can also be deducted that there is a security issue, where the ad viewers would be skeptical to click on ads directly fearing spyware infiltration or getting pop-up ads that would slow down the network. Kuwait's conservative culture refrains users from allowing cookies to be collected from them, or stored on their computer.

4.3   Findings and Analysis

Our findings reveal that most users do not find any of the ads relevant to their needs. This probably suggests that either the collection of cookies is not sufficient to do efficient RTB and hence show the right ads. A better platform that forms a promising vehicle for RTB is social networking. Consumers in Kuwait and in many other places use those extensively and a proper RTB needs to exploit the big data such platforms offer. The findings also suggest that the audience in Kuwait would be reluctant to click on the ads even if they were relevant or of interest to them, so the use of programmatic advertising is not very effective in Kuwait. Reasons may be attributed to the fact that although Programmatic Bidding is the closest thing to efficient marketing, means to increase its effectiveness and efficiency are certainly a subject of research. Those problems might be bad for the branding of a company. In principle, advertising activities either support the brand image or can be performance-related [9]. If a company's ads end up on inappropriate web site ad slots, the brand image of the company is negatively influenced. Bidders may not be provided with a full profile of the assortment of items hosted in the unit [7]. Transparency is a key issue here. Another problem that might be unintendedly caused is placing an ad in a ghost website and paying for an ad slot that might never be seen. As it is very expensive to build and host an RTB platform, it is very crucial to choose the correct ad exchange network that is most transparent, fast, has a big database and multiple suppliers. Choosing an ideal ad exchange for your business model, will insure that your ads are being placed on real website, and seen by the target audience will not only cut costs paid for traditional advertising but also generate a higher revenue.

Our investigation reveals that some companies in Kuwait do use RTB as an advertising technique but there is no Real-Time Bidding API based and built in Kuwait. Most of the ads that appear on Kuwaiti websites are for locations and business in the region mostly Qatar and Dubai. Technology in Kuwait is not as advanced as it is in other parts of the world like the United States, Europe or India. There is hardly any IT Solution building companies established or built in Kuwait, they are mostly foreign and outsourced. There are two approaches that might be seen in the future in Kuwait. The first approach avoids building own platforms for RTB as this is time consuming and expensive. Instead, it might be more beneficial in Kuwait to utilize RTB API's built by companies like Google, Yahoo or Facebook. The full potentials of the RTB approach need be understood in order for the motivation and the investment to occur. The second approach is to establish an RTB API in Kuwait that does not only serve Kuwait only but also serves the MENA region with joint MENA investment. The second approach seems to be currently farfetched as it requires Kuwait to mature technologically in order for this to succeed. Given the above, we believe that users in Kuwait will realize the full potential of RTB once relevance of displayed ads is achieved to a great extent. This also encourages proper utilization of the technique by businesses with online presence in the country to ensure the consumers are targeted with relevant ad material and hence obtain an attractive Return on Investment.

5 Conclusion

Programmatic Advertising (especially RTB) aims at cutting advertising costs and generates higher revenue by achieving efficient marketing. It is apparent that efficient marketing is the utopia of marketing and cannot be fully achieved. Having access to data by using cookies is a closer step to marketing to the right person at the right time. Newer technologies that collect user information might prove very useful in realizing the full potential of RTB. Social networking platforms, a source of big data, present a rich resource for RTB that need to be utilized to its fullest extent. There are several kinds of platforms to do RTB. So, using RTB platforms wisely and choosing the right platform is crucial to the business marketing plan. In Kuwait, RTB is not widely used as the infrastructure needs to evolve to acquire this technology and thus the data. This would provide businesses with enough encouragement to utilize RTB and thus gain the technology's full potential of offering efficient educated targeted marketing. The Kuwaiti culture is tight, so marketing techniques mainly used in Kuwait is the word of mouth, people usually trust the experiences of other people around them. Hence, it would also be an opportunity to use clips with famous social influencers, to advertise for a certain product. Doing so, the Kuwaiti market would start to trust the adverts they see online.

Appendix

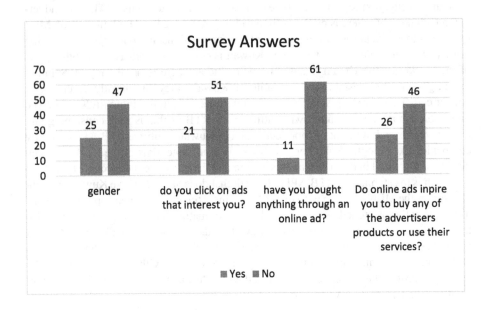

Please note that in the gender data, Red is Female and Blue is Male.

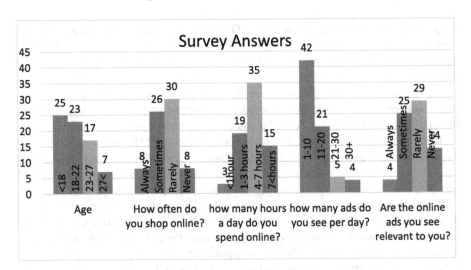

References

1. Berke, A.: State of performance marketing 2017: North America & Europe. State of Performance Marketing. Adroll (2017). https://www.adroll.com/assets/pdfs/guides-and-reports/adroll-state-of-performance-marketing-17.pdf
2. Fernandez-Tapia, J., Guéant, O., Lasry, J.: Optimal real-time bidding strategies. Appl. Math. Res. eXpress **2016**, 1–42 (2016)
3. Google Inc.: The Arrival of Real-Time Bidding and What it Means for Media Buyers. White Paper Review (2011)
4. Grether, M.: Using big data for online advertising without wastage: wishful dream, nightmare or reality? Gfk- Mark. Intell. Rev. **8**(2), 38–42 (2016)
5. Moghrabi, I.A.R., Al-Mohammed, A.R.: Social media or social business networks? In: Dwivedi, Y.K., Mäntymäki, M., Ravishankar, M.N., Janssen, M., Clement, M., Slade, E.L., Rana, N.P., Al-Sharhan, S., Simintiras, A.C. (eds.) I3E 2016. LNCS, vol. 9844, pp. 42–52. Springer, Cham (2016). doi:10.1007/978-3-319-45234-0_4
6. Münstermann, H., Würtenberger, P.: Programmatic disruption for premium publishers. In: Busch, O. (ed.) Programmatic Advertising. MP, pp. 25–36. Springer, Cham (2016). doi: 10.1007/978-3-319-25023-6_3
7. Sayedi, A.: Real-Time Bidding in Online Display Advertising. University of Washington, Washington (2017)
8. Sun, Z., et al.: The making of a good impression: information hiding in ad exchanges. MIS Q. **40**(3), 717–724 (2016)
9. Traver, C.G., Laudon, K.C.: E-Comemrce 2015: Business, Technology, Society, 11th edn. Pearson, Boston (2015)
10. Vickrey, W.: Counterspeculation, auctions, and competitive sealed tenders. J. Financ. **16**(1), 8–37 (1961)
11. Yuan, S.: Supply side optimisation in online display advertising. Doctoral dissertation, UCL (University College London) (2015)
12. Yuan, S., Wang, J.: Sequential selection of correlated ads by POMDPs. In: Proceedings of the 21st ACM International Conference on Information and Knowledge Management, pp. 515–524 (2012)
13. Zhang, W., Yuan, S., Wang, J.: Optimal real-time bidding for display advertising. In: Proceedings of the 20th ACM SIGKDD International Conference on Knowledge Discovery and Data Mining, pp. 1077–1086 (2014)

Customizable Vehicle Tracking with Intelligent Prediction System

Dhanasekar Sundararaman[1](✉) [iD], Gowtham Ravichandran[1] [iD], R. Jagadeesh[1] [iD],
S. Sasirekha[1] [iD], I. Joe Louis Paul[1] [iD], and S. Swamynathan[2] [iD]

[1] Department of IT, SSN College of Engineering, Chennai, India
dhanasekar312213@gmail.com
[2] Department of IST, Anna University, Chennai, India

Abstract. In this work, an efficient vehicle tracking with intelligent prediction system is designed and implemented for tracking the movement of any vehicle from any location. The proposed system uses an inexpensive technology that combines a smartphone application with a microcontroller. The users will be able to continuously monitor a moving vehicle on demand using the smartphone application and determine the estimated distance and time for the vehicle to arrive at a chosen destination. Apart from this, the system is designed further to account for the case of failing to catch one's vehicle by dynamically suggesting a new vehicle within one's reach with an estimated time and a route. The data collected using the tracking system is effectively used to predict the estimated arrival time of the vehicles using sophisticated machine learning technique Artificial Neural Networks (ANN). While there are other systems on vehicle tracking, we present a vehicle tracking, dynamic route suggestion on failing to catch one's vehicle and intelligent arrival time prediction system together making it a comprehensive system for users. The feasibility and effectiveness of the system are presented through experimental results of the vehicle tracking system with the advantages and challenges.

Keywords: Vehicle tracking · Prediction methods · Artificial neural networks · Global positioning system · Databases

1 Introduction

A vehicle tracking is a basic prerequisite in almost all of the organizations today ranging from academic institutions like schools and colleges to government organizations like the military. It provides the benefit of safety and assurance for both the travelers and the people concerned about them. Two of the essential components of vehicle tracking systems are Global Positioning System (GPS) and Global System for Mobile Communication (GSM).

Vehicle tracking systems are imperative in the current generation of increased transportation as the technology is growing at a fast pace resulting in the automated vehicle tracking system being used in a variety of ways to track and display vehicle locations in real-time. This paper proposes a vehicle tracking system using GPS/GSM/GPRS

A.K. Kar et al. (Eds.): I3E 2017, LNCS 10595, pp. 298–310, 2017.
DOI: 10.1007/978-3-319-68557-1_27

technology with a smartphone application to provide comprehensive service and cost effective solution for users.

The world is experiencing exponential growth in smartphone ownership. As smartphones become more familiar with finding use in the day-to-day lives of people, their influence on society continues to grow. The key force for this growth in smartphone usage is the scope of a large variety of applications to meet the needs of a variety of users. In our work, we develop a smartphone application along with the vehicle-tracking device. The two parts work together to offer the most convenience to the users as they become handy to track vehicle locations in real-time.

In vehicle tracking systems, the vehicle location is one of the most important components. The designed vehicle device works using GPS and GSM/General Packet Radio Service (GPRS) technology installed in a vehicle whose position is to be determined and tracked in real-time The time and location data anywhere on Earth is fetched using GPS technology. For wireless data transmission, GSM and Short Message Service (SMS) technologies are used. A microcontroller is used to control the GPS and GSM/GPRS modules.

The proposed customizable vehicle tracking system uses a smartphone application to monitor the vehicle location fetched from the tracking device powered by a microcontroller powered by GSM. The vehicle tracking system uses the GPS module to get geographic coordinates at regular time intervals. The GSM/GPRS module is used to transmit and update the vehicle location to a vehicle database. A smartphone application is developed for continuously monitoring the vehicle location along with a provision for setting the alarm on reaching the desired destination to make the user aware of his arrival at the destination. The Google Maps Application Programming Interface (API) displays the vehicle on the map, with the route to the destination in the smartphone application using the values in the database. The vehicle location is automatically placed on Google maps, which makes it easier for tracking a vehicle and provides users with more accurate vehicle location information. An alarm is set based on one's preference like the distance remaining to the destination to prevent them from missing their stop under any circumstances. In addition to all this, if one could not catch the vehicle because of any unfavorable circumstances, the system is designed to dynamically find the new vehicle adopting the proposed system within a range in Kms (specified by the user) which has a stop in that range to accompany that person. By customization, here we mean the ability to modify the system. Eg: Setting an alarm when the destination is 5 km away. Here the user can change the number of kilometers left. It also refers the ability to extend this system for a specific cause like averting any accidents, monitoring fuel in a vehicle etc.

To summarize in few points, we carry on the following

- Extraction of a vehicle's geographic coordinates (regarding latitude and longitude) from the GPS satellite in real time.
- Conveyance of a vehicle's location information and a vehicle's ID to a web server equipped with the database at a time interval using the wireless GSM module.
- The database is scalable and is designed to store and retrieve vehicle's location information.
- On a request of vehicle's location by a user, it can be accessed from the database and displayed on Google maps in real-time using the smartphone application

- Alarm triggers at the request of the user based on his/her preference. Say "An alarm before 2 km of my destination."
- In the case of user failing to catch the vehicle, the application finds another vehicle that has a stop near user's location. The nearness is quantified using a threshold (in Km/miles).
- The data collected over a period is used effectively to predict the estimated arrival time of the vehicle.

The paper is as follows. Section 2 compares the various other works on vehicle tracking system and intelligent arrival time prediction system with that of ours. Section 3 details the architecture and functionalities of our proposed customizable vehicle tracking system while Sect. 4 gives the implementation of our work and the results.

2   Related Works

There is a myriad of research works on automated vehicle tracking, and each has its unique methods and features. One of the earliest research work on vehicle tracking was proposed by Eliezer et al. [1]. This system did not rely on the usage of Geographical Positioning System, instead depended on various sensors installed on the vehicle and monitored by cellular transmitter sites. The position of the vehicle is found using the signal strength received on these sites from the various sensors of the vehicle. This system had clearly lacked the accuracy in vehicle's position as the location is rounded off based on the cellular transmitter sites location. Hence the need of GPS for tracking a vehicle became mandatory. One of the earliest in using GPS to locate the vehicle's location, in which CPU's were used to monitor the change in location logs and used to update them periodically using alarm was [2]. These two works were two among the earliest in attempting vehicle tracking system with and without the use of GPS.

Suleyman Eken et al. proposed work that deals with the automated vehicle tracking system by creating smart bus stops installed with Quick Response (QR) codes for the display of the location of the vehicle in [3]. Users registered with that smartphone application can decode that QR code to know about their concerned vehicle's location. This type of systems does not solve the purpose of vehicle tracking completely as the user has to be at the bus stop to know about their bus rather viewing at their convenience (by staying wherever they are). A fully automated vehicle tracking system with a smartphone application is proposed to check the location of the vehicle periodically is achieved in [4]. This system is highly correlated to our work in the way that it also uses smartphone application as the interface to the vehicle tracking system and has all the features intact such as real-time display of vehicle using GPS and vehicle statistics. We add one of the key features of suggesting an alternate vehicle with the attached vehicle tracking system when a user fails to catch one's vehicle.

A sophisticated bus tracking system with not only tracking the vehicle but also predicts the number of minutes remaining for the vehicle to arrive at the user's destination is performed in [5]. Though that system is sophisticated with a lot of features, the arrival time prediction is too trivial with just using mean trip times. A vehicle tracking system can be used for a variety of applications. An another perspective in vehicle tracking by monitoring the speed, the location of the vehicle along with the fuel left to make it easy for the owner of vehicles to monitor is done in [6]. A fully automated vehicle tracking system using GPRS, GSM and a smartphone application with Google Maps API to monitor vehicles real time is conceptualized in [7]. This work is vastly similar to that of [4] on the implementational basis, but the interface comprising lacks the provision to show the case where a user misses one's vehicle and the alternate vehicle is shown on the smartphone screen.

Zhou et al. propose an intuitive methodology to track vehicles without the use of GPS. It involves the cooperative participation of users by updating their location for other users to know. In this way, a database is built consisting various users and locations. Though this approach avoids the use of GPS, this system still requires updating of location by users in [8]. Our system has far more accuracy than this due to the fetching of exact location using GPS. The usage of vehicle tracking system as a purpose to prevent robbery and accident occurrences is done in [9]. The detection of such occurrences is evident by the trigger caused from the airbag circuitry or through a voluntary press of a panic button by the driver. Apart from preventing these unfortunate incidents, and another work goes to the next level by automatically sending updates to hospitals, police stations and civil defense about any mishappenings is implemented in [10]. These are many such applications one can think of using an automated vehicle tracking system like preventing robbery, controlling vehicle speeds to avoid overspeeding etc. These are derived solutions and our system can be easily extended to support these cases.

Though the above papers were mainly concerned about the tracking of the vehicle and the applications of automated vehicle tracking system to prevent unfortunate incidents, predicting the arrival time using the historical and live data is the need for the hour as the data collected over time can be highly beneficial. Predicting the arrival time in advance using the historical data and the live data is done in [11], where the model uses statistical concepts such as moving average that takes into account both the dynamics of traffic of live data and previous history of data. Those these models seem to predict the arrival times of the vehicles, they are statistical methods that cannot imbibe the dynamics of the vehicle (due to the computational structure of ANN) like ANN can. The data models and the various machine learning prediction models were compared and contrasted for predicting the arrival time of any vehicle which favors the use of Artificial Neural Network (ANN) for its increased accuracy over other models in [12]. It is evident that historical model and even other machine learning algorithms like Regression does not perform as well as ANN [12]. Mehmet et al. provide a comprehensive analysis of various arrival time prediction models such as average time and speed model based on historical data and statistical models like time series and Regression. Finally, an analysis of machine learning models such as ANN and Support Vector Machines (SVM) on GPS data is made in [13]. The analysis favors machine learning models for its accuracy when large datasets are available.

To summarize there are various methods [1–4, 6] for designing a vehicle tracking system and one of the cost effective methods is the use of microcontrollers. There are also many works in using the vehicle tracking system as an application to prevent mishappenings [7, 9, 10]. While there is also research works, that deals with the designing a vehicle tracking system and using the data to predict the estimated arrival time using statistical and machine learning models [5, 8, 11–13]. We are focused on the design of cost-effective customizable vehicle tracking system and in suggesting alternate routes for a user and analyzing the data gathered to create an efficient prediction model using Artificial Neural Network making a comprehensive system.

3   System Design

3.1   Physical Layer

The Physical Layer consists of all the hardware module necessary for the functioning of the vehicle tracking device such as GPS, GSM, Microcontroller (Arduino in this case), Modem and Antennas (Fig. 1).

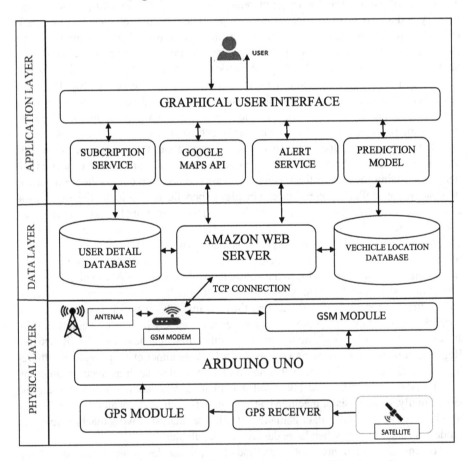

Fig. 1. Proposed vehicle tracking system architecture (three layered).

GPS module. The Global Positioning System in vehicle tracking systems are commonly used to provide users with information such as the location coordinates, speed, time, and so on, anywhere on the Earth. GPS module has the GPS receiver with an antenna. The antenna receives the location coordinates from the satellite through a receiver module.

GSM module. GSM module is responsible for establishing connections wirelessly for passing data. Here, it transmits data acquired from the GPS to a remote server for transmitting the vehicle's location information, using Transmission Control Protocol/Internet Protocol (TCP/IP) connection through the GSM network.

Arduino microcontroller. The Arduino UNO microcontroller acts as the brain behind this entire tracking system. Arduino coordinates and controls the GSM and GPS. The code responsible for collecting vehicle's location and the transmission of location coordinates to the server is compiled and saved in the microcontroller's flash memory. Upon execution, the program interacts with the GPS module to get the location coordinates and updates the data in the Vehicle Location Database.

3.2 Data Layer

The Data Layer consists of the various databases responsible for the analysis and execution of the prediction model and the tracking system. It consists of the Vehicle Location Database for storing the updated information about all vehicles that have installed the tracking system, a User Detail Database for storing credentials of the user and a Web Server for processing and retrieving vehicle's location.

Vehicle Location Database. The Vehicle Location Database consists of the location regarding latitude and longitude and the timestamp of the recent location update of various vehicles in which the proposed system is adopted. This database is the central repository using which the map is displayed in real time on the smartphone application. This is the basis for the training of the prediction model, which is used to predict the estimated arrival time

User Detail Database. The User Detail Database is used for validation of the various users subscribing the system. When a user subscribes, the credentials of that user such as username, password, and associated vehicle ID is stored in this database. This data is used for validating when the user tries to sign in to the smartphone application.

AWS Web Server. The Amazon Web Server (AWS) manages both the Vehicle Location Database and User Detail Database. A Java servlet, responsible for retrieving the associated vehicle location when the respective user requests. The Java Servlet also handles alternate bus route requests where it computes the nearby bus stops that are possible for the user to reach to another bus.

3.3   Application Layer

The Application Layer details the various features offered to the end user through the smartphone application and the prediction model that is responsible for predicting the arrival time of a vehicle in advance.

Smartphone Application. The smartphone application (app) acts as the central module that coordinates all the other modules and displays the information needed for the user intuitively. The app has a Maps Activity that displays the position of the vehicle in real-time graphically using the coordinates (latitude and longitude) from the database through Google Maps API. A feature for setting the alarm based on preferences of a user such as the distance and time remaining to reach the destination. In the case of failing to catch one's vehicle, a feature to find an alternate vehicle which has a stop within the threshold radius (as specified by the user). The path for the new vehicle is also shown on the smartphone application.

Google Maps API. Google Maps API for Android is used to display a vehicle location on a smartphone application using Google Maps real-time using a Hypertext Transfer Protocol (HTTP) request. The Google Maps API automatically handles access to the Google Maps servers, displays map, and responds to user gestures such as drags and clicks. The API can also be used to suggest paths to the destination through markers and lines. The API is modified for our convenience to display not only the location of the vehicle but also suggest other vehicle paths a user can take in the case of failing to catch one's vehicle.

Alert Service. After a user successfully signs up for the tracking system and once the system starts tracking the bus, the user need not constantly look into their phones, as the application gives timely notification updates and warnings when the bus nears the user's bus stop. The significance of our system is to avoid the constant use of the application by the user while driving on the road.

Subscription Service. When using the application for the first time, the credentials of the user are requested and added to the User Detail Database. By this way, the user chooses to subscribe the system using the smartphone application. These credentials are used every time to validate the authenticity of the user on signing in to the application.

Prediction Model. Using the data collected from the vehicle tracking device comprising of GPS and GSM powered by the microcontroller, a predictive analysis methodology is adopted when the system fails to have access to the Internet. The data collected over a period when the user used the smartphone application is recorded and structured. The data is personalized to the type of vehicle a user had used for enabling a better prediction rather having a generic prediction. The data enables a prediction of the arrival time of the next stops or the user's destination stop in seconds with a better accuracy than a generic prediction model.

The data is modeled with features as various stops to reach the destination a particular user passes by every day. The pattern within the data is analyzed with the help of ANN and extracted to produce meaningful output in some minutes/seconds left for the destination.

Graphical User Interface. The Graphical User Interface (GUI) is the core through which the user interacts with the tracking system. The GUI can show the current location of the vehicle, enable a marker for setting the alarm at the desired location, and show alternate vehicles in case of failing to catch one's vehicle, respond with an alarm on reaching the desired destination.

4 Implementation and Results

This section deals with the implementation of various services discussed in Sect. 3

The User Detail Database stores the user's credentials such as username, password, and the associated Vehicle IDs respective to the user. Table 1 is used for validation and displaying particular user's vehicle on Map in the smartphone.

Table 1. User detail database.

Username	Password	Vehicle IDs
X	*******	1, 2, 3
Y	*******	2, 6, 7
Z	*******	3, 4

Table 1 stores fields such as Username and corresponding vehicle IDs. Table 2 is of prime importance for displaying the vehicle on a smartphone in real time.

Table 2. Vehicle location database.

Vehicle ID	Timestamp	Latitude	Longitude
1	201705051721	106.2121332	104.23232
2	201705051212	105.2232323	106.12212

The Graphical User Interface consists of the following. Figure 2 describes the provision to set the alarm by pinching the location on the smartphone screen, Fig. 3 shows the shortest traversable path by the vehicle between the current location of the vehicle to the location where the alarm is set.

Fig. 2. Setting an alarm for a desired location.   **Fig. 3.** Shortest traversable route from Alarm location to current location of vehicle.

Figure 4 gives the other vehicles currently inside the radius defined by the user while Fig. 5 signifies the vehicles that have a stop in the radius with a green mark and the vehicles that don't have a stop with a red mark.

Fig. 4. Other vehicles within threshold at time 't'.   **Fig. 5.** Vehicles with stop within threshold radius (indicated in green). (Color figure online)

Table 3 shows a sample data collected for a vehicle over a period of 'n' days for the different stops it traveled. The data is in seconds to maintain the accuracy of prediction in seconds.

Table 3. Vehicle data

Day/stop point time in seconds	Stop1/start point	Stop 2	Stop 3	Stop 4	Stop 5	Stop 6/end point
Day 1	0	3000	6700	12000	14500	17000
Day 2	0	2870	6400	12200	14000	16900
Day 3	0	3450	6890	12000	13898	17253
Day 4	0	3332	6565	11879	14768	17123
Day n-1	0	2999	6875	12132	14567	17876
Day n	0	3233	7123	12899	15677	18767

Table 3 shows the Vehicle Data, where each row gives the seconds elapsed on arrival for various stops, while each column gives the various stops. The data was collected for 200 days (n = 200). The data collected is efficiently analyzed and can be used to predict the arrival time of the vehicle when the application is not connected to the Internet. All the dynamics of the vehicle is covered such as delays, traffics that is evident from the data collected. The data is mapped to the ANN model where the input neurons are the various bus stops reached in seconds. The input is centered and normalized between 0 and 1. The output neurons in the output layer give the current time in seconds to reach various stops.

Figure 6 conveys the mapping of vehicle data parameters such as the various stops and time in seconds to ANN.

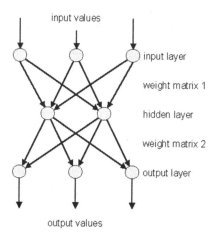

Fig. 6. Mapping vehicle data to ANN

The input values are the seconds taken for the arrival of each stop obtained from Table 3. The data of 200 such days are used. The hidden layer is responsible for

establishing the connection between input and output layers where most of the computations take place. The number of hidden layers is 1 in the figure (sample). Weight matrix
1 and 2 are the weights in floating point numbers responsible for establishing a relation
between input layer with the hidden layer and the hidden layer with the output layer.
These weights are dynamic and tend to change as the data is loaded one by one. The
ideal set of weights are obtained through Gradient Descent Optimization technique, and
the errors are calculated using backpropagation.

The data consisting of the time 't' of each stop of each day of a vehicle is randomly
generated with constraints to simulate an actual vehicle's dynamics in time when traveled over the same path multiple times. The vehicle is assumed to have six stops
including the start and destination and hence a six input and six output Neural Network
is created. The number of hidden layers is fixed after iteratively increasing the hidden
layers. The number of hidden layers cannot be too high as the training data is prone to
overfitting and the computation budget may conflict, while the number of hidden layers
cannot be too low as the network cannot imbibe the data and extract the pattern efficiently. Here the number of hidden layers is fixed as five after balancing both the conditions specified and the dimensions of the seven layers are 6×8, 8×8, 8×16, 16×16,
16×8, 8×8, and 8×6. The data is the time 't' in seconds for each of the six stops as
given in Table 3 and the output is the deviation in arrival time of each stop from the
ideal time in seconds. The training was carried on for 60000 iterations and the error
(difference in actual time delay and the predicted time delay) is obtained.

Figure 7 plots Error of training vehicle data. The data collected is split into training
and test on 80:20 ratio (ideal split ratio for training and test data) and the model is trained
on training data. The model is then run on test data to analyze its efficiency in prediction.
Thus, for a bus covering six stops daily, the data collected over a period can be modeled
using a six input six output ANN with hidden layers in between. The Network is trained
to reduce the prediction error using Gradient Descent Optimization. The data is trained
in batches to prevent any pattern in the data affecting the outcome of the prediction, and
the training error was recorded for each batch.

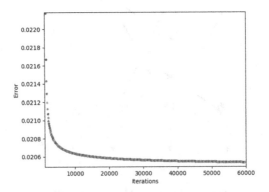

Fig. 7. Variation of error with Iterations

Table 4 shows the comparative result analysis of the features of our system with the other systems through a survey made through the works described in Sect. 2. As evident from Table 4, the proposed system is capable of working offline by using the data collected to predict arrival time using ANN and another key improvement made is the ability to find alternate vehicles that have a stop within the radius mentioned by the user as shown in Figs. 4 and 5.

Table 4. Comparative result analysis

Feature	Manual system	Automated system using GPS	Smartphone based vehicle tracking	Proposed system
Access speed	Yes	Yes	Yes	Yes
Accuracy	< 50%	< 50%	> 90%	> 90%
Interactiveness	No	No	Yes	Yes
Data management	Less efficient	More efficient	Most efficient	Most efficient
Map display	No	No	Yes	Yes
Alarm	No	No	Yes	Yes
Alternate vehicle suggestion	No	No	No	Yes
Works offline	No	No	No	Yes
Arrival prediction	No	No	No	Yes

Before concluding, we would like to brief the merits and demerits of the system. One of the key advantages of this system is its ability to work both online and offline using Intelligent Prediction. The other advantages include its features as tabulated in Table 4. Some of the challenges that we overcame include stale vehicle location in the database, Google API server call limits. On the downside, the system may fail to perform in finding alternate vehicles if the data connection is poor as this operation is server intensive. So in the case of poor data connection, the users cannot rely on our system heavily.

5   Conclusion

The results obtained for the predicted values of the arrival time of the vehicle is well consistent with the reality of the travel as all the dynamics such as traffic, bus delay is considered. The results presented can potentially support for the use of the real world intelligent vehicle tracking system. The ability to suggest alternate routes or vehicles can help many people who miss their buses frequently. Overall this system can be efficiently used for people to track their vehicle routes and alternate vehicles and for predicting the arrival time of the vehicle, even when not connected to the internet. In the future, we would like to extend this system across vehicles to support vehicle to vehicle communication to carry on tasks like routing, vehicle capacity and thereby benefitting humans by completely eliminating manual handling.

References

1. Sheffer, E.A., Thompson, M.J.: Vehicle tracking system. U.S. Patent No. 5,218,367, 8 June 1993
2. Jefferies, J., Christie, D.S.: Vehicle tracking system. U.S. Patent No. 5,898,391, 27 April 1999
3. Eken, S.: A smart bus tracking system based on location aware services and QR codes. In: IEEE International Symposium on Innovations in Intelligent Systems and Applications (INISTA) Proceedings (2014)
4. Sujatha, K.: Design and development of android mobile based bus tracking system. In: First International Conference on Networks & Soft Computing (2014)
5. Biagioni, J.: EasyTracker: automatic transit tracking, mapping, and arrival time prediction using smartphones. In: Proceedings of the 9th ACM Conference on Embedded Networked Sensor Systems (2011)
6. Yosif, S.A.E.: Design of bus tracking and fuel monitoring system. In: International Conference on Communication, Control, Computing and Electronics Engineering (2017)
7. Lee, S.J.: Design and implementation of vehicle tracking system using GPS/GSM/GPRS technology and smartphone application. In: IEEE World Forum Internet of Things (WF- IoT) (2014)
8. Zhou, P., Zheng, Y., Li, M.: How long to wait? predicting bus arrival time with mobile phone based participatory sensing. In: Proceedings of the 10th International Conference on Mobile Systems, Applications, and Services. ACM (2012)
9. Fleischer, P.B., et al.: Design and development of GPS/GSM based vehicle tracking and alert system for commercial inter-city buses. In: 2012 IEEE 4th International Conference on Adaptive Science & Technology (ICAST). IEEE (2012)
10. Tarapiah, S., Atalla, S., AbuHania, R.: Smart on-board transportation management system using gps/gsm/gprs technologies to reduce traffic violation in developing countries. Int. J. Digital Inf. Wireless Commun. (IJDIWC) 3(4), 430–439 (2013)
11. Gong, J., Liu, M., Zhang, S.: Hybrid dynamic prediction model of bus arrival time based on weighted of historical and real-time GPS Data. In: Control and Decision Conference (CCDC), 2013 25th Chinese. IEEE (2013)
12. Jeong, R., Rilett, R.: Bus arrival time prediction using artificial neural network model. In: The 7th International IEEE Conference on Intelligent Transportation Systems (2004)
13. Altinkaya, M., Zontul, M.: Urban bus arrival time prediction: a review of computational models. Int. J. Recent Technol. Eng. (2013)
14. Arduino microcontroller. http://arduino.cc
15. GPS module. https://www.sparkfun.com/products/10709
16. TinyGPS. http://arduiniana.org/libraries/tinygps/
17. GSM/GPRS module. https://www.sparkfun.com/products/9607
18. The Google Directions API. https://developers.google.com/maps/documentation/directions/

Social Media and Web 3.0 for Smartness

Density and Intensity-Based Spatiotemporal Clustering with Fixed Distance and Time Radius

Aragats Amirkhanyan$^{(\boxtimes)}$ and Christoph Meinel

Hasso Plattner Institute (HPI), University of Potsdam, Potsdam, Germany
{Aragats.Amirkhanyan,Christoph.Meinel}@hpi.de
https://hpi.de

Abstract. Nowadays, social networks produce a huge amount of spatial and spatiotemporal data that provide interesting knowledge. This knowledge can be discovered by clustering algorithms and the result of that can be used for different applications. One of such applications is the geospatial event detection based on data from social networks. Many of such detection methods rely on clustering algorithms that should provide clusters with the high level of density in space and intensity in time. Meanwhile, traditional clustering methods are not always practical for spatial and spatiotemporal data because of the specific of such data. Therefore, in this paper, we present the density and intensity-based spatiotemporal clustering algorithm with fixed distance and time radius. This approach produces the clusters that have the density-based center in space and intensity-based center in time. In the paper, we provide the description of the method from the perspective of 2 aspects: spatial and temporal. We complete the paper with the full description of the algorithm methods and detailed explanation of the pseudo code.

Keywords: Clustering · Spatiotemporal clustering · Spatial data · Spatiotemporal data · Analysis · Location-based social networks

1 Introduction

Nowadays, social media services produce a huge amount of data. A big part of them is geotagged (spatial) data, such as geotagged images, tweets, and so on. Geotagged data give more possibilities for analysis of public social data, since we can be interested not only in the content of data but also in the location, where these data are produced. Therefore, many researchers started to use geotagged data in their researches. One of the most popular cases is to use geotagged data for natural disasters prediction. For example, Sakaki et al. [21] use Twitter users as social sensors to detect earthquake shakes. Another use case of using public social data to analyze natural disasters was presented by De Longueville et al. [13]. In their paper, they showed how location-based social networks (LBSN) can be used as a reliable source of spatiotemporal information, by analyzing the

© IFIP International Federation for Information Processing 2017
Published by Springer International Publishing AG 2017. All Rights Reserved
A.K. Kar et al. (Eds.): I3E 2017, LNCS 10595, pp. 313–324, 2017.
DOI: 10.1007/978-3-319-68557-1_28

temporal, spatial and social dynamics of Twitter activity during a major forest fire event in the South of France in July 2009.

The amount of geotagged data increases, therefore, it gives the possibility to detect not only global events, such as natural disasters but also local geospatial events. In 2013, Walther et al. [24] presented the paper, where they have shown how to detect local geospatial events in the twitter stream. According to the authors, they are interested in detecting local events, such as house fires, ongoing baseball games, bomb threats, parties, traffic jams, Broadway premiers, conferences, gatherings and demonstrations in the area they monitor.

With increasing the amount of social geotagged data, detection of local geospatial events is becoming more promising. For that, there are different techniques and some of them imply the initial step - spatiotemporal clustering. This step is based on the natural assumption that if something happens in some place then the messages about that appear around this event and during some period of time. Therefore, in the case of the paper [24], as the first step of detection, they try to cluster geotagged tweets based on the specified radius and predefined time period. And then, as the second step, they apply machine learning to classify possible events. In this event detection algorithm, the first step of clustering data is very important because it affects the efficiency of the second step - machine learning classifier. And as better we do clustering, better we can classifier possible local geospatial events. Therefore, the goal of this paper is to propose a novel approach for spatiotemporal clustering of geotagged data that can efficiently produce the spatiotemporal clusters for the geospatial event detection algorithms.

The remainder of the paper is organized as follows: We start with Sect. 2, where we make an overview of related work in the scope of geo clustering and spatiotemporal clustering. Section 3 reflects the concept of our approach with the description, explanation, and analysis of the main steps and stages of the algorithm. In Sect. 4, we show in details how our algorithm works. For that, we provided the simplified pseudo code of the main parts of the algorithm. We conclude the paper and provide future directions for research in Sect. 5.

2   Related Work

In this paper, we propose the approach for spatiotemporal clustering that can be used as an initial step for geospatial event detection algorithms. Therefore, in this section, we look at existing clustering algorithms from different perspectives: geo clustering, density-based clustering, and spatiotemporal clustering.

Many existing geo clustering solutions for online maps use one of two common approaches [5]: (1) the grid-based clustering or (2) the distance-based clustering. The first approach uses the geohash concept to cluster data. Geohash[1] is a latitude/longitude geocode system invented by Gustavo Niemeyer. Thus, the grid-based clustering works on the simple principle of dividing the map into

---

[1] https://en.wikipedia.org/wiki/Geohash.

squares of a certain size and then grouping points inside of such squares [5]. Geohash allows to specify the precision of the geohash function (the accuracy of the location): from 1 up to 12 characters. So, grid-based clustering uses different levels of the precision of the geohash value to group near located points regarding a zoom level. There are different solutions that use geohash for grid-based geo clustering, but they have almost the same principle [2,4]. Main disadvantage of the grid-based clustering is that it is not accurate in the case when points are located close to the border of grids. Also, the center of the cluster is not in the center of the densest area.

The distance-based clustering is similar to the grid-based clustering. But instead of the geohash principle, the distance-based clusters are created based on the distance between the point and the center of the cluster. The center of the cluster is specified algorithmically through iteration of the existing points [5]. The distance-based clustering can provide little bit better accuracy for clustering, but it still has the problem that the center of the cluster could be not in the densest area. To overcome disadvantages of mentioned above algorithms, Amirkhanyan et al. [7] in 2015 presented the algorithm of the density-based clustering that combines grid-based and distance-based clustering with proposed parameters for trading off between the accuracy and performance.

Clustering is a well-known topic from the machine learning area and there are many existing solutions for clustering data. But not all of them are suitable for clustering spatial data (geotagged data). The most popular approaches from machine learning for clustering spatial data for online maps are based on the density-based clustering. Parimala et al. [17] provided a survey on density-based clustering algorithms for mining large spatial databases. The most popular solutions for density-based clustering are DBSCAN [15], OPTICS [11] and many of their modifications. There are many papers that use density-based clustering to cluster geotagged data for different purposes. For example, Tamura and Ichimura [23] and Sakai et al. [19] presented in their papers how they used a density-based spatial clustering algorithm for extracting attractive local regions in georeferenced documents.

Most studies on discovering clusters for ordinary data are impractical for clustering spatiotemporal data, because the knowledge discovery process for spatiotemporal data is more complex than for non-spatial and non-temporal [12]. Therefore, it requires novel approaches, in order to extract useful knowledge from such type of data. Kisikevich et al. [16], in 2010, presented the survey of spatiotemporal clustering. Their report includes the classification of different types of spatiotemporal data, the description of the state-of-the-art approaches and methods and the description of trajectory clustering as a type of spatiotemporal clustering. Additionally, they presented several possible application domains. The ST-DBSCAN approach was presented in 2006 by Birant et al. [12]. They presented their adjustment of DBSCAN algorithm for spatiotemporal data. In contrast to the existing density-based clustering algorithms, their approach has the ability to discover clusters according to non-spatial, spatial and temporal values of the objects.

We are motivated to provide the method for spatiotemporal clustering that can produce the density-based in space and intensity-based in time clusters. Such clusters would have the centers in the densest area in space and in the intensest area in time. Meanwhile, we meet the requirement of the online algorithm. It means that the algorithm should be able to process its input piece-by-piece in a serial fashion without having the entire input available from the start. With these requirements, the algorithm can be useful for clustering geotagged data from social networks to provide the clusters that can be candidates of local geospatial events. And by this way, we can support and improve the geospatial event detection algorithms.

3   Method

In this section, we describe the main concept of the proposed approach. We start with an overview of entities, which we use in our approach. In Fig. 1, we present the UML diagram of the entity classes. Understanding of them is important for the further explanation of the algorithm in the next section. The main class has the name *Cluster*. It has the following fields: *center* - the center of the cluster, *points* - the list of points that constitute the cluster, *radius* - the geographic radius of the cluster, *date* - the center date of the cluster in time space, *timeRadius* - the radius of the cluster in time space. Additionally, we have *minDistance* and *maxDistance* that show the distance to the closest and the farthest points from the center. Also, we have *minDate* and *maxDate* that show the time borders of the cluster. Another supporting entities are *Point* and *LatLng*. *LatLng* consists of latitude and longitude coordinates. *Point* consists of the *position* (*LatLng* type) and the *date*.

Once we introduced entities, we can start to describe the methods for clustering. The clustering algorithm is the spatiotemporal algorithm that has 2 aspects of clustering: spatial (geographic space) and temporal (time space). The spatial aspect of clustering is supported by the algorithm proposed by Amirkhanyan et al. [7] in 2015. We use this approach because it works in online mode and it produces the density-based clusters based on the specified radius. We use this algorithm with additional adjustments that are explained in the next section.

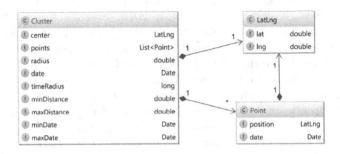

Fig. 1. Entities

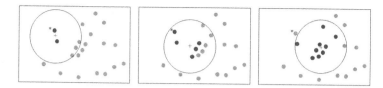

Fig. 2. Illustration of the spatial density-based clustering (Color figure online)

The detailed explanation of the geo clustering algorithm, you can find in the paper [7]. But here, we provide only the brief overview of the approach that it is needed for the complete description and understanding of the paper.

In Fig. 2, you can see the detailed illustration of the spatial aspect of the clustering. The cross reflects the center of the cluster (centroid), blue points reflect clustered points (points belong to the cluster) and red points reflect non-clustered points (points do not belong to any cluster). On the first frame, we start with the state when 2 blue points are grouped into the one cluster. We see that inside of the created cluster there are three red points, which are not clustered. We assume that these points are close to our cluster and they must be added to it. When we do it, we have 5 blue points and we recalculate the centroid. The result, you can see on the second frame. But after recalculating the centroid, the centroid moves to the more dense area. By this way, we got that new 5 red points are inside of the cluster. So, it means that we must cluster them and we do it. And as a result, we got the new cluster with new centroid illustrated on the third frame. We remind that blue points reflect clustered points and red points reflect non-clustered points. And we want to notice that the point marked with *, which was blue (clustered) on the first and on the second frames, became the red point (non-clustered) on the third frame. It is explained, that after changing the centroid, the cluster moved and the * point became out of the cluster's range and it affected that the * point was pulled from the cluster and marked as red.

Next, we consider the second aspect of clustering - temporal aspect. The straightforward (naive) method for that is to divide the timeline into fragments with the predefined size. The disadvantage of this solution is that the center of the time frame is not in the intensest area. Meanwhile, theoretically, if we suppose that some event happened then it should produce the burst time peaks that reflect the time of the main activities. In time series analysis, such time peaks provide the main interest. And usually, researchers, which work in time-serial analysis, are interested in the detection of such peaks and even in the prediction of them. From our side, we are interested in the combination of the naive fragmentation of the timeline and peak detection, in order to produce the time fragments with the high intensity of points.

For the temporal aspect of clustering, we propose to use the intensity-based fragmentation of the timeline. In this approach, the center of the fragment is calculated with the formula $\frac{\sum_{i=1}^{n} t_i * p_i}{\sum_{i=1}^{n} p_i}$, where t - time, p - the number of points.

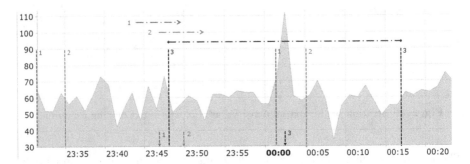

Fig. 3. The intensity-based fragmentation of the timeline (temporal clustering) (Color figure online)

With that, we have the time center in the intensest area. Also, we are interested that time fragments would have the local time peaks. Therefore, we make the approach iterative that changes the center and borders of the time fragment depending on change of the intensity distribution.

In Fig. 3, you can see the illustration of the approach. We imply that the state of the fragment changes under influence of incoming points. After each incoming point, inside of the time frame, we need to recalculate the center and move the frame to the more intense area. For explanation, we consider 2 iterations. At one point of time, we could have the time fragment with the borders and center presented by the red dash lines (1). Then we assume that new points came and they are time close to the right border. After that, we need to recalculate the center, in order to keep the center in the more intensive area. Therefore, after that recalculation, we have to move the time fragment to the new center (2 - green dash lines in the figure). By this way, new incoming points force the time frame to continuously move, in order to keep the state with the intensity-based center. Naturally, points are sorted by time and the movement goes iteratively to the right. The time frame moves until the time frame gets the stable position. In our example, it happens when the time frame reaches the position 3 (black lines), which is characterized by the time peak (00:02). This time peak forces the time frame to slow down movement and finally stop. After that, we can start to build the next intensity-based time frame.

4   Algorithm

This section is dedicated to the description of the algorithm methods that are used in our approach of spatiotemporal clustering. To simplify the explanation, we present our approach by means of describing several algorithm methods. All together, they make up the idea of the approach.

We start the description with presenting the method for calculation of the time center of the temporal part of the cluster. It is calculated by the formula $\frac{\sum_{i=1}^{n} t_i * p_i}{\sum_{i=1}^{n} p_i}$, where t - time, p - the number of points. In Fig. 4, we present the pseudo code of the implementation of this formula. You can see that the method accepts the cluster date, point date and the total weight, which is the number of the points in the cluster. Firstly, we retrieve the time in milliseconds from the dates (lines 2–3) and then we calculate the average value (line 4). New average value becomes the new cluster date (line 5). You can notice that, in statement 4, we do not apply the full formula, but we use the simplified iterative version, in which we consider the current cluster date ($clusterTime$) as an intermediate result. Such iterative simplification helps us to save the computation time and not calculate the average time over all points again.

Later, in this section, we present the algorithm for spatiotemporal clustering. But before that, we need to draw your attention that in the pseudo code we use references to the methods, which we do not explain in this section, because they are mostly supporting methods. These supporting algorithms are well-known: (1) the algorithm for calculating the distance between two geographic points [1] and (2) the algorithm for calculating the geographic center [3]. Therefore, we do not provide their implementations, but we just use the name of the methods

```
1: procedure CENTERDATE(clusterDate, pointDate, weight)
2:     clusterTime ← clusterDate.getTime()
3:     pointTime ← pointDate.getTime()
4:     newClusterTime ← (clusterTime * weight + pointTime)/(weight + 1)
5:     return newDate(newClusterTime)
6: end procedure
```

Fig. 4. The calculation of the time center of the cluster (iterative version)

```
1: procedure ADDPOINTTOCLUSTER(cluster, point)
2:     center ← cluster.center
3:     date ← cluster.date
4:     points ← cluster.points
5:     size ← cluster.points.size
6:     if center == null then
7:         center ← point.position
8:     else
9:         center ← center(center, point.position, size)
10:     end if
11:     if date == null then
12:         date ← point.date
13:     else
14:         date ← centerDate(date, point.date, size)
15:     end if
16:     points.add(point)
17:     updateMinMaxPoint(cluster, point)
18: end procedure
```

Fig. 5. Assigning the point to the cluster

to refer to them: *distance()* for the first algorithm and *center()* for the second. Another supporting method is *isInsideTime()*. This method is used to find out whether the date of the point is in the scope of the time frame of the cluster. By other words, it checks whether the time distance between 2 date points is less or equal to the time distance.

In Fig. 5, we present the algorithm for adding the point to the cluster Firstly, we retrieve some variables from the cluster that we use in the algorithm (lines 2–5). Then we check, whether the center of the cluster is *null*. If the center is *null* and the passed point is the first point in the cluster, then we set the center of the cluster as a position of the point. If the passed point is not the first, then we need to calculate a new center based on the new point and existing points. For that, we invoke the method *center()* and pass the cluster center, the point's position and the size of the points list. The same procedure we do for the date.

```
 1: procedure ADDTOCLOSESTCLUSTER(point, clusters, radius, timeRadius)
 2:     cluster ← null
 3:     distance ← radius
 4:     overlapping ← false
 5:     for each c in clusters do
 6:         if !isInsideTime(point.date, c.date, timeRadius) then
 7:             continue;
 8:         end if
 9:         d ← distance(c.center, point.position)
10:         if d <= distance) then
11:             distance ← d
12:             cluster ← c
13:         end if
14:         if cluster = null then
15:             if !clusterOverlapping then
16:                 clusterOverlapping = d < (cluster.maxDistance + radius)
17:             end if
18:         end if
19:     end for
20:     if cluster = null then
21:         if !overlapping then
22:             cluster ← newCluster(radius, timeRadius)
23:             clusters.add(cluster)
24:         else
25:             return point
26:         end if
27:     else
28:         return point
29:     end if
30:     addPointToCluster(cluster, marker)
31: end procedure
```

Fig. 6. Finding the closest spatiotemporal cluster and assigning the point to it

If the cluster does not have the date then the point date becomes the cluster date. Otherwise, we calculate the center date for the cluster with the method *centerDate()*, which we introduced above (Fig. 4). At the end, we need to add the point to the list of the points. Also, we calculate some supporting parameters, such as min and max distances between the cluster center and points, and the time borders of the clusters. We need these parameters for detecting possible overlaps among the clusters, which we show later in this section.

In Fig. 6, we present the algorithm for adding the point to the closest cluster. We go through the clusters and check the conditions. Firstly, we check whether the point is inside of the cluster's time radius. For that, we use the method *isInsideTime()*. The next step is the calculation of the distance between the point and the cluster center. By this way, we try to find the closest in space cluster that is inside of the accepted time radius. If we did not find the appropriate cluster then we can create a new one. But we can do it only if this new cluster will not have the overlapping with existing clusters (lines 14–18). For detection of overlapping, we use the *maxDistance* parameter that we calculate in the algorithm from Fig. 5. At the end, if we found the closest cluster or we are allowed to create the new cluster, which does not overlap the existing clusters (lines 20–23), we add the point to the cluster (line 30). Otherwise, we return the point to the pool and we will try to assign this point later in the next iteration (lines 25, 28).

Figure 7 presents the simplified top view of the clustering algorithm. The method takes the *points, clusters, radius* and *timeRadius*. We iterate through the points in the loop until we empty the queue. For each point, we retrieve the time close clusters (clusters that have the time frame appropriate for the considering point). Then we invoke the method *addToClosestCluster()*. This method returns some possible non-clustered points that we save into the *overlapPoints* variable for the next iteration. Also, it could be that some points become out of the spatial and temporal radius of the cluster after adjusting the spatial and temporal centers (recalculation of the cluster center and date). Therefore, we need to pull such points and pass them again into the queue. For that we use the method *pullPoints()*, which we describe below.

```
1:  procedure CLUSTER(points, clusters, radius, timeRadius)
2:      overlapPoints ← null
3:      while points.size! = 0 do
4:          point ← points.nextPoint
5:          tClusters ← retriveTimeCloseClusters(clusters, point)
6:          overlapPoints ← addToClosestCluster(point, tClusters, radius, timeRadius)
7:          if points.size == 0 then
8:              points ← pullPoints(clusters)
9:              points ← overlapPoints
10:         end if
11:     end while
12: end procedure
```

Fig. 7. The density and intensity-based spatiotemporal clustering

```
 1: procedure PULLPOINTS(cluster)
 2:     points ← cluster.points
 3:     for each point in points do
 4:         if !isInsideTime(cluster.date, point.date, cluster.timeRadius) then
 5:             pulledPoints ← cluster.points.pull(point)
 6:         end if
 7:         if !isInRadius(cluster.center, point.position, cluster.radius) then
 8:             pulledPoints ← cluster.points.pull(point)
 9:         end if
10:     end for
11:     recalculateClusterCenterAndDate(cluster, pulledPoints)
12:     return pulledPoints
13: end procedure
```

Fig. 8. Pulling the points from the clusters that are out of the cluster's range

In Fig. 8, we present the final important component of our density and intensity-based spatiotemporal clustering algorithm. In this method, we go through the clusters and check whether the points of the clusters are still inside the temporal and spatial spaces. For that, we use methods *isInsideTime()* and *isInRadius()*. If some points do not fulfill the conditions, we pull them from the points list. After that, we need to recalculate the cluster center and the cluster date. We return the pulled points back to the queue for further handling.

5   Conclusion

We have developed and presented the approach for spatiotemporal clustering. The approach meets requirements of the online algorithm and provides clusters with the center in the densest area in space and in the intensest area in time. Therefore, we call our approach - the intensity and density-based clustering algorithm. The proposed approach can be used for analysis of geotagged data from social networks. Particularly, it can be used for initial clustering geotagged data that can be used in the geospatial event detection algorithms. In this paper, we described in details the concept of the approach, provided the pseudo code of the algorithm methods and the full explanation of them. The presented algorithm was implemented and tested with collected from Twitter geotagged data.

We are interested in the future development of spatiotemporal clustering. In the current implementation, we have to specify the distance and time radius. It brings some limitations, in the case if the geospatial event covers bigger area and happens longer time than we specified. Therefore, one of possible future work is to make the algorithm with the flexible time and distance radius that can be changed depending on changeable distribution of the time intensity and spatial density.

For the case of spatiotemporal clustering data from social networks, it is important to consider also the content feature. Therefore, we would like to add new dimensional into the clustering algorithm - textual aspect. With that, we want to provide the online algorithm that can produce spatiotemporal clusters among similar topics (words). Such algorithm could provide the initial detection of local geospatial events from social geotagged data.

The result of the paper and future possible directions of research are aimed to provide the methods for discovering knowledge from spatiotemporal data and supporting the algorithms for local geospatial events detection.

References

1. Distance between geo coordinates. http://www.movable-type.co.uk/scripts/latlong.html
2. Geocluster: Server-side clustering for mapping in Drupal based on Geohash. http://dasjo.at/files/geocluster-thesis-dabernig.pdf
3. Geographic midpoint. http://www.geomidpoint.com/calculation.html
4. Geohash Clustering. http://blog.trifork.com/2013/08/01/server-side-clustering-of-geo-points-on-a-map-using-elasticsearch/
5. Google's recommendations for clustering geodata. https://developers.google.com/maps/articles/toomanymarkers
6. Ahern, S., Naaman, M., Nair, R., Yang, J.H.I.: World explorer: visualizing aggregate data from unstructured text in geo-referenced collections. In: Proceedings of the 7th ACM/IEEE-CS Joint Conference on Digital Libraries, JCDL 2007, pp. 1–10. ACM, New York, (2007). doi:10.1145/1255175.1255177
7. Amirkhanyan, A., Cheng, F., Meinel, C.: Real-time clustering of massive geodata for online maps to improve visual analysis. In: 2015 11th International Conference on Innovations in Information Technology (IIT), pp. 308–313, November 2015
8. Amirkhanyan, A., Meinel, C.: Visualization and analysis of public social geodata to provide situational awareness. In: 2016 Eighth International Conference on Advanced Computational Intelligence (ICACI), pp. 68–73, February 2016
9. Amirkhanyan, A., Meinel, C.: Analysis of data from the twitter account of the berlin police for public safety awareness. In: Proceedings of the 2017 IEEE 21st International Conference on Computer Supported Cooperative Work in Design (CSCWD 2017), April 2017
10. Amirkhanyan, A., Meinel, C.: Analysis of the value of public geotagged data from twitter from the perspective of providing situational awareness. In: Dwivedi, Y.K., et al. (eds.) I3E 2016. LNCS, vol. 9844, pp. 545–556. Springer, Cham (2016). doi:10.1007/978-3-319-45234-0_48
11. Ankerst, M., Breunig, M.M., Kriegel, H.P., Sander, J.: Optics: Ordering points to identify the clustering structure, pp. 49–60. ACM Press (1999)
12. Birant, D., Kut, A.: St-dbscan: an algorithm for clustering spatial-temporal data. Data Knowl. Eng. **60**(1), 208–221 (2007). doi:10.1016/j.datak.2006.01.013
13. De Longueville, B., Smith, R.S., Luraschi, G.: "Omg, from here, i can see the flames!': a use case of mining location based social networks to acquire spatiotemporal data on forest fires. In: Proceedings of the 2009 International Workshop on Location Based Social Networks, LBSN 2009, pp. 73–80. ACM, New York (2009). doi:10.1145/1629890.1629907
14. Duan, L., Xiong, D., Lee, J., Guo, F.: A local density based spatial clustering algorithm with noise. In: IEEE International Conference on Systems, Man and Cybernetics, SMC 2006, vol. 5, pp. 4061–4066, October 2006

15. Ester, M., Kriegel, H.P., Sander, J., Xu, X.: A density-based algorithm for discovering clusters in large spatial databases with noise, pp. 226–231. AAAI Press (1996)
16. Kisilevich, S., Mansmann, F., Nanni, M., Rinzivillo, S.: Spatio-temporal clustering. In: Maimon, O., Rokach, L. (eds.) Data Mining and Knowledge Discovery Handbook, pp. 855–874. Springer, Boston (2010). doi:10.1007/978-0-387-09823-4_44
17. Parimala, M., Lopez, D., Senthilkumar, N.: A survey on density based clustering algorithms for mining large spatial databases (2011). http://www.sersc.org/journals/IJAST/vol31/5.pdf
18. Ram, A., Jalal, S., Jalal, A.S., Kumar, M.: A density based algorithm for discovering density varied clusters in large spatial databases
19. Sakai, A., Tamura, K., Kitakami, H.: A new density-based spatial clustering algorithm for extracting attractive local regions in georeferenced documents. In: Proceedings of the International MultiConference of Engineers and Computer Scientists, IMECS 2014, pp. 360–365. Newswood Limited, Hong Kong (2014).http://www.iaeng.org/publication/IMECS2014/IMECS2014_pp360-365.pdf
20. Sakai, T., Tamura, K., Kitakami, H.: Density-based adaptive spatial clustering algorithm for identifying local high-density areas in georeferenced documents. In: 2014 IEEE International Conference on Systems, Man and Cybernetics (SMC), pp. 513–518, October 2014
21. Sakaki, T., Okazaki, M., Matsuo, Y.: Earthquake shakes twitter users: real-time event detection by social sensors. In: Proceedings of the 19th International Conference on World Wide Web, WWW 2010, pp. 851–860. ACM, New York (2010). doi:10.1145/1772690.1772777
22. Singh, S.: Spatial temporal analysis of social media data. http://129.187.45.33/CartoMasterNew/fileadmin/user_upload/Smita_Presentation.pdf
23. Tamura, K., Ichimura, T.: Density-based spatiotemporal clustering algorithm for extracting bursty areas from georeferenced documents. In: 2013 IEEE International Conference on Systems, Man, and Cybernetics (SMC), pp. 2079–2084, October 2013
24. Walther, M., Kaisser, M.: Geo-spatial event detection in the twitter stream. In: Serdyukov, P., Braslavski, P., Kuznetsov, S.O., Kamps, J., Rüger, S., Agichtein, E., Segalovich, I., Yilmaz, E. (eds.) ECIR 2013. LNCS, vol. 7814, pp. 356–367. Springer, Heidelberg (2013). doi:10.1007/978-3-642-36973-5_30

Should We Disable the Comment Function on Social Media? The Impact of Negative eWOM on Consumers' Trust in Fashion Presentations

Julian Bühler, Matthias Murawski[(✉)], and Markus Bick

ESCP Europe Business School Berlin, Berlin, Germany
{jbuehler,mmurawski,mbick}@escpeurope.eu

Abstract. Electronic word-of-mouth (eWOM) has attracted a great deal of attention in both academia and practice in recent years. Our empirical study investigates the relation of negative comments and consumers' trust in fashion presentations focusing on clothing. It is a product category characterized by a lot of online conversation and opinion sharing, but is surprisingly under-researched regarding eWOM. We calculate a multiple regression model moderated by consumers' social media experience to identify the impact of a dichotomous eWOM stimulus. We find that negative comments referring to a fashion presentation cause a significant decrease of trust. However, the more experienced a user is in dealing with social media services such as Facebook or YouTube, the weaker this effect will get. These findings contribute to the existing academic discourse about the impact of negative eWOM.

Keywords: Clothing · Moderated regression · Negative eWOM · Social media · Trust · Valence

1 Introduction

In September 2014, the famous gamer and YouTuber Felix "PewDiePie" Kjellberg, who had more than 30 million subscribers at this time, disabled the comment function for his videos as he was not satisfied with the content of most of the comments [1]. This led to an intense debate about online comments in general. In this study, we transfer this debate to a business context.

Today, the Internet is not just a mere collection of websites; it is also a platform for interactive exchange of opinions and experiences. Countless anonymous senders and receivers can communicate with one another and spread their messages [2]. Enabled by the Internet, phenomena such as the megaphone effect have emerged, meaning that ordinary customers can reach a mass audience [3], e.g. through online comments. Research shows that the majority of consumers tend to rely more on the messages of people who are similar to themselves, e.g., 61% of consumers refer to blogs or other social platforms for gathering feedback on products or services before buying [4]. In addition, there is empirical evidence validating the meaning of social media for marketing purposes, leading to an increase in sales [5].

A.K. Kar et al. (Eds.): I3E 2017, LNCS 10595, pp. 325–338, 2017.
DOI: 10.1007/978-3-319-68557-1_29

Consequently, the topic of electronic Word-of-Mouth (eWOM) becomes increasingly important for any marketing strategy [6] and has attracted remarkable attention within the academic community [7]. Besides marketing, the IS field takes a leading role in research on eWOM [8], dealing with topics such as eWOM credibility [9], trust and satisfaction in e-commerce [10], or trust-building web strategies [11].

In this study, we place the focus on three aspects of eWOM. First, we consider negative consumer reviews as a specific field of valence research [12]. Generally, research on the impact of valence shows differing results, which motivates a need for further investigation [13]. More specifically, while most studies deal with positive eWOM, or the comparison of positive and negative eWOM, we investigate the impact of negative eWOM compared to no eWOM at all. This can be considered as a relevant aspect because prominent social media services such as YouTube offer the opportunity to completely disable the comment function on their websites – as "PewDiePie" did. Although studies have started to investigate the impact of negative eWOM [14, 15], further exploration is required [7]. Second, building on an established web trust model [16], we investigate the role of eWOM on consumers' trust in a product presentation. Third, our study deals with a specific product category which is clothing. The topic of eWOM in fashion industry is rather under-researched [17], although social media in general and sharing opinions about clothing and style play a primary role in this field [18]. *Therefore, the main objective of our paper is to examine the impact of negative eWOM on consumers' trust in a clothing product presentation.* For this purpose, we have designed an online questionnaire yielding a sample of 101 participants. In an experimental setting, a dichotomous eWOM stimulus is varied and we investigate its impact on a social media display of clothing. We calculate the corresponding multiple regression model and include social media experience as a moderating factor in our statistical evaluation.

The remainder of this paper is organized as follows: Sect. 2 contains an overview of the current state of research on eWOM and trust in general before focusing on the meaning of eWOM for fashion products. In Sect. 3 we describe our research approach and in Sect. 4 we present our results. They are discussed and linked to existing research in Sect. 5, before we end with concluding remarks in Sect. 6.

2 Theoretical Foundation

2.1 Introduction to eWOM

The emergence of eWOM is based on the rise of e-commerce and social media. First definitions of eWOM aimed at the distinction to 'traditional' WOM, e.g. regarding size of network, speed of diffusion, or privacy [7]. According to Trenz and Berger [19], the most widespread definition of eWOM is the following one by Hennig-Thurau et al.:

eWOM is any positive or negative statement made by potential, actual, or former customers about a product or company, which is made available to a multitude of people and institutions via the Internet [20].

However, while emphasizing positive or negative statements, this definition does not consider neutral statements. Another limitation is that brands are not included. Thus, we follow a recent definition of eWOM proposed by Ismagilova et al. [7] which underlines that eWOM is not a static process and specifies content and sources of recommendations:

eWOM is the dynamic and ongoing information exchange process between potential, actual, or former consumers regarding a product, service, brand, or company, which is available to a multitude of people and institutions via the Internet [7].

From a technological perspective, eWOM is based on social media that is predominantly developed for private and non-commercial communication. Although senders and receivers usually do not have any commercial intentions, their messages often contain product names, or brands [18]. Firms aim to derive valuable insights from these crowds' messages and use them to design marketing campaigns or develop products, which indicates the link between eWOM and crowd-sourcing [21]. Generally, scholars have investigated different facets of eWOM, e.g., motivation to engage in eWOM [18, 20], antecedents of using online reviews [22], or the value of eWOM [23].

Our study contributes to another research stream of eWOM which is valence. Valence refers to the positive or negative rating assigned by consumers when they evaluate a product or service [12] and is found to be a significant factor for perception of a product or brand attitude [24]. In terms of theoretical foundation, the optimal arousal theory combined with the two-sided appeal [25] provide the logical reasoning for this. The two-sided appeal describes that a company allows both positive and negative reviews as this indicates a higher credibility [13]. The optimal arousal theory assumes that each person has a unique 'optimal' arousal level and when the arousal level drops below this optimal level, stimulation is required. Individuals prefer stimuli that are moderately novel over stimuli that offer too much or too little novelty [13]. Due to the two-sided appeal, the perceived novelty can be increased moderately as positive and negative reviews are allowed, thus leading to a heightened chance of consumers attention [25].

Some studies find that negative eWOM has a stronger impact on all phases of the consumer decision making process as well as on consumers' attitude of brands than positive eWOM [26, 27]. This asymmetry can be explained by the 'negativity effect' [28] which means that 'negative product attributes are believed to be more characteristic of a poor quality product, than positive attributes are for a high quality product' [26]. In other words, negative framing seems to be more effective than positive framing [29]. This is in line with the core idea of prospect theory which says that the value function is generally steeper for losses than for gains [30].

However, other studies dealing with the impact of valence draw differing conclusions and find that positive eWOM is more persuasive than negative eWOM [31] or that eWOM valence does not affect product sales at all [24]. These contrasting results indicate a clear research gap regarding valence in general and negative eWOM in particular [7]. Our study addresses this gap by investigating the impact of negative eWOM on consumers' trust in the respective product presentation.

2.2   eWOM and Trust

We define trust as 'an actor's expectation of the other party's competence and good-will' [32], because this definition includes both technical capabilities and skills ('competence') and the more abstract goodwill implying moral responsibility and positive intentions towards the other. Generally, prior research shows strong relations between eWOM, trust, and purchase intentions [8] and it is proven that eWOM has an impact on consumers' trust in a firm and its products [33]. In the context of eWOM and trust, the trust typology by McKnight et al. [16] is often adopted [8]. As illustrated in Fig. 1, trust in a web context is a complex system. In line with our research goal to investigate consumers' trust in a product presentation, we place the focus on trusting beliefs (grey box in Fig. 1). Trusting beliefs is defined as 'the confident truster per-ception that the trustee—in this context, a specific Web-based vendor—has attributes that are beneficial to the truster.' [16]. Trusting beliefs can be divided in three sub-groups: 'competence (ability of the trustee to do what the truster needs), benevolence (trustee caring and motivation to act in the truster's interests), and integrity (trustee honesty and promise keeping)' [16]. Although all three beliefs seem to play a role for our research, the most important one is probably integrity since consumers have a strong need for an 'honest' product presentation and that 'promises' made in the presentation are kept by the company.

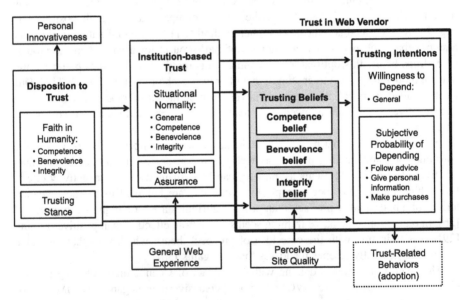

Fig. 1. Web trust model by McKnight et al. (2002, p. 341) [16]

When it comes to trust in eWOM context, most studies compare the impact of positive and negative comments [34] and consider different product types [35]. In contrast to the mostly used approach of comparing positive and negative reviews, we conduct a comparison of negative eWOM with the case of no comments at all, meaning neither positive nor negative nor neutral eWOM. This approach is similar to studies that examine the influence of complaint websites on trust in a firm or product [36, 37]. Their findings indicate that negative eWOM reduces trust [8]. However, they do not provide theoretical reasoning. Before formulating hypotheses, we describe the product type we consider in our study in Sect. 2.3.

2.3   eWOM in Fashion Industry

Individuals often define themselves and others in terms of their possessions, which serve as key symbols for personal qualities and interests. Fashion, or more specifically clothing, is seen as such a possession [38]. In addition, fashion acts as a powerful social symbol, which is used to create and communicate personal as well as group identities [39]. Wolny and Mueller [18] emphasize the network effect associated with fashion: '[fashion] trends are co-created by consumers who not only perpetuate but also adapt them along the way. Such network effects mean that when a trend is adopted success- fully by a number of people, it impacts the perceived value of the product for another user, in a positive or negative way, depending on the reference point.' [18]. That means, products that one owes determine how a person is perceived by others [40], which naturally has implications for peer-to-peer communication about fashion [18].

Fashion in general can be assigned to high-involvement products, which means 'either expensive, rarely bought, linked to personal identity, or carry high risks (social or otherwise)' [18]. Research indicates that such high-involvement products attract a lot of online conversation between customers [41]. This might be related to the complexity in determining the value of fashion, leading to increased information sharing in social media with the aim of receiving feedback regarding one's fashion choices [42].

Kulmala et al. [17] illustrate the process and elements in creating eWOM in fashion blogs. They distinguish between organic and amplified eWOM. Organic (or endoge- nous) eWOM means that a person wants to tell others about an experience, for instance with a product, and does not entail any direct intervention from the firm. In contrast, amplified (or exogenous) eWOM occurs when a firm encourages others (e.g., bloggers) to speak about their product or tries to actively influence customer-to-customer inter- action [43]. Kulmala et al. [17] find that amplified eWOM content in consumer fashion blogs resembles organic content. The main topics discussed in organic eWOM include personal style, brands, and designers and retailers, while amplified topics are products received by the blogger, brands, and designers and retailers [17]. Although amplified eWOM seems to increase in relevance, we consider organic eWOM in our study.

Apart from studies dealing with eWOM in retailing in general [14], consumers' motivation to engage in fashion-related eWOM [18], and different types of eWOM in fashion blogs [17], research on eWOM with a focus on fashion or clothing is scarce [17]. With respect to the high level of personal involvement and emotions related to fashion in general and clothing in particular [18, 41], we believe it is worth investi- gating the impact of negative comments on consumers' trust (i.e., trusting beliefs, see Fig. 1) in the presentation of clothing. This is in line with current conceptual research on the impact of eWOM on trust which is grounded in research on complaint websites [36, 37]. For instance, See-To and Ho [8] formulate the proposition 'negative eWOM will weaken the user's trusting belief on the firm'. Based on these thoughts, we develop the following hypotheses:

H1   Consumers trust a social media presentation of clothing less if it is accompanied by negative eWOM compared to the case of absence of any eWOM.

H2   The impact of negative eWOM on trust in a social media presentation of clothing is moderated by the level of social media experience

H1 clearly reflects the main objective of our study. Although considering a negative one-sided appeal, we posit that consumers trust a product presentation less if negative comments exist compared to a presentation that is free of any eWOM influence (e.g., because of disabled comment functions). Furthermore, we believe that the consumers' social media experience moderates the relation described in H1. This moderating role of experience follows the approach of established models in the field of behavioral research and technology acceptance research, such as the Unified theory of Acceptance and Use of Technology (UTAUT) [44].

3   Research Approach

Based on the two hypotheses we derived from the literature review, we can create our research model which will be validated in the empirical section (Fig. 2).

For the empirical validation of the model, we developed a questionnaire which meets the characteristics previously identified in the literature review. The first two sections contain demographic questions, i.e., age, gender, and questions addressing participants' general social media behavior, i.e., frequently used social media services and important topics on corresponding social media platforms.

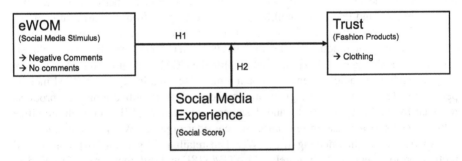

Fig. 2. Research model on eWOM

To test our hypotheses empirically, it was also necessary to select a suitable survey setting in order to measure differences regarding eWOM, specifically between its two alternative parameters *negative comments* compared to *no comments*. Experimental designs generally vary a factor called stimulus and measure its impact on a dependent variable [45]. We decided to use such an experimental approach as both comment parameters form the external eWOM stimulus which serves as an independent variable, the social media stimulus. In our research model, it impacts the way social media users perceive a product presentation online and, consequently, their trust in a product. As an instrument to measure the different impacts, we capitalized on the concept of randomization [46, 47]. At runtime, participants were allocated randomly to either group A or group B and were presented with two alternative displays, each representing the *no comments* (group A) or *negative comments* (group B) stimulus.

Thus, participants of both groups had to answer the same questions in the first two sections of the questionnaire, but received a different stimulus in the last section. As the focus of this study lies on fashion, especially on clothing, we varied a social network display that shows a young couple wearing the same type of a white t-shirt, a green jacket, and brown trousers. Group A could only see a picture of this couple whereas Group B was additionally confronted with *negative comments* on the style. Both groups were then asked to rate both the style and their level of trust on scales ranging from 'not stylish/not trustworthy' to 'really stylish/trustworthy'.

Regarding the target group, we decided to mainly ask younger adult users (18 years or older) including Millennials, but did not technically limit it to this cluster. Millennials are a suitable core target group because they can be characterized as digital natives who are often familiar with all kinds of social media services such as Facebook or Twitter [48]. Thus, they very likely have a large social media affinity and have already experienced situations where eWOM has potentially influenced their use behavior. Since we investigated social media as a stimulus as visualized in the research model, we could focus on the main social media services for acquisition purposes without causing a sample bias. The survey link was distributed through Facebook and Twitter —two of the largest social media services [49]—and additionally cross promoted through various other online (e.g., e-mail) and offline channels (notice boards). Participants took part in the survey exclusively online so that we could guarantee an accurate randomization and an identical digital presentation of both alternative displays. It was implemented with the tool Limesurvey and both the acquisition as well as the final sampling took place between November 2015 and January 2016 after initial pretests with university students.

For the analysis, we use version 23 of the statistics software IBM SPSS Statistics (SPSS). The first two sections of the survey contain dichotomous and multiple-choice questions whereas for the randomization, 5-Point Likert scales are used to measure style and trust. This scaling allows us to calculate several t-tests and a regression as we can assume equidistant items and, consequently, metrical scale levels [50]. T-tests can be used in our study to compare average means between the two stimulus groups, and we use them to make sure that our independent samples are not statistically different regarding the factors age and social media affinity. This is necessary to avoid unintentional impacts on the model caused by these factors. To predict the influence of eWOM on trust in our clothing displays, we calculate a multiple regression with and without moderation. Both models can be compared to shed light on the moderating effect of social media experience [51].

4 Results

4.1 Descriptive Results

After a period of seven weeks, we finally received 135 survey responses of which 34 had to be rejected. Plausibility checks reveal that these responses are not filled out completely, fail to meet necessary levels of accuracy such as response times or age, or

Table 1. Descriptive sample results

		Gender		Age	
Group	N	Male	Female	Mean[a]	SD
A	52	24	28	26.56	5.82
B	49	21	28	25.04	4.32

[a] p > 0.05, t-test not statistically significant between groups A and B

indicate response bias issues. Thus, the final sample size included in the model analysis is n = 101 survey participants. The initial descriptive results are presented in Table 1 and reveal a similar distribution in terms of gender and age. The intended target group of young adults and Millennials could be addressed with the questionnaire according to the average age.

We controlled the randomization process by applying a t-test for age. Results (sig. 2-tailed: .142) indicate no statistically significant differences between both groups. Taking both t-test results and the similar gender distribution, we can assume that no bias interfered with the randomization process and both groups are rather homogenous. Thus, potential differences can be linked to the variation of the stimulus rather than demographic effects.

4.2 Social Score

Because we investigate the impact of a social media stimulus in our model, we first ask the respondents to disclose their general social media usage. For the most relevant services participants can state whether they use them or not. Like in the ALEXA ranking, Facebook is the favorite service [49], and nearly all participants in the sample use it. A comparably large gap following YouTube on second place marks the cut between two dominant services on the one hand, and a portfolio of other services used less frequently on the other hand. Surprisingly, Instagram was ahead of Twitter in contrast to the order in the ALEXA ranking. The results are visualized in Fig. 3.

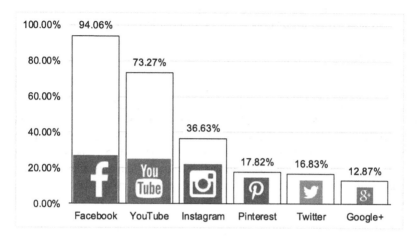

Fig. 3. Social media usage

Based on these results, we calculate a social score which we use as the moderating variable in our model. It represents the social media experience of a user and is the aggregated number of services used by a participant. A majority of participants in the sample regularly use two or three different services, mostly including Facebook and YouTube whereas 17.8% are less experienced (score: 1) or very experienced (score: 4 or 5). On average, participants reach a score of 2.51 (SD: 1.1) and t-test results again reveal no significant differences between both groups.

4.3   Multiple Regression and Moderation Results

We measure eWOM through a social media stimulus which is dichotomous. Thus, this variable is dummy-coded as 0/1 with 0 representing *no comments* and 1 representing *negative comments*. Trust in the display of a couple wearing a specific dress is measured on a 5-point Likert scale and for the moderating effect of the social media experience we use the social score. The social score forms an interaction term with the social media stimulus by multiplication of both variables. This results in two different models, one model without moderation (model 1) and another one with the interaction · effect (model 2), which can be compared to identify a moderating effect [50, 52].

Overall results indicate a significant moderating effect as the R^2 changed increased by 4.8% (Sig. Change: .027**) in the second model. The interaction effect causes the second regression model to be statistically significant in contrast to model 1 (Table 2).

Table 2. Significance of regression models[a]

Model	Sum of Squares	df	Mean Square	F	Sig.
1	4.130	2	2.065	1.807	.170[b]
2	9.674	3	3.225	2.938	.037[c] **

[a] Dependent Variable: Trust in the display
[b] Predictors: (Constant), Social Score (SC), Social Media Stimuli (ST)
[c] Predictors: (Constant), SC, ST, SCxST
** $p < 0.05$

This moderating effect can be investigated in more detail for the individual predictor variables. In model 1, the social media stimulus representing the eWOM effect is only weakly significant on the 90% confidence level whereas in the second model, it is highly significant ($p < 0.01$) as well as the moderator ($p < 0.05$). The strong negative standardized beta coefficient (-0.675) for the social media stimulus indicates a decrease in trust if *negative comments* exist. This effect is moderated in such a way that the less experienced a social media user is, the stronger the decrease in results will be (Table 3).

Table 3. Coefficients of the regression models[a]

Model		Unstandardized coefficients		Standardized coefficients		
		B	Std. Error	Beta	T	Sig.
1	(Constant)	3.541	.284		12.450	.000
	ST	−.364	.213	−.170	−1.711	.090*
	SC	−.078	.097	−.080	−.805	.423
2	(Constant)	4.148	.388		10.691	.000
	ST	−1.448	.525	−.675	−2.756	.007***
	SC	−.321	.144	−.328	−2.229	.028**
	SCxST	.431	.192	.606	2.248	.027**

[a] Dependent Variable: Trust in the display
* $p < 0.1$, ** $p < 0.05$, *** $p < 0.01$

5 Discussion

With regard to our two initial hypotheses, we can summarize our findings as follows: H1 is supported because the level of trust in the presentation of clothing is significantly lower if negative comments are linked to the display. This effect is rather weakly significant, though. H2 addresses the moderating effect of social media experience and is strongly supported. The moderation is highly significant as the negative influence of negative comments on trust mainly exists for unexperienced users. Figure 4 visualizes the strong negative slope if no moderation is considered (black line) in contrast to the nearly unchanged moderated (grey) line. This indicates that experienced social media users are hardly not influenced by negative comments of other users. Thus, eWOM

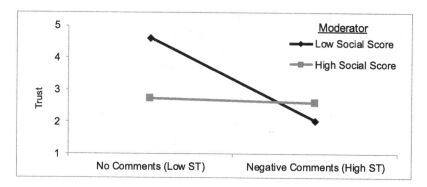

Fig. 4. Moderating effect of social media experience

plays a less important role for them. However, users who are not so familiar with the various social media services can be influenced by these negative eWOM stimuli.

Our findings support the proposition of See-To and Ho [8] that says negative eWOM will weaken the user's trusting belief on the firm. This might be explained by the fact that clothing is a high-involvement product which is very sensitive to negative comments. Furthermore, our findings seem to fit to optimal arousal theory. People need stimuli to maintain their optimal arousal level and negative stimuli are stronger than the stimuli only based on the product presentation without any eWOM. In addition, this stimulus is lower for more experienced users (H2). At first glance, our findings seem to support the negativity effect. However, the negativity effect focuses explicitly on the comparison between positive and negative eWOM. As we apply a different approach, no final statement on the negativity effect can be made.

6 Conclusion

Our study contributes to the topic of negative eWOM while focusing on a rather under-researched product category (clothing). In addition, by empirically investigating trusting beliefs, we contribute to a better understanding of the web trust model of McKnight et al. [16]. Our main finding is that the trust level is significantly lower if there is negative eWOM compared to if there is no eWOM. However, this finding alone is not sufficient to decide on questions such as enabling or disabling comment functions. There are basically two reasons for this. First, we consider negative and no eWOM, but we do not consider positive eWOM. In follow-up studies, our setting could be easily extended to a tripartite combination of positive, negative, and no comments. Consequently, the relatively small sample size of our initial experimental setting would be enlarged to allow accurate generalizations as well. Second, research shows promising results for firms with a sound response strategy on negative eWOM [7, 37]. Including these aspects in a comprehensive study would potentially lead to more concrete managerial implications. Besides these limitations, it can be concluded that negative eWOM should never be underestimated, especially when it concerns sensitive products such as clothing. Ignoring negative eWOM could harm the relationship to customers which might result in decreasing sales. As found in our study presentations within the social media environment are especially vulnerable to negative eWOM. Thus, one practical recommendation for marketers is to disable the comment function if the channel is not administrated regularly, e.g., a channel below a YouTube video, to avoid loss of consumers' trust.

Recent scientific work on eWOM offers a multitude of further research opportunities. One aspect which might be particularly relevant for our study is the quality of comments. It can be shown that the influence of eWOM varies depending on the quality of comments (i.e., high-quality vs. low-quality) [15]. Thus, as we have used the same negative comments in our survey, this distinction would be a valuable advancement of our research approach.

The final remark refers to our introductory example: "PewDiePie" re-activated the comment function for his videos one month after he disabled it.

Acknowledgment. We are grateful for the support of Mirja Frey throughout the data acquisition stage.

References

1. Stuart, K.: PewDiePie switches off YouTube comments: 'It's mainly spam'. https://www.theguardian.com/technology/2014/sep/03/pewdiepie-switches-off-youtube-comments-its-mainly-spam
2. Hettler, U.: Social Media Marketing. Oldenbourg Wissenschaftsverlag, Munich (2012)
3. McQuarrie, E.F., Miller, J., Phillips, B.J.: The megaphone effect: taste and audience in fashion blogging. J. Consum. Res. **40**, 136–158 (2013)
4. Cheung, C.M., Lee, M.K.: What drives consumers to spread electronic word of mouth in online consumer-opinion platforms. Decis. Support Syst. **53**, 218–225 (2012)
5. Mikalef, P., Giannakos, M., Pateli, A.: Shopping and word-of-mouth intentions on social media. J. Theor. Appl. Electron. Commer. Res. **8**, 5–6 (2013)
6. Eccleston, D., Griseri, L.: How does Web 2.0 stretch traditional influencing patterns? Int. J. Market Res. **50**, 591–616 (2008)
7. Ismagilova, E., Dwivedi, Y.K., Slade, E., Williams, M.D.: Electronic Word of Mouth (eWOM) in the Marketing Context. Springer International Publishing, Cham (2017)
8. See-To, E.W., Ho, K.K.: Value co-creation and purchase intention in social network sites: the role of electronic word-of-mouth and trust – a theoretical analysis. Comput. Hum. Behav. **31**, 182–189 (2014)
9. Lis, B.: In eWOM we trust - a framework of factors that determine the eWOM credibility. Bus. Inf. Syst. Eng. **5**, 129–140 (2013)
10. Kim, D.J., Ferrin, D.L., Rao, H.R.: Trust and satisfaction, two stepping stones for successful E-Commerce relationships: a longitudinal exploration. Inf. Syst. Res. **20**, 237–257 (2009)
11. Sia, C.L., Lim, K.H., Leung, K., Lee, M.K.O., Huang, W.W., Benbasat, I.: Web strategies to promote internet shopping. Is cultural-customization needed? MIS Q. **33**, 491–512 (2009)
12. King, R.A., Racherla, P., Bush, V.D.: What we know and don't know about online word-of-mouth: a review and synthesis of the literature. J. Interact. Mark. **28**, 167–183 (2014)

13. Shaw, V., Coker, B.: Keeping negative Facebook comments leads to more trust in your brand. In: The 2012 World Congress in Computer Science Engineering and Applied Computing, Las Vegas, NV (2012)
14. Davis, A., Khazanchi, D.: The influence of online word of mouth on product sales in retail e-commerce: an empirical investigation. In: Proceedings of the Thirteenth Americas Conference on Information Systems (AMCIS) (2007)
15. Lee, J., Park, D.-H., Han, I.: The effect of negative online consumer reviews on product attitude: an information processing view. Electron. Commer. Res. Appl. 7, 341–352 (2008)
16. McKnight, D.H., Choudhury, V., Kacmar, C.: Developing and validating trust measures for e-commerce: an integrative typology. Inf. Syst. Res. 13, 334–359 (2002)
17. Kulmala, M., Mesiranta, N., Tuominen, P.: Organic and amplified eWOM in consumer fashion blogs. J. Fashion Mark. Manage. 17, 20–37 (2013)
18. Wolny, J., Mueller, C.: Analysis of fashion consumers' motives to engage in electronic word-of-mouth communication through social media platforms. J. Mark. Manage. 29, 562–583 (2013)
19. Trenz, M., Berger, B.: Analyzing online customer reviews - an interdisciplinary literature review and research agenda. In: Proceedings of the European Conference on Information Systems (2013)
20. Hennig-Thurau, T., Gwinner, K.P., Walsh, G., Gremler, D.D.: Electronic word-of-mouth via consumer-opinion platforms: What motivates consumers to articulate themselves on the Internet? J. Interact. Mark. 18, 38–52 (2004)
21. Storbacka, K., Frow, P., Nenonen, S., Payne, A.: Designing business models for value co-creation. In: Vargo, S.L., Lusch, R.F., Malhotra, N.K. (eds.) Special Issue: Toward a Better Understanding of the Role of Value in Markets and Marketing, vol. 9, pp. 51–78. Emerald Group Publishing Limited, Bingley (2012)
22. Park, C., Lee, T.M.: Antecedents of online reviews' usage and purchase influence: an empirical comparison of U.S. and Korean consumers. J. Interact. Mark. 23, 332–340 (2009)
23. Dwyer, P.: Measuring the value of electronic word of mouth and its impact in consumer communities. J. Interact. Mark. 21, 63–79 (2007)
24. Davis, A., Khazanchi, D.: An empirical study of online word of mouth as a predictor for multi-product category e-Commerce sales. Electron. Mark. 18, 130–141 (2008)
25. Crowley, A.E., Hoyer, W.D.: An integrative framework for understanding two-sided persuasion. J. Consum. Res. 20, 561 (1994)
26. van Noort, G., Willemsen, L.M.: Online damage control: the effects of proactive versus reactive webcare interventions in consumer-generated and brand-generated platforms. J. Interact. Mark. 26, 131–140 (2012)
27. Lee, M., Rodgers, S., Kim, M.: Effects of valence and extremity of eWOM on attitude toward the brand and website. J. Curr. Issues Res. Adver. 31, 1–11 (2009)
28. Ahluwalia, R.: how prevalent is the negativity effect in consumer environments? J. Consum. Res. 29, 270–279 (2002)
29. Maheswaran, D., Meyers-Levy, J.: The influence of message framing and issue involvement. J. Mark. Res. 27, 361 (1990)
30. Kahneman, D., Tversky, A.: Prospect Theory. An Analysis of Decision under Risk. Econometrica 47, 263 (1979)
31. Gershoff, A.D., Mukherjee, A., Mukhopadhyay, A.: Consumer acceptance of online agent advice: extremity and positivity effects. J. Consum. Psychol. 13, 161–170 (2003)
32. Blomqvist, K.: The many faces of trust. Scand. J. Manag. 13, 271–286 (1997)
33. Dellarocas, C.: the digitization of word of mouth: promise and challenges of online feedback mechanisms. Manage. Sci. 49, 1407–1424 (2003)

34. Pan, L.-Y., Chiou, J.-S.: How much can you trust online information? Cues for perceived trustworthiness of consumer-generated online information. J. Interact. Mark. **25**, 67–74 (2011)
35. Sen, S., Lerman, D.: Why are you telling me this? An examination into negative consumer reviews on the Web. J. Interact. Mark. **21**, 76–94 (2007)
36. Bailey, A.A.: Thiscompanysucks.com: the use of the Internet in negative consumer-to-consumer articulations. J. Mark. Commun. **10**, 169–182 (2004)
37. Lee, Y.L., Song, S.: An empirical investigation of electronic word-of-mouth: informational motive and corporate response strategy. Comput. Hum. Behav. **26**, 1073–1080 (2010)
38. O'Cass, A.: Fashion clothing consumption: antecedents and consequences of fashion clothing involvement. Eur. J. Mark. **38**, 869–882 (2004)
39. Ahuvia, A.C.: Beyond the extended self: loved objects and consumers' identity narratives. J Consum. Res. **32**, 171–184 (2005)
40. Kamineni, R.: Influence of materialism, gender and nationality on consumer brand perceptions. J. Target. Meas. Anal. Mark. **14**, 25–32 (2005)
41. Gu, B., Park, J., Konana, P.: The impact of external word-of-mouth sources on retailer sales of high-involvement products. Inf. Syst. Res. **23**, 182–196 (2012)
42. Lin, T.M., Lu, K., Wu, J.: The effects of visual information in eWOM communication. J. Res. Interact. Mark. **6**, 7–26 (2012)
43. Godes, D., Mayzlin, D.: Firm-Created word-of-mouth communication: evidence from a field test. Mark. Sci. **28**, 721–739 (2009)
44. Venkatesh, V., Morris, M.G., Davis, G.B., Davis, F.D.: User acceptance of information technology: toward a unified view. MIS Q. **27**, 425–478 (2003)
45. Keppel, G., Wickens, T.D.: Design and Analysis: A Researcher's Handbook. Pearson/Prentice Hall, Upper Saddle River (2004)
46. Kirk, R.E.: Experimental design. In: Handbook of Psychology. Wiley, New York (2003)
47. Kirk, R.E.: Experimental Design: Procedures for the Behavioral Sciences. Sage Publications, Thousand Oaks (2012)
48. Statista Inc: Internet usage of Millennials in the United States. https://www.statista.com/study/19343/millennials-in-the-us-internet-und-online-shopping–statista-dossier
49. Alexa Internet, Inc: The top 500 sites on the web. http://www.alexa.com/topsites
50. Hair, J.F., Black, W.C., Babin, B.J., Anderson, R.E.: Multivariate Data Analysis. Prentice Hall, Upper Saddle River (2014, 2010)
51. Jaccard, J., Turrisi, R.: Interaction Effects in Multiple Regression. Sage, Thousand Oaks (2009)
52. Hayes, A.F.: Introduction to Mediation, Moderation, and Conditional Process Analysis. Guilford Publications, New York (2013)

The Untold Story of USA Presidential Elections in 2016 - Insights from Twitter Analytics

Purva Grover[1(✉)], Arpan Kumar Kar[1], Yogesh K. Dwivedi[2], and Marijn Janssen[3]

[1] DMS, Indian Institute of Technology, Delhi, India
groverdpurva@gmail.com
[2] School of Business and Economics, Swansea University, Swansea, UK
[3] Delft University of Technology, Delft, Netherlands

Abstract. Elections are the most critical events for any nation and paves the path for future growth and prosperity of the economy. Due to its high impact, a lot of discussions take place among all stakeholders in social media. In this study, we attempt to examine the discussions surrounding USA Election, 2016 in Twitter. Further we highlight some of the domains influencing the voter behaviour by applying the outcome of Twitter analytics to Newman and Sheth's model of Voter Choice. Through the analysis of 784,153 tweets from 287,838 users over 18 weeks, we present interesting findings on what may have affected the polarization of USA elections.

Keywords: Social media · Social media analytics · Twitter analytics · Information propagation · Public policy

1 Introduction

Every presidential election of United States of America (USA) is hugely significant for the country and as well for the world due to all the economic and trade relations USA has with other countries. United States presidential election of 2016 was held on Tuesday, November 8, 2016. The final two candidates for the presidential election of 2016 was Republican Donald Trump and Democrat Hillary Clinton. Although initially Hillary Clinton had higher visibility, Donald Trump won the 2016 election. According to Statista, out of 251 million voters in USA, there are around 67 million monthly active users in Twitter. Thus Twitter data can become a significant source of information for analyzing the impact of the election. Now days, people without meeting physically can create, share and exchange their thoughts, ideas, opinions, information, videos, images and other digital content through social media platforms like Twitter [28]. In Twitter anything tweeted by an user becomes available to others following the discussion.

The objective of this paper is to understand the impact of Twitter on the US Presidential Elections 2016. This research paper attempts to evaluate how the sentiments and topics evolving among the voters change over the period of time of the election and how there voting preferences was getting polarized over the period of election. For our study we had collected 784,153 tweets from 287,838 users on USA election over the 18 weeks,

© IFIP International Federation for Information Processing 2017
Published by Springer International Publishing AG 2017. All Rights Reserved
A.K. Kar et al. (Eds.): I3E 2017, LNCS 10595, pp. 339–350, 2017.
DOI: 10.1007/978-3-319-68557-1_30

starting from 13th of the August to 10th of December, 2016. We applied different social media analytics methods and Newman and Sheth's model of Voter Choice to get a better understanding of discussions and voting outcome.

2 Review of Literature

The first section in the review of literature highlights the importance of social media and links it to the current context. The second section, highlights some of the public policies related to social media which have been already explored in existing literature.

2.1 Importance of Social Media

Social media platforms are important for various sectors such as education [34], marketing [40], customer engagement [15], brand management [20], product and services promotions [30], recruitment [16], sales forecasting [3] and in evaluation of corporate agility [37] purposes. More and more people are joining these platforms and interacting within the virtual communities in specific interest domains and domain specific understanding may be developed by analyzing user generated content and understand market dynamics [19, 41]. Social media data (i.e. user generated content) had been extensively used for analyzing real life problems such as predicting flu trends [1], predicting electoral forecasting [5], engaging with voters [2], identifying social tensions [6], evaluating voting intentions [18] and measuring transition in organization behavior [22].

2.2 Social Media and Public Policy

Literature highlights that Twitter had been used by Chicago Department of Public Health for the campaigns of electronic cigarettes in public health policy [14]. Twitter was used for giving the early warning of the natural hazards to citizens as done by Indonesian government in 2012 [9]. Sentiments relating to "climate" had also been analyzed to understand social sensitivity towards the environment [10]. Literature indicates post on tobacco and its new products had been analyzed for policy purposes [29].

The evidences and potential of using Twitter to uncover unbiased information from user generated content was the driver for choosing Twitter data for our study.

3 Research Contribution

The contributions of this study is interdisciplinary and addresses both political science and social media literature. To develop a better understanding of the event of USA elections, some of our objectives and contributions are listed subsequently:

- What is the nature of discussions surrounding US elections?
- Which types of social discussions tend to affect outcome of elections?
- Are there indications of polarization of voting preferences during the entire period?

This study highlights a new mixed research methodology of developing insights out of the real time events and the discussion surrounding them in social media. The study lists down the four methodologies for analyzing the Twitter data such as descriptive, content, network and time-space analysis. We try to explain the insights derived out of Twitter analytics using the Newman and Sheth's model of Voter Choice Behavior [43]. In particular, the focus of how polarization happened in voting choices in social media platform, is a unique contribution of the existing study.

4   Research Methodology

The methodology had been divided into the five phase such as phase 1 identifies the search terms to extract the data from Twitter. For this study, a list of election related search terms like "USA election", "Hillary Clinton" and "Donald Trump" were identified based on listing in Twitter trends. Phase 2 of the study focuses on extracting data from Twitter. The unstructured data collected through the Twitter API using Python scripts was in JSON format. Phase 3 of the study helps in converting unstructured data to structured data, i.e. JSON to the structured excel format. The steps in phase 2 and 3 where repeated daily over the 18 weeks to extract the data from the Twitter. Phase 4 helps in digging the insights of the data through various Twitter analysis methodologies such as descriptive, content, network and time-space analysis. Table 1 illustrates an indicative list of methods for Twitter analytics. The Phase 5 explains the impact of the findings through the Newman model of voter behavior using seven concepts like issues and policies, social imagery, emotional feelings, candidate image, current events, personal events and epistemic issues. Figure 1 illustrates the flow of analysis based on Twitter analytics mapped to voter behavior model as adopted in this study.

Table 1. Overview of Twitter analytics methods

Descriptive analytics	Content analysis
Tweet statistics (Tweet, Reply, RT) [33]	Sentiment analysis [21]
User statistics (i.e. number of users) [23]	Polarity analysis [35]
URL analytics [39]	E-motion analysis [32]
Hashtags analysis [8]	Topic modelling [26]
@mentions analysis [36]	Lexical diversity [11]
Word cloud (most frequent words) [31]	
Reach metric [12]	
Network analysis	Space-time analysis
Friend-follower networks [13]	Time-trend analysis [27]
Network layout [17]	Time series comparisons [4]
Network diameter [9]	Geo-spatial analysis [42]
Centrality analysis [8]	Geo-location analysis [38]
Cluster detection [42]	Topic evolution [25]
Information flow networks [7]	

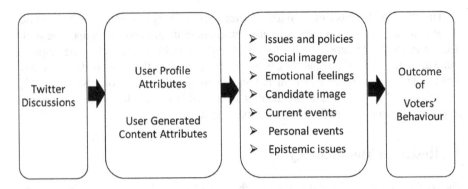

Fig. 1. Proposed model of analyzing voter behavior

Social media analytics can extract the crucial information from the user profiles, hashtags, groups, communities and search terms. Thus social media analysis can give us useful, non-biased user preferences without intruding the context. An indicative list of methods for Twitter analytics is illustrated in the Table 1.

Descriptive analysis focuses on descriptive statistics, such as the number of tweets and its types, number of unique users, hashtags, @mention and hyperlinks added in the tweets with frequency, word cloud and the reach metrics. Word clouds help us to visualize the popular words/topics tweets [31]. The "reach" metric can be used to measure the reach of the messages of the influencer [12]. Similarly reply and retweet feature in Twitter helps in assessing two way interaction and engagement [33]. The tweet can contain the hyperlinks as well to relevant resources [39]. The hashtags are used in the tweets so that the tweet opinion can be associated with a wider community of similar interest [8]. Similarly the @mentions analysis helps in identifying the influencers who had influenced the users to the extent that he/she wants to have a discussion with the influencer on the tweet topic [36].

Content analysis is used to extract the semantic intelligence from the text data. It leverages upon natural language processing (NLP) and text mining to retrieve the information from large amount of the text data. For example, sentiment analysis includes two types of the analysis such as polarity analysis and emotion analysis. Sentiment analysis is the process of computationally identifying and categorizing the opinions of the text [21]. For this study the sentiment analysis of the tweets were done using the R using syuzhet, lubridate and dplyr libraries. Polarity analysis is one of the highest used techniques for Twitter data analysis to measure the opinions of the user [35]. The e-motion analysis is one of the sentiment analysis techniques where user generated content is grouped into eight emotions categories such as anger, anticipation, disgust, fear, joy, sadness, surprise and trust. Similarly, topic modelling identifies the key themes among the tweets through mining of unstructured text [26]. Topic modelling was done in our study by using the tm and topicmodels libraries of R.

5   Findings and Interpretation

A descriptive overview of the Twitter activity of Clinton and Trump is presented in Table 2, which illustrates the degree of interaction both candidates had with the voters.

Table 2. Descriptive statistics of activity and engagement

	Retweet_count		Favorite_count	
	Clinton	Trump	Clinton	Trump
Total Tweets	2,400	1,227	2,400	1,227
Minimum activity/tweet	175	1,792	0	0
Maximum activity/tweet	665,370	345,548	1,197,489	634,112
Mean activity/tweet	4619.51	12,439.78	8,617.21	32,749.12
Std. Dev. of activity/tweet	16,190.92	14,256.63	31,359.86	37,376.37

We also tried to assess the possibility of voter's polarization in terms of their preferences. For understanding the same, the election period was divided into the two phases of 60 days each. Phase 1 was considered from August 13, 2016 to October 11, 2016 and Phase 2 was considered from October 12, 2016 to December 10, 2016. For both the phases the tweets was segregated on the basis of Clinton and Trump. The sentiment analysis was applied on tweets for identifying the polarity. Table 3 illustrates the count for users in which sentiment transition had occurred during the election period for Trump and Clinton respectively. For Trump there was around 48.18% of polarization whereas for Clinton there was around 49.66% polarization.

Table 3. Impact assessment of polarization of preferences among voters

Highlighted cells indicate polarization from Phase 1 to Phase 2		Hillary Clinton		Donald Trump	
		Phase 2		Phase 2	
		Positive	Negative	Positive	Negative
Phase 1	Positive	11236	10250	476	309
	Negative	10944	10243	485	361

In the subsequent section, we attempt to explain based insights derived from "USA Election Twitter data" by applying Twitter analytics method through the Newman and Sheth's model of voter choice, through seven distinct and separate cognitive domains which drives the voter's behavior. These factors are issues and policies, social imagery, emotional feelings, candidate image, current events, personal events and epistemic issues [43]. Validation of insights from Twitter analytics, is done by exploring news and blog articles for confirmatory evidences.

5.1   Issues and Policies

This factor tries to address the economic policy, foreign policy and social policy raised by candidate during the election period and the leadership characteristics possess by the candidate. Literature highlights the issues and policies are important component in influencing the voter behavior [43]. Voters will vote for candidate that will provide them with higher level of utility. Economy policy refers to the policies focusing on reducing inflation and budget balancing. Foreign policies include polices like increasing the defense spending. The tweets from both the presidential candidates Twitter screen where extracted and classified into four areas such as economy, foreign policy, social issues and leadership with the help of content analysis. The content analysis procedure was applied on the tweets by both the judges individually. There were 14,508 decision points (2400 tweets of Hillary Clinton, 1227 tweets of Donald Trump and four areas. Two independent judges agreed on 13,293 decisions and disagreed on 1,215 decisions with a coefficient of reliability of 91.62% which satisfies the thresholds of being over 85% [44]. Figure 2 illustrates the counts of the tweets posted by presidential candidates regarding the policies and issues.

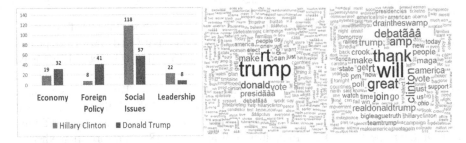

Fig. 2. Issues and policies raised by Clinton (left cloud) and Trump (right cloud)

There were around 167 tweets posted by Hillary Clinton regarding the policies and issues where as Donald Trump raised 138 tweets only. Clinton discussed various social issues surrounding the women and children related to equality, safety, empowerment and child care leave, disability, free education, career progression and mental stability. Clinton's tweets were focusing more on social issues (and Trump's policies!) whereas Trump was focusing more on economy and foreign policies like fighting against terrorism and crime, immigration, raising jobs and easing the business processes in USA.

5.2 Social Imagery

The factor refers to image of the candidate perceived by the voter in his/her mind. The candidate can have positive and negative stereotypes of the candidate depending on the various attributes such as demographic, socioeconomical, cultural, ethical, political and ideological dimensions. Figure 3 show the top 30 popular hashtags in the election period through which the social image of the candidate can be highlighted. Interestingly, Wiki-Leaks had released around 20,000 emails with almost 8,000 attachments of Democratic National Committee which indicated possibility of corruption in campaigns led by Clinton. Such discussions are indicated with hashtags like #podestaemails, #wikileaks, and #crookedhillary. However the popularity of #iamwithher was also one of the dominant among the hash tags, which indicate a huge amount support for Clinton.

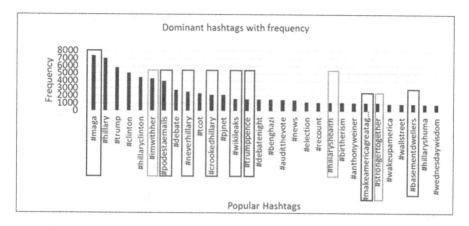

Fig. 3. Top 30 hashtags in election discussions and their dominant imagery in Tweets

The hashtags in green box indicates positive imagery of the Clinton, hashtags in red box indicates negative imagery of Clinton, the hashtag in blue box show positive imagery of Trump and no negative imagery appear among top 30 hashtags for Trump.

5.3 Emotional Feelings

Emotional feelings refer to the personal feelings possessed by the voter towards the candidate. A comparative analysis of all discussions surrounding the two candidates was conducted in terms of emotion analysis, as illustrated in Fig. 4. Higher visibility and presence among social discussions are likely to win an election through possible polarization [24]. In sheer volumes, discussions centered on Clinton surpassed all discussions surrounding Trump, in terms of all sentiments. This outcome is also comparable in the emotion comparison where the difference is highly contrasted for emotions like trust,

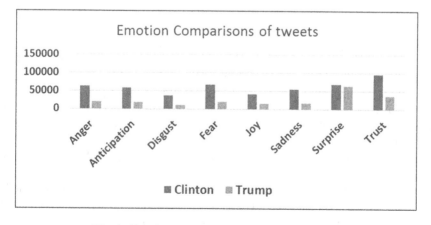

Fig. 4. Emotion analysis around Clinton and Trump

anger, anticipation, fear and disgust. In terms of surprise, however, count of tweets were somewhere comparative surrounding both the candidates.

5.4 Candidate Image

This factor refers to the salient personality traits of candidate image. However, in terms of percentage of tweets, polarity is somewhat similar. But given the difference of number of tweets, it is apparent that discussions surrounding Clinton, negative as well as more positive tweets, are more as compared to that of Trump.

Voters make up their opinion of vote on the basis of "candidate image" rather than referencing into election campaign issues, which result in interaction and engagement. Figure 5 illustrates the top 30 @mention along with their frequency over 18 weeks. Among 784,153 tweets there are 32,568 tweets which had @realdonaldtrump (around 4.15%) and 20,515 tweets had @hillaryclinton (around 2.61%). However the third popular mention was @wikileaks where a lot of debate was presented surrounding corruption of Clinton's administration. This is indicative that the role of WikiLeaks may have been significant in deciding the outcome of the final result. Further dominant mentions were from news and journalism based sources (cnn, nytimes, reuters, foxnews). Further the role of opinion leaders like Linda Suhler and Mike Cernovich is also highlighted, who actively supported Trump, is also indicative in the outcome.

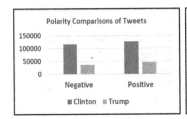
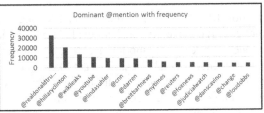

Fig. 5. Polarity analysis and top @mentions in USA election discussions

5.5 Current Events

This factor takes into the account all the events which had happened during the course of the election campaigning it includes both the domestic and international situations that would cause the voter to switch his/her voting preference. Since topic modeling is extremely computationally extensive, only the selective days when user sentiments in Twitter fluctuated significantly (i.e. mean tweet polarity $\pm 2 \times$ standard deviation), the tweets were analyzed. Then the topic identified from 18 days for creating the word cloud to identify the main concerns during the periods which enhanced user activity and resulted in major fluctuations of sentiments during the period of the elections. For topic modelling, each day top 15 topics were identified. Figure 6 illustrates the word cloud created based on the popularity of 15 topics across 18 days each, to visually present the dominance among emerged topics. Trump has 17.6 million followers on Twitter with 34,160 tweets whereas Hillary Clinton has 11.7 million followers with 9,838 tweets.

From this statistics it can be said Donald Trump had more reach than Hillary Clinton. However Fig. 6 still indicates that Twitter users are more frequently discussing about Clinton rather than Trump. Wikileaks appeared to have played an important role in the discussions surrounding around Clinton. Despite such popularity, the final outcome may be attributed to the nature of popularity in such discussions, which may have polarized the citizens of USA.

Fig. 6. Polarity analysis of USA election over 18 weeks

5.6 Personal Events

This factor refers to all events which had happened in the past of the candidate and can cause the voter to switch his/her voting preference. Some of the personal events surrounding Hillary Clinton which may had influence the voter behavior in negative sense are like deleting emails using BleachBit, WikiLeaks releasing the information regarding the governance of Hillary Clinton, FBI had released detailed interview notes of investigation of Hillary Clinton's email practices, USA WTFM, had declared Hillary Clinton as an insider. Trump in contrast did not hold a government post before winning the election, and such influence based on social discussions were not available.

5.7 Epistemic Issues

This factor refers to the issues raised by candidates to change the pace of the time and bring something new and different. The issues which raises the curiosity of the voters also come under these. In Fig. 3, the analysis highlighted that hashtag #maga contains the highest frequency among all the other hashtags which relates to the nationalist campaign "Make America Great Again". Other famous campaigns drive by Donald Trump was "Big League Truth" and "Drain The Swamp" were also popular. In contrast to this #strongertogether was launched by Hillary Clinton motivating the citizens to unity and fight against social issues, had much lesser popularity among followers. While Fig. 5 illustrates Trump's campaign got social support, Clinton's campaign did not get too much social support from Twitter retweets and mentions.

6   Concluding Discussion

Our study highlights some of the reasons which may have affected the outcome of USA elections. The study help us in understanding the possible reasons for polarization of voters among the Twitter users during the USA election. It helps us to identify the popular hashtags, @mention and the various domains influencing the voter's behavior on Twitter. However, the analysis of tweets highlights that the election outcome may have been strongly polarized by the presence of debates and opinion leaders. The study also helps us in examining the reactions of the users towards news evolving over the period of the elections. Despite Clinton having much more visibility in terms of interaction, the outcome of the election was effected by the nature of visibility and the resonance the voters had with her content. It appears that the campaigns of Clinton failed to gain popularity, though Trump's campaign gathered significant support, in terms of their presence in the descriptive analytics of hashtags, @mentions and word-cloud built of topics created. More than the campaigns and their outcome, Clinton also appeared to have spoken more about her competitor which was strongly contrasting for Trump who focused more on his policies and their outcome. Further, interestingly, as highlighted in Fig. 6, massive fluctuations in social activity happened when voters predominantly talked about Clinton, rather than any other topics.

However this study is still descriptive and may be further extended to explore the dynamics of verified and non-verified information which may be have been discussed at length in the USA elections, which may have polarized the outcome. The study also signifies in today's world Twitter handle plays the great role in the success of the election. The limitation of the study is if Twitter user gets influence by any other external events rather than Twitter discussion than that cannot be mapped. Further only if users contribute to the hashtag or topic directly, the discussion may be analyzed.

References

1. Achrekar, H., Gandhe, A., Lazarus, R., Yu, S.H., Liu, B.: Predicting flu trends using twitter data. In: IEEE Conference on Computer Communications Workshops (INFOCOM WKSHPS), pp. 702–707 (2011)
2. Adams, A., McCorkindale, T.: Dialogue and transparency: a content analysis of how the 2012 presidential candidates used twitter. Public Relat. Rev. 39(4), 357–359 (2013)
3. Asur, S., Huberman, B.A..: Predicting the future with social media. In: 2010 IEEE/WIC/ACM International Conference on Web Intelligence and Intelligent Agent Technology (WI-IAT), vol. 1, pp. 492–499 (2010)
4. Bollen, J., Mao, H., Zeng, X.: Twitter mood predicts the stock market. J. Comput. Sci. 2(1), 1–8 (2011)
5. Burnap, P., Gibson, R., Sloan, L., Southern, R., Williams, M.: 140 characters to victory? Using Twitter to predict the UK 2015 General Election. Electoral. Stud. 41, 230–233 (2016)
6. Burnap, P., Rana, O.F., Avis, N., Williams, M., Housley, W., Edwards, A., Sloan, L.: Detecting tension in online communities with computational Twitter analysis. Technol. Forecast. Soc. Chang. 95, 96–108 (2015)

7. Cha, M., Benevenuto, F., Haddadi, H., Gummadi, K.: The world of connections and information flow in Twitter. IEEE Trans. Syst. Man Cybern. Part A Syst. Hum. **42**(4), 991–998 (2012)
8. Chae, B.K.: Insights from hashtag# supplychain and Twitter analytics: considering Twitter and Twitter data for supply chain practice and research. Int. J. Prod. Econ. **165**, 247–259 (2015)
9. Chatfield, A.T., Scholl, H.J.J., Brajawidagda, U.: Tsunami early warnings via Twitter in government: net-savvy citizens' co-production of time-critical public information services. Gov. Inf. Q. **30**(4), 377–386 (2013)
10. Cody, E.M., Reagan, A.J., Mitchell, L., Dodds, P.S., Danforth, C.M.: Climate change sentiment on twitter: an unsolicited public opinion poll. PloS One **10**(8), e0136092 (2015)
11. Cohen, R., Ruths, D.: Classifying political orientation on Twitter: it's not easy!. In: ICWSM (2013)
12. Ganis, M., Kohirkar, A.: Social Media Analytics: Techniques and Insights for Extracting Business Value Out of Social Media. IBM Press, New York (2015)
13. Hale, S.A.: Global connectivity and multilinguals in the Twitter network. In: Proceedings of the SIGCHI Conference on Human Factors in Computing Systems, pp. 833–842. ACM (2014)
14. Harris, J.K., Moreland-Russell, S., Choucair, B., Mansour, R., Staub, M., Simmons, K.: Tweeting for and against public health policy: response to the Chicago Department of Public Health's electronic cigarette Twitter campaign. J. Med. Internet Res. **16**(10) (2014)
15. Heller Baird, C., Parasnis, G.: From social media to social customer relationship management. Strategy Leadersh. **39**(5), 30–37 (2011)
16. Henderson, A., Bowley, R.: Authentic dialogue? The role of "friendship" in a social media recruitment campaign. J. Commun. Manage. **14**(3), 237–257 (2010)
17. HerdaĞdelen, A., Zuo, W., Gard-Murray, A., Bar-Yam, Y.: An exploration of social identity: the geography and politics of news-sharing communities in twitter. Complexity **19**(2), 10–20 (2013)
18. Ceron, A., Curini, L., Iacus, S.M., Porro, G.: Every tweet counts? How sentiment analysis of social media can improve our knowledge of citizens' political preferences with an application to Italy and France. New Media Soc. **16**(2), 340–358 (2014)
19. Joseph, N., Kar, A.K., Ilavarasan, V., Ganesh, S.: Review of discussions on Internet of Things (IoT): insights from Twitter analytics. Forthcoming J. Glob. Inf. Manage. **25**(2), 38–51 (2016)
20. Kim, A.J., Ko, E.: Do social media marketing activities enhance customer equity? An empirical study of luxury fashion brand. J. Bus. Res. **65**(10), 1480–1486 (2012)
21. Kolchyna, O., Souza, T.T., Treleaven, P., Aste, T.: Twitter sentiment analysis (2015)
22. Lakhiwal, A., Kar, A.K.: Insights from Twitter analytics: modeling social media personality dimensions and impact of breakthrough events. In: Dwivedi, Y.K., et al. (eds.) I3E 2016. LNCS, vol. 9844, pp. 533–544. Springer, Cham (2016). doi:10.1007/978-3-319-45234-0_47
23. Lampos, V., Aletras, N., Preoţiuc-Pietro, D., Cohn, T.: Predicting and characterising user impact on Twitter. In: 14th Conference of the European Chapter of the Association for Computational Linguistics, EACL 2014, pp. 405–413 (2014)
24. Larsson, A.O., Moe, H.: Studying political microblogging: Twitter users in the 2010 Swedish election campaign. New Media Soc. **14**(5), 729–747 (2012)
25. Lau, J.H., Collier, N., Baldwin, T.: On-line trend analysis with topic models: #twitter trends detection topic model online. In: COLING, pp. 1519–1534 (2012)
26. Llewellyn, C., Grover, C., Alex, B., Oberlander, J., Tobin, R.: Extracting a topic specific dataset from a Twitter archive. In: Kapidakis, S., Mazurek, C., Werla, M. (eds.) TPDL 2015. LNCS, vol. 9316, pp. 364–367. Springer, Cham (2015). doi:10.1007/978-3-319-24592-8_36

27. Mathioudakis, M., Koudas, N.: Twittermonitor: trend detection over the twitter stream. In: Proceedings of the 2010 ACM SIGMOD International Conference on Management of Data, pp. 1155–1158 (2010)

28. Munar, A.M., Jacobsen, J.K.S.: Motivations for sharing tourism experiences through social media. Tour. Manag. **43**, 46–54 (2014)

29. Myslín, M., Zhu, S.H., Chapman, W., Conway, M.: Using Twitter to examine smoking behavior and perceptions of emerging tobacco products. J. Med. Internet Res. **15**(8) (2013)

30. Neiger, B.L., Thackeray, R., Van Wagenen, S.A., Hanson, C.L., West, J.H., Barnes, M.D., Fagen, M.C.: Use of social media in health promotion purposes, key performance indicators, and evaluation metrics. Health Promot. Pract. **13**(2), 159–164 (2012)

31. Nooralahzadeh, F., Arunachalam, V., Chiru, C.G.: 2012 presidential elections on Twitter–an analysis of how the US and French election were reflected in tweets. In: 2013 19th International Conference on Control Systems and Computer Science, pp. 240–246. IEEE (2013)

32. Ou, G., Chen, W., Wang, T., Wei, Z., Li, B., Yang, D., Wong, K.F.: Exploiting community emotion for microblog event detection. In: EMNLP, pp. 1159–1168 (2014)

33. Purohit, H., Hampton, A., Shalin, V.L., Sheth, A.P., Flach, J., Bhatt, S.: What kind of #conversation is Twitter? Mining #psycholinguistic cues for emergency coordination. Comput. Hum. Behav. **29**(6), 2438–2447 (2013)

34. Reuben, R.: The use of social media in higher education for marketing and communications: a guide for professionals in higher education, 04-420 (2008)

35. Hassan, S.; Miriam, F.;Yulan, H., and Harith, A.: Evaluation datasets for Twitter sentiment analysis: a survey and a new dataset, the STS-Gold. In: 1st International Workshop on Emotion and Sentiment in Social and Expressive Media: Approaches and Perspectives from AI (ESSEM 2013), Turin, Italy (2013)

36. Shuai, X., Pepe, A., Bollen, J.: How the scientific community reacts to newly submitted preprints: article downloads, twitter mentions, and citations. PloS One **7**(11), e47523 (2012)

37. Singh, A.: Social media and corporate agility. Glob. J. Flex. Syst. Manage. **14**(4), 255–260 (2013)

38. Singh, V.K., Gao, M., Jain, R.: Situation detection and control using spatio-temporal analysis of microblogs. In: Proceedings of the 19th International Conference on World Wide Web, pp. 1181–1182. ACM (2010)

39. Tao, K., Hauff, C., Houben, G.J., Abel, F., Wachsmuth, G.: Facilitating Twitter data analytics: platform, language and functionality. In: 2014 IEEE International Conference on Big Data (Big Data), pp. 421–430. IEEE (2014)

40. Thackeray, R., Neiger, B.L., Hanson, C.L., McKenzie, J.F.: Enhancing promotional strategies within social marketing programs: use of Web 2.0 social media. Health Promot. Pract. **9**(4), 338–343 (2008)

41. Utsuro, T., Zhao, C., Xu, L., Li, J., Kawada, Y.: An empirical analysis on comparing market share with concerns on companies measured through search engine suggests. Glob. J. Flex. Syst. Manage. **18**, 3–19 (2016)

42. Walther, M., Kaisser, M.: Geo-spatial event detection in the Twitter stream. In: Serdyukov, P., Braslavski, P., Kuznetsov, S.O., Kamps, J., Rüger, S., Agichtein, E., Segalovich, I., Yilmaz, E. (eds.) ECIR 2013. LNCS, vol. 7814, pp. 356–367. Springer, Heidelberg (2013). doi:10.1007/978-3-642-36973-5_30

43. Newman, B.I., Sheth, J.N.: A model of primary voter behavior. J. Consum. Res. **12**(2), 178–187 (1985)

44. Kassarjian, H.H.: Content analysis in consumer research. J. Consum. Res. **4**(1), 8–18 (1977)

Determining Consumer Engagement in Word-of-Mouth: Trust and Network Ties in a Social Commerce Setting

Patrick Mikalef[1(✉)], Ilias O. Pappas[1], Michail N. Giannakos[1], and Kshitij Sharma[2]

[1] Department of Computer Science, Norwegian University of Science and Technology, Sem Saelandsvei 9, 7491 Trondheim, Norway
{patrick.mikalef, ilpappas, michailg}@ntnu.no
[2] CHILI Lab, EPFL, RLC D1 740, Station 20, 1015 Lausanne, Switzerland
kshitij.sharma@epfl.ch

Abstract. Prompted by the popularity of social commerce in the past few years, this study seeks to examine how online reviews influence consumer's tendency to engage in word-of-mouth (WOM). We investigate how different aspects pertinent to online reviews affect consumers trust, and how that in turn induces WOM passing and WOM giving. The moderating influence of network ties is studied in the trust to WOM relationship. Building on survey-based study design with a sample of 385 social commerce consumers, we that specific aspects induce a sense of trust towards vendors. In turn, our study demonstrates that trust positively influences WOM passing and WOM giving and this relationship is amplified in conditions of strong network ties. We conclude the paper summarizing the findings and drawing theoretical and practical implications that arise.

Keywords: Social commerce · Survey study · Online reviews · Trust · Word-of-Mouth · Network ties

1 Introduction

Building on the popularity of social media and social networks, social commerce has managed to gain attention as a subset of e-commerce in the past few years. Social commerce sites presents certain some critical differences from conventional e-commerce stores, particularly by enabling social interactions and the creation and circulation of user generated content [1]. Inevitably, social commerce initiatives have sparked the interest of business executives and marketers due to the large user base and the interactions that develop [2]. As such, a growing number of marketers are now engaging in social commerce prompted by the promising early outcomes [3]. Nevertheless, while conventionally marketers were in control of the information they provided to consumers, in social commerce settings part of this power has been transferred to the consumer [2].

The influence of online reviews is becoming ever more important in the decision making process of individuals and has been a topic of increased relevance over the past

© IFIP International Federation for Information Processing 2017
Published by Springer International Publishing AG 2017. All Rights Reserved
A.K. Kar et al. (Eds.): I3E 2017, LNCS 10595, pp. 351–362, 2017.
DOI: 10.1007/978-3-319-68557-1_31

few years [4]. Yet, there is limited knowledge on how the reviews on social commerce websites influence consumers to engage in word-of-mouth (WOM) and pass on, or convince their fellow peers, on the importance of products found on social commerce sites. To date, the mechanisms through which online reviews affect consumer attitudes and behavior have not been explored sufficiently, particularly in relation to the trust-building mechanism they induce. In addition, the influence of network ties is largely disregarded in terms of the reach and valence that WOM communication has. As such, we build on these gaps and develop the following research question which guides our study: *How do online reviews influence social commerce users' trust, and what is the impact on WOM? What are the effects of network ties in this relationship?* To delve into this topic we build on a survey-based empirical study.

The rest of the paper is structured as follows. In Sect. 2 we overview the background which this study builds upon. In Sect. 3, we develop the research hypotheses, while in Sect. 4 the study design is described. In Sect. 5 the analysis is presented along with results from the quantitative analysis. Finally, Sect. 6 discusses the theoretical and practical implications that arise from the results.

2   Background

Past research has shown that online reviews, trust, and WOM are inextricably associated [5]. Users of social commerce websites consume the information they find online concerning a product or service they are interested in, with online reviews being an increasingly important source [6]. While literature often equated online reviews with WOM the two notions are inherently distinct. Online reviews consist of comments and ratings made by consumers towards a specific product or service which are accessible to everyone. On the other hand, WOM refers to the passing of information from one peer to another, or the process of persuasion towards a specific individual [5]. Potential consumers utilize online reviews in various forms and from a diverse background of people, which works as a mechanism of increasing their trust in the product itself or the vendor that is selling it [7]. Past research suggests that when a potential consumer senses that conditions are appropriate based on his or her understanding of information provided by online reviews that will lead to a formation of trust [8]. In turn, this positive expectation activates a sense of confidence in the potential consumer which facilitates the engagement of WOM towards others peers [9].

Hence, WOM is a result of the trust-building mechanism which is developed by consumers consuming online reviews [10]. Conversely, if a consumer is not satisfied by the context relating to online reviews, trust will be deterred, leading to an absence of outcomes that are beneficial towards marketers [11]. The effect of online reviews on purchase-related behavior has been studied in several contexts on online commerce and virtual communities [12]. Nevertheless, the indirect effect and the trust building mechanisms that online reviews facilitate have been largely under-explored, particularly in the context of social commerce [13]. Previous research in the domain of online commerce has shown that trust mediates many buying-related behaviors and is a good predictor of actions taken by consumers [14]. While the importance of online reviews has been clearly documented in several research papers in the context of social commerce, very little attention has been placed on the trust building mechanisms it enables, and specifically towards engaging consumers to partake in WOM. In the following section, we focus on online review related factors that are posited to be important predictors of inducing trust of consumers. We then proceed to explain how trust ignites the process of WOM and how this is amplified in conditions of high network ties.

3 Research Hypotheses

While developing a sense of trust towards a product or firm is a process that unfolds over time, in the context of social commerce and online reviews some factors have been found to be important determinants. In the seminal paper of McKnight et al. [14], trust is decomposed into several dimensions, with trusting beliefs being one of the most important in determining pre-action behavior. Trusting beliefs have to do with the confidence of a consumer in the attributes of the truster; in this case with vendors on social commerce sites. Thus, in this study we examine the determinants that facilitate the formation of trusting beliefs in vendors of social commerce sites. Specifically, credibility of the source has been extensively documented over time as being an important facilitator of trust-building [15]. Credible reviewers are perceived as delivering more factual reviews that outline both positive and negative aspects of the product service without having any bias [16]. Despite not knowing much personal information about individual reviewers in the social commerce context due to its globalized reach, various mechanisms have been established in order to distinguish valid and factual reviews from those that contain little useful information [17]. Furthermore, personal attributes of the consumer such as his or her propensity to read online reviews, i.e. susceptibility to reviews, and inclination to utilize information found on these (persuasiveness) are noted as important contributors of developing trust [5]. Past research has found that users that tend to rely more on online reviews are more prone to purchase and engage in other purchase-related behavior (Bailey, 2005). Other studies find that while susceptibility may be important, what dictates the subsequent actions of consumers is his or her persuasiveness from the reviews [18, 19]. While susceptibility may be influenced by a multitude of factors, it is usually a personal attribute which is rooted in a consumer's predisposition to trust, a significant aspect in the formation of trusting beliefs towards a vendor or commerce outlet [14]. Nevertheless, the online context necessitates consumers to be vigilant and be in place to recognize the validity of information found and that it has not been tampered with by unauthorized sources. Hence, perceptions of security of the online domain are regarded as important enablers or inhibitors of the trust-building mechanism [20]. From the above we hypothesize the following

H1: *A consumers' perceptions of security will have a positive impact on trusting beliefs (Social commerce vendors)*

H2: *A consumers' perceptions of general credibility will have a positive impact on trusting beliefs (Social commerce vendors)*

H3: *A consumers' persuasiveness will have a positive impact on trusting beliefs (Social commerce vendors)*

H4:   *A consumers' susceptibility to reviews will have a positive impact on trusting beliefs (Social commerce vendors)*

The trusting beliefs developed from the previously mentioned set of factors, is also argued to influence consumers purchase-related behavior [21]. The main premise developed in the work of McKnight et al. [14] is that trusting beliefs can explain trust-induced behavior. Past research in online environments has empirically shown that trusting beliefs have a direct effect on purchase intentions [22]. Trusting beliefs are accompanied with familiarity and a perceived absence of threat, which inevitably lead to lowering consumer inhibitions when making a purchase decision [23]. A similar phenomenon is noted when consumers tend to share product-related information from firms or vendors that they have formed a trusting relationship with [24–26]. Their trust bond builds a sense of ownership and promotes feelings of loyalty towards a specific brand or vendor, which in turn can lead to passing on information or influencing fellow peers [27]. From the above argumentation, we hypothesize that:

H5:   *A consumers' trusting beliefs will have a positive impact on WOM passing*
H6:   *A consumers' trusting beliefs will have a positive impact on WOM giving*

Network ties are a particularly important feature of online communities present on social media [28]. Close ties constitute a stronger relationship amongst a person's social network, while weak ties are weaker and less personal [29]. Within social commerce websites, consumer's behavior is argued to be influenced by both intimate and strong tie interactions and remotely connected weak ties [30]. Strong ties are argued to accelerate the dissemination of product-related information to peers in the network, while weak ties are posited to have a lesser impact [31]. The effect of network ties on resulting WOM behavior however is contingent upon the trust that has been developed with the respective vendor of the social commerce medium, therefore we hypothesize that:

H7:   Strong network ties positively moderate the relationship between a *consumers' trusting beliefs and WOM passing.*

H8:   Strong network ties positively moderate the relationship between a *consumers' trusting beliefs and WOM giving.*

4   Research Methodology

4.1   Data Collection

To examine the proposed research hypotheses of this study, a survey-based study was initiated using an online questionnaire which was then administered to participants between October and December 2016. To recruit participants to fill out the questionnaire, two main sources were utilized. The first was Amazon's Mechanical Turk (MTurk), which allows for a significantly socio-economically and ethnically diverse population of customers that use social commerce sites to be contacted [32]. MTurk is a digital platform through which individuals can be contracted to perform specific tasks mostly related to completing surveys. These participants are recruited based on a number of criteria that are relevant to the study at hand and are provided a pre-defined financial reward for their time. In the academic community MTurk has received growing attention as a valid method of gathering data from a diverse population [33]. Several studies have examined the effectiveness and validity of using MTurk and found that if well-defined instructions are given to the sample, MTurk participants demonstrate higher attentiveness compared to other sample groups (e.g., students) [33].

As an additional means of contacting respondents and increasing the validity of findings, we utilized a snowball sampling methodology which allowed a more representative sample. Individuals that had previous experience in social commerce were contacted through social media, such as social network sites, blogs, forums as well as peers for social circles etc. [34]. The instructions given asked participants to forward the survey to their personal or business contacts that had experience in using social commerce platforms. In order to increase participant's willingness to complete the survey, a raffle was created with gift cards. The snowball effect in the selected sample was induced by giving participants additional entries in the raffle if they invited friends and peers. Respondents that had no previous experience purchasing or even browsing on social commerce sites were disqualified from the study based on a pre-question. In addition, in both cases we provided an example of what a social commerce platform is, in order to omit respondents that were not knowledgeable or had not experience of using such a platform. The final sample consisted of 452 responses, 385 of which were complete and suitable for further analysis.

4.2   Sample Demographics

The final sample consisted of an almost equal distribution of men (55.1%) and women (44.9%). Concerning the age of respondents, the sample is relatively equally distributed with those between 35 to 45 years old accounting for 28.8% of the population, and those between 30 and 34 years old representing 27.2% of the total. Further, 21.9% belonged to the age group 25–29, 15.8% were older than 46 years old, and 6.3% were 18-24. The majority of respondents (53.8%) held a bachelor's degree, with the next biggest group being those that are high school graduates (37.2%). In addition, 9% of the respondents were post-graduates. Most respondents checked their social media accounts several times (63.6%) a day, 21.9% about once a day, and the remaining 14.5% checked their accounts a few times a week or less. Participants were also asked to estimate how much money they spend on average on online shopping in a period of month. The largest group of respondents spent between $25 and $50 (31.9%), followed by those who spent between $50 and $100 (26.9%). Finally, 17.7% spent less than $25 a month, with the remainder of the sample spending over $100 (23.5%).

4.3   Measures

The questionnaire used in this study consisted of two main parts. In the first part, respondents were asked to provide information about their demographics and spending habits in social commerce environments. In the second part, respondents were presented with several statements and questions regarding their perceptions and beliefs about various aspects related to social commerce. Specifically, for the purpose of this study the following constructs were utilized as presented in Table 1. The full list of items used to operationalize these constructs can be found in Appendix A.

Table 1. Construct definitions and supporting references

Construct	Definition	References
Perceived security	Perceived security is defined as the level of security that users feel while they are shopping on e-commerce sites.	[20]
General credibility	General credibility is defined as the perceived degree of factuality of reviews of social commerce sites.	[5]
Persuasiveness	Persuasiveness is defined as the degree to which consumers are influenced by the content of review on social commerce sites.	[5]
Susceptibility to reviews	Susceptibility to reviews is defined as the propensity of consumers to utilize product-related information in the form of reviews on social commerce sites.	[5]
Trusting beliefs	Trusting beliefs refers to the confidence of consumers that the trustee—in this context, a social commerce vendor—has attributes that are beneficial to the consumer.	[14]
WOM passing	WOM passing is defined as the propensity of individuals to forward/pass on product-related information they regard as interesting on social commerce sites.	[30]
WOM giving	WOM giving is defined as the propensity of individuals to try to exert influence on others attitudes and behaviors relating to products on social commerce sites.	[30]
Tie strength	Tie strength is defined as the potency of the bond between members of a social media network.	[30]

5   Empirical Results

5.1   Measurement Model

All the variables utilized in this study are developed as reflective latent construct, and are therefore subjected to reliability, convergent validity, and discriminant validity tests. We assessed reliability a both the construct and item level. At the construct level, Cronbach Alpha (CA) values were evaluated to confirm that they were above the threshold of 0.70. At the item level, construct-to-item loadings were examined to confirm that all scores were above the lower limit of 0.70. All CA values were above 0.83, while construct-to-item loadings exceed the minimum value and had scores above 0.73. Hence, reliability was established at both construct and item level [35]. To verify that convergent validity is established, we looked at if Average Variance Extracted (AVE) values exceeded the lower limit of 0.50 [36]. The lowest detected value was 0.73 which greatly surpasses the above mentioned threshold. We tested for discriminant validity through two ways. First, we examined if each constructs AVE square root was greater than its highest correlation with any other construct (Fornell-Larcker criterion).

Second, we checked that each indicators outer loadings on its corresponding construct was larger than any other cross-loading with other constructs [37]. After conducting all the previously mentioned measurement model tests, we can conclude that the first-order variables are valid and reliable, and that the underlying items are good indicators of their respective constructs as depicted in Table 2.

Table 2. Assessment of reliability, convergent and discriminant validity

	(1)	(2)	(3)	(4)	(5)	(6)	(7)	(8)
(1) Perceived security	**0.859**							
(2) General credibility	0.266	**0.959**						
(3) Persuasiveness	0.033	0.580	**0.946**					
(4) Susceptibility to reviews	0.037	0.518	0.836	**0.893**				
(5) Trusting beliefs	0.375	0.425	0.228	0.246	**0.896**			
(6) WOM passing	0.212	0.194	0.048	0.128	0.366	**0.958**		
(7) WOM giving	0.155	0.224	0.066	0.135	0.356	0.705	**0.950**	
(8) Tie strength	0.199	0.185	0.062	0.135	0.329	0.500	0.462	**0.908**
Mean	3.89	4.83	5.70	5.53	4.51	3.66	2.97	4.66
Standard deviation	1.27	1.45	1.39	1.71	1.84	1.45	1.52	1.60
Cronbach Alpha (CA)	0.834	0.912	0.886	0.914	0.951	0.955	0.945	0.894
Average variance extracted (AVE)	0.737	0.919	0.896	0.798	0.803	0.917	0.902	0.825

5.2   Structural Model

To put the proposed set of hypotheses to test, a partial least squares structural equation modeling (PLS-SEM) approach is applied on the collected sample. The significance of estimates (t-statistics) are obtained by running the bootstrap algorithm using 5000 resamples. Path weights are calculated by applying the PLS algorithm of SmartPLS. The structural model derived from the PLS analysis is summarized in Fig. 1, in which the explained variance of endogenous variables (R^2) and the standardized path coefficients (β) are depicted. As illustrated in Fig. 1, seven out of the eight total hypotheses are empirically supported. More specifically, we find that perceived security ($\beta = 0.285$, $t = 5.904$, $p < 0.001$), general credibility ($\beta = 0.328$, $t = 4.829$, $p < 0.001$), and susceptibility to reviews ($\beta = 0.188$, $t = 2.014$, $p < 0.05$) positively affect trusting beliefs. Contrarily, general persuasiveness is found to have negative but non-significant influence on the trusting beliefs of consumers of social commerce sites ($\beta = -0.089$, $t = 0.993$, $p > 0.05$). In turn, the trusting beliefs formed by users have a positive and significant influence on both WOM passing ($\beta = 0.231$, $t = 4.450$, $p < 0.001$), and WOM giving ($\beta = 0.234$, $t = 5.048$, $p < 0.001$). This relationship if found to be strengthened by an increased tie strength, since the moderating effect for WOM passing ($\beta = 0.104$, $t = 3.185$, $p < 0.001$), and WOM giving ($\beta = 0.127$, $t = 4.243$, $p < 0.001$) is positive and highly significant.

The structural model explains 26.0% of variance for trusting beliefs ($R^2 = 0.260$), 31.1% for WOM passing ($R^2 = 0.311$), and 28.4% for WOM giving ($R^2 = 0.284$). These coefficients of determination represent moderate to substantial predictive power of the structural model [35]. In addition to examining the R^2, the model is evaluated by looking at the Q^2 (Stone-Geisser) predictive relevance of constructs. This test is a measure of how well observed values are reproduced by the model and its parameter estimates, assessing as such the model's predictive validity through sample re-use [38]. Q^2 values greater than 0 are an indication that the structural model has sufficient predictive relevance, whereas values below 0 are an indication of insufficient predictive relevance [35]. Results of the blindfolding procedure show that trusting beliefs ($Q^2 = 0.193$), WOM passing ($Q^2 = 0.267$), and WOM giving ($Q^2 = 0.237$) have satisfactory predictive relevance [35].

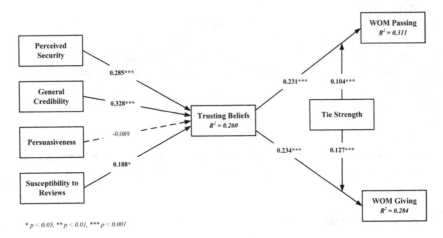

$* p < 0.05, ** p < 0.01, *** p < 0.001$

Fig. 1. Estimated causal relationships of structural model

6 Discussion

Based on prior literature we put forth a research model consisting of eight hypotheses concerning the role of perceptions about online reviews and their effect on WOM. Specifically, we examine the trust-building mechanism that online reviews have, and how they indirectly facilitate WOM passing and WOM giving. The impact of trust on the two types of WOM is investigated under the moderating influence of network ties. As such, the proposed research model and the empirical results contribute theoretically in three ways.

First, while the influence of online reviews and their various attributes has been examined in a direct manner in relation to purchase-related behavior, limited focus has been placed on the aspect of trust as an enabling condition for trust-induced behavior. Second, while WOM is usually examined as an exchange of information between two peers, we differentiated the concept in WOM passing and giving. It is important to understand the effect that trusting beliefs have not only on the simple passing on of product-related information, but also on the persuasion of other peers about the product at hand. Third, while the importance of network ties is widely acknowledged in the study of social networks and as an extension in social commerce, limited studies examine their effect on moderating WOM propensity. Our results reveal that strong network ties have positive returns or the degree to which consumers trusting beliefs influence WOM. Thus, while trusting beliefs may be important in conditioning WOM-induced behavior, this effect is amplifies for individuals who are part of a large and well-connected social circle.

From a practical point of view our findings reveal that vendors should take into account aspects of security very seriously and establish ways in which content of reviews can be verified towards its authenticity. Some social commerce vendors already have implemented such tools such as Amazon who indicates if a review comes from a verified purchase or not. Furthermore, the importance of network ties in amplifying the effect of WOM passing and giving should prompt marketers in developing strategies to connect people and intensify their interactions. By doing so they can strengthen network ties and potentially contribute to the enhancement of product-related information flow between peers.

While this research presents some novel results it does come with certain limitations. Firstly, we center of consumer-specific factors in relation with online reviews in the formation of trusting beliefs. Equally as important are product-related information that are generated by marketers. Furthermore, we do not distinguish between the various formats in which this information is presented. It is frequent for social commerce vendors to have several ways to represent online reviews in raw format or in aggregated ways. Lastly, the results of the study are based on a survey study in which further details about the constructs and notions at hand cannot be captured. Future studies could follow a qualitative approach and interview consumers during the process of browsing products online on social commerce websites. This would enable a deeper understanding of the factors they find important when trying to establish a sense of trust, and how in turn this results in trust-induced behavior.

Appendix A. Questionnaire Items

Measure	Items
Please indicate how much you agree or disagree with the following sentences (1 – totally disagree, 7 – totally agree)	
Perceived security	I believe the information I provide social commerce sites will be manipulated by inappropriate parties (R)
	I am confident that the private information I provide social commerce sites will be secured
	I believe inappropriate parties may deliberately view the information I provide social commerce sites
General credibility	I think that online product reviews are credible
	I trust product reviews provided by other consumers
Persuasiveness	Online product reviews have an impact on my purchase decisions
	Before making important purchase decisions, I consult product reviews to learn about other consumers' opinions

(continued)

(*continued*)

Measure	Items
Susceptibility to reviews	I often read other consumers' online product reviews to know what products/brands make good impressions on others
	To make sure I buy the right product/brand, I often read other consumers' online product reviews
	I often consult other consumers' online product reviews to help choose the right product/brand
	I frequently gather information from online consumer product reviews before I buy a certain product/brand
Trusting beliefs	I believe that vendors on social media would act in my best interest
	I expect that vendors on social media are well meaning
	I would characterize vendors on social media as honest
	Overall, social media platforms are effective in providing trustworthy vendors from which I can purchase
	On social media I can find excellent vendors for purchasing products/services
	Vendors on social media would keep their commitments
WOM passing	When I receive product related information or opinion from a friend, I will pass it along to my other contacts over social media
	On social media, I like to pass along interesting information about products from one group of my contacts on my 'friends' list to another
	I tend to pass along my contacts' positive reviews of products to other contacts on social media
WOM giving	I often persuade my contacts on social media to buy products that I like
	My contacts on social media pick their products based on what I have told them
	On social media, I often influence my contacts' opinions about product
Tie strength	Approximately how frequently do you communicate with the contacts on your friends list on social media (1 – never, 7 – very frequently)
	Overall, how important do you feel about the contacts on your 'friends' list on social media? (1 - Not at all important, 7 - very important)
	Overall, how close do you feel to the contacts on your 'friends' list on social media? (1 - Not at all close, 7 - Very close)

References

1. Mikalef, P., Giannakos, M., Pateli, A.: Shopping and word-of-mouth intentions on social media. J. Theor. Appl. Electron. Commer. Res. **8**, 17–34 (2013)
2. Zhou, L., Zhang, P., Zimmermann, H.-D.: Social commerce research: an integrated view. Electron. Commer. Res. Appl. **12**, 61–68 (2013)
3. Stephen, A.T., Toubia, O.: Deriving value from social commerce networks. J. Mark. Res. **47**, 215–228 (2010)
4. Ng, C.S.-P.: Intention to purchase on social commerce websites across cultures: a cross-regional study. Inf. Manag. **50**, 609–620 (2013)

5. Bambauer-Sachse, S., Mangold, S.: Brand equity dilution through negative online word-of-mouth communication. J. Retail. Consum. Serv. **18**, 38–45 (2011)
6. Cheng, Y.-H., Ho, H.-Y.: Social influence's impact on reader perceptions of online reviews. J. Bus. Res. **68**, 883–887 (2015)
7. Dellarocas, C.: The digitization of word of mouth: promise and challenges of online feedback mechanisms. Manage. Sci. **49**, 1407–1424 (2003)
8. Mikalef, P., Pappas, Ilias O., Giannakos, M.: consumer intentions on social media: a fsQCA analysis of motivations. In: Dwivedi, Yogesh K., Mäntymäki, M., Ravishankar, M.N., Janssen, M., Clement, M., Slade, Emma L., Rana, Nripendra P., Al-Sharhan, S., Simintiras, Antonis C. (eds.) I3E 2016. LNCS, vol. 9844, pp. 371–386. Springer, Cham (2016). doi:10.1007/978-3-319-45234-0_34
9. Ranaweera, C., Prabhu, J.: On the relative importance of customer satisfaction and trust as determinants of customer retention and positive word of mouth. J. Target. Meas. Anal. Mark. **12**, 82–90 (2003)
10. Kim, S., Park, H.: Effects of various characteristics of social commerce (s-commerce) on consumers' trust and trust performance. Int. J. Inf. Manage. **33**, 318–332 (2013)
11. Awad, N.F., Ragowsky, A.: Establishing trust in electronic commerce through online word of mouth: an examination across genders. J. Manage. Inf. Syst. **24**, 101–121 (2008)
12. Chan, Y.Y., Ngai, E.W.: Conceptualising electronic word of mouth activity: an input-process-output perspective. Mark. Intell. Plan. **29**, 488–516 (2011)
13. See-To, E.W., Ho, K.K.: Value co-creation and purchase intention in social network sites: the role of electronic Word-of-Mouth and trust–A theoretical analysis. Comput. Hum. Behav. **31**, 182–189 (2014)
14. McKnight, D.H., Choudhury, V., Kacmar, C.: Developing and validating trust measures for e-commerce: an integrative typology. Inf. Syst. Res. **13**, 334–359 (2002)
15. Hajli, N.: Social commerce constructs and consumer's intention to buy. Int. J. Inf. Manage. **35**, 183–191 (2015)
16. Zhu, F., Zhang, X.: Impact of online consumer reviews on sales: the moderating role of product and consumer characteristics. J. Mark. **74**, 133–148 (2010)
17. Metzger, M.J., Flanagin, A.J., Medders, R.B.: Social and heuristic approaches to credibility evaluation online. J. Commun. **60**, 413–439 (2010)
18. Lu, B., Fan, W., Zhou, M.: Social presence, trust, and social commerce purchase intention: an empirical research. Comput. Hum. Behav. **56**, 225–237 (2016)
19. Mikalef, P., Pappas, I.O., Giannakos, M.N.: Value co-creation and purchase intention in social commerce: the enabling role of word-of-mouth and trust. In: AMCIS (2017)
20. Yenisey, M.M., Ozok, A.A., Salvendy, G.: Perceived security determinants in e-commerce among Turkish university students. Behav. Inf. Technol. **24**, 259–274 (2005)
21. Moody, G.D., Galletta, D.F., Lowry, P.B.: When trust and distrust collide online: the engenderment and role of consumer ambivalence in online consumer behavior. Electron. Commer. Res. Appl. **13**, 266–282 (2014)
22. McKnight, D.H., Choudhury, V.: Distrust and trust in B2C e-commerce: do they differ? In: Proceedings of the 8th International Conference on Electronic Commerce: The New e-Commerce: Innovations for Conquering Current Barriers, Obstacles and Limitations to Conducting Successful Business on the Internet, pp. 482–491. ACM (2002)
23. Lu, Y., Zhao, L., Wang, B.: From virtual community members to C2C e-commerce buyers: trust in virtual communities and its effect on consumers' purchase intention. Electron. Commer. Res. Appl. **9**, 346–360 (2010)
24. Dwyer, P.: Measuring the value of electronic word of mouth and its impact in consumer communities. J. Interact. Mark. **21**, 63–79 (2007)

25. Kourouthanassis, P.E., Mikalef, P., Pappas, I.O., Kostagiolas, P.: Explaining travellers online information satisfaction: a complexity theory approach on information needs, barriers, sources and personal characteristics. Inf. Manage. (2017)
26. Pappas, I., Mikalef, P., Giannakos, M.: User Experience in Personalized E-Commerce: A Configurational Approach (2016)
27. Walsh, G., Mitchell, V.-W.: The effect of consumer confusion proneness on word of mouth, trust, and customer satisfaction. Eur. J. Mark. **44**, 838–859 (2010)
28. Gilbert, E., Karahalios, K.: Predicting tie strength with social media. In: Proceedings of the SIGCHI Conference on Human Factors in Computing Systems, pp. 211–220. ACM (2009)
29. Pigg, K.E., Crank, L.D.: Building community social capital: the potential and promise of information and communications technologies. J. Community Inf. **1** (2004)
30. Chu, S.-C., Kim, Y.: Determinants of consumer engagement in electronic word-of-mouth (eWOM) in social networking sites. Int. J. Adv. **30**, 47–75 (2011)
31. Brown, J.J., Reingen, P.H.: Social ties and word-of-mouth referral behavior. J. Consum. Res. **14**, 350–362 (1987)
32. Casler, K., Bickel, L., Hackett, E.: Separate but equal? A comparison of participants and data gathered via Amazon's MTurk, social media, and face-to-face behavioral testing. Comput. Hum. Behav. **29**, 2156–2160 (2013)
33. Hauser, D.J., Schwarz, N.: Attentive Turkers: MTurk participants perform better on online attention checks than do subject pool participants. Behav. Res. Methods **48**, 400–407 (2016)
34. Constantinides, E., Fountain, S.J.: Web 2.0: Conceptual foundations and marketing issues. J. Dir. Data Digital Mark. Pract. **9**, 231–244 (2008)
35. Hair Jr., J.F., Hult, G.T.M.: A primer on partial least squares structural equation modeling (PLS-SEM). Sage Publications, Thousand Oaks (2016)
36. Fornell, C., Larcker, D.F.: Evaluating structural equation models with unobservable variables and measurement error. J. Mark. Res., 39–50 (1981)
37. Farrell, A.M.: Insufficient discriminant validity: a comment on Bove, Pervan, Beatty, and Shiu (2009). J. Bus. Res. **63**, 324–327 (2010)
38. Chin, W.W.: The partial least squares approach to structural equation modeling. Mod. Meth. Bus. Res. **295**, 295–336 (1998)

#Demonetization and Its Impact on the Indian Economy – Insights from Social Media Analytics

Risha Mohan[✉] and Arpan Kumar Kar

Department of Management Studies, IIT Delhi,
IV Floor, Vishwakarma Bhavan, Hauz Khas, New Delhi 110016, India
risha.mohan@dmsiitd.org, arpan_kar@yahoo.co.in

Abstract. In recent times, twitter has emerged as a central site where people express their views and opinions on happenings surrounding their lives. This paper tries to study the general public sentiment surrounding a major break-through event for the Indian economy i.e. demonetization by capturing 1,44,497 tweets about demonetization. The paper also tries to find the impact of demone-tization on various sectors of the economy and whether there exists any correlation between the public sentiments expressed over twitter and the stock market performance of Nifty 50 companies. The industries were classified into cash dependent and independent sectors and the impact on both were separately studied. It was found there exists no significant correlation between the sentiments expressed over twitter about demonetization and the performance of various sectors in the economy and twitter sentiments alone do not necessarily predict the performance of financial market.

Keywords: Demonetization · Economic policy · Content analytics · Sentiment analytics · Stock price movement · Nifty 50 · Industry impact

1 Introduction

The advent and rapidly increasing popularity of social media has transformed various facets of our lives, be it business, politics, communication patterns around the globe, news consumption, communities, dating, parenting etc. As per latest data, nearly 50% (3.77 billion) of population uses internet while 37% (2.79 billion) use it actively which will continue to rise in near future [1]. Unlike conventional media which permitted information transfer only in one direction, digital mediums allow two- way form of communication, ensures faster dissemination and retrieval of information and hence, increasingly attracting the attention of business and research community intrigued with their affordance and reach [2].

Stock market movement and its prediction has always remained a key area of study, which is of great interest to stock investors, traders and applied researchers [3]. According to behavioral economics hypothesis, there exists correlation between public mood and market performance [4]. However, quantification of public mood is not an easy task. Before the internet era, dissemination of information regarding company's

A.K. Kar et al. (Eds.): I3E 2017, LNCS 10595, pp. 363–374, 2017.
DOI: 10.1007/978-3-319-68557-1_32

stock price, direction and general sentiments and consequently, market reaction took longer time. However, with internet and social media, getting information viral is just a click away. As such, short term sentiments play a significant role in short term performance of financial market instruments such as stocks, indexes and bonds [5]. Twitter, with an active monthly user base of 319 million in 2016, is one such social media platform which is being frequently used to study public mood and sentiment and there exists considerable support for the claim that it provides valid measurement of the same [6, 7]. Interested users post their views in form of short 140 character messages, often leading to ad hoc establishment of shared or trending 'hashtags' which forms the basis of data extraction and analysis [8].

This research revolves around a recent event which is a major breakthrough for the Indian economy i.e. demonetization by analyzing 1,44,497 tweets centered on this topic collected over a period of two months following demonetization. Each tweet captured had 16 attributes which captured user specific and user generated content specific data, which was used for subsequent analysis. The objective of this paper are as follows: Firstly, to perform sentiment analysis on the tweets extracted and analyze public mood and sentiment. Secondly, analyze the movement of stock prices of Nifty 50 companies during the same period and find a correlation, if it exists, between public sentiment and stock prices.

2   Literature Review

The literature review has been organized into two subcategories beginning with the correlation of stock prices with public sentiments and use of twitter to gauge public sentiments.

2.1   Correlation of Stock Prices with Public Sentiments

There have been multiple studies in the past which investigate the correlation between public sentiments (as captured from web data) and financial markets. A study [9] observed twitter data for emotional outbursts over a period of 5 months and found that when people expressed negative sentiments such as fear, worry, less hope etc. stock market indicators such as Dow Jones, NASDAQ and S&P 500 went down the next day. [10] also confirmed that there exists strong correlation between stock price movement and public sentiments as captured from twitter. Another research [11] studied the impact of investor sentiments on different economic sectors and found that certain sectors indexes like industry, banking, food and beverages saw more influence of investor sentiments in comparison to other sectors such as retail, telecom etc. In a recent study [12], the authors argued that the correlation between Twitter sentiment and Dow Jones Industrial Average (DJIA) index for the observed duration of 15 months is low. However, during certain 'events' which are marked by increased activity of twitter users such as quarterly announcements, macroeconomic policy announcement etc. there is significant correlation between the twitter sentiments and abnormal returns during the peaks of twitter volume. Thus, past studies confirm that web data have a bearing on stock prices.

2.2   Use of Twitter for Gauging Public Sentiments

A study [13] argued that twitter is an effective way to gauge societal interest and general public's opinion. Sentiments expressed over Twitter are being studied in numerous context. Another research work [14] studied the relationship between electoral events and expressed public sentiment during 2012 US Presidential elections and founded that tweet volume is hugely driven by campaign events. In October 2011, NM Incite and Nielson study [15] proved the correlation between twitter volume and TV ratings. Twitter has also been used to understand consumers' attitude towards global brands and how it can be leveraged while designing companies' marketing and advertising strategy [16]. Hence, the prior research confirms that Twitter is a rich source of data for mining public opinion. Its open architecture and integration to API allows easy access to data making it relevant for study.

3   Proposition

In the light of the above discussion, we can effectively state that short term public sentiments act as determinants of performance of financial market and Twitter as a social media platform can be effectively used to capture such sentiments. In this paper, we have focused on a recent event which took the whole nation by surprise i.e. demonetization leading to 86% of the currency in circulation getting extinguished at a moment's notice [17]. In a dramatic move to crackdown on unaccounted for and counterfeit cash, the Prime Minister of India announced the demonetization of Rs.500 and Rs.1000 currency notes with effect from November 8, 2016 making them invalid as legal tender. What followed the sudden announcement was acute cash crunch among citizens and businesses which resulted in a lot of social discussions. The move drew both positive as well as negative reaction with one group of people lauding the bold step to fight black money while the other group criticizing how ill-planned the move was. Social media platforms were set abuzz with people's reactions pouring in from across the nation with demonetization accounting for 6 out of 10 trending topics between November 8–24 [18]. There are divided opinions on whether demonetization had an overall positive or negative impact. As per one school of thoughts, the economy witnessed a contraction in money supply, fall in public expenditure leading to corresponding fall in production and incomes. It caused short-term impact on various sectors of the economy-payment, real estate, retail, agriculture and related sectors, BFSI, consumption related sectors like consumer durables, FMCG etc., entertainment, coal industry and tourism [19–21]. Unorganized sectors which accounts 45% of production, suffered an immediate impact with decline in both transactions and output. It had a spill- over effect on organized sectors which also saw an immediate impact, although less [22]. In a contrast to this view, the World Bank CEO, pointed that demonetization will prove effective in the long term fostering a clean and digitized economy [23].

In view of these discussions, the current study focuses on the following questions:

- What is the buzz over social media about demonetization?
- What are the general public sentiments surrounding demonetization?

- What is the impact on industries, if any, due to demonetization, captured by observing stock price fluctuations of Nifty 50 companies during the period?
- Whether the impact is restricted to companies that have heavy dependence on cash?
- Is there any correlation between the sentiments expressed in social media and industry performance as measured through stock price fluctuations?

4 Data Collection

The collection of twitter data (tweets and metadata) has been done from Twitter website using R programming language and the twitter package. This allows us to capture 1% of publically available data on twitter [8]. The keywords used were '#demonetization' and '#demonetisation'. 1, 44,497 tweets centered on these topic were collected from 12th November, 2016 to 12th January, 2017. Out of this, the total number of unique tweets was 45493. The collected data was cleansed or processed to be made ready for analysis. Figure 1 shows the process of data cleansing.

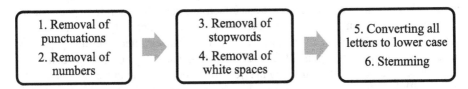

Fig. 1. Process of data cleansing

Figure 2 shows the tweet rate over an interval of 10 days. It can be seen that the maximum number of tweets were posted in the initial days of announcement of demonetization. The tweet rate follows a downward trend as the social media buzz starts to fade with the initial inconvenience situation settling in.

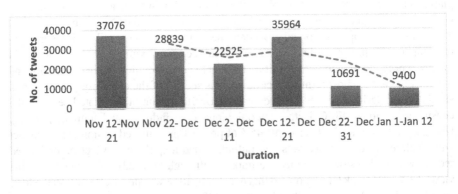

Fig. 2. Tweet Rate over a period of 10 days

In the same duration, the stock price data of Nifty 50 companies was collected from the National Stock Exchange (NSE). The Nifty 50 stock accounts for 14 sectors of the economy which include Cigarettes, Pharmaceuticals, Information Technology, Cements, Automobile, Financial Services, Metals, Energy, Telecom, Consumer Goods, Construction, Industrial Manufacturing, Media & Entertainment and Shipping [24]. In our study, we have also captured stock price data of Real Estate sector by collecting data of 4 major players namely DLF, Oberoi Realty Ltd, Jaypee Infratech and Ansal Properties & Infrastructure Ltd. This has been done as real estate was touted to take the worst hit due to high involvement of black money and cash transactions, especially in case of resale and land transactions [25].

5   Research Methodology and Findings

5.1   Exploratory Data Analysis

As part of the exploratory analysis, we looked at the most frequent words among the tweets with the help of wordcloud. The larger the word in the wordcloud, the higher will be its usage frequency. Figure 3 shows the wordcloud generated from the collected tweets. The most frequently used words are 'narendramodi', 'Modi', 'PMOIndia'. 'BlackMoney', 'India', 'Support', 'ArvindKejriwal', 'IAmwithModi' etc. A deeper look shows people's massive support to PM Narendra Modi's fight against black money. There are few negative sentiments as reflected in words like 'issue', 'failure', 'cash', 'pain', 'failed', 'old', 'died', 'queue' etc. mostly centered around the initial inconvenience caused due to cash crunch. Overall, the move successfully garnered public support. The other theme that emerges from the wordcloud is the focus on digital transactions as reflected in words like 'Paytm', 'card', 'axisbank', 'digitalIndia' which is rightly so as mobile wallet companies benefitted hugely from demonetization. Paytm, one of the largest players in mobile wallet space, saw its traffic increase by 435% and app download by 200% [26].

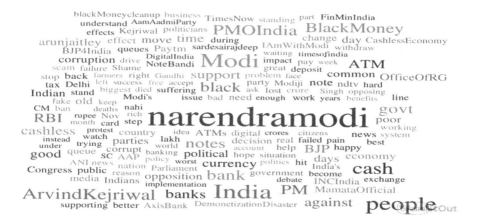

Fig. 3. Wordcloud for demonetization

5.2 Sentiment Analysis

Sentiment analysis or opinion mining has gained popularity as a more cost and time efficient and non- intrusive method of text analytics as compared to traditional market survey methods like surveys and opinion polls. For performing the sentiment analysis, Syuzhet package available in R has been used. The get_ncr_sentiment method which implements Saif Mohammad's NRC Emotion lexicon comprising of words and their associations with 8 emotions (anger, fear, anticipation, trust, surprise, sadness, joy, and disgust) and two sentiments (negative and positive) [27]. Figure 4 shows the percentage of emotions in our tweet sample. As can be seen, trust has the highest percentage (22.15%) among all emotions followed by anticipation (15.94%) and anger (13.03%). Hence, overall trust of people on PM Modi and his efforts to fight corruption outweighs the negatives caused due to initial inconvenience.

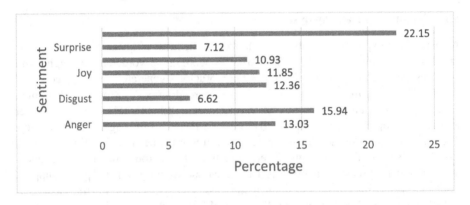

Fig. 4. Percentage emotions in tweet sample

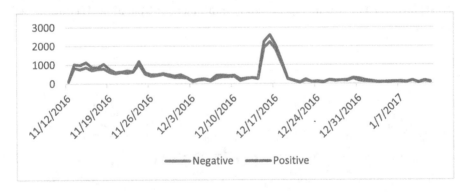

Fig. 5. Sum of positive and negative valence of tweets grouped by date

Figure 5 shows the variation in the scale of positive and negative tweets per day. This has been calculated by summing the positive/negative valence as measured using NRC Emotion lexicon of all individual tweets grouped by date. As can be seen, the positive sentiments are higher than the negative sentiments on all days. Average sentiment for a day was calculated by averaging the valence (Positive valence + (Negative valence* −1)) of all tweets on that particular day. Majority tweets (90.16%) reflect positive sentiments. One can witness a downward trend in the number of positive tweets. This can also be attributed to the declining number of tweets as the post demonetization effects started to settle.

5.3 Correlation Analysis Between Stock Prices of Nifty 50 Companies and Twitter Sentiments

In our study, we have focused on the correlation between stock accounts for 15 sectors of the economy (fourteen sectors being represented by Nifty 50 companies and real estate being the fifteenth). In order to calculate correlation between industry perform-ances and twitter sentiments, we first normalized the values of stock prices of the companies within the sector and hence, taking the average of stock prices of the compa-nies for a particular day. For calculating the normalized value, following formula has been used where z represents the normalized value of stock price, μ represents the mean of the stock prices of the companies and σ represents the standard deviation of the distribution.

$$z = (x - \mu)/\sigma \qquad (1)$$

Table 1 explains how normalized values have been calculated. For a particular date, the stock prices of the companies listed under that particular sector (information tech-nology in our case) were normalized and then averaged to find a single value for that sector for that particular day. This was done for all the sectors over our observed duration of two months.

Table 1. Calculation of normalized value of stock prices for a sample industry for a given date

Sector	Company	Stock price	Normalized value
Information Technology	HCL Technologies	770.75	−0.335192577
	Infosys	923.55	−0.104930936
	TCS	2121.3	1.700015925
	Tech Mahindra	430.95	−0.847253477
	Wipro	447.95	−0.821635362
	Average sentiment for the day	**−0.081799285**

For calculating the correlation between the stock prices and sentiments, we have eliminated the days where stock market was closed (weekends and public holidays). The results of the Pearson correlation coefficient between the average sentiment of the day and normalized value of the stock prices for the industry are illustrated in Table 2.

Table 2. Result of correlation analysis between twitter sentiments and average industry stock price

Industry	Cash dependent/ independent sector	Pearson correlation coefficient	Strength
Cigarettes	Cash dependent	0.0138673	Weakly negative
Pharmaceuticals	Cash dependent	0.1997678	Weakly positive
IT	Cash independent	0.0541927	Weakly negative
Cements	Cash independent	0.3168577	Medium positive
Automobile	Cash dependent	0.1256828	Weakly positive
Financial services	Cash independent	0.1060174	Weakly positive
Metals	Cash independent	0.1564007	Weakly positive
Energy	Cash independent	0.0942602	Weakly positive
Telecom	Cash independent	0.1134828	Weakly positive
Consumer goods	Cash dependent	0.1460163	Weakly positive
Construction	Cash dependent	0.0315842	Weakly positive
Industrial manufacturing	Cash independent	0.1517175	Weakly positive
Media & Entertainment	Cash dependent	0.0578423	Weakly positive
Shipping	Cash independent	0.0569725	Weakly positive
Real estate	Cash dependent	0.0748107	Weakly positive

It can be seen that there is no significant correlation between the sentiments expressed over twitter about demonetization and the performance of various sectors in the economy.

6 Inferences

Our initial assumption was that there will not be any significant correlation between the performances of stocks of companies belonging to sectors that have minimal or no dependence on cash. As can be seen from Table 3, the assumption holds true for such cases. However, even for cases in which sectors have heavy dependence on cash transactions, no significant correlation is observed apart from cements which shows medium correlation. Figure 6 and 7 shows the percentage change in the average stock prices from previous day of the companies within cash dependent and cash independent sectors respectively, though the public sentiments did not really correlate with the changes.

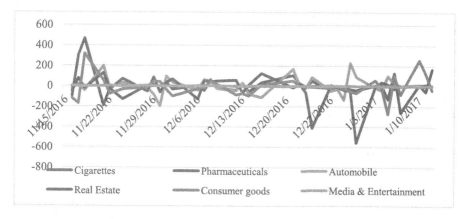

Fig. 6. Percentage change in stock prices of cash dependent sectors

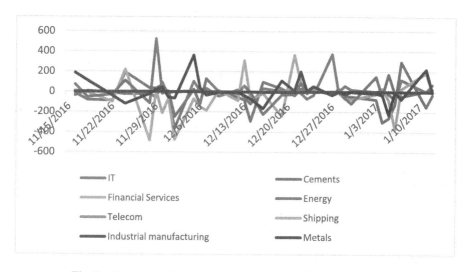

Fig. 7. Percentage change in stock prices of cash independent sectors

As can be observed, no clear trend is applicable across either cash dependent or cash independent sectors except for certain industries like real estate which showed steep decline in stock prices. Another interesting finding is that the fluctuations in stock price of cash independent sector is more than cash dependent sector. However, it is difficult to segregate whether the fluctuations are caused solely due to demonetization.

There were other short term phenomenon which affected industry performance. Some sectors like pharmaceuticals saw an increase in stock prices as old currency was accepted by chemists till 15th December, leading to significant increase in short term sale in anticipation of more problem in future [28]. Core sectors like cement, steel etc. which are not dependent on cash were negatively impacted as people deferred long term investments. Sectors like IT, FMCG etc. remained unaffected. [29] has argued that demonetization has not impacted overall market much as investors perceive the impact as temporary. Besides, there are other factors apart from demonetization such as US Presidential elections, rise is US bond yields etc. which have impacted the overall market performance.

Thus, our study shows that twitter sentiments alone do not necessarily determine the performance of financial market. There are other factors (economic, political, short term phenomenon impacting consumer behavior etc.) which need to be taken into account for determining the performance of stocks.

7   Limitations

The research in a novel approach in estimating the impact of twitter sentiments on the industrial performance post any major economic policy announcement. It assumes a direct relationship between the sentiments expressed over social media and stock prices which remains one if its limitations. Other factors which may have affected the stock prices have not been taken into account as it was not feasible to segregate the impact of all other factors. The study also suffers from self- selection bias as we have only considered the tweets with hashtags- '#demonetization' or '#demonetisation'. Contributors to the discussion who may not use similar words or hashtags would not be within the scope of the current analysis. Another limitation of the study is that user base of twitter may not necessarily comprise of industry experts of all sectors. However, despite these limitations, the research highlights intriguing relationship between public sentiments and performance of stock market post a macroeconomic phenomenon which may be taken forward in future research.

References

1. Smart Insights Homepage. http://www.smartinsights.com/social-media-marketing/social-media-strategy/new-global-social-media-research/. Last accessed 20 Apr 2017
2. Ellison, N.B.: Social network sites: definition, history, and scholarship. J. Comput.-Mediated Commun. 13(1), 210–230 (2007)
3. Nair, B.B., et al.: Stock market prediction using a hybrid neuro-fuzzy system. In: International Conference on Advances in Recent Technologies in Communication and Computing (ARTCom). IEEE (2010)
4. Makrehchi, M., Shah, S., Liao, W.: Stock prediction using event-based sentiment analysis. In: 2013 IEEE/WIC/ACM International Joint Conferences on Web Intelligence (WI) and Intelligent Agent Technologies (IAT), vol. 1, pp. 337–342. IEEE (2013)
5. Rao, T., Srivastava, S.: Analyzing stock market movements using twitter sentiment analysis. In: Proceedings of the 2012 International Conference on Advances in Social Networks Analysis and Mining (ASONAM 2012), pp. 119–123. IEEE Computer Society (2012)
6. The Statistics Portal: Number of monthly active Twitter users worldwide from 1st quarter 2010 to 4th quarter 2016 (in millions). https://www.statista.com/statistics/282087/number-of-monthly-active-twitter-users. Last accessed 25 Mar 2017
7. Mao, H., Counts, S., Bollen, J.: Predicting financial markets: Comparing survey, news, twitter and search engine data. arXiv preprint arXiv:1112.1051 (2011)

8. Lakhiwal, A., Kar, A.K.: Insights from Twitter analytics: modeling social media personality dimensions and impact of breakthrough events. In: Dwivedi, Y.K., Mäntymäki, M., Ravishankar, M.N., Janssen, M., Clement, M., Slade, Emma L., Rana, Nripendra P., Al-Sharhan, S., Simintiras, Antonis C. (eds.) I3E 2016. LNCS, vol. 9844, pp. 533–544. Springer, Cham (2016). doi:10.1007/978-3-319-45234-0_47

9. Zhang, X., Fuehres, H., Gloor, P.A.: Predicting stock market indicators through twitter "I hope it is not as bad as I fear". In: Procedia-Social and Behavioral Sciences 26, pp. 55–62 (2011)

10. Pagolu, V.S., et al.: Sentiment Analysis of Twitter Data for Predicting Stock Market Movements. arXiv preprint arXiv:1610.09225 (2016)

11. Uygur, U., Taş, O.: The impacts of investor sentiment on different economic sectors: evidence from Istanbul Stock Exchange. Borsa Istanbul Rev. 14(4), 236–241 (2014)

12. Ranco, G., et al.: The effects of Twitter sentiment on stock price returns. PLoS ONE 10(9), e0138441 (2015)

13. Khan, A.Z.H., Atique, M., Thakare, V.M.: Combining lexicon-based and learning-based methods for Twitter sentiment analysis. In: Int. J. Electron. Commun. Soft Comput. Sci. Eng. (IJECSCSE) 89 (2015)

14. Wang, H., Can, D., Kazemzadeh, A., Bar, F., Narayanan, S.: A system for real-time twitter sentiment analysis of 2012 us presidential election cycle. In: Proceedings of the ACL 2012 System Demonstrations, pp. 115–120. Association for Computational Linguistics (2012)

15. Spredfast Portal: Confirmed! Relationship between Tweet Volume and Nielsen TV Ratings. https://www.spredfast.com/social-marketing-blog/confirmed-relationship-between-tweet-volume-and-nielsen-tv-ratings. Last accessed 15 Apr 2017

16. Mostafa, M.M.: More than words: social networks' text mining for consumer brand sentiments. Expert Syst. Appl. 40(10), 4241–4251 (2013)

17. Livemint: Consequences of the demonetisation shock. http://www.livemint.com/Opinion/OBjsLy2iZn1Huoyzz1v6WP/Consequences-of-the-demonetization-shock.html. Last accessed 15 Apr 2017

18. The Economic Times: Demonetisation rules social media, most netizens leaning in favour. http://economictimes.indiatimes.com/tech/internet/demonetisation-rules-social-media-most-netizens-leaning-in-favour/articleshow/55760319.cms. Last accessed 15 Apr 2017

19. MoneyLife: How does the demonetisation affect different sectors? http://www.moneylife.in/article/how-does-the-demonetisation-affect-different-sectors/48769.html. Last accessed 15 Apr 2017

20. Steel360: Demonetization to Impact Coal Industry until Q1 FY18. http://news.steel-360.com/coal/demonetization-impact-coal-industry-q1-fy18/. Last accessed 15 Apr 2017

21. Financial Express: How demonetization will impact top six sectors of economy. http://www.financialexpress.com/economy/how-demonetization-will-impact-top-six-sectors-of-economy/490999/. Last accessed 15 Aug 2017

22. Kumar, A.: Economic consequences of demonetisation. Econ. Polit. Weekly 52(1) (2017)

23. Hindustan Times: Demonetization will have positive impact on Indian economy, says World Bank CEO, 2 March 2017. http://www.hindustantimes.com/business-news/modi-s-demonetisation-move-will-positively-impact-economy-world-bank-ceo/story-8Khb9U8UHOoEXoi75vyDfI.html. Last accessed 15 Feb 2017

24. Sharma, R.: Nifty 50 Companies – List & Sector-wise Weightage. http://www.blog.sanasecurities.com/nifty-50-companies-list-sector-wise-weightage/. Last accessed 15 Apr 2017

25. Control, M.: 7 FAQs on demonetization & its impact on home buying. http://www.moneycontrol.com/news/business/personal-finance-business/7-faqsdemonetization-038-its-impacthome-buying-928005.html. Last accessed 22 Apr 2017

26. Hindustan Times: Mobile wallets see a soaring growth post-demonetisation. http://www.hindustantimes.com/business-news/mobile-wallets-see-a-soaring-growth-post-demonetisation/story-zwdBi3UGqG1qZD92AEF9GK.html. Last accessed 22 Apr 2017

27. Jockers M.: Introduction to the Syuzhet Package. https://cran.r-project.org/web/packages/syuzhet/vignettes/syuzhet-vignette.html. Last accessed 22 Apr 2017

28. Oswal, M.: http://www.motilaloswal.com/article.aspx/1157/Demonetizations-Effect-on-Share-Market. Last accessed 22 Apr 2017

29. Live mint: How much has demonetisation affected the stock market? http://www.livemint.com/Money/hRb1noUQV17fmP0o1GNQEJ/How-much-has-demonetisation-affected-the-stock-market.html. Last accessed 15 Apr 2017

Motivations and Emotions in Social Media: Explaining Users' Satisfaction with FsQCA

Ilias O. Pappas[1($\boxtimes$)], Sofia Papavlasopoulou[1],
Panos E. Kourouthanassis[2], Patrick Mikalef[1],
and Michail N. Giannakos[1]

[1] Norwegian University of Science and Technology (NTNU),
Trondheim, Norway
{ilpappas,spapav,patrick.mikalef,michailg}@ntnu.no
[2] Ionian University, Corfu, Greece
pkour@ionio.gr

Abstract. This study aims to explain how motivations and emotions combine to influence users' satisfaction with social media. Motivations are decomposed into four attributes, entertainment, information, social-psychological, and convenience, while emotions are divided into their two main categories, that is positive and negative emotions. In order to examine the interplay of these factors and their combined effect on satisfaction, a conceptual model is developed, and validated on a data sample of 582 social media users, through fuzzy-set qualitative comparative analysis (fsQCA). The findings indicate eight configurations that lead to high satisfaction, which show the importance of high convenience, followed by entertainment and information in being satisfied with social media, while emotions and social-psychological factors are less important. This study contributes in social media literature by identifying specific patterns of users for whom these factors are important and influence greatly their satisfaction.

Keywords: Social media · Motivation · Emotions · FsQCA

1 Introduction

Social media have intruded on peoples' lives and is a main computer activity. The main characteristic of social media is that they are highly experiential media and their value depends on users' adoption through interaction. Many studies in the area focus on systems' acceptance and satisfaction from their use, through technical and interface characteristics [1, 2]. We suggest a different approach to satisfaction focusing on internal factors influencing the use of social media. As users' needs and motivations are not independent from the system they are using [3], we view users as individuals with motivations and emotions, which influence their satisfaction with social media use.

In the context of online services, affective states and their influence in behavior has been examined widely [4–6]. Emotions, like enjoyment and pleasure, may increase users' levels of satisfaction with online services [7]. Additionally, during the interaction with social media, different emotions are developed [8] affecting users' behavior and satisfaction [9]. Nonetheless, studies mainly focus on specific emotions, thus a holistic

A.K. Kar et al. (Eds.): I3E 2017, LNCS 10595, pp. 375–387, 2017.
DOI: 10.1007/978-3-319-68557-1_33

approach to the examination of emotions is needed. Here, we argue that it is needed to explore the role of motivations and emotions on increasing users' satisfaction, as the latter is a main antecedent of repeated behavior, on which social media adoption is based. As social media evolve and new types appear continuously, it is needed to understand factors that will lead to satisfied users, and by extension to loyal users.

Previous studies in the area of social media examine various ways influencing users' satisfaction or behaviour, identifying users' motivations, such as entertainment, information, social-psychological, convenience [2, 10], and various types emotions as important in influencing satisfaction or behaviour [7]. There is a lack of theories in the area and, mainly, empirical studies that examine the combined effects of the afore-mentioned factors. Users with different motivations and emotions, might not be rep-resented from the one-model-fits-all produced from the traditional variance based approaches. Such traditional approaches (e.g., multiple regression analysis, structural equation modelling) assume that relations among variables are symmetric and offer one single best solution that explains the outcome. However, a sample includes variables with asymmetric relationships among each other, not identifiable by traditional approaches [11]. Thus, multiple configurations of the examined variables lead to multiple solutions explaining the same result, while representing overall a larger part of the sample.

In this study, we build on complexity theory and configuration theory in order to identify the different causal patterns of factors that users' satisfaction with social media. To this end, we employ a fuzzy-set qualitative comparative analysis (fsQCA) [12] to explain how motivations and emotions lead to high satisfaction with social media. The findings identify multiple, different, and equally effective combinations of motivations and emotions that are able to explain high satisfaction. The paper contributes to existing literature in two main ways. First, it provides empirical evidence on the importance of motivations in satisfied customers, and second, it examines the combined influence of motivations (i.e., entertainment, information, social-psychological, con-venience) and emotions (i.e., positive and negative emotions) on satisfaction with social media.

2   Background and Conceptual Model

2.1   Motivations When Using Social Media

People using social media have various needs and their motivations may differ, influence their actions, and their fulfillment is expected to increase their satisfaction. This is inherent in the uses and gratification theory (UGT) which, in the context of social media, suggests that the use of social media is based on and motivated by users' inner needs [13]. Such motivations include socializing, entertainment, information, psychological, and hedonic motivation [2, 9, 10], and are linked with the benefits that social media may offer to their users by covering their needs [10]. People use social media to find their friends, communicate with them in a convenient way, develop a feel of belongingness, encouragement and companionship from both existing social relationships, but also create new relationships based on similar interests and preferences [2]. Also, individuals may use social media to seek information, on multiple occasions, from news to travelling information. Also, individuals may seek social and psychological benefits through social media, which may be gained as people continuously use social media [10]. Furthermore, users are likely to use social media and visit online communities because they feel they are fun or amusing [14], suggesting that emotions play in important part both in their satisfaction and their overall behaviour. The convenience and entertainment that social media offer, for example by being pleasing and easy to use [15], will increase users' intention to adopt them. The latter is directly influenced by users' satisfaction [16], highlighting its importance in forming users' motivation in social media. To improve our understanding of social media usage and explain individuals' satisfaction with them further work is needed to provide an integrated view of social media by employing new methods that are able to give more insight into the area.

2.2   Emotions and Social Media Satisfaction

Using social media is a highly experiential task, therefore different emotions occur when people use them. The link of emotions with satisfaction is inherent and one may lead to the other, or vice versa [17]. Extant research has examined the role of emotions when using online services and how users' behavior is affected by their feelings [4, 6]. Specifically in social media, affection has a positive effect on their usage [18], while the way people feel will have an influence on their satisfaction [19]. Some of the most widely studied emotions, such as enjoyment, have been found to increase users' satisfaction with online networks [7], and the majority of the studies in the area of online services either do not take into consideration emotions or focus on specific ones. However, emotions are a multidimensional factor and studying together positive and negative emotions, which are likely to coexist, may provide better understanding about their role on increasing satisfaction and formulation behaviors [5].

Positive emotions, like enjoyment and pleasure, and on the other hand, negative emotions, like anger and anxiety, were studied to explain users' satisfaction and behavior when using online services [4, 20]. In detail, previous studies have found that positive emotions will increase users' satisfaction, while negative ones will decrease it [20]. Different types of emotions appear in social networks [21] and being able to capture, analyze, and explain them will lead to improved services [8], highlighting the need for a deeper understanding of their interactions with users' motivations on social media.

2.3   Conceptual Model

With the increasing number of people using social media, it is crucial to better understand users' different motivations to identify how their satisfaction can be increased [1, 9]. Recent studies in the area build on the UGT to explain users' motivations to use social media, and how they may differ from the motivations to use traditional media [2, 13]. Towards this end, various motivations have been identified as critical when using social media, with entertainment, information, social-psychological, and convenience among the most important ones, and their effect on users' attitudes and behavior has been verified [2, 10]. However, their relationship with satisfaction needs to be explored further [1]. Also, since motivations are based on users' inner needs, the role of emotions should be examined [5]. As argued above, emotions are linked with user satisfaction, and their inclusion here will offer more insight on this relation and how it is shaped. However, there are not enough studies in the area examining motivations and emotions, and at the same time existing studies employ regression based tests, which assume a symmetric relation between the examined factors. Thus, further work needed to provide a general overview that describes the role of motivations and emotions, and their interrelations in predicting high satisfaction with social media.

To address this gap, we examine users' satisfaction with social mead by unravelling configurations of causally related sets of factors. We posit that there is a synergy among motivations and emotions in explaining satisfaction with social media, and theorize that there is not one single, optimal, configuration of such values. Instead, multiple and equally effective configurations of causal conditions exist, which may include different combinations of motivations and emotions. To conceptualize these relationships, we propose a conceptual model (Fig. 1) showing the examined constructs and their intersections. Overlapping areas represent possible combinations among factors, that is areas that one factor may exist together with the rest (e.g., combinations that explain high satisfaction are included within the outcome of interest area).

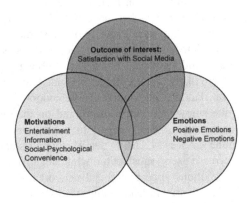

Fig. 1. Venn diagram of the conceptual model explaining satisfaction with social media

Drawing on complexity theory and the principle of *equifinality*, a result may be equally explained by alternative sets of causal conditions [22]. These conditions may be coalesced in sufficient configurations to explain the outcome [11, 23]. Motivations and emotions are important antecedents of users' satisfaction [1, 17], thus they may interact with each other in various configurations. For example, users that seek information or entertainment are more likely to be satisfied with social media if the feel happy using them, while at the same time users' may still be satisfied if they felt negative emotions due to the lack of convenience, but they managed to find the information they were looking for. Thus, high satisfaction may be achieved through various ways.

Further, configuration theory proposes the principle of *causal asymmetry*, which means that the presence or absence of a condition that explains an outcome, depends on the presence or absence of the other conditions [23]. Following the previous example, alternative configurations may include (i) high levels of information and entertainment motivations, and positive emotions in one configuration, or (ii) high levels of negative emotions, low levels of convenience, and high levels of information motivations. Thus, the same outcome may be influenced either positively or negatively by a specific factor, depending on how it combines with the other factors.

3 Research Methodology

3.1 Sampling and Measures

Our research model deals with experienced users in social media. The respondents were given a definition of social media, followed by a few examples, and they were asked to keep this in mind, while answering the questions based on their previous experience. We used a sample of 582 Greek users of social media. They were kindly asked to voluntary fill in an online questionnaire with no reward for their participation. The survey was conducted in March-April 2016 and aimed at 1800 social media users. The sample consists of more women (64%) than men (36%). The majority of the responders are between 25–34 years old (37%), 27% between 18–24, followed by 19% at the age of 35 to 44 and 12% were less than 17 years old. The rest were over 45 years old (5%). In terms of the educational status, the vast majority (50,7%) were university graduates. Almost all of our sample had experience in social media for over a year.

The first part of the questionnaire has questions about the demographic profile of the responders, and the second part had measures of the constructs chosen to be examined, selected from the proper literature review (needs, performance, confirmation, emotions, satisfaction). For the questions of the second part, a 7-point Likert scale was used, anchored from 1 ("completely agree") to 7 ("completely disagree"). Motivations include four types of motivations and explain to why people use social media [2, 10]. Positive and negative emotions, divided based on valence, refer to how users feel when using social media, and have been adopted from Scherer, Shuman, Fontaine and Soriano [24]. Satisfaction refers to users' overall satisfaction with social media [25]. In the Appendix a detailed table presents all constructs along with descriptives and loadings.

3.2 FsQCA

FsQCA is the combination of fuzzy sets and logic principles with Qualitative Comparative Analysis (QCA) [26]. It has been applied in many fields, like business and social commerce [5, 27], and takes the researcher beyond the traditional MRAs as it identifies multiple paths explaining the same outcome. These paths are combinations of variables, and may include variables influencing the outcome only in a small subset of cases, that are not identified by MRAs [11]. The combinations create multiple solutions (or configurations) offered by fsQCA, and include both necessary and sufficient conditions, which may be present or absent on a solution, or they may be on a "do not care" situation. The "do not care" situation indicates that the factor may either be present or absent and it does not play a role on a specific configuration. Necessary and sufficient conditions may be present (or absent) as core, indicating a strong causal relationship with the outcome, and peripheral elements, indicating a weaker relationship [23].

Calibration follows, all factors are transformed into fuzzy-sets with a range of values from 0–1 [12]. This may be done directly or indirectly, based on the data and underlying theory [12]. In the direct way, three qualitative thresholds (or breakpoints) are chosen, while in the indirect, the factors are calibrated following qualitative assessments. The thresholds set the full membership, full non-membership and inter-mediate membership, representing the degree that a case is part of a set [12]. We employ the direct method and the thresholds are chosen based on the survey scale; full membership threshold is set at 6; full non-membership threshold is set at 2; and, intermediate membership at 4.

Next, fsQCA produces a truth table of 2^k rows (k is the number of predictors and each row represents every possible combination), which is sorted based on frequency (i.e., the number of observations for each combination) and consistency (i.e., "*the degree to which cases correspond to the set-theoretic relationships expressed in a solution*") [12, 23]. To obtain a minimum number of observations for the assessment of the relationships a frequency threshold is set. We set at 3, and all combinations with smaller frequency are removed from further analysis [12, 23]. Also, the threshold for consistency is set at over the recommended threshold of 0.85 [28]. The combinations above the consistency threshold are those that fully explain the outcome, which means that for those combinations the outcome variable is set at 1, and for the rest is set at 0. FsQCA offers three sets of solutions (i.e., complex, parsimonious, intermediate) that need to be interpreted by the researcher. The complex solution presents all combinations of conditions when logical operations are applied, and are simplified into parsimonious and intermediate solutions, as they are simpler to interpret.

4   Findings

4.1   Measurements

The constructs are assessed for reliability based on the Cronbach alpha and Composite Reliability indicators, that show acceptable indices of internal consistency as all constructs exceed the cut-off threshold of .70. For validity, the average variance extracted (AVE) needs to be larger than .50, correlations among variables should be lower than .80 points, and the square root of each factor's AVE should be higher than its correlations with the other factors [29]. The AVE ranges between 0.57 and 0.84, all correlations are lower than 0.80, and square root AVEs are larger than corresponding correlations. Since our data are not normally distributed, we employ Kendall's tau test to measure correlation, which is generally preferred over Spearman's rho, as it is a better estimate of the corresponding population parameter, and its standard error is known [30]. The findings are presented in Table 1. Multicollinearity [31] is examined along with the potential common method bias by utilizing the common latent factor technique and the CFA marker variable technique, which are better from other control procedures (e.g., Harman's single factor test) [32]. Variance inflation factor (VIF) for all factors is lower than the recommended value (< 3), thus multicollinearity is not an issue. Common method bias is not a problem, as variance from the common latent factor technique and the CFA marker variable technique, is 0.08 and 0.21, respectively.

Table 1. Descriptive statistics and correlations of latent variables

Construct	Mean (S.D.)	CR	AVE	1	2	3	4	5	6	7
1. Entertainment	4.10 (1.49)	.82	.53	.73						
2. Information	4.64 (1.57)	.92	.74	.27	.86					
3. Social psychological	3.11 (1.22)	.87	.64	.34	.18	.80				
4. Convenience	4.75 (0.91)	.91	.70	.39	.33	.45	.84			
5. Positive emotions	3.51 (1.38)	.93	.61	.44	.33	.48	.40	.78		
6. Negative emotions	2.16 (1.64)	.93	.57	−.02	.04	.14	−.01	.19	.76	
7. Satisfaction	4.44 (1.64)	.94	.78	.39	.38	.43	.61	.53	−.14	.89

Note: Diagonal elements (in bold) are the square root of the average variance extracted (AVE). Off-diagonal elements are the correlations among constructs (all correlations higher than 0.1 are significant, $p < 0.01$;). For discriminant validity, diagonal elements should be larger than off-diagonal elements. CR; Composite Reliability.

4.2   Findings from FsQCA

The findings from the fsQCA on the configurations for high satisfaction when using social media are presented in Table 2. Each combination in the solution is able to explain the same outcome at a specific amount. In detail, the presence of a condition is presented by black circles (●), and its absence by crossed-out circles (⊗) [23]. Blank spaces indicate a "do not care" situation, which means that the condition may either be present or absent. Consistency values are presented in Table 2 for every and the overall solution, with all values being higher than the recommended threshold (> 0.75). Consistency shows the degree that a relationship has been approximated, and coverage evaluates the empirical relevance of a consistent subset [28]. The overall consistency is similar to the correlation and the overall solution coverage indicates the extent to which high satisfaction may be determined from the existing configurations, and is comparable to the R-square value reported in traditional regression analyses. The overall solution coverage of .80 indicates that a substantial amount of the outcome is explained by the eight solutions. FsQCA estimates also the empirical relevance for every solution, by calculating raw and unique coverage. The raw coverage describes the amount of the outcome that is explained by a certain alternative solution, while the unique coverage describes the amount of the outcome that is exclusively explained by a certain alternative solution. The solutions presented in Table 2 explain a great number of users' satisfaction with social media, ranging from 25% to 59% cases associated with the outcome.

Table 2. Combinations that lead to high satisfaction when using social media

Configuration	Solution							
	1	2	3	4	5	6	7	8
Motivation								
Entertainment	•			●	●		●	•
Information	●	●	●		●			•
Social Psychological		⊗		⊗	⊗	⊗	•	⊗
Convenience	●	●	●	●		●	●	
Emotions								
Positive			⊗	⊗	⊗	⊗		●
Negative			⊗		⊗	●	●	•
Consistency	.92	0.89	.93	.91	.93	.86	.95	.95
Raw Coverage	.59	0.56	.36	.41	.29	.29	.28	.25
Unique Coverage	.05	0.03	.02	.03	.01	.01	.02	.01
Overall Solution Consistency	0.86							
Overall Solution Coverage	0.80							

Note: Black circles (●) indicate the presence of a condition, and circles with "x" (⊗) indicate its absence. Large circles indicate core conditions, and small ones represent peripheral conditions. Blank spaces indicate "don't care."

Solutions 1–5 present combinations that lead to high satisfaction when using social media, when emotions are not high or not important. In detail, high information and convenience motivations will satisfy the users when (i) combined with high entertainment (Solution 1) or (ii) low social-psychological motivations (Solution 2), regardless of emotions, or (iii) when both positive and negative emotions are low (Solution 3). Next, the combination of high entertainment and convenience will lead to high satisfaction when social-psychological motivations are low, as well as emotions (Solutions 4 and 5). On the other hand, when one or both emotions are high, satisfaction may be achieved by (i) high convenience with low social-psychological motivations and positive emotions (Solution 6), (ii) high entertainment, convenience and social-psychological motivations (Solution 7), or last by (iii) high entertainment, information, with low social-psychological motivations (Solution 8).

5 Discussion

This study suggests that in social media, users' motivation and emotions combine and create configurations that explain their overall satisfaction with social media. We draw on complexity theory and configuration theory and propose a conceptual model to identify the aforementioned configurations. In detail, the model includes four users' motivations, that is entertainment, information, social psychological, convenience, and their positive and negative emotions. The findings lead to multiple recipes explaining high satisfaction with social media, with two main outcomes. First, we identify the importance of motivations when using social media over emotions, and second the ability of emotions to lead to satisfied users when motivations are less important for them.

The findings show that convenience is the most important factor, since it is present (i.e., high) in 6 out of 8 solutions, always as a core factor. People tend to choose solutions that make their life easier, especially with the advancement in mobile devices, thus using social media because it is simple and easy will increase their satisfaction. Also, convenience is critical as it is linked with the other motivations, because it can make it easier or simpler to access information, seek entertainment, and communicate with others more efficiently. This is also verified by our findings, on which entertainment and information are present in 5 out of 8 solutions, except for social-psychological motivation which is mainly absent (i.e., low). The latter is explained by the relatively low level of responses of the users, as shown in the Appendix. However, this indicates that users do not actively seek to fulfil such needs when using social media, raising the question if the way people use social media has changed over the past 15 years.

As social media are both utilitarian and high experiential systems thus and much attention should be given to internal factors, our findings indicate that emotions and social-psychological factors are less important than entertainment, information, and convenience. Nonetheless, we identify specific patterns of users for whom these factors are important and influence greatly their satisfaction. This verifies the fact that people have different motivations when using social media and extends previous findings by highlight how motivations and emotions combine to lead to high satisfaction [1, 2].

This research has both theoretical and practical implications towards satisfaction with social media. First, it complements extant research in the area [1, 2] by offering an alternative view on how motivations and emotions combine with each other to predict high satisfaction. Second, we provide empirical support on how different levels of motivations and emotions may explain satisfaction of the users', a relation that has not been examined deeply in the past [1]. Finally, we extend the literature on social media by examining emotions as a multidimensional concept studying together positive and negative emotions, as they are likely to overlap and one may diminish the other [5]. Although emotions were found to be important in certain occasions in leading to satisfaction, we are not able to fully verify previous findings in the area of online services, that emotions to be critical in formulating users' attitude, satisfaction and behavior [1, 4, 5], increasing the need for further studies into the area.

Following the results of this study, practitioners can gain insight on how their highly satisfied customers are motivated and how they feel. This can help them improve or revise their online strategies and business models, by optimizing the services they offer as they can choose the optimal mix of motivations and emotions to target their customers accordingly. Since new social media appear quite frequently, practitioners may exploit the identified paths to understand the rationale of users' decisions, and by extension focus on specific functionality or create more effective communication strategies, to satisfy users and increase adoption and use. For example, a new social media that has only built a mobile application should focus on convenience and either entertainment or information, depending on the services and functionality it supports.

This paper contributes to methodology, as it differs from previous studies in the area, employing regression-based analyses to examine users' motivations, satisfaction and behaviour. Here, a configuration analysis is performed with the use of fsQCA, to examine the asymmetric relationships among the factors. This methodology has recently received increased attention in online services and social media [9, 27, 33], and if applied together with complexity theory and configuration theory, can contribute to the creation of new hypotheses, models, and theories [11, 22]. Thus, we propose a conceptual model to identify highly satisfied users of social media based on their motivations and emotions, and the findings show complex causal patterns among the variables and highlight asymmetric relationships that may lead to the same outcome (i.e., high satisfaction). Thus, future studies, should examine direct and indirect effects of motivations and emotions on users' satisfaction, and complement or extend our findings by contrasting findings from both fsQCA and regression-based analyses.

As with all empirical studies, there are some limitations. First, the sampling method may limit the generalization of the findings since snowball sampling was used to recruit respondents. Further, the findings are based on self-reported data. Future studies may combine self-reported data with real data from using social media, and extend them with semi-structured interviews, observations, which may provide deeper insight on user satisfaction. Also, here we only examine value motivations and emotions as antecedents of satisfaction. Researchers may include more variables that have been found to influence users' satisfaction as well as examine their effect on behaviour.

Appendix

Scale items with mean, standard deviation and standardized loading

Construct and scale items	Mean	S.D.	Loading
Entertainment			
I use social media to forget about work or other things	3.01	1.77	0.61
I use social media to relax	4.82	1.64	0.83
I use social media to feel excited.	3.37	1.56	0.75
I use social media to pass the time	5.18	1.62	0.70
Information			
I use social media to learn about unknown things	4.94	1.57	0.88
I use social media to do research	4.00	1.92	0.78
I use social media to learn about useful things	4.69	1.68	0.92
I use social media to get new ideas	4.93	1.57	0.86

(*continued*)

(*continued*)

Construct and scale items	Mean	S.D.	Loading
Social Psychological			
I use social media to seek identity	2.39	1.47	0.74
I use social media to keep relationship with members	4.26	1.84	0.82
I use social media to seek a sense of belonging	2.36	1.52	0.78
I use social media to get involved with members	3.40	1.75	0.86
Convenience.			
I use social media anytime, anywhere	4.01	1.97	0.80
I use social media conveniently	5.01	1.58	0.90
I use social media easily	5.41	1.51	0.87
I use social media and get what I want for less effort	4.57	1.74	0.79
Satisfaction			
I am satisfied with the experience of using social media	4.66	1.38	0.90
I am pleased with the experience of using social media	4.54	1.35	0.91
My decision to use social media was a wise one	4.05	1.50	0.83
My feeling with using social media was good	4.50	1.39	0.90

Emotions

	Mean	SD	Loading		Mean	SD	Loading
Positive							
Pleasure	4.13	1.64	0.88	Contentment	3.69	1.70	0.87
Joy	3.90	1.61	0.86	Admiration	2.99	1.66	0.79
Pride	2.49	1.57	0.73	Love	2.69	1.64	0.75
Amusement	4.63	1.55	0.77	Relief	2.59	1.58	0.71
Interest	4.44	1.46	0.66				
Negative							
Anger	2.42	1.58	0.78	Disappointment	2.87	1.89	0.81
Hate	1.80	1.32	0.77	Shame	2.08	1.56	0.80
Contempt	2.31	1.63	0.76	Regret	1.87	1.35	0.68
Disgust	2.27	1.65	0.86	Guilt	1.71	1.27	0.62
Fear	1.95	1.44	0.67	Sadness	2.30	1.63	0.80
				Compassion	2.71	1.67	0.69

References

1. Kim, J.H., Kim, M.-S., Nam, Y.: An analysis of self-construals, motivations, Facebook use, and user satisfaction. Intl. J. Hum.-Comput. Interact. **26**, 1077–1099 (2010)
2. Kim, Y., Sohn, D., Choi, S.M.: Cultural difference in motivations for using social network sites: a comparative study of American and Korean college students. Comput. Hum. Behav. **27**, 365–372 (2011)
3. Au, N., Ngai, E.W., Cheng, T.E.: Extending the understanding of end user information systems satisfaction formation: an equitable needs fulfillment model approach. MIS Q. **32**, 43–66 (2008)
4. Pappas, I.O., Kourouthanassis, P.E., Giannakos, M.N., Chrissikopoulos, V.: Shiny happy people buying: the role of emotions on personalized e-shopping. Electronic Markets **24**, 193–206 (2014)
5. Pappas, I.O., Kourouthanassis, P.E., Giannakos, M.N., Chrissikopoulos, V.: Explaining online shopping behavior with fsQCA: the role of cognitive and affective perceptions. J. Bus. Res. **69**, 794–803 (2016)
6. Pappas, I.O., Kourouthanassis, P.E., Giannakos, M.N., Chrissikopoulos, V.: Sense and sensibility in personalized e-commerce: how emotions rebalance the purchase intentions of persuaded customers. Psychology & Marketing (2017)
7. Kang, Y.S., Hong, S., Lee, H.: Exploring continued online service usage behavior: the roles of self-image congruity and regret. Comput. Hum. Behav. **25**, 111–122 (2009)
8. García-Crespo, Á., Colomo-Palacios, R., Gómez-Berbís, J.M., Ruiz-Mezcua, B.: SEMO: a framework for customer social networks analysis based on semantics. J. Inf. Technol. **25**, 178–188 (2010)
9. Krishen, A.S., Berezan, O., Agarwal, S., Kachroo, P.: The generation of virtual needs: recipes for satisfaction in social media networking. J. Bus. Res. **69**, 5248–5254 (2016)
10. Chung, J.Y., Buhalis, D.: Information needs in online social networks. Inf. Technol. Tourism **10**, 267–281 (2008)
11. Woodside, A.G.: Embrace•perform•model: complexity theory, contrarian case analysis, and multiple realities. J. Bus. Res. **67**, 2495–2503 (2014)
12. Ragin, C.C.: Redesigning Social Inquiry: Fuzzy Sets and Beyond. Wiley (2008)
13. Raacke, J., Bonds-Raacke, J.: MySpace and Facebook: applying the uses and gratifications theory to exploring friend-networking sites. CyberPsychol. Behav. **11**, 169–174 (2008)
14. Wang, Y., Fesenmaier, D.R.: Modeling participation in an online travel community. J. Travel Res. **42**, 261–270 (2004)
15. Lin, K.-Y., Lu, H.-P.: Why people use social networking sites: an empirical study integrating network externalities and motivation theory. Comput. Hum. Behav. **27**, 1152–1161 (2011)
16. Shin, D.-H.: Analysis of online social networks: a cross-national study. Online Inf. Rev. **34**, 473–495 (2010)
17. Oliver, R.L.: Satisfaction: a behavioral perspective on the consumer. Routledge (2014)
18. Xu, C., Ryan, S., Prybutok, V., Wen, C.: It is not for fun: an examination of social network site usage. Inf. Manag. **49**, 210–217 (2012)
19. Chang, Y.P., Zhu, D.H.: The role of perceived social capital and flow experience in building users' continuance intention to social networking sites in China. Comput. Hum. Behav. **28**, 995–1001 (2012)
20. Kuo, Y.-F., Wu, C.-M.: Satisfaction and post-purchase intentions with service recovery of online shopping websites: Perspectives on perceived justice and emotions. Int. J. Inf. Manage. **32**, 127–138 (2012)

21. Van Zalk, N., Van Zalk, M., Kerr, M., Stattin, H.: Social anxiety as a basis for friendship selection and socialization in adolescents' social networks. J. Pers. **79**, 499–526 (2011)

22. Fiss, P.C.: A set-theoretic approach to organizational configurations. Acad. Manag. Rev. **32**, 1180–1198 (2007)

23. Fiss, P.C.: Building better causal theories: a fuzzy set approach to typologies in organization research. Acad. Manag. J. **54**, 393–420 (2011)

24. Scherer, K.R., Shuman, V., Fontaine, J.R., Soriano, C.: The GRID meets the Wheel: assessing emotional feeling via self-report. Components of emotional meaning: a sourcebook, pp. 281–298 (2013)

25. Lu, H.-P., Hsiao, K.-L.: The influence of extro/introversion on the intention to pay for social networking sites. Inf. Manag. **47**, 150–157 (2010)

26. Ragin, C.C.: Fuzzy-set social science. University of Chicago Press (2000)

27. Mikalef, P., Pappas, Ilias O., Giannakos, M.: Consumer intentions on social media: a fsQCA analysis of motivations. In: Dwivedi, Yogesh K., Mäntymäki, M., Ravishankar, M.N., Janssen, M., Clement, M., Slade, Emma L., Rana, Nripendra P., Al-Sharhan, S., Simintiras, Antonis C. (eds.) I3E 2016. LNCS, vol. 9844, pp. 371–386. Springer, Cham (2016). doi:10. 1007/978-3-319-45234-0_34

28. Ragin, C.C.: Set relations in social research: evaluating their consistency and coverage. Political Anal. **14**, 291–310 (2006)

29. Fornell, C., Larcker, D.F.: Structural equation models with unobservable variables and measurement error: Algebra and statistics. J. Marketing Res., 382–388 (1981)

30. Howell, D.C.: Statistical Methods for Psychology. Cengage Learning (2012)

31. O'brien, R.M.: A caution regarding rules of thumb for variance inflation factors. Qual. Quant. **41**, 673–690 (2007)

32. MacKenzie, S.B., Podsakoff, P.M.: Common method bias in marketing: causes, mechanisms, and procedural remedies. J. Retail. **88**, 542–555 (2012)

33. Kourouthanassis, P.E., Mikalef, P., Pappas, I.O., Kostagiolas, P.: Explaining travellers online information satisfaction: a complexity theory approach on information needs, barriers, sources and personal characteristics. Inf. Manage. **54**, 814–824 (2017)

Online Reviews or Marketer Information?
An Eye-Tracking Study on Social Commerce Consumers

Patrick Mikalef[1(✉)], Kshitij Sharma[2], Ilias O. Pappas[1], and Michail N. Giannakos[1]

[1] Department of Computer Science, Norwegian University of Science and Technology,
Sem Saelandsvei 9, 7491, Trondheim, Norway
{patrick.mikalef,ilpappas,michailg}@ntnu.no
[2] CHILI Lab, EPFL, RLC D1 740, Station 20, 1015, Lausanne, Switzerland
kshitij.sharma@epfl.ch

Abstract. Driven by the increasing popularity of social commerce sites, this study seeks to examine the information sources and formats that influence consumer intentions to purchase. Specifically, we build on uses and gratifications theory and dual-process theory to determine how user-generated content and marketer-generated content are consumed by users when making a purchase decision. Using an eye-tracking approach on a popular social commerce site with a sample of 23 consumers, we find significant differences in the types of information used for product purchase compared to those omitted. Our study demonstrates that the format and source of information that consumers utilize, as well as the gaze transitions they make between different types of content when browsing, follow different patterns depending on if a product is bought or rejected. We conclude the paper summarizing the findings and drawing theoretical and practical implications that arise.

Keywords: Social commerce · Eye-tracking · Dual-process theory · User-generated content

1 Introduction

Prompted from the popularity of social media and social networks, social commerce has managed to quickly gain momentum as a subset of e-commerce in the past few years. Social commerce presents certain differences from conventional e-commerce activities by enabling social interactions and the creation and circulation of user generated content on social media platforms [1]. Not surprisingly, social media have attracted the interest of business executives and marketers regarding their potential in gaining a competitive edge [2]. An increasing number of firms are now launching social commerce initiatives, sparked by the promising early outcomes [3]. Yet, while traditionally marketers were in control of the information they provided to consumers through their online venues, in social commerce settings part of this power has been transferred to the consumer [2].

The influence of user generated content is becoming ever more important in the decision-making process of individuals and has been a subject of growing interest in

© IFIP International Federation for Information Processing 2017
Published by Springer International Publishing AG 2017. All Rights Reserved
A.K. Kar et al. (Eds.): I3E 2017, LNCS 10595, pp. 388–399, 2017.
DOI: 10.1007/978-3-319-68557-1_34

research [4]. As more people utilize user generated content on social commerce sites, the process by which they evaluate the credibility and importance of it becomes more complex [5]. This is because user generated content is developed from a very large number of unknown participants world-wide, and the presentation of such a vast amount of information makes decision making an intricate task [6]. In addition, such user generated content is usually presented in several different formats, from extensive reviews, to aggregated information and summarized product ratings [4]. Adding to this, marketers also tend to present product related information in various formats [7].

This vast amount of information, both from individual consumers and marketers, render the buying decision process as quite complicated, since users need to navigate through all content and select the appropriate ones to base their selection [5]. As such, this study builds on uses and gratifications and dual-process theory to understand what type of information users tend to rely on when faced with a purchase dilemma. We use an eye-tracking approach on a popular social commerce site to identify the differences in information consumption between the products selected compared to those that are omitted. Results show that there are significant differences in the utilization of information when consumers are in the process of formulating purchase-related decisions.

The rest of the paper is structured as follows. In Sect. 2 we review the theoretical background which this study builds upon. Next, we develop the research hypotheses, while in Sect. 4 the study design is described. In Sect. 5 the analysis is presented along with results from the eye-tracking experiment. Finally, Sect. 6 discusses the theoretical and practical implications that arise from the results.

2 Background

Social commerce websites present unique characteristics compared to physical, or even conventional, online shops. The simultaneous presence of user-generated content (UGC) and content of marketer of products, or else producer-generated content (PGC), creates an interesting environment for consumers who are faced with making purchase decisions based on the different types of information available [5]. While marketers have been able to control the product related information from their side, the affordances present on social commerce sites enable consumers to have strong opinions about products or services and express the openly, without being bound by standards of objectivity [8]. It is widely noted that UGC when negative can have harmful consequences for building and sustaining a brands image, an issue which is compounded since consumers often rely more heavily on UGC when making purchase decisions [9]. While there has been much attention towards the significance of UGC in shaping consumer's behavior, there are very few studies addressing the issue of decision making under the concurrent presence of UGC and PGC. Even more, there is a lack of understanding on how the various formats in which these types of information are presented are utilized by consumers when making purchase decisions [10].

To this end we investigate the usefulness of the different forms of information under the uses and gratification theory (UGT). Uses and gratification theory is concerned with how individuals use media, thus, centering on the individual as the main unit of analysis.

It has been applied extensively in online environments since it provides one of the most concrete perspectives to explain psychological and behavioral dimensions in mediated communication [11]. The main objective of the uses and gratification theory is to explain the psychological needs that shape why people use media, and what stimuli engage them in performing certain media-based behaviors [11]. One of the main assumptions of UGT is that users are goal-oriented, consequently, when they are faced with a decision choice they select the appropriate media to gratify their goals or needs [12]. In the context of social commerce studies, UGT has been the principal theoretical lens in understanding motives, benefits, and values of consumers [1, 13]. While UGT has been mostly focused on explaining the propensity of use of certain affordances on social commerce websites, there is still limited empirical understanding on the consumption of information sources depending on their origin.

Furthermore, the forma that these information sources are presented in is commonly aggregated at a high level as either UGC or PGC. Yet, many social commerce sites present such information in various formats which result in different means of consuming it when making purchase decisions. Dual-process theory has been widely applied to explain how people are influenced by the different forms of information they are provided with [14]. In the context of online shopping, dual-process theory distinguishes between two different types of influences, normative factors and information factors. Information factors are based on the content of user experiences or marketer descriptions, while normative factors reflect the impact of social aggregation mechanisms available on social commerce websites [4]. According to dual-process theory, informational and normative factors work in parallel in shaping consumers' opinions about products online and finally making purchase-related decisions [4]. In the present study, dual-process theory is applied as the theoretical grounding in explaining the extent to which these two types of information influence the purchase decisions of users of social commerce websites. As such, it provides an influence model based on both the consumers' self-judgment of the information provided by marketers and consumers, and the normative power of aggregated information. Informational influence is derived from information obtained as evidence about reality, and therefore is present in the content, source, and visual cues relating to the product at hand, whether UGC or PGC. On the other hand, normative influence is apparent in aggregated evaluations of the opinions of others [15].

3   Research Hypothesis

According to Yale's model, source, message, and receiver are three important informational components in message evaluation [16]. Product related information such as description, price, and technical characteristics are important elements of the message, while visual cues such as images of the product are also found to play a significant role in communication judgment in terms of PGC [17, 18]. It is also noted that thumbnail images produce further stimuli to consumers who tend to enlarge them to identify more information about the product and increase enjoyment [19]. Similarly, consumers tend to rely increasingly more on UGC to gain more information about a product they are interested in, and identify how other users have evaluated it. Such reviews have been subject of much attention since their content, whether positive or negative, is shown to have a significant impact on consumers' intentions to purchase [20]. Despite the significance of such informational components, consumers tend to rely on the opinion of the masses, making normative factors such as average score or ratings of other consumers, an easily accessible resource on which they can safely base their decisions [21]. Hence, we consider the previously mentioned informational and normative factors as important determinants of consumers' intention to make purchase-related decisions.

3.1 Informational Factors

Producer Generated Content Producer-generated content usually presents some commonalities in terms of presentation and content including several key elements. Firstly, price is a critical component of any purchase decision, with consumers comparing characteristics of products and attempting to determine the ideal price/characteristic balance. Price in combination with brand recognition have been shown to mitigate the risk and influence perception of product quality [21]. In online environments such as that of social commerce, it noted that additional aspects pertinent to the product can help consumers avoid risky purchases [22]. Chen et al. [23] find that the availability of information in a multitude of formats positively contributes to consumers' intentions to purchase online. Product-related information nevertheless can be presented in various formats. Pictures of the product have been found to influence consumers' behavioral intentions by evoking different levels of emotional imagery [24]. Specifically, Yoo and Kim [25] find that the ability to interact with visual cues, such as zooming into the product, has a significant effect on consumers' buying-related behavior. Consequently, we can infer that the behavior of consumers who are likely to purchase a specific product will demonstrate significant differences in the abovementioned areas compared to when they decide to eliminate it. As such we hypothesize the following:

H1: *User gaze on the details of the selected product will be more extensive compared to the ones eliminated.*

H2: *User gaze on the price of the selected product will be more extensive compared to the ones eliminated.*

H3: *User gaze on the product description of the selected product will be more extensive compared to the ones eliminated.*

H4: *User gaze on the product info table of the selected product will be more extensive compared to the ones eliminated.*

H5: *User gaze on the image of the selected product will be more extensive compared to the ones eliminated.*

H6: *User gaze on the zoomed image of the selected product will be more extensive compared to the ones eliminated.*

User Generated Content While producer generated content has been the predominant means of evaluating the appropriateness of a product with regard to consumer preferences, user generated content on online media have gained increased importance in the decision-making process [5]. Such content can range from negative reviews of the product or service to highly positive, and have been a subject of considerable attention [26]. Evidence to date has been mixed on how consumers factor both positive and negative reviews when making purchase-related decisions [27]. Chevalier and Mayzlin [26] found that products with more positive user generated content had higher sales, although negative user generated content had a stronger impact on sales than positive ones. Similar findings have been noted in other studies where more positive reviews by consumers tended to generate increased sales [28]. On the other hand, negative reviews have been found to be helpful for the decision-making process of consumers since low quality products can be easily detectable and thus eliminated from selection [29]. We therefore hypothesize the following:

H7: *User gaze on negative reviews will be more extensive for the eliminated products compared to the selected one.*

H8: *User gaze on positive reviews will be more extensive for the selected product compared to the ones eliminated.*

3.2   Normative Factors

Although informational determinants, as discussed above, partially explain how consumers assess and evaluate the product at hand, these do not take into account the aspect of normative influence. In the context of social commerce, various representations of aggregated user generated content are present which are aimed at structuring the opinions of previous buyers. Product rating is a measure which aims to calculate the mean score given by all past buyers towards a specific product, most commonly, on a 5-level scale. In some cases consumers also have access to the number, or percentage of consumers, who rated the product on each score (i.e. how many rated on a level of 1, 2 etc.). These types of representing information generated by users are some of the most important factors when it comes to decision making [28]. Past studies have shown that normative factors such as user generated product rating act on perceived product quality, which in turn influences purchase intention [21]. These findings highlight the importance of social influence mechanisms in the decision making process of consumers on social commerce platforms [30–33]. We therefore hypothesize that:

H9: *User gaze on review summary will be more extensive for the selected product compared to the ones eliminated.*

4   Experiment and Variables

4.1   Procedure

There were 23 participants in the experiment. There were 10 females. The average age was 27.5 years (age std. dev. 7.15 years). All of them had average to high experience with shopping at Amazon. The participants were provided with three Amazon products (electronic fans with remote controls). The products were chosen to be gender neutral so that the gender bias could be eliminated. The simple experimental task was to select one of the fans after carefully examining the information given on each of the pages. All the participants took 10–15 min to decide which product they would have bought. During this whole process their gaze was recorded using three SMI eye-tracking glasses at 60 Hz and two Tobii eye-tracking glasses also at 60 Hz. After careful examination of the data, we excluded four participants from the analysis.

4.2 Dependent Variable

We distinguish between the products that the participants chose and the others they eliminated. We subsequently call them "selected" and "eliminated", respectively.

4.3 Process Variables

We extracted a few variables from the eye-tracking data while the participants were selecting the product to buy. We computed the proportion of the total time spent on the specific Area of Interest (AOI). For the rest of the paper, we will use the notion "time spent on…" for the "proportion of time spent on…".

In this section, we present the different AOIs that we used to differentiate the gaze behavior between bought and eliminated products. For the following descriptions, we will refer to the Figure x1. The actual details in Figure x1 might vary from the details at the time of data gathering because of time difference between data gathering and writing this contribution.

Gaze on Reviews: We distinguished between the time spent on the review summary (Figure x1) and the individual reviews. We further grouped the individual reviews into positive and negative reviews based on the sentiments they expressed. Following are exemplar reviews:

Example of positive review (4 stars): *"Living in So. Cal. I need a fan on me while sleeping. The Optimus does the job, comes with a remote and has a sleep timer. This is easy to clean and has performed well for two years. Why anyone would buy a fan that you cannot easily clean is beyond me. Some of the pricy tower fans cannot be cleaned at all without a major disassembly. The Optimus is reasonably quiet and puts out a good breeze. I own two."*

Example of negative review (1 star): *"I brought this fan thinking I would not have to buy another. I received this Fan and was very pleased with the look, set up was easy. The first day was fine so I brought another for my sister. Why did I do that this fan started clicking and clicking. I adjusted the head every which way this was the hottest part of the summer. Now here I am needing another fan because this one is driving me CRAZY, My sister asked that I not waste my money she'll get her own. REGRET, Don't do it to yourself."*

Gaze on product specifications: We distinguished between the time spent on the following parts of the website under product specifications (Fig. 1): image, zoomed image, details, product information table, and product description.

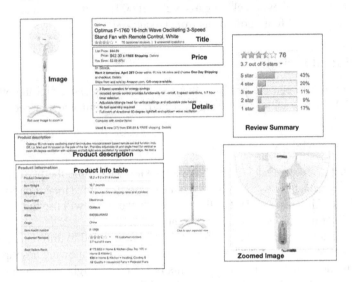

Fig. 1. The different Areas Of Interests (AOIs) defined for the analysis of the eye-tracking data. Most of the AOIs are self-explanatory except a few, for example, the "image" is the image of the product, while the "zoomed image" is the image that pops out when the user hovers the mouse over the image. In addition to these AOIs, we also defined two more AOIs for the positive and negative reviews.

Gaze Transitions: Alongside the individual AOIs, we also computed the proportions of the attention shift between different AOIs as the gaze transitions (The complete list of gaze transitions considered in this contribution is provided in Table 1.). These gaze

Table 1. Descriptive statistics and the t-test results for the comparison of time spent on the various AOIs for the selected and eliminated products.

AOI	Selected mean (Std. dev)	Eliminated mean (Std. dev)	t-test statistic	p-value
Image	0.05 (0.04)	0.02 (0.02)	2.43	0.02
Details	0.08 (0.04)	0.05 (0.02)	2.84	0.01
Zoomed image	0.004 (0.01)	0.002 (0.005)	0.81	0.42
Product description	0.007 (0.01)	0.007 (0.01)	0.04	0.96
Product info. table	0.03 (0.02)	0.03 (0.03)	−0.43	0.67
Review summary	0.09 (0.08)	0.11 (0.07)	−0.92	0.37
Positive reviews	0.05 (0.07)	0.06 (0.04)	−0.17	0.86
Negative reviews	0.03 (0.04)	0.07 (0.06)	−2.34	0.03

transition provide use with additional information about the information processing behavior. For example, an attention shift among the positive and negative reviews could depict the behavior of comparing the good and bad qualities of the product to have a trade-off between them.

5   Results

5.1   Gaze on Individual AOIs

Negative reviews: participants spent significantly less time on the negative reviews of eliminated products as compared to the negative reviews of the selected product. (t[31.66] = −2.34, p = 0.02, Fig. 2).

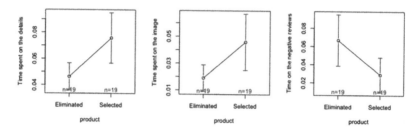

Fig. 2. Gaze on individual AOIs, blue bars show 95% confidence intervals. (Color figure online)

Positive reviews: we observed no difference in the time spent on the positive reviews of eliminated products and the time spent on the positive reviews of the selected product (t[= 31.67] = −0.17, p = 0.86).

Review summary: Similar to the positive reviews for the products there was no significant difference in the time spent on the review summaries of the eliminated and selected products (t[32.77] = −1.10, p = 0.27).

Details: time spent on the details of the selected products was significantly more than that for eliminated products (t[27.68] = 2.84, p = 0.008, Fig. 2).

Images: similar to the details, participants spent more time on the image of selected product than the images of eliminated products (t[25.58] = 2.42, p = 0.02, Fig. 2).

Zoomed images: there was no significant difference between the times spent on the zoomed images of the products (t[29.01] = 0.80, p = 0.42).

Product info. table: we observed no significant difference between the times spent on the products' information tables (t[34.00] = 0.04, p = 0.96).

Product description: there was no significant difference between the times spent on the products' descriptions (t[35.29] = −0.43, p = 0.66).

5.2 Gaze Transitions

Among reviews (negative-positive): the gaze transitions among the positive and the negative reviews for the eliminated products were significantly more than those for the selected product (t[26.80] = −2.07, p = 0.05, Fig. 3) (Table 2).

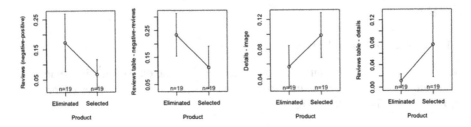

Fig. 3. Gaze transitions between AOIs, 95% confidence intervals.

Table 2. Descriptive statistics and the t-test results for the comparison of gaze transitions between the various AOIs for the selected and eliminated products.

Transition	Selected mean (Std. dev)	Eliminated mean (Std. dev)	t-test statistic	p-value
Reviews (positive-negative)	0.07 (0.10)	0.17 (0.20)	−2.07	0.05
Review summary-positive review	0.16 (0.23)	0.09 (0.13)	1.02	0.31
Review summary-negative review	0.11 (0.16)	0.23 (0.16)	−2.29	0.03
Review summary-price	0.01 (0.04)	0.01 (0.03)	0.42	0.67
Price-details	0.22 (0.23)	0.22 (0.15)	0.13	0.90
Price-image	0.13 (0.12)	0.14 (0.15)	−0.41	0.68
Image-details	0.10 (0.06)	0.06 (0.06)	2.14	0.04
Review summary-details	0.08 (0.12)	0.01 (0.02)	2.30	0.03

Positive reviews and review table: there was no significant difference between transitions between the review table and the positive reviews (t[27.93] = 1.02, p = 0.31).

Negative reviews and review table: the transitions between the negative reviews and the review table for the eliminated products were significantly higher than those for the selected product (t[35.99] = −2.29, p = 0.03, Fig. 3).

Price and review table: there was no difference in gaze transitions between the price and the review table for eliminated and selected products (t[34.82] = 0.42, p = 0.67).

Details and review table: the transitions between the details and the review table for the selected product were significantly higher than those for the eliminated products (t[19.55] = 2.30, p = 0.03, Fig. 3).

Image and details: the transitions between the image and the details for the eliminated products were significantly lower than those for the selected product (t[35.87] = 2.30, p = 0.04, Fig. 3).

Price and details: we observed no difference in the gaze transitions between the price and the details for the eliminated and selected products (t[30.62] = 0.13, p = 0.90).

Price and image: there was no difference in the gaze transitions between the price and the review table for the eliminated and selected products (t[35.13] = −0.41, p = 0.68).

6 Discussion

We presented the results from 19 participants deciding over three products to choose from. The participants were presented with both the PGC (title, price, image, details, product info. table) and UGC (positive and negative reviews). The information presented on the Amazon pages for the three products could also be divided in informative (PGC and UGC) and normative (review summary) factors.

The results show that a few of the informative, both PGC and UGC, factors play an influential role in product selection. For PGC, the participants spent more time on the details (*H1 confirmed*) and the image (*H5 confirmed*) of the selected products than the eliminated ones. However, there was no difference between the times spent on the product info. table (*H4*), the price (*H2*), the zoomed image (*H6*), or the product description (*H3*). The root cause for this could be attributed to the information content of these PGC. The details, product description, and the product info. table, had replicated information. The easiest way to receive information was to read the details of products, as it was easy to compare the details with the image of the product. This fact is evident from the analysis of gaze transitions between the details and image, which were higher for the selected product than the eliminated ones. This could also be the reason that almost nobody paid much attention to the zoomed image as well.

Concerning the UGC, we found that the negative reviews had more influence while eliminating a product (*H7 confirmed*) than the influence of positive reviews while selecting one (*H8*). One plausible reason for this could be the difference in the amount of information provided in the negative and positive reviews. All the three products had comparable number of both types of reviews. However, the negative reviews for all the products were extensive in terms of problems faced by the users and were often accompanied by the phrases like *"REGRET"* and *"BUYER BEWARE"* in the title of the reviews. On the other hand the positive reviews were shorter than the negative reviews and often contained the satisfactory sentences about the products.

The results show that while considering the individual information pieces the time spent on normative factor is not a distinctive influential mechanism in our study (*H9 not supported*). However, the combination of the normative information with the informational factors had an influence on the choice of the product. For example, gaze transitions between the review summary (normative) and the negative reviews (informational, UGC) helped eliminating the products. While the gaze transitions between the review summary (normative) and the product details (informational, PGC) helped selecting the product.

References

1. Mikalef, P., Giannakos, M., Pateli, A.: Shopping and word-of-mouth intentions on social media. J. Theor. Appl. Electron. Commer. Res. **8**, 17–34 (2013)
2. Zhou, L., Zhang, P., Zimmermann, H.-D.: Social commerce research: an integrated view. Electron. Commer. Res. Appl. **12**, 61–68 (2013)
3. Stephen, A.T., Toubia, O.: Deriving value from social commerce networks. J. Mark. Res. **47**, 215–228 (2010)
4. Cheung, M.Y., Luo, C., Sia, C.L., Chen, H.: Credibility of electronic word-of-mouth: Informational and normative determinants of on-line consumer recommendations. Int. J. Electron. Commer. **13**, 9–38 (2009)
5. Cheong, H.J., Morrison, M.A.: Consumers' reliance on product information and recommendations found in UGC. J. Interact. Adv. **8**, 38–49 (2008)
6. Mikalef, P., Giannakos, M.N., Pateli, A.G.: Exploring the business potential of social media: an utilitarian and hedonic motivation approach. In: Bled eConference, p. 21. (2012)
7. Yadav, M.S., De Valck, K., Hennig-Thurau, T., Hoffman, D.L., Spann, M.: Social commerce: a contingency framework for assessing marketing potential. J. Interactive Mark. **27**, 311–323 (2013)
8. Bruhn, M., Schoenmueller, V., Schäfer, D.B.: Are social media replacing traditional media in terms of brand equity creation? Manage. Res. Rev. **35**, 770–790 (2012)
9. Luo, X., Zhang, J., Duan, W.: Social media and firm equity value. Inf. Syst. Res. **24**, 146–163 (2013)
10. Trusov, M., Bucklin, R.E., Pauwels, K.: Effects of word-of-mouth versus traditional marketing: findings from an internet social networking site. J. Mark. **73**, 90–102 (2009)
11. Ko, H., Cho, C.-H., Roberts, M.S.: Internet uses and gratifications: a structural equation model of interactive advertising. J. Advertising **34**, 57–70 (2005)
12. Limayem, M., Cheung, C.M.: Predicting the continued use of Internet-based learning technologies: the role of habit. Behav. Inf. Technol. **30**, 91–99 (2011)
13. Tsai, W.-H.S., Men, L.R.: Consumer engagement with brands on social network sites: a cross-cultural comparison of China and the USA. J. Mark. Commun. **23**, 2–21 (2017)
14. Cheung, C.M., Thadani, D.R.: The impact of electronic word-of-mouth communication: a literature analysis and integrative model. Decis. Support Syst. **54**, 461–470 (2012)
15. Filieri, R.: What makes online reviews helpful? a diagnosticity-adoption framework to explain informational and normative influences in e-WOM. J. Bus. Res. **68**, 1261–1270 (2015)
16. Hovland, C.I., Janis, I.L., Kelley, H.H.: Communication and persuasion; psychological studies of opinion change (1953)
17. Chang, T.-Z., Wildt, A.R.: Price, product information, and purchase intention: an empirical study. J. Acad. Mark. Sci. **22**, 16–27 (1994)
18. Wells, J.D., Valacich, J.S., Hess, T.J.: What signal are you sending? How website quality influences perceptions of product quality and purchase intentions. MIS Q. **35**, 373–396 (2011)
19. Kim, J., Fiore, A.M., Lee, H.-H.: Influences of online store perception, shopping enjoyment, and shopping involvement on consumer patronage behavior towards an online retailer. J. Retail. Consum. Serv. **14**, 95–107 (2007)
20. Pan, Y., Zhang, J.Q.: Born unequal: a study of the helpfulness of user-generated product reviews. J. Retail. **87**, 598–612 (2011)
21. Flanagin, A.J., Metzger, M.J., Pure, R., Markov, A., Hartsell, E.: Mitigating risk in ecommerce transactions: perceptions of information credibility and the role of user-generated ratings in product quality and purchase intention. Electron. Commer. Res. **14**, 1–23 (2014)

22. Chiu, C.M., Wang, E.T., Fang, Y.H., Huang, H.Y.: Understanding customers' repeat purchase intentions in B2C e-commerce: the roles of utilitarian value, hedonic value and perceived risk. Inf. Syst. J. **24**, 85–114 (2014)

23. Chen, J., Teng, L., Yu, Y., Yu, X.: The effect of online information sources on purchase intentions between consumers with high and low susceptibility to informational influence. J. Bus. Res. **69**, 467–475 (2016)

24. Flores, W., Chen, J.-C.V., Ross, W.H.: The effect of variations in banner ad, type of product, website context, and language of advertising on Internet users' attitudes. Comput. Hum. Behav. **31**, 37–47 (2014)

25. Yoo, J., Kim, M.: The effects of online product presentation on consumer responses: a mental imagery perspective. J. Bus. Res. **67**, 2464–2472 (2014)

26. Chevalier, J.A., Mayzlin, D.: The effect of word of mouth on sales: Online book reviews. J. Mark. Res. **43**, 345–354 (2006)

27. Dhar, V., Chang, E.A.: Does chatter matter? The impact of user-generated content on music sales. J. Interact. Mark. **23**, 300–307 (2009)

28. Forman, C., Ghose, A., Wiesenfeld, B.: Examining the relationship between reviews and sales: the role of reviewer identity disclosure in electronic markets. Inf. Syst. Res. **19**, 291–313 (2008)

29. Lee, J., Park, D.-H., Han, I.: The effect of negative online consumer reviews on product attitude: an information processing view. Electron. Commer. Res. Appl. **7**, 341–352 (2008)

30. Flanagin, A.J., Metzger, M.J.: Trusting expert-versus user-generated ratings online: the role of information volume, valence, and consumer characteristics. Comput. Hum. Behav. **29**, 1626–1634 (2013)

31. Mikalef, P., Pappas, I.O., Giannakos, M.N.: Value co-creation and purchase intention in social commerce: the enabling role of word-of-mouth and trust. In: Americas Conference on Information Systems AMCIS (2017)

32. Pappas, I.O, Mikalef, P., Giannakos, M,N., Pavlou., P.A.: Value co-creation and trust in social commerce: an fsQCA approach. In: European Conference on Information Systems ECIS (2017)

33. Mikalef, P., Pappas, Ilias O., Giannakos, M.: Consumer intentions on social media: a fsQCA analysis of motivations. In: Dwivedi, Y.K., et al. (eds.) I3E 2016. LNCS, vol. 9844, pp. 371–386. Springer, Cham (2016). doi:10.1007/978-3-319-45234-0_34

Consumer Satisfaction Rating System Using Sentiment Analysis

Kumar Gaurav[⊠] and Prabhat Kumar

Department of Computer Science and Engineering,
National Institute of Technology Patna, Patna, India
kumargaurav.nitp@gmail.com, prabhat@nitp.ac.in

Abstract. Owing to the inclination towards e-Commerce, the importance of consumer reviews has evolved significantly. Potential consumers exhibit sincere intents in seeking opinions of other consumers who have already had a usage experience of the products they are intending to make a purchase decision on. The underlying businesses also deem it fit to ascertain common public opinions regarding the quality of their products as well as services. However, the consumer reviews have bulked over time to such an extent that it has become a highly challenging task to read all the reviews, even if limiting to only the top ones, to reach an informed purchase decision or have an insight regarding how satisfied or not the consumers of a particular product are. Since most of the reviews are either unstructured or semi-structured, information classification is employed to derive knowledge from the reviews. However, most classification methods based on sentiment orientation of reviews do not detect which features of a product were specifically liked or disliked by a reviewer. This constitutes itself into another problem since most consumers are on the lookout for certain prerequisite features while viewing the products. The paper proposes a Consumer Satisfaction Rating System (CSRS) based on sentiment analysis of consumer reviews in context of the features of a product. The system aims at providing a summary that represents the extent to which the consumers were satisfied or unsatisfied with the specific features of a product.

Keywords: e-Commerce · Online reviews · Product features · Sentiment analysis · Opinion mining

1 Introduction

The Internet has paved several alternate ways for tasks and transactions which could be conducted only through the levels of physical contact or communication in the yesteryears. With the recent advances in e-Commerce, there has been a catastrophic surge in the number of people conducting their commercial transactions over the Internet. They shop, book, rent, sell, etc. on various e-Commerce platforms that have taken the reigns of marketing from their offline counterparts. However, contrary to traditional shopping in which consumers purchase from physical stores and gain an actual experience of the product such as how a cloth material actually feels especially in cases when they are looking for good quality fabric, online marketing is received with much skepticism since there is absence of any such tangible or physical contact

© IFIP International Federation for Information Processing 2017
Published by Springer International Publishing AG 2017. All Rights Reserved
A.K. Kar et al. (Eds.): I3E 2017, LNCS 10595, pp. 400–411, 2017.
DOI: 10.1007/978-3-319-68557-1_35

during initial product showcasing. One cannot have an insight into how a product actually feels or performs like unless one receives it after waiting for a requisite period of time post placing the order on an online shopping platform. The same stands true for services such as booking a hotel online or buying tickets for a bus ride. And this is when consultation from reviews is sought. The most cardinal objective of the reviews is to bridge the gap between product experience and potential consumers [1]. While surfing through the product details listed on the online e-Commerce websites, the one prominent element which the consumers are mostly looking for is assurance in terms of product quality and usage experience indicial of consumer satisfaction. Consumers tend to read reviews posted by other consumers who have had an experience of the product or have something to share regarding it. These attempts are primarily focused on gaining insight on product and its features and whether the product actually succeeded in delivering the level of performance it claimed. The businesses underlying e-Commerce platform also consider such reviews as an effective information source for ascertaining whether the consumers of its products or services are actually satisfied with them or not. However, maneuvering through the large quantities of information provided in the product reviews poses as a very tricky as well as a tiresome task for consumers seeking to make an informed purchase decision. Figure 1 depicts the huge bulk of consumer reviews that are available on an e-Commerce website such as Amazon [2]. It can be further inferred from the aforementioned figure that even if the consumers narrow their review-reading to encompass only the top reviews, they would still have to read a considerably large number of reviews before deducing information catalytic in reaching to their decision regarding the purchase of that product or service.

Fig. 1. Availability of consumer reviews in bulk

It is therefore a necessary improvisation to seek ways through which information provided in the consumer reviews can be classified or the most vital elements of a review that help in the decision making can be extracted and effectively represented in the form of a summary. Since most of the reviews are generally in the form of unstructured or semi-structured text, it becomes but a necessity to involve Natural Language Processing techniques to extract usable information.

Various machine learning algorithms such as Naïve Bayes, Decision Tree and Support Vector Machines are employed along with the Natural Language Processing techniques to detect the sentimental orientation of the reviews and thereby provide an overview depicting the consumers liking or disliking the product or service [3]. However, most of such review summarization methods reflect the fraction of consumers which have liked or not liked the product as a whole. They do not delve into answering questions such as what were those salient features which the consumers particularly liked or disliked in the product.

Detection of sentiment orientation of reviews is conducted on document level, sentence level and feature/aspect level [3]. Most of the research works have considered searching opinions on the former two levels [4, 5]. Less focus has been laid on the feature/aspect level of sentiment analysis. This paper proposes a Consumer Satisfaction Rating System based on sentiment analysis of consumer reviews in context of the aspects/features of a product or a service. The objective is to mine opinions of consumers from their reviews in regard of the features of a product or a service. This will help the consumers as well as the manufacturers in conceiving which features or aspects of a product or a service were particularly liked or disliked. It reflects how many consumers were satisfied with which particular features of the product or service.

The paper has been organized in the following manner. Section 2 provides an overview of the related work in this domain. Section 3 explains the proposed work. Section 4 sheds light on the results obtained and related analysis. Lastly, conclusion and future scope have been provided in Sect. 5.

2   Related Work

Sentiment Analysis integrates an intersection of various disciplines of study such as Data Mining, Computational Linguists and Natural Language Processing. As previously mentioned, sentiment analysis can be processed at document, sentence and feature levels [3]. The characteristic feature of sentiment analysis at document level is that, here, the aggregate opinion orientation of the document, as a whole, is considered for classifying it. This is different from conducting sentiment analysis at sentence level where the sentimental orientation of each sentence is considered for its classification into being negative, neutral or positive. Further, aspect/feature level sentiment analysis incorporates determination of opinion orientation regarding the aspects/features of the product [4].

Most of the previous research works based on detecting sentiment orientation of consumer reviews have concentrated on document and sentence levels. The most notable contribution which also happens to be the pioneering research work in the domain of application of sentiment analysis and opinion mining techniques is that of Hu and Liu [6]. They proposed a technique for conducting summarization of reviews. Their work was mainly focused on searching the frequent features from the consumer reviews and detecting opinion orientation in their regard. The works succeeding it subjected subjective phrases for determining opinion polarity of reviews.

In [7], OPINE, an information extraction system using unsupervised learning, has been proposed by Popescu and Etzioni. It mines the reviews and builds a model of the important features. Further, it checks for how these features are evaluated by the reviewers and also compares their quality with other products. However, OPINE's major focus is limited to finding the features rather than detecting opinion orientation of the reviews corresponding to those features.

Pang et al. [8] attempted to discern whether determination of sentiment and its classification could be simply categorized into two categories of positive sentiment and negative sentiment. The work does not extend to consideration of how positive or negative a sentiment was in its true orientation.

Peñalver-Martinez et al. [9] proposed an improvement in the contemporary method of sentiment analysis. The proposed method involves ontology in selection of features. Further, it uses a sentiment analysis method based on vector analysis. Several prominent works have followed in the recent years [10–14].

It can be concluded from the literature survey that major emphasis has been laid on feature extraction and, therefore, development of a system for reflecting summarized feedback of the consumers regarding the features of a product is a domain in need of further exploration.

3   Proposed Work

Several instances have been evident where a customer seeks only for a particular feature or set of features while making a purchase decision. As of now, a customer has to read a bulk of reviews in order to ascertain the satisfaction level of the customers who have submitted their reviews. Even in cases where one is looking only for a selected feature such as battery life or performance of a mobile phone, one has no alternative to reading all the reviews related to the aforementioned mobile phone, regardless of whether the review has anything to mention about that particular feature or not. None of the popular e-Commerce platforms have introduced any provision for reducing the efforts invested by the customers while looking to make a purchase decision after finding the satisfaction levels of the reviewers with a particular feature or feature set.

Our proposed method consists of the following steps, as represented in Fig. 2. First, the system scrapes all of the customer reviews available online for a particular product at a specified point of time. It applies various preprocessing techniques on the customer review sentences and subsequently adds them in a review database created by the system. Then the system scrapes the product description provided for the given product. It preprocesses the data and prepares a filtered description table containing the aspects/features of the product. After constructing the review database and the filtered description table, the system searches the reviews for obtaining a match with the aspects/features listed in the filtered description. Once matches are obtained, opinion phrases/words are detected for those matched features. Each opinion phrase/word

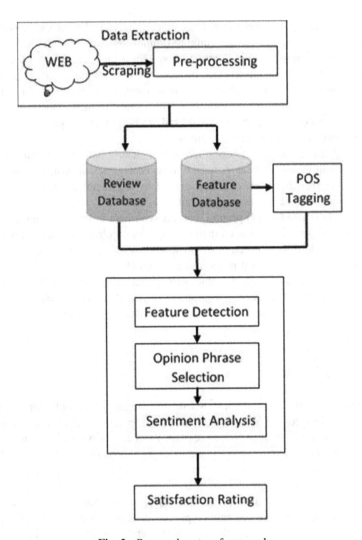

Fig. 2. Proposed system framework

carries a sentiment polarity value between the range [−1, 1]. The system involves a dictionary-based approach. Therefore, it uses a lexical database for obtaining sentiment polarity scores.

After obtaining a cumulative sentiment score for each aspect/feature listed in the filtered description table, it is utilized to rate the customer satisfaction level for the specific aspect/feature. Lastly, these ratings are represented along the product description on the e-Commerce webpage.

3.1 Data Extraction

The product reviews are extracted from the e-Commerce website using a web scraper. A web scraper can be a crawler or an HTML parser. In either case, the webpages containing the reviews are fetched and parsed in order to extract targeted content. Since the system is primarily focused at obtaining customer satisfaction levels, it scrapes reviewer name and review content. Further, a review database is created and the extracted reviews are saved in it.

3.2 Preprocessing and Review Database Creation

The data collected from the e-Commerce website contains noise. Therefore, it becomes important that such unnecessary data be removed. Also, data that do not contribute in the sentiment analysis detection needs to be removed. Preprocessing involves steps related to detection of stop word, stemming and tokenization.

Stemming refers to reduction of a word into its root form. Stop word demarcates the end of a sentence. Tokenization refers conversion of words into tokens. The aforementioned preprocessing methods alleviate convenience in effective implementation of Parts of Speech (POS) tagging [15], discussed in the following section, and sentiment analysis processes. The data obtained after conducting preprocessing is saved in a review database featuring mainly two columns, one containing the name of the reviewers and the other containing the review text.

3.3 POS Tagging and Feature Selection

The objective of the proposed work necessitates detection of product features and opinions regarding them. Product features are generally nouns and immediate pronouns and their opinions are contained in adjectives, adverbs or related phrases. Therefore, tagging of the words dominant in the reviews becomes a necessary step in determination of feature opinion pairs. Table 1 represents a Feature Opinion pair.

Table 1. Review sentence and feature opinion pair

Review	
Sentence	The display is bright
Feature opinion pair	(display, bright)

In POS tagging, words are classified and labeled according to their parts of speech [15]. The associated tags have been represented with their parts of speech counterpart in Table 2.

Table 2. POS tagging

Tag	Description	Tag	Description
CC	Coordinating conjunction	PRP$	Possessive pronoun
CD	Cardinal number	RB	Adverb
DT	Determiner adverb	RBR	Adverb, comparative
EX	Existential *There*	RBS	Adverb, superlative
FW	Foreign word	RP	Particle
IN	Preposition/subordinating conjunction	SYM	Symbol
JJ	Adjective	TO	To
JJR	Adjective, comparative	UH	Interjection
JJS	Adjective, superlative	VB	Verb, base form
LS	List item marker	VBD	Verb, past tense
MD	Modal	VBG	Verb, gerund/present participle
NN	Noun, singular/mass	VBN	Verb, past participle
NNS	Noun, plural	VBP	Verb, non 3rd person singular present
NNP	Proper noun, singular	VBZ	Verb, 3rd person singular present
NNPS	Proper noun, plural	WDT	Wh-Determiner
PDT	Predeterminer	WP	Wh-Pronoun
POS	Possessive ending	WP$	Possessive Wh-Pronoun
PRP	Personal pronoun	WRB	Wh-Adverb

The POS tagging method is utilized in mining features of product from the product description provided on the webpage of the e-Commerce platform. These features are saved in a separate table post which these features are searched for matches in the review text stored in the review database.

3.4 Sentiment Analysis and Representation

Sentiment analysis integrates an intersection of computational linguistics, natural language processing and text analysis with the objective of subjectivity determination and information extraction [3]. It detects the opinion polarity of a natural language element to ascertain whether it reflects a negative, neutral or positive opinion [16]. Regular opinions are elements of expression that exhibit opinion on a particular entity, here, for products or services [4]. As for example, "The processor of this palmtop is sluggish". They are mostly subjective in nature. On the other hand, opinions involving comparisons include depictions of two or more entities and how they fare against each other on certain parameters. As for example, "X processor is faster than Y processor." Such opinions can be either objective or subjective. The basic components of an opinion are as follows:

- Opinion holder: It refers to the individual/organization that has an opinion regarding an entity.
- Entity: It refers to the subject regarding which the opinion is.
- Opinion: It is the assumption, conclusion, notion or view of an opinion holder regarding an entity.

As stated in Eq. 1, an opinion has been defined as a quintuple or an expression formed through combination of five essential elements:

$$\left(e_x, a_{xy}, so_{wxyz}, h_w, t_z\right) \tag{1}$$

where

- e_x represents target entity.
- a_y represents aspect of entity e_x.
- so_{wxyz} represents sentiment value of the opinion holder h_w on aspect a_{xy} of entity e_x at time t_z. so_{wxyz} is +ve, −ve, or neutral, or a more granular rating.
- h_w represents opinion holder.
- t_z represents time of opinion expression.

After finding a match for the extracted feature in the review text, its immediate adjective/adverb phrase is considered as the opinion phrase. Since the proposed work employs a dictionary-based approach, we relate the text considered as opinion phrase with the synonym/antonym sets provided in the dictionary. The dictionary stores sets of synonyms and antonyms and values depicting the levels of positivity/negativity. Thus, sentimental orientation of the opinion phrases for the product features are determined as neutral, positive or negative along with their numerical representations.

Algorithm 1. Proposed Algorithm for CSRS
Input : List of all reviews (review[]),   List of all features present in description (fil_desc[]) **Output**: List of sentiment values for features
Initialization; 1.   Pre-processing and subsequent POS tagging 2.   desc_sent[]=[0]*length(fil_desc) 3.   for i=1 to length(review) 4.   for j=1 to length(sentences_in_review) 5.   for k=1 to length(fil_desc) 6.   if fil_desc[k] is in sentences_in_review[j] 7.   desc_sent[k]=sentiment(sentences_in_review[j])

Now, opinions for each product feature contained in the product feature table, discussed in Sect. 3.3, have been obtained. The proposed method for developing the Consumer Satisfaction Rating System has been provided in Algorithm 1. The concluding objective of the proposed work is to represent the results obtained for these product features in the product description section provided on the webpage of the e-Commerce portal.

4 Implementation and Results

The experiments were conducted on the Linux platform with a system configuration of i5-2430 M CPU and 3 GB RAM. The proposed system was implemented on Python for detecting sentiment orientation of opinion phrases associated with specific product features provided in the product description. Over 53,291 reviews were extracted from Amazon during the period of October 2016 – January 2017. The reviews belonged to the Electronics category of the website and were concentrated around 4 products, namely two smartphones (Moto G4 Plus and Redmi Note 3) and two laptops (Apple Macbook Air and Dell Inspiron 3558 Notebook). Further, a review database was created and the aforementioned reviews were appended after initial preprocessing. The review database consisted of fields containing reviewer's name and review text.

In succession to the aforementioned steps of preprocessing, product features were extracted from the product description text scraped from the webpage and saved in a CSV file. The product description text was mined to obtain product features from it by first tagging the text according to their parts of speech. The concept that product features are most likely to be nouns and the more detailed ones are likely to be proper nouns was exploited. For example, in case of a smartphone, processor is a noun whereas a detail such as it being a Snapdragon is a proper noun. Thus, a final feature database containing a table of product features mined from the product description text was obtained. Further, a search was conducted in the review database for a match with the features dominant in our final feature database.

After obtaining a match, the related opinion phrases were marked and the sentiments involved were analyzed using a pattern library. The module Pattern Analyzer was utilized for pattern based processing. For POS tagging, wherever required, NLTK's standard TreeBank tagger has been utilized [17]. The aforementioned tagger requires NumPy [18], another module aiding in scientific processing. Since the proposed method uses a dictionary-based approach for text analysis, we rely on the synsets and sentiment scores provided in publicly available lexical databases named WordNet [19] and SentiWordNet [20]. Figure 3 and 4 represent the results obtained through sentiment analysis of reviews based on the product features of smartphones and laptops, respectively.

The most significant aspects of the results obtained are that they are concentrated around conducting sentiment analysis at the aspect/feature level and the results are cumulative in nature i.e. the results show that the features which have higher instances of dominance in the reviews have higher values in comparison to the features which have been mentioned minimally. Besides being informative for consumers, the results

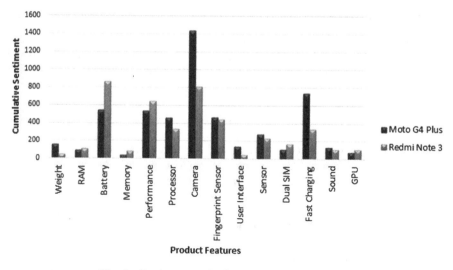

Fig. 3. Sentiment results for features of smartphones

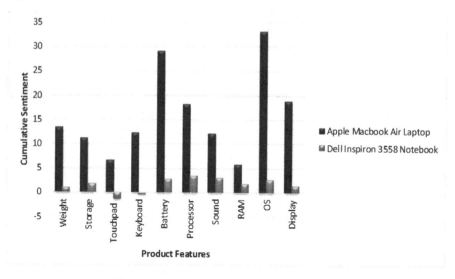

Fig. 4. Sentiment results for features of laptops

also aim at benefitting business forerunners since they will be able to acknowledge which features of their product have been more prominently liked by the consumers.

Also, they will also be able to get insights into how their product fares in comparison to their competitors and that how they have been received by the consumers.

4.1   Validation

The accuracy of the proposed system can be evaluated by computing a ratio between the summation of truly positive (TP) and truly negative (TN) sentiment for feature f and the summation of truly positive, falsely positive (FP), truly negative and falsely negative (FN) sentiment for feature f, as shown in Eq. 2.

$$Accuracy(f) = (TP + TN)/(TP + FP + TN + FN) \qquad (2)$$

The accuracy is represented between 0 and 1, where 0 represents minimum accuracy i.e. 0% and 1 represents maximum accuracy i.e. 100%. On an average, an accuracy of 0.908 was obtained for the proposed system.

5   Conclusion and Future Work

It can be inferred from the results mentioned in Sect. 4 that a Consumer Satisfaction Rating System, which detects how satisfied or not the consumers are with respect to the individual features of a product, has been developed. This, indeed, is helpful for consumers who are intending to make decisions regarding purchasing a product based on whether it actually contains that one feature they have been looking for and that it has satisfied its previous users or not. Besides the fact that the proposed work processes sentiment analysis targeted at the specific features of a product, the unique aspect of the work is that the results obtained through it are cumulative and not simply comparative. This means that a few instances of a particular feature such as camera of a smartphone being mentioned as good does not necessitate its association with a higher satisfaction value. If many users are satisfied with a particular feature then that particular feature is given a higher value even if the satisfaction value hadn't been one of the soaring ones individually.

Research efforts in future may be levied at improving mining of features and integrating the application of features provided by the manufactures on the webpage as well as those mentioned by the consumers in the reviews. Also, research may be extended further to detect deceptive reviews, which are aimed at conducting socio-economic attacks [21], and eventually nullify their contribution in the average consumer satisfaction rating. Efforts can also be levied at developing a visualization method that would be an improvement in the comprehension levels offered by the contemporary alternatives.

References

1. Bollen, J., Mao, H.: Twitter mood predicts the stock market 2, pp. 1–8 (2011)
2. Amazon. www.amazon.com
3. Pang, B., Lee, L.: Opinion mining and sentiment analysis. found. trends®. Inf. Retr. 1, 91–231 (2006)

4. Liu, B.: Sentiment analysis and opinion mining. Synth. Lect. Hum. Lang. Technol. **5**, 1–167 (2012)
5. Srivastava, A., Singh, M.P., Kumar, P.: Supervised semantic analysis of product reviews using weighted k-NN classifier. In: 11th International Conference on Information Technology: New Generations (ITNG), pp. 502–507. IEEE, Las Vegas (2014)
6. Hu, M., Liu, B.: Mining and summarizing customer reviews. In: ACM SIGKDD International Conference on Knowledge Discovery and Data Mining KDD 04, pp. 168–177 (2004)
7. Popescu, A.-M., Etzioni, O.: Extracting product features and opinion from reviews. Hum. Lang. Technol. Empir. Methods Nat. Lang. Process. Vancouver, Br. Columbia, pp. 339–346 (2005)
8. Pang, B., Lee, L., Vaithyanathan, S.: Thumbs up? Sentiment classification using machine learning techniques. In: ACL-02 Conference on Empirical Methods in Natural Language Processing - EMNLP 2002 (2002)
9. Peñalver-Martinez, I., Garcia-Sanchez, F., Valencia-Garcia, R., Rodríguez-García, M.Á., Moreno, V., Fraga, A., Sánchez-Cervantes, J.L.: Feature-based opinion mining through ontologies. Expert Syst. Appl. **41**, 5995–6008 (2014)
10. Fan, Z.-P., Che, Y.-J., Chen, Z.-Y.: Product sales forecasting using online reviews and historical sales data: a method combining the Bass model and sentiment analysis. J. Bus. Res. **74**, 90–100 (2017)
11. Tiwari, P., Mishra, B.K., Kumar, S., Kumar, V.: Implementation of n-gram methodology for rotten tomatoes review dataset sentiment analysis. Int. J. Know. Discov. Bioinf. **7**, 30–41 (2017)
12. Liu, Y., Bi, J.-W., Fan, Z.-P.: Ranking products through online reviews: a method based on sentiment analysis technique and intuitionistic fuzzy set theory. Inf. Fusion **36**, 149–161 (2017)
13. Villaroel Ordenes, F., Ludwig, S., Grewal, D., de Ruyter, K., Wetzels, M.: Analyzing online reviews through the lens of speech act theory: implications for consumer sentiment analysis. J. Consum. Res. **189**, 227–246 (2016)
14. Qiu, G., Liu, B., Chen, C.: Opinion word expansion and target extraction through double propagation. Assoc. Comput. Linguist. **37**, 9–27 (2011)
15. Santorini, B.: Part-of-speech tagging guidelines for the Penn Treebank Project (3rd revision) (1990)
16. Kumar, S., Kumar, P., Singh, M.P.: A generalized procedure of opinion mining and sentiment analysis. In: International Conference on Recent Trends in Communication and Computer Networks (ComNet), pp. 105–108, Hyderabad (2013)
17. Bird, S., Loper, E., Klein, E.: Natural Language Processing with Python. O'Reilly Media Inc. (2009)
18. Walt, S., Colbert, S.C., Varoquaux, G.: The Numpy array: a structure for efficient numerical computation. Comput. Sci. Eng. **13**, 22–30 (2011)
19. WordNet. http://wordnet.princeton.edu
20. Baccianella, S., Esuli, A., Sebastiani, F.: SentiWordNet 3.0: an enhanced lexical resource for sentiment analysis and opinion mining. In: 7th Conference on International Language Resources and Evaluation (LREC 2010), pp. 2200–2204 (2010)
21. Kumar, P., Dasari, Y., Nath, S., Sinha, A.: Controlling and mitigating targeted socio-economic attacks. In: Dwivedi, Y.K., et al. (eds.) I3E 2016. LNCS, vol. 9844, pp. 471–476. Springer, Cham (2016). doi:10.1007/978-3-319-45234-0_42

Forecasting the 2016 US Presidential Elections Using Sentiment Analysis

Prabhsimran Singh[1(✉)], Ravinder Singh Sawhney[2],
and Karanjeet Singh Kahlon[1]

[1] Department of Computer Science,
Guru Nanak Dev University, Amritsar, India
{prabh_singh32, karanvkahlon}@yahoo.com
[2] Department of Electronics Technology, Guru Nanak Dev University,
Amritsar, India
sawhney.ece@gndu.ac.in

Abstract. The aim of this paper is to make a zealous effort towards true prediction of the 2016 US Presidential Elections. We propose a novel technique to predict the outcome of US presidential elections using sentiment analysis. For this data was collected from a famous social networking website (SNW) Twitter in form of tweets within a period starting from September 1, 2016 to October 31, 2016. To accomplish this mammoth task of prediction, we build a model in WEKA 3.8 using support vector machine which is a supervised machine learning algorithm. Our results showed that Donald Trump was likely to emerge winner of 2016 US Presidential Elections.

Keywords: Forecasting · Twitter · Sentiment analysis · Support vector machine · WEKA

1 Introduction

Accurate future prediction of an event has always been a tedious task for researchers, but with advancement in technologies and availability of powerful computing devices researchers have started taking keen interest in this research area. One of the key factor in these advancement has been the popularity of social networking websites (SNW) especially Twitter. Twitter is one of the most popular social networking media, with 695,750,000 registered users till date and approximately 135,000 new users are registering every day [1]. This large audience is responsible for tons of tweeting happening everyday i.e. sharing their view in relatively fewer words and hence providing researchers a large pool of tweets, which may contain anger or love towards an entity like an election. Using the concept of sentiment analysis as suggested by Liu [2], we can extract their sentiments from these tweets and use these in predicting the outcome of any event, be it elections. Since US is a developed country [3], with an established fact that 88.5% of the population has access to the internet [4] and approx 67 million Twitter users in the US [5], all these factors give us a perfect platform to carry out our research on 2016 US Presidential Elections.

© IFIP International Federation for Information Processing 2017
Published by Springer International Publishing AG 2017. All Rights Reserved
A.K. Kar et al. (Eds.): I3E 2017, LNCS 10595, pp. 412–423, 2017.
DOI: 10.1007/978-3-319-68557-1_36

For this research paper, we have collected the tweets through Twitter. Then we synthesized these tweets using sentiment analysis that helped us to have a better insight into the outcome of 2016 US Presidential Elections. We would be discussing our approach towards our predicted results in the upcoming sections.

2 Background of US Presidential Elections

US Presidential elections were scheduled to be held on November 8, 2016 to elect the new President of United States of America for the next 4 years, as the second term of the current President Mr. Barack Obama was going to expire on January 2017. Since Obama was holding the presidential chair for the second term, so as per the US presidential ordinances he could not contest these elections. The event became more engaging, as both the candidates contesting the election were first timers. As we know Democratic Party and Republican Party were the two main parties, so the entire paper has been focused on these parties as well as their Presidential candidates.

The selection of both presidential candidates was made through primaries held between February to June 2016. In the Democratic Party Presidential primaries Ms. Hillary Clinton defeated Mr. Bernie Sanders, thus becoming the first female Presidential candidate in the history of United States, to be nominated by a major political party. While the Republican Party Presidential primaries saw 17 candidates were entering the primaries, making it the largest ever presidential primary contesting for any political party in United States history. In the finals Mr. Donald Trump, a businessman manages to defeat Mr. Ted Cruz to be selected as Republican Party Presidential candidate.

None of the candidates had an absolute cakewalk, and both faced their respective ups and downs during the course of their campaign and debates. Donald Trump had easy primaries while Hillary Clinton had a tough fight with Bernie Sanders. During debates, Hillary Clinton always had an edge over Donald Trump. Donald Trump was highly criticized for various comments and attitude toward other nations during campaigns and speeches while Hillary Clinton had tough times for her email controversies. So even up to week before the elections, there was ambiguity about the winner and the lead was constantly swinging among both candidates.

3 Related Work

Twitter and Elections share a strong bond since a longtime now. With advancement in technology and increase in a number of people using Twitter, the researchers working in this domain have a perfect opportunity to work on Twitter based emotions towards election predictions. Though this approach was rather crude and had many flaws yet it provided useful insights that helped us towards making a realistic prediction with some modern prediction tools the task seems realistic.

Tumasjan et al. [6] were the first to make use of Twitter to predict the results of German Federal election held in September 2009. They collected 104,003 tweets over the period of 27 days for the six popular political parties of Germany. Their technique was quite simple and dependent on a basic counting of the number of tweets that a party or its prominent leaders get. Using this simple technique, they were successful in predicting the winner of 2009 German Federal Elections. However this simple technique faced huge criticism, in particular, Jungherr et al. [7] pointed the lack of methodological justification while Gayo-Avello [8, 9] stressed on the need to make true prediction i.e. predictions made prior to the actual election. Another point highlighted by Gayo-Avello [8, 9] was to make use of sentiment analysis in order to know the sentiment of the tweet, which indeed will help to produce more accurate results. The subsequent studies DiGrazia et al. [10], Franch [11], Ceron et al. [12], Caldarelli et al. [13], Burnap et al. [14] have all taken the advice of Gayo-Avello and made use of sentiment analysis in order to produce more accurate results.

Our work is also influenced by the advice of Gayo-Avello [8, 9]. We made a true prediction for 2016 US Presidential elections, instead of simply relying on the amount of tweets for making the prediction we have used sentiment analysis in our methodology along with some scientific tools to make predictions.

4 Proposed Methodology

Data collection is a trivial task and in our case as well the initial hurdle was efficient data collection. So we gathered data from Twitter in form of tweets. For this, we built a system in ASP.Net 2012. Since a person can post multiple tweets on Twitter, so in order to avoid biased results, we have first removed multiple tweets from single source so that only one tweet could be considered from one person. Next we applied sentiment analysis to obtain polarity (positive or negative) of each tweet using WEKA 3.8. All these phases are discussed with suitable explanation in the upcoming sections. The flowchart of the process is given in Fig. 1.

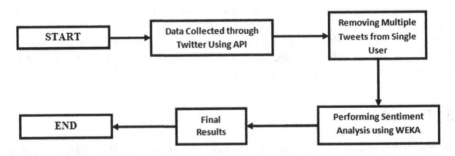

Fig. 1. Flowchart of proposed methodology

5 Data Collection

Data for our research was collected from Twitter. For this purpose, a system was developed in ASP.Net using visual studio [15]. For tweet fetching we used tweetinvi API [16] which is freeware and can be easily integrated with Dot. Net framework. The tweets were fetched using this system based on the hashtags (#) for both the respective candidates. Table 1 shows the hashtags (#) that were used for fetching tweets from Twitter.

Table 1. Hashtags (#) used for fetching tweets

Candidates	Hillary Clinton	Donald Trump
Hashtags(#)	#Hillary, #HillaryClinton, #ClintonKaine, #Votehillary	#DonaldTrump, #TrumpPence16, #Trump, #VoteTrump

A total of 327,127 tweets were collected from September 1, 2016 to October 31, 2016 daily from the USA. This time period was chosen because the election campaigns were in full swing so it was possible to get data from all type of Twitter users at this time. Out of the 327,127 tweets collected from the USA, 194,753 (59.53%) of tweet mentions were in favor of Donald Trump, while 132,374 (40.47%) of tweet mentions were in favor of Hillary Clinton. Table 2 shows the daily tweet collection for both the candidates.

Table 2. Daily tweet collection for both candidates

Date	Donald Trump	Hillary Clinton
01-09-16	3512	1356
02-09-16	2728	1499
03-09-16	2757	1329
04-09-16	2319	1160
05-09-16	2548	1122
06-09-16	2361	2638
07-09-16	2722	1520
08-09-16	3587	2193
09-09-16	2638	1475
10-09-16	1919	1644
11-09-16	2410	4649
12-09-16	2748	1667
13-09-16	2152	1552
14-09-16	2661	1596
15-09-16	3483	1803
16-09-16	3771	2027
17-09-16	3369	1554
18-09-16	3184	1548
19-09-16	2280	1604
20-09-16	2818	1678
21-09-16	3253	4226

(continued)

Table 2. (*continued*)

Date	Donald Trump	Hillary Clinton
22-09-16	2960	1524
23-09-16	2902	1392
24-09-16	2617	1454
25-09-16	2729	1640
26-09-16	3717	2491
27-09-16	1822	4344
28-09-16	3870	2073
29-09-16	3643	1775
30-09-16	4017	2028
01-10-16	3178	1814
02-10-16	3309	1672
03-10-16	3084	1978
04-10-16	2398	2008
05-10-16	3018	2326
06-10-16	2742	1468
07-10-16	3289	1841
08-10-16	4039	3078
09-10-16	3790	2299
10-10-16	4205	3666
11-10-16	3903	2574
12-10-16	3998	3379
13-10-16	4279	3247
14-10-16	4198	2705
15-10-16	3858	2442
16-10-16	3868	2120
17-10-16	1502	954
18-10-16	3769	2150
19-10-16	4255	2705
20-10-16	3897	2938
21-10-16	3441	2195
22-10-16	3144	2090
23-10-16	3035	2312
24-10-16	2775	2688
25-10-16	3575	2966
26-10-16	3485	2145
27-10-16	3813	2492
28-10-16	2918	1760
29-10-16	3530	2753
30-10-16	3596	2520
31-10-16	3365	2528
Total	*194,753*	*132,374*

Since in the actual elections, a person can vote only once. We have also applied a similar restriction, that only one tweet would be considered per person. The reason for this restriction was that nowadays many companies and agencies are being hired by the candidates in order to make the analysis bias. To rule out this anomaly, we had simply used the coding skills that if a person who tweeted multiple times, then the first tweet by that person would be considered for evaluation of results. Table 3 shows an example how this restriction works. In this "Roy" has tweeted 3 tweets, while "Sheral" has tweeted 2 tweets. So we set flag '1' for all tweets except the initial/first tweet. So for "Roy" and "Sheral" only one tweet will be counted, hence eliminating the effect of multiple tweets.

Table 3. Example for applying restriction of one tweet per person

Sr. No.	Tweet	Sender	Flag
1	I support Donald Trump	Roy	0
2	Trump you are my hero	Roy	1
3	Hillary we win this elections	Sheral	0
4	Trump: Make US Great again	Roy	1
5	Hillary we support you	Sheral	1

After applying this restriction, we were left with 136,192 (41.64%) tweets, while 190,935 (58.36%) duplicate tweets were removed. This highlights an important point that the number of people posting multiple tweets was quite high. Out of the 136,192 tweets collected from the USA, 81,946 (60.16%) of tweet mentions were in favor of Mr. Donald Trump, while 54,246 (39.84%). Table 4 shows the daily tweet collection for both candidates after applying the restriction of one tweet per person. Our entire experimentation was to be dependent on these 136,192 tweets.

Table 4. Daily tweet collection (With Restriction)

Date	Donald Trump	Hillary Clinton
01-09-16	1372	554
02-09-16	1097	564
03-09-16	1054	523
04-09-16	892	451
05-09-16	966	506
06-09-16	1540	1529
07-09-16	1013	600
08-09-16	1302	823
09-09-16	1063	594
10-09-16	832	668
11-09-16	926	1686
12-09-16	1040	718
13-09-16	927	682

(continued)

Table 4. (*continued*)

Date	Donald Trump	Hillary Clinton
14-09-16	1073	712
15-09-16	1306	638
16-09-16	1547	1963
17-09-16	1257	607
18-09-16	1161	590
19-09-16	945	641
20-09-16	1163	690
21-09-16	1277	2058
22-09-16	1237	643
23-09-16	1219	583
24-09-16	1119	542
25-09-16	1171	627
26-09-16	1666	918
27-09-16	1016	1973
28-09-16	1547	895
29-09-16	1466	716
30-09-16	1623	756
01-10-16	1315	725
02-10-16	1334	635
03-10-16	1313	874
04-10-16	1038	772
05-10-16	1418	939
06-10-16	1299	643
07-10-16	1540	762
08-10-16	1786	1064
09-10-16	1679	918
10-10-16	1854	1506
11-10-16	1685	1009
12-10-16	1677	1100
13-10-16	1802	1111
14-10-16	1828	995
15-10-16	1655	963
16-10-16	1604	863
17-10-16	791	515
18-10-16	1500	900
19-10-16	1676	1120
20-10-16	1659	1193
21-10-16	1362	904
22-10-16	1285	793
23-10-16	1294	757

(*continued*)

Table 4. (*continued*)

Date	Donald Trump	Hillary Clinton
24-10-16	1213	892
25-10-16	1444	930
26-10-16	1593	944
27-10-16	1585	966
28-10-16	1360	888
29-10-16	1557	1068
30-10-16	1498	992
31-10-16	1485	1055
Total	*81,946*	*54,246*

6   Results and Findings

As mentioned earlier, volume of tweets is not the deciding factor for the victory of any specific candidate, we computed polarity (positive or negative) for each tweet by applying sentiment analysis. Sentiment analysis is the study of analyzing people's opinions, sentiments, evaluations, appraisals, attitudes and emotions towards entities such as products, services, organizations, individuals, issues, events, topics, and their attributes [2].

For this, we developed a classification model in WEKA 3.8 [17], which is open source software and consists of a collection of machine learning algorithms for data mining tasks. Further we applied support vector machines (SVM) which is a supervised machine learning approach for performing the sentiment analysis. The SVM is a learning machine for two-group classification problems that transforms the attribute space into multidimensional feature space using a kernel function to separate dataset instances by an optimal hyperplane [18]. The reason for building the model using SVM was that it is often regarded as one of the best classification algorithm [19].

The training data set was same as used by Kotzias et al. [20], which contains reviews and scores from three different datasets i.e. Amazon [21], IMDb [22], Yelp [23]. Each dataset contains a total of 500 positive and 500 negative sentences, so in total the dataset had 1500 positive and 1500 negative sentences. The data set contained two columns first the sentence and second the sentiment of each sentence in form of "0" (negative) and "1" (positive).

For classification, we used filtered classifiers, which enable us to build a classifier with a filter of our choice. As discussed earlier SVM is used as classifier while "String To Word Vector" is used as a filter which convert a string attribute to a vector that represents word occurrence frequencies. In addition to this we used 10 fold cross validation which is also known as rotation estimation to analyze how a predictive model would perform on an unknown dataset. The training set got an efficiency of 79.26%, this means 2378 instances from the training set were correctly classified while 622 instances were incorrectly classified. According to the confusion matrix 1191 negative instances (Class a) were correctly classified while 1167 positive instances

(Class b) were correctly classified. The detailed results along with confusion matrix are shown in Fig. 2, while Fig. 3 shows the graph showing area under the curve (ROC = 0.793).

For testing set, we used the tweets collected from Twitter. Before testing we preprocessed the data in order to remove unwanted Html tags, web links and special symbols (, " ! ' ; : @ #) so that we should not get biased results. The task of data

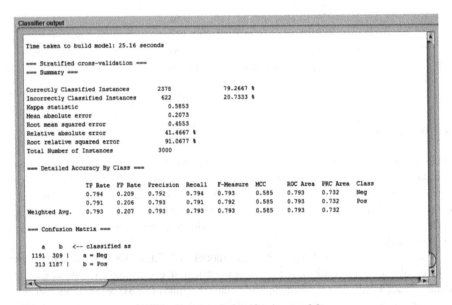

Fig. 2. Results of classification model

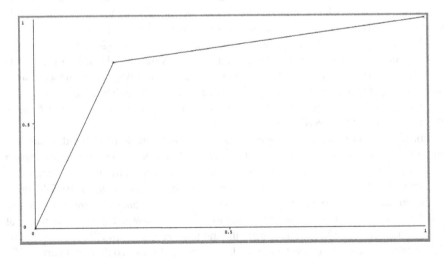

Fig. 3. Area under the Curve (ROC = 0.793)

preprocessing was performed in an automated fashion. Once preprocessing was done, we passed the testing set through the classification model developed earlier and it gave us the classification results i.e. polarity of each tweet. From these results we calculated net positive score (NPS), which is simply the difference between the total number of positive tweets and total number of negative tweets received by a candidate. The results of the same have been shown in Table 5.

Table 5. Result of Sentiment Analysis for both candidates

	Number of Tweets	
	Donald Trump	Hillary Clinton
Positive	42518	27582
Negative	39428	26664
Net positive score (NPS)	3090	918

Out of the total 81,946 tweet for Donald Trump got, 42,518 (51.88%) tweets were positive and 39428 (48.12%) tweets were negative. Similarly out of the total 54,246 tweets Hillary Clinton got, 27,582 (50.84%) tweets were positive and 26,664 (49.16%) tweets were negative. The net positive score (NPS) of Donald Trump was observed to be significantly higher than that of Hillary Clinton. Based upon our experimental results it was evident that Donald Trump would be winning the 2016 US Presidential Elections. Figure 4 shows the results of the same in graphical form.

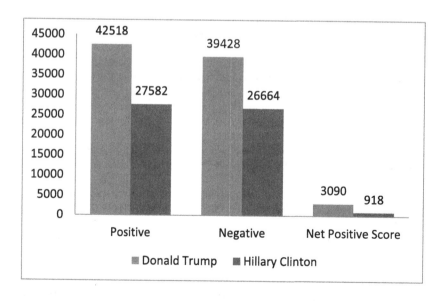

Fig. 4. Final results

7 Conclusions and Future Work

Predicting an event is always an uphill task. There are lots of factors that ought to be considered for making a truthful prediction. The aim of this paper was to predict the winner of 2016 US Presidential Elections. For this we collected data from Twitter. Further we applied a restriction that only one tweet per person will be considered for evaluation. Finally, we build a classification model in WEKA using SVM for performing sentiment analysis. Based upon the results of sentiment analysis we calculated the NPS. The results of our experiments clearly indicate that Donald Trump would be winning the 2016 US Presidential Elections.

Our experiments gave us the probability that the winner will be Donald Trump, however the actual winner in the US presidential election is based on the electoral vote and not the percentage of votes, and we should build a mathematical model that can convert the results of sentiment analysis into electoral votes which indeed will be our future aim.

References

1. Statisticbrain Twitter Facts. http://www.statisticbrain.com/Twitter-statistics/
2. Liu, B.: Sentiment analysis and opinion mining. Synth. Lect. Hum. Lang. Technol. **5**(1), 1–167 (2012). doi:10.2200/S00416ED1V01Y201204HLT016
3. IMF Report. http://www.imf.org/external/pubs/ft/weo/2015/01/weodata/groups.htm
4. CIA Internet User Report. https://www.cia.gov/library/publications/resources/the-world-factbook/rankorder/2153rank.html
5. Statisticbrain US Twitter Facts. https://www.statista.com/statistics/274564/monthly-active-Twitter-users-in-the-united-states/
6. Tumasjan, A., Sprenger, T.O., Sandner, P.G., Welpe, I.M.: Predicting elections with Twitter: what 140 characters reveal about political sentiment. In: ICWSM, vol. 10, pp. 178–185 (2010)
7. Jungherr, A.: Tweets and votes, a special relationship: the 2009 federal election in germany. In: Proceedings of the 2nd Workshop on Politics, Elections and Data, pp. 5–14 (2013). doi:10.1145/2508436.2508437
8. Daniel, G.A., Metaxas, P.T., Mustafaraj, E.: Limits of electoral predictions using twitter. In: Proceedings of the Fifth International AAAI Conference on Weblogs and Social Media. Association for the Advancement of Artificial Intelligence (2011)
9. Daniel, G.-A.: I Wanted to Predict Elections with Twitter and all I got was this Lousy Paper A Balanced Survey on Election Prediction using Twitter Data. arXiv preprint arXiv:1204.6441 (2012)
10. DiGrazia, J., McKelvey, K., Bollen, J., Rojas, F.: More tweets, more votes: social media as a quantitative indicator of political behavior. PLoS ONE **8**(11), e79449 (2013). doi:10.1371/journal.pone.0079449
11. Franch, F.: (Wisdom of the Crowds) 2: 2010 UK election prediction with social media. J. Inf. Technol. Polit. **10**(1), 57–71 (2013). doi:10.1080/19331681.2012.705080
12. Ceron, A., Curini, L., Iacus, S.M., Porro, G.: Every tweet counts? How sentiment analysis of social media can improve our knowledge of citizens' political preferences with an application to Italy and France. New Media Soc. **16**(2), 340–358 (2014). doi:10.1177/1461444813480466

13. Caldarelli, G., Chessa, A., Pammolli, F., Pompa, G., Puliga, M., Riccaboni, M., Riotta, G.: A multi-level geographical study of Italian political elections from Twitter data. PLoS ONE **9** (5), e95809 (2014). doi:10.1371/journal.pone.0095809
14. Burnap, P., Gibson, R., Sloan, L., Southern, R., Williams, M.: 140 characters to victory? Using Twitter to predict the UK 2015 General Election. Electoral. Stud. **41**, 230–233 (2016). doi:10.1016/j.electstud.2015.11.017
15. Visual Studio 2012. https://www.visualstudio.com/en-us/downloads/download-visual-studio-vs.aspx
16. Tweetinvi API. https://www.nuget.org/packages/TweetinviAPI/
17. Frank, E., Hall, M.A., Witten, I.H.: The WEKA Workbench. Online Appendix for "Data Mining: Practical Machine Learning Tools and Techniques", 4th edn. Morgan Kaufmann (2016)
18. Hearst, M.A., Dumais, S.T., Osuna, E., Platt, J., Scholkopf, B.: Support vector machines. IEEE Intell. Syst. Their Appl. **13**(4), 18–28 (1998). doi:10.1109/5254.708428
19. Petrova, N.V., Cathy, H.: Prediction of catalytic residues using Support Vector Machine with selected protein sequence and structural properties. BMC Bioinf. **7**(1), 312 (2006). doi:10.1186/1471-2105-7-312
20. Kotzias, D., Denil, M., De Freitas, N., Smyth, P.: From group to individual labels using deep features. In: Proceedings of the 21th ACM SIGKDD International Conference on Knowledge Discovery and Data Mining, pp. 597–606. ACM (2015). doi:10.1145/2783258.2783380
21. McAuley, J., Leskovec, J.: Hidden factors and hidden topics: understanding rating dimensions with review text. In: Proceedings of the 7th ACM Conference on Recommender Systems, pp. 165–172. ACM (2013). doi:10.1145/2507157.2507163
22. Maas, A.L., Daly, R.E., Pham, P.T., Huang, D., Ng, A.Y., Potts, C.: Learning word vectors for sentiment analysis. In: Proceedings of the 49th Annual Meeting of the Association for Computational Linguistics: Human Language Technologies, vol. 1, pp. 142–150. Association for Computational Linguistics (2011)
23. Yelp Dataset. https://www.yelp.com/dataset_challenge

Smart Solutions for the Future

Cities and Urban Living at the Crossroads

Jeremy Millard[(⊠)]

Danish Technological Institute, Taastrup, Denmark
jeremy.millard@3mg.org

Abstract. Cities need to look again at their approach to evolving the smart city concept to addresses the challenges of urbanization. This concept paper highlights the European approach along with the need for social, technological and economic innovation to make such an objective feasible and sustainable.

Keywords: Smart cities · Urbanization · Public policy · Governance

1 The Urbanization Challenge

In 2014, for the first time in human history, more than half of the world's population lived in urban areas, a proportion that is expected to increase to 66% by 2050. Projections show that urbanization combined with the overall growth of the world's population could add another 2.5 billion people to urban areas by 2050. And, although this trend is global, almost 90% of the increase is expected to be concentrated in Asia and Africa [1]. In real terms, the number of urban residents is growing by nearly 60 million people every year. As the planet becomes more urban, cities need to become smarter. Major urbanization requires new and innovative ways to manage the complexity of urban living. It demands new ways to target problems like overcrowding, energy consumption, resource management and environmental protection, as well as to address issues like the social cohesion, wellbeing and prosperity of city inhabitants.

The seemingly irreversible trend of urbanization poses both immense challenges as well as fantastic opportunities for human and planetary development. We need to take a 'glass-half-full' optimist approach in order to successfully address these challenges, but without being blind to the many so-called 'wicked' problems that city growth and city life bring in its wake. The main reason for this optimism is that cities are, in principle, at the perfect 'sweet spot' balancing the myriad ways it is possible for populations to govern, organize and run their lives.

2 Cities at the 'Sweet Spot'

Why are cities at the 'sweet spot'? On the one hand, most cities are large enough to access and wield significant political power, financial and other resources together with the people, communities, firms and institutions located in them. They are also generally large enough to have resilience through their internal diversity, strength in depth and

© IFIP International Federation for Information Processing 2017
Published by Springer International Publishing AG 2017. All Rights Reserved
A.K. Kar et al. (Eds.): I3E 2017, LNCS 10595, pp. 427–433, 2017.
DOI: 10.1007/978-3-319-68557-1_37

strategic competence. These attributes are essential for well-run human societies. On the other hand, however, and in contrast to central governments in all but very small countries, cities are at the same time geographically, culturally and historically close enough to these same actors to understand their needs, collaborate meaningfully with them and take and implement appropriate decisions on the ground. They are also generally small enough to be nimble, flexible, dynamic and responsive, certainly when compared to most national and international institutions. In many ways, therefore, cities can balance these two contrasting sets of attributes, thereby in principle functioning as the most efficient and effective form of human organization that we have yet devised for a global population now numbered in the billions.

It is important to underline that this is the potential of cities – many if not most cities exhibit a large number of these qualities, whilst too many do not. The challenge, therefore, is to better understand and spread good ideas, and build knowledge about successful city development in a collaborative way across the globe as well as within countries and regions. Although every city is faced with a highly unique set of challenges and opportunities, mutual learning between cities in terms of good practices and how these might be adapted to fit specific contexts, is absolutely paramount. This is, of course, already happening on a large scale through a plethora of city networks and communities of practice.

3   Re-thinking the 'Smart City' Label

The 'smart city' label, although currently the most prominent, is by no means the only game in town. There are, for example, networks and/or concepts focusing on digital cities, sustainable cities, innovative cities, intelligent cities, creative cities, open cities, energy cities, cities of tomorrow, as well as cities as launch pads for transformation. More recently, other city networks have also flourished, such as so-called Fab Cities, shareable cities, cities of nature, green cities, resilient cities, and not least the so-called C40 network of the world's megacities committed to addressing climate change.

It would be mistaken to imagine that the 'smart city' label is an umbrella term that somehow embraces all the others. Many of these networks eschew the description of 'smart' as it might be perceived as being too technology-deterministic, whilst others see technology as an absolutely essential enabler if we are to live in well-functioning, fair and prosperous settlements. It is thus clear that mutual learning and cross-fertilization is essential to align such different views. Cities need to redouble their efforts to examine and compare the most important, striking and valuable developments and trends from many of the different strands of experience and discussion.

4   The European Approach

The European approach reflects these complexities and the emergence of new city concepts and networks. A recent study on smart cities in the EU for the European Parliament [2] concluded that the smart city concept has emerged not just as an innovative modus operandi for future urban living in Europe but as a key strategy to tackle poverty and inequality, unemployment and energy management. Despite much discussion and debate on the value, function and future of smart cities, as a concept it resists easy definition. At its core, the idea of smart cities is rooted in the creation and connection of human capital, social capital and Information and Communication Technology (ICT) infrastructure in order to generate greater and more sustainable economic development and a better quality of life. The European approach to smart cities is further defined along six axes or smart dimensions [3] related to: economy, mobility, environment, people, living and governance. The coordination of policies along these dimensions reflects the positive feedback between city development and urbanization; cities attract people whilst the availability of populations and infrastructure facilitates economic and societal development. But this feedback alone and the growth to which it gives rise are not sufficient to produce the hoped for benefits, as the problems associated with the uncontrolled growth of many mega-cities amply demonstrate [4]. The linkages between economic, societal and environmental development are not easily scalable as cities expand and are difficult to predict precisely, let alone control. Their beneficial evolution must therefore be facilitated by a combination of framework conditions and ICT infrastructures. In this way a platform needs to be provided on which governments, businesses and citizens can communicate and work together, and track the evolution of the city.

The move towards an increasingly smart, green and sustainable city agenda
During the preparation for and in the run up to the UN's global agreement on the Sustainable Development Goals (SDGs) in September 2015, including SDG11 on 'inclusive, safe, resilient and sustainable cities', and not least the Climate Change Agreement in December of that same year, both research and policy attention has turned to the green and sustainable agenda. It would be a mistake, however, to perceive this as purely about environmental protection, as the 'sweet spot' which the city occupies is increasingly understood as the most effective crucible in which environmental concerns can be successfully wedded to social, economic and governance imperatives to provide wins across all four dimensions. Indeed, it has been the large number of medium-sized and large cities in the USA which have declared that their President's withdrawal from the UN Climate Accord will have no affect on their climate agendas. These cities have their own resources and powers to continue to implement their chosen initiatives, regardless of the policies of their federal government.

In Europe, the 'Fab City' agenda and network, developed in Barcelona in 2016, has an ostensibly technological, economic and manufacturing purpose but proposes and develops its raison d'être also on the basis of its social and environmental credentials: "Newly created cities and the urbanization process in rural areas replicates a lifestyle based on consumerism and the linear economy, causing destructive social and economic impact, while compromising the ecological systems of the planet. We are losing livelihoods through both offshoring and automation, and this in turn leads to the demise of dynamic hubs of practical and cultural knowledge, where things are made. Extreme industrialization and globalization have turned cities into the most voracious consumers of materials, and they are overwhelmingly the source of carbon emissions through both direct and embodied energy consumption; we need to reimagine the cities and how they operate." [5] Since its launch in 2016, the Fab City network has grown to sixteen practicing cities, encompassing all continents, with the following objectives:

- To move from current linear industrial production, i.e. importing raw materials and products and exporting waste and pollution
- To move to spiral innovation ecosystem: i.e. where materials flow within cities whilst information and data on how things are made circulate globally
- To move from centralized mass production to decentralized distributed manufacturing and mass customization.

The Fab City concept is perhaps the most ambitious, as well as most recent, attempt to join up new forms of inclusive and low carbon economic growth based on the knowledge economy through the deployment of ICT. However, Barcelona's experience has not been without its challenges, the most intractable of which is how such strategies are inserted into the wider political economy and, in particular, the political ecology of urban transformation. Despite the undoubted benefits that Barcelona's smart and Fab City endeavors have brought, the smart city utopian discourse, intentionally or unintentionally, is seen by some as having been mobilized in ways that serve to depoliticize urban redevelopment and environmental management. There is some evidence that the techno-political language adopted has made it difficult for ordinary citizens to participate, let alone understand what is going on. There are calls to repoliticize the smart city discourse and "put citizens back at the center of the urban debate" [6]. This is of course not just an issue in Barcelona, but one which pervades most attempts to develop smart cities.

The need for smart cities based on social as well as technological and economic innovations

The European Commission is reflecting such calls to put citizens back at the center in some of its recent research and innovation programmes, most notably the science with and for society initiative [7] and the nature-based solutions for inclusive urban regeneration initiative [8]. The latter cites the "growing recognition and awareness that nature can help provide viable solutions that use and deploy the properties of natural ecosystems and the services that they provide in a smart, 'engineered' way." "Furthermore nature-based solutions, by reshaping the built environment, can enhance the inclusivity, equitability and liveability of the cities, regenerate deprived districts, improve mental and physical health and quality of life for the citizens, reduce urban violence, and decrease social tensions through better social cohesion particularly for the most vulnerable groups e.g. children, elderly and people of low socioeconomic status."

Such approaches are clearly top-down policy pushes, part of a number of strategic initiatives in response to the UN's SDG and the Climate Change agendas. But there are also a large number of genuine examples and practical approaches taking place on the ground developed by individual city authorities, social and commercial organizations in response to local demands as well as market forces, many of which are also linking up through some of the city networks cited above. For example, the 'new Nordic scalable model for city development', implemented at various sites around Copenhagen and developed by a small Danish architectural company [9]:

- Attempting to move away from tackling climate change issues, such as water, using bigger sewers, harder surfaces and technological 'fixes', but instead focusing on the intricate design of topography, soil, trees, flowers, vegetation, natural seepage and drainage woven into the urban fabric
- Focusing on inter-linking three extremely site-specific circuits: the hydrological, the biological and the social
- Deploying social innovation approaches and methods, like co-creation, dialogue and humanistic nature-based solutions, through continuous collaboration with residents, school children and local civil organizations, where the results are claimed to be greener, happier, more sensuous and varied local cultures that promote neighborhood identity and empower inhabitants.

5   Smart Cities and Social Innovation

The above policies and examples illustrate attempts to apply both ecological and social innovation concepts and approaches to the smart city bandwagon. In a 2014 blog for an open source European project [10], the author pointed out that the focus of the smart city movement to date, in which the city authorities and other organizations deploy sensors, networks, data and data analytics to improve the efficiency and effectiveness of urban systems (like transport, utilities, etc.) and services, is indeed only half the story. From this perspective on its own, there is the danger of a one-size fits all, top-down view of urban development. The diverse needs of the inhabitants as individuals, households, neighborhoods, communities, organizations and businesses that bring the city to life are just as important.

Thus, any adequate model for the smart city must also focus on the smartness of its citizens and encourage the processes, and especially social innovation processes, that make cities important: those that sustain very different – sometimes conflicting – activities. Cities are, by definition, engines of diversity, so focusing solely on stream-lining utilities, transport, construction and unseen government processes can be massively counter-productive. This is in much the same way that the 1960's penchant for social-housing in tower blocks, based on their apparent economic efficiency in Le Corbusier style, was ultimately found to be socially and culturally unsustainable and highly damaging. Instead, "smart cities will be smart because their citizens have found new ways to craft, interlink and make sense of their own and each other's assets, data and other resources" [11].

The 2014 European Parliament study showed that currently one of the most common types of so-called smart city initiatives across Europe is, in fact, about 'smart neighborhoods', and is especially concerned with using data and coordinating local assets of all types to improve the lives of local inhabitants in terms of improved physical environments, mobility as well as community cohesion to tackle many of their own problems. Indeed, the conclusions of this study are that inclusion and participation are important targets for successful smart city programmes to avoid polarization between the urban elite and low income areas. The study's case studies highlight that it is often inspiring leaders ('city champions') behind many successful initiatives, many of whom are local activists. In the most successful cases, citizens are being empowered through active participation to create a sense of ownership and commitment, so it is important to foster participative environments that facilitate and stimulate citizens, businesses and the public sector to contribute.

The strategic objective of the most successful smart neighborhood projects in Europe to date is to develop better public services hand-in-hand with community cohesion. This is based on input from citizens obtained by providing digital so-called 'ideation platforms' to develop a better city (e.g. the Amsterdam Smart City Platform), or competitions to take advantage of open public data to develop apps, useful data mash-ups or new services. This includes ICT-enabled citizen participation open data strategies, crowdsourcing and co-creation platforms. For example, the city of Helsinki, Finland, is finding new ways to encourage developers to exploit open data in order to create digital services and useful applications for and with citizens. One underlying theme of the Helsinki project is transparency of city decision-making and enabling better feedback from citizens to civil servants. Smart city services are thereby tested in the Helsinki Metropolitan area as part of people's everyday life.

A 'smart city' has both everything and nothing to do with technology

Smart cities started out as wishing to exploit the power of new ICT to improve the efficiency and effectiveness of city performance and wellbeing, and did so with notable success. Like many other areas it soon realized that technology is not a panacea and can have negative consequences, even sometimes with dystopian overtones, both for the environment as well as the conditions of human life, if the human dimension does not become an integral part of any urban strategy – indeed it should be the driving force of such strategies. "Whether smart cities descend into a dystopian fantasy or forge a new cooperative relationship between the human and the non-human world" is a critical issue going forward [6]. Indeed there is much research already which demonstrates, empirically as well as conceptually, that much better results are achieved when people and technology work together, than when operating on their own [13]. This applies as much to so-called smart cities as in every other aspect of human life.

References

1. http://www.un.org/en/development/desa/news/population/world-urbanization-prospects-2014.html
2. European Parliament: Mapping Smart Cities in the EU, Brussels (2014). http://www.europarl.europa.eu/RegData/etudes/etudes/join/2014/507480/IPOL-ITRE_ET(2014)507480_EN.pdf
3. Smart Cities, Ranking of European Medium-Sized Cities. http://www.smart-cities.eu/
4. These problems also occur in the developing world, perhaps more acutely such as in Nigeria, as well as in the emerging economies of China, India and Brazil
5. The Fab City Whitepaper: locally productive, globally connected, self-sufficient cities, 15 April 2016. http://fab.city/whitepaper.pdf
6. March, H., Ribera-Fumaz, R.: Smart contradictions: the politics of making Barcelona a self-sufficient city. Eur. Urban Reg. Stud. **23**(4), 816–830 (2016)
7. https://ec.europa.eu/programmes/horizon2020/en/h2020-section/science-and-society

8. http://ec.europa.eu/research/participants/portal/desktop/en/opportunities/h2020/topics/scc-02-2016-2017.html
9. http://sla.dk/files/2914/9449/3217/SLA_Ramboll_HansTavsensPark_UK.pdf
10. http://siresearch.eu/blog/smart-cities-and-social-innovation
11. See also Usman Hague's article in Wired Magazine in April 2012: Surely there's a smarter approach to smart cities? http://www.wired.co.uk/article/potential-of-smarter-cities-beyond-ibm-and-cisco
12. McAfee, A., Brynjolfsson, E.: Machine, Platform, Crowd: Harnessing Our Digital Future. W.W. Norton and Company, New York (2017)

Digitized Residential Address System: A Necessity Towards the Faster Service Delivery and Smart Cities Development in India

Harish Kumar[✉], Manoj Kumar Singh, M.P. Gupta, and J. Madaan

Department of Management Studies, Indian Institute of Technology, IIT Delhi,
New Delhi 110016, India
harishkr08@gmail.com, manojksiet@gmail.com,
{mpgupta,jmadaan}@dms.iitd.ac.in

Abstract. The Economic development of the country also depends on its IT enabled services available to common citizens. The cost effective services, delivery mode and delivery time make the governance friendly to the citizens. But the conflicting and lengthy house's address system in India causes a lot of delays in services delivery. A house or building address can be used for various purposes like postal services, courier services, logistics services delivery, meetings, party venue etc. A high degree of failed service deliveries provide a gap to digitize the house address system to deliver accurate and faster services to the citizens. The paper proposes a conceptual method to digitize the house address system which may be stored electronically into a centralized database to reduce the time consuming process of writing and storing a lengthy address repeatedly for delivering the various services. The paper also explores the possibilities of how this digitized address could be integrated with the aadhaar database system to make it more potentially applied in terms of citizens' oriented applications and services. The digitized address would contribute significantly to transform India into a digitally empowered society and knowledge economy.

Keywords: Digitized residential address · Smart city · Faster services · Digital India · Aadhaar card

1 Introduction

The variety and quality urban services [5] lead to social and economic sustainability of urban living [17]. The smart cities are defined as ICT based cities which have a promise of providing better services and quality of life to its citizens. The development of physio-socio-digital infrastructure in the cities are the base condition for the smart cities program. The government of India has taken a lot of initiatives to digitalize the city data, information and infrastructure like digital India campaign, digital India platform, and open data platform to innovative, quality and timely services and efficient delivery of services to its citizens. To digitize the services, web2.0, mobile platforms, cloud, aadhaar and payment gateways can be integrated. A lot of difficulties usually being faced by city

A.K. Kar et al. (Eds.): I3E 2017, LNCS 10595, pp. 434–441, 2017.
DOI: 10.1007/978-3-319-68557-1_38

governments while planning for the city development [3]. A home or building address can be used for administrative, emergency response, marketing, GIS, routing and navigation, and many other purposes and services. The information based services [3, 11] must be focused of the smart cities infrastructure which provide opportunities to make cities digitally empowered. The success of digital address program will stands India as a leading nation in terms of developed and advanced facilities.

1.1 Digital Initiatives to Make Digitally Empowered Country

Digital India initiatives are preparing India to become a knowledge economy and digitally empowered country through synchronized and coordinated engagement of the all levels of the government. A digital government can be defined as regular patterns of growth in a particular country [8]. The Digital India campaign primarily focuses on the inclusive growth of use smart devices, facilitating electronic services, products, manufacturing and job opportunities etc. The program also includes the development of digital infrastructure in the country. The digital government landscape shows the government initiatives to innovate and provide digital solutions to social, economic, political and other pressures [8]. The increasing population and high demand of services have created pressure on government and logistics supplier to deliver the services in a fast and accurate manner. The government is trying to integrate services across various departments to pace the service delivery speed with in the city and across the cities. The trust, security, privacy, accessibility and quality of public services are some of the major issues [7] in providing e-services to the citizens.

The cloud computing, big data, ICT applications and smart devices have created the platform for digitally empowered citizens. Access to services, quality of services, information privacy and security could be enhanced through cloud solutions. Some policy initiatives have been undertaken by government of India like e-kranti framework for electronic delivery of service, e-infrastructure for delivery of e-services, policy on adoption of open source software, policy on use of IT resources, collaborative way of development, use of cloud big data, securing India's cyber space, knowledge network to enhance India's role in global platforms of internet governance and service deliveries.

1.2 Service Delivery System in Cities

The high rate of urbanization and increasing population worldwide are creating a huge pressure on city infrastructure and services. The cities are competing each other to attract resources, cultural advancements and increased quality of life [9, 14, 19]. There is a lot of pressures on service providers to meet the service demand and delivery of the services at right time. The growing volume of packets, mail, increasing competition from private courier industry, administered prices, poor technology [16] and confusing addresses are some main causes for the failures, lost and delays in services [6]. Usually, the service providers are unable to locate the lengthy, conflicting and unorganized addresses provided by citizens, resulting inefficient government and commercial service deliveries [6]. The growing rate of urbanization creates a lot of confusion to locate the exact address to deliver the critical urban services. The personalization of the cities [11] can be done to improve the efficiency of their local services.

The smart cities are defined as ICT enabled cities which would provide the high quality services, improved life styles and happy living to its citizens. The smart city transformation would enhance the communication among citizens, government and service providers that may require the changes in city operations, including government, buildings, mobility, energy, environment and services. The main focus of smart cities development are to fulfill the needs of citizens, providing local services, and digital infrastructure [3]. The delivery of services accurately, quality of services and time consumed in service delivery could be main focus of service providers in smart cities. For that house or building needs a digital address that could be integrated with smart technologies like internet of things (IoT) devices, smart phones and cloud applications. To manage the digital addresses city wide or country wide, a centralized address database would be needed. Whenever a person uses digital address, the database should decode the complete physical address of the same. The address intelligence [18] can be used for area-specific solutions to increase the timely service delivery. The innovative planning, implementation of policies and some regulations are required [16] to design the digital address to make Indian society completely digital in terms of services.

2   Literature Studies

The cities and societies which have future vision and advanced development plan tend to show better economic and societal health [10]. The governments are adopting the new technological solutions to respond the current pressures [8] of service demands and to provide services for all the citizens in a hassle free environment. The digital India campaign will promote e-governance and Indian economy to a new heights in near future. Easy access to public services, cashless transactions and smooth service delivery would develop a digitally advanced societies and cities in India. The role of governance have been signified [10, 12] in improving the various services provided to citizens. A huge range of information and services [7] can be provided online through e-government and mobile government. The services provided by government should be based on the demand and requirement of its citizens which would help government to improve its accountability and responsibilities [13] towards the citizens. Citizens' perceptions and participation should be considered while developing new services. ICT [1] can alter the way individuals, organizations, and governments usually works. Implementation of ICTs can improve quality of life for citizens especially living in the less developed countries [2]. The use of ICT has been vastly promoted [13] in government in last few years. It has been found that managing a coherent address system can be difficult for a city government even under the best circumstances [6]. A lot of frauds [8] have been reported related with failed service deliveries in the cities which causes insecurity among the citizens to use digital services and putting orders online. The validation is required for the correctness of the mentioned place before start delivering the service. The address validation techniques should be implemented to check for consistency among address components and corrects them [16]. The provided address further cross checked for any inconsistency or mis-spelt. Therefore, to deliver the services to its citizens in a proper fashion, a digital address system is required.

In previous studies, performed in various countries, the street address was main concern while designing the house or building addresses. Street was divided into primary, secondary, and third order streets based on use and importance [6]. Some streets were categorized into even and odd number streets and number usually increases towards the moving direction from the reference point [6]. The most important street normally gets the most important name. Some authors have used directional conventions in designing the address systems. But now a days, this type of addressing system cannot be deployed. The feature address might have any syntax, but city, state, and pin code were separated from the rest of the address. House address must be applied effectively to inform to the public especially to the children. Naming convention should be proposed for the new developments at the time of developing sector layouts in a particular city. If a person feed digital address string, the exact and verified location should be shown correctly. Thus, the integration of national digital address system database with GIS and aadhaar database will solve such issues and would promote automation in addressing system.

3   Proposal for the Digitized Address System

The effective use of technology is the need of this competitive era in terms of development and modern infrastructure. ICT has totally changed the way of living in urban as well rural areas. The smart digital address could be a combination of technology, information and data to make digital infrastructure and better delivery of services. Assigning and management of buildings address could be done via digital address system. A house or building address usually contains house/building number, area name, city/village name, district name, state name, country name, pin code [16].

The paper proposes the concept of digitizing residential and commercial addresses. An address database should be developed to record and maintain all physical addresses. Whenever the digitized address string is used electronically or scanned, it would automatically show or print the complete address of that person or organization from the central address database (Fig. 1). This would also make the citizens smart to maintain an automated personal digital address book and fast accessibility to house services. The service and billing addresses might not be always identical. In such cases more than one digitized string can be used clearly indicating which one should be used for service delivery.

The centralized digital address database could be linked with aadhaar card database. Integration of aadhaar card would provide biometric authentication, eKYC and verified address information (Fig. 1) to reduce the address frauds and confusions in services deliveries. Compulsion of providing Aadhaar number of sender (in case of courier/postal service) would give the auto-verification of person who wish to send the particulars. Requesting aadhaar number with digital sign of recipient at the time of service delivery would make the system more robust and will control the frauds. The digital address

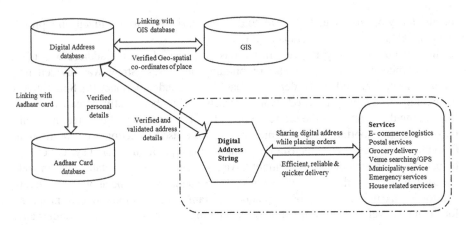

Fig. 1. Service delivery using digital address system and linking digital address with Aadhaar card

database can also be linked with GIS database to find the geospatial information of a particular address.

The residential or commercial address could be digitized into a string of alphabets and numbers like vehicle number, phone number, bank account number, passport number or aadhaar card number. Followings are some suggestions to design a digital address (Table 1). The followings are the assumptions in proposed digitized residential address system:

1. Each city and village should be assigned a unique code or number in respective district (like Indian railway has given a unique code to all stations)
2. Unique pin code system (already exist in India which signifies region, district and postal office of a particular area)
3. Each sub locality, sector, colony, society or village area should be assigned a unique number by concern authority.
4. Each house/building/tower/bhulekh/plot number should be assigned a unique number (Most of the cities/village are already have this).

Table 1. The proposed guidelines for digitization of house address system

Particular	Data type	Examples
City code/Railway station code/Tehsil code	String (4 digits)	For Ghaziabad – GZB
Pin Code	Numeric (6 digits)	201001
Sub locality/sector/colony/village/society code	Numeric (3 digits)	Nehru nagar = 067, Sector 144 = 144, Shiv colony = 052
House/Building/Tower/Bhulekh/plot number	String (4 digits)	House = C073, Flat = Z401, Plot = 0132

Thus from Table 2, the digital address of House number C-73, Nehru Nagar, Ghaziabad, Gautam Buddha Nagar, India-21001 would be GZB201001067C073.

The use of city/village code (as per Indian railway standard) will provide a better readability to the service providers in terms of understanding because a city code can be remembered easily as compared to interpreting the postal code digits or scanning the whole string to get the details every time. This would help in sorting and arranging order materials or delivery packets in city wise clustering during the transit. After city code, the pin code will provide the direction till to the post office of a locality. Then rest part of the string will direct the service provider till to the recipient. The locality could be further divided into sub section codes based on city/village's special requirements. If a particular is not applicable for some areas, in such cases, 00 could be assigned in digital string. If a village, society, town, city, district or state formed newly, the same standards should be follow in a regular pattern to digitize the new addresses. Whenever a person shifts from one address to another, the digitalized address must be updated with new address string in a centralized address database system. The address change may be notify to the contacts associated with the person's contact book. It might be optional alerts if a person wants to notify his new address to his relatives or known persons.

Table 2. Example of a digital address

Address particulars	City/Village	Pin code	Locality	House number
Current address system	Ghaziabad	201001	Nehru nagar	C073
Digital address	GZB ↓	201001 ↓	067 ↓	C073 ↓
	City/Village code	Pin code	Sector code	House number

The hospitals, police station, fire brigade stations, army cant area, historically important area could be assigned a special code while digitizing their addresses to make them distinguished which could be navigate faster in an area with their special code.

4   Benefits of Digitized Address System

The residential digitized address system will have a lot of benefits like address standardization and faster navigation of any location. The digital address could be stored or scanned electronically for various service deliveries rather writing a lengthy address every time. Whenever a person feeds this digital address string, global positioning system should also indicate the exact location physically. This system would reduce the address duplication efforts, resolving conflict and confusing addresses, improving the service delivery quality, quicker reach of emergency services, more efficient wide range service delivery, facilitating housing census, and would help e-commerce firms and government organizations to expend their services especially in tier-II and tier-III cities to make the lives of citizen easier and more comfortable in a digitally empowered era.

5 Conclusions

The house address system must be more consistent citywide as well as country wide. A digital address of a house or building would make address location simpler for residents and businesses. The digital address system would improve the navigation and search to find the exact location in cities or towns. The emergency services would response in a lesser time to deliver emergency services like health, fire, and resolving security issues. The digitized house address system will enhance the digital empowerment of citizens and collaborative digital platforms for participative governance with services, policies and best practices. The national digital address system will enhance the readiness of government to develop smart cities and digital empowered India.

6 Limitations and Further Research

The basic need for the digital address system will be high speed secured internet. Setting up the broadband and maintaining Wi-Fi connectivity throughout the city and country is a big challenge to the government. Maintaining digital infrastructure with the advancement in technology, security and privacy of individual details would be crucial challenge for the concern authority. The digital divide [15] can affect the quality aspects of service accessibility and usability. The digital divide is a relative concept measuring the gap in access and use of ICT systems between individuals, groups and countries [4]. The government should take some initiatives to reduce digital divide among the citizens. The use of digital address would vary on age of citizens, geography, education level, language and physical disability of the citizens. The facility to write address and displaying address in Indian local languages must be required to make the complete use of digital address system to highlights the transformative impact in citizens' life through digitalization. In the present study, we have not included details of a recipient like name, mobile number as we can see in current address system in India. To identify the recipient, the study has suggested to link address with aadhaar database. This would increase the complexity at digital infrastructure level. But by integrating this, a verified personal details and valid address will enhance the faster service delivery to the citizens. In future, a more holistic and generalized digital address system could be designed to make India a digitally empowered country in a real sense.

References

1. Alawneh, A., Al-Refai, H., Batiha, K.: Measuring user satisfaction from e-Government services: lessons from Jordan. Gov. Inf. Q. 30(3), 277–288 (2013)
2. Ayanso, A., Lertwachara, K.: An analytics approach to exploring the link between ICT development and affordability. Gov. Inf. Q. 32(4), 389–398 (2015)
3. Belanche, D., Casaló, L.V., Orús, C.: City attachment and use of urban services: benefits for smart cities. Cities 50, 75–81 (2016)
4. Brännström, I.: Gender and digital divide 2000–2008 in two low-income economies in Sub-Saharan Africa: Kenya and Somalia in official statistics. Gov. Inf. Q. 29(1), 60–67 (2012)

5. Gupta, M.P., Jana, D.: E-government evaluation: a framework and case study. Gov. Inf. Q. **20**(4), 365–387 (2003)

6. Infrastructure, G.S.D.: Street Addressing Standards and Guidelines for the State of Georgia (2000)

7. Jaeger, P.T.: The endless wire: e-government as global phenomenon. Gov. Inf. Q. **20**(4), 323–331 (2003)

8. Janowski, T.: Digital government evolution: from transformation to contextualization. Gov. Inf. Q. **32**(3), 221–236 (2015)

9. Jung, T.H., Lee, J., Yap, M.H., Ineson, E.M.: The role of stakeholder collaboration in culture-led urban regeneration: a case study of the Gwangju project, Korea. Cities **44**, 29–39 (2015)

10. Khalil, O.E.: e-Government readiness: does national culture matter? Gov. Inf. Q. **28**(3), 388–399 (2011)

11. King, S., Cotterill, S.: Transformational government? The role of information technology in delivering citizen-centric local public services. Local Gov. Stud. **33**(3), 333–354 (2007)

12. Lee, H., Irani, Z., Osman, I.H., Balci, A., Ozkan, S., Medeni, T.D.: Research note: toward a reference process model for citizen-oriented evaluation of e-government services. Transforming Gov. People Process Policy **2**(4), 297–310 (2008)

13. Linders, D.: From e-government to we-government: defining a typology for citizen coproduction in the age of social media. Gov. Inf. Q. **29**(4), 446–454 (2012)

14. Miles, S., Paddison, R.: Introduction: the rise and rise of culture-led urban regeneration. Urban Stud. **42**(5–6), 833–839 (2005)

15. Mutula, S.M.: Digital divide and economic development: case study of sub-Saharan Africa. Electron. Libr. **26**(4), 468–489 (2008)

16. Nagabhushan, P., Angadi, S.A., Anami, B.S.: A knowledge based fast PIN code validation system for dispatch sorting of postal mail. In: International Conference on Cognitive systems New Delhi, 14th and 15th December (2004)

17. Neirotti, P., De Marco, A., Cagliano, A.C., Mangano, G., Scorrano, F.: Current trends in Smart City initiatives: some stylised facts. Cities **38**, 25–36 (2014)

18. Van Duin, J.H.R., de Goffau, W., Wiegmans, B., Tavasszy, L.A., Saes, M.: Improving home delivery efficiency by using principles of address intelligence for B2C deliveries. Transp. Res. Procedia **12**, 14–25 (2016)

19. Zhong, S.: Artists and Shanghai's culture-led urban regeneration. Cities **56**, 165–171 (2015)

Multi-homing and Software Firm Performance

Towards a Research Agenda

Sami Hyrynsalmi[1]([✉]) [iD], Matti Mäntymäki[2] [iD], and Aaron W. Baur[3]

[1] Tampere University of Technology, Pori, Finland
sami.hyrynsalmi@tut.fi
[2] Turku School of Economics, University of Turku, Turku, Finland
matti.mantymatki@tse.fi
[3] ESCP Europe Business School Berlin, Berlin, Germany
abaur@escpeurope.eu

Abstract. Joining or leaving a platform ecosystem is a key strategic decision for software developers. *'Multi-homing'* is strategy in which a company distributes its products via more than one platform ecosystem in parallel. *'Single-homing'* is an opposite strategy in which the software is being distributed exclusively via a single platform ecosystem. On one hand, multi-homing can increase customer reach in markets where customers typically single-home. On the other hand, creating a new version of the software product for multi-homing purposes generates, e.g., conversion, maintenance, and marketing cost. Interestingly, multi-homing as a strategic choice in software business has thus far have received surprisingly little academic scrutiny. In particular, there is very little information on whether multi-homing is an economically viable distribution strategy. To fill in this void, we explore the financial performance between single-homers and multi-homers in mobile application ecosystems. We investigate how the decision to multi-home affects firm performance with a sample of mobile application developers. The results imply that the revenue growth has been faster among single-homers while our dataset is biased towards single-homers. This calls for additional research comparing the two distribution strategies. This paper acts as a starting point for a research agenda in order to better understand multi-homing a strategic choice in software business.

Keywords: Multi-homing · Platforms · Software ecosystems · Strategic management · Two-sided markets

1 Introduction

Ecosystems and platforms are nowadays core building blocks of business [16]. Whereas terminology in this field is not yet stabilized and some terms are used interchangeably [c.f. 11, 23], we follow the view that a technological *platform* is a core of an *ecosystem* that enables its formation [5]. An ecosystem itself consists of a platform and its owner, as well as from complements and their providers, and from customers [8]. Well-known

A.K. Kar et al. (Eds.): I3E 2017, LNCS 10595, pp. 442–452, 2017.
DOI: 10.1007/978-3-319-68557-1_39

examples of such ecosystems include marketplace-centred mobile application ecosystems (e.g., Apple's App Store for iOS devices and Google Play for Android operating system devices).

As ecosystems and platforms have become a major distribution channels in software business [14], the decision to single-home or multi-home is a key strategic decision for a large number of software companies. In economic theory, *multi-homing* refers to participating more than one competing marketplace in parallel [20]. In today's software development and software business, multi-homing typically means distributing a product via more than one competing platforms such as Android and iOS at the same time whereas *single-homing* refers to distribution the product via only one platform [4].

As ecosystems typically have entry barriers [19], a multi-homing strategy incurs costs to the software developer. In software ecosystems, typical entry barriers are fees for participation, ecosystem-specific development tools that are not interchangeable or specific skills needed. For example, Google Play features a 25 USD registration fee and an official development tool is Android software development kit (SDK). For App Store, a membership is 99 USD and the official tool is iOS SDK. The iOS SDK and Android SDK are not cross-compatible.

While nowadays there are tools that reduce the costs of cross-platform software development such as Apache Cordova and Titanium [1, 6], multi-homing always generates some additional costs related to e.g. development, maintenance, product management and marketing of a new platform-specific version. Thus, the decision to multi-home a firm's products to more than one ecosystem requires careful balancing between the potential for gaining a larger market share [22] as well as reducing dependency on a single ecosystem orchestrator [15] against to the increased costs [7].

Against this backdrop, it is surprising that the outcomes of adopting a multi-homing vs. single-homing strategy in terms of software developer's performance remains largely opaque in software business literature [8]. Most of the extant literature on multi-homing focuses on the ecosystem level analysis while company-investigations of multi-homing as a strategic distribution choice and its outcomes on firm performance remain largely absent. However, choosing between multi-homing and single-homing is a strategic decision for practically any independent software vendor.

As a result, we put forward a fundamental question for software developers: *Does it pay off to multi-home?*

To shed light into this looming, yet thus far unanswered question, we sampled a set of 10,000 mobile application developers from Apple's App Store, Google Play and Microsoft's Windows Phone Store. We then investigated their product offerings to identify the companies that multi-home and acquired their financial information from the ORBIS database. Finally, we compare the turnover growths of 812 mobile application vendors to detect if multi-homing pays off or not.

The remainder of the paper is structured as follows. In the second section, we present an overview of prior research on multi-homing in software business. In Sect. 3, we describe the research approach and data collection, followed by the results in the fourth section. In Sect. 5, we discuss the findings, unveil the limitations and put forward suggestion for future research.

2 Multi-homing in Software Platforms

Multi-homing can have a profound effect on platform competition dynamics and thus ultimately the very structure of the entire market [5, 7, 9, 20–22, 24]. With respect to software platforms, in presence of several competing platforms the structure of the market depends on multi-homing patterns of application developers [22]. According to Sun and Tse [22], extensive multi-homing among application developers enables competition between platforms whereas single-homing eventually turns the market towards a single dominant ecosystem.

Landsman and Stremersch [18] in turn studied multi-homing in the gaming console market. They showed that initially a multi-homing strategy hurts the sales of the hardware consoles but this effect fades away when the ecosystem ages. Landsman and Stremersch [18] further divided multi-homing into two different categories: (1) *Seller-level* multi-homing that refers to a situation where the same producer, e.g. application developer works for several ecosystems. (2) *Platform-level* multi-homing refers to a situation where a developer, or someone else, distributes the same product via several ecosystems.

While the two forms of multi-homing are likely to be correlated, it is also possible that a developer offers different products to different ecosystems — or different developers offer a certain product to different ecosystems. As an example of the latter, the Facebook apps in Google Play and Apple Store were developed by Facebook whereas the Facebook app in Windows Store was developed and published by Microsoft a few year ago.

According to Hyrynsalmi et al. [10], the overall number of multi-homing is small in mobile application markets. However, the most popular applications are available in all competing ecosystems and the producers of these applications largely multi-home [14]. Hyrynsalmi et al. [14] describe this situation as a multi-level two-sided market to underscore the difference between the level of multi-homing in general and multi-homing among the most popular applications.

Despite the theoretical contributions to the areas, empirical studies 1 assessment remains low. Idu et al. [15] analysed multi-homing inside Apple's three different subecosystems. The found 17.2% platform-level multi-homing in their set of 1,800 mobile applications. In their empirical analysis of multi-homing in the three leading (Android, iOS, and Windows Phone) mobile application ecosystems, Hyrynsalmi et al. [14] found that only 1.7–3.2% of all applications (i.e. platform-level) and 5.8–7.2% all developers (i.e., seller-level) in the three mobile application operating systems were multi-homing. Interestingly, however, from the most popular applications 41–58% were multi-homing. Similarly, 42–69% of the keystone developers, i.e. producers of the most popular applications, were multi-homing.

Whereas the multi-homing rate is a significantly higher than one showed by Hyrynsalmi et al. [14] it is worth of noting that entry barrier into a different sub-ecosystem inside Apple's ecosystem is lower (e.g., development tools are same). Furthermore, it should be noted that there are numerous different Android devices while Apple has only a limited number of different iOS phone and tablet versions. In addition, for a comparison, Burkard et al. [3] studied popularity of multi-homing strategy in SaaS business solutions market. They found only 70 multi-homers (ca. 3.5%) in their dataset of over two thousand software vendors.

Nevertheless, the surveys on the popularity of multi-homing strategy shows that often only a small part has adopted the publication strategy. However, it seems that number of adopters are rising. For example, when the results of Hyrynsalmi et al. [14] and Idu et al. [15] are compared against Boudreau's [2] results, who found less than 1% overall multi-homing rate, a decade earlier in the mobile application markets, a clear growth in the number of multi-homing strategy adopters can be seen. This might be a result of either the growth of mobile application market's value [c.f. 8], the development of technological tools for multi-homing [c.f. 1] or due to a wider understanding of the platform economy and its rules [c.f. 16].

A number of studies addressing the impacts of multi-homing to a single software company are low. To the best of the authors' knowledge, only one prior study has examined this topic. In a cross-segment approach, Hyrynsalmi et al. [12] analysed multi-homing of Finnish computer game companies. In their study, they included all game companies ranging from mobile game and social media add-ons to AAA class video game developers. Out of the 208 active game companies, they found that a majority (54.8%) were multi-homers. However, they did not found any major differences between multi-homers' and single-homers' financial performances.

To summarize, a clear majority of existing work focuses on a market-level analysis and on the impacts of multi-homing to a market as a whole [e.g. 5, 18, 22]. However, there is a dearth of studies addressing *how* multi-homing affects to individual companies. While there are arguments for and against of using multi-homing publishing strategy [7, 14, 15] and importance of multi-homing to development of whole market [5, 7, 22], it is surprising that there is a little empirical evidence whether is worth or not, for a single developer to multi-home.

Therefore, this study focuses on this question and aims to uncover are there quantitative evidence that multi-homing would be a better choice for a single developer than single-homing strategy. We select mobile application ecosystems as the case environment as it is currently a swiftly developing market with multiple different, non-compatible among each other, operating systems. Furthermore, there is a plethora of application developers, small as well as big ones, joined in the market. Thus, there is a potentially rich information available in the domain.

3   Empirical Research

In this study, we focus on the question whether it pay off or not to multi-home. We chose revenue growth of our focal indicator of the financial viability of multi-homing *vs.* single-homing. As multi-homing increases the number of potential customers, it should lead to increasing revenues compared to single-homing. As an example, Gartner's latest report[1] states that in the last quarter of 2016, 81.7% of the new smart phones were using Android operating system and 17.9% were using iOS devices. Despite this, it is reported

---

[1] Gartner Says Worldwide Sales of Smartphones Grew 7 Percent in the Fourth Quarter of 2016. http://www.gartner.com/newsroom/id/3609817 Accessed May 5th, 2017.

that applications in the Apple's App Store are generating higher revenue than the ones in Google Play store[2],[3]. Thus, for a mobile application developer gain the largest audience, he should select the Android operating system whereas it is likely that higher revenue is generated in Apple's App Store.

Revenue growth as an indicator does not take into account the increased costs associated to multi-homing. However, as obtaining information about these costs from financial statements is practically impossible, we concluded that revenue growth is an appropriate measure to extrapolate the pay-off of multi-homing.

In this study, we utilized a simple three-steps research process illustrated in Fig. 1. In the first step, to gather the starting data, we employed a web crawler that collected a sample 10,000 mobile application vendors from three mobile application marketplaces, Google Play, Apple's AppStore and Windows Phone Store. From each vendor, we collected the name that the vendor used to presents itself in the marketplace and the number of applications the vendor has published in that marketplace. We then manually double-checked the data and e.g. in case of slightly different names between the marketplaces matched the data. The dataset and the multi-homing information was collected in the beginning of 2013.

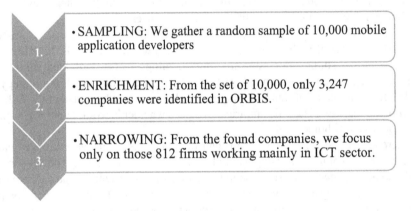

Fig. 1. The process flow of research in this study.

In the second step, to acquire financial information regarding the vendors, we used the ORBIS financial information database by Bureau van Dijk. The ORBIS database contains financial information on over 200 million companies globally. We uploaded the list of 10,000 software vendor names for the batch search and used the database's matching logic to identify corresponding companies. As the database allows selecting between various levels of matching accuracy, to maximize the quality of our data, we decided to only accepted matches where the matching quality was given the highest 'A'.

[2] App Annie 2015 Retrospective. http://go.appannie.com/report-app-annie-2015-retrospective Accessed May 5th, 2017.
[3] App Annie 2016 Retrospective. http://go.appannie.com/app-annie-2016-retrospective Accessed May 5th, 2017.

From the 10,000 software vendor names in our query, a match was found for 3,247 (32.5%). As the mobile application developers are known to be a rather heterogeneous set ranging from commercial developers with financial interests to hobbyist and non-profit organizations [13], it was expected that only a minority of the developers would have founded and registered a company for collecting the income and paying taxes from the applications sales.

Our subscription of ORBIS did not cover financial information of 34 companies, and thus those were excluded from performance analyses. From the identified 3,247 companies, there were companies and organizations from various fields. For example, we found several European airports multi-homing, i.e. providing their apps via all marketplaces.

For all companies, we acquired operating revenue information from the years 2013, 2014 and 2015. Naturally, only for a few companies the financial information of the year 2016 have been registered; thus, this year is omitted. The financial performance is studied through the growth of a company's revenue from the year 2013 to 2014 and 2015. We use three intervals for measuring the performance growth. The reason is that the impact of multi-homing in the revenue of the company might take more than a year. The starting point is 2013 as the multi-homing information of the year 2013 was acquired from the marketplaces.

In the third step of the process, to focus deliberately on companies that are in software business, we added a further constraint to narrow down our results to companies that have defined 'Information and Communication' as their main business domain classification. We thereafter omitted companies with missing revenue information. The final set of ICT companies consisted of 538 companies.

4   Results

The identified 3,247 companies are from various fields as shown in Fig. 2. The largest sections in our dataset are *'Information and Communication'* (808 firms, 30% of all), *'Wholesale and retail trade'* (440, 16%), and *'Professional, scientific and technical activities'* (387, 14%). For 200 companies, no information was stored in under the field 'NACE Rev. 2 main section'. The companies are from 39 different countries while Great Britain, France, Italy and Germany being the biggest country of origin.

The financial indicators are infrequently reported to the database. For example, it is quite common in the dataset that a company might not have any financial indicators stored for a certain year whereas they are available for previous and next years. For example, our full dataset contains financial information of over 3,200 companies. From those, only 1,102 companies have revenue information available for the years 2013 and 2014. Thus, in the forthcoming performance analysis, the number of companies used in each analysis varies.

The average turnover growths for the studied firms are shown in Table 1. When looking our sample of companies as a whole, the average revenue growth rate from 2013 to 2014 was 80 per cent and 2014 to 2015 it was 79 per cent. At the same, the companies in the ICT field growth averagely only 54% and 13%.

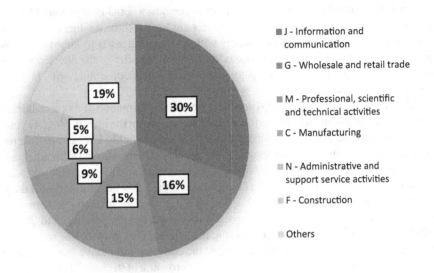

Fig. 2. Distribution of studied companies NACE Rev 2. classifications.

Table 1. Average turnover growths and the size of sample

Strategy	2013–2014	(n)	2014–2015	(n)	2013–2015	(n)
All companies	80%	(1,102)	79%	(881)	118%	(836)
Single-homing	86%	(1,008)	85%	(806)	126%	(763)
Multi-homing	14%	(94)	11%	(75)	39%	(73)
Information and Communication field	54%	(304)	13%	(244)	57%	(229)
Single-homing	59%	(271)	14%	(218)	51%	(205)
Multi-homing	14%	(33)	1%	(26)	26%	(24)

We identified 209 (6.4%) companies multi-homing in our set. Out of those, 78 were classified as ICT companies (i.e. belonging NACE Rev. 2 class 'J – Information and communication') and 131 into other fields. Thus, 9.6% of ICT companies are multi-homing whereas only 6.2% of non-ICT companies are multi-homers. While ICT companies are more keen to multi-home based than non-ICT companies, the multi-homing rates still remain low.

In the final step of the analysis, we focused on the performance of ICT companies. In this, we excluded non-ICT companies as there are likely more factors explaining their growth of revenue than decision to publish multi-homed application. Thus, here we focus on the 812 companies belonging into 'Information and communication' category.

Interestingly, and contrary to our assumptions, the results imply that single-homing ICT companies had stronger growth rates than multi-homers (59% vs. 14% in 2013–2014, 14% vs. 1% in 2014–2015, and 51% vs. 26% in 2013–2015) as depicted in Table 1. While the number of multi-homers remain small in each studied set, they are growing considerably slower than single-homers. The similar phenomenon can be seen also by looking the average growths of all companies – here also single-homing companies outperform multi-homing companies with a reasonable big margin.

To summarize, as Table 1 shows the turnover growth is faster among single-homers than multi-homers during the studied periods. However, the final sample was heavily biased towards single-homers as less than ten per cent of the companies are multi-homing. Furthermore, due the sparse availability of financial information, the number of multi-homing ICT-companies remain remarkable low. This largely inhibits drawing far-reaching conclusions from the data.

5   Discussion

In the following, we will first discuss on the implications of this study. It is followed by a discussion of limitations and some ideas for future work.

5.1   Implications

This study was motivated to shed some empirical light on a key question in software business *does it pay off to multi-home?* To this end, we concluded an extensive empirical study to identify relevant companies and used the ORBIS financial information database of obtain the relevant financial figures.

While multi-homing is generally considered a desirable strategic choice in prior software business literature [14], based on the findings from this study, we cannot empirically corroborate, or reject, this notion. While our initial results show that single-homers are performing better in the terms of revenue growth, the number of multi-homing companies, with financial information, included into the sample remain too low to draw a statistically reasonable conclusion.

We started by hypothesizing that multi-homing would incur more cost due to the entry barriers as well as the need of maintaining alternative versions. However, a larger potential buyer population would ultimately payback the investments. Our initial results support these hypotheses only weakly, if at all, as the single-homers are collecting remarkably better revenues. In other words, based on this analysis, it seems that multi-homing does not pay off. However, due to the missing financial information and dominance of single-homing companies in our dataset, far-reaching decision cannot be made.

Yet our ultimate research question remains unanswered, our approach in empirically investigating issue is nevertheless a definite contribution to software business literature [c.f. 8, 15] by setting forward the research agenda towards a better understanding of multi-homing as a strategic choice in software business. To this end, our study clearly demonstrates that relying on publically available financial information as the only source of data is not a sufficient approach to investigate the bottom-line financial effect of multi-homing.

From a practice-oriented perspective, while the effect of multi-homing on turnover development remains unanswered, multi-homing remains a viable strategy to reduce software developers' dependency on a single client platform. Hence, the decision whether to multi-home or not is not solely a matter of maximizing revenue but essentially about managing risks.

5.2   Limitations and Future Research

Like any other piece of empirical research, our study is subject to a number of limitations. First of all, it is evident that our current data is by no means sufficient to provide answer to a pivotal research question such as the one posed in this study. Thus, we strictly advice against drawing far-reaching conclusions from the present study. There are two main reasons for this: (1) Publicly available financial information has remarkable amount of missing fields for all companies, and (2) partially due to the previous reason, the number of multi-homers with reported performance measures remained low for a statistically significant analysis.

As a result, additional research with a new data collection is needed. Furthermore, due to the limitations of the current dataset and the exploratory stance of the study, further studies in the area should control for the potential confounding effects of the various factors that may influence growth rates to meaningfully isolate the potential influence of multi-homing. Nevertheless, we demonstrated a decent sampling strategy for a selection of mobile application vendors that can be turn out to be useful for other kinds of studies.

Alternative option would be to change the research stance from quantitative analysis towards a qualitative work. As this study presents, finding statistically relevant results might be problematic (e.g., the selection of performance measures), thus a qualitative case study on multi-homing and single-homing companies could create a better picture of the benefits and drawbacks of multi-homing publishing strategy.

Finally, in future work, also the type of the market or apps should be reconsidered as they might also play a role in the performance analyses. For example, the console gaming market is mature and relationships within the ecosystem are more complex than in the mobile application markets. Several games are exclusively published for a certain console and only after a delay of months, they are ported to the other consoles. Furthermore, the development of freemium mobile games features its unique characteristics [cf. 17]. Thus incorporating a wider selection of different markets and ecosystems would be an advisable course for future research.

6   Conclusion

The purpose of the paper was to be a starting point for a research agenda in order to better understand multi-homing as a strategic choice in software business. The market tendency either towards multi-homing or single-homing has been linked in the extant theories on the future development of the whole market. However, only little has been research on the impact of multi-homing to companies.

We performed a quantitatively study of over 3,200 companies that had published a mobile application. Single-homing companies (93.6% of all) dominate the set. While only a small amount of them were found to be multi-homers, it seemed that on average single-homers are performing better than multi-homers. However, due to the small amount of multi-homing companies with available financial information, we advice against of doing far-reaching decisions based on this. Nevertheless, this is among to first to address the question do multi-homing pay off to the companies.

References

1. Ahti, V., Hyrynsalmi, S., Nevalainen, O.: An evaluation framework for cross-platform mobile app development tools: a case analysis of Adobe PhoneGap framework. In: Rachev, B., Tegolo, D., Kalmukov, Y., Smrikarova, S., Smrikarov, A. (eds.) Proceedings of the 17th International Conference on Computer Systems and Technologies 2016, pp. 41–48 (2016)
2. Boudreau, K.: Too many complementors? Evidence on software developers. Technical report hal-00597766, HEC-Paris School of Management (2007). https://hal-hec.archives-ouvertes.fr/hal-00597766
3. Burkard, C., Widjaja, T., Buxmann, P.: Software ecosystems. Bus. Inf. Syst. Eng. **4**(1), 41–44 (2012)
4. Caillaud, B., Jullien, B.: Chicken & egg: competition among intermediation service providers. RAND J. Econ. **34**(2), 309–328 (2003)
5. Cusumano, M.A.: Staying Power: Six Enduring Principles for Managing Strategy and Innovation in an Uncertain World (Lessons from Microsoft, Apple, Intel, Google, Toyota and More). Oxford University Press, Oxford (2010)
6. Dhillon, S., Mahmoud, Q.H.: An evaluation framework for cross-platform mobile application development tools. Softw. Pract. Exp. **45**(10), 1331–1357 (2015)
7. Eisenmann, T., Parker, G., Van Alstyne, M.W.: Strategies for two-sided markets. Harvard Bus. Rev. **84**(10), 92–101 (2006)
8. Hyrynsalmi, S.:. Letters from the war of ecosystems — an analysis of independent software vendors in mobile application marketplaces. TUCS Dissertations No 188. University of Turku, Turku, Finland (2014)
9. Hyrynsalmi, S., Linna, P.: The role of applications and their vendors in evolution of software ecosystems. In: Biljanovic, P. (ed.) Proceedings of the 40th International Convention on Information and Communication Technology, Electronics and Microelectronics, pp. 1686–1691. IEEE (2017)
10. Hyrynsalmi, S., Mäkilä, T., Järvi, A., Suominen, A., Seppänen, M., Knuutila, T.: App Store, Marketplace, Play! an analysis of multi-homing in mobile software ecosystems. In: Jansen, S., Bosch, J., Alves, C. (eds.) Proceedings of the Fourth International Workshops on Software Ecosystems, CEUR Workshop Proceedings, CEUR-WS, vol. 879, pp. 59–72 (2012)
11. Hyrynsalmi, S., Seppänen, M., Nokkala, T., Suominen, A., Järvi, A.: Wealthy, healthy and/or happy — what does 'ecosystem health' stand for? In: Fernandes, J.M., Machado, R.J., Wnuk, K. (eds.) ICSOB 2015. LNBIP, vol. 210, pp. 272–287. Springer, Cham (2015). doi: 10.1007/978-3-319-19593-3_24
12. Hyrynsalmi, S., Suominen, A., Jansen, S., Yrjönkoski, K.: Multi-homing in ecosystems and firm performance: does it improve software companies' ROA? In: IWSECO 2016 – Proceedings of the International Workshop on Software Ecosystems, CEUR Workshop Proceedings, CEUR-WS, vol. 1808, pp. 56–69 (2016)
13. Hyrynsalmi, S., Suominen, A., Mäkilä, T., Järvi, A., Knuutila, T.: Revenue models of application developers in android market ecosystem. In: Cusumano, M.A., Iyer, B., Venkatraman, N. (eds.) ICSOB 2012. LNBIP, vol. 114, pp. 209–222. Springer, Heidelberg (2012). doi:10.1007/978-3-642-30746-1_17

14. Hyrynsalmi, S., Suominen, A., Mäntymäki, M.: The influence of developer multi-homing on competition between software ecosystems. J. Syst. Softw. **111**, 119–127 (2016)
15. Idu, A., van de Zande, T., Jansen, S.: Multi-homing in the Apple ecosystem: why and how developers target multiple Apple App Stores. In: Proceedings of the International Conference on Management of Emergent Digital EcoSystems, pp. 122–128. ACM, New York (2011)
16. Kenney, M., Zysman, J.: The rise of the platform economy. Issues Sci. Technol. **32**(3), 61–69 (2016)
17. Koskenvoima, A., Mäntymäki, M.: Why do small and medium-size freemium game developers use game analytics? In: Janssen, M., Mäntymäki, M., Hidders, J., Klievink, B., Lamersdorf, W., van Loenen, B., Zuiderwijk, A. (eds.) I3E 2015. LNCS, vol. 9373, pp. 326–337. Springer, Cham (2015). doi:10.1007/978-3-319-25013-7_26
18. Landsman, V., Stremersch, S.: Multi-homing in two-sided markets: an empirical inquiry in the video game console industry. J. Mark. **75**(6), 39–54 (2011)
19. McAfee, P., Mialon, H.M., Williams, M.A.: What is a barrier to entry? Am. Econ. Rev. **94**(2), 461–465 (2004)
20. Rochet, J.C., Tirole, J.: Platform competition in two-sided markets. J. Eur. Econ. Assoc. **1**(4), 990–1029 (2003)
21. Rochet, J.C., Tirole, J.: Two-sided markets: a progress report. RAND J. Econ. **37**(3), 645–667 (2006)
22. Sun, M., Tse, E.: When does the winner take all in two-sided markets? Rev. Netw. Econ. **6**(1), 16–40 (2007)
23. Suominen, A., Hyrynsalmi, S., Seppänen, M.: Ecosystems here, there, and everywhere. In: Maglyas, A., Lamprecht, A.-L. (eds.) Software Business. LNBIP, vol. 240, pp. 32–46. Springer, Cham (2016). doi:10.1007/978-3-319-40515-5_3
24. Teixeira, J., Hyrynsalmi, S.: How do software ecosystems co-evolve? A view from OpenStack and beyond. In: Ojala, A. (ed.) Software Business: 8th International Conference, ICSOB 2017, pp. 1–15. Springer, Cham (2017)

Paradigm Shift of Indian Cash-Based Economy to Cash-Less Economy: A Study on Allahabad City

G.P. Sahu and Naveen Kumar Singh[(✉)]

Motilal Nehru National Institute of Technology, Allahabad, India
gsahu@mnnit.ac.in, rajput.naveen07@gmail.com

Abstract. This paper is an attempt to study the important factors responsible for successful implementation of digital payment (e-Payment) system in India. Examine the status of e-Payment at Allahabad city (Uttar Pradesh, Indian) and to conduct an analysis of imitation of e-Payment in other regions of India. A qualitative study with extensive literature review, interview and expert opinion was adopted to conduct the study. To analyse the result and to identify the success factor NVivo 11 Pro software is used. With the help of software 13 success factors identify namely: Anonymity, Bank Involvement, Drawer, Infrastructure, Mobility, Parties, Popularity, Range of Payment, Risk, Security, Transfer limit, Transfer mode, and Transfer time for successful implementation of digital payment at Allahabad city. The outcome will be helpful for implementation of digital payment in various other cities of India.

Keywords: Digital payment · NVivo 11 Pro · Cashless economy · Cashbased economy · Demonetisation

1 Introduction

Government of India declared demonetisation as a "Shock Therapy" on 8th November 2016. Government ceased the legal tender of 500 and 1000 currency notes and launched new 2000 and 500 rupee notes in circulation. With this step of demonetization, India lost 86% of its monetary base [15]. The total value of old currency notes of Rs. 500 and Rs. 1000 in the circulation is to the tune of Rs. 14.2 trillion, which is about 85 per cent of total value of circulated currency in the country [11]. After demonetization the currency now pass through the formal banking channel to get legality. From the market perspective this is a welcome move by the Indian government. Government of India tackled issues which affected the economy like, parallel economy, tax evasion, counterfeit currency in circulation and terror financing [15].

The outlook for cashless economy appears highly controversial and unsettled in India. E-payment defines as, any exchange of funds initiated via an electronic communication channel [26] or a payment made through electronic signals linked directly to deposit or credit accounts [9]. E-payment represents any kind of non-cash payment that does not involve a paper cheque [14]. A cashless economy is one in which currency notes are not used as a medium of transaction [19]. It is a hypothetical stage or situation

© IFIP International Federation for Information Processing 2017
Published by Springer International Publishing AG 2017. All Rights Reserved
A.K. Kar et al. (Eds.): I3E 2017, LNCS 10595, pp. 453–461, 2017.
DOI: 10.1007/978-3-319-68557-1_40

in favour of alternative means of exchange. All the transactions are done through cards, wallets, or digital medium with minimal physical circulation of currency. In other terms, cashless economy can be defined as a situation in which the flow of cash within the economy become zero and all the transactions must be through electronic means like, credit cards, debit cards, money wallets, IMPS, RTGS, NEFT etc.

> "Non-cash payments are not accomplished merely by exchanging the payment instrument between payer and payee, but transferring deposit money between the payer's bank and the payee's bank. Non-cash payment instruments provide the mechanism for this bank-to-bank transfer. Non-cash payment instruments, such as cheques, NEFT, RTGS, must specify the payment amount, the names of the payer and the payee and their banks."
>
> – World Bank

The primary objective of this study is to identify factors influencing successful implementation of digital payment in India. An extensive literature review, interview and expert opinion have been conducted to identify the success factors of digital payment. Using NVivo 11 Pro software 13 success factors were recognized and validated namely: Anonymity, Bank Involvement, Drawer, Infrastructure, Mobility, Parties, Popularity, Range of Payment, Risk, Security, Transfer limit, Transfer mode, and Transfer time. This study will helpful in implementation of digital payment in other region of India. As well as this will help the researches to their studies on digital payment.

1.1   The Payment Environment – An Overview

A report of The Boston Consulting Group [25] estimates that, consumer are 90% likely to use digital payments for offline and online transactions, and around 60% of the total value of such payments will come from offline merchants such as unorganised retailers, fast food corners and transport. Moving against backdrop of, overflow of currency, and black money in the country; the adoption of electronic payment channels that include cards, ATMs, POS terminals, mobile phones and Internet flow the secure, convenient and cheapest transactions that are not only provide the transparency but also provide the easy way for global transaction. Payment system is one of the substantial changes policies in all over the world. Initially, trading through barter system was common, a system where people exchange their livestock from food, crop or goods [1]. But the present concept of cashless economy is completely different; here the cashless transactions are made through digital currencies. Cashless banking strengthens monetary policy effectiveness and that the current level of e-money usage does not pose an intimidation to the stability of the financial system [21].

Cashless Transactions system was introduced in the 1950s and now become the essential form of "ready money", which reduces the risk of cash handling, theft by pickpocket etc. During 1990's, the growing popularity of e-banking made the use of cashless transactions popular among the technologically advanced countries. In 2010 the digital payment methods became well established in most of the countries across the world. Internet banking is eminent example of IT in the service industry; it is convenient and time saving in comparison to traditional banking [30]. Earlier, online tools like Paypal, NFC payments by smartphone or electronic cards, digital wallet system operated by Apple, electronic banking and bill payment system helped the users towards cashless transactions online. There were different types of payment systems exist before the emergence of modern banking system in India [25]. Banking operations was done through manually, which lead to slow transactions. This system involves "Book-Keeping", i.e., posting of transactions from one ledger to another ledger manually without using any machine. Computer and electronic machines was used for figure or counting of money. It takes a lot of time and effort to do manually work. Banks having more than one computer are like "triton among the minnows" and that single computer helps to improve the crawling working condition. A local study [4] mentioned that, "Payment through cash is an expensive proposition for government". There are many factors which influence users to adopt technology [5], and two factors are important in these factor. First, "utility", in which people are likely to use or not use an application to the extent they believe it will help them to perform their job better. Second, "convenient", in which people perceive that if the technology is too hard to use, they likely not to adopt and not to use it even though they believe that the technology is useful.

Advantages of a Cashless Economy

The foremost advantage of having no cash is to reduce the use of paper, cost, elimination of carrying and managing problem etc. A Study by Hirschman [13] used focus groups to identify 11 payment characteristics salient to the preference and usage of payment instruments. Such included budgeting, control of spending, documentation, reversibility, transaction record, acceptability, leverage potential, transaction time, security, social desirability/prestige, and transfer time. Central bank in the Netherlands identified four overarching payment system characteristics: safety (financial risk by using digital instrument), speed (time needed to complete the transaction), costs (that the consumer carries for the possession and actual use of a payment instrument), and ease of use (effort of consumer to complete the payment process with a electronic medium).

Challenges of Cashless Economy

Every reforms has some pros and cons, hence, there are few challenges to proposed cashless economy. Study [40] suggested that there are basic ICT literacy is necessary to enjoy the benefits of e-payment but cash and cheques will remain popular because consumers are not convinced of the benefits of using e-payment [12]. Prior adoption of IT had an identifiable impact because customers will usually adopt a new service only when they have similar experiences before [6]. A very high and unbreakable security system needed to secure the transactions from hackers and cyber criminals [3, 7, 8, 16, 18, 22–24, 29, 31–33, 35, 38]. The central bank of Malaysia [20] cites lack of awareness as one of the reasons why consumers are not using e-payment. Cashless economy won't be readily popular among the region where the people not much literate or aware.

However, till FY 2016-17, Indian government introduced lots of methods to digital payment like, Banking Cards (Debit/Credit/Cash/Travel/Other); Unstructured Supplementary Service Data (USSD); Aadhaar Enabled Payment System (AEPS); Unified Payments Interface (UPI); Mobile Wallet; Banks Pre-Paid Cards; Point of Sale (PoS); Internet Banking including, National Electronic Fund Transfer (NEFT), Real Time Gross Settlement (RTGS), Electronic Clearing System (ECS), Immediate Payment Service (IMPS); Mobile Banking; Micro ATMs. Very few literatures are available on factors affecting successful implementation and functionality of digital payment in India. This paper is an attempt to fill this gap with reference to Allahabad city and to conduct a feasibility analysis of imitation of digital payment on other cities and rural areas of India.

2 Research Methodology

To conduct the study a qualitative approach with in-depth literature review followed by interview and expert opinion through which comments/perceptions were recorded. The collected data were analyzed by using NVivo 11 Pro software (a qualitative software), which helps to provide systematize and order data with visual result. Nvivo facilitate careful and faithful qualitative research analysis [2, 10]. NVivo is Qualitative Data Analysis (QDA) application software developed by QSR International. NVivo not only help the researcher to managing and categorization of data according to the need and requirement of the researcher, but also it is convenient, efficient, effective and more user friendly in comparison to manual task for qualitative research [27]. NVivo 11 helps the researcher to visualise the result through cloud analysis, word tree map, node analysis etc. For primary data, vendors from Allahabad city and experts from Motilal Nehru National Institute of Technology (MNNIT) Allahabad has been interviewed and recorded for analysis using transcript command. On the other hand various journal, magazine, internet, newspaper etc. has been reviewed to collect secondary data. After-wards, with the help of coding process, both primary and secondary data imported to the NVivo 11 Pro software. With the help of coding process 13 success factors were analysed namely: Anonymity, Bank Involvement, Drawer, Infrastructure, Mobility, Parties, Popularity, Range of Payment, Risk, Security, Transfer limit, Transfer mode, and Transfer time for successful implementation of digital payment in India.

Case Study of Allahabad City

Allahabad is one of the member districts of "KAVAL towns" which are also known as "Panchpuri Nagar" (five biggest cities) of Uttar Pradesh. KAVAL towns include; Kanpur, Agra, Varanasi, Allahabad, and Lucknow. According to census 2011, the popu-lation of Allahabad is 5,954,391 which is highest population [42] out of total 71 districts of Uttar Pradesh. It is situated at the confluence (Sangam) of three rivers Ganga, Yamuna and the mythological Saraswati. Allahabad is known for academic ambience and pres-ently houses six national level Institutes/Universities. The literacy rate of Allahabad [42] is 72.32% which slightly lower than the literacy rate of India i.e. 74%. There are 125 bank branches (commercial & cooperative) and around 181 ATMs in Allahabad city. By interview of respondents it is observed that, shopkeepers are using cash as well as digital equipments for transaction. Some shopkeepers are using electronic devices/ digital equipments from long time, while some have started after demonetisation. Paytm, internet banking, card swipe machine etc. are the medium of digital transaction. Customers are also demand and encourage digital medium of transaction. However, they face various problems like, internet connectivity, lack of trust in online services, threat of online theft etc.

3   Analysis and Interpretation

Coding involves collecting all the material about a particular study in a node for further exploration. In this study the coding was carried out in 2 phases: first, Video and Audio recorded during the interview of expert and respondent, and second, literature review available as a secondary source of data. Coding process includes analyse of data with the help of "count" and "frequency of occurrence" of word from the data collected from primary and secondary source.

Number and Frequency Table

Following table shows the word frequency of occurrence under the different factors during the interview as well as in the literature review of the study.

From Table 1, it is evident that the factor like Infrastructure, transfer mode, risk and security are used maximum times and most commonly, whereas factors like drawer, parties, transfer limit, and bank involvement are used minimum and less commonly by the respondents.

Table 1.   Number of world count and frequency

Factors	Count	Weighted %
Anonymity	115	4.92
Bank involvement	58	2.48
Drawer	33	1.41
Infrastructure	572	24.48
Mobility	154	6.59
Parties	56	2.39
Popularity	176	7.53
Range of payment	65	2.78
Risk	271	11.6
Security	260	11.13
Transfer limit	57	2.44
Transfer mode	449	19.26
Transfer time	70	2.99

It may therefore be said that infrastructure is most concern part of digitalisation including, transfer mode, risk, and security. So the government need to more focus on the infrastructure of the system which includes, internet connectivity, methods of payment, availability of internet enabled phones, awareness and ICT literacy.

Bar Graph of Nodes

Bar graph shows the maximum and minimum count of the factors used by the respondent. Tallest plot shows the maximum repetition while shortest plot shows the minimum repetition of word.

From Fig. 1 it can be said that Infrastructure, transaction mode and risk are having higher range of codes and on other side Drawer, Parties and Range of Payment having less higher range of codes in the chart.

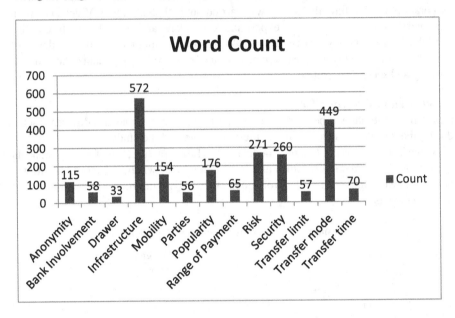

Fig. 1. Bar graph of nodes

4   Result and Discussion

With the help of number and frequency table and Bar Graph of Nodes, it is observed that Infrastructure [34], Security [3, 7, 8, 16, 18, 22–24, 29, 31–33, 35, 38] and Risk are the major factors of adoption of digital payment in Allahabad city. Subsequently, Awareness [40], Habit of use cash [12], ease of use [5, 17, 36, 37], cost effective [4, 39] are another factors, to implement the digital payment system in India. Without sufficient infrastructure, risk management and security solutions of digital payment, system could not be achieved the goal of study. Cashless system is not only requirement but also a need of the society [38]. The transformation from a cash-centric economy to electronic one would need more time and awareness; people should trust and have faith on the cashless system with [8]; ease to use [5, 17, 36, 37], minimal charges [4, 39], high level of security [18], and accessible to all [24]. Apart from the selected 13 factors, there are few more factors that respondent discussed like, government policies, market, type of card, type of mobile device, need and usage of e-payment system etc., but these factor were not included in the study because they were not important or marginally important than the others. There are multiple digital payment systems exist in the Indian market like, NEFT/RTGS, IMPS, Plastic money, Mobile banking, UPI, AEPS, BHIM, USSD, m-wallets [28]. In order to increase the penetration and popularity of an electronic payment system, government as well as non-government organisations need to alliances with other industries such as telecommunications, television, advertising agencies, financial and retail firm will be needed with regular awareness and synergy specially in rural and semi-urban areas. For internet connectivity government need to establish tower or internet connections in rural and semi-urban area of the country. Government provide awareness also, among the users through advertisement and awareness program.

5   Limitation and Conclusion

The study indentified 13 factors namely: Anonymity, Bank Involvement, Drawer, Infrastructure, Mobility, Parties, Popularity, Range of Payment, Risk, Security, Transfer limit, Transfer mode, and Transfer time for successful implementation of digital payment system at Allahabad city. It is also evident that the replication of digital payment system at other cities are possible after resolving few issues like, infrastructure, awareness, management of risk and security issues. There are some limitations with the study that, this is a city based analyses which is limited to Allahabad city only. Result may differ if large geographical area has been taken as sample area. Subsequently, the longitudinal study in terms of time as well as money may differ the result.

References

1. Achor, P.N., Robert, A.: Shifting policy paradigm from cash-based economy to cashless economy: the Nigeria experience. Afro Asian J. Soc. Sci. 4(4) (2013)
2. Andrade, A.D.: Interpretive research aiming at theory building: adopting and adapting the case study design. Qual. Rep. 14(1), 42–60 (2009). Retrieved from http://nsuworks.nova.edu/tqr/vol14/iss1/3/
3. Chellappa, R., Pavlou, P.: Perceived information security, financial liability and consumer trust in electronic commerce transactions. Logistics Inf. Manage. 15(5), 358–368 (2002)
4. Das, A., Agarwal, R.: Cashless Payment System in India- A Roadmap, Technical Report, Indian Institute of Technology Bombay, Department of Mathematics, Bombay (2010)
5. Davis, F.D.: Perceived usefulness, perceived ease of use, and user acceptance of information technology. MIS Q. 13(3), 319–340 (1989)
6. Eastin, M.J.: Diffusion of e-commerce: an analysis of the adoption of four ecommerce activities. Telematics Inform. 19(3), 251–267 (2002)
7. Fatimah, M.A., Kusairi, M.N., Mohd, F.A.: E-commerce adoption in Malaysia: Problems and barriers from the firms' perspective. In: Proceedings of International Conference on Electronic Commerce (2000)
8. Friedman, B., Kahn, P.H., Howe, D.C.: Trust online. Commun. ACM 43(12), 34–40 (2000)
9. Gans, J.S., Scheelings, R.: Economic Issues Associated with Access to Electronic Payment Systems (1999)
10. Ghauri, P.: Designing and conducting case studies in international business research. In: Handbook of Qualitative Research Methods for International Business, pp. 109–124 (2004)
11. Group, HDFC Bank Investment Advisory. Demonetization and Its Impact, Event Update (2016). Retrieved 11 Nov 2016. https://www.hdfcbank.com/assets/pdf/Event_Update_Demonetization_and_its_impact.pdf
12. Hataiseree, R.: Development of e-Payments and Challenges for Central Banks: Thailand's Recent Experience. In: Working Paper, pp. 1–53 (2008)

13. Hirschman, E.C.: Consumer payment systems: the relationship of attribute structure to preference and usage. J. Bus. **55**(4), 531–545 (1982)
14. Hord, J.: How Electronic Payment Works (2005)
15. INSIGHTS: The Big Picture- Impact of Demonetization, InsightsIAS (2016). Retrieved 11 Nov 2016. http://www.insightsonindia.com/2016/11/16/big-picture-impact-demonetization/
16. Kousaridas, A., Parissis, G., Apostolopoulos, T.: An open financial services architecture based on the use of intelligent mobile devices. Electron. Commer. Res. Appl. **7**(2), 232–246 (2008)
17. Legris, P., Ingham, J., Collerette, P.: Why do people use information technology? A critical review of the technology acceptance model. Inf. Manage. **40**(3), 191–204 (2003)
18. Linck, K., Pausttchi, K., Wiedemann, D.G.: Security issues in mobile payment from the customer viewpoint. In: Proceedings of the 14th European Conference on Information System (ECIS 2006), pp. 1–11 (2006)
19. Livemint: Making India a cashless economy (2016). Retrieved 2 Apr 2017. http://www.livemint.com/Opinion/XGbavEnoeP7dZITeh21MRM/Making-India-a-cashless-economy.html
20. Malaysia, C.B.: Payment and Settlement Systems Report (2009)
21. Marco, A., Bandiera, L.: Monetary Policy, Monetary Areas and Financial Development with Electronic Money. IMF Working Study, IMF (2004)
22. Johar, M.G.M., Ahmad, A.J.: The role of technology acceptance model in explaining effect on e-commerce application system. Int. J. Managing Inf. Technol. **3**(3), 1–14 (2011)
23. Oh, S., Kurnia, S., Johnston, R.B., Lee, H., Lim, B.: A stakeholder perspective on successful electronic payment systems diffusion. In: Proceeding of the Hawaii International Conference on Systems Sciences, (HICSS-39), Hawaii (2006)
24. Poon, W.C.: Users' Adoption of e-banking services: the Malaysian perspective. J. Bus. Industr. Mark. **23**(1), 59–69 (2008)
25. Shah, A., et al.: Digital Payments 2020: The Making of a $500 Billion Ecosystem in India. The Boston Consulting Group (2016)
26. Shon, T.H., Swatman, P.M.: Identifying effectiveness criteria for internet payment system. Internet Res. Electron. Netw. Appl. Policy **8**(3), 202–218 (1998)
27. Siccama, C.J., Penna, S.: Enhancing validity of a qualitative dissertation research study by using NVIVO. Qual. Res. J. **8**(2), 91–103 (2008)
28. Singh, S.: The Economic Times, Why Mobile Wallets will Die Lucknow, p. 14 (2017)
29. Singh, S.: Helping consumers realise the potential of the e-commerce revolution. In: Centre for International Research on Communication and Information Technologies (1998)
30. Siu, N.Y.M., Mou, J.C.W.: Measuring service quality in internet banking: the case of Hong Kong. J. Int. Consum. Mark. **17**(4), 99–116 (2005)
31. Streeter, W.: Could e-cash threaten payment integrity? Am. Bankers Assoc. (ABA) J. **89**(11), 58–68 (1997)
32. Stroborn, K., Heitmann, A., Leibold, K., Frank, G.: Internet payments in Germany: A classificatory framework and empirical evidence. J. Bus. Res. **57**(12), 1431–1437 (2004)
33. Sumanjeet, S.: Emergence of Payment System in the Age of Electronic Commerce: The State of Art (2009)
34. Tim Jones: The future of digital money. Eur. Bus. Rev. **99**(4), 261–264 (1999)
35. Tsiakis, T., Sthephanides, G.: The concept of security and trust in electronic payments. Comput. Secur. **24**(1), 10–15 (2005)
36. Venkatesh, V., Davis, F.D.: A theoretical extension of the technology acceptance model: four longitudinal field studies. Manage. Sci. **46**(2), 186–204 (2000)

37. Wang, W.T., Li, H.M.: Factors influencing mobile services adoption: a brand-equity perspective. Internet Res. **22**(2), 142–179 (2011)
38. Wang, Y.S., Wang, Y.M., Lin, H.H., Tang, T.I.: Determinants of user acceptance of internet banking: an empirical study. Int. J. Serv. Ind. Manage. **14**(5), 501–519 (2003)
39. Williamson, S.: Costly monitoring, financial intermediation and equilibrium credit rationing. J. Monetary Econ. **18**(2), 159–179 (1986)
40. Worku, G.: Electronic-banking in Ethiopia-practices, opportunities and challenges. J. Internet Bank. Commer. **15**(2), 1–8 (2010)
41. http://cashlessindia.gov.in/
42. http://census2011.co.in/
43. https://www.rbi.org.in/
44. http://www.npci.org.in/

Benefits and Challenges of a Reference Architecture for Processing Statistical Data

Agung Wahyudi[✉][iD], Ricardo Matheus[iD], and Marijn Janssen[iD]

Faculty of Technology, Policy and Management, Delft University of
Technology, Jaffalaan 5, 2628 BX Delft, The Netherlands
{a.wahyudi, r.matheus, m.f.w.h.a.janssen}@tudelft.nl

Abstract. Organizations are looking for ways to gain advantage of big and
open linked data (BOLD) by employing statistics, however, how these benefits
can be created is often unclear. A reference architecture (RA) can capitalize
experiences and facilitate the gaining of the benefits, but might encounter
challenges when trying to gain the benefits of BOLD. The objective of the
research to evaluate the benefits and challenges of building IT systems using a
RA. We do this by investigating cases of the utilization of a RA for Linked
Open Statistical Data (LOSD). Benefits of using the reference architecture
include reducing project complexity, avoiding having to "reinvent the wheel",
easing the analysis of a (complex) system, preserving knowledge (e.g. proven
concepts and practices), mitigating multiple risks by reusing proven building
blocks, and providing users a common understanding. Challenges encountered
include the need for communication and learning the ins and outs of the RA,
missing features, inflexibility to add new instances as well as integrating the RA
with existing implementations, and the need for support for the RA from other
stakeholders.

Keywords: Reference architecture · Open government · e-Government · Open
Data · Big data · BOLD · Statistical data · LOSD · Data processing · Data cube

1 Introduction

Large amounts of data are available due to pervasiveness of data-generation and related
technologies such as mobile computing, internet-of-things (IoT), and social media. This
all results in big and open linked data (BOLD) in which some data is opened and the
linking of data creates value [2].

Todays' massive data have been publicly available by government initiates to open
data. The underlying motivations are to create transparency, enable participation and to
stimulate innovation [3–7]. The data may represent government's spending, parliament
meeting record, as well as Government's IoT such as GPS data from public trains and
buses, weather data, and environment data. This extends the existing published statistical data, such as census data, demography data, education data, etc. Moreover,
academia, businesses and individuals also start opening their data [8]. Research data,
company's supply chain data, crowd-sourced data are examples of publicly available
data from non-government parties. Open data refers to datasets that are published under

© IFIP International Federation for Information Processing 2017
Published by Springer International Publishing AG 2017. All Rights Reserved
A.K. Kar et al. (Eds.): I3E 2017, LNCS 10595, pp. 462–473, 2017.
DOI: 10.1007/978-3-319-68557-1_41

an open license, access to and (third-party) use of the datasets is without any restrictions [9]. According to Janssen, et al. [4], the primary goal of open data initiatives is to minimize the constraints on and efforts of reusing data.

Combining a dataset with other datasets is easy if the dataset are published in a structured way and are linked to each another [10]. Data can be sourced from multiple providers, interlinked each other, and retrieved using semantic queries. Linked data principles has been adopted by a growing number of data providers (both public and private) over the years, leading to the development of a global data space (i.e. the Web of Data) that consists of billions of assertions across multiple sectors. According to the statistics provided by LOD stats, the Web of Data contains 149 billion RDF triples from 2973 datasets[1].

The combination of big data, open data and the linking of data results in *linked open statistical data* (LOSD). A number of studies argue that organizations gain various benefits from LOSD, including improving economic growth, creating innovation, assisting to develop new or crafting better products and services [11–13]. The interest using LOSD is considerably growing [14], and a number of new business models for LOSD adoption is introduced [15–17].

The use of LOSD encounters a number of hurdles [18]. Gantz and Reinsel [19] found that even two thirds of businesses across North America and Europe failed to create value from their data. According to LaValle et al. [20], those challenges is not caused by the data only, but also by the IT systems capturing and processing the data, and the people who conduct operation on the data. Data users need to tackle issues such as metadata availability, connectivity between datasets, data quality, data ownership, privacy constraint, interoperability between applications, data standardization, and so on [21].

A reference architecture (RA) which serves as a guide to develop IT system has been developed to support the implementation of LOSD. A RA describes the highest level of abstraction and does not convey the design for an actual system or even a detailed diagram of the interconnection, but rather provides architectural guidance [22]. In this way a RA can support a smoother implementation.

The OpenCube Toolkit (OCT) serves as an instance of a reference architecture of IT system development for processing LOSD. OCT was built upon an underlying data processing lifecycle. Each process in the lifecycle is performed by certain applications. Those involved applications are then built and bundled in an integrated platform, i.e. Information Workbench[2].

A RA can help IT system developers to manage the complexities, and also deliver a number of benefits such as knowledge management, common understanding, risk mitigation, easing the analysis of systems, increasing reusability and connectivity, and reducing errors and mistakes [22, 23]. However, possible drawbacks are overhead projects and stifling creative and innovative solutions to problems [24]. Hence, the experiences with RA provide mixed outcomes.

---

[1] http://stats.lod2.eu/.

[2] https://github.com/opencube-toolkit/.

The objective of this paper is to evaluate the benefits and challenges of building IT system using a RA. This paper is organized as follows. First, we describe the research background. Thereafter the research approach is presented. This is followed by the presentation of the RA. In Sect. 4, we describe the cases of developing IT system for processing LOSD using the RA. Using the cases, we discussed the benefit and challenges of using an instance of RA (i.e. OCT) that will be covered in Sect. 5. Finally, conclusions are drawn.

2 Research Approach

We aim at investigating the benefits and challenges of building IT system using a RA. First, challenges and benefits of RAs were derive from literature. The findings were then used to investigate cases using OCT for developing LOSD applications (Fig. 1).

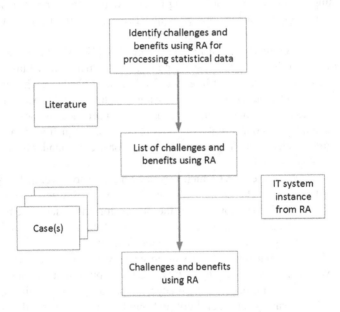

Fig. 1. Research approach in this study

OCT provided by OpenCube Consortium was used as the primary RA. Its use was investigated by analyzing eleven cases from an assignment given to students from Delft University of Technology (TU Delft), The Netherlands. The assignment was to create an IT system for combining LOSD that takes seven weeks to complete. Reports included mistakes, challenges and issues. We conducted content analysis to the groups' reports to identify benefits and challenges of using RA for building IT systems. We identified, coded and analyzed the benefits and challenges using NViVo. They were grouped based on the ICT architecture layers, i.e. business, business process, application, information, and infrastructure.

3   OpenCube Toolkit (OCT) Reference Architecture

The OpenCube Toolkit (OCT) is open source software developed by Open Cube Project[3]. The project aimed at developing software tools that facilitate (a) producing high-quality LOSD and (b) reusing distributed LOSDs in data analytics and visualizations. As a reference OCT takes a data processing lifecycle as the foundation. The OCT projects describe three main processes, i.e. Create, Expand, and Exploit. In the *creation phase*, the data users ingest raw data, pre-process the data, and then convert the data to linked data format in the data cubes forms. Data cube is a way to describe multi-dimensional variables contained in the data. For example, a 4-dimensional data cube may contains income, population, age, and year of observation from a certain country.

Three activities are defined in the *expansion phase*, i.e. (1) Discover and pre-process raw data; (2) Define structure & create cube; and (3) Publish cube. The outcome of this phase is a linked data cube. The cube can be expanded using new data. For this two activities need to be executed; (1) identify compatible cubes and (2) expand cube. Expansion of the cube could be caused by aggregating different cubes to accomplish a certain objective.

The last phase is the *exploitation phase* in which data users process, analyze and visualize the data, communicate the result, and/or make decision from the result. Therefore, three activities are defined in this phase, namely (1) discover and explore cube, (2) analyze cube, and (3) communicate results.

The components of OCT were selected and/or developed based on the proposed data processing lifecycle. There are number of open source components corresponding to certain process. In the *creation phase*, the goal is to transform raw data to linked data so that the proposed RA applications include data converting software such as JSON-stat2qb, Grafter, D2RQ, TARQL, and R2RML. The applications were developed by the members of OCT consortium. Most of them are used in the integrated platform, but some are stand-alone such as Grafter. TARQL creates RDF data cubes from legacy tabular data, such as CSV/TSV files. D2RQ produces RDF data cubes from relational databases. JSON-stat2qb converts JSON-stat files into RDF data cubes. R2RML transforms tabular data to linked data cubes.

The objective in the *expansion phase* is to expand the linked data cube. The corresponding applications proposed in the RA are the OpenCube Compatibility Explorer, OpenCube Aggregator, and OpenCube Expander. Given an initial cube in the RDF store, the main role of the OpenCube Compatibility Explorer is to search into the Linked Data Web and identify cubes that are relevant to expand the initial cube, and create typed links between the local cube and the compatible ones. The role of OpenCube Aggregator is twofold. First, given an initial cube with n dimensions the aggregator creates $(2n - 1)$ new cubes taking into account all the possible combinations of the n dimensions. Second, given an initial cube and a hierarchy of a dimension, the aggregator creates new observations for all the attributes of the hierarchy. OpenCube Expander creates a new expanded cube by merging two compatible cubes.

---

[3] http://www.opencube-toolkit.eu.

Data users create value from the data in *Exploitation* phase. OCT RA proposes a number of accessing, processing, analytics, visualization applications such as Data Catalogue Management, SPARQL console, OpenCube Browser, DataCube Grid View, Spreadsheet Builder, OpenCube OLAP Browser, R Statistical Analysis, Choropleth Map View, OpenCube Map View, and Interactive Chart Visualization. Data catalogue management serves as user interface (UI) templates for managing metadata on RDF data cubes and supporting search and discovery. OpenCube Browser is a table-based visualization of RDF data cubes. Data users could perform OLAP operations (e.g. pivot, drill-down, and roll-up) on top of multiple linked data cubes using OpenCube OLAP Browser. R statistical analysis enables execution of R data analysis scripts from the OpenCube Toolkit, visualization of results or their integration as RDF triples. Interactive chart serves as visualization widgets, i.e. visualization of the RDF data cube slices with charts. OpenCube MapView is map-based visualizations of linked data cubes with a geo-spatial dimension.

The software building blocks are integrated and bundled in a single platform, namely Information Workbench Community Edition platform. This is an open source application that serves as an architectural backbone of the toolkit. Information Workbench provides the SDK for building customized applications and realizing generic low-level functionalities such as shared data access, logging and monitoring (Fig. 2).

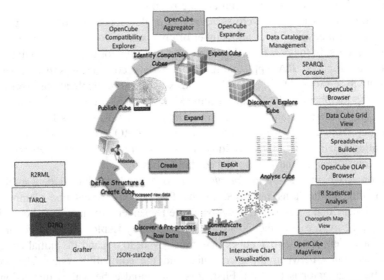

Fig. 2. Open cube toolkit processes and systems components RA [25]

OCT meets the attributes of a RA because (1) it comprises a prescriptive architecture that is built based on data processing lifecycle and includes the corresponding system elements (i.e. applications and infrastructure), and (2) it serves as a guidance for implementations (principles, guidelines, or technical positions).

4   IT Architecture for Processing LOSD Using OCT

Our objective is to investigate the experiences of the use of the RA for building a concrete IT system for processing LOSD. For that purpose, we exploit OCT as a reference architecture for combining LOSD. An assignment solving a business problem using LOSD was given to a number of Master students from Delft University of Technology (TU Delft), The Netherlands. There were eleven cases created by eleven groups that consist of 3–4 persons each, as listed in the Table 1.

Table 1. LOSD use cases from Master students of Delft University of Technology

Group	Project
1	Not-so-funda: A Linked Open Data analysis of house prices and education in Utrecht
2	Location Analysis for the Automotive Industry after the Brexit in the EU: Designing a decision-making process for reallocating assembly plants of Nissan, Toyota and Honda within European Union
3	Matching human capital supply and demand in Europe
4	OpenUN: An architectural design for measuring a Sustainable Development Goal
5	E-Doctor Platform: Healthcare services for integrating immigrants in the Netherlands
6	Linking the data - Where to invest?: A research in a Linked open data architecture on investment regions within the municipality of Amsterdam
7	Amsterdam parking app
8	Raising Awareness About GHGs Emission Among EU Citizens with the Use of Open Data
9	Primary School Recommendation System
10	Attractiveness of countries' living situations
11	The European Gender Inequality Indicators

5   Benefits and Challenges of the Reference Architecture

The benefits and challenges faced by the groups were analyzed. The benefits as found in the literature were used to evaluate the assignment and the results are shown in Table 2. The benefits are categorized using architecture layers [26] as shown in the left column in the table.

In the *business process* layer, the majority of the groups mentioned OCT helped them to reduce project complexity due to the availability of pre-defined data processing lifecycle as part of OCT. They did not need to reinvent the processes but were able to directly fit the processes to their objectives. Some customization of the data processing lifecycle probably took place, but the effort was much less than building the processes from scratch. This finding confirms the benefit mentioned in the literature, i.e. RA is supposed to help IT architects to reduce complexity [22].

In the *application* layer, several groups noted the benefit originating from reusing the building blocks in OCT. The blocks were designed to support the data processing

Table 2. Benefits of using OCT as a reference architecture

Architecture layer	Benefit	Mentioned by group
Overall architecture	• Not having to start from scratch • More efficient development (less time) • Decomposing the complex problem into smaller parts • Providing a common knowledge (and improving understandability)	#2–#4, #7–#9, #11
Business process	• Using the process of data lifecycles	#1,#2, #4, #5–#11
Application	• Use of proven interconnected building blocks • Knowledge transfer of building blocks • Reduce risks of failure	#2, #5, #7, #9
Information	• Variety of involved information is pre-defined as a template • Templates are knowledge repository	#2, #4, #7, #11
Infrastructure	• Effective on implementing the system (hardware and software)	#1–#4, #6, #8, #10, #11

lifecycle. The interrelation (i.e. between the business process and the related applications) eases the architecture's users to understand and breakdown the system. This finding confirm the benefit stated by Gong [23], that a RA should ease the analysis of a (complex) system. The building blocks were also proven to do the specified job and they are interoperable with each other. The groups found the building blocks were very helpful and replicable for the functions they needed to accomplish their objectives. This confirms the findings of Cloutier et al. [22], that a RA should preserve knowledge (e.g. proven concepts and practices) that can be reused and replicated for future projects. Reusing proven building blocks will also reduce failure risk that is a benefit from a RA [22].

In the *information* layer, a number of pre-defined information were found useful for several groups. Using these as templates, they did not need to design types of information to be used, stored, and archived. The templates act as a knowledge repository for the information architects.

Most of the groups found that OCT helped them to execute the systems implementation project better. Using the hardware and software components that are proven to work and interoperate, the implementation project became effective which means the amount of available resources such as investment and labor were properly utilized. Consequently, risk from the architecture project such as delay and the resulting overrun project cost could be properly mitigated, as Cloutier et al. [22] mentions.

As illustrated in the OCT case, a RA provides IT architects the common language to speak about the business process and the corresponding applications, information, and infrastructure. For example, OCT users interpret the meaning of expand process as the updating process for any current data cubes with a recent corresponding incoming data, not other definitions. This confirms common understanding advantage from using a RA as described by Cloutier et al. [22].

We also identified a number of challenges from the groups' report. Those challenges create hurdles and impediments of using the RA. We listed the identified challenges in Table 3.

Table 3. Challenges of using OCT as a reference architecture

Architecture layer	Challenge	Mentioned by group
Overall architecture	–	–
Business process	1. Using building blocks from OCT is not straightforward due to lack of documentation (e.g. uploading CSV files, converting CSV to RDF) 2. It's not clear how to create data pipelines in OCT (i.e. placing output of a building block as inputs of the others) 3. No clue how to automate the process (e.g. processing streaming of data, visualizing real-time output) 4. OCT does not provide assessment of data quality support 5. Lack of community involvement	1. #1–#11 2. #2, #3, #6, #11 3. #3, #10 4. #1, #2 5. #10
Application	1. Users find it difficult to use the menu and interface in the Information Workbench because they are not intuitive 2. Certain dependencies are required (e.g. Oracle Java 8); OCT does not work with updated version of the dependencies 3. Very often applications outside OCT are utilized due to OCT limitation (e.g. OpenRefine, Google Fusion) 4. Data visualization using OCT is challenging because the installed R packages are limited by default while OCT users are impossible to install packages 5. Only support R for visualization; Difficult to connect other visualization applications to OCT	6. #2,#5,#7, #10 7. #3, #4, #7, #10 8. #2, #4, #9 9. #1, #2, #6, #8, #11 10. #7, #11
Information	1. OCT does not provide mechanism to store the data in the different machine (e.g. data center, data lake) from the one where OCT is installed 2. Which linked data vocabularies that OCT supports is not documented clearly 3. SPARQL queries is challenging to use 4. Since linked data is not human-readable, it's difficult to understand the benefit	11. #1, #3, #10 12. #3, #7, #8, #11 13. #2 14. #1, #5
Infrastructure	1. OCT could be installed only in Unix-based environment 2. No clue how to implement OCT in a cluster of computers	15. #2, #6, #8 16. #10, #11

In the *business process* layer, all groups reported that understanding the RA was somewhat difficult due to a lack of documentation. This hindered them to use the OCT better. After effortful try-and-error activities that stuck the progress, many of them finally used other applications beyond OCT, such as OpenRefine, Perl, R, Python, awk,

Tableau, etc. They have gone a number of unsuccessful trials of building their IT system using the menu in the Information Workbench. There was also no guideline how to automate the process, such as scheduling of retrieving raw data from the data sources, processing streaming of data, or visualizing real-time data. Some groups also noted that data quality was difficult to be assessed using the Information Workbench. Incorporating multiple datasets mean that the data users should take variety of data quality into account. Therefore, some additional applications beyond OCT were used to assess and improve data quality. The use of OCT was also difficult because there was very few example of successful OCT implementation. We hardly found community involvement for OCT improvement such as forum, user groups, mailing lists, etc.

In the *application* layer, the groups found it's difficult to use the menu and interface in the Information Workbench because they are too simple and not intuitive enough. Dependencies of OCT applications were also too rigid, for example OCT works only with Oracle Java 8. Very often applications outside OCT are utilized due to OCT limitation (e.g. Open-Refine, Google Fusion). Data visualization using OCT is challenging because the installed R packages are limited by default while OCT users are impossible to install packages. Only support R for visualization; Difficult to connect other visualization applications to OCT.

There are also a number of challenges found in the *information* layer. First, OCT does not provide mechanism to export and store the data to other machines (e.g. data center or data lake). Second, which linked data vocabularies that OCT supports is not documented clearly. Currently there are many varieties of linked data vocabularies with which data creators could confuse. Third, SPARQL syntax is quite different from standard SQL/PL. Some groups found it's quite challenging to understand and use SPARQL. Fourth, since linked data is not human-readable, it's difficult to understand the benefit. Some groups questioned the need to convert the raw data to linked data. They preferred to exploit the raw data directly without having spent additional effort to publish linked data.

The groups mentioned several challenges in the *infrastructure* layer such as OCT could be installed only in Unix-based environment and no clue how to implement OCT in a cluster of computers. As the data size and number of users grows, the most common approach is to deploy a cluster of regular hardware. Building an OCT instance in a parallel environment was not described in the documentation and currently OCT does not support cluster implementation.

From the OCT cases, we derived challenges coping with a RA in general. First, proper documentation is needed to fully exploit the RA. It means that a RA needs the optimum amount of documentation. Too few guidelines will cause the RA difficult to concretize and implement. Issues mentioned in the cases, i.e. difficult to use the RA components and confusing what standards to be followed (e.g. LOD vocabularies) reflect the consequences of lack of documentation. Proper documentation is also required to introduce new or unpopular technologies adopted by the RA, for example linked data principles and SPARQL syntax in our cases. On the other hand, too much information in the documentation will lead the high level users such as business managers and customers troublesome to get the helicopter view.

Second challenge is that missing important features will make the RA irrelevant. Those important features should exist in every RA because they constitute the functionalities a RA must have. We noted several missing important features from OCT cases, i.e.: (1) process automation that is mandatory for a RA in data processing; (2) intuitive and sufficient user interface that strictly important for helping the users to master the RA; (3) proper authority that ensures the user to fit the tools with the jobs (e.g. users unable to install R packages in the R statistical analysis in OCT, meanwhile the packages are required to accomplish the data objective).

The need for proper documentation for full exploitation of RA, missing important features from a RA that makes it irrelevant, inflexibility to add a new instance as well as integrate it in existing implementation, and RA still island without future support and collaboration among stakeholders.

Every user has different data objectives with different kind of problems (e.g. issues with data quality, privacy, etc.), initial conditions (e.g. having legacy system), and constraints (e.g. budget, time, management approval, etc.). Consequently, there should be many customizations in implementation of a RA. Systems customization could be also resulted due to adoption of emerging technologies, such as cloud computing, parallel processing, in-memory analytics, etc. Therefore, a RA should be flexible to add a new instance (e.g. a process, application, information, or an infrastructure component) as well as to integrate the instance in existing implementation. From our cases, some groups require features beyond OCT capability such as data quality assessment, data wrangling, web service, storing the data in a location besides OCT machine, and implementing in a cluster. As we observed, these available features from OCT were not feasible to perform the task. Although the features could be deployed in the machine where OCT resides, but integrating it within OCT environment was troublesome.

The last challenge is that OCT is still a stand-alone without future support and collaboration between users and developers, among users, and among developers for massive use. The collaboration is stimulated and incubated in an ecosystem. Good collaboration will result in proven components of RA, richness of RA implementation cases, and crowd-solutions for many architectural problems. From our cases, after the groups found the documentation of OCT was not helpful, they tried to search relevant cases and find the answers for their questions in the Internet. However, those were neither useful because useful knowledge was hardly available on the internet.

6 Conclusion

The objective of the research presented in this paper is to evaluate the benefits and challenges of using a reference architecture for building IT systems. The OpenCube Toolkit was used as a reference architecture for developing Linked Open Statistical Data applications. We investigated the experiences by observing the development in eleven cases. A range of benefits using OCT as a reference architecture were identified. The RA helps to (1) reduce project complexity and need not "reinvent the wheel", (2) eases the analysis of a (complex) system, (3) preserves knowledge (e.g. proven concepts and practices) that can be reused and replicated for future projects, (4) mitigates multiple risks such as failure risk, delay and the resulting overrun project cost by reusing proven building blocks, and (5) provides common understanding.

Implementing IT system using OCT seems to be initially straightforward, but in a reality a number of challenges needs to cope with, i.e. (1) the need for proper documentation for full exploitation of RA, (2) missing important features from a RA that makes it irrelevant, (3) inflexibility to add a new instance as well as integrate it in existing implementation, and (4) RA is a blueprint that could only be widely used with support and collaboration among stakeholders. Although generalization of the results is difficult, our findings suggest when developing a RA the users should have clear guidelines on how to use the RA and what the limitations of its use are.

Acknowledgement. Part of this work is funded by the European Commission within the H2020 Programme in the context of the project OpenGovIntelligence (www.opengovintelligence.eu) under grant agreement No. 693849.

We would like to thank PT. Telekomunikasi Indonesia, Tbk. for their support during the study as well as the students who participated in the practical work.

References

1. Mayer-Schönberger, V., Cukier, K.: Big Data: A Revolution That Will Transform How We Live, Work, and Think. Houghton Mifflin Harcourt, Boston (2013)
2. Janssen, M., Kuk, G.: Big and Open Linked Data (BOLD) in research, policy, and practice. J. Organ. Comput. Electron. Commer. **26**(1–2), 3–13 (2016)
3. Charalabidis, Y., Psarras, J.: Combination of interoperability registries with process and data management tools for governmental services transformation. In: Hawaii International Conference on System Sciences (HICSS-42), pp. 5–8, January 2009
4. Janssen, M., Charalabidis, Y., Zuiderwijk, A.: Benefits, adoption barriers and myths of open data and open government. Inf. Syst. Manag. **29**(4), 258–268 (2012)
5. Zhang, J., Dawes, S.S., Sarkis, J.: Exploring stakeholders' expectations of the benefits and barriers of e-government knowledge sharing. J. Enterp. Inf. Manag. **18**(5), 548–567 (2005)
6. Zuiderwijk, A., Jeffery, K., Janssen, M.: The potential of metadata for linked open data and its value for users and publishers. J. eDemocracy **4**(2), 222–244 (2012)
7. Manyika, J., Chui, M., Groves, P., Farrell, D., Van Kuiken, S., Doshi, E.A.: Open data: unlocking innovation and performance with liquid information. McKinsey&Company (2013)
8. Zuiderwijk, A., Janssen, M., van de Kaa, G., Poulis, K.: The wicked problem of commercial value creation in open data ecosystems: policy guidelines for governments. Inf. Polity **21**(3), 223–236 (2016)
9. Open Knowledge Foundation: Open Data Handbook Documentation (Release 1.0.0) (2012)
10. Heath, T., Bizer, C.: Linked Data: Evolving the Web into a Global Data Space, 1st edn., vol. 1, no. 1. (2011)
11. Janssen, K.: The influence of the PSI directive on open government data: an overview of recent developments. Gov. Inf. Q. **28**(4), 446–456 (2011)
12. Lundqvist, B.: Digital agenda: turning government data into gold: the regulation of public sector information–some comments on the compass-case (2012). SSRN 2148949
13. Martin, C.: Barriers to the open government data agenda: taking a multi-level perspective. Policy Internet **6**(3), 217–240 (2014)
14. GovLab: Open Data 500 US (2015). http://www.opendata500.com/us/

15. Ferro, E., Osella, M.: Eight business model archetypes for PSI Re-Use. In: Open Data on the Web Workshop, Google Campus, Shoreditch, London (2013)
16. Janssen, M., Zuiderwijk, A.: Infomediary business models for connecting open data providers and users. Soc. Sci. Comput. Rev. **32**(5), 694–711 (2014)
17. Magalhaes, G., Roseira, C., Manley, L.: Business models for open government data. In: Proceedings of the 8th International Conference on Theory and Practice of Electronic Governance, pp. 365–370 (2014)
18. Zuiderwijk, A., Janssen, M., Choenni, S., Meijer, R., Alibaks, R.S.: Socio-technical impediments of open data. Electron. J. e-Gov. **10**(2), 156–172 (2012)
19. Gantz, J., Reinsel, D.: Extracting value from Chaos State of the universe: an executive summary. IDC iView, pp. 1–12, June 2011
20. LaValle, S., Lesser, E., Shockley, R., Hopkins, M.S., Kruschwitz, N.: Big data, analytics and the path from insights to value. MIT Sloan Manag. Rev. **21** (2013)
21. Janssen, M., Estevez, E., Janowski, T.: Interoperability in Big, Open, and Linked Data—Organizational Maturity, Capabilities, and Data Portfolios. IEEE Computer Society (2014)
22. Cloutier, R., Muller, G., Verma, D., Nilchiani, R., Hole, E., Bone, M.: The concept of reference architectures. Syst. Eng. **13**(1), 14–27 (2010)
23. Gong, Y.: Engineering Flexible and Agile Services: A Reference Architecture for Administrative Processes. TU Delft, Delft University of Technology (2012)
24. Windley, P.J.: Digital Identity. O'Reilly Media, Inc., Sebastopol (2005)
25. Kalampokis, E., Roberts, B., Karamanou, A., Tambouris, E., Tarabanis, K.: Challenges on developing tools for exploiting linked open data cubes. In: CEUR Workshop Proceedings, vol. 1551 (2015)
26. Lankhorst, M.: Enterprise Architecture at Work: Modelling, Communication and Analysis. The Enterprise Engineering Series (2009)
27. Janssen, M.: Framing enterprise architecture: a meta-framework for analyzing architectural efforts in organizations. In: Coherency Management: Using Enterprise Architecture for Alignment, Agility, and Assurance, pp. 99–118 (2009)

IT Consulting: A Systematic Literature Review

Abhishek Kumar[1], Purva Grover[1(✉)], Arpan Kumar Kar[1], and Ashis K. Pani[2]

[1] Indian Institute of Technology Delhi, New Delhi, India
groverdpurva@gmail.com
[2] XLRI School of Management, Jamshedpur, India

Abstract. Today information technology has become integral part of every kind of business. Organizations often need experts who have great insights in solving their business problems through information technology. This has led to development of a new field: information technology consulting (or IT consulting). This field has matured quite well in last 20 years. This study is an attempt to identify major focus of IT consulting practices and the challenges associated with them. 123 peer-reviewed academic research papers in field of IT consulting were considered for this systematic literature review. After filtering these papers, eventually 36 papers were selected. A number of major focus of IT consulting in last 20 years and challenges associated with them were identified (Education/IT Training, Auditing, Project Management, Knowledge Transfer, IT Economics, Security, Competitiveness, Applications). This review paper provides valuable information for business executives who are seeking to use IT practices for their business problems. It also provides directions for future research in IT consulting.

Keywords: IT consulting · Literature review · Consulting · Information systems

1 Introduction

Among all developments, the biggest impact on management consulting has been made by Information Systems (IS) in general and Information Technology (IT) in particular (Nolan and Bennigson 2002). It has become a major tool for management consulting companies to deal with central issues of organizations like scenario analysis in strategic planning consulting, managing information of organization in data warehouse, data driven decision making through data mining and business intelligence techniques (Galliers and Leidner 2014). Systems like Customer Relationship Management (CRM) and Enterprise Resource Planning (ERP) introduced by IT consulting firms, have played key roles in management improvements. IS has become de facto necessity for any management firm to achieve sustainable competitive advantage (Clemons 1986).

This study is an attempt to identify key areas for which IT consulting have been used and for achieving a specific outcome. Till now, there is no review article on this inter-disciplinary domain, which the current study addresses. The rest of the paper has been structured as follows: Sect. 2 discusses the methodology adopted, Sect. 3 discusses the emerging themes whiles Sect. 4 concludes with directions for future research.

© IFIP International Federation for Information Processing 2017
Published by Springer International Publishing AG 2017. All Rights Reserved
A.K. Kar et al. (Eds.): I3E 2017, LNCS 10595, pp. 474–484, 2017.
DOI: 10.1007/978-3-319-68557-1_42

2 Methodology for Systematic Review

This section provides outline for systematic literature review. These outlines include development of review protocol, selection of academic papers and extraction of data.

Protocol development is the first step and this step determines the search criteria for academic papers for the purpose of review. Research papers for review were extracted from Scopus database. Specific keywords were used to search these papers. The keywords used for searching Scopus database are Information Technology Consulting, Information Systems Consulting and IT Consulting. In order to extract all possible combinations of search keywords, the Boolean operator "OR" was used. The second step in this process is to take the Inclusion decision on the basis of title of the research paper. This step involved the independent readings of titles of the papers by both authors. Irrelevant papers were filtered out. Many non-English, duplicate, news and commentaries were eliminated in this step. After this step, 75 papers were kept for further filtering process. The third step in this process was creating the inclusion decision on the basis of abstract. This step involved the independent readings of titles of the abstracts by both authors. Despite of the fact that many search keywords appeared in these paper, focus of many papers were found not to be in IS/IT consulting. Such papers were filtered out. After this step, 52 papers were kept for further filtering process. 123 peer-reviewed academic research papers in field of IT consulting were considered for this systematic literature review. After filtering these papers, eventually 52 papers were selected. For the final selection, the two authors read the papers independently. Following criteria were decided for final selection:

- Does the study address core aspects of IT/IS consulting?
- Are more than one factors from technological factors, management factors, social factors, human factors and organizational factors considered in these studies?

The above criteria lead to shortlisting of 36 papers which could be used for this study. The selection process and the total number of papers identified in each step are illustrated in Fig. 1.

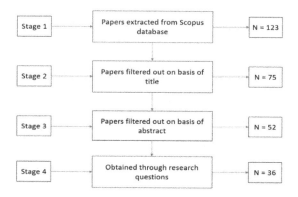

Fig. 1. Stages of the paper selection process

3   Results

Using the 36 research studies selected by the protocol mention in Sect. 2, the title and keywords of the selected research study word cloud was formed as illustrated in Fig. 2 to identify dominant themes in such studies. The key terms in the word clouds are consultants, management, knowledge, information, system and technology. The objective of such an exploration is to visualize how the themes connect with each other among the studies, using tools for text mining.

Word cloud of the title of selected research studies for this systematic review   **Word cloud of the keywords of selected research studies for this systematic review**

Fig. 2. Word cloud of the keywords and title of selected research studies

Subsequently, the association among the words present in the title of selected research studies is identified and illustrated in Fig. 3 using association rule mining. The rules found with the help of Apriori algorithm indicates the nature of association of focus areas within IT consulting literature. The network illustration indicates that focus in such

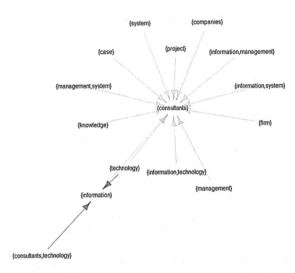

Fig. 3. Association among the words present in the title of selected research studies

studies is strongly on the consultants along with information technology (or systems) and information management.

The year wise distribution of the selected studies shown in Fig. 4. The highest number of studies had been published in 2016, by looking at the graph it can be said IT consulting is one of the trending topics.

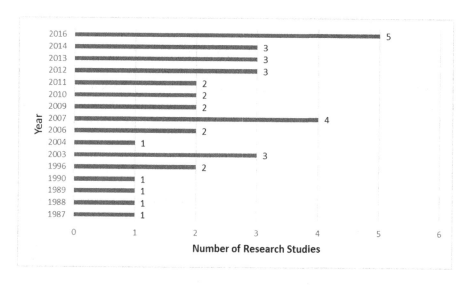

Fig. 4. Year wise distribution of selected research studies

Selected research papers have been reviewed and classified into eight broad categories of trends in IT & IS consulting. This categorization is based on the thematic focus in individual studies. It also provides scope of consulting practices in light of these eight

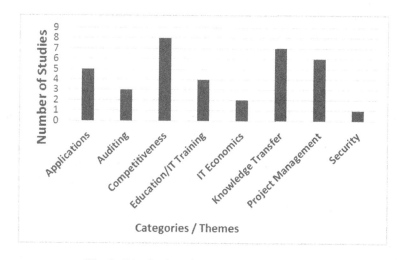

Fig. 5. Distribution of final papers across 8 fields

areas. Figure 5 shows distribution of papers across several areas. It is evident from the graphical representation that most popular context touched upon by studies in IT consulting surrounds domains like competitiveness, knowledge transfer and project management. In later subsections, greater exploration would be conducted in each individual area of interest.

3.1 Education/IT Training

New technologies are emerging rapidly in field of IS. People seeking to work in IS to update their knowledge regularly. Most of university students focus on either business or information technology. Those who wish to launch career in MIS or related fields need to have specific skills both in business management and IS. Consulting practicum has potential to help students acquire skills in both areas, thereby enabling smooth transition from university to a professional career in MIS field (Akpan 2016). However it remains interesting to see how this can help people already working in some other fields like sociology, psychology etc. who have good understanding of business environment and wish to move to IS.

Universities offer wide range of courses to business executives to help them understand latest updates in MIS. Often times they focus on more on either business perspective or technical perspective. It lacks proper synergy between research and practice. A framework for integrated approach based on design science research methodology has been developed for teaching professionals IT management and IT consulting (ITMC). This framework has potential to transfer knowledge from researchers working in academia and industries to companies (Boehm et al. 2011).

The Further Education Maturity Model (FEMM) has been developed to aid young IT professionals in selecting right training offerings for them based on their maturity level and quality of training offerings (Boehm et al. 2013).

An Educational Integration Platform Solution (EIPS) which conceptualizes the teaching of IT management and IT consulting as hybrid package of products and services offers a new perspective of ITMC teaching (Boehm et al. 2011). However, impacts of social factors like motivation level of instructors and students remain to be seen.

3.2 Auditing

Information technologies are being deployed in almost every division of organizations i.e. sales, finance, research etc. to aid decision making. So, organizations need to examine and evaluate their IT infrastructure, policies and operations. IT auditing helps organizations in deciding their IT controls. IT auditing requires people who are experts in information security (Felley and Dornberger 2016). It is recommended for students pursuing IS Bachelor or Masters programs to get trained in IT auditing and security aspects of IS as well.

Traditionally role of IT auditors was limited to application control reviews (ACRs) and general control reviews (GCRs). The role has expanded to provide consulting and assurance services on enterprise governance of IT. Therefore, IT auditors should understand business processes and frameworks like COBIT 5 as guideline (Zororo 2014).

Change management and change auditing can be integrated into IT consulting firm's methodology in order to deal with risks and uncertainties caused by unexpected demands during project period (Chou and Chou 2009).

3.3 Project Management

IT project management deals with planning, organization and delineation of responsibility for successful completion of IT goals of the firm. Traditionally Project Management Information System focused only on scheduling and resource management but now its role is be a comprehensive system that supports the entire project life-cycle, project program and project portfolios. However, such PMIS is expensive, thereby beyond reach of small and medium enterprises (SME). Teixeira et al. 2016 proposes the design process of a PMIS which can improve performance of investment projects and incentives of the firm. This design process can easily be replicated by firms which have similar projects. However, this design process should be tested and validated against other non-investment projects. For successful completion of IT project, establishing effective communication among all stakeholders are of utmost importance. PMIS takes care of this. But now-a-days firms have multiple IT consulting projects at any time. Project teams lacking in multiple task management skills can not deliver desired outcomes on right time. Therefore, adapted techniques of project portfolio management based on portfolio project management, PMIS and project communication management can help in tackling this issue (Kaewta and Chutima 2014).

The hurdle model can been applied to three categories of the IT consulting services such as Idea generation (before the hurdle), Idea execution (after the hurdle) and Project management (both sides) and with effective communication skills IT consultants can better meet their objective (Djavanshir and Agresti 2007). The quality of the consulting services received by the customers can be measure on the basis of the six dimensions such as reliability, responsiveness, assurance, empathy, process and education (Yoon and Suh 2004). Information technology and human resource management oriented tools can be integrated to give rise to knowledge production and it is necessary for the success of knowledge management (Koch 2003). Selection of an appropriate development strategy and the assessment of risk associated with the project are the two major functions for the planning an IS development project (Lesusky et al. 1987).

3.4 Knowledge Transfer

IT project Knowledge transfer deals with transferring knowledge from one part of the firm to the other. It aims to increase productivity by making learning process easier and quicker, thereby reducing the training time. Since learning is social action, social network in addition to incentives have been successfully utilized in knowledge transfer thereby increasing productivity in the ERP sector (Bologa and Lupu 2014). Firms should focus on managing their knowledge network on levels of individual, group, organization and collectives of organizations to facilitate transfer process effectively. IT and organization culture play critical role in this (Liu and Zhao 2009). Knowledge management in consultancies industry had been key to competitive advantage (Kautz and Mahnke 2003).

Knowledge management models: reuser, stabilizer, explorer and innovator, can been developed on the basis of the knowledge and service type (Kim and Trimi 2007).

To enable smooth knowledge transfer inside the firm, employees must be willing to share their knowledge with other employees. Therefore, firms should focus on changing perception of their employees about knowledge sharing and provide them motivation and proper communication channel to do so (Hidayanto et al. 2013).

Knowledge management systems help the organization in building the social capital along the three dimensions such as structural, relational and cognitive and enabling the organization for creating and transferring of knowledge (Sherif et al. 2006). The process based on the complex adaptive systems can be used for the creation of knowledge within the organization. This process first identifies attributes for the knowledge assets, than finds relationship among them through association, aggregation, generalization and specialization (Sherif and Xing 2006).

Usually IT users are not familiar with company's knowledge management framework but till the framework had been used by 2/3 respondents to search for the general information (Kautz and Mahnke 2003). So, the company should focus on its efforts of making its framework familiar to the users.

3.5   IT Economics

Many multinational companies are utilizing IT consulting practices which have been successful in developed economies to developing ones. For successful deployment of such practices in developing economies, complexities of unknown contexts with various risks should be taken into consideration (Wang 2012).

In transitional economies like Serbia, Ukraine, management and IT consulting face problems due to lack of managerial and restructuring experience in a free-market economy. Therefore, important innovation, managerial education and improvement in IT infrastructure are necessary to deal with major problems (Fuxman and Ivanovic 2012).

3.6   Security

Data breaches to firm may lead to business opportunities to IT consulting firms. But it has limitations. It has been highlighted that effects of such security breaches are not limited to the affected firm but also the market value of security consultants are positively associated with the disclosure of security breaches by other firms. Reputation of IT consulting firms can be adversely affected if the number of records breaches is massive (Cavusoglu et al. 2004). This impact becomes even more severe if clients belong to certain industries such as technology and retail sectors.

According to information transfer theory and capital market expectation, clients and investors may hold IT consultation providers responsible for IT security breaches, thereby leading to negative returns (Chen et al. 2012). So, IT firms should have experts for dealing with cyber threat, data breaches or system hacks as advisory to pre-empt such security breaches in organizations. However, this is a less explored domain and is likely to become more critical as an area for exploration in the wake of digitization and the development of cyber-physical systems.

3.7 Competitiveness

IT consulting firms use their resources and capabilities strategically in order to achieve competitive advantage. Among these resources, firm's knowledge on human resources and their relationship with customers are crucial ones (Calicchio and Marcondes 2016). They also seek to hire top performing consultants. Top performing IT consultants should be able to deliver a good balance of technical skills, functional skills for economic viability and communication skills (Joshi et al. 2010).

Information asymmetry between clients and IT firms lead them to behave in their self-interests. This affects legal and social constraints of engagement between clients and IT firms. Dawson et al. 2010 explains how levels of information symmetry affect the adopted constraint mechanism for engagement between clients and IT firms. Both parties use signal and screen to negotiate. This asymmetry highly affects tacit knowledge-centric projects (Dawson et al. 2016). National culture also play major role in effects of information asymmetry (Dawson et al. 2013).

To move up in career, IT consultants need recognize and build a skill set that can satisfy both personal and other stakeholders' expectations. It has been noted that top performing IT consultants seems to favor masculinity (Joshi and Kuhn 2007).

The project phases can been divided into seven phases such as pre-project system analysis, project initialization, problem analysis, solution development, solution implementation, project close and post-project system analysis (Becker 2007).

Organizations use information technology to achieve the competitive advantage over the others. So to achieve this, project managers need to plan, select the tools for tracking and monitoring purposes, organize the project for decision making and troubleshoot the project when it is undergoing the difficult phase (Aitcheson 1989).

3.8 Applications

Information is regarded as the major asset by many organizations with can help the organization in long term planning, problem solving, product development and innovation (Harling 1988).

Concurrent-convergent strategy in IT consulting can be used for increasing the client efficiency and for deriving the insights from other information based applications (Liao and Cheung 2003). Both business systems managers along with IS managers should design the new information flows across the enterprises and how it can be used for achieving the business goals (Monheit and Tsafrir 1990). IS facilities the communication of information among the people such as organization are assisting their customers to solve their problems related to services and products offered by the organization (Harling 1988).

Global positioning systems, geographic information systems and remote sensing technologies has been integrated to address the surface environmental issues such as assessment of the groundwater resources (Gibas-Tracy 1996). IS for consulting the passengers with the help of the tools has also been developed (Gance 1996).

4   Conclusion and Future Direction

The main objective of this study was to find IT practices adopted by IT firms for consulting with their clients and issues associated with them. To accomplish this objective, this literature review attempted to identify challenges faced in IT consulting and their solutions to deal with them by various firms and researchers, both in industry and academia. This review found out that majority of research papers follow empirical methodology. Papers which provide conceptual frameworks and theoretical analysis are lacking. Problems like negotiations between IT firms and clients, signaling among firms etc. are challenging to solve using empirical approach. They lack a proper framework which could serve as foundation of any further application. With innovation in IT technologies, malicious practices like fraud, data breach etc. are also increasing, thereby making roles of IT auditors. Currently, there is no proper framework for IT auditors and their roles are vaguely defined. Responsibilities and qualifications of IT auditors need to be clearly identified. Further research needs to be done on cognitive aspects of IT consulting practices because cognitive aspects play key role in acquiring new knowledge and deciding how to design training modules for company employees. Also, many papers provide recommendations for students who wish to work in IT field. More research needs to be done in designing modules/recommendations for people working in non-IT fields and wish to switch to IT fields.

References

Akpan, I.J.: The efficacy of consulting practicum in enhancing students' readiness for professional career in management information systems: An empirical analysis. Decis. Sci. J. Innov. Educ. **14**(4), 412–440 (2016)

Boehm, M., Stolze, C., Breitschwerdt, R., Zarvic, N., Thomas, O.: An integrated approach for teaching professionals IT management and IT consulting. In: AMCIS (2011)

Felley, G., Dornberger, R.: How to Efficiently Conduct an IT Audit–in the Perspective of Research, Consulting and Teaching (2016)

Chou, D.C., Chou, A.Y.: Integrating change management and change auditing into information technology consulting practice. Int. J. Inf. Syst. Change Manage. **4**(1), 15–41 (2009)

Zororo, T.: IT governance assurance and consulting: A compelling need for today's IT auditors. EDPACS **49**(6), 1–9 (2014)

Teixeira, L., Xambre, A.R., Figueiredo, J., Alvelos, H.: Analysis and design of a project management information system: Practical case in a consulting company. Procedia Comput. Sci. **100**, 171–178 (2016)

Kaewta, S., Chutima, P.: Improvement of project portfolio management in an information technology consulting company. In: IOP Conference Series: Materials Science and Engineering, Vol. 58(1), p. 012012. IOP Publishing (2014)

Bologa, R., Lupu, A.R.: Organizational learning networks that can increase the productivity of IT consulting companies. A case study for ERP consultants. Expert Syst. Appl. **41**(1), 126–136 (2014)

Liu, H., Zhao, L.: Knowledge transfer in knowledge network of IT consulting company. In: 2009 International Conference on Information Management, Innovation Management and Industrial Engineering, Vol. 1, pp. 490–495. IEEE (2009)

Hidayanto, A.N., Hapsari, I.C., Alfina, I., Sucahyo, Y.G.: Knowledge sharing perception: Multiple case studies in Indonesian IT consulting companies. JCP **8**(10), 2719–2723 (2013)

Wang, Y.: Existing system solutions redeployment in remote developing country: lessons learnt from a multi-national IT consulting firm. In: Cusumano, Michael A., Iyer, B., Venkatraman, N. (eds.) ICSOB 2012. LNBIP, vol. 114, pp. 279–284. Springer, Heidelberg (2012). doi: 10.1007/978-3-642-30746-1_25

Fuxman, L., Ivanovic, A.: International applications of knowledge intensive services of management and IT consulting in transitional countries. In: Service Science Research, Strategy and Innovation: Dynamic Knowledge Management Methods, pp. 499–518. IGI Global (2012)

Chen, J.V., Li, H.C., Yen, D.C., Bata, K.V.: Did IT consulting firms gain when their clients were breached? Comput. Hum. Behav. **28**(2), 456–464 (2012)

Cavusoglu, H., Mishra, B., Raghunathan, S.: The effect of internet security breach announcements on market value: Capital market reactions for breached firms and internet security developers. Int. J. Electron. Commerce **9**(1), 70–104 (2004)

Dawson, G.S., Watson, R.T., Boudreau, M.C.: Information asymmetry in information systems consulting: toward a theory of relationship constraints. J. Manage. Inf. Syst. **27**(3), 143–178 (2010)

Calicchio, A.C., Marcondes, R.C.: Relevant factors for competitiveness in information technology consulting businesses. Gestão & Produção 23(3), 625–637 (2016)

Joshi, K.D., Kuhn, K.M., Niederman, F.: Excellence in IT consulting: Integrating multiple stakeholders' perceptions of top performers. IEEE Trans. Eng. Manage. **57**(4), 589–606 (2010)

Boehm, M., Stolze, C., Thomas, O.: Understanding IT-management and IT-consulting teaching as product service system: Application of an engineering model. In: EMISA, pp. 219–224 (2011)

Boehm, M., Jasper, M., Thomas, O.: The Further Education Maturity Model: Development and Implementation of a Maturity Model for the Selection of Further Education Offerings in the Field of IT Management and IT Consulting (2013)

Dawson, G., Li, Y., Zhang, H., Huang, W.W., Watson, R.: Assessing the Relevancy of National Culture in Predicting the Efficacy of Constraints in the Information Systems Consulting Domain (2013)

Liao, Z., Cheung, M.T.: Concurrent-convergent strategy in IT consulting. Commun. ACM **46**(9), 103–104 (2003)

Gibas-Tracy, D.R.: Cost-effective environmental consulting using geographic information systems and remote sensing. In: 1996 International Geoscience and Remote Sensing Symposium, IGARSS 1996 Remote Sensing for a Sustainable Future, Vol. 4, pp. 2234–2236. IEEE (1996)

Gance, D.: A new generation of passenger information systems: a single core database and easy tools for consulting (1996)

Monheit, M., Tsafrir, A.: Information systems architecture: a consulting methodology. In: Proceedings of the 1990 IEEE International Conference on Computer Systems and Software Engineering, CompEuro 1990, pp. 568–572. IEEE (1990)

Harling, B.S.C.: Information Systems At Bicardo Consulting Engineers (No. 885155). SAE Technical Paper (1988)

Joshi, K.D., Kuhn, K.M.: What it takes to succeed in information technology consulting: Exploring the gender typing of critical attributes. Inf. Technol. People **20**(4), 400–424 (2007)

Becker, J., Niehaves, B., Klose, K.: Political dimensions in IT consulting projects: a governance theory approach. Int. J. Inf. Syst. Change Manage. 2(2), 109–124 (2007)

Aitcheson, G.: Consulting the oracle: A future role for expert systems in IT project management. Int. J. Project Manage. 7(1), 39–41 (1989)

Kim, S.K., Trimi, S.: IT for KM in the management consulting industry. J. Knowl. Manage. 11(3), 145–155 (2007)

Sherif, K., Hoffman, J., Thomas, B.: Can technology build organizational social capital? The case of a global IT consulting firm. Inf. Manage. 43(7), 795–804 (2006)

Sherif, K., Xing, B.: Adaptive processes for knowledge creation in complex systems: The case of a global IT consulting firm. Inf. Manage. 43(4), 530–540 (2006)

Kautz, K., Mahnke, V.: Value creation through IT-supported knowledge management? The utilisation of a knowledge management system in a global consulting company. Informing Sci. 6, 75–88 (2003)

Djavanshir, G.R., Agresti, W.W.: It consulting: Communication skills are key. IT Prof. 9(1) (2007)

Yoon, S., Suh, H.: Ensuring IT consulting SERVQUAL and user satisfaction: a modified measurement tool. Inf. Syst. Front. 6(4), 341–351 (2004)

Galliers, R.D., Leidner, D.E.: Strategic Information Management: Challenges and Strategies in Managing Information Systems. Routledge, New York (2014)

Koch, C.: Knowledge management in consulting engineering–joining IT and human resources to support the production of knowledge. Eng. Constr. Architectural Manage. 10(6), 391–401 (2003)

Lesusky, F.M., Rhudy, R.L., Wiginton, J.C.: The development of a knowledge-based system for information systems project development consulting. Comput. Industr. Eng. 13(1–4), 29–33 (1987)

Nolan, R.L., Bennigson, L.: Information technology consulting. Division of Research, Harvard Business School (2002)

Clemons, E.K.: Information systems for sustainable competitive advantage. Inf. Manage. 11(3), 131–136 (1986)

Dawson, G., Watson, R.T., Boudreau, M.C., Pitt, L.F.: A knowledge-centric examination of signaling and screening activities in the negotiation for information systems consulting services. J. Assoc. Inf. Syst. 17(2), 77 (2016)

The Role of Contemporary Skills in Information Technology Professionals: An FsQCA Approach

Michail N. Giannakos[✉], Ilias O. Pappas, and Patrick Mikalef

Norwegian University of Science and Technology, Trondheim, Norway
michailg@ntnu.no

Abstract. Information Technology (IT) industries' knowledge and ability to innovate, heavily relies in the skills of the IT professionals. In particular, inefficiencies usually come from the lack of skills or IT professionals' inability to apply them in a way that allows a firm to adapt and evolve concurrently with business demands. In order to examine the interplay of skills related with data analysis, entrepreneurship, business, communication and collaboration, and their combined effect in enhancing employees' perceived work performance, a conceptual model is developed and examined on a data sample of 72 IT professionals, through fuzzy-set qualitative comparative analysis (fsQCA). The findings indicate five configurations that lead to high perceived work performance. The outcomes of the analysis show the importance of collaboration and entrepreneurship, since they appear in most of the configurations/solutions; but also the importance of data analysis, which can lead to high work performance even with the absence of all the other skills. This study also confirms that the identified skills portray to a good extend IT professionals' work performance, which is critical for a firm to evolve and innovate.

Keywords: Data analytics skills · Entrepreneurial Skills · Business Skills · Communication Skills · Collaboration Skills · Work Performance · IT professionals

1 Introduction

IT firms' performance and competitiveness depends to a great extent on IT professionals' knowledge and expertise towards the software development process [28] as well as their non-technical skills (e.g., management, communication) [7]. Prior research guides how to manage the organizations [10], and highlights the importance of both technical and non-technical skills and competences [7, 22]. Related work however do not incorporate skill related with the 21st century technological developments [35], like understanding/analyzing big data and entrepreneurship amongst others [1, 3, 23]. Despite the fact that those technological developments provide a way forward for solving the global challenges of the 21st century, building sustainable development, and advancing human welfare [35], it is still unclear how those skills might benefit IT professionals' evolvement and performance.

© IFIP International Federation for Information Processing 2017
Published by Springer International Publishing AG 2017. All Rights Reserved
A.K. Kar et al. (Eds.): I3E 2017, LNCS 10595, pp. 485–496, 2017.
DOI: 10.1007/978-3-319-68557-1_43

IT professional's performance has been investigated considering different skills, however, mainly, without studying the existence of different combinations among these skills, which may lead to different models explaining IT professionals performance. Such approaches (e.g., multiple regression analysis, structural equation modelling) assume that relations among the variables are symmetric and offer one single best solution explaining the outcome. This may be misleading as within a sample the variables may also have asymmetric relationships, not identifiable by variance based approaches [36]. Multiple configurations of the examined skills that lead to multiple solutions, explaining the same result, representing a larger part of the sample, need to be identified. This paper complements prior work by utilize multiple configurations to explain how various skills might combine to result high work performance of IT professionals.

This exploratory study draws data from 72 IT professionals, to better understand how selected important skills (namely: data analytics, entrepreneurial, collaborative, communication and business skills) influence perceived work performance. Thus, we build on complexity theory and configuration theory and employ the novel fuzzy-set Qualitative Comparative Analysis (fsQCA) [5] in order to identify multiple solutions of the various skills that result high work performance of the IT professionals. FsQCA is appropriate for explaining the complex interrelations among variables, as their combinations and interdependencies lead to the desired outcome and is suitable because it may offer valid responses in studies with small samples [5]. FsQCA has received increased attention in different areas, such as business [20], learning analytics [18] and others [19], and we build and expand on their contributions. The paper contributes to the literature first, by offering empirical evidence on the important role of data analytics, communication, collaborative, entrepreneurial and business skills on the development of IT professionals performance in today's demanding and continuously evolving IT firms; through the lens of the fsQCA approach.

The rest of the paper is structured as follows. In the next section we present the background and related work upon which the conceptual model is built. In Sect. 3 the methodology is outlined, and in Sect. 4 the findings of the study are presented. In closing, Sect. 5 provides a discussion on research directions and areas of future interest.

2 Background and Conceptual Model

In today's IT industry, hard skills, like software development, architecture, testing and maintenance are essential for professionals to take on an entrepreneurial role and focus on innovation. However, the complete spectrum of needed skills for IT professionals is determined by the tasks that are required in their work environment [12], and as the complexity of technology increases, the skills of related professionals must also increase and evolve [37]. Thus, in addition to hard skills, 21st century IT professionals must pose a robust understanding of skills related to data understanding and analysis [9], entrepreneurship and business as well as communication and collaboration with other professionals but also the end users [22]. These skills allow them to utilize resources and, understand needs and opportunities in order to gain innovative outcomes and competitive advantages. Today's challenges of IT industry faced by IT professionals go beyond solving technical problems and the expected skillset requires knowledge in relation to business functionality, decision making strategy and evolving environment, especially in an increasingly turbulent business and technological context [37].

Kim et al. [8] describe IT expertise skills as "professional skills and knowledge of technologies, technology management, business functions, and relational (or interpersonal) areas necessary for IT staff to undertake assigned tasks effectively" (p. 492). Related work in the area of technical skills and abilities (hard skills) of IT professionals based on their training and expertise in specific technical areas, and these skills can advance the development or configuration of IT-related services [4]. In order to develop IT-applications that satisfy today's increased demands, IT professionals must have the abilities to communicate with the end user and understand the tasks of other functions in addition to their technical skills [34]. In this study, we combine data analytics, entrepreneurship, business, collaboration and communication to offer an empirical evidence about the critical role of those emerging skills in IT professionals' work performance, and ultimately in the IT industry as a whole.

To address this gap, we examine IT professionals' perceived work performance (we hereinafter refer to it as work performance) by unravelling configurations of causally related sets of the five aforementioned skills. Relationships between two skills (e.g., X, Y) are complex, and the presence of one (X) may lead to the presence of the other (Y), indicating sufficiency. Also, skill Y may be present even with skill X being absent, thus the presence of X is a sufficient but unnecessary condition for Y to occur. With the presence of additional factors, X may be necessary but insufficient for Y to occur. We posit that there is a synergy between the five skills in explaining work performance of IT professionals. We theorize that there is not one single, optimal, configuration of such skills. Instead, multiple and equally effective configurations of causal conditions exist, which may include different combinations these skills. Depending on how they combine they may or may not explain IT professionals high work performance.

To conceptualize these relationships, we propose a theoretical model (Fig. 1) illustrating six constructs (five types of skills and work performance) and their intersections. The overlapped areas represent possible combinations among factors, that is areas that one factor may exist together with the rest (e.g., combinations that explain high purchase intentions are included within the outcome of interest area).

Drawing on complexity theory and the principle of equifinality, a result may be equally explained by alternative sets of causal conditions [5]. These conditions may be combined in sufficient configurations to explain the outcome [36]. IT-related skills, especially the skills possessed by the IT professionals, can be viewed as complimentary to each other. If IT personnel have adequate set of skills, they can combine those skills to develop, improve or adjust IT applications efficiently and effectively in order to increase the quality and innovation of the produced products and services [30, 33]. Demands from the IT industry indicates the need for various sets of skills; for instance, drawing from both IT personnel job advertisements but also the guidelines for IT curriculum design [29, 31]. For example, after analyzing job advertisements for IT professionals (e.g., software engineers) across two decades; it became clear that business skills, if one of the most important knowledge areas for hiring IT personnel [34]. Along the same lines, IT curriculum guidelines - developed by the Association for Computing

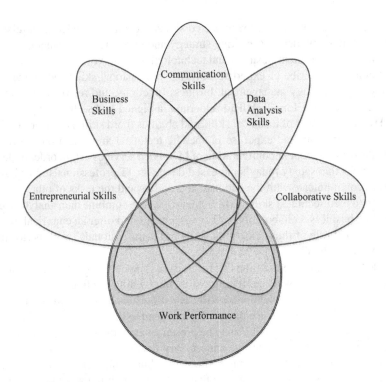

Fig. 1. Venn diagram illustrating the conceptual model explaining work performance

Machinery (ACM), the Association for Information Systems (AIS) and the IEEE-Computer Society [29, 31] - suggested that IT professionals should be equipped with: business skills and business domain fundamentals. Business skills and business domain fundamentals includes leadership, collaboration and communication skills as well as knowledge and skills regarding general business models, key business specializations, and the evaluation of business performance [34]. Thus, high work performance may be achieved in more than one combination of skills in the IT industry and therefore configuration theory and fsQCA approach are essential in the realization of our research.

Configuration theory proposes the principle of causal asymmetry, which means that, for an outcome to occur, the presence and absence of a causal condition depends on how this condition combines with the other conditions [5]. Also, causal asymmetry suggests that the causal conditions that explain the presence of an outcome, cannot be assumed as mirror pictures of conditions explaining the absence of the same outcome [5]. For instance, alternative configurations of high work performance in IT professionals may include high data analysis skills in one configuration and low communication skills in a different configuration. Thus, the same outcome may be influenced either positively or negatively by a specific factor, depending on how it combines with the other factors. Furthermore, high data analysis skills might be part of a combination that explains high work performance, and might also be part of another combination that explains medium work performance (in this study we focus only in high work performance). Thus, configurations that explain the presence of an outcome do not suggest that their reverses are also able to explain the absence of the same outcome.

3   Research Methodology

3.1   Sampling

To actualize the objectives of this study a custom-built questionnaire was developed and sent to respondents to fill out electronically (online questionnaire). Our target population consisted of IT graduates from Norway's primary university for technological education, with respondents filling out the questionnaire required to be in an active IT position. The survey was conducted between February and March 2016. In order to recruit participants, we distributed the online survey via the IT graduates' alumni mailing list. A raffle was created with gift cards as a reward to the participants. In total, 72 responses were gathered.

The sample consists of 63 men (87.5%) and 9 women (12.5%), with relatively long experience in the IT industry, which range from 2 to 33 years with an average of 13.21 years (S.D.: 7.35 years). Although the participants of the study had formal IT education and hold IT positions, there is a variation in their expertise and job titles; in particular, 16 are developers (e.g., software engineer, mobile developer), 6 directors (e.g., CTOs, strategy directors, business development), 14 project managers, 21 IT consultants, 8 software architects, 3 in R&D positions and 5 with responsibilities in various stages. The majority of firms operated in the IT sector (54.2%), with companies from oil and gas (9.7%) and telecommunications (9.7%) following, there was also a small proportion of firms from utilities, consumer goods and healthcare (approx. 3–5% from each sector). The vast majority (59.7%) belonged to SME size-class (1–249 employees), with 40.3% being large enterprises (250+ employees). More specifically, from the SME grouping, micro firms (0–9 employees) accounted for 15,3%, small firms (10–49 employees) for 23,6%, and medium-sized (50–249 employees) firms for 20,8%. The majority of the firms were active in the national level (91.7%) with most of them being also active in the inter-national arena (65.3%).

3.2   Measures

The questionnaire comprised of three parts. First the respondents were presented with different questions about their demographics and personal work experience, followed by the second part which included questions in relation to the size, orientation and focus of their firm, the third part included measures of the constructs related with their Data Analysis Skills (DAS), Entrepreneurial Skills (ES), Business Skills (BS), Communication Skills (ComS), Collaborative Skills (ColS) and Work Performance (WP) as those were identified in the literature. The survey included scales for all the constructs that were used in this study with a seven-point Likert-type scale. The operational definitions of all constructs are presented in Table 1, along with their source in the literature.

Table 1. Operational definitions of the constructs

Construct	Operational definition	Source
Data Analysis Skills (DAS)	DAS is the degree to someone's capacity to make sense, extract intelligence and make decisions from big data	[32]
Entrepreneurial Skills (ES)	ES indicates how confident respondents are in their possession of a high-enough level of certain skills related to entrepreneurship (e.g., feel capable to start a firm, higher personal attraction)	[13]
Business Skills (BS)	BS is the degree to someone's capacity to understand business functions, problems, needs, policies and plans	[2]
Communication Skills (ComS)	ComS is the degree to someone's capacity to listen, communicate and present ideas in a clear and concise manner	[13]
Collaborative Skills (ColS)	ColS is the degree to someone's capacity work and coordinate group problem solving activities and utilize the proper degree and type of participation	[2]
Work Performance (WP)	WP is the degree to which employees are indicating their performance	[11]

3.3 Data Analysis

The constructs of this study were evaluated in terms of their reliability and validity. Reliability testing, based on Composite Reliability and Cronbach alpha, showed acceptable indices of internal consistency in that all constructs exceeded the cut-off threshold of 0.70. For validity, the average variance extracted (AVE) should be higher than .50, and the correlations among the variables in the confirmatory model should not exceed .8 points, the latter because exceeding 0.8 suggests low discrimination. The square root of each factor's AVE needs to be greater than its correlations with the other factors [6]. The AVEs for all constructs ranged between 0.55 and 0.80, all correlations were lower than 0.80, and the square root AVEs for all constructs were larger than their correlations. Next, we tested for multicollinearity [16] along with the potential common method bias by utilizing Harman's single-factor test. The variance inflation factor for each variable was under 3, suggesting multicollinearity is not an issue. Findings indicate an absence of common method bias as the first factor did not account for the majority of the variance and no single factor occurred from the factor analysis.

3.4 FsQCA

To address its objective this study employs fsQCA using fs/QCA 2.5 [24], which was developed through the integration of fuzzy sets and fuzzy logic principles with Qualitative Comparative Analysis (QCA) [25]. By using fsQCA researchers go beyond traditional regression based analyses, as they identify multiple pathways that explain the same outcome [27]. These pathways or combinations include variables that are not identified by regression based analyses because they influence the outcome only for a small number of cases. The aforementioned combinations create to multiple solutions, offered by fsQCA, and each variable (or condition) may be present or absent on a solution, or it may be on a "do not care" situation. The "do not care" situation indicates that the variable may either be present or absent and it does not play a role on a specific configuration [5].

Data calibration

The next step is to calibrate all factors into fuzzy sets with values ranging from 0 to 1 [28]. This procedure may be direct or indirect. In the direct, the researcher chooses three qualitative breakpoints, while in the indirect, the factors should be rescaled based on qualitative assessments. Either method may be chosen depending on data and the underlying theory [28]. The direct method of setting three values that correspond to full-set membership, full-set non-membership and intermediate-set membership is recommended [28].

Data calibration here was done based on the direct method. Since our data is skewed to the right, choosing the three qualitative anchors for the calibration based on the survey scale (seven-point Likert scale) [17, 20] would not lead to meaningful results [21]. Thus, data calibration is done by using percentiles, that is the 80th percentile is the full-set membership, the 20th percentile is the full-set non-membership, and the 50th percentile is the intermediate set membership. Next, the values of each variable are calibrated on a linear function to fit into the three aforementioned breakpoints.

Truth table analysis

Next, fsQCA produces a truth table of 2k rows, on which k represents the number of outcome predictors and each row represents every possible combination. The truth table should be sorted based on frequency and consistency [20, 27]. Frequency describes the number of observations for each possible combination, and consistency refers to "the degree to which cases correspond to the set-theoretic relationships expressed in a solution" [5]. A frequency threshold should be set to ensure that a minimum number of empirical observations is acquired for the assessment of the relationships. For samples larger than 150 cases the threshold should be set at 3, while for smaller samples the threshold may be set at 2 [26], thus all observations with smaller frequency are removed from further analysis. Also, the threshold for consistency is set at .80, higher than the recommended threshold of 0.75 [27]. Observations above the consistency threshold are the ones that fully explain the outcome.

4   Findings

The findings from the fsQCA on the configurations for high work performance of IT professionals is presented in Table 2. Every possible combination in the solution is able to explain the same outcome at a specific amount. In detail, the presence of a condition is depicted by black circles (●), while its absence by crossed-out circles (⊗) [5].

The blank spaces indicate a "do not care" situation, meaning that the causal condition may either be present or absent. FsQCA identifies both core and peripheral elements, core conditions are represented with large circles, and peripheral ones with small circles. Table 2 also presents consistency values for every configuration as well as for the overall solution. All values are above the recommended threshold (>0.75). Consistency measures the degree to which a subset relationship has been approximated, while coverage assesses the empirical relevance of a consistent subset [27]. The overall consistency is similar to the correlation. The overall solution coverage indicates the extent to which high work performance of IT professionals may be determined from the existing configurations, and is comparable to the R-square value reported in traditional regression analyses. The overall solution coverage of .96 indicates that a substantial amount of the outcome is explained by the five solutions. FsQCA estimates also the empirical relevance for every solution, by calculating raw and unique coverage. The raw coverage describes the amount of the outcome that is explained by a certain alternative solution, while the unique coverage describes the amount of the outcome that is exclusively explained by a certain alternative solution. The solutions presented in Table 2 explain a great number of IT professionals perceived work performance, ranging from 19% to 39% cases associated with the outcome.

Table 2. Combinations that lead to high work performance

Configuration	Solution				
	1	2	3	4	5
Skills					
Entrepreneurial	●		●	●	⊗
Business		⊗	⊗	●	⊗
Communication		⊗	⊗	●	⊗
Collaborative	●	●		●	⊗
Data Analysis	⊗	⊗	⊗		●
Consistency	0.98	0.96	0.96	0.99	0.98
Raw Coverage	0.39	0.29	0.34	0.32	0.19
Unique Coverage	0.06	0.03	0.07	0.09	0.03
Overall Solution Consistency	0.63				
Overall Solution Coverage	0.96				

Note: Black circles (●) indicate the presence of a condition, and circles with "x" (⊗) indicate its absence. Large circles indicate core conditions, and small ones represent peripheral conditions. Blank spaces indicate "don't care."

For high work performance, the five solutions present different combinations of the five different skills (Table 2). In detail, IT professionals have high work performance, when they have entrepreneurial and communications skills, without having data analysis skills; regardless of business and communication skills (Solution 1). When business, communication and data analysis skills are absent, the IT professional can still has high work performance if one of the entrepreneurial or collaborative skills is present, regardless of the other (Solutions 2 and 3). Further, solution 4 explains that an IT professional with entrepreneurial, business, communication and collaborative skills, has high work performance, regardless of his/her data analysis skills (Solution 4). Finally, when entrepreneurial, business, communication and collaborative skills are absent, the IT professional can still have high work performance, as long as the data analysis skills are present (Solution 5).

5 Discussion

Developing various skills for IT firms has gained enormous attention from executives, as noted by Luftman et al. [14] in the Society for Information Management. Rather than focusing on traditional soft and hard skills for general employees, we targeted IT professionals and examined factors related with the 21st developments, like data-driven decisions and entrepreneurship amongst others. Unlike previous research which focused on skills as static characteristics of the employee, this study considers the state-of-the-art skills and their contribution to firms' competitiveness in a more dynamic and realistic manner.

The present study proposes that entrepreneurial, business, communication, collaborative and data analysis skills combine with each other to form configurations that explain work performance of IT professionals. Building on complexity theory and configuration theory a conceptual model is created to identify such configurations. The model includes six constructs, that is the five types of skills and work performance. By employing the model to IT firms we collected data from 72 IT professionals and test the proposed model. The findings identify five solutions leading to high work performance, and showcase the significance of the five types of skills. The findings also indicate that there is an important interplay between the five types of skills and employees' work performance.

In detail, the five solutions present how an IT professional with a good set of these skills is productive (e.g. Solution 4 where four out of the five skills are present). In addition, the solutions indicate that IT professionals who are mastering few or even one of these skills, even with the absence of all the others (i.e. Solutions 2, 3 and 5), are able to overcome low disposition to some of the skills and be productive. Another important observation is the central role of today's data analysis skills, in solution 5 we can see that even with the absence of every other skill, data analysis skills can lead the professional to high work performance. This can be explained, by the fact that IT professionals with strong data analysis skills are the cornerstone for a company to move from competitive parity to competitive advantage [9]. In summary, the results show that the five types of skills are all important for IT professionals, and under different combinations can make IT professionals feel confident and productive (perceived work performance).

Based on related work and 21st century technological developments, we selected to include a specific-range of skills and consider their influence on the personnel of IT firms. While we carefully selected those skills, the study might have been benefited from the inclusion of some more traditional skills (e.g., traditional hard and soft skills). Moreover, there may be other predicting factors other relationships between them might be discovered by using regressions techniques (e.g. SEM). Future research could establish other relationships by combining the proposed model with other potential predictors but also alternative data analysis approach; this can be addressed in a future large scale study.

Moreover, this study included only limited demographic variables (e.g., gender, experience) and due to the relative small sample size, we could not use them as configuration variables. Given prior research [15], individual characteristics, such as specific job-related skills, may result significant differences. In particular, employees who have higher levels of job-related skills will have a deeper understanding of the specific tasks [15]. Future research might also examine how these factors affect IT professionals' intention to learn new skills. A more detailed investigation of these skills and how these skills differ between specific department in an IT firm and their relation to firm's strategy, are also important directions for future research. Finally, the findings are based on self-reported data. Future studies may combine self-reported data with real data from firms' performance and strategy, as well as triangulate them with more qualitative data from interviews and observations. Although, this is pioneering study, and one of the first who attempted to explain the role of contemporary skills in IT firms. The collected data are from a limited number of IT professionals, from a specific country in a specific time. Thus, further research is needed, in a large scale context collecting longitudinal evidence, in order to enhance our current understanding of the relationships among different skills and their role in IT firms.

Acknowledgments. The authors would like to express their gratitude to all of the IT professionals for volunteering their time. Our very special thanks go to Unni Kringtrø Eide for supporting us with the data collection. This work is part of the Centre for Excellent IT Education (Excited - http://www.ntnu.edu/excited).

References

1. Boyles, T.: 21st century knowledge, skills, and abilities and entrepreneurial competencies: a model for undergraduate entrepreneurship education. J. Entrep. Educ. **15**, 41 (2012)
2. Byrd, T.A., Turner, D.E.: An exploratory examination of the relationship between flexible IT infrastructure and competitive advantage. Inf. Manag. **39**(1), 41–52 (2001)
3. Davenport, T.H., Patil, D.J.: Data scientist: the sexiest job of the 21st century. Harvard Bus. Rev. **90**(10), 70–76 (2012)
4. Finch, D.J., Peacock, M., Levallet, N., Foster, W.: A dynamic capabilities view of employability: exploring the drivers of competitive advantage for university graduates. Educ. Train. **58**(1), 61–81 (2016)
5. Fiss, P.C.: Building better causal theories: a fuzzy set approach to typologies in organization research. Acad. Manag. J. **54**(2), 393–420 (2011)
6. Fornell, C., Larcker, D.F.: Structural equation models with unobservable variables and measurement error: algebra and statistics. J. Mark. Res. **18**(3), 382–388 (1981)
7. Gallagher, K.P., Kaiser, K.M., Simon, J.C., Beath, C.M., Goles, T.: The requisite variety of skills for IT professionals. Commun. ACM **53**(6), 144–148 (2010)
8. Kim, G., Shin, B., Kim, K.K., Lee, H.G.: IT capabilities, process-oriented dynamic capabilities, and firm financial performance. J. AIS **12**(7), 487–551 (2011)
9. Kiron, D., Prentice, P.K., Ferguson, R.B.: The analytics mandate. MIT Sloan Manag. Rev. **55**(4), 1–25 (2014)

10. Lee, M.S., Trauth, E.M., Farwell, D.: Critical skills and knowledge requirements of IS professionals: a joint academic/industry investigation. MIS Q. **19**(3), 313–340 (1995)
11. Leftheriotis, I., Giannakos, M.N.: Using social media for work: losing your time or improving your work? Comput. Hum. Behav. **31**, 134–142 (2014)
12. Leitheiser, R.L.: MIS skills for the 1990s: a survey of MIS managers' perceptions. J. Manag. Inf. Syst. **9**(1), 69–91 (1992)
13. Linan, F.: Skill and value perceptions: how do they affect entrepreneurial intentions? Int. Entrep. Manag. J. **4**(3), 257–272 (2008)
14. Luftman, J., Kempaiah, R., Henrique, E.: Key issues for IT executives 2008. MIS Q. Exec. **8**(3), 151–159 (2009)
15. Morgeson, F.P., Delaney-Klinger, K., Hemingway, M.A.: The importance of job autonomy, cognitive ability, and job-related skill for predicting role breadth and job performance. J. Appl. Psychol. **90**(2), 399–406 (2005)
16. O'brien, R.M.: A caution regarding rules of thumb for variance inflation factors. Qual. Quant. **41**(5), 673–690 (2007)
17. Ordanini, A., Parasuraman, A., Rubera, G.: When the recipe is more important than the ingredients a Qualitative Comparative Analysis (QCA) of service innovation configurations. J. Serv. Res. **17**(2), 134–149 (2014)
18. Pappas, I.O., Giannakos, M.N., Sampson, D.G.: Making sense of learning analytics with a configurational approach. In: Book Making Sense of Learning Analytics with a Configurational Approach (2016)
19. Pappas, I.O., Giannakos, M.N., Jaccheri, L., Sampson, D.G.: Assessing student behavior in computer science education with an fsQCA approach: the role of gains and barriers. ACM Trans. Comput. Educ. (TOCE) **17**(2) (2017)
20. Pappas, I.O., Kourouthanassis, P.E., Giannakos, M.N., Chrissikopoulos, V.: Explaining online shopping behavior with fsQCA: the role of cognitive and affective perceptions. J. Bus. Res. **69**(2), 794–803 (2016)
21. Plewa, C., Ho, J., Conduit, J., Karpen, I.O.: Reputation in higher education: a fuzzy set analysis of resource configurations. J. Bus. Res. **69**, 3087–3095 (2016)
22. Poston, R.S., Dhaliwal, J.: IS human capital: assessing gaps to strengthen skill and competency sourcing. Commun. AIS **36**(1), 34 (2015)
23. Power, D.J.: Using 'Big Data' for analytics and decision support. J. Decis. Syst. **23**(2), 222–228 (2014)
24. Ragin, C.C., Davey, S.: fs/QCA [Computer Programme], version 2.5. University of California, Irvine (2014)
25. Ragin, C.C.: Fuzzy-Set Social Science. University of Chicago Press (2000)
26. Ragin, C.C.: Redesigning Social Inquiry: Fuzzy Sets and Beyond. Wiley Online Library (2008)
27. Ragin, C.C.: Set relations in social research: evaluating their consistency and coverage. Polit. Anal. **14**(3), 291–310 (2006)
28. Rivera-Ibarra, J.G., Rodríguez-Jacobo, J., Serrano-Vargas, M.A.: Competency framework for software engineers. In: Proceedings of the 23rd IEEE Conference on Software Engineering Education and Training, CSEE&T, pp. 33–40 (2010)
29. Sahami, M., Danyluk, A., Fincher, S., Fisher, K., et al.: Computer Science Curricula 2013: Curriculum Guidelines for Undergraduate Degree Programs in Computer Science. Association for Computing Machinery (ACM). IEEE Computer Society (2013)
30. Sambamurthy, V., Bharadwaj, A., Grover, V.: Shaping agility through digital options: reconceptualizing the role of information technology in contemporary firms. MIS Q. **27**(2), 237–263 (2003)

31. Topi, H., Valacich, J.S., Wright, R.T. et al.: Curriculum guidelines for undergraduate degree programs in information systems. ACM/AIS Task Force (2010)
32. Wamba, S.F., Gunasekaran, A., Akter, S., et al.: Big data analytics and firm performance: effects of dynamic capabilities. J. Bus. Res. **70**, 356–365 (2016)
33. Wang, E.T.G., Chiu, C.-H., Chen, K.-X.: Effect of IT skills on IT capabilities and IT-business alignment. In: PACIS 2013 Proceedings (2013). Paper 113
34. Wang, Y.Y., Lin, T.C., Tsay, C.: Encouraging IS developers to learn business skills: an examination of the MARS model. IT People **29**(2), 381–418 (2016)
35. Wilson, K.E., Vyakarnam, S., Volkmann, C., et al.: Educating the next wave of entrepreneurs: unlocking entrepreneurial capabilities to meet the global challenges of the 21st century. In: World Economic Forum: A Report of the Global Education Initiative (2009)
36. Woodside, A.G.: Embrace perform model: Complexity theory, contrarian case analysis, and multiple realities. J. Bus. Res. **67**(12), 2495–2503 (2014)
37. Yu, P.L., Fang, S.C., Wang, Y.L.: Improving IT professionals job skills development: the use of management styles and individual cultural value orientation. Asia Pac. Manag. Rev. **21**(2), 63–73 (2016)

Service Complexity and Service Productivity in E-Mobility: New Insights from Emergency and Roadway Breakdown Services

Aaron W. Baur[1]([⊠]), Bastian Sander[2], Robert Kummer[2], Jörg von Garrel[3], and Markus Bick[1]

[1] ESCP Europe Business School Berlin, Berlin, Germany
abaur@escpeurope.eu
[2] Fraunhofer Institute for Factory Operation and Automation IFF,
Magdeburg, Germany
[3] SRH Fernhochschule – The Mobile University,
Riedlingen, Germany

Abstract. The introduction and wide-spread adaptation of e-mobility influences emergency and roadway breakdown service firms. Service complexity and service productivity are important constructs to measure and monitor where the industry is headed and where firms need to quickly adapt.

The purpose of this paper is to investigate effects on service complexity and service productivity of emergency and roadway breakdown services on the back of a growing market penetration of electric vehicles in industrialized countries.

The study is grounded on expert interviews and a quantitative analysis of 325 questionnaires that have been distributed among roadside assistant service providers in Germany. It reveals the increasing complexity of an important service industry that had only been studied scarcely in the past. With its large-scale quantitative design, it adds significantly to the body of knowledge available and can be the basis for further advanced research in other geographical settings. The research supports practitioners in the field of roadside assistant services in rethinking their service offering and the handling of increasingly heterogeneous propulsion technologies such as electric drives. In order to keep the service productivity high and the complexity low, assistance systems and targeted qualification and training concepts for the roadway personnel have to be developed and rolled out.

The research setting is focused on the German market, but links are provided to apply the study design to other countries and further investigate respective market singularities.

Keywords: E-Mobility · Services · Service complexity · Service productivity

1 Introduction and Background

Individual mobility is still the prime way of transportation for the majority of people in the Western world. For instance, more than 80% of transport performance in Germany, measured in passenger-kilometers, is delivered through cars and motorbikes [1].

© IFIP International Federation for Information Processing 2017
Published by Springer International Publishing AG 2017. All Rights Reserved
A.K. Kar et al. (Eds.): I3E 2017, LNCS 10595, pp. 497–513, 2017.
DOI: 10.1007/978-3-319-68557-1_44

Although many innovations have been introduced, such as the antilock braking system, lane assistance or start/stop systems, the use of combustions engines as the primary way of propulsion has remained almost untouched. This continuity of technology ensured a quick emergency response and optimized processes in case of an accident or roadway breakdown.

However, negative news about the climate change and the harmful effects of the oxides of nitrogen and other constituents of exhaust fumes call for action. The political will for a comprehensive introduction of innovative technology and mobility concepts exists in some areas of the world. Pending discussions are on to stop registration of cars with combustion engines within the next decade (e.g., Netherlands and Norway 2025, Germany, India, and California 2030) [2]. E-mobility can be regarded the prime way to reduce local exhaust fumes. Hence, it is now a priority in many industrialized countries globally.

The higher number of hybrid or fully electrical driven vehicles (EVs) on the roads also expectedly increases the likelihood of road accidents and breakdowns which involve electric vehicles. To deliver users of electric vehicles emergency and breakdown services of high quality and timeliness, new concepts and services have to be developed, operationalized and tested that enable effective and secure – but also productive – handling of such situations. The main actors have to be comprehensively sensitized and educated of how to handle electric vehicles after non-planned situations such as breakdowns or accidents.

Thus, we want to shed light with this research on the effects of service complexity and service productivity important roadside assistance firms report, on the back of a growing market penetration of electric vehicles.

The remainder of our paper is structured as follows: section two introduces the theoretical background and framework of peculiarities of electric vehicles and how they affect service complexity and service productivity. Nine hypotheses are developed based on analyzed literature and interviews with experts in the field. Section three explains the research method applied including data gathering and data analysis. In section four, we analyze the data and discuss the results, before we conclude the paper with implications, limitations, and areas of future research in section five.

2   Theoretical Framework and Hypotheses Development

Our research framework is built on the concepts of service productivity and service complexity in the context of e-mobility.

2.1   Characteristics of Electric Vehicles in Emergency Service Contexts

In this paper, we follow the definition of the German government that defines electric vehicles as passenger cars, light-duty commercial vehicles, motorbikes and micro cars which use electricity as the primary means of fuel [3]. In detail, these are so-called battery electric vehicles (BEV), range-extended electric vehicles (REEV) and plug-in hybrid electric vehicles (PHEV). All of them use a high-voltage (HV) system with up to 1,000 V (alternating current, AC) or 1,500 V (direct current, DC). If they flow through the human body, these voltages can lead to apnea, ventricular fibrillation or death. Although the OEMs have developed various safety features that shut down or isolate the critical components after an accident, residual risks remain. This causes serious implications for emergency rescue or roadside assistance personnel who need to help drivers of EVs. In order to safely deliver the respective services on an EV, the German DEKRA (the European market leader specialized in the inspection of motor vehicles and other technical systems) recommends the use of additional safety equipment for emergency personnel, such as electrical protection gloves, safety helmets with full visors and voltage testers. Because of these new technical developments and a lack of experience, emergency and roadside assistance firms express uncertainty of how to handle electric vehicles in breakdown or accident situations. Additionally, the incident of an EV of the US National Highway Traffic Safety Administration (NHTSA) that started burning three weeks after a conducted crash test, damaging three additional vehicles and a warehouse, increases this uncertainty [4].

The missing standardization across manufacturers is another issue. For instance, some vehicles are clearly marked as electric, others are not; safety cards that show the HV components are included in some vehicles, but not in others; or some vehicles can be towed, others have to be picked up. Finally, there are technological peculiarities of EVs that in the case of a non-planned event cause risks to safety personnel that cannot be completely controlled, no matter how advanced the safety and cut off provisions are. For example, the electro-chemical accumulators cannot be completely turned off and contain health hazardous substances or reaction products [5], which pose a risk to personnel especially when accidents cause mechanical deformations on the high voltage components. Hence, the service firms perceive a lack of process stability when it comes to electric vehicles in general, but in particular when handling non-planned operational situations.

2.2 Excellence of Service

To ensure the success of the politically enforced electric mobility, the quality, safety and productivity of rescue services must be ensured through efficient work processes and a profound qualification of service providers and (end) users of electric vehicles. The concepts of excellence of services, service complexity and service productivity and can be used to characterize these roadside services (cf. [6]).

Excellence of service is made up of the service provider which is based on the factors service productivity and service complexity, and the service consumer, based on service quality (Fig. 1).

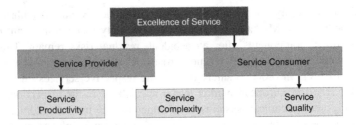

Fig. 1. Breakdown of excellence of service (Source: own visualization)

Service productivity. Productivity describes the ratio of output to input [7]. When measuring productivity of services, the integration of the external factor, i.e., the customer, and its immateriality pose the greatest difficulties [8]. To just transfer the classical understanding of productivity into an interactive and integrative service process will not pay off [9]. Authors therefore focus on the efficiency of external processes [10], and the effectiveness of delivering the service (customer satisfaction, customer benefit and economic success). Measures to design service productivity thus entail aspects of efficiency, effectiveness, and their possible interdependencies [6, 11].

In this paper, we follow the model of [12] and define service productivity as a function of (1) how effectively input resources into the service (production) process are transformed to outputs in the form of services (internal efficiency), (2) how well the quality of the service process and its outcome is perceived (external efficiency or effectiveness) and (3) how effectively the capacity of the service process is utilized (capacity efficiency).

For instance, the construct of service productivity is comprised of efficiency and effectiveness, the effectiveness being defined as the external efficiency while the efficiency is comprised of internal and capacity efficiency (see Fig. 2). The effective and efficient delivery of services is characterized by (1) the efficient input of production resources and the ability of the service provider to integrate its customers as value-adding actors into the service delivery process (internal efficiency), (2) the handling of demand (capacity efficiency) and (3) the resulting customer benefit and the

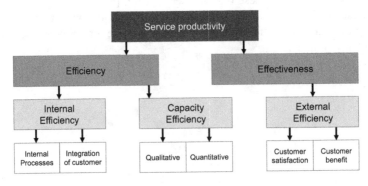

Fig. 2. Breakdown of service productivity (Source: based on [13])

degree of perceived service quality that a firm can generate with a pre-set input of resources (external efficiency) [13].

2.3 Hypotheses Development

Understanding service productivity as the combined effect of how well a service provider manages the cost efficiency of its service production resources [14], its processes (internal efficiency) and the perceived quality of its services (external efficiency), leads to several hypotheses.

Employee Base of the Firm. In order to be able to deliver roadside assistance services, the providers have to hold a certain number of employees available. Of them, some are administrative, but the majority naturally ought to be roadside assistants that actually deliver the service to customers on the road. Larger firms can normally afford to purchase more modern technical equipment and potentially provide a more thorough qualification to their employees. Especially factors regarding the capacity efficiency should be positively influenced. We therefore hypothesize:

Hypothesis 1a.   There is an interrelation between *service productivity* and number of employees within the firm.

Hypothesis 1b.   There is an interrelation between *service productivity* and number of roadside assistants within the firm.

Qualification Base of Employees. As discussed before, for workers to deliver roadside services to electric vehicles, the peculiarities of these new types of vehicles have to be known and trained. One of the most-common and most-suited qualification is the so-called BGI8686[1] certificate, which gives the non-electric basics in handling EVs, e.g., switching tires, doing an oil exchange, or any other mechanical task.

Hypothesis 2.   The BGI 8686 certificate increases the likelihood of whether the service provider has already delivered roadside assistance to EVs.

Similarly, employees that enjoy a higher degree of training in the context of EVs may be suited to judge the higher level of service complexity and service productivity that electric vehicles cause.

Hypothesis 3a.   Respondents who have the BGI 8686 qualification judge the service complexity of EVs higher than those that do not have it.

Hypothesis 3b.   Respondents who have the BGI 8686 qualification judge the service productivity of EVs higher than those that do not have it.

---

[1] The certificate BGI/GUV-I 8686 is issued by the "Deutsche Gesetzliche Unfallversicherung", i.e., the German Casualty Insurance. It has been renamed to "DGUV Information 200-005 - Qualifizierung für Arbeiten an Fahrzeugen mit Hochvoltsystemen" (qualification to work with vehicles with high-voltage systems).

Level of Experience. A higher degree of experience with the emergency and break-down service for electric vehicles may change the way employees judge service complexity and service productivity. We hypothesize:

Hypothesis 4a.   Firms which have already delivered roadside assistance to EVs judge service complexity of EVs higher than those firms that did not deliver such services.

Hypothesis 4b.   Firms which have already delivered roadside assistance to EVs judge service productivity of EVs higher than those firms that did not deliver such services.

Current Level of Action. Many firms have realized the necessity to adapt to an increasing installed base of electric vehicles and have started to get ready for the change. Consequently, we hypothesize:

Hypothesis 5a.   There is a difference between the judgement of service complexity of roadside assistance for EVs of firms which have implemented certain measures regarding e-mobility and those that did not implement these measures.

Hypothesis 5b.   There is a difference between the judgement of service productivity of roadside assistance for EVs of firms which have implemented certain measures regarding e-mobility and those that did not implement these measures.

These hypotheses will be tested below, bringing the characteristics of electric vehicles and the concepts of service productivity and service complexity together.

3   Research Method

In order to shed light on the service phenomenon of roadside assistance services with electric vehicles, the research has been conducted based on a qualitative sample and statistical calculations.

3.1   Research Setup

A multi-step approach has been taken to analyze how electric vehicles today already impact the services of roadway breakdown firms.

In a first step, an approximation on the construct of excellence of a service was conducted based on a theory-driven conceptualization (see Sect. 2). Through further research and analyses, the three factors service productivity, service complexity and service quality could be operationalized. An initial interview guideline was set up and used as a basis for conversations and interviews with experts of two large roadside assistance clubs. The content analysis of these interviews then lead to a first formu-lation of items that enabled the measurement of the respective factors and thus the excellence of a roadside service.

In a second step, to measure the abovementioned service productivity, the operationalized and validated item battery of [13] has been used. Analogous to that battery, a total of 25 items were formulated that were adapted to the processes, work organization and the industry language of roadside breakdown services in terms of comprehensibility and clearness. Items that were less relevant were partially reformulated or replaced by more exact ones.

3.2 Data Gathering and Analysis

Following a project-internal test of the questionnaire (clearness, structure and logic of questions, time needed to complete it), a pre-test was conducted at IFBA, the leading European professional towing and rescue trade fair, held in Kassel (Germany)[2]. Overall, 48 roadside assistants were questioned. Through discussions with some of the questioned individuals, further important bits of information could be gathered. Based on the results, the questionnaire was updated and optimized/validated using factor analysis. The update has again been tested internally to then issue the final version, which was comprised of 4 areas with 16 item blocks, containing a total of 91 items (e.g., what services are offered, experience with electric vehicles and judgements of the complexity and productivity of the services offered).

The paper-based questionnaires were then sent out across Germany to the members of two large automobile clubs/assistance services. The survey method has been deemed most appropriate for gaining a high, representative number of data across the whole

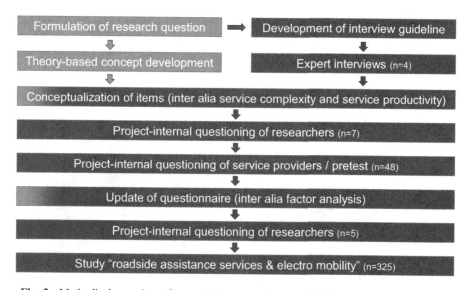

Fig. 3. Methodical overview of quantitative research approach (Source: own visualization)

---

[2] http://www.ifba.eu/index.html.

country which consists of different hierarchy and qualification levels of the emergency service companies [15, 16]. An overview of the approach is given in Fig. 3.

Of the 325 collected surveys, 314 could be used for data analysis (11 surveys were taken out of the sample, as they were from the same firm and had identical answers, leaving the impression they were all filled in by the same person). The data were recorded and coded (primarily binary) in Microsoft Excel to be analyzed in IBM SPSS Statistics v24 [17]. Multiple imputations were then calculated with this software to replace missing data and to minimize the effects of non-response bias on certain questions.

With the final data set, we conducted a factor analysis (VariMax rotation). Based on the Eigenwerte, we kept three factors and tested the internal consistency afterwards with a reliability analysis. Service productivity reached a Cronbach's Alpha of 0.721, displaying a fair reliability. Service complexity, on the other hand, reached an even slightly higher internal consistency with an Alpha of 0.740.

4 Results and Discussion

In this section, the results and implications of the aforementioned research process are presented and discussed.

4.1 Descriptive Analysis

In order to get a better view of the sample, we analyzed several important descriptive statistics. The number of employees averaged 13, with a minimum of 1 and a maximum of 220, thereof 42% were roadside assistants.

As a proxy for job experience, we asked about the number of years the person has been employed at the current company and which position he has got. The distribution and ratio of executives/owners to employees points towards a good quality of the sample (Fig. 4).

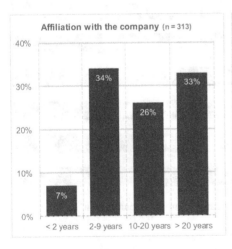

Fig. 4. Duration of company affiliation and current position

As for the qualification of the respondents, the questionnaire asked for the professional background and additional certificates proofing knowledge of how to handle roadside accidents and the recovery of electric vehicles. More than 61% of respondents had the qualification "towing and recovery professional", and 47% had an apprenticeship as a motor mechanic. 30% have acquired the "BGI 8686 certificate for high-voltage vehicles", which is important in our research context.

4.2 Hypothesis Testing and Discussion

In H1a, we hypothesized the number of employees having an effect on the service productivity. According to Spearman's rank correlation coefficient (rho, ρ) of 0.06 and a p-value of 0.307 (two-tailed), respectively, we cannot refuse the null-hypothesis. The number of employees neither influences the internal or external efficiency, nor the capacity efficiency.

In part b of Hypothesis 1, the number of roadside assistants within the firm had been checked. With rho = 0.106 and the p-value = 0.069*[3] (two-tailed), we can refuse the null-hypothesis and find a significant, positive effect on the 10-percent-level. Looked on the different statements separately, significant relationships can be noticed in the following efficiencies (framed in red, Table 1):

Table 1. Three pillars of service productivity with rho and p-values

		rho	p-value	Statement to be evaluated
Internal	A	-0.065	0.257	Easy transfer of process-relevant information to the roadside assistant
	B	-0.048	0.403	Optimal supply of process-relevant information to the employees
	C	0.020	0.738	Trouble-free operation through structuring of usage of resources
Capacity	D	0.199	0.000***	Adapted service offering to altered conditions
	E	0.113	0.047**	Suitable technical equipment to solve upcoming tasks
	F	0.179	0.002***	Excellent qualification of employees to master future demands
External	G	0.027	0.646	Enabling of journey continuation on the location of breakdown
	H	-0.080	0.168	Compliance with scheduled (arrival) times
	I	-0.201	0.000***	Rare confrontation of firm with complaints

The service productivity hence increases especially with capacity factors. It decreases if the number of complaints decreases.

Service productivity is not related to the overall number of employees in the service firms. However, there is a significant effect of the number of roadside assistants delivering the service. Especially the capacity efficiency is higher, resulting from

---

[3] For the remainder of this paper, the level of significance is represented with asterisks: * = 10%, ** = 5%, *** = 1%.

greater financial possibilities of larger firms, which increases service offerings, equipment and qualification of employees. For smaller players in the field, this is bad news: With an increasing number of propulsion technologies on the market, they may not be able to keep pace with developments, leading to lower service productivity of their roadside staff and to potentially lower profits in the mid- to long-term.

With H2, it has been tested if the *BGI 8686 certificate* increases the likelihood of whether the service provider has *already delivered roadside assistance* to EVs. With a Chi-Quadrat (Pearson) of $p = 0.000***$, value = 38.963 and after an exact Fisher test (one-tailed $0.000***$), the null hypothesis can be refused.

Hence, certificates/qualifications like the BGI 8686 are decisive whether roadside assistance is delivered or not (see Table 2).

Table 2. Number of respondents with and without BGI 8686 certificate

		Roadside breakdown services for electric vehicles		
		No	Yes	Total
Qualification BGI 8686	No	109	109	218
	Yes	12	83	95
	Total	121	192	313

Companies with qualified employees are therefore more likely to offer services to electric vehicle than companies with less qualified staff.

In H3a, we tested whether respondents that have the BGI 8686 qualification judge the *service complexity* of EVs higher than those that do not have it. The result of a Mann-Whitney-U-Test (p-value = 0.786) leads to a non-rejection of the null hypothesis, i.e., the qualification BGI 8686 of respondents does <u>not increase</u> the judgment of service complexity. The more heterogeneous approach, a higher variety of work tasks, and the demands to meet the more sophisticated technology are evaluated without differences. A significant difference can only be observed in regard to judgement of the employee qualifications (employee complexity, see Table 3). Here, BGI 8686 qualified workers appreciate that a higher qualification is needed.

Table 3. Analysis of different statements of H3a

	p-value	Statement to be evaluated	
A	0.502	More heterogenous approach/procedure	
B	0.554	Higher variety of work tasks	
C	0.350	More sophisticated technology	
D	0.038**	Higher qualification of employees	

In the second part of this hypothesis, H3b, we checked whether the BGI 8686 qualification increases the judgment of *service productivity*. The Mann-Whitney-U-Test showed a p-value of 0.002***, the hypothesis can be accepted. The qualification BGI 8686 of respondents <u>increases</u> the judgment of service productivity.

When looking at the different statements separately, two of three capacity efficiency factors show significant p-values (Table 4). Firms of respondents which have got the BGI 8686 qualification have got a higher service productivity, especially regarding the service offering adaptation and the employee qualification.

Table 4. Analysis of different statements of H3b

		p-value	Statement to be evaluated
Internal	A	0.641	Easy transfer of process-relevant information to the roadside assistant
	B	0.853	Optimal supply of process-relevant information to the employees
	C	0.189	Trouble-free operation through structuring of usage of resources
Capacity	D	0.000***	Adapted service offering to altered conditions
	E	0.106	Suitable technical equipment to solve upcoming tasks
	F	0.000***	Excellent qualification of employees to master future demands
External	G	0.277	Enabling of journey continuation on the location of breakdown
	H	0.212	Compliance with scheduled (arrival) times
	I	0.169	Rare confrontation of firm with complaints

In terms of experience, we tested in H4a whether personnel of firms with EV roadside service experience judge *service complexity* higher to those that do not have experience. As can be seen in Fig. 5, service providers, which have already delivery roadside breakdown services to EVs, judge these services as being more complex in

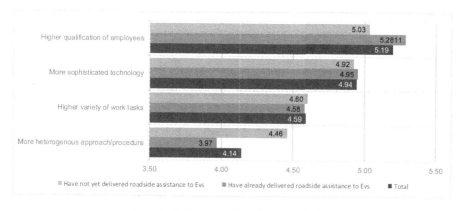

Fig. 5. Judgement of service complexity

regard to qualification and technology when compared to conventional vehicles. The differences are not significant, though.

The Mann-Whitney-U-Test resulted in a p-value of 0.214, hence the null hypothesis cannot be rejected. The evaluation of service complexity seems not to be related to the level of experience with services for electric vehicles. Only one statement lead to a significant value, i.e., the complexity regarding the approach/procedure is seen higher by staff with experience than by those without (Table 5).

Table 5. Analysis of different statements of H4a

	p-value	Statement to be evaluated
A	0.016**	More heterogenous approach/procedure
B	0.772	Higher variety of work tasks
C	0.947	More sophisticated technology
D	0.116	Higher qualification of employees

On the other hand, the questioned items in regard to *service productivity* (H4b) lead to a p-value of 0.02**, hence the null hypothesis can be rejected. Service productivity depends on the experience of services with EVs, this is visible especially in the items that make up the capacity factor (Fig. 6). Firms with EV experience show a higher service productivity judgement.

The absolute values for the different statements are confirmed by the Mann-Whitney-U-Test (Table 6):

Table 6. Analysis of different statements of H4b

		p-value	Statement to be evaluated
Internal	A	0.892	Easy transfer of process-relevant information to the roadside assistant
	B	0.430	Optimal supply of process-relevant information to the employees
	C	0.177	Trouble-free operation through structuring of usage of resources
Capacity	D	0.000***	Adapted service offering to altered conditions
	E	0.025	Suitable technical equipment to solve upcoming tasks
	F	0.000***	Excellent qualification of employees to master future demands
External	G	0.068	Enabling of journey continuation on the location of breakdown
	H	0.102	Compliance with scheduled (arrival) times
	I	0.928	Rare confrontation of firm with complaints

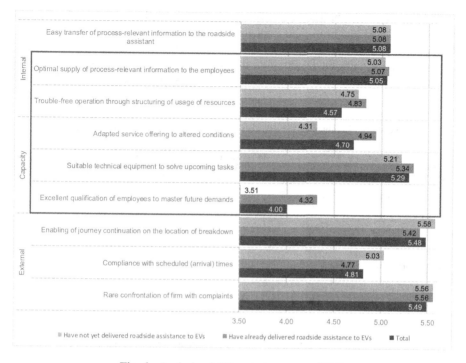

Fig. 6. Analysis of different statements of H4b

The comparison of both groups (*experience* and *no experience*) validates these significant differences. The whole concept of service productivity as well as the capacity efficiency deliver significant p-values (Table 7).

Table 7. Comparison of means of two different groups (H4b)

	Mean if *no services* for EVs	Mean if *services* for EVs	p-value (Mann-Whitney-U-test)
Self Evaluation	4.314 N=121	4.396 N=192	0.564
Service Productivity	4.847 N=112	5.028 N=182	0.002***
Internal Efficiency	4.814 N=120	4.962 N=191	0.082*
Capacity Efficiency	4.351 N=115	4.888 N=184	0.000***
External Efficiency	5.336 N=118	5.225 N=188	0.087*

Finally, we asked the professionals regarding the complexity and productivity in the light of whether the firms have implemented certain measures related to e-mobility. Regarding hypotheses H5a and H5b, the Kruskal-Wallis-Test for service complexity did not deliver significant results, i.e., the null hypothesis cannot be rejected. The measures have no influence on the evaluation of service complexity (Table 8).

Table 8. P-values of service complexity on different measures (H5a)

Measures	p-values of service complexity
Training of employees	0.841
Flexibilization of workforce	0.105
Extension of vehicle fleet	0.137
Purchase of technical equipment	0.317
Technical adaptation of vehicle fleet	0.729

On the other hand, the Kruskal-Wallis-Test for *service productivity* revealed significant differences between the groups that have taken the measures, have planned to do so or are not planning to take them (besides the measure "flexibilization of workforce[4]"). Therefore, the null hypothesis can be rejected.

When looking at the different efficiencies of service productivity, the significant differences are – again – mainly in the capacity efficiency (Table 9).

Table 9. Comparison of means of two different groups (H5b)

Measures	p-values of service complexity
Training of employees	0.000***
Flexibilization of workforce	0.278
Extension of vehicle fleet	0.005***
Purchase of technical equipment	0.000***
Technical adaptation of vehicle fleet	0.000***

To summarize the empirical findings, we got a mixed picture of accepted and rejected hypotheses based on the underlying data set. Some hypothesized assumptions

---

[4] This exception may be due to the respondents' improper understanding of the meaning of this item.

could not be confirmed, but overall, our analyses confirmed the results of our factor and subsequent reliability analysis.

Table 10 shows the correlation of constructs regarding service productivity.

Table 10. Correlation of constructs (service productivity)

	Self Evaluation [a]	Service Productivity [b]	Internal Efficiency	Capacity Efficiency	External Efficiency
Self Evaluation	1 N=313	0,269*** N=254	0,287*** N=311	0,200*** N=299	0,154*** N=306
Service Productivity		1 N=294	0,766*** N=294	0,752*** N=294	0,643*** N=294
Internal Efficiency			1 N=311	0,381*** N=298	0,442*** N=304
Capacity Efficiency				1 N=299	0,172*** N=295
External Efficiency					1 N=306

a) Self evaluation of service productivity.
b) Mean of internal, external and capacity efficiency

Service complexity measured with 4 items resulted in a Cronbach's Alpha $\alpha = 0.740$.

As frequently mentioned above, the data reveals again that service productivity is mainly defined by capacity and internal aspects. Looking at the internal consistency, it resulted in 9 items with a Cronbach's Alpha α of 0.721.

5   Conclusion

5.1   Implications and Recommendations

It was our research aim to investigate how roadside traffic service providers experience service complexity and service productivity [18] on the back of an increasing installation base of electric vehicles.

As detailed above, the higher number of electric vehicles on the roads calls for new or – at the least – an adaption of roadside assistance and breakdown services. By now, most providers have realized that. More qualifications and trainings for employees and the acquisition and use of more advanced technical equipment are measures that have been partially taken by the players in the field.

The contribution of our research is twofold: In the scientific community, there is very little service research in the context of roadside assistants and e-mobility. The research presented here can help to stimulate discussion in order to ignite further necessary investigation. Service literature states that an optimal balance between perceived service quality and productivity has to be maintained by the service provider's inputs in the process, in order to guarantee excellent performances [19].

From a managerial point of view, roadside assistant providers get valuable insights on how to adapt to future disruptive changes in technology, which result in fluctuating demand for roadside assistance services. However, through an ongoing adaption process, service providers can find and maintain an optimal balance between perceived quality and internal efficiency.

Service providers must learn from their customers how to meet their demands and adequately adjust to their value systems. By doing so, service productivity is improved over time.

Only if the quality and quantity/availability of e-mobility roadside assistance services keeps up the high standards they used to have with combustion engines, will the e-mobility be adapted quickly and successfully.

5.2   Limitations and Future Research

The study also contains certain limitations which we would like to address. First, the research has been conducted in the German roadside assistance market only. Questions of external validity, i.e., generalization of the findings, may be problematic at this point in time. Second, the questioned individuals were only from two roadside assistance clubs, there are many more in Germany, whose members may have a different view and different issues when delivering their services to electric vehicles. Third, some relations to other upcoming technology trends such as autonomous cars have not been addressed in this study. These trends might interfere with each other, leading to an even higher service complexity in the future. Fourth, the focus of this study was put on the technological aspects of e-mobility. Even though legal and political aspects were not ignored, they are not in the center of our research, but may have an influence on the development of service complexity and service productivity of e-mobility.

We recommend that future research addresses these shortcomings. A wide-spread dissemination of the survey to other (European or global) contexts could validate the findings, discover respective market singularities and/or bring up new and more detailed insights into this important but neglected application of service research. We think that it should be seen as a starting point to initiate more research and to speed up the adaptation process of service firms to get them ready for the heavy acceleration of electric car penetration that has been on the political agenda for quite some time.

Acknowledgement. The research project "Szenariengestützte Entwicklung des Dienstleistungssystems »Sichere Versorgung bei Unfällen und Pannen mit Elektrofahrzeugen« (SafetE-car)" has been partially funded by a grant from the German Ministry for Education and Research (Bundesministeriums für Bildung und Forschung - BMBF) and has ben supervised by the project owner Karlsruhe (PTKA). The responsibility for the content of this publication lays with the authors.

References

1. Radke, S.: Verkehr in Zahlen 2016/2017 (Traffic in Numbers 2016/2017). DVV Media Group, Hamburg (2016)
2. SPIEGEL: Diesel-Pkw stoßen teils mehr Stickoxide aus als Lkw (Diesel cars sometimes emit more nitric oxides than heavy trucks). http://www.spiegel.de/diesel-pkw-stossen-teils-mehr-stickoxide-1128839.html
3. Bundesregierung: Nationaler Entwicklungsplan Elektromobilität (National development plan electric mobility of the German government) (2009)
4. Smith, B.: Chevrolet volt battery incident overview report (2012)
5. Warner, J.: The Handbook of Lithium-Ion Battery Pack Design. Chemistry, Components, Types and Terminology. Elsevier, Amsterdam (2015)
6. Chase, R.B., Haynes, R.M.: Service operations management: a field guide. In: Swartz, T.A., Iacobucci, D. (eds.) Handbook of Services Marketing & Management, pp. 455–472. Sage Publications, Thousand Oaks (2000)
7. Walsh, G., Walgenbach, P., Evanschitzky, H., Schaarschmidt, M.: Service productivity: what stops service firms from measuring it? J. Organ. Transform. Soc. Chang. 13, 5–25 (2016)
8. Bullinger, H.-J., Scheer, A.-W., Schneider, K. (eds.): Service Engineering. Entwicklung und Gestaltung innovativer Dienstleistungen (Service Engineering: Development and Design of Innovative Services). Springer, Berlin (2006)
9. Ojasalo, K.: Conceptualizing productivity in services, Helsinki (1999)
10. Corsten, H., Gössinger, R.: Dienstleistungsmanagement (Service Management). Oldenbourg Wissenschaftsverlag, München (2014)
11. Wacker, J., Hershauer, J., Walsh, K.D., Sheu, C.: Estimating professional service productivity. Theoretical model, empirical estimates and external validity. Int. J. Prod. Res. 52, 482–495 (2013)
12. Grönroos, C., Ojasalo, K.: Service productivity. Towards a conceptualization of the transformation of inputs into economic results in services. J. Bus. Res. 57, 414–423 (2004)
13. von Garrel, J., Tackenberg, S., Seidel, H., Grandt, C.: Dienstleistungen produktiv erbringen (Productively Delivering Services). Springer Gabler, Wiesbaden (2014)
14. Cocca, S.: Significance of qualitative factors for a deeper understanding of service productivity. Int. J. Serv. Sci. Manag. Eng. Technol. 4, 46–59 (2013)
15. Denzin, N.K., Lincoln, Y.S.: The Sage Handbook of Qualitative Research. Sage, Thousand Oaks (2011)
16. Hair, J.F., Wolfinbarger, M., Money, A.H., Samouel, P., Page, M.J.: Essentials of Business Research Methods. M.E. Sharpe, Armonk (2011)
17. Hair, J.F., Black, W.C., Babin, B.J., Anderson, R.E.: Multivariate Data Analysis. Prentice Hall, Upper Saddle River (2014)
18. Demmelmair, M.F.: Essays on Service Productivity: Theoretical Foundation and Selected Empirical Studies. FGM-Verlag, München (2015)
19. Calabrese, A.: Service productivity and service quality. A necessary trade-off? Int. J. Prod. Econ. 135, 800–812 (2012)

Internet Use by Elderly People in the Czech Republic

Martina Hedvicakova and Libuse Svobodova[✉]

Faculty of Informatics and Management, University of Hradec Kralove,
Rokitanskeho 62, 50003 Hradec Kralove, Czech Republic
{Martina.Hedvicakova,libuse.svobodova}@uhk.cz

Abstract. The number of information technology users increases as fast as new information technology develops. This paper aims to analyse Internet users older than 65 years and focusing on the Czech Republic, the Visegrad group (also referred to as V4) and the European Union. Elderly people use the Internet the least from all age groups. The partial aim of this paper is to analyse whether, since 2009, there has been a constant increase in Internet users in the elderly age group in the Czech Republic and also the EU. The second scientific issue deals with the confirmation that the number of Internet users in the 65+ age group is similar to the EU-28 and V4. The analysis showed that the number of 65+ users has been steadily increasing since 2009. In the Czech Republic only 28.4% elderly people used internet in 2015 and 26.7% in 2014. According to Eurostat methodology the Internet is used in the 65–74 years age group by 33% of users. More than one third (38%) of elderly aged 65–74 used the internet at least once a week in the EU-28.

Keywords: Elderly people · Technologies · Internet · Utilization · Statistics

1 Introduction

This millennium is marked by constant change and dynamic development. People must constantly learn new things and acquire advanced technology. This places great demands on the knowledge and also we must not neglect the psychological aspect of the matter. More and more people connect via various social networks or use the Internet for shopping, reading messages or making phone calls etc. It puts greater and greater demands on people regarding the technical and social skills. As shown by A. Toffler an optimal approach would be for the individual to acknowledge first the limits of his capacities and then go through the change.

Thus, elderly people, same as young and adult persons are submitted to a process of continuous adjustment and they need a support for that. It is rather difficult than easy, even more when a defining feature of this century is demographic ageing, growth of number of elderly people with needs. (Nistor [4]). People learn all the time during lifetime; still, it is possible that "no one is learning at the level, with the intensity and the speed necessary for facing the complexity of modern world" (Botkin, Elmandjira, Malița, 1981, in Paloş et al. [5]). Communication using cyber technology is innate to generations that grew up along with it [1].

© IFIP International Federation for Information Processing 2017
Published by Springer International Publishing AG 2017. All Rights Reserved
A.K. Kar et al. (Eds.): I3E 2017, LNCS 10595, pp. 514–524, 2017.
DOI: 10.1007/978-3-319-68557-1_45

Internet is an ever-growing communication net that connects the most computer systems of the world. It is also the growing technology which is used by people like "the information storage, sharing, and easy access". Computer and internet are large communication vehicles of nowadays and future that provide an easy, quick, cheap and safe access to a lot of information. Germany, the Netherlands are the most represented by the website dedicated to old people, where you can get different information from legal aid to purchase online [2, 3].

Boll and Brune [22] argued in favor of an integrated online service and social network platform to support elderly people in their everyday life.

1.1 Literature Review

All around the world analysis and research is performed to investigate the current status of internet use by elderly and to explore their opinions toward factors associated with internet use.

Smarn [6] study was conducted with 385 elderly living in Khon Khaen Municipality, Khon Khaen Province. The finding revealed that most elderly did not use the Internet (80.7%). Numbers of female elderly who did not use the Internet were higher than male ones while the majority of elderly who were older than 70 years of age did not use the Internet at all.

Reisenwitz et al. [21] found that 52.8% of the elderly used the Internet less than 5 h a week and 54.0% of them had been using the Internet for more than one year. [6]

Results revealed that those seniors with higher levels of nostalgia proneness used and accessed the internet less, purchased less online, had less online experience and felt less comfortable using the internet. There is also support for the impact of innovativeness on mature consumers' internet use, frequency, online purchases, experience, comfort level with the internet, and satisfaction with the internet. In terms of risk aversion, seniors with more online experience report a lower level of risk aversion to the internet than other mature consumers [7].

Hogeboom et al. [8] revealed that 62.0% of people who were between 50–64 years old were using the Internet, but only 33.0% of people who were 65 and upper who were still using the Internet [6, 13].

1.2 Broadband Development

The European Commission's Digital Agenda forms one of the seven pillars of the Europe 2020 Strategy which sets objectives for the growth of the European Union (EU) by 2020. Europe needs competitively priced fast and ultra fast Internet access for all. To achieve this, the EU must establish next generation access networks (NGAs). The Commission is channelling some of its public funds, via different instruments, to invest in broadband infrastructure.

The EU must exploit the potential offered by the use of ICTs in the following areas:

- climate change, through partnerships with emitting sectors,
- managing ageing population, through e-health and telemedicine systems and services,

- digitisation of content, through Europeana,
- intelligent transport systems, by applying the proposed Directive [16].

Main aims for broadband development

The Czech Republic's national broadband strategy, called Digital Czech Republic v.2.0, has been adopted in 2013 and is valid until 2020.

Due to the technical limitations that mobile broadband technologies entail, the focus lies on fixed broadband networks to provide nation-wide coverage with at least 30 Mbps until 2020. Regarding the utilization of the sort of fixed broadband technologies, the Czech government's position seems neutral. Regional conditions vary, appropriate infrastructure is being discussed by the government; the infrastructure is supposed to be future proof in the long term with guaranteed high–speed connection to the Internet.

Current coverage of broadband networks (2015)

Fixed: 98.5%

NGA: 72.9% [14, 17] (Table 1)

Table 1. Broadband technologies (2014)

Technologies	Coverage of homes
DSL	97%
VDSL	46%
FTTP	14%
WIMAX	71%
STANDARD CABLE	33%
DOCSIS 3 CABLE	32%
HSPA	97%

Source: Broadband coverage in Europe in 2014 by IHS and VVA [14]

Based on available data from the Czech Telecommunication Office and Czech Statistical Office, the Ministry of Industry and Trade has developed a model of availability to broadband Internet access through optic networks with speeds of at least 30 Mbit/s (see Table 2). This table illustrates the very low penetration of optic networks in the Czech Republic. Moreover, in the Czech Republic unlike other countries in the EU, the formerly monopolistic operator nor the other big players in the market invest in these networks. Development of the optical network is therefore just the domain of local operators, who began as community wireless service providers in medium-sized municipalities. An important role is also currently played by cable TV network operators, who allow some of their customers to reach speed excessing 100 Mbit/s. Problematic, however, are mainly small municipalities and localities with low population densities, because the return on investment for the private sector is very limited out of localities with high densities of people (such as housing estate) [14].

Table 2. The availability of broadband Internet access through optic networks with speeds of at least 30 Mbit/s in the Czech Republic, the source MIT, CTO, CSO.

Basic indicators (excluding Prague)	Total	To 199	200–499	500–999	1000–1999	2000–4999	5000–9999	10000 and more
Number of municipalities	6249	1524	1975	1356	723	400	140	130
Population	9275612	189334	645742	953015	1009378	1219378	960042	4298626
No. of households	3068385	64732	179976	289841	311408	398343	324983	1499102
No. of households without access to high-speed network in%		100	100	100	100	95	90	80
No. without free access to high-speed network in%		67	47	25	5	0	0	0

Source: [14]

The foregoing indicated that it's meaningful to promote opportunities for the effective use of co-financing a construction from public funds as a possible complementary mechanism generating the necessary incentives for private investment in infrastructure for high-speed access to the Internet and the emergence of projects that would probably not have been implemented at all without this support [14].

The present shares of different technologies on the retail market for Internet access and the long-term development are documented in the following Fig. 1 [23].

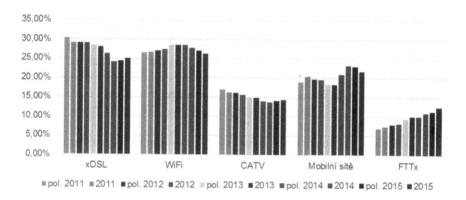

Fig. 1. The development of the share of high-speed access by individual technological solutions on the Czech retail market, including mobile network access, CTO Source: Ministry of Industry and Trade [23]

2 Goals and Methods

This paper aims to analyse the use of the Internet in the Czech Republic and its comparison with EU-28 and V4 in connection with the use of advanced technologies by elderly people.

The research procedure followed two phases:

- The first phase deals with: the number elderly people using the Internet in the Czech Republic, at least at the average level as in EU-28.
- The second phase: every year (since 2009) the number of elderly people using the Internet has been increasing.

First it is necessary to define the term "elderly people". According to World Health Organisation: Most developed world countries have accepted the chronological age of 65 years as a definition of 'elderly' or older person. At the moment, there is no United Nations standard numerical criterion, but the UN agreed cut-off is 60+ years to refer to the older population [9].

For further analysis the distribution according to age 65+ will be used.

2.1 Development of Population in the Czech Republic

The share of seniors in the Czech population has been steadily increasing since 1985 (from the level of 12%). By the end of the 20th century, the growth was slow (to 13.9% in 2000–2003), but thereafter it accelerated. The share significantly rose especially since 2007, in the connection with baby boomers born in the 40 s of the 20th century across the border 65 years of age. During the years 2004–2014, the share of seniors increased from 14% to almost 18%. The last presented data (to 31. 12. 2014) states that the proportion of people over 65 years of age is in the general population 17.8% (see Table 3). The current number of 1.88 million is about 243 thousands higher than at the beginning of 2011. Also the highest increases in the age groups were concentrated in the population of the age group of seniors over 65 years. Those increased by 54,900 during 2014 [2, 10].

Due to the aging population this issue is very serious in solving economic, social and other areas.

Table 3. The characteristics of the age composition of 1984, 1994, 2004 and 2014 (to 31. 12.)

Index	1984	1994	2004	2014
The share of seniors (in%)	11,8	13,1	14	17,8
The share of persons aged 80+ on 65+ years (in%)	17,9	21,0	21,5	22,3
Age index	50,3	69,6	94,0	117,4
Average age (in years)	35,6	37,0	39,8	41,7
Median age (in years)	33,9	36,2	38,7	41,1
The number of seniors aged 65+ years (in mil.)	1,22	1,36	1,43	1,88
The number of seniors aged 80+ years (in thousands)	219	285	308	419

Source: [2]

Despite the fact that ten years ago, there was no usual use of ICT by elderly people, the situation is in recent years evolving and changing.

Learning and using information and communication technologies (ICT) such as computer technologies and internet by the elderly is seen as an important demand for their integration in daily life and as a factor related to active aging [11].

The number of seniors over 65 was in Europe in 2016 from 8.2% (in Turkey) to 22% (in Italy). In all countries there was an increase in the number of seniors compared to 2000. The Czech Republic is with 18.3% of the seniors on the average of Europe [25].

Population changes in the Czech Republic are shown in Fig. 2.

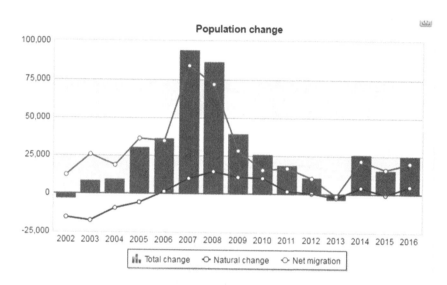

Fig. 2. Population change in the Czech Republic Source: Czech Statistical Office [24]

After the end of the economic crisis in the Czech Republic in 2013, net migration started to grow. This trend is in line with the development of GDP in the Czech Republic, which declined from 2007 to 2013.

3   Results

3.1   Elderly Population and Using the Internet in EU-28

Statistics were obtained from Eurostat sources. Data are always stated for years that were statistically processed. Always refer to all "All Individuals". Data only for 65+ are not available at the moment. Selected data for the EU 28 and the Czech Republic together with the countries of the Visegrad Group were chosen for comparison because those countries are close to the Czech Republic. Data are always given in %. Tables are completed with graphs which will help in faster-after straightening.

It is recorded in the statistics of the statistical office of the European Union (Eurostat) relating to information and communication technologies (ICTs) that 38% which is slightly more than one third of the elderly people aged 65 to 74 in the EU-28 used the internet at least once a week. Ten years ago there were only 7% of the elderly people using the internet regularly, at least once a week.

Figure 3 illustrates the share of the elderly people who use the internet daily. It is revealed in these statistics that if elderly people become acquainted with ICT and consequently reach a desirable computer competency they begin to use the internet actively, like younger generations. In 2004 there were 57% of the elderly using the internet weekly, ten years later there were already three quarters (76%) of elderly people utilizing the internet at least once a week. [12]

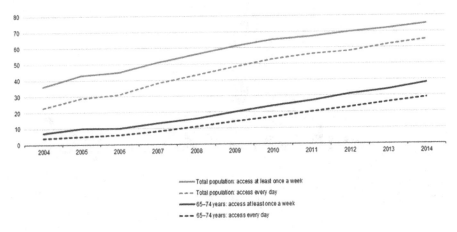

Fig. 3. Proportion of the population accessing the internet, by age and frequency of use, EU-28, 2004–14 (%) Source: Eurostat [12]

Figure 4 analyses the situation in the field of utilisation of using the Internet by elderly people in the Czech Republic and to compare the use of social networks in the Czech Republic with other countries of EU-28 and V4. (Visegrad group /V4/is the association composed of Czech Republic, Slovak Republic, Poland and Hungary focuses on foreign policy activities and the group aims to promote co-operation and stability in the broader region of Central Europe) and EU28 [20].

Figure 4 shows that in comparison with the average the Czech Republic is more or less at the same level as EU-28 as well as V4 in the use of the Internet by overall population and elderly. The elderly age group in the Czech Republic is more active than in the other V4 countries. Compared to the average of the EU-28 however, the use by the elderly age group is lower by 5%.

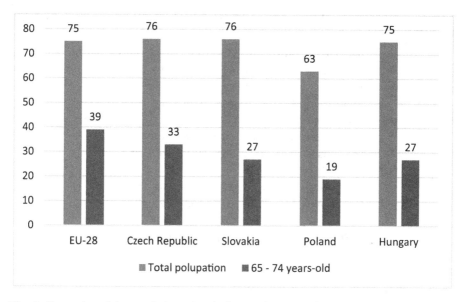

Fig. 4. Proportion of the population using the internet in Visegrad group in 2014 (in %) Source: own elaboration based on Eurostat [12]

3.2 Individuals Using the Internet in the Czech Republic

99% of students use the Internet, 93.9% of housewives use the Internet. Only 32.8% elderly people use it. The difference is also among employed people who use the Internet 17.7% more than the unemployed. The results are comparable with other international studies (e.g. Lian and Yen [18]).

Only 32.8% of pensioners in the Czech Republic use the Internet, which is 61.1% less than in the group of students (see Table 4). Elderly people in the Czech Republic are mostly represented in the lowest-income quartile.

Since 2015, the Czech Statistical Office moved to a similar methodology for calculating elderly people. Previously it distinguished 65+ age group, currently it uses the same age group as Eurostat, i.e. 65–74 years and 74+. This leads to different values in % of users using the Internet. After the division into two age groups, the results from the Czech Republic match the results from Eurostat.

Figure 5 shows the data for the 65+ age group regarding the use of mobile phones, personal computers and Internet for a period of 2005–2015.

While in 2005 landline telephones were more commonly used and mobile phones were used only by approximately thirty percent of the population, in 2008 more than half of this group already used a mobile phone, and in 2015 it reached the provisional maximum of 88.5%. Regarding the use of computers and the Internet, there has also been a significant change. Of the original 2.2% using a computer, the use increased to 27.7% and for the internet from 2.2% to 28.4%. From the results it can be expected that

Table 4. Individuals using the Internet in the Czech Republic (in %) Source: Czech Statistical Office [19]

Indicator	2010	2011	2012	2013	2014	2015[2]
Total	61,8	65,5	69,5	70,4	74,2	75,7
Males	65,8	69,2	72,3	72,8	77,3	77,9
Females	58,1	61,9	66,8	67,7	71,3	73,5
Age group						
55–64 years	42,1	46,3	56,0	57,6	64,0	68,0
65+ years	13,2	16,2	16,8	18,9	26,7	28,4
Economic activity status						
Employed	77,8	81,0	87,5	87,9	90,4	91,7
Unemployed	53,8	62,2	63,7	66,2	79,4	74,0
Pensioners	16,5	19,7	20,5	23,5	30,8	32,8

(1) Share in the total number of individuals in a given group.
(2) Preliminary data.

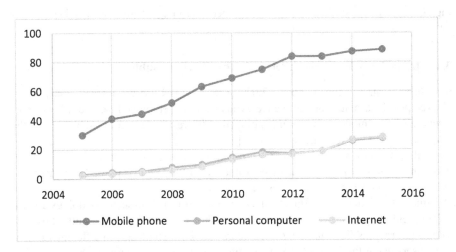

Fig. 5. Individuals aged 65+ years (in %) Source: Czech Statistical Office

elderly people do not always own a computer, and that they also connect to the Internet from public computers. The trend in the use of computers and the Internet is very similar.

It can also be interesting to watch the frequency of the Internet use. While according to the Eurostat statistics in the EU-28 the internet in 2014 was used by 65% of individuals aged 16 to 74 daily on average and 10% at least once a week. In the Czech Republic, the ratio is 60% a day and 15% at least once a week. In the Slovak Republic, Hungary and Poland the use is lower. The lowest usage is in Poland, where 51% of citizens use the Internet daily and 12% at least once a week.

4 Conclusion and Discussion

There is always a share of elderly people who are rather cautious or distrustful about utilization of new technologies, in particular computers and the internet. Anyway the proportion of senior citizens who go online is increasing; younger generations who used the internet are getting old and move to the older age category and beside that there is a significant group of elderly people willing to learn and gain computer skills and benefit from the internet with its numerous new opportunities and services.

In 2015, more than 3.1 million Czech households (73%) were equipped with a computer and the Internet. In 2015, the Internet was used for the first time by more individuals than the computer. "In terms of the proportion of Internet users in the Czech adult population in 2014 it even exceeded the EU-28 average. The Internet was used in the Czech population aged 16–74 years by 79.7% people, while the average of EU countries amounted to 78.0%", said by President of CSO Iva Ritschelová. [15]

The analysis showed that the number of users older than 65 years has been steadily increasing since 2009. In the Czech Republic the Internet was used only by 28.4% elderly people in 2015 and 26.7% in 2014. More than one third (38%) of the elderly aged 65–74 used the internet at the least once a week in the EU-28.

The question for the discussion is whether the increasing number of elderly people in the Czech Republic will lead to the increase in the number of the Internet users and social networks in the 65+ group, or a personal communication will be still a bigger benefit.

Population has been increasing since 2013 due to migrants. The next question is whether an increased number of migrants in the mid-year will affect this surveyed group.

It will also depend on the health status of older people and the economic situation whether they will be able to afford a computer and an Internet connection.

Elderly people can use the internet to improve their lives e.g. for home care, eHealth and the treatment of their illness.

Another question is whether a greater impact on the number of users will be the growing number of population in the group of 55–64 or natural aging of population of users who at this moment use the Internet 40% more than the 65+ age group.

Further research will analyse how busy the use of the Internet is in connection with the use of social networks.

The paper was written with the support of the specific project 6/2017 grant "Determinants affecting job satisfaction" granted by the University of Hradec Králové, Czech Republic and thanks to help students Veronika Domšová.

References

1. Nistor, G.: New educational strategies regarding quality of life for elderly people. Procedia Social Behav. Sci. **142**(14), 487–492 (2014). doi:10.1016/j.sbspro.2014.07.653
2. Ramazan, A., Kazaz, N., Basa, B.: The internet addiction of Kosovo and Turkey Elderly People. Procedia Social Behav. Sci. **103**, 1104–1117 (2013)
3. Kaliterna-Lipovčan, L., Tomek-Roksandić, S., Perko, G., Mihok, D., Radašević, H., Puljak, A., Turek, S.: Gerontehnologija u Europi i u Hrvatskoj, Medicus, vol. 14, no. 2, pp. 301–304, Zagreb (2005)

4. Nistor, G.: Quality of live for elderly people – a new approach to social-medical problems in family context. In: Volume II of International Conferences Contemporary Issues Facing Families: Psychological, Social and Spiritual Perspectives in Dialogue, 2012. Universitatea de Vest din Timişoara, Timişoara (to appear)

5. Paloş, R., Sava, S., Ungureanu, D., (coord.). Educaţia adulţilor. Baze teoretice şi repere practice. Iaşi: Editura Polirom (2007)

6. Smarn, L.: Thai elderly behavior of internet use. Procedia Social Behav. Sci. **147**(25), 104–110 (2014)

7. Reisenwitz, T., Iyer, R., Kuhlmeier, D.B., Eastman, J.K.: The elderly's internet usage: an updated look. J. Consum. Mark. **24**(7), 406–418 (2007)

8. Hogeboom, L.D.: Internet use and social networking among middle aged and older adults. Educ. Gerontol. **36**, 93–111 (2010)

9. World Health Organization: Definition of an older or elderly person. http://www.who.int/healthinfo/survey/ageingdefnolder/en/

10. Statistika & MY, Praha už není nejstarším krajem. http://www.statistikaamy.cz/2015/05/praha-uz-neni-nejstarsim-krajem/

11. Sitti, S., Nuntachampoo, S.: Attitudes towards the use of ICT training curriculum for Thai elderly people. Procedia Social Behav. Sci. **103**, 161–164 (2013)

12. Eurostat: People in the EU – statistics on an ageing society. http://ec.europa.eu/eurostat/statistics-explained/index.php/People_in_the_EU_%E2%80%93_statistics_on_an_ageing_society

13. Hedvicakova, M., Pozdilkova, A., Stranska, P.K., Svobodova, L.: Analysis of mobile social networks using clustering. Adv. Sci. Lett. **22**(5–6), 1273–1277 (2016)

14. European Commission: Digitální Česko v. 2.0 - Czech Broadband Strategy. https://ec.europa.eu/digital-single-market/en/news/digit%C3%A1ln%C3%AD-%C4%8Desko-v-20-czech-broadband-strategy

15. Czech Statistical Office: Počtem uživatelů internetu jsme přeskočili Evropu. https://www.czso.cz/csu/czso/poctem-uzivatelu-internetu-jsme-preskocili-evropu

16. European Commission: Europe 2020 strategy. https://ec.europa.eu/digital-single-market/en/europe-2020-strategy

17. European Commission: Country information - Czech Republic. https://ec.europa.eu/digital-single-market/en/country-information-czech-republic

18. Lian, J.W., Yen, D.C.: Online shopping drivers and barriers for older adults: age and gender differences. Comput. Hum. Behav. **37**, 133–143 (2014)

19. Czech Statistical Office (2015). https://www.czso.cz/csu/czso/cinnosti-provadene-jednotlivci-na-internetu

20. Svobodová, L., Hedvicakova, M.: Doing business in the countries of Visegrad group. Procedia Econ. Fin. **34**, 453–460 (2015). 8s. Elsevier, Amsterdam. ISSN 2212-5671

21. Reisenwitz, T., Iyer, R., Kuhlmeier, D.B., Eastman, J.K.: The ederly's internet usage: an updated look. J. Consum. Mark. **24**, 406–418 (2007)

22. Boll, F., Brune, P.: Online support for the elderly – why service and social network platforms should be integrated. Procedia Comput. Sci. **98**, 395–400 (2016)

23. Ministry of Industry and Trade: National Plan for the Development of Next Generation Networks (2016). https://www.mpo.cz/assets/cz/e-komunikace-a-posta/elektronicke-komunikace/koncepce-a-strategie/narodni-plan-rozvoje-siti-nga/2016/11/NPRSNG_EN_final-copy_1.pdf

24. Czech Statistical Office: Senior citizens (2017). https://www.czso.cz/csu/czso/seniori

25. Eurostat: Data, Database (2017). http://ec.europa.eu/eurostat/data/database

Correction to: Selected Aspects in Searching for Health Information on the Internet Among Generation Y

Petra Maresova and Blanka Klimova

Correction to:
Chapter "Selected Aspects in Searching for Health Information on the Internet Among Generation Y" in: A. K. Kar et al. (Eds.): *Digital Nations – Smart Cities, Innovation, and Sustainability*, LNCS 10595, https://doi.org/10.1007/978-3-319-68557-1_20

The book was inadvertently published with an incorrect grant number in the acknowledgement at the end of chapter 20. "No. 15330/16/AGR" should read correctly "No. 17- 03037". Correction has been updated in chapter.

The updated version of this chapter can be found at
https://doi.org/10.1007/978-3-319-68557-1_20

Author Index

Printed in the United States
By Bookmasters